A House Divided

DEDICATED TO

SUSAN COLTRANE LOWANCE

AND TO THE

UNIVERSITY OF MASSACHUSETTS STUDENTS

IN

"RACE AND SLAVERY IN AMERICAN CULTURE"

A House Divided

THE ANTEBELLUM SLAVERY DEBATES

IN AMERICA, 1776–1865

· *EDITED BY MASON I. LOWANCE, JR.* ·

PRINCETON UNIVERSITY PRESS

PRINCETON AND OXFORD

Library of Congress Cataloging-in-Publication Data

A house divided : the antebellum slavery debates in America, 1776–1865 / edited by
Mason I. Lowance, Jr.

p. cm.

ISBN 0-691-00227-4 (cl : acid-free paper) — ISBN 0-691-00228-2 (pb : acid-free paper)
1. Slavery—Political aspects—United States—History—Sources. 2. Antislavery
movements—United States—History—Sources. 3. Slavery—United
States—Justification—History—Sources. 4. United States—Politics and
government—1775–1783—Sources. 5. United States—Politics and
government—1783–1865—Sources. 6. United States—Race relations—Political aspects—
History—Sources. I. Lowance, Mason I., 1938–

E441 .H86 2002
326′.0973′09033—dc21
2002072853

British Library Cataloging-in-Publication Data is available

This book has been composed in Adobe Caslon

Printed on acid-free paper. ∞

www.pupress.princeton.edu

Printed in the United States of America

1 3 5 7 9 10 8 6 4 2

· CONTENTS ·

put on comp us t (handwritten annotation)

put on
comp list

[handwritten annotation: "put on comp list"]

The title of this volume, *A House Divided*, is taken from Abraham Lincoln's famous speech delivered on June 16, 1858. This address served not only as a prophecy of the coming Civil War, but as a metaphor for the Lincoln household itself. Abraham Lincoln was married to a Kentucky slaveowner's daughter, Mary Todd, whose brother was later killed fighting for the Confederacy against the Union army of which Lincoln was commander in chief. In the "House Divided" speech, the President argued that

> "A house divided against itself cannot stand." I believe this government cannot endure permanently half slave and half free. I do not expect the Union to be dissolved—I do not expect the house to fall—but I do expect it will cease to be divided. It will become all one thing, or all the other. Either the opponents of slavery will . . . place it where the public mind shall rest in the belief that it is in the course of ultimate extinction; or its advocates will put it forward, till it shall become alike lawful in all the States, old as well as new—North as well as South.

In 1862, before Lincoln's transformation into a moral crusader against slavery with the conviction that the Union could only be salvaged by crushing the rebellion of the South, he wrote to the journalist Horace Greeley concerning his views of the relationship of slavery to the Union cause. The "House Divided" principle reappeared as the president attempted to secure a Union victory that would preserve the United States without necessarily ending slavery. It is significant that he also considered the possibility that colonization would be a solution for ending the bloodshed and ideological conflict between the North and the South, that is, that the freed slave population would be returned to Africa rather than allowed to remain in the United States.

To the Hon. Horace Greeley
From the Executive Mansion, August 22, 1862

> . . . As to the policy I "seem to be pursuing," as you say, I have not meant to leave anyone in doubt. I would save the Union. I would save it the shortest way under the Constitution. The sooner the national authority can be restored; the nearer the Union will be to the Union as it was. If there be those who would not save the Union, unless they could at the same time save slavery, I do not agree with them. If there be those who would not save the Union unless they could at the same time destroy slavery, I do not agree with them. My paramount object in this struggle is to save the Union, and is not either to save or to destroy slavery. If I could save the Union without freeing any slave, I would do it, and if I could save it by freeing all the slaves I would do it; and if I could save it by freeing some and leaving others alone I would also do that. What I do about slavery, and the colored race, I do because I believe it helps to save the Union; and what I forbear, I forbear because I do not believe it would help to save the Union. I shall do less whenever I shall

believe what I am doing hurts the cause, and I shall do more whenever I shall believe doing more will help the cause. I shall try to correct errors when shown to be errors; and I shall adopt new views so fast as they shall appear to be true views.

In the Second Inaugural Address, which Lincoln delivered on March 4, 1865, just weeks before his assassination, the president clearly shows, even more than in his earlier addresses, the rhetorical power of the Bible and its influence on his own rhetorical style. The historian David Herbert Donald has noted that in the "House Divided" speech, Lincoln appropriated a metaphor which was entirely biblical; "the 'house divided' quotation was one familiar to virtually everybody in a Bible-reading, churchgoing state like Illinois; it appeared in three of the [four New Testament] Gospels."[1] But in the Second Inaugural Address, Lincoln expressed his conviction that the crusade against slavery was now a holy cause, an apocalyptic moment in history from which the nation, as he had stated in 1858, would turn either all slave or all free. He even remarks on the historical irony of Northerners and Southerners "praying to the same God": "Both read the same Bible . . . each invokes His aid against the other." But he turns immediately to the subject of slavery as a national offense against the Divine will, which gives Divine sanction to the Union cause and the crusade against Robert E. Lee's army.

> The prayers of both could not be answered; that of neither has been answered fully. The Almighty has His own purposes. "Woe unto the world because of offences! For it must needs be that offences come; but woe to that man by whom the offence cometh." If we shall suppose that American Slavery is one of those offences which, in the providence of God, must needs come, but which, having continued through His appointed time, He now wills to remove, and that He gives to both North and South, this terrible war, as the woe due to those by whom the offence came, shall we discern therein any departure from those divine attributes which the believers in a Living God always ascribe to Him? Fondly do we hope—fervently do we pray—that this mighty scourge of war may speedily pass away. Yet, if God wills that it continue until all the wealth piled by the bond-man's two hundred and fifty years of unrequited toil shall be sunk, and until every drop of blood drawn with the lash, shall be paid by another drawn with the sword, as was said three thousand years ago, so still it must be said, "the judgments of the Lord are true and righteous altogether."
>
> With malice toward none; with charity for all; with firmness in the right, as God gives us to see the right, let us strive on to finish the work we are in; to bind up the nation's wounds; to care for him who shall have borne the battle, and for his widow, and his orphan—to do all which may achieve and cherish a just and lasting peace among ourselves, and with all nations. [March 4, 1865]

This apocalyptic rhetoric is not only biblical; it is derived from the rhetorical strategies of the prophets of the Old Testament. By associating slavery with "wrong," and the will of God with "right," Lincoln asserts that the Union cause will prevail in the contemporary conflict because it is the will of God and His

Providence. Ultimately, right will triumph over wrong and good will win over evil. Thus Abraham Lincoln's final posture on slavery and the secession crisis was a fusion of purposes, a forging of causes: the preservation of the Union through a victory over the secessionist Southern states would also insure the end of slavery, which was abolished by the Congress of the United States by a slim House of Representatives margin of three votes. If Lincoln asserted the preservation of the Union as his highest priority in his early addresses, even to the sacrifice of the antislavery cause, he was able, after 1863 and the Emancipation Proclamation, to understand how antislavery principles could be joined to the cause of preserving the Union, and this was a more moral, less pragmatically political position. Just as the nation had been divided by slavery and secession, Abraham Lincoln's rhetoric from 1858 to 1865 shows a movement toward reconciliation between a determination to preserve the Union at all costs and an awareness of the necessity of abolishing slavery in the process. The antebellum slavery debates show a similar complexity; it would be reductive to assign proslavery sentiments to the South and abolitionist persuasion to the North. While the Southern cotton economy depended on slave labor and the abolitionists condemned the institution, both regions shared the ideological conflict.

1. David Herbert Donald, *Lincoln* (New York: Simon and Schuster, 1995), 206.

CHARLES-TOWN,

TO BE SOLD,

On WEDNESDAY the 29th Inftant,

A CARGO of 𝕿𝖜𝖔 𝕳𝖚𝖓𝖉𝖗𝖊𝖉 and 𝕹𝖎𝖓𝖊𝖙

SLAVES

REMARKABLY HEALTHY.

JUST arrived in the Ship Sally, Capt. George Evans, from CAPE MOUNT ☞ A RICE COUNTRY ☜ on the WINDWARD COAST, after a SHORT Paffage of Five Weeks.

Thomas-Loughton & Roger Smith.

CHARLES-TOWN, March 18, 1769.

TO BE SOLD,

On WEDNESDAY the 29th Inftant,

A CARGO of 𝕺𝖓𝖊 𝕳𝖚𝖓𝖉𝖗𝖊𝖉 and 𝕿𝖍𝖎𝖗𝖙𝖞=𝕰𝖎𝖌𝖍𝖙

SLAVES,

REMARKABLY HEALTHY:

JUST arrived in the Brigantine Shelburne, Capt. James Clark, after a SHORT Paffage of Thirty-two Days from SENEGAL, and EQUAL to any NEGROES imported.

Thomas-Loughton & Roger Smith.

Printed at TIMOTHY's Office, in BROAD-STREET.

Slave auction broadside, by permission of Georgia Barnhill, Mellon Curator of Graphic Arts, American Antiquarian Society, Worcester, Mass.

The antebellum slavery debates in America were paralleled by arguments concerning slavery that were taking place throughout the western world in the eighteenth and nineteenth centuries. Antislavery societies in the United States were closely allied with antislavery societies in Great Britain, and abolitionists on both sides of the Atlantic regularly traveled to the opposite shore to promote emancipation and to share concerns. Eighteenth century arguments concerning "natural rights" were based on Enlightenment principles that were vigorously debated in Europe and in the Americas. Nevertheless, the antebellum debates in America were special because the United States, contrasted with the monarchial governments of Europe, were "conceived in liberty and dedicated to the proposition that all men are created equal." From the founding of the United States in the American Revolution and in the drafting of the Constitution, the issue of slavery in the former colonies was a burning question that would not go away. *A House Divided* has been organized to illuminate the arenas of debate surrounding this fundamental inconsistency in the early history of the United States, and to provide the reader, whether scholar or beginning student of American history, with primary texts that articulate each argument, whether proslavery or antislavery. Some of the materials that follow, especially those documents in chapter 7 concerning contemporary race theory, are what we now call "racist" and are offensive to the modern sensibility concerning race relations. But these were the views held by a majority of Americans in the period between the American Revolution and the Civil War. The arguments that developed for and against slavery eventually led to the bloodshed on the battlefields of Atlanta and Gettysburg. Secession and the political arguments about preservation of the Union were of course critical in the generation of the Civil War; however, the antebellum slavery debates were equally important and provided a moral rationale for the hostilities. It is the basic purpose of this volume to bring together the complex strands of the slavery debates, and to weave some meaning from the diverse views presented by these controversial texts.

The pages that follow contain significant slavery-related texts developed by American thinkers between the Revolutionary War (and the subsequent drafting of the Constitution) and the Civil War of 1861–65. Because the charter document, the Constitution, failed to adequately treat or even confront the question of slavery, the legacy of the early importation of Africans to North America to serve as laborers on Southern plantations and as domestic servants and laborers in some Northern colonies was transmitted to the nineteenth century, just as the new nation, "conceived in liberty and dedicated to the proposition that all men are created equal," as Abraham Lincoln would eloquently rephrase it in his Gettysburg Address of 1863, was attempting to define its objectives and establish its identity. Remarkably, the flexibility of the Constitution as an ever-changing charter, whose amendment system permits alteration of the original plan, gave opponents of slavery the opportunity not only to argue the moral degradation of humanity brought about by the "peculiar institution," but to set forth an objective of immediate and unconditional emancipation of the slaves through an amendment to the Constitution itself, the Thirteenth Amendment of 1865. This volume contains primary sources for the fundamental arenas of debate. Included from among the numerous speeches in the United States Congress are those by Horace Mann and Charles Sumner, one from the House of Representatives and one from the Senate. A thorough account and analysis of the antebellum Congressional debates is available in William Lee Miller, *Arguing about Slavery: the Great Battle in the United States Congress* (New York: Alfred P. Knopf, 1995). Similarly, the easily available antebellum slave narratives, extremely important voices in the debates, have been omitted because they are better understood when read and analyzed in full, and many are now in paperback. (The most complete collections have been edited by Willie Lee Rose, *A Documentary History of Slavery in North America*, New York: Oxford University Press, 1976, and Yuval Taylor, *I Was Born a Slave* [2 vols.], New York: Lawrence, 1999.) The Introduction to this volume contains an analysis of the slave narratives in their historical contexts.

A House Divided has been developed out of a decade of teaching the materials of the antebellum slavery debates, and it has benefited greatly from the contributions of many students in both graduate and undergraduate courses in "Race and Slavery in Nineteenth-Century American Culture." Moreover, a number of institutions and individuals have been instrumental in bring *A House Divided* into being. I first became interested in slavery and civil rights while working as an instructor in the Upward Bound Program at Morehouse College, 1964–67, where President Benjamin E. Mays and Dr. Arthur Banks, the first African-American to receive the Ph.D. from Johns Hopkins University (1955) and my department head, welcomed us as colleagues with something to contribute to an understanding of African-American history. The Morehouse campus was deeply engaged in the civil rights movement, and Martin Luther King, Jr., was a member of the Religion faculty at the time. At the University of Massachusetts, I have learned much from my English department colleagues, particularly Joseph Skerrett, and from the historian Steven Oates, all of whom have read bits and pieces of *A House Divided* over the years. The late Sidney Kaplan, whose *The Black Presence in the Era of the American Revolution* is now a classic, was an inspiration for civility and civil rights long before the 1960s, when both became fashionable. For a sabbatical semester in 1997, I participated in the Wednesday lunch seminars at the W. E. B. Du Bois Institute of Harvard University, where Henry Louis Gates, Jr., presided over one of the most informative, stimulating, and controversial series of meetings I have ever attended. When most humanities enterprises are uncertain of their voices and conflicted about objectives, this seminar was clearly organized around historical themes with discussions that left everyone wanting to remain for the whole afternoon. Professors Larry Buell, Kenneth Silverman, Emory Elliott, David Watters, A. Walton Litz, Dean Grodzins, William Pannapacker, David Reynolds, James McPherson, and Daniel

Kevles have listened patiently, read portions of the introductory materials, composed references, or all of the above. One accrues many debts in working through this much material over many years, and one's colleagues in the profession are a constant source of encouragement and discourse.

Of course this book could not have been completed or even started had it not been for the availability of resources on antebellum America. I have worked some in the Library of Congress, where our tax dollars support one of the finest computer databases for bibliographical investigations available anywhere in the world. My excursions to Washington have been met with courtesy, efficiency, and prompt response even though I was unknown to the staff. At the Newberry Library in Chicago, I directed two NEH Summer Seminars for College Teachers (1992 and 1995) on "*Uncle Tom's Cabin* and Antebellum American Culture." The facilities and collections of the Newberry are exceptional for such seminars, and Directors of Education Richard Brown and Fred Hoxie were extremely helpful. The American Antiquarian Society, in Worcester, Massachusetts, provided fellowship support in the spring of 1990 when the resource gathering began. The AAS collections are stunning, and former President Marcus McCorison, one of America's foremost bookmen, was extremely supportive and courteous in the formative years of this study. The Widener Library of Harvard University has many volumes on its open shelves concerning American slavery that would be in any other library's rare book collection. Widener's many rows of pro- and antislavery volumes form the core of the materials presented in *A House Divided*. In addition, the stacks also contain most of the titles listed in Dumond's *Bibliography of Antislavery Writings in America* (1961), all available for the scholar's browsing. The Robert Frost Library of Amherst College and the W. E. B. Du Bois Library of the University of Massachusetts at Amherst have been invaluable resources for secondary materials, although the primary documents came from the Newberry, the AAS, and Widener.

I am deeply grateful to the scholars of nineteenth-century American culture who have contributed their expertise to this volume. Professor Len Gougeon of the University of Scranton, Pennsylvania, an expert on Ralph Waldo Emerson as a reformer and the author of several works about Emerson and antislavery, has contributed an essay on Emerson and Thoreau as antislavery thinkers. Christopher Hanlon of the English department at Eastern Illinois University has authored the introduction to O. S. Fowler in chapter 7, and has edited Fowler's phrenological texts for this volume. Similarly, Melba Jensen has turned her dissertation from the American Studies program at the University of Massachusetts into an essay on the New York abolitionists, especially Gerrit Smith and Lewis Tappan. William Pannapacker, assistant professor in the department of English at Hope College, Holland, Michigan, authored the introductory essays on both Emerson and Walt Whitman, and Dean Grodzins, assistant professor at Meadville-Lombard Theological Seminary in Chicago, prepared the essay and materials on Theodore Parker, the Transcendentalist philosopher who was also a prominent Unitarian minister in Boston. Both Pannapacker and Grodzins completed their doctoral work at Harvard University, where they were lecturers in history and literature and regularly taught courses in nineteenth-century American culture. I thank each of the contributors whose "labor of love" has added significantly to our understanding of antebellum America, and whose cooperation in meeting seemingly arbitrary deadlines is much appreciated.

Finally, I wish to thank Walter Lippincott, director of the Princeton University Press, for patience and understanding during the completion of this project, and to say a special thanks to Thomas Lebien, the editor assigned to this volume, for his thorough work in preparing the book for publication, and for his suggestions as he read through several versions of the typescript. His editorial skills are matched by his gracious manner and intelligent arguments for revision. Jodi Beder, an experienced copyeditor, has turned clutter into clarity throughout the typescript. My wife, Susan, has patiently listened as this project moved from inception to completion, gracefully tolerating my many mood swings as the book progressed. The hundreds of students in "American Identities," "American Romanticism," and "Race and Slavery in Nineteenth-Century American Culture" have contributed more to this volume than they will ever know. To Susan, and to my students in these University of Massachusetts courses, this volume is hereby dedicated.

Mason I. Lowance, Jr.
Amherst and Boston
June 2001

Slave Burrell and John Wallace Comer, by permission of Henry Howell, Atlanta, Ga.

This photograph was made from a plate taken in 1861 of John Wallace Comer and his personal slave, Burrell, who, during the course of the Civil War, not only fought against the Union Army alongside his master, but also rescued Comer twice from the field of battle.

Wallace, as John Wallace Comer was known, was only sixteen at the outbreak of the Civil War, and he enlisted on April 1, 1863, in the Fifty-Seventh Alabama Infantry. He participated in the Battle of Peachtree Creek during the Atlanta campaign, where he was wounded and pulled from the conflict by Burrell.

The courageous slave then managed to construct a crude raft, which he used to transport Wallace Comer down the Chattahoochee River to Columbus, Georgia, from which Burrell took him to the ancestral home at Spring Hill, near Troy, Alabama.

Source Note: Anne Kendrick Walker, *Braxton Bragg Comer: His Family Tree from Virginia's Colonial Days* (Richmond: The Dietz Press, 1947), pp. 167–70.

The purpose of this book is to provide the scholar, student, and general reader with resource materials for study of the antebellum slavery debates in America from the Revolutionary era, when the institution of chattel slavery was first seriously challenged and defended, to the Civil War, when it was finally overthrown. American slavery was introduced into the colonies in 1621, when the Jamestown settlement, then in its infancy, gradually began the importation of African slaves to sustain the labor force needed to operate the small farms and plantations necessary to survival in the agricultural economy. The Virginia Colony operated under a charter from the king of England; many British colonies institutionalized slavery during the seventeenth century, and in the West Indies, slavery was utilized to operate the sugar cane plantations of the French colonies. As a historical practice, institutionalized chattel slavery can be traced to ancient times, to the Greeks and Romans, and, as the documents in this book will clearly show, to biblical times, both in the Old and New Testaments. In sum, slavery had deep historical and intellectual roots in western culture. It is important to realize that in antebellum America, not everyone regarded slavery as un-American, and that the period 1776–1865 was an era of intellectual debate and conflict, when proslavery arguments were not only possible, but often were mainstream thinking, North and South.

What exactly was slavery in the United States? According to *[George] Stroud's Compendium of Laws of Slavery*,[1] (published in 1843 but also containing a summary of legal practices in the thirteen colonies during the seventeenth and eighteenth centuries), the slave had no rights whatsoever. The "chattel property" of his master, the slave had no claim to any property, no right to vote in any election, no right of inheritance, no right to a legal marriage, no claim for his children, who were often sold to new owners over his protests, no legal redress should he be unjustly treated by a white owner or overseer, absolutely no control over his time; and he was legally prohibited from ever striking a white man for any offense whatsoever. He was subjected to cruel and unusual punishments for the slightest violations of plantation obedience codes, and he had no legal or moral redress for any actions taken against him by owner or overseer, even if his wife and family were violated by actions perpetrated by whites.

He was also denied the right to an education. South Carolina enacted legislation prohibiting slave literacy in its Slave Code of 1740, and Georgia adopted the code in 1755. The progression of this prohibition against literacy among the slaves was to intensify after the American Revolution; indeed, by the early nineteenth century it was illegal to teach a slave to read and write in nine Southern states. However, in most of the colonies, the teaching of reading was associated with the promotion of Christianity, and schools for the slaves were developed for the specific purpose of training slaves to read the Scriptures. Jennifer Monaghan put it this way: "There are several implications to be drawn from these schools for the enslaved. First, at no school was writing taught, even though only two colonies legally proscribed it before the American Revolution. Second, and a function of the first, no white male taught at any of them. All instruction was provided by the politically disenfranchised—women or [literate] slaves. Third, reading instruction was motivated by the Christian requirement that children be taught to read the Scriptures. Reading was taught purely to inculcate Christianity; Christianity was believed to inculcate docility and obedience."[2] From the beginning, in colonial America the teaching of reading was separated from training in writing, which was considered a commercial skill and associated with masculine enterprise rather than domestic cultivation of the arts and letters. Slave narratives and novels like *Uncle Tom's Cabin* (1852) are filled with examples of benevolent plantation mistresses who inculcate what Horace Bushnell would call "Christian Nurture" by teaching selected slave children how to read. Some missionary societies specifically called for literacy training among the slaves as a way of spreading the gospel of Christianity.

But literacy among the slaves came to be a serious threat to the slave power of slaveholding Southerners. By the early nineteenth century, measures were developed to curtail the development of literacy among the slaves, even though this meant that the spread of Christianity among the American slave population would be achieved primarily through sermons and oral tradition. "We may identify four main factors that led, in many Southern states, to the passage of laws that attacked the teaching of any kind of literacy, reading as well as writing: first, the fear on the part of Southerners of what was called 'illegal assembly'; second, the rise of abolitionism; third, the writings of free African Americans; and fourth, the consequences of revolts led by literate Christian slaves."[3]

Miscegenation was also prohibited by law, although many slaveowners and overseers slept with their female slaves and produced offspring "mulattos," such as the brilliant and powerful Frederick Douglass. Douglass's 1845 autobiographical *Narrative* contains many examples of these oppressive practices and offers the modern reader an excellent "insider picture" of life on a Southern plantation. His mixed parentage is the source of an identity crisis from the first chapter: "My father was a white man. He was admitted to be such by all I ever heard speak of my parentage. The opinion was also whispered that my master was my father; but of the correctness of this opinion, I know nothing; the means of knowing was withheld from me." For Frederick Douglass as for many others, miscegenation resulted in identity anxiety and a determined effort to establish parental genealogy.

Another perspective on American slavery is found in a demographic analysis of the larger institution. The computer-generated facts about slavery now being provided by such organizations as the Atlantic Slave Trade Project of the Du Bois Institute of Harvard University make available to readers alarming statistics that dramatize the brutality and horror of the American slave trade. For example, in 1790, George Washington's administration conducted a primitive census of the population and produced some important, if general, figures. In 1776, the year of the Declaration of Independence, there were some 700,000 black slaves in the United States, and some 20 percent of the population of the Colonies was enslaved. In 1790 there were approximately 55,000 free blacks living in the North, and by 1820, this figure had risen to 250,000. By 1820 there were over 1,000,000 African slaves living in the South, and by 1860, this figure had risen to 3,954,000. Congress had outlawed the importation of slaves in 1808; however, thousands of slaves were imported illegally long after the slave trade was legally ended, and natural increase accounted for the remainder of this growth. By the mid-nineteenth century, calculated as a percentage of population, the United States was one of the largest slaveholding societies in the world.

Essentialist arguments about African inferiority became a prominent source of attitudes and values in the culture of antebellum America. "Racism" was a term that did not exist in the vocabulary of Americans until the twentieth century, but its meaning was well understood by writers and critics of nineteenth-century literature. Mark Twain, James Russell Lowell, John Greenleaf Whittier, and Harriet Beecher Stowe were among the nineteenth century's most outspoken literary critics of slavery. Stowe's novel, *Uncle Tom's Cabin* (1852), reached total worldwide sales of 4.5 million by 1860, and translation into sixteen languages by that year gave it a world readership estimated at 20 million. Twain's popular *Huckleberry Finn* (1885) and *Pudd'nhead Wilson* (1894), both set in antebellum America, demonstrate an intense preoccupation with issues of race, ethnicity, and the essentialist arguments about African character and quality that had been advanced by Josiah Clark Nott and George Gliddon fifty years earlier. Both of Twain's works are searing social satires, taking apart the masks of an American society that did not fully understand itself or the racial issues that divided it. Some would argue that works of fiction have little influence on the practical affairs of government and social policy. But novelists like Twain and Stowe have forced Americans of the antebellum and reconstruction United States to take a careful, clear look at the race problem that the institution of slavery produced, a problem derived from the importation of slaves for profit and labor, and a problem that has not been fully resolved in American society as we enter the twenty-first century. Modern critics like Jane Tompkins have shown the cultural work that fiction can do, and it is clear that both Stowe and Mark Twain had considerable influence in shaping America's ideology of race during the nineteenth century.

THE HISTORICAL CONTEXTS FOR THE ANTEBELLUM SLAVERY DEBATES, 1700–1865

Americans began debating the slavery issue in the late seventeenth century, when the Quakers, who had opposed slavery in Great Britain, developed arguments against the expansion of chattel slavery in North America, although their voices were muted compared to the calls for economic development of the plantation system in the Southern colonies. Early opponents of slavery were primarily religious figures, like the founder of Methodism, John Wesley, who wrote, in the 1750s, a treatise attacking the inhumanity of the institution. The Quaker meetings collectively opposed slavery, and one lone voice among them, John

Woolman, eloquently told of the anguish of conscience he suffered when required by his employer, a New Jersey lawyer, to write an indenture for the purchase of a slave. Moreover, slavery was challenged by natural rights theorists of the Enlightenment, and it is one of the ironies of American history that the most eloquent articulation of those principles composed by an American, the Declaration of Independence (1776), should have been authored by Thomas Jefferson, master of Monticello, a large Virginia plantation, and the owner of slaves. The early voices of opposition to slavery employed primarily religious arguments and pointed to biblical precedents, particularly the New Testament ethical teachings of Jesus, but proslavery advocates found many examples of slaveholding by the Israelites in the Old Testament texts.

Slavery in the early years was by no means isolated to the Southern states. Before Massachusetts outlawed slavery in the 1780s, both Cotton Mather and Increase Mather, the president of Harvard College, held household slaves, and the Reverend Jonathan Edwards, minister of the Great Awakening in New England in the 1730s and 1740s, owned a household servant named Venus. In the nineteenth century, the period with which this collection is primarily concerned, national attention to the problems of slavery was more regionally focused on the South because it had been abolished in many Northern states (New York not among them). However, the debates concerning its place in American society raged in pulpits, newspapers, and lecture halls both North and South as well as in the United States Congress and Supreme Court, so that chattel slavery was always an American, national problem rather than a simple regional issue. The passing of the Fugitive Slave Law as part of the Compromise of 1850 made all citizens of the United States participants in the institutionalization of chattel slavery, and the arguments throughout the 1850s concerning the admission of new states as "free soil" or slave kept alive the vigorous debates on both sides of the Mason-Dixon line.

Three distinct phases of the antislavery movement may be distinguished. First, religious voices extended from 1688, when a Quaker meeting issued a treatise opposing slavery on moral and religious grounds. (This type of argument is represented in this volume by Samuel Sewall's *The Selling of Joseph* [1700] and John Saffin's response to Sewall.) This phase of argumentation was also characterized by abstract moral and philosophical discourse concerning the "natural rights" of man. In England's Parliament, the debates focused also on the moral injustices of the slave trade itself. William Wilberforce and the British abolitionists mounted a well-organized campaign late in the eighteenth century that led to the outlawing of the slave trade in 1807. The United States Congress followed soon after, outlawing the trade effective January 1, 1808. This century and a half of argumentation focused more on the evils of the slave trade and less on the inhumanity of slavery as an institution. Consequently, the slave population of the Southern states continued to grow, even as Northern states were abolishing slavery, one by one. Economic pressure and the worldwide demand for cotton products entrenched the "peculiar institution" as a labor supply as never before.

The second major phase of antislavery reform extended from the abolition of the slave trade in 1808 to 1830, when William Lloyd Garrison and David Walker commenced the abolitionist crusade. This second phase was characterized by an emphasis on "gradualism," the argument that slavery should be tolerated for the existing slave population, but that the status of the mother should no longer determine the status of the child—for example, children born to slaves after a certain predetermined date should be free rather than slave. This second phase also saw the formation of the American Colonization Society in 1816–17, an organization that assumed the essential inferiority of the African to the American white, and proposed the exportation of all Africans following their emancipation. It is significant that even Garrison should have temporarily embraced colonization as a solution to America's slavery problem, a position he soon repudiated publicly. In the throes of the Civil War, as early as 1852 and as late as 1863, President Abraham Lincoln also seriously considered colonization as a solution to the problem of a divided Union. The problems associated with colonization were numerous, and included the moral argument against what was tantamount to deportation of a population only a small portion of whom had been imported from Africa. There were also immense practical problems associated with colonization, such as the enormous costs. By the 1820s, the slave population of the United States exceeded one and one-half million, and the free black population brought this figure to nearly two million.[4] By 1860, the slave population in the United States was about 3,954,000 out of a total population of only 31 million, so that the deportation of Africans to Liberia or any other African nation would have cost more than the gross national product of the new nation for an entire year. Finally, no one bothered to ask the opinion of the Africans themselves, slave or free. Most likely those who were born in the United States would have been opposed to a forced return to Africa, and while preliminary inquiries were made to the tribal governments of Liberia, the most often cited destination for the deported African-Americans, formal agreements for the absorption of millions of Africans by countries on the African continent were not made.

The significance of the demographic figures becomes clear when they are placed in a historical context and interpreted in social and political terms. For example, in 1856, the free states in the North had 144 members in the U.S. House of Representatives, while the slave states of the South had 90 members. This means that one Northern, free-state congressman represented 91,958 white men and women while one Southern, slave-state congressman represented 68,725 white men and women. Thus fewer Southern proslavery advocates than Northern antislavery representatives were required to exercise equivalent, representative power in the House of Representatives. The Southern "slave power" was a function of congressional representation, and the Southern members of Congress exercised this power regularly to perpetuate the institution of slavery on which the Southern economy was dependent.

Similarly, in the United States Senate in 1856, the sixteen free states in the North had a white population of 13,243,000 and had 32 senators. The fifteen slave states in the South, with a population of only 6,185,248, held 30 Senate seats. This translates into an unfavorable ratio for the Northern free citizens: 413,813 free citizens in the North enjoyed the same power and privilege in the Senate given to only 206,175 citizens of the slave states. Clearly, the Southern "slave power" voice could dominate the discourse. The geographical area of the fifteen slave states was 851,508 square miles, while the geographical area of the free Northern states was 612,597. Slave power held the geographical advantage, and the legislative advantage of the slaveholding states was a serious restriction on the advance of antislavery sentiment among the members of Congress.

The organized antislavery colonizationists could never command a sufficient following to oppose the "slave power" of the Southern states and their proslavery representatives in Congress. As the historian John Thomas put it,

> Some Southern planters supported the American Colonization Society in the hope that exporting free Negroes would strengthen the institution of slavery, while Northern philanthropists endorsed colonization in the equally futile expectation that it would purify American democracy by ridding the country of slaves. Thus Colonization embraced two irreconcilable points of view. On one crucial issue, however, both Northern and Southern colonizationists were agreed—the Negro was inherently inferior to the white man and had no place in a democratic society. It was precisely this sweeping assumption of inferiority and unfitness, which the pioneer abolitionists rejected. Their argument proved devastatingly simple: slavery was a sin and a crime, a sin because it denied to the African the status of human being, a crime because it violated the natural rights to life, liberty, and the pursuit of happiness guaranteed in the Declaration of Independence. These two beliefs—in the spiritual equality of all believers and the political equality of all Americans—served as the chief moral weapons in the attack on slavery.[5]

The "gradualists" and antislavery colonizationists lacked the antislavery power of the abolitionist crusade, a militant and well-organized movement that led eventually to the Thirteenth Amendment abolishing the institution of chattel slavery. The abolitionist crusaders, led by William Lloyd Garrison, Frederick Douglass, and others, dominated this third and final phase of the antislavery movement. We shall see much more of them shortly.

RACE AND THE ARGUMENTS AGAINST SLAVERY

The context of a commercial culture provided proslavery advocates with a free-trade argument for continuing the institution—indeed, for its expansion. Slaves were commercial property, and a pervasive acceptance of race theory empowered the continuation and extension of slavery into the Western territories. As the historian Barbara Fields has suggested, "ideas about color are always mediated by prevailing social relations. To assume, by intention or default, that race is a phenomenon outside history is to take up a position within the terrain of racialist ideology and to become its unknowing, and therefore uncontesting, victim."[6] The nineteenth century in America became a battleground for race and slavery discourse long before it became a literal battlefield at Gettysburg and Atlanta.

Originally, the slavery debate was a debate about the slave trade. Numerous versions of the argument in favor of the slave trade appeared, paralleling those few voices such as the Quaker John Woolman, who argued against slavery and for the natural rights of individuals. But even Woolman, in *Some Considerations on the Keeping of Negroes*,[7] condemned the trade more than the inhumanity of slavery: "Though there were Wars and Desolations among Negroes, before the Europeans began to trade there for Slaves, yet now the Calamities are greatly increased, so many thousands being annually brought from thence, and we, by purchasing them, with Views of self interest, are become Parties with them, and accessory to that Increase." The central slave-trade questions were raised rhetorically in a text by James Swan of England, whose *Discourse to Great Britain* (1772) was more a critique of the presence of slavery in an enlightened society than it was a religious argument. For Swan and other British opponents of the slave trade, the advocates of slavery had not developed a sufficiently rational argument to justify the cruelty of the trade itself. It would require a later fusion of moral suasion and religious rhetoric by the nineteenth-century abolitionists and other writers to bring about a reconsideration of the whole ideology of slavery, including race theory. As the historian Philip Gould observes, "for the eighteenth century, *the slave trade as a corrupt commercial activity* became a means of defining negatively the ideal of enlightened society and thereby a way of legitimizing the mores of a modern commercial society once the slave trade issue had been resolved."[8] The slave trade was abolished in England in 1807, and by the United States Congress on January 1, 1808. Until these political acts were taken, the debate concerning slavery focused less on the status of slaves as a racially inferior people and more on the evils of the trade itself. As late as 1820, Daniel Webster would argue against the evils of the slave trade with little emphasis on the inhumanity of slave ownership itself. Antislavery critiques of the brutal "Middle Passage" were common in the late eighteenth and early nineteenth centuries.

The abolitionist crusade in America changed the focus to the horrors of the institution of slavery itself. The moral inconsistencies of a nation founded on principles of human equality while permitting chattel slavery through its Constitution and legislative processes became pivotal arguments for the antislavery advocates after 1808 and the legal ending of the transatlantic trade.

But in the early nineteenth century, another major obstacle developed for the antislavery movement, namely, the rise of scientific or pseudoscientific theories of race and the classification of humanity into a hierarchy of racial groups. It is this pseudoscientific movement that installed the searing stereotypes in the American imagination. No sooner had the slave trade been outlawed as unchristian and uncivilized for an "enlightened west," than racial classification theories were developed to maintain the institution of chattel slavery and to degrade the African.

In 1831, the slave Nat Turner led a rebellion in Virginia that had wide-ranging effects on the debate on slavery.[9] Turner's revolutionaries butchered the bodies of over sixty white people, resulting in his capture and execution. The savage insurrection and the equally savage repression of the revolt fueled anxiety about emancipation, especially in the South where the African-American population was large. While the revolt momentarily retarded the influence of the abolitionist societies in New England, it also contributed to the debate concerning the essential nature of the African and his future role in American society. At precisely this moment in American history, Tocqueville was asserting that the very future of the democracy itself rested on the ability of the white population to assimilate equally with the African slave population following emancipation, which he saw as inevitable. But the Richmond debates of 1831–32 turned things around, highlighting the potential violence of slave insurrections.

While Tocqueville's discussion centered on the issue of racial equality and emancipation, at Richmond, Virginia, the debate focused on the proposal of Thomas Jefferson Randolph—grandson to the president—who called for a referendum on emancipation, arguing that slavery itself had produced the Nat Turner rebellion. A racist, repatriation argument itself, Randolph's proposal nevertheless was met with hostility in the South.[10] Professors and educators entered the dialogue vigorously. Their influence extended not only over their students, but far more widely through their publications concerning racial inequality. Thomas R. Dew's *Review of the Debate* (1832) argued that emancipation would be catastrophic, even apocalyptic, because Africans were "utterly unfit for a state of freedom among the whites. . . . the emancipated black carries a mark which no time can erase; he forever wears the symbol of his inferior condition; the Ethiopian cannot change his skin, nor the leopard his spots." As Reginald Horsman puts it, "Blackness, not slavery, was the essential cause of the Negro condition," according to Dew, who "avoided the more scientific species question, but his general theme was clear; blacks could not be free to participate in white society, for all men and all races were not created equal."[11]

It is important to remember that in the historical context, there was often confusion and ambiguity when a document did not specifically sanction or condemn slavery. For example, while antislavery advocates could point to the Declaration of Independence and its assertion that "all men are created equal" to validate their arguments, they were less able to use the Constitution as a resource because the framers of that document avoided all mention of slavery and thus left enormous uncertainty as to its application to the African slave or freeman. Similarly, just as most proslavery advocates turned to their Bibles, especially the Old Testament, to find support for their arguments, so antislavery abolitionists turned to Scripture to find support for their moral positions. Most Southerners and a sizable number of abolitionists saw the Constitution as proslavery, especially after Garrison and Phillips had written analyses of the Constitution as a proslavery compact, and many abolitionists would have regarded the essential message of the Bible to be antislavery, its Old Testament examples notwithstanding.

One example among many captures this inherent ambiguity and the passions of the times. In 1857, Abraham Lincoln became outraged by the publication of a volume authored by the Reverend Frederick A. Ross, pastor of the Presbyterian Church in Huntsville, Alabama. The book, *Slavery Ordained of God*, was a collection of Ross sermons that took very extreme positions to argue the natural and biblical inferiority of the African, using reasoning based on Old Testament models of slaveholding (Abraham and Hagar, for example) as well as the genealogical descent of Africans from Cain and Canaan, who are both cursed in the Book of Genesis. A staunch defender of the "rightness" of slavery and an opponent of abolitionism, Ross was a believer in the essential, natural inferiority of the African. With characteristic precision and logic, Lincoln wrote: "Suppose it is true, that the Negro is inferior to the white, in the gifts of nature, is it not the exact reverse of justice that the white should, for that reason, take from the Negro, any part of the little which has been given him? 'Give to him that is needy,' is the Christian rule of charity; but 'Take from him that is needy,' is the rule of slavery."

As the historian Mark Neely has made clear, Lincoln "did not tackle the Biblical argument."[12] But Lincoln made extremely clear his division of proslavery and antislavery arguments into the two camps of "right" and "wrong," a moral position which is easily dissociated from biblical reasoning and exegesis. Lincoln argued:

> The sum of proslavery theology seems to be this: "Slavery is not universally right, nor yet universally wrong; it is better for some people to be slaves, and, in such cases, it is the Will of God that they be such." Certainly there is no contending with the Will of God; but still there is some difficulty in ascertaining and applying it to particular cases—for instance, we will suffer the Rev. Dr. Ross has a slave named Sambo, and the question is, "Is it the Will of God that Sambo shall remain a slave or be set free?" The Almighty gives no available answer to the question, and His revelation,—the Bible—gives none or none but such as admits of a squabble as to its meaning. No one thinks of asking Sambo's opinion on it, so, at last, it comes to this, that Dr. Ross is to decide the question. And while he considers it, he sits in the shade with gloves on his hands and subsists on the bread that Sambo is earning in the burning sun. If he decides that God wills Sambo to continue a slave, he thereby retains his own comfortable position, but if he decides that God wills Sambo to be free, he thereby has to walk out of the shade, throw off his gloves, and labor for his own bread. Will Dr. Ross be activated by that imperfect partiality, which has ever been considered not favorable to correct visions?

Lincoln's anecdotal style in this imaginative response to Ross, and his use of the Sambo example to destroy the arguments from biblical precedent advanced by Ross and his contemporaries, juxtapose the moral argument of human example with the absurd logic of historical, biblical reasoning. Lincoln was clearly no biblical "fundamentalist," taking Scripture to be literally the word of God; rather, he sought the "spirit behind the letter," and as he does in the Ross response, he argued the spiritual content of Christian doctrine rather than the literal, historical precedent of Scripture.

This is only one of many such examples. The Reverend Thornton Stringfellow of Virginia developed elaborate strategies for claiming African inferiority

based primarily on scriptural example, arguments from Nature, and examples
taken from the "family of man," an almost Jungian appeal to the universal subordination of children to their parents worldwide, claiming in the end that the
African never actually achieves the status of an adult and should therefore always be subordinated to the European. Stringfellow elaborately examined Paul's
letter to Philemon, which treats the problem of the runaway slave, Onesimus,
and concluded that Paul himself endorsed slavery as it would be practiced in the
United States in the 1840s. The Reverend Alexander McCaine also argued for
the institution of slavery, not only from the many examples of slavery found in
the Old Testament but also from the absence of sanctions in Christ's teachings
in the New Testament.

In many antebellum documents, moral and philosophical arguments were
separated from biblical precedents, and while the proponents of slavery were
hard-pressed to find "moral" support for the "peculiar institution" in America,
the Bible provided abundant examples of slavery that made it difficult for the
abolitionists to turn to Scripture as a primary text in support of their cause.
Nevertheless, some courageous ministers ventured into the murky waters of
Scripture to find support for their antislavery positions. One of these, Alexander
McLeod, was a Scotsman who ministered to the Reformed Presbyterian Church
in New York in the decades before the Civil War. His powerful sermon, *Negro
Slavery Unjustifiable* (1802 and 1846), is an example of the rhetorical strategies
that ministers who opposed slavery utilized when they turned to the Bible for
historical and scriptural support. Moral and biblical arguments were advanced
by James Freeman Clarke, whose *Slavery in the United States*, a Thanksgiving
Day sermon for 1842, was an early and popular example of antislavery rhetoric.
Clarke also wrote a jeremiad against the organized church in its support of
slavery, *The Church As It Was, As It Is, and As It Ought to Be* (1848). This
document follows the tradition of Puritan denunciations of communal sin dating back to the seventeenth century. Clarke's sermon is accompanied in this
volume by selections from his contemporary, William Ellery Channing, minister
of the Arlington Street Church in Boston, who used his pulpit to oppose the
increasing support for the institution of slavery that was growing steadily inside
the organized church, both North and South. Although Channing was not a
militant abolitionist like William Lloyd Garrison, he spoke frequently and
effectively against slavery from one of the most prominent pulpits in New
England. His 1835 publication of a comprehensive study, *Slavery*, provided a
historical, moral, biblical, and political perspective on antebellum America's
most pressing social issue.

NINETEENTH-CENTURY RACE THEORY ARGUMENTS

It is impossible to understand the antebellum slavery debates without some
command of the race theories that were advanced to promote and defend the
institution. The slavery debates are complex and often confusing because they
encompass so many venues of argumentation, from moral, philosophical, and
biblical arguments to emerging challenges to Scripture from science, such as

Charles Darwin's *On the Origin of Species* (1859) and the investigations of Josiah Clark Nott and George R. Gliddon, *Indigenous Races of the Earth, or, New Chapters of Ethnological Inquiry* (1857). Darwin eventually had more influence over the science of social and cultural anthropology, but before the Civil War, Nott and Gliddon's scientific anthropological study exerted significant influence on American thinking about the status of the African in American society. The scientists argued "polygenesis" or multiple creations throughout the world, which gave the proslavery advocates a new platform for their view of African inferiority and the "rightness" of slavery as ordained by God. Those abolitionists who advanced the argument that the races were equal used the biblical version of Creation, the "monogenic" theory, which stated that while Adam and Eve may not have been the true, literal parents of all humankind, there was nevertheless a single creation from which all persons derive, thereby establishing an argument that cultural differences and environment constitute the major mutations in the development of a diverse, multicultural population. But even among the abolitionists there were very few advocates of racial equality, and the "race theory" documents in this volume are overwhelmingly supportive of the view that the African is essentially inferior to the white.

Relying on earlier Renaissance investigations into racial grouping, the "scientists" of race theory, like James Cowles Pritchard in England and Josiah Friedrich Blumenbach in Germany, developed five major racial groups:

Caucasian-Aryan-white
American–Native American
Mongoloid–East Asian
Malay–Pacific Islander
Negroid-African-black

American researchers like Samuel F. B. Morse (inventor of the Morse code), Samuel Morton, J. B. Turner, Josiah Nott, George R. Gliddon, J. H. Van Evrie, and O. S. Fowler, the phrenologist, advanced particularly strong challenges to the doctrine that "all men are created equal" as they sought to establish this "hierarchy of races" not only in the scientific literature, but also in the popular cultural assumptions about race. As allies of the proslavery advocates, the scientific community posited equally unsubstantiated theories of race arguing the natural, essential inferiority of the African that were widely accepted in antebellum culture, appearing in political discourse and in the racial stereotyping of minstrel entertainment and in fictional representations from Stowe's *Uncle Tom's Cabin* (1852) to Margaret Mitchell's *Gone with the Wind* (1936).

Numerous widely circulated publications were spawned by these investigations, which advanced the belief in polygenesis—that there were multiple origins in creation—and that physical, moral, and intellectual differences and other distinctions among the races constituted a classification system that could not be altered through emancipation or educational advancement, or any change in the social order. There were "essential" or "natural" qualities in race theory that were irrevocable; individuals might excel or achieve greatness, but one's racial and ethnic grouping had a determining influence on ability and character. Blumen-bach paved the way for later cranial and phrenological theories of human intelligence.

As Reginald Horsman has noted,[13] one such publication was Samuel George Morton's *Crania Americana* (1839), which was based on the author's collection of human skulls. "Comparing cranial size, capacity, and structure, Morton em-phasized the basic physical differences between races. By the end of the 1840s, he contended that there had been various creations of human beings in different parts of the world" at different historical moments, a polygenic theory that was welcomed by literary proslavery advocates such as John Pendleton Kennedy. Morton's research, though controversial, was regarded as basic to an understand-ing of human racial origins until Darwin shattered the work of the American school with his publication of *On the Origin of Species* in 1859 and *The Descent of Man* in 1871 (Horsman, p. 125). But the damage had been done. Popular cultural assumptions about race took support from the writings of Josiah Clark Nott and George R. Gliddon, a professor of anthropology and a doctor of medicine who contributed *Indigenous Races of the Earth, or, New Chapters of Ethnological Inquiry* (1857) and the influential polygenic treatise, *Types of Man-kind* (1843). The floodgates were open, and minstrel show caricatures were not far behind these pseudoscientific arguments, with their harsh stereotypes and role models that were widely embraced in popular culture. As the historian Thomas Cassirer notes,

> In the first decade of the 1800s, a major intellectual shift occurred. Some scholars and scientists, particularly in France, began to introduce the idea that humanity was divided into a permanent hierarchy of races, with each race having immutable physi-ological, intellectual, and moral characteristics of its own. White Europeans were at the very top; the African at the very bottom. The enlightenment "unity of mankind" ideal was thus repudiated. This meant that it was no longer necessary to deny black people's humanity in order to enslave them; blacks were simply an inferior race of humans and would always be so. Their fate was to remain subordinate to white Europeans who alone had the ability to master knowledge and rule the world. Such theories, relying on bias and selective evidence, would inspire the European view of the world for the following century and a half and provide the ideological frame-work for the next wave of colonial imperialism.[14]

The essentialist tenets of race theory influenced nearly all antebellum slavery debates. As was argued when slave literacy posed a threat to social order, race theorists developed an ideology that claimed the inferiority and brutality of the African contrasted with the reasoned intelligence of the Caucasian.

If these racist theories served to justify slavery, they also frequently coexisted with abolitionist sentiments that assumed the inferiority of Africans while op-posing slavery. Indeed, among the abolitionists themselves, there were only iso-lated voices for full racial equality, such as those of Garrison, Wendell Phillips, Gerrit Smith, and Lydia Maria Child. Even the prominent abolitionist Theodore Parker has been shown to have embraced the theories of race that permeated antebellum American society.

Alongside the abolition movement was the movement for colonization, which assumed essential racial differences, and advocated a mass exodus of all persons of African origin to Liberia or other destinations on the African continent. Thinkers as diverse as Thomas Jefferson and Abraham Lincoln embraced the idea temporarily. Indeed, during the Civil War, President Lincoln developed elaborate schemes for the emancipation of the American slaves, which would be immediately followed by colonization or deportation to Latin America, Africa, the Caribbean, and other locations outside the United States. Even William Lloyd Garrison had an early flirtation with colonization, in an 1829 speech to the American Colonization Society, a view he later repudiated publicly in an editorial in *The Liberator*.

Perhaps no American so poignantly captures the ease with which race theory and abolition could coexist as Abraham Lincoln, the Moses of emancipation. In the Lincoln-Douglas debates of 1858, the future president said:

> I say that I am not, nor ever have been, in favor of bringing about in any way the social and political equality of the white and black races. I am not now, nor ever have been, in favor of making voters or jurors of Negroes, nor of qualifying them to hold office, nor to intermarry with white people, and I will say in addition to this that there is a physical difference between the white and black races which I believe will forever forbid the two races living together on terms of social and political equality. And inasmuch as they cannot so live, while they do remain together, there must be the position of superior and inferior, and I as much as any other man am in favor of having the superior position assigned to the white race.

Here, Lincoln echoed a view held by most Americans at mid-century.

United States Supreme Court Chief Justice Roger B. Taney (1777–1864) put race theory to work as legislative power of the most influential kind, namely, as supporting arguments for his opinions in *Groves v Slaughter* (1841), *Prigg v Pennsylvania* (1842), *Strader v Graham* (1850), and *Dred Scott v Sandford* (1857). A few lines from the latter decision will make the point:

> The legislation and histories of the times, and the language used in the Declaration of Independence, show that neither the class of persons who had been imported as slaves, nor their descendants, whether they had become free or not, were then acknowledged as part of the people to be included in the general words used in that memorable instrument. It is difficult at this day to realize the state of public opinion in relation to that unfortunate race, which prevailed in the civilized and enlightened portions of the world at the time of the Declaration of Independence, and when the Constitution of the United States was framed and adopted. They had for more than a century before been regarded as beings of an inferior order, and altogether unfit to associate with the white race, either in social or political relations; and so far inferior, that they had no rights which the white man was bound to respect; and that

the Negro might justly and lawfully be reduced to slavery. He was bought and sold, and treated as an ordinary article of merchandise and traffic, whenever a profit could be made by it. This opinion was at that time fixed and universal in the civilized portion of the white race.

In this blanket justification of the continuation of slavery, penned at the time of the Compromise of 1850 and its infamous Fugitive Slave Law, the chief justice of the Supreme Court of the United States endorsed passionately the race theory arguments of Blumenbach, Pritchard, Nott, Gliddon, Van Evrie, and O. S. Fowler.

It is into this climate of hostile race-theory opinion that the courageous abolitionists and antislavery authors ventured. At the tender age of twenty-six, in 1831, in his first editorial for *The Liberator*, William Lloyd Garrison made clear his position: "*I am in earnest—I will not equivocate—I will not excuse—I will not retreat a single inch—and I will be heard.*" Garrison's courage was matched by his determination to bring an end to chattel slavery, and unlike Lincoln, he lived to see the passage of the Thirteenth Amendment to the Constitution in 1865, and of subsequent civil rights legislation. Having no power, the abolitionists sought to exert moral influence, what came to be known as "moral suasion." Whether or not they also embraced contemporary race theory, the abolitionists and antislavery writers were united in their opposition to the institution of chattel slavery, and most criticized or satirized the race-theory extremes of Pritchard, Blumenbach, Nott, and Gliddon. For example, at the century's end, Mark Twain published *Pudd'nhead Wilson*, in which the whole "essentialist" theory of race is inverted and savagely attacked. Twain shows how Tom Driscoll, the slave master's child who has been mistakenly raised as a slave, is wholly unfit to return to white society on the discovery of his "true" parentage, precisely because he had been a slave for two decades and was therefore shaped by his environment in spite of his essential or natural attributes. Twain's concluding portrait of Driscoll is that of a pathetic man who is a displaced person, a man without a country, *not because he is naturally inferior, but precisely because he has been mistreated for so long as a slave.* As Tom Driscoll returns to white society, we are told that the institution of slavery has completely destroyed him, body and soul:

> He could neither read nor write, and his speech was the basest dialect of the Negro quarter. His gait, his attitudes, his gestures, his bearing, his laugh—all were vulgar and uncouth; his manners were the manners of a slave. . . . The poor fellow could not endure the terrors of the white man's parlor, and felt at home and peace nowhere but in the kitchen. The family pew was a misery to him, yet he could nevermore enter into the solacing refuge of the "nigger gallery."

This is a very clear statement of the influence of environment over heredity, of social condition over essential character. It is a damning critique of biological race theory, and an even harsher judgment of social Darwinism, by which it was argued that regardless of social conditions and education, Nature would perpetuate the survival of only the fittest and the overpowering of the weak by the strong, the subordination of the naturally, essentially inferior to the naturally, essentially superior. Tom Driscoll, the all-white son of the master, has been turned into a pitiful spectacle of humanity, proving that his decline was the direct influence of the institution of slavery on its victims, regardless of genetic makeup or lineage. Frederick Douglass also challenged race theory in a speech at Western Reserve Academy on July 12, 1854, where the ex-slave confronted the pseudoscience issue in an address called "The Claims of the Negro Ethnologically Considered." But it was Stowe and Twain who reached the widest audience with representations of race that challenged the fundamental tenets of race theory.

THE STOWE DEBATE

Not only did the literary abolitionists of the nineteenth century struggle with racial values and attitudes that were shaped by the legalization of chattel slavery in the Southern states, but they also worked to correct the essentialist arguments of the antebellum scientific community. There is a very long history of resistance to slavery among the novelists and poets of the nineteenth century, coupled with an espousal of the equality argument in the decades following the Civil War. If Harriet Beecher Stowe developed racial stereotypes in *Uncle Tom's Cabin* that would cause James Baldwin to castigate her method, she clearly also developed one of the most powerful antislavery arguments mounted in the decades before 1861, and the sales figures of her novel in the United States alone show the enormous influence of her work in a culture that was uncertain of its democratic objectives and struggling to resolve the moral inconsistencies posed by the presence of chattel slavery.

In 1861, the total population of the United States was some 32 million persons. Of these, some 4 million were chattel slaves, about 90 percent illiterate and most certainly prohibited from reading Stowe's inflammatory novel. In many Southern states, the book had been effectively banned, further reducing the available reading population. At the time, the literacy rate throughout the Northern states was only about 50 percent, so the target group for Stowe's novel numbered some 12 or 13 million men, women, and children, among whom several million copies of *Uncle Tom's Cabin* were circulated. This is an astonishing figure, and it is for this reason that Stowe's novel must be read not only for its obvious racial stereotyping but also for the influence it had in turning the national conscience against chattel slavery. To be sure, the stereotypes are there, from Topsy the pickaninny to the sacrificial and nurturing Uncle Tom himself. But Stowe reached the masses of Northern readers with her sentimental novel that dramatized the plight of the plantation slave in ways that few political addresses could.

An assessment of Stowe's method should rest on two arguments. First, she should not be held responsible for the post–Civil War abuses of her characters by the manufacturers of Topsy dolls or the minstrel show dramatizations of her work, including nine simultaneous productions of chapters of the novel in New York City alone in the year 1859. Second, the novel is not only structured as a politically powerful sentimental narrative with insertions of sermonizing and moralizing by the narrator; it is also filled with satiric elements that inspire the reader to outrage, revulsion, agreement, or action.

In his noted critique of Stowe's book, "Everybody's Protest Novel" (1949), James Baldwin wrote: "*Uncle Tom's Cabin* is a very bad novel, having, in its self-righteous, virtuous sentimentality, much in common with *Little Women*. Sentimentality, the ostentatious parading of excessive and spurious emotion, is the mark of dishonesty, the inability to feel; the wet eyes of the sentimentalist betray his aversion to experience, his fear of life, his arid heart and is always, therefore, the signal of secret and violent inhumanity, the mask of cruelty." This is obviously a powerful statement. However, when Baldwin begins to attack Stowe's characters, one by one, he misses the point of the satirical method Stowe employed as a wake-up call to her readers and their values. Moreover, Stowe places herself squarely in the context of the novel's stereotypes. In the 1853 *Key to Uncle Tom's Cabin*, a document exhaustively drafted comprising all of Stowe's sources for the novel itself, she suggests that the stereotypical, sanctimonious Aunt Ophelia is a version of herself, from the moral righteousness Ophelia enforces on St. Clare's plantation to her revulsion at having to love and nurture Topsy, when the child is given to her by St. Clare as a personal slave. Baldwin himself acknowledges this self-portrait when he declares that "Miss Ophelia, as we may suppose, was speaking for the author." With characteristic New England reserve and reluctance, perhaps even a revulsion, Ophelia overcomes her prejudices and "race theory" biases to provide what Horace Bushnell would call "Christian Nurture," but not before St. Clare has confronted her with some of her own prejudices. In chapter 20, "Topsy," we find the classic separation of the races accepted by most antebellum Americans:

> There stood the two children, representatives of the two extremes of society. The fair, high bred child, with her golden head, her deep eyes, her spiritual, noble brow, and prince-like movements; and her black, keen, subtle, cringing, yet acute neighbor. They stood the representatives of their races. The Saxon, born of ages of cultivation, command, education, physical and moral eminence; the Afric, born of ages of oppression, submission, ignorance, toil, and vice!

This trope, vigorously attacked by African-American criticism since 1852 and exploited by proslavery advocates, Reconstruction race-theorists, and minstrel dramatists, has provided the centerpiece of "The Stowe Debate" since the novel first appeared. But the passage should be contextualized. It is, first, part of a local debate between St. Clare and Ophelia about "Nurture" versus "Nature" in Topsy's character. Recalling slave master Shelby's patronizing treatment of young Harry in the Jim Crow sequence in chapter 1, Stowe asks readers to examine carefully the prejudices and biases they harbor toward their African brothers and sisters. Especially in this chapter, the book holds up a satirical mirror to the readership and challenges the cultural assumptions concerning race so pervasive in mid-century America. Like the best of Jonathan Swift's satirical writing, these searing stereotypes require that readers come to terms with them, precisely by evaluating how powerfully they create in themselves agreement or revulsion. Stowe employs the technique of satirical writing present in literature from Lucian and the Book of Job to Swift, Pope, and Dickens. Stowe's novel, then, is not only a moral and spiritual call to arms concerning the social and political institution of chattel slavery; it is also a satirical masterpiece requiring nineteenth-century readers to look carefully at their attitudes toward everything from women in marriage to race theory.

Stowe's racial stereotypes are crucial to her method of critical discourse, and to the resolution of ideological conflict contained in the novel's drama. Fundamentally, Stowe not only relies on the tradition of sentiment and the rhetoric of sermons familiar to her reading audience, she also exaggerates all of her characters precisely in order to make them appear larger than life, unreal, and "representative" of racial, religious, or moral values. Josiah Henson, on whom Tom is based, conducted a large party of slaves from Maryland to Kentucky, with some of their journey passing through the free state of Ohio, delivering his entire group to his master as promised. But Tom is even more conciliatory, obedient, and forgiving than Henson. Tom's exaggerated character becomes that of a Christ-like martyr who must be sacrificed on the altar of man's greed for power. Similarly, Simon Legree, now a synonym for debauchery and cruelty, must be developed as a modern Satan figure, the embodiment of evil and decadence, so that their eventual and inevitable confrontation in the "crucifixion" scene gives the reader no moral ambivalence: evil confronts good, only this time, Black is good and White is Satanic.

Uncle Tom's Cabin is a classic, textbook example of Wolfgang Iser's "reader response" theory, where the audience participates as much in the creation of meaning as the author. The final paragraphs of the novel are a sermonic jeremiad and a wake-up call for a sinful, decadent nation. Like Mark Twain, Stowe shows a preference for Nurture over Nature and essentialism, though she often seems to want to have it both ways, to argue against the institution of chattel slavery with her fellow abolitionists, but to simultaneously observe that Nurture will have to work hard to overcome Nature. Indeed, the ambiguities of the final chapter in the book have led Baldwin and others to judge the stereotyping in the novel as supportive of a racist agenda. But once again: our modern, so-called enlightened perspective should not dismiss Stowe's immensely powerful and satirical arguments for the termination of chattel slavery, regardless of how we may also wish to view the racial values she inherited from the race theorists so pervasive in antebellum America. To do so would be to view her work ahistorically, out of context, and without a full consideration for the value of that work in its own time.

While Stowe and the literary abolitionists did not produce the polemical diatribes of William Lloyd Garrison, the militant abolitionists, or the slave narrators, their work clearly reflected the issues of the antebellum slavery debates, and they reached a much larger audience than did *The Liberator* and other antislavery society documents. And it is to the literary abolitionists that readers in later centuries owe a significant debt, for the "canonization" of their works in college and university American literature curricula has popularized the slavery issue when the writings of the abolitionist crusade were largely ignored or forgotten.

SLAVE NARRATORS AND THE ANTEBELLUM SLAVE NARRATIVE

Any balanced and thorough account of the antebellum slavery debates must begin with the slave narratives themselves. These long-neglected accounts are, in a word, the original "literary responses" to slavery, which was an established political, social, and economic institution long before it was the subject of moral and religious debate. The slave narratives provided much authenticity for the antebellum debates, and it is slave narratives that also provide the foundation for twentieth-century literary representations of slavery. The slave narrators are the original response group because these narratives were written by victims of the system, persons who examine the experience of slavery from an insider's point of view. Some of the most prominent titles include:

The Interesting Narrative of the Life of Olaudah Equiano, or Gustavas Vassa, the African, Written by Himself (1789), an eighteenth-century slave narrative that includes a graphic description of the infamous "Middle Passage," a description Steven Spielberg utilized in his account of the Amistad mutiny.

An Autobiography of the Rev. Josiah Henson (1842), ostensibly the prototype for the character of Uncle Tom in Stowe's 1852 novel.

The three autobiographical accounts authored by Frederick Douglass, including Narrative of the Life of Frederick Douglass, an American Slave, Written by Himself (1845); My Bondage and My Freedom (1855); and The Life and Times of Frederick Douglass (1881).

Harriet Jacobs, Linda: Incidents in the Life of a Slave Girl, composed in 1857–59 but not published until 1861, just as the Civil War commenced.

These are, of course, only a few of over one hundred such titles. Most antebellum slave narratives contain these conventional patterns of spiritual, autobiographical narration:

1. A journey motif in which the narrator's personal experience is metaphorically paralleled by a spiritual awakening to freedom.

2. A sense of the narrator's isolation in a hostile environment that imposes barriers which must be crossed in the journey to freedom, barriers which preclude a full realization of the self.

3. Several prominent episodes along the way where transformations occur, such as the gaining of literacy or an awareness of the importance of literacy to freedom.

4. An escape structure, in which the predator and prey are always closely linked in an intense pursuit.

5. The presence of multiple narrative voices, as the adult narrator recapitulates earlier experiences in slavery and then provides commentary both moral and interpretative, as viewed from an adult perspective on past events.

6. A litany of gothic representations of the horrors of slavery, including flogging and auction scenes.

7. An emphasis on the slave's family, including attempts to establish an authentic genealogy where possible.[15]

These features, many of them shared with the antecedent models of Puritan spiritual autobiography, constitute a "typology" for the American antebellum slave narrative. However, it would be historically and politically incorrect for critics to argue that these qualities prove that the abolitionist editors like William Lloyd Garrison and Lydia Maria Child actually composed the slave narratives, simply because the documents appear to follow a common formula. Rather, all slave narratives shared the common objective of bringing an end to the institution of chattel slavery, and whatever emphases seemed to work with the reading public, the narrators utilized in realizing this objective. Both Garrison and Child edited slave narratives, but they were not the authors of the documents they edited.

The antebellum slave narratives have gained much prominence since the 1960s, with the introduction of African-American history courses, programs, and departments. Similarly, postwar scholarship has focused on the experience of the slave in America.[16] This wealth of recent scholarship makes some distinctions necessary, in particular between the antebellum slave narratives, which followed conventional literary models, and the reminiscences by former slaves written after 1865, especially those orally delivered by elderly former slaves to WPA workers during the 1930s. These reminiscences are generally unstructured accounts in which some episodes are highly romanticized; and few could be characterized as having the determined agenda of illuminating the horrors of slavery. Kenneth Rawick's multivolume edited collection of these oral testimonials is now widely available in libraries. However, it is the antebellum slave narrative that has so significantly influenced nineteenth- and twentieth-century writing. *Beloved*, by the African-American Nobel Prize–winning author Toni Morrison, follows closely the typology of the antebellum narratives, while violating the historical chronology; and in Ralph Ellison's *The Invisible Man*, the narrative voice closely resembles that of a Douglass narrative. These modern writers have recreated the slave narrative either through plot, characterization, voice, or some combination of these narrative elements.[17]

Morrison's *Beloved* provides an excellent example of the continuing relevance of these narratives, and in the process, it challenges the idea that the legal end of institutional slavery "brings about freedom by depicting the emotional and psychological scars of slavery as well as the persistence of racism."[18] Morrison especially has suggested that the horrors of chattel slavery can only be known through historical research into extant antebellum slave narratives and through some of the primary sources written by whites. Out of this, she has recreated the emotional and psychological as well as the historical experience of slavery for twentieth-century audiences. For example, *Beloved* recounts the common phenomenon of infanticide, basing its story on the nineteenth-century Margaret Garner episode. Like William Faulkner's fiction, Lisa Siegman observes, Morrison's novel does not follow the strictly chronological order of the antebellum narrative but uses multiple points of view to suggest that historical time is less important than the ethical and moral issues raised by a society where the taking of the life of one's own child is preferable to allowing it to live a life of slavery.[19] (Mark Twain had his central character, Roxy, wrestle briefly with the same question, in *Pudd'nhead Wilson*.) Morrison is clearly indebted to Harriet Jacobs's *Incidents* (1861), in which Jacobs observes, "If God has bestowed beauty upon her, it will prove her greatest curse. That which commands admiration in the white woman only hastens the degradation of the female slave."[20]

Ultimately, *Beloved*, as it recapitulates nineteenth-century slave culture, struggles to answer the question of how the individual, the family, the community, and indeed the reader, are supposed to reconcile an act of motherhood which would value taking the life of the child over allowing the child to live as a slave. By drawing on the narrative devices of James Joyce and William Faulkner, and by setting the murder in free Ohio, Morrison's novel transcends time, and a nineteenth-century ethical dilemma becomes a formidable twentieth-century moral issue. The antebellum slave narratives clearly provided not only theme and material for twentieth-century African-American authors, but also a moral landscape out of which the arguments of these fictional accounts could be fashioned. As Raymond Hedin put it, "More generally, the open-ended quality which characterizes so much twentieth-century black fiction is less a reflection of the concurrent mainstream tendencies than a means of suggesting, as the slave narratives did, that the larger story of the race, which black writers have continued to represent in their narratives, is still very much undecided."[21]

PROSLAVERY FICTION

We must not assume that the only "literary responses" to slavery were attacks on the system like *Beloved* or *Uncle Tom's Cabin*. Popular proslavery novels such as John Pendleton Kennedy's *Swallow Barn* (1832) and Mary Eastman's *Aunt Phillis's Cabin* (1852)—a direct response to Stowe—developed highly romanticized visions of Southern plantation life, graphically captured by Currier and Ives in "Old Times on the Plantation," reproduced in this volume. This illustration was widely circulated and was eventually engraved for *Harper's Illustrated Weekly*. It compares with another proslavery illustration, also for *Harper's*, entitled "The Happy Slaves; or Life on the Plantation" (1854). In this picture, we find well-dressed slave children wearing handsome dresses, gingham skirts, and aprons, gaily playing in front of the small slave cabin, which has a stone chimney with hearth, window boxes adorned with flowers, and mullioned glass windows and doors insulating the cabin from the elements. The parents are at leisure to attend to domestic tasks in the yard of the house, while in the background, far in the distance, rising on a hill toward an earthly heaven, is the "big house" with its columns and grandeur, where the master sits comfortably on the porch observing the behavior of his docile and obedient slave children. This paternalistic, idealized version of Southern plantation life follows the typology of the extended slave family, branching out from slaveowner George Washington's theory of the master's benevolence, and gave proslavery advocates a positive image to put before the public.

Kennedy and Eastman presented widely read and accepted views of plantation life, so that antislavery writers such as Stowe and James Russell Lowell and poets such as John Greenleaf Whittier had an uphill struggle to convince the reading public of what Theodore Dwight Weld had called *American Slavery As It Is* (1839). It would take the powerful arguments of the abolitionist crusade to bring the slavery issue into such national prominence that it ultimately overwhelmed the proslavery arguments that had perpetuated the "peculiar institution" for nearly two centuries.

THE ABOLITIONIST CRUSADE, 1830–1865

Freedom is and has always been America's root concern, a concern
that found dramatic expression in the abolitionist movement. The
most important and revolutionary reform in our country's past, it
forced the American people to come to grips with an anomaly that
would not down—the existence of slavery in the land of the free.
Benjamin Quarles, *The Black Abolitionists*, 1969

In contrast to the antislavery movement as a whole, the "abolitionist movement" or "abolitionist crusade" was a specific, historical group action that is associated with the publication of David Walker's *Appeal* in 1830 and the appearance of William Lloyd Garrison's *The Liberator* in 1831. Walker, an African-American, was an early proponent of racial equality, with special emphasis on political and social equality, and he was joined by the Garrisonians, who not only argued for equality and for an end to racial prejudice, but also emphatically called for "immediate, unconditional emancipation," without compensation to the slaveowners. These abolitionists were characterized by a militant tone, and by exceptional organizational skills. Their message of reform was naturally evangelical, and they adopted many of the tactics of the American Tract Society, whose expansion and missionary zeal had reached all corners of the new nation through national, regional, and local organizations.

William Lloyd Garrison (1805–79) is generally regarded to have been the most prominent leader of the abolitionist movement in the United States. Influenced early in his life by the Quaker rejection of chattel slavery and its inhuman practices, Garrison became one of the earliest and most outspoken advocates of the complete and total emancipation of the slaves, which he first articulated in Benjamin Lundy's newspaper, *The Genius of Universal Emancipation*. With the publication of the first issue of *The Liberator* on January 1, 1831, Garrison became identified with his searing admonition, "I am in earnest—I will not equivocate—I will not excuse—I will not retreat a single inch—and I will be heard." He was a brilliant organizer, and founded two antislavery societies to carry on his work, making a modest living by directing their programs and spreading the gospel of antislavery through the regional and local chapters of the national organizations. In 1833, when the Garrisonians formed the American Antislavery Society, they immediately developed local chapters to represent the objectives of the national organization, and the principal players in the national movement traveled frequently to meetings of the local groups. Thus abolitionism and Christian reform paralleled each other in method and scope if not in objectives and message, at a time when the American culture was well used to oratory by reformers whose causes were well known.

At the same time, during the 1820s and 1830s, American women were beginning to perceive the parallels between their own oppressed condition and that of the African slaves, so that the aggressive abolitionist movement led by Garrison and his followers provided them an opportunity to develop arguments for female emancipation. The antislavery movement gave them a constituency and a political alliance on which they were able to rely until the Civil War. The Garrisonians encouraged American feminists, and at an antislavery convention in London, Garrison himself climbed to the gallery to sit with the women observers when they were not allowed on the convention floor as delegates. As Ellen Dubois put it,

> By contrast with the moral reform movement, Garrisonian abolitionism provided women with a political framework that assisted the development of the feminist movement. As Garrisonians, women learned a way to view the world and a theory and practice of social change that they found most useful in elaborating their pro-feminist insights. In addition, the antislavery movement provided them with a constituency and a political alliance on which they were able to rely until the Civil War. Thus, American feminism developed within the context of abolitionism less because abolitionists taught women that they were oppressed than because abolitionists taught women what to do with that perception, how to develop it into a social movement. Two aspects of the way that Garrisonians approached social reality were particularly important to the development of nineteenth-century American feminism: the ability to perceive and analyze entire institutions, and the assumption of absolute human equality as a first principle of morality and politics. Both habits of mind, though seemingly abstract, were derived from the concrete task facing abolitionists, to make slavery a burning issue for northern Whites. The women who built the women's rights movement borrowed these approaches and found them eminently useful in overcoming obstacles that had stopped other proto-feminists. The habit of institutional analysis permitted Garrisonian women to escape the control of the clergy and move beyond pietistic activism. The principle of absolute human equality freed them from the necessity of justifying all their duties in terms of woman's sphere.[22]

The role of women abolitionists is exceptionally well represented by Lydia Maria Child's *Appeal in Favor of that Class of Americans Called Africans* (1833), which was an early and militant call for unconditional emancipation without compensation to slaveowners and an argument for full political and social equality of blacks and whites. Like Garrison, Child blatantly defied the cultural customs, political system, and social conventions of both the North and South, and like Garrison, she suffered disapproval not only from her fellow Bostonians, but also from her own family. It was the crucial issue of equality that brought the abolitionists of the 1830s and 1840s together with the early feminists.

> The principle of absolute human equality was the basic philosophical premise that American feminism borrowed from Garrisonian abolitionism. Because the abolitionists' target was northern racial prejudice and their goal the development of white empathy for the suffering of the slave, the core of their argument was the essential unity of whites with blacks. Although many Garrisonians believed in *biological* differences between the races, their politics ignored physical, cultural, and historical characteristics that might distinguish blacks from whites. They stressed instead the common humanity and the moral identity of the races. They expressed this approach as a moral abstraction, a first principle, but its basis was the very concrete demands of the agitational task they faced.[23]

Today, abolitionists and early antislavery advocates stand out as luminaries in a firmament of change that on reflection looks extremely moral and right. However, it is important to remember that in the 1820s to 1840s, some of these figures were considered a radical, even dangerous, fringe element, and were often regarded as violent insurrectionists. They posed a serious threat to the political and social order of the United States, especially for those Southern states whose economy depended almost entirely on slave labor. By 1850, "King Cotton" was the leading export of the United States, and a disruption of this production was rightly feared to be a threat to the larger economy of the country. For Garrison, Phillips, Child, Weld, and Walker, this meant taking extremely unpopular and often confrontational stands against slavery and race prejudice (which the Garrisonians saw as inextricably linked), with significant physical risks and exposure of one's home and family to retaliation by the often-violent opposing groups. William Lloyd Garrison was nearly lynched by an angry Boston mob that opposed his racial equality doctrines, and in 1830 he was convicted of libel and imprisoned. These antebellum slavery debates were not abstractions; they were frequently heated confrontations that erupted into violent interaction between the proslavery and antislavery camps.

The most prominent vehicles for this confrontation were the abolitionist newspaper and the sermonic tract, combined with the powerful oratory of the lyceum or speaker's platform. Wendell Phillips was particularly well regarded as an abolitionist speaker, and he and Garrison became the leading voices of the antebellum abolitionist cause. They were joined by prominent black abolitionists such as Frederick Douglass and David Walker, and by early feminist advocates and abolitionists like Lydia Maria Child, and the sisters from South Carolina, Angelina Grimké Weld and Sarah Moore Grimké, who embraced abolitionism and became extremely vocal opponents of America's national sin. The "wrongfulness" and "sinfulness" of slavery had long been an argument of antislavery thinkers; now the more contemporary rights of women and the scientific arguments that developed around the theory of evolution were also employed in the slavery debates.

For example, the abolitionists were faced with proslavery arguments by polygenesists, whose explanations for the multiple creations of races ideally suited contemporary race theory and social segregation by race. Equally formidable were the proslavery arguments of ministers who used their Bibles to establish a precedent in ancient history by which the peculiar institution was justified in Scripture by God Himself. The proslavery arguments were not confined to the South; according to the historian Larry Tise, of the fifty-five proslavery sermons published in the decade of the 1830s, thirty-seven were authored by Northern ministers.[24] The abolitionists vigorously opposed these views, and they joined the moral suasion of earlier antislavery advocates to the more militant and aggressive arguments of crusaders like Garrison and Phillips.

The abolitionist movement in antebellum America is best reviewed through the writings of two prominent groups: the white, militant antislavery advocates like Garrison, Wendell Phillips, John Brown, Henry David Thoreau, Lydia Maria Child, and Harriet Beecher Stowe, and the African-American abolitionists, represented in this volume by Frederick Douglass, David Walker, Alexander Crummell, and James McCune Smith. But readers should also consider the widely available slave narratives by Jupiter Hammond, William Wells Brown, Josiah Henson, Henry Bibb, and Harriet Jacobs, who told the story of the hardships, injustices, oppression, and horrors of slavery from a first-person perspective. The voices that appear in these slave narratives, which should be read in conjunction with the abolitionist documents contained in this volume, differ markedly from the demanding, hostile, and often uncompromising tone of some of the white abolitionist writing, such as Garrison's first editorial for *The Liberator*. The slave narrators told an intensely personal story, often filled with pathos, but always focused on the dual objective of attaining personal freedom and achieving emancipation and equality for all African-Americans. This contrast may be seen clearly by comparing any of the Garrison texts, or Lydia Maria Child's 1833 *Appeal in Favor of that Class of Americans Called Africans*, with the tone and style of Douglass's first of three autobiographical accounts, *A Narrative of the Life of Frederick Douglass, an American Slave, Written by Himself* (1845), or Harriet Jacobs's autobiographical narrative, *Incidents in the Life of a Slave Girl* (1861).

Although a full historical treatment of this movement lies outside the scope of this book, the story of the unsung heroes of the Underground Railroad, who risked imprisonment and even their lives to provide security and safety to escaped slaves who were making their way from the plantation South to the free North, is central to antislavery history. The Fugitive Slave Law of 1850, part of the Compromise of 1850, required that all escaped slaves be returned as property to their rightful owners in the South, regardless of the conviction of the Northern antislavery sympathizers. Thus it became a federal crime, punishable by fines and jail sentences, to harbor an escaped slave or to participate in the

work of the Underground Railroad. Despite this federal injunction, many workers continued to assist runaway slaves either into safe sanctuary in the North or
into further escape into Canada.

The abolitionists represented in this volume were opposed to the objectives of
the American Colonization Society, which had been organized in 1817 with the
goal of removing all of the Africans in America to Liberia. The abolitionists
opposed colonization for two primary reasons. First, it was clear from the outset
that the colonization societies were all white, all male, and had no intention of
consulting the victims of slavery themselves about their wishes concerning removal to Africa. The first reason derives from the second, that the colonizationists were usually race theorists who regarded the African to be inferior to the
white.

For the abolitionists, the two decades preceding the publication of *Uncle Tom's
Cabin* were crucial, and they divided along the watermark year of 1840.[25] By
1840, both moderate antislavery advocates and militant abolitionists were calling for immediate emancipation, but Garrison's camp had declared war on the
U.S. Constitution itself, labeling it a proslavery document, a "compact with
Satan," and "an agreement with hell." Garrison had early called for "no union
with slaveholders," effectively declaring that the North should secede from the
South. The division among abolitionists resulted in the formation of a new
political party, with the selection of James Birney and Thomas Earle, a Philadelphia Quaker, as the candidates for president and vice president. The Liberty
Party and the Free-Soil Party represented antislavery interests when it was perceived that the two national parties no longer adequately opposed chattel slavery
(Thomas, pp. 3–4). With the Garrisonians still calling for "no union with slaveholders," the concept of party politics as usual within the Union was inconceiv-
able. As Louis Ruchames put it:

> A decisive event in abolitionist history was Garrison's decision, in 1843, that slavery
> could not be eliminated as long as the North remained in the Government of the
> United States and thereby cooperated with the South, under the Constitution, in
> the maintenance of slavery. The Constitution, Garrison came to believe, assumed
> the existence of slavery, gave the institution its sanction, and could not be changed
> without the consent of a considerable portion of the slave states themselves, which
> therefore made the abolition of slavery by constitutional means impossible. The
> Constitution, he concluded, was—in the words of the prophet Isaiah[,] whom he
> quoted—"a covenant with death and an agreement with hell." Indeed, the "free
> states[,]" by upholding the Constitution, "are guardians and essential supports of
> slavery. We are the jailers and constables of the institution." The only moral and just
> course for the North was disunion or secession, which would ultimately result in the
> fall of slavery.[26]

Thus William Lloyd Garrison distanced himself from those very charter documents the abolitionist movement had sought to reconcile with current events
through a vigorous debate over slavery and freedom. After all the dust had settled
and the Civil War was at an end, the Emancipation Proclamation had been

written, and the Thirteenth Amendment to the Constitution debated, Abraham Lincoln paid high tribute to Garrison in a public statement on April 5, 1865: "I have been only an instrument," he said. "The logic and moral power of Garrison and the anti-slavery people of the country and the Army, have done all."[27]

Like Frederick Douglass and Wendell Phillips, Garrison sought radical change in America's social and political structure, and he argued for a complete overhaul of the democratic form of government to include African-Americans as full citizens. He espoused doctrines of full racial equality, a position which some of his fellow abolitionists, like Theodore Parker, were not prepared to accept. Primarily, however, it was his opposition to the United States Constitution that made him controversial, even among his followers. For example, at an abolitionist gathering on Independence Day, 1854, in Framingham, Massachusetts, Garrison publicly burned the Constitution of the United States, crying out, "So perish all compromises with tyranny."[28] Garrison was a strident and sometimes monotonous speaker, but his message was always clear: "I hate slavery as I hate nothing else in this world. It is not only a crime, but the sum of all criminality." In his personal anger and sense of outrage he was often less balanced and controlled than Wendell Phillips, or Douglass, who had scars on his back from the floggings of his youth and suffered discrimination his entire life. A highly controversial leader of the abolitionist movement, Garrison managed to hold together the militant wing of the abolitionist crusade for three decades by continuous weekly publication of *The Liberator* and by denouncing slavery at every opportunity.

Wendell Phillips (1811–84) was perhaps the most eloquent orator of the abolitionist lecture circuit, although Frederick Douglass was easily his rival. Phillips was a Boston Brahmin, attended the Boston Latin School and Harvard Law School, and could trace his heritage back to the founding of the Massachusetts Bay Colony in 1630. He married a wealthy woman and never developed much of a law practice; rather, he spent his hours fighting slavery. In 1837, at a meeting in Faneuil Hall, the site of gatherings of the first patriots and a favorite speaking venue for Boston abolitionists and women's rights organizers, Phillips denounced the murder of Elijah Lovejoy, an abolitionist editor in Alton, Illinois, and the first white man to be martyred arguing for the cessation of slavery. Phillips's speeches were often called passionate and eloquent, and "caught the imagination of his audience."[29]

The center of abolitionist activity in the 1840s, after the fragmentation of the American movement into warring factions, was not New England, but Great Britain, and both Garrison and Phillips were delegates to the World Antislavery Convention held in London in 1840. Both men denounced the Constitution of the United States as a proslavery compact. Following Garrison's twenty-seven years as president of the American Antislavery Society, Phillips succeeded his friend and colleague. Like Garrison, Phillips linked the issues of women's rights and antislavery, but he was not as radical a thinker or as passionate a critic as his mentor, and his writings lack the invective that characterizes Garrison's tracts and the rhetorical strategies that give the Douglass writings so much power.

Frederick Douglass was born into slavery in 1818, the son of a slave mother and a white man, possibly his mother's master. He was originally named Frederick Augustus Washington Bailey, but would later take the name "Douglass" from a character of Sir Walter Scott whom he admired. His adolescent years were miserable ones, with much suffering as a plantation hand, and he was early separated from his mother, who worked as a field hand some twelve miles distant. His recollection of the few meetings he ever had with his mother are some of the most moving lines of his *Narrative of the Life of Frederick Douglass* (1845). Douglass was not only an accomplished orator in the abolitionist cause, but also a skilled writer. His speeches held audiences spellbound, his use of direct address and the personal pronoun "you" and "your" in his "What to the Slave Is the Fourth of July?" (1852) reflect his ability to create a personal identity with his audience. It is significant that exactly ten years later, on July 4, 1862, Douglass delivered an address in which he referred to the Fourth of July as "my celebration," indicating the progress he felt had been made in the past decade, and the optimism he felt for an apocalyptic Union victory over Southern slaveholding.

Douglass had a clear sense of the dramatic force of his delivery. Once, during the opening moments of a lecture in London, an audience expressed hostile disbelief in his past as a chattel slave, his oratory and elocution were thought to be so beyond the abilities of a former slave. Douglass promptly stripped off his shirt, without speaking another word, and turned his flayed back to the incredulous audience to show the scars of his floggings. The veracity of his testimony was authenticated by the exposure of his body as a textual testimony to his slave past.

Douglass was a staunch Garrisonian abolitionist in the 1840s. However, his association with Garrison soured when he independently founded his own newspaper, *The North Star*, later to be called *Frederick Douglass's Paper*. Douglass also favored working within the constitutional system of amendments, while Garrison rejected the Constitution as an immoral instrument of oppression that could never permit adequate civil rights to the African slave. This dispute over control of the media for the abolitionist crusade continued throughout their careers, and the two men contributed mightily to the cause from wholly different perspectives.

Douglass, who along with William Wells Brown was one of the most prominent slave narrators to participate in the abolitionist movement, developed a keen political instinct, which governed his published and spoken comments on the relationships between slavery and the United States government, women's rights, and the United States Constitution. Unlike the Garrisonians, Douglass argued that the Constitution was potentially an antislavery document which, when properly amended, would allow emancipation. He was, however, powerfully radical in his critique of America's hypocrisy concerning the Declaration of Independence. In this volume, Douglass's critique, "What to the Slave Is the Fourth of July?" is presented not only as a response to Thomas Jefferson's Declaration of Independence, but also as a wake-up call to an errant nation that has abandoned its charter principles and has allowed slavery to coexist with annual proclamations and celebrations of individual rights. The hypocrisies and inconsistencies of American democratic government are castigated severely.

Douglass was a prominent speaker at the first American suffragette convention, held at Seneca Falls, New York, in 1848—the year that marked revolutions throughout Europe. Indeed, on the day of his death, February 20, 1895, Douglass had just spoken at a women's rights meeting. He was politically very influential, writing regularly for the *Washington Evening Star*, *Harper's Weekly*, *Woman's Journal*, and the *London Times*, in addition to editing *Frederick Douglass's Paper* and the *National Era* (which had originally published Harriet Beecher Stowe's *Uncle Tom's Cabin* serially). Like Garrison, Douglass was a man of strong principles, and he voiced his opinions freely and powerfully. He fought most of his life for the emancipation of the slaves, then turned to related issues including opposition to the migration of freed blacks to the North. He was the friend and confidant to several presidents, including Abraham Lincoln, and he was appointed by President Benjamin Harrison to be consul general to the Republic of Haiti. Under President James Garfield, he was given charge of the Office of Recorder of Deeds. The political patronage appointments and public appearances rendered Douglass what we would call today a "public intellectual"; however, Douglass never abandoned his abolitionist rhetoric, and toward the end of the Civil War, with characteristic awareness of the struggle ahead in the Reconstruction and the Jim Crow South, he pronounced that "the work of freedom is not here concluded; it has only begun."

William Wells Brown (1814–84) was another slave narrator who, like Douglass, espoused the abolitionist cause and articulated its connection with women's rights. His autobiographical slave narrative, *Narrative of William W. Brown, a Fugitive Slave, Written by Himself* (1847), was complemented by a literary work, *Clotel, or, The President's Daughter: Narrative of Slave Life in the United States* (1853, reissued in 1860 as *Miralda, or the Beautiful Quadroon*). He also authored a refutation of the pseudoscience of polygenesis that was prominent among proslavery advocates, called *The Black Man: His Antecedents, His Genius, and His Achievements* (1863). Brown was often compared to Douglass, his contemporary; while Douglass controlled the journalistic and political end of the ex-slave abolitionist spectrum, Brown was a prominent contributor to its literature. Brown spent his adult life as a fugitive slave, in the service of the abolitionist movement as a speaker and writer. Brown's popular works joined Harriet Beecher Stowe's *Uncle Tom's Cabin* as "nonfiction novels" that dramatized the damning effects of slavery on both owners and slaves. As Stowe's work clearly shows, and as *Clotel* also argues, the institution of slavery is the "demonic other" that must be ended; individual characters, both oppressed and oppressor, are subordinated in these novels to the pervasive evils of the "system," that "peculiar institution" that threatened the very fabric of American democracy.

To view the antebellum abolitionist movement as a collection of eminent lives and the writings of those figures may seem peculiar to some readers. Historians, for example, might stress the internecine wars of the 1840s in which Garrison opposed certain types of political actions among his followers, who in turn opposed his more radical leadership; or the serious differences that developed between the prominent black and white leaders of the abolitionist cause, Douglass and Garrison. These disputes have been amply treated in scores of historical studies about antebellum antislavery activity, the best known of which are listed in the "Suggestions for Further Reading." They are represented here by primary texts authored by the leading figures of the Garrisonian wing of the abolitionist movement, and by some of the more moderate voices that also struck out against chattel slavery. What is important, however, is that an active minority of both black and white Americans were obsessively dedicated to the abolition of chattel slavery in the United States, and that two of these spokesmen, Garrison and Douglass, were sufficiently united in their opposition to the sanctioning of slavery by the federal government and the endorsement of the Fugitive Slave Act of 1850 to cry out against this national disgrace. They were joined by the nonfiction novelists William Wells Brown and Harriet Beecher Stowe and by the slave narrator Harriet Jacobs in a crusade that contributed significantly to the emancipation of the slaves in the Thirteenth Amendment to the Constitution (1865), but also paved the way for the Civil Rights Act of 1875 and the civil rights movement of the 1960s.

SUMMARY

It required the influence of Stowe's novel, the slave narrators, the abolitionists, Abraham Lincoln, and the Civil War, all working at the same time, if not working together, to bring an end to the national disgrace of chattel slavery. As Ken Burns's effective Public Broadcasting System series "The Civil War" has shown, one cannot truly understand the history of the United States without having some grasp of the issues that preceded the coming of the most devastating conflict in our nation's history, one where some 670,000 lives (including some 50,000 civilians) were lost on both sides, more than have been lost in all the other American wars combined, including the First and Second World Wars, the Spanish-American War, the Korean War, the Vietnam War, and the Gulf War.

Historians have argued endlessly whether the Civil War was caused by slavery or by the Confederacy's right to secede from the Union; however, there can be little doubt that Alexis de Tocqueville was correct when, in the 1830s, he predicted that the success or failure of American democracy would rest entirely on how effectively the relationships between African-Americans and white Americans developed. The problems that Tocqueville cited in 1835 are still present in American society, and while the issue of slavery is no longer a prominent subject of political debate, the subtle and pernicious legacy of race prejudice, which Garrison clearly saw as the root cause of slavery, remains unresolved. As we enter the twenty-first century, the issue of race prejudice continues to plague the nation whose founding fathers declared that "all men are created equal."

ABOUT THIS BOOK

A House Divided provides the reader with extremely important primary documents that were familiar to Mark Twain, Harriet Beecher Stowe, and other nineteenth-century writers, arguments that had significant influence on decisions in the Congress of the United States, and speeches and sermons that reached thousands of Americans who were coming to terms with the institution of slavery. In the materials that follow, the reader will find a roadmap through the vast jungle of discourse, documents that were often hastily published to advance a pro- or antislavery position. The basic arenas of debate were many, though they are subdivided here to provide a historical perspective. The documents fall into arguments concerning the Bible and slavery; economic, political, legal, and constitutional questions about slavery; abolitionist arguments; and issues from science and pseudoscience. The readings and critical essays are organized around the overarching question of the "rightness" or "wrongness" of slavery in an experimental democracy that articulated "all men are created equal" in one of its primary charter documents. More specifically, the readings illustrate the important arenas of slavery discourse that dominated American culture from the Revolution through the Civil War, 1776–1865. These representative selections are historically driven by the antebellum period itself, and they illustrate the rich rhetorical power of the Second Great Awakening, the antislavery sermons of William Ellery Channing, the oratory of Wendell Phillips, the antislavery writings of Ralph Waldo Emerson and James Russell Lowell, and the published editorials of William Lloyd Garrison, to name a few examples.

The collection is organized on historical principles, and each "debate" is located in its historical context. For example, the proslavery writings of Alexander McCaine, *Slavery Defended from Scripture against the Attacks of the Abolitionists* (1842), are opposed here by antislavery critics such as James Freeman Clarke, *Slavery in the United States* (1843), and Robert Dale Owen, *The Wrong of Slavery* (1864). There are several examples where pro- and antislavery voices are directly opposed to each other. Samuel Sewall's *The Selling of Joseph* (1700) was answered almost immediately by John Saffin, in *A Brief, Candid Answer to The Selling of Joseph* (1700), and two lawyers, Lysander Spooner and Wendell Phillips, differ in their interpretations of the United States Constitution. In other cases, examples are included which are responses not to specific opponents but to pro- and antislavery positions as they were advanced during the antebellum period. This "pronouncement and response" technique gives ample representation to both sides in all of the arenas of debate. By organizing each of the debates as a dialogue between opposing sides, the editor has sought to foreground the complexity of the years between 1776 and 1865, a period of rapid growth and change in the American population.

There is significant overlap among the topical divisions, and the anthology cross-references texts where necessary and appropriate. Introductory essays by the editor for each selection combine with new, interpretative essays by leading scholars, located strategically throughout the volume, to provide the reader with a clear view of all facets of each category of discourse.

Literary representations of slavery and arguments for and against the institution were numerous, particularly following the passage of the Fugitive Slave Law in 1850. Slave narrators composed retrospective, autobiographical accounts of their sufferings in slavery as a way exposing the brutal horrors of plantation life from the perspective of its victims. Accounts by Frederick Douglass, Josiah Henson, and Harriet Jacobs are representative antebellum slave narratives and are readily available in paperback. Although not included here, they should be read as part of the literature of the slavery debates. In 1852, Harriet Beecher Stowe's *Uncle Tom's Cabin* was published as a direct response to the Fugitive Slave Law, and in describing Eliza's pitiable escape across the Ohio River, the novel dramatized the regional association of slavery with the southern states.

In the "literary debates" represented here, James Russell Lowell, Walt Whitman, John Greenleaf Whittier, and Ralph Waldo Emerson developed powerful arguments against slavery, while writers like John Pendleton Kennedy (*Swallow Barn*) and Mary Eastman (*Aunt Phillis's Cabin*) wrote tales of plantation life that were designed to counteract the enormous influence of Stowe's harsh critique of it in *Uncle Tom's Cabin*. Stowe's work prevailed, and the historian George Fredrickson estimates that her fictional work, together with Helper's *The Impending Crisis of the South and How to Meet It* (1857), were the two most important antislavery documents to appear before the Civil War. Although Helper was a North Carolinian, he examined slavery as a social institution, including the economic debates it generated, and concluded that abolition and emancipation were not only inevitable but that the need was urgent.

The documents in this volume trace the history of the Enlightenment doctrines of the Declaration of Independence, through the turbulent antebellum period when Americans were seeking a new identity as a nation founded on principles of equality and brotherhood rather than caste and inherited position. These documents show the passion of liberators like Garrison, Child, and Douglass who sought to reform the American system of government to reflect the ideological principles on which the nation had been founded. With the flexibility of the Constitution's amendment system, and the doctrine of free speech protected by the First Amendment to the Constitution, the abolitionists set about changing the United States forever, by eradicating the ideological inconsistency of chattel slavery in a republic founded on doctrines of individual freedom and inalienable rights.

The book has grown out of a decade of teaching "Race and Slavery in Nineteenth-Century American Culture," at the University of Massachusetts, Amherst, and at the Harvard Extension School. *A House Divided* provides the reader, whether student or scholar, with essential primary texts that articulate the arenas of the antebellum slavery debates, introduced by essays that frame these debates in their historical and cultural contexts. The debates concerning "race and slavery" will no doubt continue both in and out of the classroom for many decades to come.

Mason I. Lowance, Jr.
Amherst and Boston,
2001

1. George Stroud, *Stroud's Compendium of the Laws of Slavery* (Boston, 1843).

2. Jennifer Monaghan, James Russell Wiggins Lecture, American Antiquarian Society, Nov. 6, 1998.

3. Monaghan, "Reflections on Liberty and Literacy," *Proceedings of the American Antiquarian Society*, vol. 108, part II, 309–41.

4. The total black population in 1820 was 1,772,000, consisting of 234,000 free blacks and 1,538,000 slaves. See the U.S. Department of Commerce, Bureau of the Census web site for further information.

5. John Thomas, "Introduction," *Slavery Attacked: the Abolitionist Crusade* (Englewood Cliffs, NJ: Prentice-Hall, 1963), p. 14.

6. Barbara Fields, "Ideology and Race in American History," in *Region, Race and Reconstruction: Essays in Honor of C. Vann Woodward*, ed. J. Morgan Kousser and James McPherson (New York: Oxford University Press, 1982), p. 144.

7. See John Woolman, *Some Considerations on the Keeping of Negroes* (New York, 1754).

8. Phillip Gould, "The Eighteenth-Century Slave Trade" (unpublished manuscript, Brown University Department of American Studies, 1999), p. 27.

9. See the December 15, 1999, *New Yorker*, where the Nat Turner rebellion is thoroughly discussed and revisionist historians examine the events from a new perspective, and Kenneth Greenberg, ed., *The Nat Turner Rebellion* (Boston: Bedford Books of St. Martin's Press, 1997), a collection of documents concerning the Nat Turner rebellion and essays interpreting the event, both historical and contemporary.

10. George Fredrickson, *The Black Image in the White Mind, 1500–1900* (Madison: University of Wisconsin Press, 1972).

11. See Reginald Horsman, *Race and Manifest Destiny* (Cambridge: Harvard University Press, 1981), chapters 2 and 3.

12. See Mark Neely, *The Last Best Hope of Earth* (Cambridge: Harvard University Press, 1995), chapters 1 and 2. Neely provides a full transcription of the Lincoln letter.

13. Horsman, *Race and Manifest Destiny*, chapters 2 and 3 and pp. 125–27.

14. Thomas Cassirer and J. Brière, eds., *On the Cultural Achievements of Negroes, by Henri Grégoire* (Amherst: University of Massachusetts Press, 1996), p. xxxix.

15. For a full discussion of the typology of slave narrative characteristics and an analysis of the major antebellum slave narratives, see Lowance, "The Slave Narrative in American Literature," in *African-American Writers*, ed. Lea Baechler and A. Walton Litz (New York: Charles Scribner's Sons, 1991 and 2001).

16. Benjamin Quarles and John Hope Franklin were pioneers in this scholarship who, as African-Americans themselves, were often denied access to university libraries where important resources were held. In spite of these restrictions, Franklin produced the magisterial *From Slavery to Freedom* in 1947, which has been revised six times since and in 1999 had sold over one million copies. Scholarly and critical studies include William Andrews, *To Tell a Free Story: The First Century of African-American Autobiography, 1760–1865* (Urbana: University of Illinois Press, 1986); Charles Davis and Henry Louis Gates, Jr., *The Slave's Narrative* (New York: Oxford University Press, 1985); and John Sekora and Darwin Turner, *The Art of the Slave Narrative* (Macomb: Western Illinois University Press, 1982).

17. As Hazel Carby has observed, "the idea that the ex-slaves wrote themselves into being through an account of the condition of being a slave is woven into the very fabric of the Afro-American literary imagination and its critical reconstruction." Hazel Carby, "Ideologies of Black Folk: The Historical Novel of Slavery," in Deborah McDowell and

Arnold Rampersad, eds., *Slavery and the Literary Imagination: Selected Papers from the English Institute, 1987* (New York: Oxford University Press, 1989), p. 125; see also Lisa Siegman, "The Slave Narrative as Influence on Twenty African-American Writers" (unpublished essay, University of Massachusetts, 2000), p. 10.

18. See Linda Krumholz, "The Ghosts of Slavery," in *Toni Morrison's Beloved: A Casebook*, ed. William Andrews and Nellie McKay (New York: Oxford University Press, 1999), p. 108.

19. Siegman, "The Slave Narrative," p. 12.

20. Harriet Jacobs, *Incidents in the Life of a Slave Girl, Written by Herself*, ed. Lydia Maria Child (1861), newly edited by Jean Fagan Yellin (Cambridge: Harvard University Press, 1987), p. 28.

21. Raymond Hedin, "Strategies of Form in American Slave Narratives," in John Sekora and Darwin Turner, eds., *The Art of the Slave Narrative: Original Essays in Criticism and Theory* (Macomb: Western Illinois University Press, 1982), p. 34. See also Siegman, "The Slave Narrative," p. 15.

22. Ellen Dubois, "Women's Rights and Abolition: the Nature of the Connection," in *Feminism and Suffrage: The Emergence of an Independent Women's Movement in America, 1848–1869* (Ithaca, NY: Cornell University Press, 1978).

23. Ibid., pp. 245–46.

24. Larry E. Tise, *Proslavery: A History of the Defense of Slavery in America, 1701–1840* (Athens: University of Georgia Press, 1987), p. 262.

25. John Thomas noted that "by 1840, the Abolitionists were engaged in a civil war of their own, with both political abolitionists and Garrisonians struggling for control of the nearly moribund national society. . . . Thus the year 1840 marked a turning point in the Abolitionist crusade. Its institutional phase was over. Although Garrison's 'Old Organization' (as his followers called themselves) and the secessionist 'New Organization' (as they contemptuously referred to their opponents) continued to agitate for immediate emancipation, an effective national organization ceased to exist after 1840." Thomas, *Slavery Attacked*, pp. 3–4.

As Thomas has shown, the abolitionists relied almost exclusively on moral persuasion and aggressive rhetorical strategies to develop their arguments and spread their beliefs.

> To destroy the power of slavery the Abolitionists relied on the equally simple strategy of conversion. In the beginning, they tried to change the minds of slaveholders and gain sympathizers by appealing directly to the individual conscience. They broadcast their indictment in their own press, organized societies and wrote pamphlets, compiled statistics and circulated petitions, all with the purpose of bringing their moral argument directly to bear on the presumed guilt of the American people. The American Antislavery Society functioned chiefly as a clearinghouse for a huge propaganda campaign mounted by agents and agitators who looked to moral suasion for their power. Its program however, variously interpreted in later years, originally called for moral agitation directed at individual citizens in both sections of the country to make them see and feel the sinfulness of slavery. Change people's hearts, they believed, and the people would soon change their habits. [pp. 1–2]

The Garrisonians embraced "moral suasion" in the early years, but later separated from those abolitionists who sought reform from within the system by public debate and Constitutional amendments. They added potent tactics to the rhetoric of moral reform.

A smaller but more militant group of abolitionists, led by William Lloyd Garrison and Wendell Phillips, took another and—so they believed—a higher road to emancipation. Insisting that proscription and repression branded the American church and state as hopelessly corrupt, they demanded that abolitionists have "no union with slaveholders." They refused to seek office, vote for anti-slavery candidates, or in any way support the political abolitionists whom they denounced as traitors to the cause of moral suasion. With their intransigent "come outer" beliefs, the Garrisonians carried moral suasion to its limits in Christian non-resistance and women's rights. The logic of their position, if not all their activities, pointed towards secession. [Thomas, *Slavery Attacked*, p. 3]

26. Louis Ruchames, *The Abolitionists: A Collection of Their Writings* (New York: G. P. Putnam's Sons, 1960), p. 23.

27. Ibid., p. 24. See also Truman Nelson, *Documents of Upheaval: Selections from William Lloyd Garrison's "The Liberator," 1831–1865* (New York: Hill and Wang, 1966), p. vii. Lincoln is cited in both of these sources as the author of this statement.

28. See Henry Mayer, *All on Fire: William Lloyd Garrison and the Abolition of Slavery* (New York: St. Martin's Press, 1998), chapters 1–3.

29. See the essay on Wendell Phillips in the *Dictionary of American Biography* (New York: Oxford University Press, 1995), p. 546.

Sandra Duvivier is completing a Ph.D. in African-American studies at the University of Massachusetts, Amherst.

Len Gougeon is professor of American literature at the University of Scranton. He has published widely on antebellum reform and the literature of the period. His articles have appeared in *American Literature, New England Quarterly, South Atlantic Review, Studies in the American Renaissance*, and other journals. He is the author of *Virtue's Hero: Emerson, Antislavery, and Reform* (University of Georgia Press, 1990), and coeditor, with Joel Myerson, of *Emerson's Antislavery Writings* (Yale University Press, 1995). He currently serves as president of the Ralph Waldo Emerson Society.

Dean Grodzins is on the faculty of the Mead-Lombard Theological Seminary in Chicago. Formerly a visiting scholar at the Charles Warren Center for Studies in American History and lecturer in history and literature at Harvard University, he is now editor of the *Journal of Unitarian-Universalist History*. He received his Ph.D. in history from Harvard in 1993 with his dissertation "Theodore Parker and Transcendentalism," which was awarded the Alan Nevins Prize, the DeLancey K. Jay Prize, and the Harold K. Gross Prize. He has written a biography of Theodore Parker, which will be published by the University of North Carolina Press.

Christopher Hanlon has taught courses in American literature and culture at the University of Massachusetts (Amherst and Lowell campuses) and North Carolina State University at Raleigh. He currently is assistant professor of English at Eastern Illinois University. His current work concerns the intersections of American pragmatist philosophy and continental psychoanalytic theory, but his research ranges more widely over American intellectual history, critical theory, and especially the literature and culture of the antebellum period. He has published his work in *New Literary History, Journal X*, and *Jouvert*, and is currently developing a book-length work entitled *Pragmatism and the Unconscious*.

Melba Jensen is completing her graduate work in English at the University of Massachusetts, Amherst. Her dissertation examines the writings and ideology of the New York abolitionists, Gerrit Smith, Arthur Tappan, and Lewis Tappan. In addition to editing the section on the New York abolitionists, she authored the introductory essay on George Fitzhugh for this volume and served as the book's editorial assistant.

Arthur F. Kinney is Thomas W. Copeland Professor of Literary History and director of the Massachusetts Center for Renaissance Studies at the University of Massachusetts, Amherst. He is the editor most recently of *Renaissance Drama* (1999) for Blackwell, *The Witch of Edmonton* (1998) for New Mermaids, and the *Cambridge Companion to English Literature, 1500–1600* (2000). He is the author of the recently published *Lies Like Truth: Shakespeare, Macbeth, and the Cultural Moment* (2001) and *Shakespeare by Stages* (forthcoming).

Adam Linker is completing a Ph.D. in African-American studies at the University of Massachusetts, Amherst.

Mason Lowance, editor, is professor of English and American literature at the University of Massachusetts, Amherst, where he has taught since 1967. His books include *Increase Mather* (1974); *Early Vermont Broadsides* (1975); *Massachusetts Broadsides of the American Revolution* (1976); *The Language of Canaan: Metaphor and Symbol in New England Writing from the Puritans to the Transcendentalists* (1980); *The Typological Writings of Jonathan Edwards* (1993); *The Stowe Debates: Rhetorical Strategies in Uncle Tom's Cabin* (1994); and *Against Slavery: An Abolitionist Reader* (2000). He is a member of the American Antiquarian Society, where he has been an NEH fellow, and has been fellow of the National Humanities Institute, Yale University, and a Guggenheim fellow.

William Pannapacker is assistant professor of English at Hope College, Holland, Michigan, where he teaches courses in American literature and history. He holds a Ph.D. in American civilization from Harvard University focusing on the autobiographical writings of Frederick Douglass, P. T. Barnum, and Walt Whitman. He won the Bell Prize for the best graduate essay in the Department of English, and the Bowdoin Prize for the best essay in American literature, and he held the prestigious Whiting Fellowship at Harvard. He has taught at Brandeis University and has also taught in the Harvard History and Literature program and in the Harvard Extension School.

Additional suggestions on specific topics are given throughout this volume, at the end of many of the headnotes and essays.

GENERAL SOURCES

Abzug, Robert. *Cosmos Crumbling: American Reform and the Religious Imagination.* New York: Oxford University Press, 1994.

———. *Passionate Liberator: Theodore Dwight Weld and the Dilemma of Reform.* New York: Oxford University Press, 1980.

Adams, Nehemiah (1806–78). *A South Side View of Slavery: Three Months at the South.* Savannah, GA: Beehive Press, 1974.

Agassiz, Louis. "The Diversity of Origin of the Human Races," *Christian Examiner* 49 (July 1850).

Allison, Robert J. *The Interesting Narrative of the Life of Olaudah Equiano, Written by Himself.* Boston: Bedford Books of St. Martin's Press, 1995.

Andrews, William L. *To Tell a Free Story: The First Century of Afro-American Autobiography, 1760–1865.* Urbana: University of Illinois Press, 1986.

———, ed. *Critical Essays on Frederick Douglass.* Boston: G. K. Hall, 1991.

———, ed. *The Frederick Douglass Reader.* New York: Oxford University Press, 1996.

Aptheker, Herbert. *Abolitionism: A Revolutionary Movement.* Boston: Twayne Publishers for G. K. Hall, 1971.

Bachman, J. *The Doctrine of the Unity of the Human Race Examined on the Principles of Science.* Charleston, SC, 1850.

Baker, Houston. *Long Black Song: Essays in Black American Literature and Culture.* Charlottesville: University Presses of Virginia, 1972.

Barnes, Gilbert Hobbs. *The Antislavery Impulse, 1830–1844.* New York: D. Appleton Century, 1933.

Bartlett, Irving. *Wendell and Ann Phillips: The Community of Reform, 1840–1880.* New York: W. W. Norton, 1979.

Berlin, Ira. *Many Thousands Gone: The First Two Centuries of Slavery in North America.* Cambridge: Belknap Press of Harvard University Press, 1998.

Beyan, Amos I. *The American Colonization Society and the Creation of the Liberian State: A Historical Perspective, 1822–1900.* Lanham, MI: University Press of America, 1991.

Blackson, Charles L. *The Underground Railroad.* New York: Prentice-Hall, 1987.

Blassingame, John. *The Slave Community. Plantation Life in the Antebellum South.* New York: Oxford University Press, 1979.

———. *Slave Testimony.* Baton Rouge: Louisiana State University Press, 1977.

Blight, David W. *Frederick Douglass's Civil War: Keeping Faith in Jubilee*. Baton Rouge: Louisiana State University Press, 1989.

Bloom, Harold, ed. *Modern Critical Interpretations: Frederick Douglass's Narrative of the Life of Frederick Douglass, an American Slave*. New York: Chelsea House, 1988.

Brown, William Wells (1815–84). *The Travels of William Wells Brown, Including the Narrative of William Wells Brown, a Fugitive Slave, and the American Fugitive in Europe*. Edited by Paul Jefferson. New York: M. Weiner, 1991.

Burns, Roger, ed. *Am I Not a Man and a Brother: The Antislavery Crusade of Revolutionary America, 1688–1788*. New York: Chelsea House, 1977.

Cain, William, ed. *William Lloyd Garrison and the Fight against Slavery: Selections from The Liberator*. Boston: Bedford Books of St. Martin's Press, 1995.

Caldwell, Charles. *Thoughts on the Original Unity of the Human Race*. New York, 1830.

Ceplair, Larry, ed. *The Public Years of Sarah and Angelina Grimké: Selected Writings, 1835–1839*. New York: Columbia University Press, 1989.

Chesebrough, David B. *Frederick Douglass: Oratory from Slavery*. Westport, CT: Greenwood Press, 1998.

Child, Lydia Maria (1802–80). *An Appeal in Favor of That Class of Americans Called Africans*. Edited with introduction by Carolyn Karcher. Amherst: University of Massachusetts Press, 1996.

———. *A Lydia Maria Child Reader*. Edited by Carolyn Karcher. Durham: Duke University Press, 1997.

Colfax, Richard H. *Evidence against the Views of the Abolitionists, Consisting of Physical and Moral Proofs of the Natural Inferiority of the Negroes*. New York, 1833.

Commager, Henry Steele. *Theodore Parker: An Anthology*. Boston: Beacon Press, 1960.

Cooper, William James. *The South and the Politics of Slavery, 1828–1856*. Baton Rouge: Louisiana State University Press, 1978.

Cott, Nancy F. *The Bonds of Womanhood. Woman's Sphere in New England, 1780–1835*. New Haven: Yale University Press, 1977.

Countryman, Edward. *How Did American Slavery Begin?* Boston: Bedford Books of St. Martin's Press, 1999.

Cunliffe, Marcus. *Chattel Slavery and Wage Slavery: The Anglo-American Context, 1830–1860*. Athens: University of Georgia Press, 1979.

Davis, Charles T., and Henry Louis Gates, Jr., eds. *The Slave's Narrative*. New York: Oxford University Press, 1985.

Davis, David Brion. *From Homicide to Slavery: Studies in American Culture*. New York: Oxford University Press, 1986.

———. *The Problem of Slavery in Western Culture*. 1966.

Delaney, Martin Robinson (1812–1885). *Blake or the Huts of America: A Novel*. Edited with introduction by Floyd J. Miller. Boston: Beacon Press, 1970.

Dew, Thomas R. *Review of the Debate in the Virginia Legislature of 1831 and 1832*. Richmond, 1832.

Dictionary of Afro-American Slavery. Edited by Randall Miller and John David Smith. New York: Greenwood Press, 1988.

Dillon, Merton L. *The Abolitionists: The Growth of a Dissenting Minority*. Dekalb: Northern Illinois University Press, 1974.

Douglass, Frederick (1818–95). *The Frederick Douglass Papers*. Edited by John W. Blassingame. New Haven: Yale University Press, 1979.

————. *The Life and Times of Frederick Douglass: His Early Life as a Slave, His Escape from Bondage, and His Complete History, Written by Himself*. Edited with new introduction by Rayford W. Logan. New York: Bonanza Books, 1972.

————, *My Bondage and My Freedom*. Edited with an introduced by William Andrews. Urbana: University of Illinois Press, 1987.

————. *Narrative of the Life of Frederick Douglass, an American Slave, Written by Himself*. Edited by David W. Blight. Boston: Bedford Books of St. Martin's Press, 1993.

Dubois, Ellen, "Women's Rights and Abolition: The Native and the Connection." In *Feminism and Suffrage, 1848–1869*. Ithaca: Cornell University Press, 1968.

Du Bois, W. E. B. *Writings of W. E. B. Du Bois*. New York: Viking Press. 1986.

Dumond, Dwight Lowell. *Antislavery: The Crusade for Freedom in America*. Ann Arbor: University of Michigan Press, 1961.

————. *Antislavery Origins of the Civil War in the United States*. Ann Arbor: University of Michigan Press, 1964.

————. *A Bibliography of Antislavery in America*. Ann Arbor: University of Michigan Press, 1961.

Edwards, Jonathan, Jr. *The Injustice and Impolicy of the Slave Trade, and the Slavery of the Africans*. Boston: Wells and Lilly, 1822.

Elkins, Stanley. *Slavery: A Problem in American Institutional and Intellectual Life*. Chicago: University of Chicago Press, 1976.

Ellis, Joseph. *Founding Brothers: The Revolutionary Generation*. New York: Alfred Knopf, 2001.

Emerson, Everett. *The Authentic Mark Twain: A Literary Biography of Samuel L. Clemens*. Philadelphia: University of Pennsylvania Press, 1984. See especially the discussion of *Puddn'head Wilson*, pp. 180–90.

Essays and Pamphlets on Antislavery. Westport, CT: Negro Universities Press, 1970.

Faust, Drew Gilpin. *Mothers of Invention: Women of the Slaveholding South in the American Civil War*. Chapel Hill: University of North Carolina Press, 1996.

Filler, Louis. *The Crusade against Slavery, 1830–1860*. New York: Harper and Row, 1960.

————. *Wendell Phillips on Civil Rights and Freedom*. Washington, DC: University Press of America, 1982.

Finkleman, Paul, ed. *Articles on American Slavery*. 18 vols. New York: Garland Publishing, 1989.

————. *Dred Scott v Sandford: A Brief History with Documents*. Boston: Bedford Books, 1997.

Fitzhugh. George. *Cannibals All! or, Slaves without Masters*. Edited by C. Vann Woodward. Cambridge: Harvard University Press, 1964.

Flournoy, J. Jacobus. *An Essay on the Origins, Habits of the Negro Race: Incidental to the Propriety of Having Nothing to Do with Negroes*. New York, 1835.

Fogel, Robert William. *Without Consent or Contract: The Rise and Fall of American Slavery*. New York: W. W. Norton, 1989.

Foner, Eric. *Nothing but Freedom: Emancipation and Its Legacy*. Baton Rouge: Louisiana State University Press, 1983.

———. *Politics and Ideology in the Age of the Civil War*. New York: Oxford University Press, 1980.

———. *Slavery, the Civil War, and Reconstruction*. Washington, DC: American Historical Association, 1990.

Foner, Philip. *Three Who Dared: Prudence Crandall, Margaret Douglass, Myrtilla Miner: Champions of Antebellum Black Education*. Westport, CT: Greenwood Press, 1984.

Fowler, Orson S. *Phrenological Chart*. Baltimore, 1836.

Fox-Genovese, Elizabeth. *Within the Plantation Household: Black and White Women of the Old South*. Chapel Hill: University of North Carolina Press, 1988.

Franklin, John Hope. *From Slavery to Freedom: A History of Negro Americans*. New York: Alfred A. Knopf, 1968.

———. *A Southern Odyssey: Travelers in the Antebellum North*. Baton Rouge: Louisiana State University Press, 1976.

Fredrickson, George M. *The Arrogance of Race: Historical Perspectives on Slavery, Racism, and Social Inequality*. Middletown, CT: Wesleyan University Press, 1988.

———. *The Black Image in the White Mind. The Debate on Afro-American Character and Destiny, 1817–1914*. New York: Harper and Row, 1971.

Freehling, William W. *The Reintegration of American History: Slavery and the Civil War*. New York: Oxford University Press, 1994.

Garfield, Deborah, and Rafia Zafar, eds. *Harriet Jacobs and Incidents in the Life of a Slave Girl: New Critical Essays*. New York: Cambridge University Press, 1996.

Genovese, Eugene D. *From Rebellion to Revolution: Afro-American Slave Revolts in the Making of the Modern World*. Baton Rouge: Louisiana State University Press, 1979.

———. *Roll, Jordan, Roll: The World the Slaves Made*. New York: Random House, 1994.

Gougeon, Len. *Emerson's Antislavery Writings*. Athens: University of Georgia Press, 1988.

———. *Virtue's Hero: Emerson, Antislavery, and Reform*. Athens: University of Georgia Press, 1990.

Greenberg, Kenneth S. *The Confession of Nat Turner and Related Documents*. Boston: Bedford Books of St. Martin's Press, 1996.

Grégoire, Henri. *On the Cultural Achievements of Negroes* (Paris, 1808). Translated and introduced by Thomas Cassirer and Jean François Brière. Amherst: University of Massachusetts Press, 1996.

Hanson, Debra Gold. *Strained Sisterhood: Gender and Class in the Boston Female Antislavery Society*. Amherst: University of Massachusetts Press, 1993.

Harold, Stanley. *The Abolitionists and the South, 1831–1861*. Lexington: University of Kentucky Press, 1995.

Hawkins, Hugh, and Lawrence Goodheart, eds. *The Abolitionists: Means, Ends, and Motivations*. Lexington, MA: D. C. Heath and Co., 1995.

Helper, Hinton Rowan (1829–1909). *The Impending Crisis of the South: How to Meet It*. Edited by George Fredrickson. Cambridge: Harvard University Press, 1968.

Hildreth, Richard. *Despotism in America: An Inquiry into the Nature, Results, and Legal Basis of the Slave-Holding System in the United States*. Reprint of 1854 edition. New York: Augustus Kelley, 1970.

Hinks, Peter P. *To Awaken My Afflicted Brethren: David Walker and the Problem of Antebellum Slave Resistance*. University Park: Pennsylvania State University Press, 1996.

Horton, James, and Lois Horton. *In Hope of Liberty*. New York: Oxford University Press, 1997.

Huggins, Nathan Irvin. *Black Odyssey: The Afro-American Ordeal in Slavery*. New York: Pantheon Books, 1977.

Jacobs, Harriet A. (1813–97). *Incidents in the Life of a Slave Girl, Written by Herself*. Edited by Lydia Maria Child. Newly edited with a new introduction by Jean Fagan Yellin. Cambridge: Harvard University Press, 1987, 1991.

Johannsen, Robert Walter. *Lincoln: the South, and Slavery: The Political Dimension*. Baton Rouge: Louisiana State University Press, 1991.

Jones, Howard. *Mutiny on the "Amistad": The Saga of a Slave Revolt and Its Impact on American Abolition, Law, and Diplomacy*. New York: Oxford University Press, 1987.

Jordan, Winthrop. *White over Black: American Attitudes toward the Negro, 1550–1812*. New York: W.W. Norton, 1968.

Karcher, Carolyn. *Shadow over the Promised Land: Slavery, Race, and Violence in Melville's America*. Baton Rouge: Louisiana State University Press, 1980.

Kemble, Fanny (1809–93). *Journal of a Residence on a Georgia Plantation in 1838–1839*. Edited with introduction by John A. Scott. New York: Alfred A. Knopf, 1970.

Kevles, Daniel. *In the Name of Eugenics*. New York: Alfred A. Knopf, 1993.

Kolchin, Peter. *American Slavery, 1619–1877*. New York: Hill and Wang, 1995.

———. *Unfree Labor: American Slavery and Russian Serfdom*. Cambridge: Belknap Press of Harvard University Press, 1987.

Kraditor, Aileen S. *Means and Ends in American Abolitionism: Garrison and His Critics on Strategy and Tactics, 1834–1850*. New York: Pantheon Books, 1960.

Lacy, Dan. *The Abolitionists*. New York: McGraw-Hill, 1978.

Lane, Ann J., ed. *The Debate over Slavery: Stanley Elkins and His Critics.* Urbana: University of Illinois Press, 1971.

Leary, Lewis. *John Greenleaf Whittier.* New Haven: College and University Press, 1961.

Lloyd, Arthur Young. *The Slavery Controversy, 1831–1860.* Chapel Hill: University of North Carolina Press, 1939.

Lowance, Mason, Jr. "Biography and Autobiography in Early America." In *The Columbia Literary History of the United States*, ed. Emory Elliott. New York: Columbia University Press, 1988.

———. "Frederick Douglass." In *African-American Writers*, ed. Lea Baechler and A. Walton Litz. New York: Charles Scribner's Sons, 1991.

———. "The Slave Narrative in American Literature." In *African-American Writers*, ed. Lea Baechler and A. Walton Litz. New York: Charles Scribner's Sons, 1991. Revised 2001.

———. "Spirituals." In *Encyclopedia of American Poetry*. Chicago: Fitzroy-Dearborn, 1998.

———, ed. *Against Slavery: An Abolitionist Reader.* New York: Penguin-Putnam, 2000.

———, et al., eds. *The Stowe Debate: Rhetorical Strategies in Uncle Tom's Cabin.* Amherst: University of Massachusetts Press, 1994.

Lowell, James Russell (1819–91). *James Russell Lowell's The Biglow Papers, First Series, a Critical Edition.* Edited by Thomas Wortham. Dekalb: Northern Illinois University Press, 1977.

Martin, B. Edmon. *All We Want Is Make Us Free: La Amistad and the Reform Abolitionists.* Lanham, MD, and New York: University Press of America, 1986.

Martin, Waldo E. *The Mind of Frederick Douglass.* Chapel Hill: University of North Carolina Press. 1984.

Mathews, Donald G. *Slavery and Methodism: a Chapter in American Morality, 1780–1845.* Princeton: Princeton University Press, 1965.

Mayer, Henry. *All on Fire: William Lloyd Garrison and the Abolition of Slavery.* New York: St. Martin's Press, 1998.

McFeely, William S. *Frederick Douglass.* New York: W. W. Norton, 1991.

McGary, Howard. *Between Slavery and Freedom: Philosophy and American Slavery.* Bloomington: Indiana University Press, 1992.

McInerney, Daniel John. *The Fortunate Heirs of Freedom: Abolition and Republican Thought.* Lincoln: University of Nebraska Press, 1994.

McKittrick, Eric. *Slavery Defended: The Views of the Old South.* Englewood Cliffs, NJ: Prentice-Hall, 1963.

McKivigan, John R., and Mitchell Snay, eds. *Religion and the Antebellum Debate over Slavery.* Athens: University of Georgia Press, 1998.

McPherson, James M. *The Struggle for Equality: Abolitionists and the Negro in the Civil War and Reconstruction.* Princeton: Princeton University Press, 1964.

Miller, William Lee. *Arguing about Slavery: The Great Battle in the United States Congress.* New York: Alfred A. Knopf, 1995.

Moore, Wilbert Ellis. *American Negro Slavery and Abolition: A Sociological Study.* New York: Third Press, 1971.

Nelson, Truman, ed. *Documents of Upheaval: Selections from William Lloyd Garrison's "The Liberator," 1831–1865.* New York: Hill and Wang, 1966.

New Perspectives on Race and Slavery in America: Essays in Honor of Kenneth M. Stampp. Edited by Robert Abzug and Stephen E Maizlish. Lexington: University Press of Kentucky, 1986.

Nichols, Charles. *Many Thousands Gone: The Ex-Slave's Account of Their Bondage and Freedom.* New York: Athenaeum, 1974.

Parish, Peter J. *Slavery: History and Historians.* New York: Harper and Row, 1989.

Parker, Theodore (1810–60). *The Slave Power.* New York: Arno Press and *New York Times*, 1969.

Patterson, Orlando. *The Ordeal of Integration: Progress and Resentment in America's Racial Crisis.* New York: Civitas/Counterpoint, 1998.

Pease, Jane, and William Pease. *The Antislavery Argument.* Indianapolis: Bobbs-Merrill, 1965.

———. *Bound with Them in Chains: A Biographical History of the Antislavery Movement.* Westport, CT: Greenwood Press, 1972.

———. *Ladies, Women, and Wenches: Choice and Constraint in Antebellum Charleston and Boston.* Chapel Hill: University of North Carolina Press, 1990.

———. *They Who Would Be Free: Blacks Search for Freedom, 1830–1861.* New York: Athenaeum Press, 1974.

Perry, Lewis. *Radical Abolitionism: Anarchy and Government of God in Antislavery Thought.* Ithaca: Cornell University Press, 1973.

Perry, Lewis, and Michael Felman. *Antislavery Reconsidered: New Perspectives on the Abolitionists.* Baton Rouge: Louisiana State University Press, 1979.

Quarles, Benjamin. *The Black Abolitionists.* New York: Oxford University Press, 1969.

Rice, Charles Duncan. *The Rise and Fall of Black Slavery.* Baton Rouge: Louisiana State University Press, 1975.

Richard, Leonard. *Gentlemen of Property and Standing: Anti-Abolition Mobs in Jacksonian America.* New York: Oxford University Press, 1970.

Ripley, C. Peter, et al., eds. *The Black Abolitionist Papers.* 5 vols. Chapel Hill: University of North Carolina Press, 1985–93.

———, eds. *Witness for Freedom: African American Voices on Race, Slavery, and Emancipation.* Chapel Hill: University of North Carolina Press, 1993.

Rose, Willie Lee Nichols. *Slavery and Freedom.* Edited by William Freehling. New York: Oxford University Press, 1982.

———. ed. *A Documentary History of Slavery in North America.* New York: Oxford University Press, 1976.

Rodriguez, Junius, ed. *The Historical Encyclopedia of World Slavery.* Santa Barbara: ABC-CLIO, 1997.

Rozwenc, Edwin, ed. *Slavery as a Cause of the Civil War.* Boston: D. C. Heath, 1963.

Ruchames. Louis. *The Abolitionists: A Collection of Their Writings*. New York: G. P. Putnam's Sons, 1960.

———. *Racial Thought in America: From the Puritans to Abraham Lincoln*. Amherst: University of Massachusetts Press, 1969.

Sekora, John, and Darwin Turner, eds. *The Art of Slave Narrative: Original Essays in Criticism and Theory*. Macomb: Western Illinois University Press, 1982.

Smith, John David. *An Old Creed for the New South: Proslavery Ideology and Historiography, 1865–1918*. Athens: University of Georgia Press, 1991.

Smith, Samuel Stanhope. *An Essay on the Causes of the Variety of Complexion and Figure in the Human Species*. Edited by Winthrop Jordan. Cambridge: Harvard University Press, 1965.

Smith, Valerie. *Self-Discovery and Authority in Afro-American Narrative*. Cambridge: Harvard University Press, 1987.

Snay, Mitchell. *The Gospel of Disunion: Religion and Separatism in the Antebellum South*. New York: Cambridge University Press, 1993.

Sorin, Gerald. *Abolitionism: a New Perspective*. New York: Praeger, 1972.

Stampp, Kenneth M. *The Peculiar Institution: Slavery in the Antebellum South*. New York: Alfred A. Knopf, 1961.

Stanton, William R. *The Leopard's Spots: Scientific Attitudes toward Race in America, 1815–1859*. Chicago: University of Chicago Press, 1960.

Stepto, Robert B. *From Behind the Veil: A Study of Afro-American Narrative*. Urbana: University of Illinois Press, 1979.

Stewart, James B. *Holy Warriors and the Abolitionists and American Slavery*. New York: Hill and Wang, 1976.

———. *Wendell Phillips, Liberty's Hero*. Baton Rouge: Louisiana State University Press, 1986.

Stowe, Harriet Beecher (1811–96). *Uncle Tom's Cabin*. New York: New American Library, 1981.

———. *Uncle Tom's Cabin*. Critical edition, ed. Elizabeth Ammons. New York: W. W. Norton, 1994.

Strane, Susan. *A Whole-Souled Woman. Prudence Crandall and the Education of Black Women*. New York: W. W. Norton, 1990.

Stuckey, Sterling. *Slave Culture, Nationalist Theory and the Foundations of Black America*. New York: Oxford University Press, 1987.

Sumner, Charles (1811–74). *The Selected Letters of Charles Sumner*. Edited by Beverly Wilson Palmer. Boston: Northeastern University Press, 1990.

Sun, Tung-Hsun. *Historians and the Abolitionist Movement*. Taipei: Institute of American Culture, Academia Sinica, 1976.

Sundquist, Eric. *To Wake the Nations: Race in Nineteenth-Century American Literature*. Cambridge: Harvard University Press, 1986.

———, ed. *Frederick Douglass: New Literary and Historical Essays*. New York: Cambridge University Press, 1990.

Tadman, Michael. *Speculators and Slaves: Masters, Traders, and Slaves in the Old South*. Madison: University of Wisconsin Press, 1989.

Takaki, Ronald. *From Different Shores: Perspectives on Race and Ethnicity in America*. New York: Oxford University Press, 1987.

———. *Iron Cages: Race and Culture in Nineteenth-Century America*. New York: Alfred A. Knopf, 1979.

———. *Lewis Tappan and the Evangelical War against Slavery*. Cleveland: Case Western Reserve University Press, 1969.

Thomas, John L. *The Liberator: William Lloyd Garrison, a Biography*. Boston: Little, Brown, 1963.

———. *Slavery Attacked: The Abolitionist Crusade*. Englewood Cliffs, NJ: Prentice Hall, 1963.

Tise, Larry E. *Proslavery: A History of the Defense of Slavery in America, 1700–1740*. Athens: University of Georgia Press, 1987.

Tracy, Susan J. *In the Master's Eye: Representations of Women, Blacks, and Poor Whites in Antebellum Southern Literature*. Amherst: University of Massachusetts Press, 1995.

Tragle, Henry Irving. *The Southampton Slave Revolt of 1831: A Compilation of Source Material*. Amherst: University of Massachusetts Press, 1971.

Underground Railroad. Produced by the Division of Publications, National Park Service, Department of the Interior, Washington, DC: 1998. Available through the Government Printing Office, Washington, DC.

Ven Deburg, William L. *Slavery and Race in American Popular Culture*. Madison: University of Wisconsin Press, 1984.

Walker, Peter F. *Moral Choices: Memory, Desire, and Imagination in Nineteenth-Century American Abolition*. Baton Rouge: Louisiana State University Press, 1978.

Walters, Ronald G. *The Antislavery Appeal: American Abolitionism after 1830*. Baltimore: Johns Hopkins University Press, 1976.

Weinstein, Allen, and Frank O. Gatell. *American Negro Slavery: A Modern Reader*. New York: Oxford University Press, 1968.

White, Deborah. *Ain't I a Woman: Female Slaves in the Plantation South*. New York: W. W. Norton, 1985.

Wish, Harvey, ed. *Antebellum Writings of George Fitzhugh and Hinton Rowan Helper on Slavery*. New York: Capricorn Books, 1960.

———, ed. *Slavery in the South; First-Hand Accounts of the Antebellum American Southland from Northern and Southern Whites, Negroes, and Foreign Observers*. New York: Farrar, Straus, 1964.

Wood, Betty. *The Origins of American Slavery: Freedom and Bondage in the English Colonies*. New York: Hill and Wang, 1997.

Yellin, Jean F. *Women and Sisters: The Antislavery Feminists in American Culture*. New Haven: Yale University Press, 1989.

———, ed. *Linda: Incidents in the Life of a Slave Girl, Harriet Jacobs*. Cambridge: Harvard University Press, 1985.

———, and John Van Home, eds. *The Abolitionist Sisterhood: Women's Political Culture in Antebellum America*. Ithaca, NY: Cornell University Press, 1994.

A House Divided

The Historical Background for the Antebellum Slavery Debates, 1776–1865

The introduction to this volume has shown how the abolitionist crusade of 1830–65 grew out of an earlier antislavery movement that was largely religious in origin and character, and lacked the aggressive, demanding resolve of William Lloyd Garrison, Lydia Maria Child, Frederick Douglass, and Wendell Phillips. The documents that follow include representative texts from this antislavery debate during the year 1700, when Judge Samuel Sewall penned *The Selling of Joseph*, an antislavery pamphlet that criticized American chattel slavery by invoking biblical precedents. The final documents included here are Thomas Jefferson's Declaration of Independence (1776) and Frederick Douglass's "What to the Slave Is the Fourth of July?" (1852), a critique of Jefferson's assertion that "all men are created equal" in the context of chattel slavery for African-Americans.

The antebellum slavery debates intensified early in the nineteenth century, particularly following the formation of the New England Antislavery Society in 1831 and the American Antislavery Society in 1833. The publication of David Walker's *Appeal* in 1830 and the commencement of William Lloyd Garrison's *The Liberator* on January 1, 1831, marked a new era in abolitionist rhetoric and thought. The early antislavery advocates had generally argued for "gradualism," a deliberate evolutionary change in American society that would require the prohibition of the importation of slaves but would allow the gradual abolition of slavery through attrition and even colonization. In the eighteenth century, the religious and moral arguments that were mounted against slavery used scriptural texts to counter the biblical precedents of the Old Testament which proslavery advocates had used to support the institution. Garrisonians called for immediate and unconditional emancipation of the slaves, with no compensation for the slaveowners.

The moral and religious arguments were advanced well before the abolitionist crusade of the 1830s, but these pioneering voices were often, like John the Baptist's, "voices crying in the wilderness," speaking out in a society that was either opposed to any form of emancipation or simply indifferent to the moral ramifications of the issue. Prior to 1776, when Jefferson's Declaration of Independence argued the equality of mankind, a natural rights principle that grew out of Enlightenment doctrine, the eighteenth-century antislavery arguments were primarily developed out of scriptural texts or religious doctrine. The Enlightenment had effectively challenged the monarchies of Europe with a radically new view of humanity that disabled essentialist arguments concerning the nature of man, and these natural-rights views were fused with antislavery biblical reasoning to advance an early argument for emancipation. Ironically, it was this very biblical precedent, particularly the Old Testament practice of enslaving captured enemies and the polygamous practice of holding female slaves during the Age of the Patriarchs (Genesis), that gave nineteenth-century proslavery advocates examples from Scripture to use against the abolitionists who demanded an immediate end to chattel slavery in the United States. The charter documents of the new nation set individual freedoms and human rights as the highest priority; biblical precedent included not only Christ's humane teachings but also the Old Testament slavery precedents and St. Paul's letter to Philemon, in which certain forms of slavery are clearly condoned. Moreover, several prominent founding fathers who were architects of the new government and authors of these charter documents, including George Washington and Thomas Jefferson, were themselves slaveholders, creating an inconsistency between theory and practice that plagued the nineteenth-century Congress as well as the framers of the Constitution.

For example, at the age of eleven, George Washington inherited ten slaves when his father died. Until the Revolutionary War, Washington really did not question slavery; there is no record of his having protested its existence or having written anything in opposition to it. He continued to hold slaves at Mount Vernon after his inauguration as president of the United States, and Martha Washington's dowry included slaves. Like most Southern plantation owners, Washington needed slave labor to develop his landholdings. When he was only nineteen years old, he already owned over fourteen hundred acres of Virginia farmland west of the Blue Ridge Mountains, having received much of this land in lieu of payment for his services as a land surveyor. Washington was paternalistic toward his slaves. He often referred to them as "my family" and considered Mount Vernon, his palatial Potomac estate, as their home. He even saw to their health maintenance and the care of their teeth, not because this was "good business" and would protect the investment in his property, but because he considered himself the patriarch of a large plantation family. It is significant that Washington did not participate in the selling of slaves, although he did purchase slaves for his estate. After the Revolution, Washington came to hate slavery and wrote, "it being among my first wishes to see some plan adopted by the Legislature by which slavery in this Country may be abolished by slow, sure, and imperceptible degrees."

This "gradualist" approach to the termination of slavery was prominent in the tracts produced in the eighteenth century. The antislavery writers of the seventeenth and eighteenth centuries included here used moral suasion and the Bible in different ways, but primarily to establish a moral position against the inhumanity of slavery as a societal institution. For example, Samuel Sewall argues that "manstealing" is morally wrong, a violation of God's ordinances, and he cites Exodus 21.16, which reads, "He that Stealeth a man and Selleth him, or if he be found in his hand, he shall surely be put to Death."

Similarly, Cotton Mather argues the Christian value of the African, his capacity for salvation, and the urgency for slaveholders to redeem themselves by Christianizing their slaves. "Who can tell but that this Poor Creature may belong to the Election of God! Who can tell but that God may have sent this

Poor Creature into my hands, so that one of the Elect may by my means be called; by my Instruction be made wise unto Salvation! The Glorious God will put an unspeakable glory upon me, if it may be so! The Consideration that would move you, to Teach your Negroes the Truths of the Glorious Gospel, as far as you can, and bring them, if it may be, to live according to those Truths, a Sober, and a Godly life. . . ." The Mathers owned slaves in Massachusetts before the new state outlawed slavery in 1783; Cotton Mather here essentially argues that Christian slaves would make better slaves for their having been introduced to the principles of the Christian faith.

In 1754, the Quaker John Woolman returned to the religious argument for the humane treatment of Africans, and writing some fifty years after Sewall and Mather, he argued for the emancipation of slaves if not for the equality of blacks and whites. "Why should it seem right to honest Men to make Advantage by these People [Africans] more than by others? Others enjoy Freedom, receive wages, equal to their work, at, or near such Time as they have discharged these equitable Obligations they are under to those who educated them. These have made no Contract to serve; been more expensive in raising up than others, and many of them appear as likely to make a right use of freedom as other People; which Way then can an honest man withhold from them that Liberty, which is the free Gift of the Most High to His rational creatures?" Woolman argues the humanity of the African, a conventional eighteenth-century Enlightenment doctrine which was challenged in the early nineteenth century by scientific and pseudoscientific theories about the natural inferiority of the black race. Woolman concludes: "Negroes are our fellow creatures, and their present condition amongst us requires our serious Consideration. We know not the time when those Scales, in which Mountains are weighed, may turn. The Parent of Mankind is gracious; His Care is over the smallest Creatures; and Multitudes of Men escape not this."

Thomas Jefferson, like John Woolman, was troubled greatly by the obvious inhumanity of chattel slavery. However, Jefferson was also a product of his times, and, like George Washington, owned a large Virginia plantation which required labor to maintain. His *Notes on the State of Virginia* (1782) reveal that he was deeply divided over the slavery issue. On the one hand, he argued that slavery was wrong and that emancipation should be gradually adopted in the United States. Although he did not emancipate any of his own slaves until after his death, when some of his slaves were manumitted by the terms of his will, and although he is now known to have sired a child by a female slave, Sally Hemings, his argument in the *Notes on the State of Virginia* reflects an ambivalence toward the institution because of its inhuman practices. Still, Jefferson also outlines the racial differences between blacks and whites in *Notes*, and he concludes that these differences are immutable and eternal. Jefferson's recapitulation of contemporary race theory arguments is not unusual. Henri Grégoire, a French scientist, countered Jefferson's essentialist position in 1808, in his *On the Cultural Achievement of Negroes*. The British anthropologist James Cowles Pritchard (1788–1848) articulated widely influential views on race classification, by which a hierarchy of races was established, and in Germany, Johann Friedrich Blumenbach (1742–1840) argued that there were five basic racial types, placing the Anglo-Saxon at the pinnacle of the polygenic chain, and the African at the bottom.

This development was, in retrospect, extremely important in establishing the European conception of the African. The eighteenth-century Age of Enlightenment had embraced theories of race that stressed the unity of humanity, while recognizing that there were vast differences between specific persons, including racial differences, but it considered these differences to be variations or mutations on a common origin, and all humans were regarded to be developing progressively. Until the late eighteenth century, it was not difficult to establish the "humanity" of the African, even if it was problematic to establish his equality with the European. But with the rise of scientific reasoning and "race classification," and the methodology of nineteenth-century researchers like Samuel Morton, J. B. Turner, Josiah Nott, George R. Gliddon, J. H. Van Evrie, and O. S. Fowler, serious challenges to the notion that "all men are created equal" were authoritatively advanced. A hierarchy of races was established not only in the scientific literature, but also in the popular cultural assumptions about race. Politically and socially, these perceived differences stripped the African of his freedom in chattel slavery, and among free blacks, of his right to vote and, in some instances, to own property, which was a precondition for enjoying the franchise. The historical debates about the "rightness" and "wrongness" of slavery would continue until the Civil War and the Thirteenth Amendment to the Constitution abolished slavery forever. However, the debates concerning the biological, social, and political equality of the African in America continued during Reconstruction and into the late nineteenth century, in such literary works as Mark Twain's *Pudd'nhead Wilson* (1894), and into the twentieth century in such studies as Herrnstein and Murray's *The Bell Curve* (1993).

Several information sources follow this introduction. First, there is a summary of the "Civil Condition of the Enslaved," found in *Stroud's Compendium*. Second, United States Census figures from 1790 to 1860, slave and free, are provided. Third, from the W. E. B. Du Bois Institute of Harvard University, Atlantic Slave Trade Project, is a summary of the number of slave voyages taken to the Americas between 1595 and 1867, a time frame in which there were a total of 26,807 known voyages. These data were compiled as of April 23, 1997. Readers should note that census statistics even today are inexact and, in some densely populated areas, rely heavily on estimates and projections. The census, taken every decade since the first United States Census was established in 1790, provides reliable but inexact data concerning the slave population. More exact data was obtained by the Atlantic Slave Trade Project concerning the number of transatlantic slavery voyages and the number of chattel slaves transported on each voyage, because the "cargo" was considered chattel or property of owners and investors, so that "bills of lading" and "inventory records" were meticulously kept to account for the sale of the cargo at the end of the voyage. Commercial accountability, in short, inadvertently provides the modern reader with more than rough estimates about the extent and brutality of the transatlantic slave trade and its infamous "Middle Passage." These are a few of the many statistical information sources now available, both in libraries and on-line, concerning the almost three centuries of slavery in North America. Readers are urged to make an on-line "Google" search using the keywords "slavery" and "middle passage" to obtain further information about this important phase of the history of slavery in the United States. Also, the Library of Congress web page provides sources for population data concerning slavery (www.loc.gov). The three sources contained here provide an overview of the three centuries of slavery in the Americas, with a focus on the United States, 1621–1865.

Stroud's Compendium of the Laws of Slavery

Number of Americans Enslaved

The increase of the slave population in these United States, for the fifty years ending in 1830, has been as follows:

Census of	Slaves	Total Population
1790	697,697	3,929,827
1800	896,849	5,305,925
1810	1,191,364	7,289,314
1820	1,538,064	9,638,181
1830	2,010,436	12,856,407
1860	3,954,000 +	31,513,000 +

Hence, it appears that, according to the ratio of increase between 1820 and 1830, there must have been in 1835, not less than 2,245,144 slaves in these United States.

CIVIL CONDITION OF THE ENSLAVED

1. The master may determine the kind, and degree, and time of labor, to which the slave shall be subjected.

2. The master may supply the slave with such food and clothing only, both as to quantity and quality, as he may think proper.

3. The master may, at his discretion, inflict any punishment upon the person of his slave.

4. Slaves have no legal right to any property in things real or personal; but whatever they may acquire, belongs in point of law to their masters.

5. The slave, being personal chattel, is at all times liable to be sold absolutely, or mortgaged, or leased, at the will of his master.

6. He may also be sold by process of law, for the satisfaction of the debts of a living, or the debts and bequests of a deceased master, at the suit of creditors of legatees.

7. A slave cannot be a party before a judicial tribunal, in any species of action, against his master, no matter how atrocious may have been the injury received from him.

8. Slaves cannot redeem themselves, nor obtain a change of masters, though cruel treatment may have rendered such change necessary for their personal safety.

9. Slaves can make no contracts.

10. Slavery is hereditary and perpetual.

11. The benefits of education are withheld from slaves.

12. The means of moral and religious instruction are not granted to the slave; on the contrary, the efforts of the humane and charitable to supply these wants are discountenanced by law.

13. Submission is required of the slave, not to the will of his master only, but to that of all other white persons.

14. The penal codes of the slaveholding states bear much more severely upon slaves than upon white persons.

15. Slaves are prosecuted and tried upon criminal accusations, in a manner inconsistent with the rights of *humanity*.

Source Note: Stroud's *Compendium of the Laws of Slavery* (Boston, 1843).

Population Statistics from the U.S. Census for 1790–1860

Census Year	Number of Slaves	Total Population
1790	694,207	3,893,874
1800	887,612	5,084,912
1810	1,130,781	6,807,786
1820	1,529,012	10,037,323
1830	1,987,428	12,785,928
1840	2,482,546	16,987,946
1850	3,200,600	23,054,152
1860	3,950,546	31,183,582

The discrepancies between these official United States Census figures, which were taken from the Department of Commerce, Bureau of the Census, and those provided by George Stroud's *Compendium* may, in part, be reconciled by applying a uniform standard for counting citizens. In 1790, for example, the African slaves were counted as three-fifths of a person for the purpose of inflating the population figures for the slaveholding South, even though these persons were not allowed to vote or hold political office or own property. Even allowing for these differences in methods of computation, the ratio of non-slave to slave population for any given decade is remarkably similar in the two tables. The editor recommends that readers who wish further information consult the web site for the Department of Commerce, Bureau of the Census, Washington, D.C.

Summary from The Atlantic Slave Trade Project

*Summary of the information contained in the consolidated data
as of 23 April 1997*

Type of information	Number of voyages for which information is known
Places of ship's departure	19,899
Places of trade on the African coast	14,904
[Only intended places of trade reported]	[4,079]
Total voyages indicating African places of trade	18,983
Places of trade in the Americas	18,259
Places of trade in both Africa and the Americas	13,803
Numbers of Africans embarked on Coast	8,550
Average number [of slaves] per slave ship [embarkation]	330
Average number of slaves per slave ship [disembarkation]	284
At least one owner known	16,177

Notes: Number of voyages carrying slaves in the data-set (1595–1867): 26,807. Of the 11 million slaves transported to the New World following Sir John Hawkins's first transatlantic slave voyage in 1567, over half were carried by English slavetraders.

Source Note: Atlantic Slave Trade Project, W. E. B. Du Bois Center for African-American Studies, Harvard University, 1997.

The European Origins of American Slavery
by Arthur Kinney

One of the most tragic legacies of the Renaissance was the reinstitution of the slave trade. Gomes Eannes de Zurana, a member of the court of Portugal, attached to the king's brother, the famed Prince Henry the Navigator who has been given credit for the compass, is one of our earliest witnesses. He noted the arrival of a half-dozen hundred-ton caravels on the southwest point of the Algarve in Portugal. It was "very early in the morning" of August 8, 1444, when he saw the ships unloading a cargo of African slaves. They were placed in a large field, "a marvellous sight," according to an observer, "for, amongst them were some white enough, fair enough, and well-proportioned; others were less white, like mulattoes; others again were black as Ethiops, and so ugly, both in features and in body, as almost to appear . . . the images of a lower hemisphere." But Gomes thought differently. "What heart could be so hard," he notes in his chronicle,

> as not to be pierced with their faces bathed in tears, looking one upon another.
> Others stood groaning very dolorously, looking up to the height of heaven, fixing
> their eyes upon it, crying out loudly, as if asking help from the Father of nature;

others struck their faces with the palms of their hands, throwing themselves at full length upon the ground; while others made lamentations in the manner of a dirge, after the customs of their country. . . . But to increase their sufferings still more, there now arrived those who had charge of the division of the captives, and . . . then was it needful to part fathers from sons, husbands from wives, brothers from brothers. No respect was shown to either friends or relations, but each fell where his lot took him.

Gomes prayed to Fortune, but Prince Henry, standing by, watched impassively, claimed his "royal fifth," forty-six of the slaves there, and gave thanks to his God for allowing him to save their souls for the Lord.

The slaves had been captured on an expedition through what is now the modern state of Sahara, or the northern part of Mauritania, led by Lancarote de Freitas, who had been brought up in the household of Prince Henry and had formerly been a collector of taxes. The practice of seizing slaves, or *razzias*, the practice of man-stealing, had long been carried out by Muslims and Christians in Spain and in Africa, but de Freitas's was the first serious commercial venture sponsored in West Africa by Prince Henry. The merchants at Lisbon who had initiated the voyage had hoped for gold, but Prince Henry thought slaves just as good: the money he received from their sale could finance further expeditions, including those of pure discovery.

The demand for African slaves likewise grew in Spain. In 1462, Diogo Valarinho, a Portuguese merchant, was given permission to sell slaves in Seville, most of them from the river Senegal and Sierra Leone. By 1475, there were enough black slaves in Spain to require a special magistrate for them. The trade was not popular with all the Portuguese, who preferred black labor to drain their marshes and work their plantations of sugar, but the king of Portugal found such trade in Spain lucrative. One Czech traveler, Vaclav Sasek, noted in 1466 that the king of Portugal was, in fact, making more money selling slaves to foreigners "than from all the taxes levied on the entire kingdom."

An even more infamous slave dealer was the Englishman John Hawkins, who established a famous trade triangle by taking slaves to the New World in exchange for gold, for "hides, ginger, sugars, and some quantity of pearls," and then bringing these goods back to England. In his first voyage, his speculation was supported by his father-in-law, Benjamin Gonson, treasurer of the navy; Sir Thomas Lodge, who was lord mayor of London and a governor of the Russia Company as well as a trader to Morocco, North Africa, and Holland; and Sir William Winter, master of the naval ordinance; among others, Queen Elizabeth herself gave the voyage her blessing.

Hawkins sailed with three ships, leaving England in 1562. He picked up a pilot at the Canary Islands and then in Sierra Leone he captured at least 300 blacks "by the sword, and partly by other means." In fact, however, he raided six Portuguese slaveboats. Hawkins then sailed across the Atlantic to Isabela, Puerto de la Plata, and Monte Cristi on the north side of Hispaniola, where he sold the slaves for rich hides, spices, and pearls. Illegally, he sent such smuggled

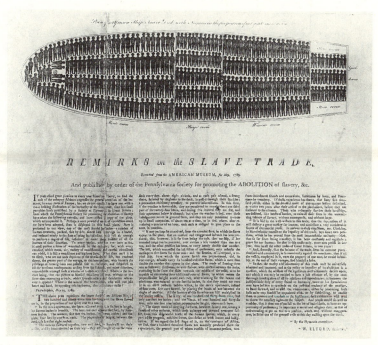

"Remarks on the Slave Trade," showing a slave ship cross-section, by permission of Georgia Barnhill, Mellon Curator of Graphic Arts, American Antiquarian Society, Worcester, Mass.

goods to Spain for sale, returning to England in 1563, after nine months at sea, his friend making "a good profit." In 1564, he set sail again, with more of England's nobility as his backers. Again he went to the river of Sierra Leone and on the land "to take inhabitants . . . burning and spoiling their towns." With four hundred African captives, he again crossed the Atlantic, this time to ports along the Venezuelan coast. Again he bought rare goods with the currency of slaves. He returned to England by way of Florida, "with great profits to the venturers of the said voyage, as also to the same realm, in bringing home both gold, silver, pearls and other jewels" worth 50,000 ducats in gold, according to the Spanish ambassador in London. This time Queen Elizabeth had less pretense: even as Hawkins boasted he made a 60 percent profit, the Queen knighted him. In response, the slave trader took for his crest the image of a black female African. Hawkins's shamelessness was identical, except, perhaps, in degree, to the English court of the Renaissance and to the Queen "of glorious memory" herself.

Source Note: The script of this "Renaissance Moment" was broadcast on NPR's "Morning Edition," hosted on WFCR by Bob Paquette, on February 6, 2002, in acknowledgment of Black History Month, by Arthur F. Kinney.

SAMUEL SEWALL (1632–1730) AND JOHN SAFFIN (1632–1710)

Samuel Sewall and John Saffin engaged in one of the earliest "slavery debates" framed in the Americas. Sewall was a Massachusetts judge, and he was also an outspoken opponent of slavery as an institution. He was not only one of the Massachusetts Bay Colony's most distinguished jurists and lawyers; he was also a successful merchant and an early American political figure. His prominence was also controversial: in 1692, he participated actively in the Salem Witchcraft trials that sent the accused to the gallows. However, in 1696, Sewall had the courage to recant his actions in a public confession while his colleagues and fellow jurists remained silent. The following excerpts are from his tract, *The Selling of Joseph*, which was published on June 12, 1700, and stands as one of the first antislavery pamphlets printed in America. (A Quaker document protesting the slave trade had appeared as early as 1687; however, Sewall's tract opposes not only the horrors of the slave trade but the injustices of the institution itself, and is one of the very earliest objections to the "peculiar institution.")

The full text of *The Selling of Joseph* shows clearly that Sewall condemned chattel slavery; however, it also reveals a writer who was familiar with contemporary race theory and who accepted the inherent inferiority of the African to the white. Modern readers should consider what Sewall meant when he regarded the African in America as a type of "extravasat Blood," or a separate biological group within the "Body Politick." But he sets out the arguments not only about slavery as an institution, but also concerning full racial equality, that would be debated throughout the nineteenth century.

John Saffin was Samuel Sewall's contemporary, and a vocal critic of Sewall's position on slavery. He was a successful merchant, a slave dealer and slave trader, and, in 1701, at the time of his writing a response to Sewall's pamphlet, he was a member of the same judicial court as Sewall. Sewall condemned Saffin privately, and Saffin replied publicly to Sewall in *A Brief Candid Answer to a Late Printed Sheet Entitled, The Selling of Joseph* (1701). Saffin's document is one of the earliest defenses of the institution on record. It had been lost until George H. Moore (1823–92) discovered a copy and published it in an appendix to his *Notes on the History of Slavery in Massachusetts* (1866). The most comprehensive account of the controversy between Sewall and Saffin is Lawrence W. Towner's "The Sewall-Saffin Dialogue on Slavery" (see "Suggestions for Further Reading" at the end of this headnote). See also Louis Ruchames, *Racial Thought in America from the Puritans to Abraham Lincoln*.

According to Larry Tise, John Saffin, who owned slaves and was a trader himself, was very annoyed by Sewall's accusations that he was, in the biblical sense of the term, a "mansteater," so he developed some twenty arguments in defense of slavery, all of which were used, with a dozen or so others, to defend the institution right up to the time of the Civil War.

After upholding his right of ownership of the slave in question, Saffin appealed directly to Biblical sanction, and the example set by the Hebrew patriarchs. Since Abraham owned slaves, "our Imitation of him in his Moral Action, is as warrantable as that of adopting his Faith." Not choosing to argue that "Blackamores are of the Posterity of Cham, and therefore under the Curse of Slavery," Saffin held that "any lawful Captives of Other Heathen Nations may be made Bond men." But "Tis unlawful," he admitted, "for Christians to Buy and Sell one another for slaves." [p. 17]

In other words, ownership of human beings is only sanctioned by God in the Old Testament when those humans are heathen and therefore inferior. This traditional argument was used regularly in the six decades before the Civil War, and it was coupled with another proslavery argument, that the transportation of the heathen Africans to the Americas afforded them the opportunity to become "civilized Christians," which they would not have had by remaining in Africa. Tise continues,

Saffin then turned to the rights of man and challenged Sewall's notion that the sons of Adam "have equal right to Liberty, and all other Comforts of Life." By no means an equalitarian, Saffin argued that God had intentionally set "different Orders and Degrees of Men in the World," and that any push toward equality would be "to invert the Order that God had set." Phrasing a statement that was repeated endlessly in the proslavery literature on the eve of the Civil War, Saffin wrote that God had ordained "some to be High and Honourable, some to be Low and despicable; some to be Monarchs, Kings, Princes, and Governours, Masters and Commanders, others to be Subjects, and to be Commanded; Servants of sundry sorts and degrees, bound to obey; yea, some to be born Slaves, and so to remain during their lives." [p. 17]

Besides upholding slavery as a blameless and natural social institution, Saffin used cynically and unnecessarily cruel phrasing that is degrading to the African. The poem that appears at the end of Saffin's excerpt is an example of this writing and has been included for that reason.

SUGGESTIONS FOR FURTHER READING

Ruchames, Louis. *Racial Thought in America from the Puritans to Abraham Lincoln*. Amherst: University of Massachusetts Press, 1964.

Tise, Larry. *Proslavery: A History of the Defense of Slavery in America, 1701–1840*. Athens: University of Georgia Press, 1987.

Towner, Lawrence W. "The Sewall-Saffin Dialogue on Slavery." *William and Mary Quarterly* 3:21 (Jan. 1964): 40–52.

Von Frank, Albert J. "John Saffin: Slavery and Racism in Colonial Massachusetts." *Early American Literature* 29 (1962): 254–73.

Winslow, Ola E. *Samuel Sewall: A Life*. New York: Hill and Wang, 1963.

The Selling of Joseph: A Memorial
by Samuel Sewall

Forasmuch as LIBERTY *is in real value next unto* LIFE: *None ought to part with it themselves, or deprive others of it, but upon most mature Consideration.*

The Numerousness of Slaves at this day in the Province, and the Uneasiness of them under their Slavery, hath put many upon thinking whether the Foundation of it be firmly and well laid; so as to sustain the Vast Weight that is built upon it. It is most certain that all Men, as they are the Sons of *Adam*, are Coheirs; and have equal Right unto Liberty, and all their outward Comforts of Life. God *hath given the Earth* [with all its Commodities] *unto the Sons of Adam, Psal.* 115.16. *And hath made of One Blood, all Nations of Men, for to dwell on all the faces of the Earth, and hath determined the Times before appointed and the bounds of their habitation; That they should seek the Lord. Forasmuch then as we are the Offspring of God, Acts* 17.26, 27, 29. Now, although the title given by the last ADAM, doth infinitely better Men's Estates, respecting GOD and themselves; and grants them a most beneficial and inviolable Lease under the Broad Seal of Heaven, who were before only Tenants at Will; Yet through the Indulgence of GOD to our First Parents after the Fall, the outward Estate of all and every of their Children, remains the same, as to one another. So that Originally, and Naturally, there is no such thing as Slavery. *Joseph* was rightfully no more a Slave to his Brethren, than they were to him; and they had no more Authority to *Sell* him, than they had to *Slay* him. And if *they* had nothing to do to Sell him, the *Ishmaelites* bargaining with them, and paying down Twenty pieces of Silver, could not make a Title. Neither could *Potiphar* have any better Interest in him than the *Ishmaelites* had. *Gen.* 37.20, 27, 28. . . .

And seeing GOD hath said, *He that Stealeth a man and Selleth him, or if he be found in his hand, he shall surely be put to Death. Exod.* 21.16. This Law being of Everlasting Equity, when Man Stealing is ranked amongst the most atrocious of the Capital Crimes: What louder Cry can there be made of that Celebrated Warning, *Caveat Emptor?*

And all things considered, it would conduce more to the Welfare of the Province, to have Slaves for Life. Few can endure to hear of a Negro's being made free; and, indeed, they can seldom use their freedom well; yet, their continual aspiring after their forbidden Liberty, renders them Unwilling Servants. And there is such disparity in their Conditions, Colour & Hair, that they can never embody with us, and grow up into orderly Families, to the Peopling of the Land still remain in our Body Politick as a kind of extravasat Blood.

Moreover, it is too well known what Temptations Masters are under, to connive at the Fornication of their Slaves; lest they should be obligated to find them Wives, or pay their Fines.

It is likewise most lamentable to think, how in taking Negros out of *Africa*, and Selling of them here, That which GOD ha's joined together men do boldly render asunder; Men from their Country, Husbands from their Wives, Parents from their Children. How horrible is the Uncleanness, Mortality, if not Murder, that the ships are guilty of that bring great Crouds of the miserable men, and women. Methinks, when we are bemoaning the barbarous usage of our Friends and Kinsfolk in *Africa*: it might not be unreasonable to enquire whether we are not culpable in forcing the *Africans* to become Slaves amongst our selves. . . .

Obj. 1. *These Blackamores are of the Posterity of Cham, and therefore are under the Curse of Slavery. Gen.* 9.25, 26, 27.

Answ. Of all Offices, one would not beg this, *viz.* Uncalled for, to be Executioner of the Vindictive Wrath of God; the extent and duration of which is to us uncertain. If this ever was a Commission; How do we know but that it is long since out of Date? Many have found it to their Cost, that a Prophetical Denunciation of Judgment against a Person or People, would not warrant them to inflict that Evil. If it would, *Hazel* might justify himself in all he did against his Master and the *Israelites*, from 2 *Kings* 8.10, 12. . . .

But it is possible that by cursory reading, this Text may have been mistaken. For *Canaan* is the person Cursed three times over, without the mentioning of *Cham*. Good expositors suppose the Curse entailed on him, and that this Prophesie was accomplished in the Extirpation of the *Canaanites*. . . .

Obj. 2. *The* Nigers *are brought out of Pagan Country, into places where the Gospel is Preached.*

Answ. Evil must not be done, that good may come of it. The extraordinary and comprehensive Benefit accruing to the Church of God, and to *Joseph* personally, did not rectify his brethren's Sale of him. . . .

Obj. 3. *The Africans have Wars one with another; Our ships bring lawful Captives taken in those Wars.*

Answ. For ought is known, their Wars are much such as were between *Jacob's* Sons and their Brother *Joseph*. An Unlawful War can't make lawful Captives. And by Receiving, we are in danger to promote, and partake in their Barbarous Cruelties. *Therefore all things whatsoever ye would that men should do to you, do ye even to them: for this is the Law and the Prophets. Matt.* 7.12. . . .

Obj. 4. Abraham *had Servants bought with his Money, and born in his House.*

Answ. Until the Circumstance of *Abraham's* purchase be recorded, no Argument can be drawn from it. In the mean time, Charity obliges us to conclude that he knew it was lawful and good. . . .

It is Observable that the Israelites were strictly forbidden the buying or selling of one another for Slaves. Levit. 25.39, 56. Jer. 34.8 . . . 22. And GOD gauged His Blessing in lieu of any loss they might conceit they suffered thereby. *Deut.* 15.18. And since the partition Wall is broken down, inordinate Self love should likewise be demolished. GOD expects that Christians should be of a more Ingenuous and benign frame of spirit. Christians should carry it to all the World, as the *Israelites* were to carry it towards another. And for men obstinately to persist in holding their Neighbors and Brethren under the Rigor of perpetual Bondage, seems to be no proper way of gaining Assurance that God ha's given them Spiritual Freedom. . . .

Source Note: Louis Ruchames, *Racial Thought in America from the Puritans to Abraham Lincoln* (Amherst: University of Massachusetts Press, 1964), with permission of Bruce

Wilcox, Director. Originally printed by Bartholomew Green and John Allen, June 24, 1700.

A Brief, Candid Answer to a Late Printed Sheet, Entitled, The Selling of Joseph
by John Saffin

That Honourable and Learned Gentleman, the Author of a Sheet, Entitled, *The Selling of Joseph, A Memorial,* seems from thence to draw this conclusion, that because the Sons of *Jacob* did very ill in selling their Brother *Joseph* to the *Ishmaelites,* who were Heathens, therefore it is utterly unlawful to Buy and Sell Negroes, though among Christians; which Conclusion I presume is not well drawn from the Premises, nor is the case parallel; for it was unlawful for the *Israelites* to sell their Brethren upon any account, or pretence whatsoever during life. But it was not unlawful for the Seed of *Abraham* to have Bond men, and Bond women either born in their House, or bought with their Money, as it written of *Abraham, Gen.* 14.14 & 21.10 *& Exod.* 21.16 *& Levit.* 25.44, 45, 46. After the giving of the Law: And in *Josh.* 9.23. That famous Example of the Gibeonites is a sufficient proof where there [is] no other. . . .

So God hath set different Orders and Degrees of Men in the World, both in Church and Common weal. Now, if this Position of parity should be true, it would then follow that the ordinary Course of Divine Providence of God in the World should be wrong, and unjust (which we must not dare to think, much less to affirm) and all the sacred Rule, Precepts and Commands of the Almighty which he hath given the Son of Men to observe and keep in their respective Places, Orders and Degrees, would be to no purpose; which unaccountably derogate from the Divine Wisdom of most High, who hath made nothing in vain, but hath Holy Ends in all his Dispensation to the Children of men. . . .

Our Author doth further proceed to answer some Objections of his own framing, which he supposes some might raise.

Object. 1. *That these Blackamores are of the Posterity of* Cham *and therefore under the Curse of Slavery. Gen.* 9.25, 26, 27. The which the Gentleman seems to deny, saying, *they were the Seed of the Canaan that were Cursed.*

Answ. Whether they were so or not, we shall not dispute: this may suffice, that not only the seed of *Cham* or *Canaan,* but any lawful Captives of other Heathen Nations may be made Bond men as hath been proved. . . .

Obj. 2. *That the Negroes are brought out of Pagan Countreys into places where the Gospel is Preached.* To which he Replies, *that we must not doe Evil that good may come of it.*

Answ. To which we answer, That it is no Evil thing to bring them out of their own Heathenish Country, where they may have the Knowledge of the True God, be Converted and Eternally saved. . . .

Obj. 3. *The* Africans *have Wars one with another;* our Ships bring lawful Captives taken in those Wars.

To which our Author answers Conjecturally, and Doubtfully, *for ought we know,* that may or may not be; which is insignificant and proves nothing. He also compares the Negroes with another, with the Wars between *Joseph* and his Brethren. But where doth he read of any such War? . . .

By all which it doth evidently appear both by Scripture and Reason, the practice of the People of God in all Ages, both before and after the giving of the Law, and in the times of the Gospel, that there were Bond men, Women and Children commonly kept by holy and good men, and improved in Service: and therefore by the Command of God, *Lev.* 25.44, and their venerable Example, we may keep Bond men, and use them in our Service still; yet with all candour, moderation and Christian prudence, according to their state and condition consonant to the Word of God. . . .

THE NEGROES CHARACTER.

Cowardly and cruel are those Blacks *Innate,*
Prone to Revenge, Imp of inveterate hate.
He that exasperates them, soon espies
Mischief and murder in their very eyes.
Libidinous, Deceitful, False and Rude,
The Spume Issue of the Ingratitude.
The Premeses consider'd, all may tell,
How near good Joseph *they are parallel. . . .*

Source Note: Louis Ruchames, *Racial Thought in America from the Puritans to Abraham Lincoln* (Amherst: University of Massachusetts Press, 1964), with permission of Bruce Wilcox, Director.

JOHN WOOLMAN (1720–1772)

John Woolman was born in Burlington County, New Jersey, near Mount Holly, a settlement of Quakers. Because Woolman attended school in Mount Holly, his early views were deeply influenced by Quaker doctrines of nonviolence, passive resistance, and opposition to slavery. It is significant that the first antislavery pamphlet published in America was a Quaker document, issued in 1687. Woolman rejected the Calvinist concept of "innate depravity" or "original sin" and the doctrines of "election" and "predestination," which had characterized the Great Awakening ministry of Jonathan Edwards. Instead, Woolman's simple theology advocated universal redemption through Christ and a belief in the "inner light" through which individual believers might come to know God. But like Quakers throughout history, Woolman found his conscience in conflict with the theocracy of New England Puritanism, and he was uncomfortable as a businessman because of the profit motive and particularly because one commodity was slaves. His *Journal* was first published in 1774, and it is a deeply sensitive and personal account of the struggles of his conscience, from the killing of a robin when he was quite young to his later distress over having drafted an indenture for the sale of a slave, a task he resolved never to repeat. The latter decision would govern his later life, namely, that he would never again participate in the institution of slavery and that he would work to end its practice.

Woolman was essentially self-educated, and practiced surveying early in his adult life; then he became a scrivener in a lawyer's office where he was responsible for the drafting of wills, indentures, bills of sale, and other legal documents. He was an extremely popular writer because of his intensely personal style. Woolman's *Journal* was preceded by his mid-century publication, *Some Considerations on the Keeping of Negroes*, in which he argued that "the Colour of a Man avails nothing, in Matters of Right and Equity." The manuscript of this book was completed by 1747, but it was not published until 1754.

SUGGESTIONS FOR FURTHER READING

Critical and analytical studies include Daniel Shea, *Spiritual Autobiography in Early America* (Princeton: Princeton University Press, 1968), and Mason Lowance, "Biography and Autobiography in Early America," in Emory Elliott, ed., *The Columbia Literary History of the United States* (New York: Columbia University Press, 1988). See also the following.

Banes, Ruth A. "The Exemplary Self: Autobiography in Eighteenth Century America." *Biography—An Interdisciplinary Quarterly* 5 (1982): 226–39.

Cope, Jackson I. "Seventeenth Century Quaker Style." *PMLA* 71 (1956): 724–54.

David, Marianna W. "The Connatural Ground of John Woolman's Triangle." *CLA Journal* 9 (1965): 132–39.

Hedges, William L. "John Woolman and the Quaker Utopian Vision." In *Utopias: The American Experience*, ed. Gairdner B. Moment and Otto F. Kraushaar. Metuchen, NJ: Scarecrow, 1980, 87–102.

Medeiros, Patricia M. "Three Travelers: Carver, Bartram, and Woolman." In *American Literature, 1764–1789: The Revolutionary Years*, ed. Everett Emerson. Madison: University of Wisconsin Press, 1977, 195–211.

Rosenblatt, Paul. *John Woolman*. New York: Twayne, 1969.

Sox, David. *John Woolman: Quintessential Quaker, 1720–1772*. Richmond, IN: Friends United Press, 1999.

Stewart, Margaret E. "John Woolman's 'Kindness beyond Expression': Collective Identity vs. Individualism and White Supremacy." *Early American Literature* 26 (1991): 251–75.

Some Considerations on the Keeping of Negroes
by John Woolman

To consider mankind otherwise than Brethren, to think Favours are peculiar to one Nation, and exclude others, plainly supposes a Darkness in the Understanding: for as God's Love is universal, so where the Mind is sufficiently influenced by it, it begets a Likeness of itself, and the Heart is enlarged towards all Men. . . .

CONSIDERATIONS

ON KEEPING

Sam.ᵈ Allinson's

NEGROES;

Recommended to the PROFESSORS of CHRISTIANITY, of every *Denomination.*

PART SECOND.

By *JOHN WOOLMAN.*

Ye shall not respect Persons in Judgment ; but you shall hear the Small as well as the Great : You shall not be afraid of the Face of Man ; for the Judgment is GOD's. Deut. i. 17.

PHILADELPHIA:

Printed by B. FRANKLIN, and D. HALL. 1762.

"Considerations on Keeping Negroes," the title page of John Woolman's treatise, printed by Benjamin Franklin, by permission of Georgia Barnhill, Mellon Curator of Graphic Arts, American Antiquarian Society, Worcester, Mass.

Through the Force of long Custom, it appears needful to speak in Relation to Colour. Suppose a white Child, born of Parents of the meanest Sort, who died and left him an Infant, fall into the Hands of a Person, who endeavours to keep him a Slave, some men would account him an unjust Man in doing so, who yet appear easy while many Black People of honest Lives, and good Abilities, are enslaved, in a Manner more shocking than the case here supposed. This is owing chiefly to the Idea of Slavery being connected with the Black Colour, and Liberty with the White: And where false Ideas are twisted into our Minds, it is with Difficulty we get fairly disentangled. . . .

The Colour of a Man avails nothing, in Matters of Right and Equity. Consider Colour in Relation to Treaties; by such Disputes betwixt nations are sometimes settled. And should the Father of us all so dispose Things, that Treaties with black Men should sometimes be necessary, how then would it appear amongst the Princes and Ambassadors, to insist on the Prerogative of the white Colour?

The Blacks seem far from being our Kinsfolk, and did we find an agreeable Disposition and sound Understanding in some of them, which appeared as a good Foundation for a true Friendship between us, the Disgrace arising from an open Friendship with a Person of so vile a Stock, in the common Esteem, would naturally tend to hinder it. . . .

So that, in their present Situation, there is not much to engage the Friendship, or move the Affection of selfish Men: But such who live in the Spirit of true Charity, to sympathise with the Afflicted in the lowest Stations, is a Thing familiar to them. . . .

Though there were Wars and Desolations among *Negroes*, before the *Europeans* began to trade there for Slaves, yet now the Calamities are greatly increased, so many Thousands being annually brought from thence; and we, by purchasing them, with Views of self-interest, are becoming Parties with them, and accessory to that Increase.

In the present Case, relating to Home-born *Negroes*, whose Understandings and Behaviour are as good as common among other People, if we have any Claim to them as Slaves, that Claim is grounded on their being Children or Offspring of Slaves, who, in general, were made such through Means as unrighteous, and attended with more terrible Circumstance than the Case here supposed. . . .

Why should it seem right to honest Men to make Advantage by these People more than by others? Others enjoy Freedom, receive Wages, equal to their Work, at, or near, such Time as they have discharged these equitable Obligations they are under to those who educated them. These have made no Contract to serve; been no more expensive in raising up than others, and many of them appear as likely to make a right Use of Freedom as other People; which Way, then, can an honest Man withhold from them that Liberty, which is the free Gift of the Most High to his rational Creatures?

The *Negroes* who live for Plunder, and the Slave-Trade, steal poor innocent Children, invade their Neighbours' Territories, and spill much Blood to get these Slaves: And can it be possible for an honest Man to think that, with a View to Self-interest, we may continue Slavery to the Offspring of these unhappy Sufferers, merely because they are the Children of Slaves, and not have a Share of this Guilt. . . .

Negroes are our Fellow Creatures, and their present Condition amongst us requires our serious Consideration. We know not the Time when those Scales, in which Mountains are weighed, may turn. The parent of Mankind is gracious. His Care is over his smallest Creatures; and a Multitude of Men escape not His Notice: And though many of them are trodden down, and despised, yet He remembers them; He seeth their affliction, and looketh upon the spreading increasing Exaltation of the Oppressor. . . . And wherever Gain is preferred to Equity, and wrong Things Publickly encouraged to that Degree, that Wickedness takes root, and spreads wide amongst the Inhabitants of a Country, there is real Cause for Sorrow to all such, whose love to Mankind stands on a true Principle, and wisely consider the end and Event of Things.

Source Note: Louis Ruchames, *Racial Thought in America from the Puritans to Abraham Lincoln* (Amherst: University of Massachusetts Press, 1964), with permission of Bruce Wilcox, Director.

Acts of Congress Relating to Slavery

Included in this chapter are portions of important historical documents relating to slavery in the United States: the Constitution, the Ordinance of 1787, the Fugitive Slave Act of 1793, the Missouri Compromise of 1820, the Wilmot Proviso of 1847, and the long and exhaustive Fugitive Slave Law of 1850. In these documents may be seen the transformation of the Congress's willingness to prohibit slavery in the western territories in the Compromise of 1820, known as the "Missouri Compromise," to the more conservative and aggressively pro-slavery Compromise of 1850, with its extremely punitive Fugitive Slave Law. It is significant that many of the congressional acts and constitutional amendments concerning slavery between 1800 and 1865 contained caveats and language that required the return of fugitive slaves to their "rightful owners," even when they were found in the free North, to which they had escaped, or in the western territories, where slavery had been prohibited. These continuous concessions to the "slave power" of the Southern states placed the Underground Railroad in direct violation of federal statutes and increased tension between proslavery and antislavery forces throughout the United States and its territories.

Sections 6 and 8 of the Fugitive Slave Law of 1850 show clearly the obligations of all United States citizens, regardless of geography, to return escaped and fugitive slaves to their "rightful owners," and they outline the punishments awaiting those citizens who violate the law, including a thousand-dollar fine and six months in jail for aiding fugitive slaves in their escape to freedom. A clear concession to the slave power of the Southern slaveholding states, and a rebuke to the Underground Railroad organization, this law contained language present in all congressional acts concerning slavery since the Ordinance of 1787, namely, that even where slavery was prohibited by law, as in the western territories, escaped slaves should always be returned to their owners. It would not be legally possible, therefore, for a slave to "escape" to freedom in the free states and to enjoy this status because he had arrived in a free state where slavery was abolished or prohibited. He would always be a fugitive under federal law, and he would always be subject to a return to slavery for appropriate punishment for having attempted escape. This series of federal laws implicated the free states of the North in the institution of slavery practiced in the slaveholding states of the South, even in states like Massachusetts and Connecticut where slavery had been abolished under state law. Larry E. Tise writes:

> Neither the Constitution nor the Northwest Ordinance of 1787 abolished slavery in lands north of the Ohio River. The abolition of slavery in the area was to be decided by the individual states. In territories south of the Ohio, there was no legal encumbrance to affect either the introduction or perpetuation of slavery. Although

Congress had oversight of these territories, it did not intervene to determine the future of slavery in any western territory until the Missouri debates. Hence, as an extension of the debates that occurred during the first emancipation in northeastern states, each state carved out of frontier lands argued the future of slavery [for that territory]. Between 1790 and 1820 fervid local debates on slavery occurred in Tennessee, Kentucky, Ohio, Indiana, and Illinois whenever constitutional questions arose. By the early 1820s, after thirty years of sporadic struggles, slavery was finally abolished in the states north of the Ohio [River] and firmly entrenched in those to the south. [p. 55]

The Missouri debates, well cited in William Lee Miller's *Arguing about Slavery*, an anthology of materials from congressional arguments concerning slavery, transformed the antebellum slavery debates from a sectional dispute into one that transcended regional and sectional boundaries, invoking proslavery and antislavery sentiments on both sides of the Mason-Dixon line. "The Missouri controversy intervened in a long-lived and ongoing dispute about the admission of Negroes into the newer states and territories and brought the debate for the first time to national attention. But instead of pitting North against South, antislavery against proslavery, and egalitarian against racist, the Missouri debates rearranged and muddled the traditional argument regarding the morality of slavery" (Tise, p. 56). Even the antislavery congressmen and moderates who attacked slavery's extension into the Western territories were often unwilling to question the "right or propriety of perpetual slavery in the South." This kind of argumentation, with its "caveats of compromise" found throughout the emerging constitutional amendments and other legislative documents, insured the continuation of slavery in the Southern states while it was federally sanctioned and as long as the debate pitted the antislavery "moralists" against the proslavery "legalists." The debates over the extension of slavery into the territories west of the Mississippi River were immensely important in framing questions concerning the "legal" versus the "moral" aspects of the issue. The territorial debates also taught the nation that slavery was a national rather than an exclusively Southern issue. These debates would continue in Congress and in state legislatures throughout the first six decades of the nineteenth century, even during the Civil War.

SUGGESTIONS FOR FURTHER READING

Miller, William Lee. *Arguing about Slavery*. New York: Knopf, 1996.
Tise, Larry E. *Proslavery: A History of the Defense of Slavery in America, 1701–1840*. Athens: University of Georgia Press, 1987.

A Declaration by the Representatives of the United States of America, in General Congress Assembled. July, 1776
by Thomas Jefferson

Thomas Jefferson, the third president of the United States, was the primary author of the Declaration of Independence, 1776. His famous phrase, "all men

THE

CONSTITUTION

OF THE

UNITED STATES

WITH THE

ACTS OF CONGRESS

RELATING TO

SLAVERY

EMBRACING, THE CONSTITUTION, THE FUGITIVE SLAVE ACT

OF 1793, THE MISSOURI COMPROMISE ACT OF 1820,

THE FUGITIVE SLAVE LAW OF 1850, AND THE

NEBRASKA AND KANSAS BILL
CAREFULLY COMPILED

ROCHESTER

PUBLISHED BY D. M. DEWEY,

ARCADE HALL.

1856

"Acts of Congress Relating to Slavery," the title page of a book containing these documents.

---

are created equal," long stood as a challenge to American democratic principles in the nineteenth century, and it occasioned several rebuttals, including Frederick Douglass's speech, "What to the Slave Is the Fourth of July?" delivered in Rochester, New York, on July 5, 1852. (See also the headnote for Thomas Jefferson in chapter 7 of this volume.)

When, in the course of human events, it becomes necessary for one people to dissolve the political bands which have connected them with one another and assume among the powers of the earth the separate and equal station to which the laws of nature and of nature's God entitle them, a decent respect to the opinions of mankind requires that they should declare the causes which impel them to the separation.

We hold these truths to be self-evident: that all men are created equal; that they are endowed by their Creator with inherent and unalienable rights; that among these are life, liberty, and the pursuit of happiness; that to secure these rights, governments are instituted among men, deriving their just powers from the consent of the governed; that whenever any form of government becomes destructive of these ends, it is the right of the people to alter or to abolish it, and to institute new government, laying its foundation on such principles, and organizing its powers in such form, as to them shall seem most likely to effect their safety and happiness. . . . But when a long train of abuses and usurpations . . . evinces a design to reduce them under absolute despotism, it is their right, it is their duty to throw off such government, and to provide new guards for their future security. . . .

Source Note: Mason Lowance, Jr., and Georgia Bumgardner, eds., *Massachusetts Broadsides of the American Revolution* (Amherst: University of Massachusetts Press, 1976), p. 80.

The Ordinance of 1787 Passed by Congress Previous to the Adoption of the New Constitution, and Subsequently Adopted by Congress, Aug. 7th, 1789

ENTITLED—An ordinance for the Government of the Territory of the United States North West of the River Ohio. . . .

[*All the articles of this ordinance previous to article VI relate to the organization and powers of the government of the territory. Only the following section relates to slavery.*]

Article VI.

There shall be neither slavery nor involuntary servitude in the said Territory, otherwise than in punishment of crimes whereof the party shall have been duly convicted: Provided always, that any person escaping into the same, from whom labor or service is lawfully claimed in any one of the original States, such fugitive may be lawfully reclaimed and conveyed to the person claiming his or her labor or service as aforesaid.

Done by the United States in Congress assembled the thirteenth day of July, in the year of our Lord, 1787, and of the sovereignty and Independence, the twelfth.

WILLIAM GRAYSON, Chairman.
CHARLES THOMPSON, Sec'y.

The Fugitive Slave Law of 1793, Second Congress.—Session 2, Chapter 7, 1793 Statute 2, February 12, 1793

CHAP. VII—AN ACT respecting fugitives from justice, and persons escaping from the service of their masters.

SEC. 1. Be it enacted by the Senate and House of Representatives of the United States of America in Congress assembled, That whenever the executive authority of any state in the Union, or of either of the territories, northwest or south of the river Ohio, shall demand any person, as a fugitive from justice, or the executive authority of any such state or territory to which such person shall have fled, and shall, moreover, produce the copy of an indictment found, or an affidavit made before a magistrate of any state or territory as aforesaid, charging the person so demanded with having committed treason, felony, or other crime, certified as authentic by the governor or chief magistrate of the state or territory from whence the person so charged fled, it shall be the duty of the executive authority of the state or territory to which such person shall have fled, to cause him or her to be arrested and secured, and notice of the arrest to be given to the executive authority making such demand, or to the agent of such authority appointed to receive the fugitive, and to cause the fugitive to be delivered to such agent when he shall appear.—But if no such agent shall appear within six months from the time of the arrest, the prisoner may be discharged. And all costs or expenses incurred in the apprehending, securing, and transmitting such fugitive to the state or territory making such demand, shall be paid by such state or territory.

SEC. 2. And be it further enacted, That any agent appointed as aforesaid, who shall receive the fugitive into his custody, shall be empowered to transport him or her to the state or territory from which he or she shall have fled. And, if any person or persons shall by force set at liberty, or rescue the fugitive from such agent while transporting as aforesaid, the person or persons so offending, shall, on conviction, be fined not exceeding five hundred dollars, and be imprisoned not exceeding one year.

SEC. 3. And be it also enacted, That when a person held to labor in any of the United States, or in either of the territories on the northwest or south of the river Ohio, under the laws thereof, shall escape into any other of the said states or territory, the person to whom such labor or service may be due, his agent or attorney is hereby empowered to seize or arrest such fugitive from labor, and to take him or her before any judge of the Circuit or District Courts of the United States, residing or being within the state, or before any magistrate of a county, city or town corporate, wherein such seizure or arrest shall be made, and upon proof to the satisfaction of such judge or magistrate, either by oral testimony or affidavit taken before, and certified by, a magistrate of any such state or territory from which he or she fled, owe services or labor to the person claiming him or her, it shall be the duty of such judge or magistrate to give a certificate thereof to such claimant, his agent or attorney which shall be sufficient warrant for removing the said fugitive from labor, to the state or territory from which he or she fled.

SEC. 4. And be it further enacted, That any person who shall knowingly and willingly obstruct or hinder such claimant, his agent or attorney, in so seizing or arresting such fugitive from labor, or shall rescue such fugitive from such claimant, his agent or attorney, when so arrested pursuant to the authority herein given or declared; or shall harbor or conceal such person after notice that he or she was a fugitive from labor as aforesaid, shall for either of the said offences, forfeit and pay the sum of five hundred dollars. Which penalty may be recovered by and for the benefit of such claimant, by action of debt, in any court proper to try the same; saving, moreover, to the person claiming such labor or service, his right of action for or on account of the said injuries, or either of them.

Approved February 12, 1793.

The Missouri Compromise of 1820, Sixteenth Congress.—Sess. 1, Chap. 22, 1820 Statute 1, March 6, 1820

AN ACT to authorize the people of the Missouri territory to form a Constitution and State Government, and for the admission of such State into the Union on an equal footing with the original State, and to prohibit slavery in certain territories. . . .

[All the previous sections of this act relate entirely to the formation of the Missouri Territory in the usual form of territorial bills. Only the eighth section relates to the slavery question.]

SEC. VIII. And be it further enacted, That, in all that territory ceded by France to the United States, under the name of Louisiana, which lies north of thirty-six degrees, and thirty minutes north latitude, not included within the limits of the state contemplated by this act, slavery and involuntary servitude, otherwise than in the punishment of crimes, whereof the parties shall have been duly convicted, shall be, and is hereby, forever prohibited. Provided always that any person escaping into the same, from whom labor or service is lawfully claimed, in any state or territory of the United States, such fugitive may be lawfully reclaimed and conveyed to the person claiming his or her labor or service as aforesaid.

Approved March 6, 1820.

The Wilmot Proviso, 1847, House of Representatives, February 1, 1847

(The Chair allowed the Hon. Preston King to read as a part of his argument [upon the appropriation of $3,000,000 to enable the President to conclude a treaty of peace with Mexico,] the amendment which was prepared by Mr. Wilmot and which is commonly called the Wilmot Proviso, viz:)

—And be it further enacted, that there shall be neither slavery nor involuntary servitude in any Territory on the Continent of America, which shall hereafter be acquired by, or annexed to, the United States, except for crimes whereof the party shall have been duly convicted: Provided always, that any person escaping into such Territory, from whom labor or service is lawfully claimed, in any one of the United States, such fugitive may be lawfully reclaimed and conveyed out of said territory to the persons claiming his or her labor or service.

The Fugitive Slave Law of 1850, Thirty-First Congress—Sess. I, Chap. 60, 1850. Sept. 18, 1850

AN ACT to amend, and supplementary to, the Act entitled, "An Act respecting Fugitives from Justice, and Persons escaping from the Service of their Masters," approved February twelfth, one thousand seven hundred and ninety-three.

SEC. 1. Be it enacted by the Senate and House of Representatives of the United States of America in congress assembled, That the persons who have been, or may hereafter be, appointed Commissioners, in Virtue of any Act of Congress, by the Circuit Courts of the United States, and who, in consequence of such appointment, are authorized to exercise the powers that any justice of the peace, or other magistrate of any of the United States, exercise in respect to offenders for any crime or offence against the United States, by arresting, imprisoning, or bailing the same under and by virtue of the thirty-third section of the act of the twenty-fourth of September, seventeen hundred and eighty-nine, entitled "An Act to establish the judicial courts of the United States," shall be, and are hereby, authorized and required to exercise and discharge all the powers and duties conferred by this act.

SEC. 2. And be it further enacted, That the Superior Court of each organized Territory of the United States shall have the same power to appoint commissioners to take acknowledgments of bails and affidavits, and to take depositions of witnesses in civil causes, which is now possessed by the Circuit Court of the United States; and all commissioners who shall hereafter be appointed for such purposes by the Superior Court of any organized Territory of the United States, shall possess all the powers, and exercise all the duties, conferred by law upon the commissioners appointed by the Circuit Courts of the United States for similar purposes, and shall moreover exercise and discharge all the powers and duties conferred by this act.

SEC. 3. And be it further enacted, That the Circuit Court of the United States, and the Superior Courts of each organized Territory of the United States, shall from time to time enlarge the number of Commissioners with a view to afford reasonable facilities to reclaim fugitives from labor, and to the prompt discharge of the duties imposed by this Act.

SEC. 4. And be it further enacted, That the Commissioners above named shall have concurrent jurisdiction with the judges of the Circuit and District Courts of the United States, in their respective circuits and districts within the several States, and the judges of the Superior Courts of the Territories severally and collectively, in term-time and vacation; and shall grant certificates to such claimants upon satisfactory proof being made, with authority to take and remove such fugitives from service or labor, under the restrictions herein contained, to the State or Territory from which such persons may have escaped or fled.

SEC. 5. And be it further enacted, That it shall be the duty of all marshals and deputy marshals to obey and execute all warrants and precepts issued under the provisions of this act, when to them directed; and should any marshal or deputy marshal refuse to receive such warrant, or other process, when tendered, or to use all proper means diligently to execute the same, he shall, on conviction thereof, be fined in the sum of one thousand dollars, to the use of such claimant, on the motion of such claimant, by the Circuit or District Court for the district of such marshal; and after arrest of such fugitive, by such marshal or his deputy, or whilst at any time in his custody, under the provisions of this act, should such fugitive escape, whether with or without the assent of such marshal or his deputy, such marshal shall be liable, on his official bond, to be prosecuted for the benefit of such claimant, for the full value of the service or labor of said fugitive in the State, Territory, or District whence he escaped; and the better to enable said commissioners, when thus appointed, to execute their duties faithfully and efficiently, in conformity with the requirements of the Constitution of the United States, and of this act, they are hereby authorized and empowered, within their counties respectively, to appoint, in writing under their hands, any one or more suitable persons, from time to time, to execute all such warrants and other process as may be issued by them in the lawful performance of their respective duties; with authority to such commissioners, or the persons to be appointed by them, to execute process as aforesaid, to summon and call to their aid the bystanders, or posse comitatus of the proper county, when necessary to insure a faithful observance of the clause of the Constitution referred to, in conformity with the provisions of this act; and all good citizens are hereby commanded to aid and assist in the prompt and efficient execution of the law, whenever their services may be required, as aforesaid, for that purpose; and said warrants shall run, and be executed by said officers, anywhere in the State within which they are issued.

SEC. 6. And be it further enacted, That when a person held to service or labor in any State or Territory of the United States, has heretofore or shall hereafter escape into another State or Territory of the United States, the person or persons to whom such service or labor may be due, or his, her, or their agent or attorney, duly authorized by power of attorney, in writing acknowledged and certified under the seal of some legal officer or Court of the State or Territory in which the same may be executed, may pursue and reclaim such fugitive person, either by procuring a warrant from some one of the Courts, judges, or commissioners aforesaid, of the proper circuit, district, or county, for the apprehension of such fugitive from service or labor, or by seizing and arresting such fugitive where the same can be done without process, and by taking, or causing such person to be taken forthwith before such Court, Judge, or Commissioner, whose duty it shall be, to hear and determine the case of such claimant in a summary manner; and upon satisfactory proof being made, by deposition or affidavit, in writing, to be taken, and certified by such Court, Judge, or Commissioner, or by other satisfactory testimony, duly taken and certified by some Court, Magistrate, Justice of the Peace, or other legal officer authorized to administer an oath and take depositions under the laws of the State or Territory from which such person owing service or labor may have escaped, with a certificate of such magistracy, or other authority as aforesaid, with the seal of the proper Court or officer thereto attached, which seal shall be sufficient to establish the competency of the proof, and with proof, also by affidavit, of the identity of the person whose service or labor is claimed to be due as aforesaid, that the person so arrested does in fact owe service or labor to the person or persons claiming him or her, in the State or Territory from which such fugitive may have escaped as aforesaid, and that said person escaped, to make out and deliver to such claimant, his or her agent or attorney, a certificate setting forth the substantial facts as the service or labor due from such fugitive to the claimant, and of his or her escape from the State or Territory in which such service or labor was due to the State or Territory in which he or she was arrested, with authority to such claimant, or his, or her agent, or attorney, to use such reasonable force and restraint as may be necessary, under the circumstances of the case, to take and remove such fugitive person back to the State or Territory whence he or she may have escaped as aforesaid. In no trial or hearing under this Act shall the testimony of such alleged fugitive be admitted in evidence; and the certificates in this and the first section mentioned, shall be conclusive of the right of the person or persons in whose favor granted, to remove such fugitive to the State or Territory from which he escaped, and shall prevent all molestation of such person or persons by any process issued by any Court, Judge, Magistrate or other person whomsoever.

SEC. 7. And be it further enacted, That any person who shall knowingly and willingly obstruct, hinder, or prevent such claimant, his agent or attorney, or any person or persons lawfully assisting him, her or them, from arresting such a fugitive from service or labor, either with or without process as aforesaid, or shall rescue or attempt to rescue such fugitive from service or labor from the custody of such claimant, his, or her agent, or attorney, or other person or persons lawfully assisting as aforesaid, when so arrested pursuant to the authority herein given, and declared, or shall aid, abet, or assist such person so owing service or labor as aforesaid, directly or indirectly, to escape from such claimant, his agent, or attorney, or other person or persons legally authorized as aforesaid; or shall harbor or conceal such fugitive so as to prevent the discovery and arrest of such person, after notice or knowledge of the fact that such person was a fugitive from service or labor as aforesaid, shall, for either of said offences, be subject to a fine not exceeding One thousand dollars, and imprisonment not exceeding six months, by indictment and conviction before the District Court of the United States, for the district in which such offence may have been committed, or before the proper Court of Criminal jurisdiction, if committed within any one of the organized territories of the United States, and shall moreover forfeit and pay, by way of civil damages to the party injured by such illegal conduct, the sum of One thousand dollars, for each fugitive so lost as aforesaid, to be recovered by action of debt in any of the District or Territorial Courts aforesaid, within whose jurisdiction the said offence may have been committed.

SEC. 8. And be it further enacted, That the Marshals, their deputies, and the clerks of the said District and Territorial Courts, shall be paid for their services the like fees as may be allowed to them for similar services in other cases; and where such services are rendered exclusively in the arrest, custody, and delivery of the fugitive to the claimant, his or her agent or attorney, or where such supposed fugitive may be discharged out of custody for the want of sufficient proof as aforesaid, then such fees are to be paid in the whole by such claimant, his agent or attorney, and in all cases where the proceedings are before a Commissioner, he shall be entitled to a fee of Ten dollars in full for his services in each case, upon the delivery of the said certificate to the claimant, his or her agent or attorney; or a fee of Five dollars in cases where the proof shall not, in the opinion of said Commissioner, warrant such certificate and delivery, inclusive of all services incident to such arrest and examination to be paid in either case, by the claimant, his or her agent, or attorney. The person or persons authorized to execute the process to be issued by such Commissioner for the arrest and detention of fugitives from service or labor as aforesaid, shall also be entitled to a fee of five dollars each, for each person he or they may arrest and take before any such Commissioner, as aforesaid, at the instance and request of such claimant, with such other fees as may be deemed reasonable by such Commissioners for such other additional services as may be necessarily performed by him or them; such as attending the examination, keeping the fugitive in custody, and providing him with food and lodging during his detention and until the final determination of such Commissioner; and, in general, for performing such other duties as may be required by such claimant, his or her attorney, or agent, or Commissioner in the premises. Such fees to be made up in conformity with the fees usually charged by the officers of the courts of justice within the proper district or county, as near as may be practicable, and paid by such claimants, their agents or attorneys, whether such supposed fugitives from service or labor be ordered to be delivered to such claimants by the final determination of such Commissioner or not.

SEC. 9. And be it further enacted, That, upon affidavit made by the claimant of such fugitive, his agent or attorney, after such certificate has been issued that he has reason to apprehend that such fugitive will be rescued by force from his or her possession before he can be taken beyond the limits of the State in which the arrest is made, it shall be the duty of the officer making the arrest to retain such fugitive in his custody, and to remove him to the State whence he fled, and there to deliver him to said claimant, his agent or attorney. And to this end, the officer aforesaid is hereby authorized and required to employ as many persons as he may deem necessary to overcome such force, and to retain them in his service so long as circumstances may require. The said officer and his assistants while so employed to receive this same compensation, and to be allowed the same expenses as are now allowed by law for transportation of criminals, to be certified by the judge of the district within which the arrest is made, and paid out of the treasury of the United States.

SEC. 10. And be it further enacted, That when any person held to service or labor in any State or Territory, or in the District of Columbia shall escape therefrom, the party to whom such service or labor may be due, his, her, or their agent or attorney, may apply to any court of record therein, or judge thereof in vacation, and make satisfactory proof to such court, or judge in vacation, of the escape aforesaid, and that the person escaping owed service or labor to such party. Whereupon the court shall cause a record to be made of the matters so proved, and also a general description of the person so escaping with such convenient certainty as may be; and a transcript of such record authenticated by the attestation of the clerk and of the seal of the said court, being produced in any other State, Territory or district in which the person so escaping may be found, and being exhibited to any judge, commissioner, or other officer authorized by the law of the United States to cause persons escaping from service or labor to be delivered up, shall be held and taken to be full and conclusive evidence of the fact of the escape, and that the service or labor of the person escaping is due to the party in such record mentioned. And upon the production by the said party of other and further evidence if necessary, either oral or by affidavit, in addition to what is contained in the said record of the identity of the person escaping, he or she shall be delivered up to the claimant. And the said court, commissioner, judge, or other person authorized by this act to grant certificates to claimants or fugitives, shall, upon the production of the record and other evidence aforesaid, grant to such claimant a certificate of his right to take any such person identified and proved to be owing service or labor as aforesaid, which shall authorize such claimant to seize or arrest and transport such person to the State or Territory from which he escaped: Provided, That nothing herein contained shall be construed as requiring the production of a transcript of such record as evidence as aforesaid. But in its absence the claim shall be heard and determined upon other satisfactory proofs, competent in law.

Approved September 18, 1850.

The Thirteenth Amendment to the U.S. Constitution

Section 1. Neither slavery nor involuntary servitude, except as a punishment for crime whereof the party shall have been duly convicted, shall exist within the United States, or any place subject to their jurisdiction.

Section 2. Congress shall have power to enforce this article by appropriate legislation.

Proposal and Ratification

The thirteenth amendment to the Constitution of the United States was proposed to the legislatures of the several States by the Thirty-eighth Congress, on the 31st day of January, 1865, and was declared, in a proclamation of the Secretary of State, dated the 18th of December, 1865, to have been ratified by the legislatures of twenty-seven of the thirty-six States. The dates of ratification were: Illinois, February 1, 1865; Rhode Island, February 2, 1865; Michigan, February 2, 1865; Maryland, February 3, 1865; New York,

February 3, 1865; Pennsylvania, February 3, 1865; West Virginia, February 3, 1865; Missouri, February 6, 1865; Maine, February 7, 1865; Kansas, February 7, 1865; Massachusetts, February 7, 1865; Virginia, February 9, 1865; Ohio, February 10, 1865; Indiana, February 13, 1865; Nevada, February 16, 1865; Louisiana, February 17, 1865; Minnesota, February 23, 1865; Wisconsin, February 24, 1865; Vermont, March 9, 1865; Tennessee, April 7, 1865; Arkansas, April 14, 1865; Connecticut, May 4, 1865; New Hampshire, July 1, 1865; South Carolina, November 13, 1865; Alabama, December 2, 1865; North Carolina, December 4, 1865; Georgia, December 6, 1865.

Ratification was completed on December 6, 1865.

The amendment was subsequently ratified by Oregon, December 8, 1865; California, December 19, 1865; Florida, December 28, 1865 (Florida again ratified on June 9, 1868, upon its adoption of a new constitution); Iowa, January 15, 1866; New Jersey, January 23, 1866 (after having rejected the amendment on March 16, 1865); Texas, February 18, 1870; Delaware, February 12, 1901 (after having rejected the amendment on February 8, 1865); Kentucky, March 18, 1876 (after having rejected it on February 24, 1865).

The amendment was rejected . . . by Mississippi, December 4, 1865.
[*Mississippi ratified the Thirteenth Amendment in 1995.*]

Source Note: Thirteenth Amendment to the U.S. Constitution. Martin Luther King, Jr., National Historic Site Interpretive Staff.

SLAVERY AND THE 1787 CONSTITUTION

The Thirteenth Amendment to the Constitution was necessary to confirm that slavery would not be permitted in the United States and to clarify the ambiguities of the 1787 Constitution. Historians have long argued over the role of slavery in the original 1787 Constitution and in the debates that followed. A recent clear and authoritative treatment of these issues may be found in *Founding Brothers: The Revolutionary Generation*, by Joseph Ellis, especially in chapter 3, "The Silence," pp. 81–120. The two charter documents, the Declaration of Independence and the Constitution, were at odds on the question of chattel slavery. "If the Bible were a somewhat contradictory source when it came to the question of slavery, the Declaration of Independence, the secular version of American scripture, was an unambiguous tract for abolition" [Ellis, p. 89]. But it was the Constitution, not the Declaration of Independence, that actually governed the new nation, and in 1787, at the conclusion of the Constitutional Convention in Philadelphia, the long-debated charter for government did not adequately address slavery, thus effectively postponing the more heated arguments until the nineteenth century.

Neither side got what it wanted at Philadelphia in 1787. The Constitution contained no provision that committed the newly created federal government to a policy of gradual emancipation, or in any clear sense placed slavery on the road to ultimate extinction. On the other hand, the Constitution contained no provisions that specifically sanctioned slavery as a permanent and protected institution south of the Potomac or anywhere else. The distinguishing feature of the document when it came to slavery was its evasiveness. It was neither a "contract with abolition" nor a "covenant with death," but rather a prudent exercise in ambiguity. The circumlocutions required to place a chronological limit on the slave trade or to count slaves as three-fifths of a person for purposes of representation in the House [of Representatives], all without ever using the forbidden word, capture the intentionally elusive ethos of the Constitution. The underlying reason for this calculated orchestration of non-commitment was obvious: Any clear resolution of the slavery question one way or the other rendered ratification of the Constitution virtually impossible. [Ellis, p. 93]

In fact, the Constitution was a document of postponement, again for purposes of ratification by the slaveholding states. The Constitution "specifically prohibited Congress from passing any law that abolished or restricted the slave trade until 1808. (Article I, Section 9, paragraph 1, read: 'The Migration or Importation of such Persons as any of the States now existing shall think proper to admit, shall not be prohibited by the Congress prior to the year one thousand eight hundred and eight.' . . . The federal government could not tamper with the slave trade during the first twenty years of the nation's existence" [Ellis, p. 82].

In spite of these restrictions, Quaker opponents of slavery had been writing against the "peculiar institution" since their first printed tract in 1687. Quakers continued to petition the new Congress to abolish not only the slave trade but chattel slavery itself. A vital part of the debate process, the Quaker petitions were variously ignored by the Congress or given prominence depending on sponsorship. In the winter of 1790, the Pennsylvania Abolition Society urged Congress to "take such measures in their wisdom, as the powers with which they are invested will authorize, for promoting the abolition of slavery, and discouraging every species of traffic in slaves." This petition was personally endorsed by Benjamin Franklin, which insured that at least it would be heard by the Congress. Both John Adams and Franklin had opposed slavery publicly, but Adams made concessions to the "slave power" that Franklin was unwilling to make. Moreover, Franklin was the most respected and beloved American in 1790, well known both in Europe and the United States. His long publishing career (*Poor Richard's Almanac*) and his ambassador's role in France assured his prominence as America's Voltaire. Although the Quaker petitions against slavery were ultimately tabled in the 1790 debates, Franklin's support for the Pennsylvania Abolition Society's petition and his own writings against slavery were important antislavery voices in post-Revolutionary America. Ellis maintains that the new petition achieved the objective of linking slavery itself with the evils of the slave trade, so that future debates about the one would necessarily have to incorporate aspects of the other.

This new petition made two additional points calculated to exacerbate the fears of [proslavery advocates]. First, it claimed that both slavery and the slave trade were incompatible with the values for which the American Revolution had been fought, and it even instructed the Congress on its political obligation to "devise means for removing this inconsistency from the Character of the American people." Second, it challenged the claim that the Constitution prohibited any legislation by the federal government against the slave trade for twenty years, suggesting instead that the "general welfare" clause of the Constitution empowered the Congress to take whatever action it deemed "necessary and proper" to eliminate the stigma of traffic in human beings and to "Countenance the Restoration of Liberty for all Negroes." Finally, to top it all off and heighten its dramatic appeal, the petition arrived under the signature of Benjamin Franklin, whose patriotic credentials and international reputation were beyond dispute. Indeed, if there were an American pantheon, only Washington would have had a more secure place in it than Franklin. [Ellis, p. 83]

The congressional arguments of the 1790s were important in advancing the antebellum slavery debates because each side forced the other to articulate its views and to clarify its objectives. While the Constitution itself had skirted the issue of slavery in 1787, the slavery debates that followed the Constitutional Convention were crucial as everyone awaited the lifting of the prohibition against further constitutional legislation until 1808. The antislavery petitions to Congress, particularly those of the Quakers with support of public figures such as Benjamin Franklin, set the stage for those nineteenth-century arguments that would ultimately result in secession and civil war. Political prudence was necessary because full ratification of the 1787 Constitution was the highest priority of the early Congress. No one, including antislavery advocates like John Adams, wished to instigate an early secession movement, so many concessions concerning slavery were made at the Convention to appease the slaveholding states. Moreover, there were serious practical considerations in the implementation of "immediate and unconditional" emancipation of the slaves, such as compensation to slaveholders for their economic losses, the huge problem of colonization and the removal of all Africans from America to Africa, and the problem of a labor shortage caused by emancipation. These issues were set against the immorality of slavery as part of a new government, "conceived in liberty" and dedicated to principles of equality.

SUGGESTIONS FOR FURTHER READING

Ellis, Joseph. *Founding Brothers: The Revolutionary Generation.* New York: Knopf, 2000.

FREDERICK DOUGLASS (c. 1818–1895)

Frederick Augustus Washington Bailey was probably born about 1817, as determined from the information supplied in his three autobiographies, and he died

HARPER'S WEEKLY.

JOURNAL OF CIVILIZATION.

Vol. XXVII.—No. 1405.
Copyright, 1883, by Harper & Brothers.

NEW YORK, SATURDAY, NOVEMBER 24, 1883.

TEN CENTS A COPY.
WITH A SUPPLEMENT.

Frederick Douglass on the cover of *Harper's Illustrated Weekly*, National Portrait Gallery, Smithsonian Institution.

in Anacostia Heights, Washington, D.C., on February 20, 1895. His career is legendary and is symbolized in the title of John Hope Franklin's study, *From Slavery to Freedom*. Douglass's journey was indeed a determined trajectory from slavery to freedom, and as represented in his autobiographical narratives, he learned at an early age that the "pathway to freedom" lay in literacy and education. The three autobiographies all reflect the dual purpose of Douglass's life-writing: to tell a personal story and to represent the plight of enslaved brothers and sisters in order to bring an end to the horrors of chattel slavery.

These are masterful documents. The first, *A Narrative of the Life of Frederick Douglass, an American Slave, Written by Himself* (1845), is the most powerfully written. *My Bondage and My Freedom* (1855) carries the narrative through another decade while making significant stylistic and some substantive changes to the earlier account. The final autobiography, *The Life and Times of Frederick Douglass* (1881), is the longest and most detailed of the three accounts, and it lacks the narrative qualities of the 1845 version while it supplies more information about Douglass's adult life. Douglass was married twice: once to a black woman, Anna Murray, who had assisted in his escape into the North, and the second time to a white woman, Helen Pitts. Born of a slave mother and (possibly) her white master, Douglass remarked that his first marriage honored his mother and his second, his father. This casual dismissal of objections to his racially mixed second marriage covers the anguish evident in the first chapters of the 1845 *Narrative*, where identity for the narrator is a frustrating and hopeless genealogical task. The *Narrative* is a rhetorically sophisticated evocation of Douglass's experience. In chapter 1, he describes the flogging of "Aunt Hester," a woman in her mid-twenties, that Douglass witnesses at the age of seven. This account of an assault on a female slave is graphically portrayed, and the language of the episode indicates that what Douglass may have witnessed that morning was the rape of Aunt Hester in addition to the flogging. This poignant moment was the "birthing into the hell of slavery" that he later recapitulates for the reader in the process of "writing himself into being." Later in the *Narrative*, Douglass recounts another developmental moment, the two-hour fight with the slave-breaker, Covey. Here, the sixteen-year-old slave, who was by then fully grown physically, determined to defend himself although the consequences of such a decision could have been fatal. He beat Covey in a lengthy fight in the presence of the assembled slaves and was never flogged again. In the adult voice that recapitulates the narrative episode, Douglass remarked to the reader, "You have seen how a man became a slave; now you shall see how the slave became a man." Throughout Douglass's writings, his personal experience as a slave and freeman is paralleled by the broader experience of his "brothers and sisters" in bondage, so that the Douglass autobiographies serve two purposes simultaneously: the recapitulation of his life experience and the presentation of a well-developed argument against the institution of slavery. The combination is a rhetorically powerful narrative that became a model for later antebellum slave narratives.

Following his escape from a Maryland plantation, Douglass attended an abolitionist meeting on Nantucket in 1841, where he was invited to speak about his experiences as a slave. His manner, physical height and appearance, powerful voice, and eloquent delivery led William Lloyd Garrison and Wendell Phillips to invite him to join the abolitionist lecture circuit as a public speaker, which he did for several years, often enduring the criticism that one so eloquent and articulate could not possibly have been an uneducated slave. On one of these occasions, he did not reply verbally, but using his body as a text, turned his back to the audience, took off his shirt, and showed the scars on his back from the beatings he had endured as a young man. His 1845 *Narrative* was in part a response to public challenges to the veracity of his assertion that he was an escaped slave.

His career was remarkable. After publication of this confessional document, he toured England as an abolitionist lecturer to avoid recapture under the Fugitive Slave Laws of the United States, which had been on the books since 1793 and were reinforced with the Fugitive Slave Law of 1850, but he returned to the United States to continue lecturing and to edit *The North Star*, with Martin Delaney. Although Douglass had long been associated with William Lloyd Garrison's *Liberator*, his publication of his own antislavery newspaper strained their relationship, as did their later disagreement over the role of the U.S. Constitution in the abolition of slavery. While Garrison favored discarding the Constitution as an "agreement with hell" and a proslavery document, Douglass argued that abolition should come through the amendment process articulated in the Constitution, as indeed it did, in 1865, with the Thirteenth Amendment. As is often the case with reform movements, the leadership fragmented, the Garrisonians representing a militant direction while Douglass developed a more conservative role. Both groups continued to demand the abolition of slavery, but where Garrison argued for "no compensation for slaveholders," Douglass allowed his freedom to be purchased by British abolitionists. In 1851, the name of his newspaper was changed to *Frederick Douglass's Paper*. In 1859, he was once again forced to leave the country, this time for Canada, because he had been accused of plotting John Brown's raid on the armory at Harper's Ferry, Virginia, that year. One of his greatest public achievements was suggesting that Abraham Lincoln form a regiment of African-American Union soldiers, and in 1863, the Fifty-Fourth Massachusetts Regiment was born, including two of Douglass's sons. Under the command of Robert Gould Shaw of Boston, this unit served with distinction in several Civil War battles until, when leading the attack on Fort Wagner, outside Charleston, South Carolina, the group was decimated by Confederate artillery and canister fire from the fort, and Shaw himself was killed. The story of the Fifty-Fourth was told in the film *Glory* (1989).

Critical and historical analyses of Frederick Douglass have always been available because Douglass was probably the most prominent African-American of the nineteenth century. (Numerous excellent analyses and essay collections have appeared since 1975, and many are listed in the accompanying "Suggestions for Further Reading.") His career began in slavery; at the time of his death, he had been adviser to four United States presidents, including Abraham Lincoln, and he had been appointed to several federal posts, including marshall of the District of Columbia and, from 1889 to 1891, U.S. minister to Haiti, an appointment by President Benjamin Harrison. Douglass also joined his antislavery pronouncements to the fight for women's suffrage, and it is significant that he was invited to give an important address at the 1848 Seneca Falls Convention in New York, where the "Declaration of Sentiments," the charter document of the nineteenth-century women's movement, was drafted. On the day of his death in 1895, he had just delivered an address at a women's rights convention.

Douglass spoke eloquently and often against oppression, even after the Emancipation Proclamation and the end of the Civil War, declaring that "the work of freedom is not ended; it has only begun." He protested the treatment of African-Americans during Reconstruction, and was particularly vocal in his support for anti-lynching legislation. He joins Booker T. Washington and W. E. B. Du Bois as the third member of a powerful and influential triumvirate who not only articulated opposition to slavery, but also designed the roadmap for the African's movement from slavery to freedom.

When he was invited to speak at the Rochester, New York, Antislavery Society meeting on July 4, 1852, Douglass accepted on the condition that he could deliver the address on July 5, since the Fourth of July was a meaningless date for the American slave. It also fell on a Sunday in 1852. His "What to the Slave Is the Fourth of July?" is a rhetorical masterpiece that responds plainly to the inconsistency of slavery in a new democracy founded on Jefferson's argument that "all men are created equal," a natural-rights principle of the Enlightenment that framed the revolutionary debate with Great Britain. That inconsistency had shadowed the evolution of the U.S. Constitution throughout the antebellum decades. Douglass spoke plainly to his audience in 1852, laying bare the hypocrisy and inconsistency that allowed slavery in a republic dedicated to the principles of individual rights and personal freedom.

SUGGESTIONS FOR FURTHER READING

Andrews, William, ed. *Critical Essays on Frederick Douglass*. Boston: Hall, 1991.

Blight, David. *Frederick Douglass's Civil War*. Baton Rouge: Louisiana State University Press, 1928.

Bontemps, Arna W. *Free At Last: The Life of Frederick Douglass*. New York: Dodd Mead, 1971.

Douglass, Frederick. *The Life and Times of Frederick Douglass* (1881). Secaucus, NJ: Citadel, 1983.

———. *My Bondage and My Freedom*. Ed. William Andrews. Urbana: University of Illinois Press, 1987.

———. *A Narrative of the Life of Frederick Douglass, An American Slave, Written By Himself*. Ed. Houston Baker. New York: Penguin, 1982.

Foner, Philip S. *Frederick Douglass, a Biography*. New York: Citadel, 1964.

———. *The Life and Writings of Frederick Douglass*. 5 vols. New York: International, 1970–75.

Huggins, Nathan. *Slave and Citizen: The Life of Frederick Douglass.* Ed. Oscar Handlin. Boston: Little, Brown, 1980.

Lowance, Mason, Jr. "Frederick Douglass." In *African-American Writers*, ed. Lea Baechler and A. Walton Litz (New York: Charles Scribner's Sons, 1991, rev. 2001).

———. "The Slave Narrative in American Literature." In *African-American Writers*, ed. Lea Baechler and A. Walton Litz (New York: Charles Scribner's Sons, 1991, rev. 2001).

Martin, Waldo. *The Mind of Frederick Douglass.* Chapel Hill: University of North Carolina Press, 1984.

What to the Slave Is the Fourth of July?
by Frederick Douglass

The fact is, ladies and gentlemen, the distance between this platform and the slave plantation, from which I escaped, is considerable—and the difficulties to be overcome in getting from the latter to the former, are by no means slight. That I am here to-day is, to me, a matter of astonishment as well as of gratitude. You will not, therefore, be surprised if in what I have to say I evince no elaborate preparation, nor grace my speech with any high sounding exordium. With little experience and with less learning, I have been able to throw my thoughts hastily and imperfectly together; and trusting to your patient and generous indulgence, I will proceed to lay them before you.

This, for the purpose of this celebration, is the 4th of July. It is the birthday of your National Independence, and of your political freedom. This to you is what the Passover was to the emancipated people of God. It carries your minds back to the day, and to the act of your great deliverance; and to the signs, and to the wonders, associated with that act, and that day. This celebration also marks the beginning of another year of your national life; and reminds you that the Republic of America is now 76 years old. I am glad, fellow-citizens, that your nation is so young. Seventy-six years, though a good old age for a man, is but a mere speck in the life of a nation. Three score years and ten is the allotted time for individual men; but nations number their years by thousands. According to this fact, you are, even now, only in the beginning of your national career, still lingering in the period of childhood. I repeat, I am glad this is so. There is hope in the thought, and hope is much needed, under the dark clouds which lower above the horizon. The eye of the reformer is met with angry flashes, portending disastrous times; but his heart may well beat lighter at the thought that America is still young, and that she is still in the impressible stage of her existence. . . . Were the nation older, the patriot's heart might be sadder, and the reformer's brow heavier. Its future might be shrouded in gloom, and the hope of its prophets go out in sorrow. . . .

Fellow Citizens, I am not wanting in respect for the fathers of this republic. The signers of the Declaration of Independence were brave men. They were great men too—great enough to give frame to a great age. It does not often happen to a nation to raise, at one time, such a number of truly great men. . . . They were statesmen, patriots and heroes, and for the good they did, and the principles they contended for, I will unite with you to honor their memory. They loved their country better than their own private interests; and, though this is not the highest form of human excellence, all will concede that it is a rare virtue, and that when it is exhibited, it ought to command respect. They were peace men; but they preferred revolution to peaceful submission to bondage. They were quiet men; but they did not shrink from agitation against oppression. They showed forbearance; but they knew its limits. They believed in order; but not in the order of tyranny. With them, nothing was "settled" that was not right. With them, justice, liberty and humanity were "final;" not slavery and oppression. You may well cherish the memory of such men. They were great in their day and generation. Their solid manhood stands out the more as we contrast it with these degenerate times. . . .

Fellow-citizens, pardon me, allow me to ask, why am I called upon to speak here to-day? What have I, or those I represent, to do with your national independence? Are the great principles of political freedom and of natural justice, embodied in that Declaration of Independence, extended to us? And am I, therefore, called upon to bring our humble offering to the national altar, and to confess the benefits and express devout gratitude for the blessings resulting from your independence to us?

Would to God, both for your sakes and ours, that an affirmative answer could be truthfully returned to these questions! . . . But, such is not the state of the case. I say it with a sad sense of the disparity between us. I am not included within the pale of this glorious anniversary! Your high independence only reveals the immeasurable distance between us. The blessings in which you, this day, rejoice, are not enjoyed in common. The rich inheritance of justice, liberty, prosperity and independence, bequeathed by your fathers, is shared by you, not by me. The sunlight that brought life and healing to you, has brought stripes and death to me. This Fourth of July is *yours, not mine.* You may rejoice, I must mourn. To drag a man in fetters into the grand illuminated temple of liberty, and call upon him to join you in joyous anthems, were inhuman mockery and sacrilegious irony. Do you mean, citizens, to mock me, by asking me to speak to-day? If so, there is a parallel to your conduct. And let me warn you that it is dangerous to copy the example of a nation whose crimes, towering up to heaven, were thrown down by the breath of the Almighty, burying that nation in irrecoverable ruin! I can to-day take up the plaintive lament of a peeled and woe-smitten people! "By the rivers of Babylon, there we sat down. Yea! we wept when we remembered Zion. We hanged our harps upon the willows in the midst thereof. For there, they that carried us away captive, required of us a song; and they who wasted us required of us mirth, saying, Sing us one of the songs of Zion. How can we sing the Lord's song in a strange land? If I forget thee, O Jerusalem, let my right hand forget her cunning. If I do not remember thee, let my tongue cleave to the roof of my mouth." [Psalm 137.1–6]

. . . Would you have me argue that man is entitled to liberty? that he is the rightful owner of his own body? You have already declared it. Must I argue the wrongfulness of slavery? Is that a question for Republicans? . . . How should I look to-day, in the presence of Americans, dividing, and subdividing a discourse, to show that men have a natural right to freedom? . . .

What, am I to argue that it is wrong to make men brutes, to rob them of their liberty, to work them without wages, to keep them ignorant of their relations to their fellow men, to beat them with sticks, to flay their flesh with the lash, to load their limbs with irons, to hunt them with dogs, to sell them at auction, to sunder their families, to knock out their teeth, to burn their flesh, to starve them into obedience and submission to their masters? Must I argue that a system thus marked with blood, and stained with pollution, is wrong? . . . What, then, remains to be argued? Is it that slavery is not divine; that God did not establish it; that our doctors of divinity are mistaken? There is blasphemy in the thought. That which is inhuman, cannot be divine! Who can reason on such a proposition? They that can, may; I cannot. The time for such argument is past. At a time like this, scorching irony, not convincing argument, is needed. O! had I the ability, and could I reach the nation's ear, I would, to-day, pour out a fiery stream of biting ridicule, blasting reproach, withering sarcasm, and stern rebuke. For it is not light that is needed, but fire; it is not the gentle shower, but thunder. We need the storm, the whirlwind, and the earthquake. The feeling of the nation must be quickened; the conscience of the nation must be roused; the propriety of the nation must be startled; the hypocrisy of the nation must be exposed; and its crimes against God and man must be proclaimed and denounced.

What, to the American slave, is *your* 4th of July? I answer: a day that reveals to him, more than all other days in the year, the gross injustice and cruelty to which he is the constant victim. To him, your celebration is a sham; your boasted liberty, an unholy license; your national greatness, swelling vanity; your sounds of rejoicing are empty and heartless; your denunciations of tyrants, brass fronted impudence; your shouts of liberty and equality, hollow mockery; your prayers and hymns, your sermons and thanksgivings, with all your religious parade, and solemnity, are, to him, mere bombast, fraud, deception, impiety, and hypocrisy—a thin veil to cover up crimes which would disgrace a nation of savages. *There is not a nation on the earth guilty of practices, more shocking and bloody, than are the people of these United States, at this very hour.*

. . . But a still more inhuman, disgraceful, and scandalous state of things remains to be presented. By an act of the American Congress [the Fugitive Slave Law of 1850], not yet two years old, slavery has been nationalized in its most horrible and revolting form. By that act, Mason and Dixon's line has been obliterated; New York has become as Virginia; and the power to hold, hunt, and sell men, women, and children, as slaves, remains no longer a mere state institution, but is now an institution of the whole United States. The power is coextensive with the star-spangled banner and American Christianity. Where these go, may also go the merciless slave-hunter. Where these are, man is not sacred. He is a bird for the sportsman's gun. By that most foul and fiendish of all human decrees, the liberty and person of every man are put in peril. Your broad republican domain is hunting ground for men. Not for thieves and robbers, enemies of society, but for men guilty of no crime. Your lawmakers have commanded all good citizens to engage in this hellish sport. . . . I take this law to be one of the grossest infringements of Christian Liberty, and, if the churches and ministers of our country were not stupidly blind, or most wickedly indifferent, they, too, would so regard it. At the very moment that they are thanking God for the enjoyment of civil and religious liberty, and for the right to worship God according to the dictates of their own consciences, they are utterly silent in respect to a law which robs religion of its chief significance, and makes it utterly worthless to a world lying in wickedness. . . . The fact that the church of our country (with fractional exceptions) does not esteem the Fugitive Slave Law as a declaration of war against religious liberty, implies that that church regards religion simply as a form of worship, an empty ceremony, and not a vital principle, requiring active benevolence, justice, love and good will towards man. . . . But the church of this country is not only indifferent to the wrongs of the slave, it actually takes sides with the oppressors. It has made itself the bulwark of American slavery, and the shield of American slave-hunters. Many of its most eloquent Divines, who stand as the very lights of the church, have shamelessly given the sanction of religion and the Bible to the whole slave system. They have taught that man may, properly, be a slave; that the relation of master and slave is ordained of God; that to send back an escaped bondman to his master is clearly the duty of all the followers of the Lord Jesus Christ; and this horrible blasphemy is palmed off upon the world for Christianity. For my part, I would say, welcome infidelity! welcome atheism! welcome anything! in preference to the gospel, as preached by those Divines! They convert the very name of religion into an engine of tyranny and barbarous cruelty and serve to confirm more infidels, in this age, than all the infidel writings of Thomas Paine, Voltaire, and Bolingbroke, put together, have done! . . . In prosecuting the anti-slavery enterprise, we have been asked to spare the church, to spare the ministry; but how, we ask, could such a thing be done? We are met on the threshold of our efforts for the redemption of the slave, by the church and ministry of the country, in battle arrayed against us; and we are compelled to fight or flee. From what quarter, I beg to know, has proceeded a fire so deadly upon our ranks, during the last two years, as from the Northern pulpit? As the champions of oppressors, the chosen men of American theology have appeared men honored for their so-called piety, and their real learning. . . . My spirit wearies of such blasphemy; and how such men can be supported, as the standing types and representatives of Jesus Christ is a mystery which I leave others to penetrate. . . .

Fellow-citizens! I will not enlarge further on your national inconsistencies. The existence of slavery in this country brands your republicanism as a sham, your humanity as a base pretense, and your Christianity as a lie. It destroys your moral power abroad; it corrupts your politicians at home. It saps the foundation of religion; it makes your name a hissing, and a byeword to a mocking earth. It is the antagonistic force in your government, the only thing that seriously disturbs and endangers your Union. It fetters your progress; it is the enemy of improvement; the deadly foe of education; it fosters pride; it breeds insolence; it promotes vice; it shelters crime; it is a curse to the earth that supports it; and yet, you cling to it, as if it were the sheet anchor of all your hopes. Oh! be warned! be warned! A horrible reptile is coiled up in your nation's bosom; the venomous creature is nursing at the tender breast of your youthful republic; *for the love of God, tear away, and fling from you the hideous monster, and let the weight of twenty millions crush and destroy it forever!* . . . In the fervent aspirations of William Lloyd Garrison, I say, and let every heart join in saying it:

> God speed the year of jubilee
> The wide world o'er!
> When from their galling chains set free,
> Th' oppress'd shall vilely bend the knee,
> And wear the yoke of tyranny
> Like brutes no more.
> That year will come, and freedom's reign,
> To man his plundered fights again Restore.
>
> God speed the day when human blood
> Shall cease to flow!
> In every clime be understood,
> The claims of human brotherhood,
> And each return for evil, good,
> Not blow for blow;
> That day will come all feuds to end
> And change into a faithful friend
> Each foe.
>
> God speed the hour, the glorious hour,
> When none on earth
> Shall exercise a lordly power,
> Nor in a tyrant's presence cower;
> But all to manhood's stature tower,
> By equal birth!
> That hour will come to each, to all,
> And from his prison-house, the thrall
> Go forth.
>
> Until that year, day, hour, arrive,
> With head, and heart, and hand I'll strive,
> To break the rod, and rend the gyve,
> The spoiler of his prey deprive—
> So witness heaven!
> And never from my chosen post,
> Whate'er the peril or the cost,
> Be driven.

JUSTICE JOSEPH STORY (1779–1845)

The "Charge to the Grand Jury" of Maine, May 8, 1820, that follows is unusual because of its early date. Two New Englanders, Joseph Story and Daniel Webster (1782–1852), were early-nineteenth-century critics of slavery, and both practiced law in Massachusetts, though Webster was born in Salisbury, New Hampshire. In the year 1820, the year of the Missouri Compromise by which that state was admitted to the Union as a slave state while territories west of the Mississippi were to be admitted as free states, both men argued publicly against slavery.

The year 1820 was also the bicentennial of the Pilgrims' landing at Plymouth, and celebrations of this event were particularly important in New England, although Plymouth Rock had by this time become a national symbol, an icon of freedom and the "new beginning" experienced by those first settlers. Daniel Webster was chosen to deliver the bicentennial oration at Plymouth in December of that year, exactly two hundred years after the Pilgrims had landed. For a short time, early in the century, Webster had practiced law in Portsmouth, New Hampshire, at a bar where Joseph Story was a prominent figure. However, the inextricable link between the two men was less personal than it was ideological. Their opposition to slavery was declared in these two public addresses in 1820, and the power of their rhetoric signaled the beginning of the antebellum slavery debates that would continue through the Emancipation Proclamation to the ratification of the Thirteenth Amendment to the Constitution in 1865.

Webster's speech was essentially a celebration of Plymouth Rock, its long and significant history, its value as a national symbol of freedom, and its meaning to Americans. When he delivered his speech, Webster was familiar with Justice Story's "Charge," which had been delivered on May 8 of the same year. What Webster did was to challenge Americans at the beginning of their new century to espouse the values of the Puritan forefathers and to terminate the institution of chattel slavery. Historian John Seelye put it this way:

> It was against this dark background that Webster, toward the end of his Plymouth oration . . . finally admitted that the long and shining record of American progress did have one blot upon it, caused by the "traffic" whose "contamination" inspired the "revolt" of every feeling of humanity . . . I mean the African slave trade. He called upon "all the true sons of New-England, to cooperate with the laws of man, and the justice of heaven. If there be, within the extent of our knowledge or influence, any participation in this traffic, let us pledge ourselves here, upon the Rock of Plymouth, to extirpate and destroy it. It is not fit, that the land of the Pilgrims, should bear the shame longer." . . . Indeed, one of Webster's major themes in his oration was a generic map tracing the evolution of "liberty," from the "love of religious liberty" associated with the Pilgrims to a love of "freedom" in its most exalted form, which gives men of "conscience" the courage to resist the "hand of power" when it becomes restrictive: "Nothing can stop it, but to give way to it; nothing can check it, but indulgence." [Seelye, p. 81]

Clearly, Webster had received inspiration from Story's "Charge," and he went on to demand that the slave trade be eradicated "from the land of the Pilgrims." Suggesting that contemporary America had lost some of the innocence of early New England, he argued: "let that spot be purified, or let it cease to be of New England. Let it be purified, or let it be set aside from the Christian world; let it be put out of the circle of human sympathies and human regards, and let civilized man henceforth have no communion with it" (Seelye, p. 83). The language here is uncompromising and forceful, foreshadowing the insistent demands of William Lloyd Garrison over the following decades. It was a landmark performance, as John Seelye has convincingly argued, and together with Justice Story's "Charge" gave rise to increasing demands for the termination of slavery in the land of the free and the home of the brave.

Justice Story's "Charge" was a different type of document from Webster's acclaimed public address. The state of Maine was newly minted in 1820, and it was admitted to the Union as a free state in part to balance the admission of Missouri as a slave state, under the terms of the Missouri Compromise. Story's "Charge" is technically a speech to the first grand jury assembled in the new state, but its publication and its rhetorical force gave it added exposure and influence. One of the most prominent features of Story's challenge to the grand jury is a long and graphic narrative account of the infamous Middle Passage on board slave ships crossing the Atlantic from Africa to the West Indies and the east coast of the United States. This description, provided here, echoes the account written in 1782 by Olaudah Equiano, or Gustavas Vassa, whose slave narrative is one of the few to include a full account of the Middle Passage. Story's recounting of the African's transatlantic voyage to the new world is moving and disturbing, not only for its detailing of the horrors suffered on board those slave ships, but also for the power of its language to move readers to action. It concludes with some rhetorical terms that would become very familiar in the emerging arguments for abolition in the decades to come: "Our constitutions of government have declared that all men are born free and equal, and have certain unalienable rights, among which are the right of enjoying their lives, liberties and property, and of seeking and obtaining their own safety and happiness. May not the miserable African ask, 'Am I not a man and a brother?'" (For a full discussion of Story's "Charge," see Seelye, pp. 81–82.)

SUGGESTIONS FOR FURTHER READING

McClellan, James, and Stephen Presser. *Joseph Story and the American Constitution: A Study in Political and Legal Thought with Selected Writings.* Norman: University of Oklahoma, 1990.

Newmyer, R. Kent. *Supreme Court Justice Joseph Story, Statesman of the Old Republic.* Chapel Hill: University of North Carolina Press, 1985.

Seelye, John. *Memory's Nation: The Place of Plymouth Rock.* Chapel Hill: University of North Carolina Press, 1998.

Shade, William G. "The Slave Question." In *Democratizing the Old Dominion:*

Virginia and the Second Party System, 1824–1861 (Charlottesville: University Press of Virginia, 1996).

Watson, Alan. *Joseph Story and the Comity of Errors: A Case Study in Conflict of Laws.* Athens: University of Georgia Press, 1992.

A Charge Delivered to the Grand Jury of the Circuit Court of the United States at its First Session in Portland for the Judicial District of Maine, May 8, 1820
by Joseph Story

The circumstances under which I address you at the present moment are perhaps without a parallel in the annals of the other quarters of the world. This District has just been admitted into the union as a free, sovereign and independent state, possessing in common with all the others an equality of national rights and honors, and protected by an excellent constitution framed, by its own deliberations, upon principles of justice and equity.

And in what manner has this been accomplished? Not by the course, in which the division of empires has been usually sought and obtained—by civil dissension and warfare—by successful resistance wading through the blood of friends and foes to its purpose—or by the terror of the sword, whose brightness has been stained by the sacrifice of innocence, or rusted by the tears of suffering and conquered virtue. Unhappily for mankind, a change of government has rarely taken place without involving evils of the most serious nature. It has been but the triumph of tyranny in the overthrow of liberties of the people; or the sudden reaction of popular resentment, indignant at wrongs and stimulated to criminal excesses.

Here a different scene—a scene of peace and good order has been presented. The separation has been the result of cool deliberation and cautious examination of the interests of both parties. It has been conducted in a spirit of mutual conciliation and friendship, with an anxious desire to promote the real happiness and prosperity of the people. . . .

Nor let us indulge the vain hope that we shall escape a like fate, if we neglect to preserve those institutions in their purity, which sustain the great interests of society. If we grow indifferent to the progress of vice; if we silently wink at violations of the laws; if we habitually follow the current of public opinion without pausing to consider its directions; if we cherish a sullen irreverent disregard of the constitution of government, under which we live, or resign ourselves to factious discontent under the exercise of its legitimate power; the time is not far distant when we shall be separated into rival states, engaged in furious contests for paltry objects, and ultimately become the prey of some unprincipled chieftain, who will first arrive at power by flattering popular prejudices, and then secure his bad eminence by the destruction of the liberties of his country. . . .

But there are other acts, which the laws of the United States have declared piracy—which are punishable as such only when committed on board of Amer-

A

CHARGE

DELIVERED TO THE GRAND JURY OF THE

Circuit Court of the United States

AT ITS FIRST SESSION IN PORTLAND

FOR THE

JUDICIAL DISTRICT OF MAINE

MAY 8, 1820,

AND PUBLISHED AT THE UNANIMOUS REQUEST OF THE GRAND JURY

AND OF THE BAR

BY THE HON. JOSEPH STORY

PORTLAND

PRINTED BY A. SHIRLEY

1820

"A Charge Delivered to the Grand Jury of the Circuit Court of the United States,"
title page.

---

ican ships, or by persons who are justly amenable to our criminal jurisdictions. . . .

2. A second declared piracy by our Laws, is the piratically and feloniously running away with any ship or vessel or any goods or merchandise to the value of fifty dollars, or the voluntarily yielding up any ship or vessel to any pirate. . . .

3. A third act of piracy by our laws is the laying of violent hands by any seaman upon his commander, thereby to hinder and prevent his fighting in defence of his ship or the goods committed to his trust. . . .

4. A fourth act of piracy by our laws is the making of a revolt by a mariner on board of the ship to which he belongs.

It is not easy to enumerate all the various circumstances, which constitute a "revolt," a word which in this clause is used in the sense of mutiny or rebellion—a mere act of disobedience to the lawful commands of the officers of the ship by the crew does not of itself constitute a revolt. But if there be a general combination of the crew to resist the lawful commands of their officers to usurp their authority on board of the ship; and any overt acts are done by the crew in the pursuance of such design; such as the confinement of their officers, or depriving them of the control and management of the ship, these and the like acts seem properly to constitute a revolt.

From this clause it is apparent how deeply involved in guilt are those of our citizens who enlist themselves in the armed ships of foreign states, and commit hostilities upon their countrymen, or plunder their property, since the law declares that they shall be "adjudged and taken to be pirates, felons, and robbers," and shall on conviction suffer death. . . .

And in the next place, gentlemen, let me call your attention to that most detestable traffic, the *Slave Trade*.

The existence of Slavery under any shape is so repugnant to the natural rights of man and the dictates of justice, that it seems difficult to find for it any adequate justification. It undoubtedly had its origin in times of barbarism, and was the ordinary lot of those who were conquered in war. It was supposed that the conqueror had a right to take the life of his captive, and by consequence might well bind him to perpetual servitude. But the position itself on which this supposed right is founded, is not true. No man has a right to kill his enemy except in cases of absolute necessity; and this absolute necessity ceases to exist even in the education of the conqueror himself, when he has spared the life of his prisoner. . . .

It is also made an offence for any citizen or other person as master, owner, or factor, to build, fit, equip, load, or otherwise prepare any vessel in any of our ports, or to cause any vessel to sail from any port whatsoever for the purpose of procuring any negro, mulatto, or person of color from any foreign country to be transported to any port or place whatsoever, to be held, sold or disposed of, as a slave, or *to be held to service or labor*. It is also made an offence for any citizen or *other person resident within our jurisdiction* to take on board, receive or transport in any vessel from the Coast of Africa or any other foreign country, or from sea, any negro, mulatto or person of color not an inhabitant of, or held to service in the United States, for the purpose of holding, selling or disposing of such person as a slave, or to be held to service or labor. . . .

And, Gentlemen, how can we justify ourselves or apologize for an indifference to this subject? Our constitutions of government have declared that all men are born free and equal, and have certain unalienable rights, among which are the right of enjoying their lives, liberties and property, and of seeking and obtaining their own safety and happiness. May not the miserable African ask, "Am I not a man and a brother?" . . .

We believe in the Christian religion. It commands us to have good will to all men; to love our neighbors as ourselves, and to do unto all men as we would they should do unto us. It declares our accountability to the Supreme God for all our actions, and holds out to us a state of future rewards and punishments as the sanction by which our conduct is to be regulated. And yet there are men calling themselves Christians who degrade the negro by ignorance to a level with the brutes, and deprive him of all the consolations of religion. He alone of all the rational creation, they seem to think, is to be at once accountable for his actions, and yet his actions are not to be at his own disposal; but his mind, his body, and his feelings are to be sold to perpetual bondage.—To me it appears perfectly clear that the slave trade is equally repugnant to the dictates of reason and religion and is an offence equally against the laws of God and man. . . .

I have called this an *inhuman* traffic, and, gentlemen, with a view to enlist your sympathies as well as your judgments in its suppression, permit me to pass from those cold generalities to some of those details, which are the ordinary attendants upon this trade. Here indeed there is no room for the play of imagination. The records of the British Parliament present us a body of evidence on this subject, taken with the most scrupulous care while the subject of the abolition was before it; taken too from persons who had been engaged in, or eye witnesses of the trade; taken too, year after year in the presence of those whose interests or passions were most strenuously engaged to oppose it. . . .

The number of slaves taken from Africa in 1768 amounted to one hundred and four thousand; and though the numbers somewhat fluctuated in different years afterwards, yet it is in the highest degree probable that the average, until the abolition, was not much below 100,000 a year. England alone in the year 1786, employed 130 ships, and carried off about 42,000 slaves. . . .

The whole number transported, consists of *kidnapped people.*—This mode of procuring them includes every species of treachery and knavery. Husbands are stolen from their wives, children from their parents, and bosom friends from each other. . . .

The second class of slaves, and that not *inconsiderable*, consists of those, whose villages have been depopulated for obtaining them. The parties employed in these predatory expeditions go out at night, set fire to the villages, which they find, and carry off the wretched inhabitants, thus suddenly thrown into their power, as slaves. . . .

The third class of slaves consists of such persons as are said to have been convicted of crimes, and are sold on this account for the benefit of their kings. . . .

The fourth class includes prisoners of war captured sometimes in ordinary wars, and sometimes in wars originated for the very purposes of slavery.

The fifth class comprehends those who are slaves by birth; and some traders on the coast make a practice of breeding from their own slaves, for the purpose of selling them, like cattle, when they are arrived at a suitable age.

The sixth class comprehends such as have sacrificed their liberty to the spirit of gaming. . . .

They are sold immediately upon their arrival on the rivers or coasts, either to land-factors at *depots* for that purpose, or directly to the ships engaged in the trade.—They are then carried in boats to the various ships whose captains have purchased them. The men are immediately confined two and two together either by the neck, leg, or arm, with fetters of solid iron.—They are then put into their apartments, the men occupying the fore part, the women the after part, and the boys the middle of the vessel. The tops of these apartments are grated for the admission of light and air; and the slaves are stowed like any other lumber, occupying only an allotted portion of room.—Many of them while the ships are waiting for their full lading in sight of their native shore, manifest great appearance of distress and oppression; and some instances have occurred where they have sought relief by suicide, and others where they have been afflicted with delirium and madness.—In the day time, if the weather be fine they are brought upon deck for air.—They are placed in a long row of two and two together, on each side of the ship, a long chain is then made to pass through the shackles of each pair, and by this means each row is secured to the deck. In this state they eat their miserable meals, consisting of horse-beans, rice and yams, with a little pepper and palm oil.—After their meals, it is a custom to make them jump for exercise as high as *their* fetters will allow them; and if they refuse they are whipped until they comply. This the slave merchants call dancing, and it would seem literally to be the dance of death.

When the number of slaves is completed, the ships begin what is called the middle passage, to transport the slaves to the colonies. The height of the apartment in the ships is different according to the size of the vessel, and is from six feet to three feet, so that it is impossible to stand erect in most of the vessels, and in some scarcely to sit down in the same posture. In the best regulated ships, a grown person is allowed but sixteen inches in width, thirty-two inches in height, and five feet eleven inches in length, or to use the expressive language of a witness, not so much room as a man has in his coffin.—They are indeed so crowded below that it is almost impossible to walk through the groups without treading on some of them; and if they are reluctant to get into their places they are compelled by the lash of a whip.—And here their situation becomes wretched beyond description. The space between decks, where they are confined, often becomes so hot that persons who have visited them there have found their shirts so wetted with perspiration that water might be wrung from them; and the steam from their confined bodies comes up through the gratings like a furnace.—The bad effects of such confinement and want of air are soon visible in the weakness and faintness which overcomes the unhappy victims. . . .

When the scuttles in the ship's side are shut in bad weather, the gratings are not sufficient for airing the room; and the slaves are then seen drawing their breath with all that anxious and laborious effort for life, which we observe in animals subjected to experiments in foul air or in an exhausted receiver of an air pump.—Many of them expire in this situation crying out in their native tongue "we are dying."—During the time that elapses from the slaves being put on board on the African coast to their sale in the colonies about one fourth part, or twenty-five thousand per annum are destroyed—a mortality which may be easily credited after the preceding statement.

At length the ship arrives at her destined port, and the unhappy Africans who have survived the voyage are prepared for sale. Some are consigned to Brokers who sell them for the ships at private sale. With this view they are examined by the planters, who want them for their farms, and in the selection of them, friends and relations are parted without any hesitation; and when they part with mutual embraces they are severed by a lash. . . .

The scenes which I have described are almost literally copies from the most authentic and unquestionable narratives published under the highest authority. They present a picture of human wretchedness and human depravity, which the boldest imagination would hardly have dared to portray, and from which (one should think) the most profligate would shrink with horror. Let it be considered that this wretchedness does not arise from the awful visitations of providence in the shape of plagues, famines or earthquakes, the natural scourges of mankind; but is inflicted by man on man from the accursed love of gold.—May we not justly dread the displeasure of that Almighty being, who is the common father of us all, if we do not by all means within our power endeavor to suppress such infamous cruelties. . . .

I make no apology, Gentlemen, for having detained you so long upon this interesting subject. In vain shall we expend our wealth in missions abroad for the promotion of Christianity; in vain shall we rear at home magnificent temples to the service of the most High; if we tolerate this traffic, our charity is but a name, and our religion little more than a faint and delusive shadow.

Source Note: Joseph Story, *A Charge Delivered to the Grand Jury of the Circuit Court of the United States at its First Session in Portland for the Judicial District of Maine, May 8, 1820, and Published at the Unanimous Request of the Grand Jury and of the Bar* (Portland, ME: A. Shirley, 1820).

Biblical Proslavery Arguments

Early Americans took the Bible very seriously. It is a gross misunderstanding to argue that Puritans took the Scriptures literally; most read their Bibles allegorically and typologically. But as a source of revealed authority governing human history, the Bible was rivaled only by the rapid rise of science as a means of perceiving truth. Therefore, both proslavery and antislavery advocates turned to the Bible to justify their causes. The readers and congregations of the eighteenth and nineteenth centuries in America would have been much more familiar with the types and figures of the Old Testament than modern Americans, so that centering one's argument for or against slavery on the precedents of the Bible would have provided instant recognition and a powerful moral force.

There are two prominent sources in the Bible used repeatedly by proslavery advocates between 1776 and 1865. First is the precedent-setting Old Testament. Not only was polygamy sanctioned and practiced among the patriarchs, but concubinage and the enslavement of enemies following battle were common practices. Abraham and Sarah were unable to conceive a child even though Abraham had been made the supreme patriarch of Israel, destined to bless the world through his line of succession. He does, however, impregnate Hagar, Sarah's slave maid and Abraham's concubine, and their child is Ishmael, patriarch of the Ishmaelites. When Sarah and Abraham later conceive Isaac, Hagar and Ishmael are cast out into the wilderness (see Genesis, chapters 10–22). The Old Testament account of Noah's flood and the succession of his sons also provides a curse on Canaan, Ham's son, that reinforces the "mark of Cain" (which was actually a protective symbol), found earlier in Genesis, chapter 4:15. The mark of Cain and the curse on Canaan were considered to be distinguishing marks, possibly designating African skin color, so that these puzzling marks were widely considered to be racial designations by the biblical proslavery advocates, who associated the Africans with God's disfavor. White was metaphorically associated with good, while blackness was considered a representation of evil.

A second prominent argument developed out of St. Paul's letter to Philemon. An escaped slave, Onesimus, is in the care of Philemon, a Christian, who writes to Paul to learn what he should do with the escaped slave. As the Fugitive Slave Laws of 1793 and 1850 were being hotly debated in antebellum America, the Pauline doctrine concerning Onesimus became a central text in determining the Christian response to this legislation. In chapter 9 of *Uncle Tom's Cabin*, Senator and Mrs. Bird engage in a lengthy discussion concerning the morality of the Fugitive Slave Law, for which Senator Bird has just voted. Mrs. Bird directs a pointed moral argument against her husband's action, citing the "moral" rather than the literal value of the Bible, but she is unable to use the Pauline text because it is regarded to be supportive of the Fugitive Slave Law. Paul's response is not ambiguous, though it is lengthy and its language confusing. Paul argues that the "right thing to do" is to return Onesimus to his owner, but only after he has been sufficiently exposed to salvation through Christ and turned into a Christian.

This argument would frequently resurface in support of the Fugitive Slave Law of 1850, by which all states in the Union were made accomplices in the institution of chattel slavery, although most Northern states had abolished slavery long before 1850. By making it a federal crime to harbor a fugitive slave such as Frederick Douglass, the Fugitive Slave Law invoked the precedent of Paul's letter to Philemon as sanction for a secular and constitutional practice. (See chapter 2, "Acts of Congress Relating to Slavery," where the texts of both the 1793 and 1850 Fugitive Slave Laws are excerpted.) The Pauline letter to Philemon was also used by proslavery advocates to sanction slavery independent of the clear association with the Fugitive Slave Laws that became part of the system of laws supported by the United States Constitution during the nineteenth century. William Lloyd Garrison and his followers were strong opponents of the Constitution, which they regarded to be a "covenant with Hell" and a proslavery compact with evil.

In the documents that follow, the Reverend Thornton Stringfellow of Virginia uses both the Old and the New Testaments to defend slavery. In *A Brief Examination of the Scripture Testimony of the Institution of Slavery* (1841), Stringfellow argued primarily from the Old Testament by showing how "Cursed be Canaan" (*Genesis* 9) is a sign that God intended for Ham's posterity to be held in abject, perpetual bondage. In *Slavery, Its Origin, Nature, and History Considered in the Light of Bible Teachings, Moral Justice, and Political Wisdom* (1861), he examined the Pauline letter to Philemon in detail and shows that "Among all the covenants made by nations involving the obligations of morality and good neighborship up to the eighteenth century, there was none to deliver up fugitive slaves to their owners." He then goes on to show that Paul "little thought, when writing this letter about a fugitive slave, and returning him to his Christian master (who was a minister of the Gospel) and most affectionately entreating that Christian master to receive this fugitive again and to forgive him . . . that it [would] induce thirteen sovereign States, seventeen hundred and twenty-nine years after that letter was written, to copy his example, and bind themselves in a solemn covenant to imitate him in their future course of national conduct." He concluded by condemning abolitionism: "How painful it is to see the moral power of this inspired example dying away under the sway of infidelity, which repudiates the Bible, and proclaims 'freedom and equality,' where God in his word teaches there is none."

Stringfellow provides a superb example of the Bible arguments used by proslavery ministers between the American Revolution and the Civil War. When these debates were at their zenith, the decades of the 1830s, 1840s, and 1850s, they were waged both North and South, although chattel slavery was an ac-

cepted institution in the fifteen slaveholding Southern states and had been abolished in most of the sixteen Northern states. In fact, Larry Tise, in *Proslavery: A
History of the Defense of Slavery in America, 1701–1840*, shows that "of the fifty-
five known defenses published between 1830 and 1840, thirty-seven were written by northern ministers" (p. 262). Sectional identification with slavery resulted
from the South's continued practice long after it had been abolished in the
North, and because the move to secede from the Union isolated the South as a
rebellious, slaveholding region where the institution received strong support.

The Tise study outlines several misconceptions concerning the regional identification of slavery with the Southern states, where the "peculiar institution" of
chattel slavery was a foundation of the cotton and agricultural economy. The
common assumption that slavery was exclusively a Southern problem was
changed forever by the Fugitive Slave Laws dating from 1793 to the most notorious proslavery provisions incorporated into the Compromise of 1850. Ironically, William Lloyd Garrison, a Bostonian, had early advocated "secession,"
but that the Northern states should dissociate themselves from the morally degraded Southern slaveholding states; however, he also regarded the Constitution
itself to be a morally tainted document because of its failure to confront the
issue of chattel slavery. Both the South and the North were governed by the
federal Constitution, and it would be incorrect to assume that slavery was exclusively a regional, Southern problem.

As Tise argues, "an examination of American proslavery literature from 1701
until the nineteenth century will suggest that Americans had a rich and telling
proslavery history throughout their colonial and revolutionary years prior to the
emergence of the Old South" (p. 10). Indeed, the concept of the "Old South" as
a distinct, proslavery region emerges naturally from the slaveholding states'
maintenance of chattel slavery long after it had been abolished by Northern
legislatures. However, proslavery sentiments were national, not regional, and
especially in the first two decades of the nineteenth century, the arguments for
and against slavery, now largely confined to the South and the newly emerging
territories of the west and southwest, were national in scope. "During those
years, colonizers and emancipators were busy at work forming societies to rid
the nation of both slavery and the Negro and most slaveholders, out of conscience, felt relatively comfortable with the efforts. Any analysis of the period
will indicate that proslavery sentiments were present in a multiplicity of national
concerns, wherever people talked about the nature and future shape of American society. Throughout the period, most of the defending of slavery was left to
social critics far removed from the scene of slaveholding" (Tise, p. 10).

While the slave trade had been abolished by England's Parliament in 1807
and by the United States Congress in 1808, the importation of slaves to the
Americas continued throughout the nineteenth century, and it has been estimated that some 250,000 slaves were brought from Africa to the United States
after the 1808 legal prohibition of the slave trade. Proslavery arguments for the
continuation of the institution in the Southern states were developed on both
sides of the Mason-Dixon line, and these arguments were essentially the same

ones used anywhere in the western world "wherever one found slaveholding on the defensive" (Tise, p. 10). Tise develops fully the argument that proslavery defenses were almost universal and not restricted to Southern legislators or ministers. "Another myth is the belief that southerners rallied around a notion that slavery was a positive good both for master and slave and such a perspective made the Old South unique among slaveholding societies. A close examination of the thesis and of pertinent related literature from other periods and other lands will suggest that the thesis is without basis in fact" (p. 10). Indeed, one of the most prominent proslavery arguments in colonial Great Britain was that "Christianizing" and "civilizing" the heathen African was a justification for the institution of slavery and for a continuation of the slave trade. Antislavery arguments were developed in Parliament by William Wilberforce and his followers, but the notion that the slave somehow benefited from exposure to western, Christian civilization was not unique to proslavery arguments in the United States.

The popular belief that most proslavery arguments were unique to Southern, slaveholding Americans does not hold up under scrutiny. "A composite biographical study of nearly three hundred individuals who published defenses of slavery in the United States suggests that the pursuit was almost without geographical distinction" (Tise, p. 10). Similarly, proslavery and antislavery debates from 1800 to 1865 transcended periodization just as they transcended regionalization.

> If proslavery ideology is seen without reference to racism, class consciousness, sectionalism, or some other factor that prejudges the issue, the problem of periodization becomes simpler. If equated with racism, perceived alterations in proslavery history would end with the rise of race consciousness in the early colonial period. If identified as class oriented, proslavery history would reach fruition with the rise of class consciousness in the middle of the nineteenth century. If connected with sectionalism, proslavery history would begin and terminate with the rise of southern consciousness in the 1820s and 1830s. But if proslavery is viewed as merely one strand of social thought with various emphases at different points in American history, its history can be traced as that independent mode of thought distinct, if not entirely separable, from the movements with which it became associated. [Tise, p. 13]

For example, in the early decades of the nineteenth century, some of the race theory arguments developed in Europe and Great Britain were used by the colonizationists as well as the proslavery advocates as they attempted to implement a scheme for returning all Africans in America back to Africa.

Colonization societies were predominately Northern institutions, and, as Benjamin Quarles has noted, were generally accepting of the tenets of contemporary race theory, by which it was argued that the African was inferior to the white American. Finally, proslavery arguments were developed simply as a means of preserving the status quo, the order of society, and by proponents, both North and South, who feared the inevitable social upheaval that might result from the emancipation of several million African slaves by a white society that had oppressed them. When emancipation finally came through the Thirteenth Amendment to the Constitution in 1865, other oppressive measures emerged to keep the African from full participation in the predominately white society. Reconstruction brought with it the rise of the Ku Klux Klan and the subsequent Jim Crow legislation with its emphasis on states' rights, literacy tests and the intimidation of voter registrants, and the segregation of public systems of transportation, accommodation, and most importantly, education, reinforced by the *Plessy v. Ferguson* Supreme Court ruling of 1896. The ideology of pro slavery, with its underlying race theory arguments as well as the arguments from economic necessity and biblical precedent, continued long after the Civil War and the abolition of the institution of slavery by Congress.

The debates represented in these readings do have the character of regional association; however, they have been selected and edited for their arguments rather than their regional representation. Stringfellow is Southern, for example, and James Freeman Clarke is Northern. However, the biblical debates were waged intensely on both sides of the Mason-Dixon line before the Civil War. Anti-abolitionist feeling ran strong both North and South, especially as the abolitionists grew more militant and after the Harpers Ferry Raid led by John Brown on October 16, 1859. The force advocated by militant abolitionists and demonstrated by Brown's raids on Kansas and Harpers Ferry ran counter to perceived ethical Christian doctrine, so that Northern sentiments were frequently addressed by ministers who saw in the Bible justifications for the continuation of slavery.

Fears of massive rebellions among the emancipated slaves of the South, as the Nat Turner rebellion had already demonstrated, were fueled by ministers who used their Bibles to show that God sanctioned slavery in the ancient world as a precedent for modern practices. When reviewing the texts that follow here as the biblical proslavery arguments, and when comparing these to the biblical antislavery arguments of chapter 4, the reader will find that the proslavery ministers used their Bibles with scholarly authority and dexterity, whereas the antislavery ministers were restricted to moral and ethical arguments developed primarily from Christ's teachings, which were less specific and often evasive concerning chattel slavery. Slavery had been a common practice in the ancient world, and the failure of the New Testament to oppose it morally gave proslavery advocates license to employ the Old Testament precedents widely in support of their side of the debate. This comparison shows how extremely difficult it was for the antislavery ministers to develop scholarly, exegetical arguments from scripture texts. Rather, like Harriet Beecher Stowe and Frederick Douglass, they relied heavily on rhetorical strategies and moral principles to develop their antislavery arguments. The texts in this section should be read in conjunction with the biblical antislavery texts, and with the political pro- and antislavery arguments developed by members of Congress.

ESSENTIAL BIBLICAL TEXTS USED BY PROSLAVERY ADVOCATES

Both proslavery and antislavery advocates used the Bible effectively to argue their views (see Tise, *Proslavery*, chapter 5, especially "The Morality of Slavery," pp. 116–20). However, because slavery is clearly sanctioned in the ancient world and especially in the Old Testament among the Israelites, abolitionists were constrained in their use of the Bible to the moral teachings of Jesus and to a handful of Old Testament references. Many of the Old Testament texts clearly show, in graphic detail, how slavery was practiced by God's chosen people, the Hebrews. The texts that follow are often proslavery or antislavery; many are ambiguous, as the accompanying commentary suggests. These texts were compiled by students in "Race and Slavery in Nineteenth-Century American Culture" at the University of Massachusetts, spring 2001. See also *The Interpreter's Bible* (Nashville: Abingdon Press, 1980); *The Oxford Bible Concordance* (Oxford and New York: Oxford University Press, 1986); I. Mendelsohn, *Slavery in the Ancient Near East*; and Walter A. Elwell, gen. ed., *Encyclopedia of the Bible* (London: Marshall Pickering, 1988).

Genesis 17. The Covenant with Abraham designates him as the patriarch of God's chosen people. Ishmael, his son by the slave-concubine Hagar, was his only offspring until his wife by marriage, Sarah, conceived and bore Isaac, who received the covenant blessing and continued the line. Initially, however, Ishmael was initiated into the Hebrew tribe by the ritual of circumcision, Genesis 17:23. "Then Abraham took his son Ishmael and all of the slaves born in his house or bought with his money, every male among the men of Abraham's house, and he circumcised the flesh of his foreskin."

Exodus 21:16 and Deuteronomy 24:7. The Old Covenant law banned kidnapping (manstealing), punishable by death. "Whosoever kidnaps a person, whether that person has been sold or is still held in possession, shall be put to death." "If someone is caught kidnapping another Israelite, enslaving or selling the Israelite, then that kidnapper shall die. So you shall purge the evil from your midst." However, the proslavery advocates focused on the distinction between enslaving one of the tribe, an Israelite, and enslaving a person from another tribal group, such as a Canaanite. Antislavery advocates seized this unusual Old Testament opportunity to argue against slavery of any kind.

Exodus 21:2 and Leviticus 25:10, 54. The Old Testament recognizes a distinction between "servitude" of the indentured variety and "chattel slavery." According to Hebrew law, indentured "servitude" was permitted even among the Hebrews, provided that both master and slave agreed to the terms of the indenture. According to Exodus 21:2, "When you buy a male Hebrew slave, he shall serve six years, but in the seventh he shall go out a free person, without debt." Even indentured slaves bought from heathens were freed by the fifty-year jubilee. As stated in Leviticus 25:10 and 25:54, "And you shall hallow the fiftieth year and you shall proclaim liberty throughout the land to all its inhabitants. It shall be a jubilee for you; you shall return every one of you, to your property and every one of you to your family." "And if they have not been redeemed in any of these ways, they and their children with them shall go free in the jubilee year."

Exodus and Deuteronomy on Strangers. A particularly vexing question for American slaveowners relying heavily on the Old Testament for precedents to justify chattel slavery, was the Covenant injunction concerning the treatment of "strangers." The Old Testament is very clear on this subject; strangers are to receive special treatment, as guests, not as chattel slaves. Exodus 22:21: "You shall not wrong or oppress a resident alien, for you were aliens in the land of Egypt." Exodus 23:9: "You shall not oppress a resident alien; you know the heart of an alien, for you were aliens in the land of Egypt." Leviticus 19:33–35: "When an alien resides with you in your land, you shall not oppress the alien. The alien who resides with you shall be to you as the citizen among you; you shall love the alien as yourself, for you were aliens in the land of Egypt: I am the Lord your God." Deuteronomy 1:16 is particularly clear concerning the matter of equal treatment under the law: "I charge your judges at that time, Give the members of your community a fair hearing, and judge rightly between one person and another, whether citizen or resident alien." See also Deuteronomy 10:17–19, "For the Lord your God is God of gods and Lord of lords, the great God, mighty and awesome, who is not partial and takes no bribe, who executes justice for the orphan and the widow, and who loves the strangers, providing them food and clothing. You shall also love the stranger, for you were strangers in the land of Egypt." Deuteronomy 27:19: "Cursed be anyone who deprives the alien, the orphan, and the widow of justice."

Exodus 21:7–11 and Leviticus 25:39–46. Old Testament Covenant law cherished the family unit, and the breakup of the family was scheduled for particularly harsh punishment. Strict regulations governed remarriage by widows and interfamily relationships. See Exodus 21:7–11: "When a man sells his daughter as a slave, she shall not go out as the male slaves do. If she does not please her master, who designated her for himself, then he shall let her be redeemed; he shall have no right to sell her to a foreign people, since he has dealt unfairly with her. If he designates her for his son, he shall deal with her as with a daughter. If he takes another wife to himself, he shall not diminish the food, clothing, or marital rights of the first wife. And if he does not do these three things for her, she shall go out without debt, without payment of money." In Leviticus 25:39–46, the Covenant law articulates specific treatment of slaves, who may own slaves, and the circumstances under which one becomes a slave.

> If any who are dependent on you become so impoverished that they sell themselves to you, you shall not make them serve as slaves. They shall remain with you as hired or bound laborers [indentured servants]. They shall serve with you until the year of the jubilee. Then they and their children with them shall be free from your authority; they shall go back to their own family and return to their ancestral property. For they are my servants, whom I brought out of the land of Egypt, they shall not be sold as slaves are sold. You shall not rule over them with harshness, but shall fear

your God. As for the male and female slaves whom you may have, it is from the nations around you that you may acquire male and female slaves. You may also acquire them from among the aliens residing with you, and from their families that are with you, who have been born in your land; and they may be your property. You may keep them as a possession for your children after you, for them to inherit as property. These you may treat as slaves, but as for your fellow Israelites, no one shall rule over the other with harshness.

These very prescriptive regulations are only the beginning of a long section of laws concerning slavery, and the reader should consult Leviticus and Deuteronomy for further examples from which proslavery and occasionally antislavery advocates would draw their evidence.

Deuteronomy 6:1–9. These verses contain the charges to the nation Israel concerning its obligations under the Covenant. "Keep these words that I am commanding you today in your heart. Recite them to your children and talk about them when you are at home and when you are away, when you lie down and when you rise. Bind them as a sign on your hand, fix them as an emblem on your forehead, and write them on the doorposts of your house and on your gates." Chapter 5 of Deuteronomy contains an almost exact repetition of the Decalogue, or "Ten Commandments," that also appears in Exodus 20:2–17. Slaveowners disregarded these Old Testament regulations when it was convenient to do so.

Exodus 21:20–21 and Leviticus 19:20–22. Although the Old Testament is emphatic in its requirement that all citizens be given equal treatment under the law, the proslavery advocates saw loopholes in the Old Testament precedents because not all persons living in Israel were "citizens." Again, Leviticus and Deuteronomy clearly argue legal equality for persons living in Israel, including "aliens" and "strangers," but in the antebellum United States, the law did not include rights for Africans, who were not citizens. As chief justice of the Supreme Court of the United States, Roger B. Taney, would declare, in *Dred Scott v Sandford*, 60 US 393, 407; 15 L Ed 691(1857), "[The African slave] had no rights which the [slavemaster] is bound to respect."

The proslavery defense would include ancient precedents as well as biblical arguments and examples. Slavery had been an essential component of the economy of the ancient world; however, for all the brutality of slavery in any historical time or place, the laws of the ancient world did protect the rights of slaves in ways that the slaveholding states of the United States did not. According to the Nuzi Tablets of Mesopotamia, for example, slaves and even their descendants were granted recourse to the law when they were mistreated by masters. And in the Old Testament, the punishment of slaves was regulated by law just as it was in the slaveholding states: "When a slaveowner strikes a male or female slave with a rod and the slave dies immediately, the owner shall be punished. But if the slave survives a day or two, there is no punishment [of the owner]; for the slave is the owner's property" (Exodus 21:20–21).

The treatment of slave women posed special problems for slaveowners because mulatto children were often the results of liaisons between masters and their slaves. Both Frederick Douglass's *Narrative* (1845) and Harriet Jacobs's *Incidents in the Life of a Slave Girl* (1861) contain episodes showing the brutal treatment reserved for the illegitimate children of such liaisons, especially when the slave's mistress lived daily with the evidence of her husband's infidelity. Old Testament laws offered little assistance: "And if a man has sexual relations with a woman who is a slave, designated for another man but not ransomed or given her freedom, an inquiry shall be held. They shall not be put to death, since she has not been freed; but he shall bring a guilt offering for himself to the Lord, at the entrance of the tent of meeting, a ram as guilt offering. And the priest shall make atonement for him with the ram of guilt offering before the Lord for his sin that he committed; and the sin he committed shall be forgiven him" (Leviticus 19:20–22).

Genesis 9:20–27. Perhaps the most frequently quoted biblical text used by the slaveholders and proslavery advocates to justify chattel slavery was the passage where a curse is placed upon Canaan, the son of Ham, son of Noah. This passage has the tone and style of myth; however, it was often used to explain the African's fate as a chattel slave of his white master, and it became the central biblical defense of slavery used by ministers and proslavery advocates in the United States:

> Noah, a man of the soil, was the first to plant a vineyard. He drank some of the wine and became drunk, and he lay uncovered in his tent. And Ham, the father of Canaan, saw the nakedness of his father, and told his two brothers outside. Then Shem and Japheth took a garment, laid it on both their shoulders, and walked backward and covered the nakedness of their father; their faces were turned away, and they did not see their father's nakedness. When Noah awoke from his wine and knew what his youngest son had done to him, he said,
>
> > "Cursed be Canaan;
> > lowest of slaves shall he be to his brothers."
> > He also said, "Blessed by the Lord my God be Shem;
> > and let Canaan be his slave.
> > May God make space for Japheth,
> > And let him live in the tents of Shem;
> > And let Canaan be his slave."

The narrative assumes that both Ham and Noah's grandson, Canaan, were guilty of seeing their father's nakedness; the curse placed on Canaan was used to explain the assumed inferiority of the African, which was designated by his blackness, the sign of this curse.

These biblical texts were frequently cited by ministers, both North and South, in the proslavery arguments for perpetuation of the institution of chattel slavery. (Larry Tise shows that in the decade of the 1830s there were some fifty-five biblical defenses of slavery published, and two-thirds were written by Northern ministers.)

Throughout the nineteenth century, the arguments concerning slavery and its precedents in the Old Testament continued. For example, the Reverend John Furman, a Baptist from South Carolina, declared that "The right of holding slaves is clearly established in the Holy Scriptures, both by precept and example." The Reverend Alexander Campbell stated that "There is not one verse in the Bible inhibiting slavery, but many regulating it. It is not, then, we conclude, immoral." Finally, no less a figure than Jefferson Davis, the president of the Confederate States of America, resorted to the biblical argument to frame his defense of slavery: "Slavery was established by the decree of Almighty God. . . . It is sanctioned in the Bible, in both Testaments, from Genesis to Revelation. . . . it has existed in all ages, has been found among the people of the highest civilization, and in nations of the highest proficiency in the arts." (See also the analysis of the Reverend Ross–Abraham Lincoln debate in the introduction to this volume.)

The Old Testament provided numerous examples of slaveholding sanctioned by Hebrew law, however regulated. Antislavery thinkers and abolitionists were more inclined to use moral arguments developed in the eighteenth century, the "natural rights" arguments of the Enlightenment, than to turn to Old Testament examples in support of their arguments. The teachings of Jesus in the four Gospels were sufficiently moral in their doctrines of love of neighbor as self and in the articulation of basic principles of human dignity, especially those precepts found in the Sermon on the Mount in Matthew 5:3–16. The simple "beatitudes" convey a populist inversion of authority, noting that in the Kingdom of God, the "last shall be first," and the humble shall be made mighty. This notion that the kingdoms of the earth shall be made subservient to the Kingdom of God has historically appealed powerfully to oppressed peoples, and the slaves of the United States found in the Bible a message of hope and salvation that promised deliverance to a "promised land" free from their earthly suffering and oppression. Nineteenth-century African spirituals reflect this kind of yearning for future fulfillment and release from the agony of present suffering. "Nobody Knows the Trouble I've Seen" and "Swing Low, Sweet Chariot" both show the slave's meditation on future glory, as contrasted with the agonies of present suffering.

But it is a long way from the teachings of Jesus, which do not adequately confront the issue of slavery, to the "natural rights" arguments of the 1840s. Moreover, the New Testament also contains the teaching of Saint Paul, who authored the letter to Philemon, a work that specifically addresses the issue of slavery and shows how a runaway slave, Onesimus, should be returned to his owner after he had been Christianized. While Paul does not address the general issue of slavery as a social institution—he rather assumes its legitimacy by arguing the finer points of the treatment of a runaway slave—he does argue that Onesimus should be received back into the household of his master, Philemon, and received into the church as an equal member with Philemon's family. The issue of whether or not Onesimus should be set free is *not* addressed in the text of Paul's letter, but, like most of the New Testament treatment of slavery, is subordinated to the larger questions of Christian conversion and acceptance into the community of Christ.

It was therefore difficult, though certainly not impossible, for antislavery advocates to frame their arguments in purely biblical terms, and they turned more frequently to the Declaration of Independence for its moral imperatives. While they could occasionally use passages from both the Old and the New Testament to suggest humane treatment of slaves or the human worth of individual persons, their primary arguments would come from Enlightenment "natural rights" doctrine, because the biblical texts were so weighted with examples of polygamy and chattel slavery practiced throughout the early books of the Old Testament, and because the New Testament teachings concerning slavery are both vague and ambiguous when not specifically supportive of slavery. As the next chapter on the biblical antislavery arguments clearly shows, there is a fusion of moral arguments taken from the Bible and the natural rights principles even when antislavery advocates are developing their doctrines with Scripture texts as examples.

SUGGESTIONS FOR FURTHER READING

Tise, Larry E. *Proslavery: A History of the Defense of Slavery in America, 1701–1840*. Athens: University of Georgia Press, 1987.

Thornton Stringfellow (1788–1869)

The two texts that follow were written by one of the most influential proslavery voices in the antebellum South. Stringfellow was a Virginian by birth and by cultural heritage, born in Fauquier County and becoming minister to a Baptist church in Culpepper, Virginia. In 1846, when the Southern Baptist Convention separated from the Northern Baptist Church over the issue of slavery, Stringfellow supported this division, and he was an ardent secessionist and "Southern sectionalist." Today, the Southern Baptist Convention which Stringfellow helped to found is one of the largest Christian churches in the world, with membership well into the millions worldwide.

Rural ministers like Stringfellow were often "circuit riding" preachers, ministering to several congregations in a county or region by "riding the circuit" every Sunday. Stringfellow employed a variety of arguments to defend slavery, citing the Bible as his primary authority, the law of nature as a secondary source, and the governance of the family of man as a concluding argument. Like many antebellum Southerners, Stringfellow firmly believed in a hierarchical, segregated society established by God through His revelation in the Old Testament, and meant for mankind to follow thereafter. The plantation society in which Stringfellow was raised and lived all of his life depended mightily on a caste system for social order. According to Peter Wallenstein, "Culpepper County's population in 1850 was 42 percent white, 54 percent slave, and four percent free black. Stringfellow himself, the son of a slaveowning family, owned about 60 slaves. He resembled his Northern counterparts in many respects, but in the defense of slavery, he resembled George Fitzhugh, another eastern Virginian" (Wallenstein, p. 615). Unlike his contemporaries George Gliddon and Josiah Nott, whose race-theory arguments established a "scientific" foundation for the antebellum social order Stringfellow endorsed, he grounded his analysis in history and in biblical precedent, arguing that Abraham had over 300 slaves and that in the New Testament, neither Jesus nor Paul mounted an effective challenge to the slave system of their time. By also suggesting that the laws of Nature, which Enlightenment philosophers had used to establish the equality of men, were in fact another example of the inequality of men by virtue of their inherited differences, Stringfellow attempted to fuse biblical precedent with the scientific racial theory of his day. It is clear that he accepted, if he did not specifically articulate, the hierarchical race categories established by Blumenbach in Germany, Pritchard in England, and Nott and Gliddon in the United States. Stringfellow vigorously countered the Jeffersonian natural rights principle that "all men are created equal" with a lengthy discussion of how, throughout history, all men have not been created equal. "The essential particulars of slavery in the Old Testament and in the Old South, that it was 'involuntary' if we would secure the well-being of both races" (Wallenstein, p. 615) and "hereditary," were all that mattered—but then there was race. "The guardianship and control of the black race, by the white," he argued in *Scriptural and Statistical View in Favor of Slavery* (1841), "is an indispensable Christian duty, to which we must yet look if we would secure the well-being of both races" (Wallenstein, p. 615). The reader should consult chapter 7 in this volume for a full discussion of antebellum race theory, not only which influenced Thornton Stringfellow, but to which his writings contributed.

The texts here are from *A Brief Examination of the Scripture Testimony on the Institution of Slavery* (1841) and *Slavery, Its Origin, Nature, and History Considered in the Light of Bible Teachings, Moral Justice, and Political Wisdom* (1861). These documents are important proslavery arguments in their own right; however, they also represent a type of argument that characterized much of the proslavery discourse. First, the 1861 document is introduced by a prominent Northerner, in this case, Samuel F. B. Morse, inventor of the Morse code and a sometime Yale College professor. Morse provided a logician's analysis of the "rightness" and "wrongness" of the slavery question which is followed by Stringfellow's exhaustive historical and biblical argument. Second, the lengthy excerpt represents a much longer work that comprehensively examines the biblical, moral, social, political, and historical evidence supportive of slavery, making it one of the most complete antebellum proslavery documents available. In antebellum America, Stringfellow's treatises on slavery were regarded to be the most extensive and most representative of the proslavery arguments. Therefore, some of Stringfellow's proslavery positions were included in E. N. Elliot's *Cotton Is King, and Proslavery Arguments* (1860). Stringfellow's life was fraught with controversy, often physical and political as well as ideological. As Drew Gilpin Faust observes, "When the Civil War broke out, Stringfellow found his two-thousand acre property near Fredericksburg under almost constant military threat. In 1863, he and his wife were held prisoners in their home for several months while Union armies supplied themselves from his plantation. Even when his seventy slaves ran away to the Yankees, however, Stringfellow's faith in the justice and benevolence of human bondage did not falter. But his health began to fail, and he remained almost constantly bedridden until his death in 1869" (Faust, p. 137).

SUGGESTIONS FOR FURTHER READING

Faust, Drew Gilpin. "Evangelicalism and the Meaning of the Proslavery Argument: The Reverend Thornton Stringfellow of Virginia." *Virginia Magazine of History and Biography* 85 (January 1977), pp. 3–17. As Faust notes, most of Stringfellow's papers were destroyed, but a diary remains in the possession of the family.

Faust, Drew Gilpin, ed. *The Ideology of Slavery: Proslavery Thought in the Antebellum South, 1830–1860*. Baton Rouge: Louisiana State University Press, 1992.

Snay, Mitchell. *Gospel of Disunion: Religion and Separatism in the Antebellum South*. Cambridge: Cambridge University Press, 1993.

Wallenstein, Peter. "Thornton Stringfellow." In *The Historical Encyclopedia of Slavery*, ed. Junius Rodriguez (Santa Barbara and Oxford: ABC-CLIO, 1997), p. 165.

A Brief Examination of the Scripture Testimony on the Institution of Slavery
by Thornton Stringfellow

The first recorded language which was ever uttered in relation to slavery, is the inspired language of Noah. In God's stead he says, "Cursed be Canaan;" "a servant of servants shall he be to his brethren." "Blessed be the Lord God of Shem; and Canaan shall be his servant." "God shall enlarge Japheth, and he shall dwell in the tents of Shem; and Canaan shall be his servant." Gen. ix. 25, 26, 27. Here language is used, showing the *favor* which God would exercise to the posterity of Shem and Japheth, while they were holding the posterity of Ham in a state of abject bondage. May it not be said in truth, that God decreed this institution before it existed; and has he not connected its *existence*, with prophetic tokens of special favor, to those who should be slave owners or masters? He is the same God now, that he was when he gave these views of his moral character to the world; and unless the posterity of Shem and Japheth, from whom have sprung the Jews and all the nations of Europe and America, and a great part of Asia, (the African race that is in them excepted,)—I say, unless they are all dead, as well as the Canaanites or Africans, who descended from Ham, then it is quite possible that his favor may now be found with one class of men, who are holding another class in bondage. Be this as it may, God *decreed slavery*—and shows in that decree, tokens of good-will to the master. The sacred records occupy but a short space from this inspired ray on this subject, until they bring to our notice a man, that is held up as a model, in all that adorns human nature, and as one that God delighted to honor. This man is Abraham, honored in the sacred records with the appellation, "Father" of the "faithful." . . .

But, says the spirit of abolition, with which the Bible has to contend, you are building your house upon the sand, for these were nothing but hired servants; and their servitude designates no such state, condition, or relation, as that, in which one person is made the property of another, to be bought, sold, or trans-ferred forever. To this, we have two answers in reference to the subject, before giving the law. In the first place, the term, servant, in the schedules of property among the patriarchs, *does designate* the state, condition, or relation in which one person is the legal property of another, as in Gen. xxiv. 35, 36. Here Abraham's servant, who had been sent by his master to get a wife for his son Isaac, in order to prevail with the woman and her family, states, that the man for whom he sought a bride was the son of a man whom God had greatly blessed with riches. . . .

Again, in Gen. xvii., we are informed of a covenant God entered into with Abraham; in which he stipulates, to be a God to him and his *seed,* (not his servants,) and to give to his *seed* the land of Canaan for an everlasting posses-sion. He expressly stipulates, that Abraham shall put the token of this covenant upon every servant born in his house, and upon every servant *bought with his money of any stranger.* . . .

In addition to the evidence from the context of these, and various other places, to prove the term servant to be identical in the import of its essential particulars with the term slave among us, there is unquestionable evidence, that, *in the patriarchal age*, there are two distinct states of servitude alluded to, and which are indicated by two distinct terms, or by the same term, and an adjective to explain. . . .

Now, with the previous light shed upon the use and meaning of these terms in the *patriarchal Scriptures*, can any man of candor bring himself to believe that two states or conditions are not here referred to, in one of which, the highest reward after toil is mere rest; in the other of which, the reward was wages? And how appropriate is the language in reference to these two states. The slave is represented as earnestly desiring the shadow, because his condition allowed him no prospect of anything more desirable; but the hireling is looking for the re-ward of his work, because that will be an equivalent for his fatigue. . . .

I have been tedious on this first proposition, but I hope the importance of the subject to Christians as well as to statesmen will be my apology. I have written it, not for victory over an adversary, or to support error or false-hood, but to gather up God's will in reference to holding men and women in bondage, in the patriarchal age. And it is clear, in the first place, that God decreed this state before it existed. Second. It is clear that at the highest manifestations of good-will which he ever gave to mortal man, was given to Abraham, in that covenant in which he required him to circumcise all his male servants, which he had bought with his money, and that were born of them in his house. Third. It is certain that he gave these servants as property to Isaac. Fourth. It is certain that, as the owner of these slaves Isaac received similar tokens of God's favor. Fifth. It is certain that Jacob, who inherited from Isaac his father, received like tokens, of divine favor. Sixth. It is certain, from a fair construction of language, that Job, who is held up by God himself as a model of human perfection, was a great slaveholder. Seventh. It is certain, when God showed honor, and came down to bless Jacob's posterity, in taking them by the hand to lead them out of Egypt, they were the owners of slaves that were bought with money, and treated as property; which slaves were allowed of God to unite in celebrating the divine goodness to their masters, while hired servants were excluded. Eighth. It is certain that God interposed to give Joseph the power in Egypt, which he used, to create a state, or condition, among the Egyptians, which substantially agrees with patriarchal and modern slavery. Ninth. It is certain that in reference to this institution in Abraham's family, and the surrounding nations, for five hundred years, it is never censured in any communication made from God to men. Tenth. It is certain when God put a period to that dispensation, he recognized slaves as property on Mount Sinai. If therefore it has become sinful since, it cannot be from the nature of the thing but from the sovereign pleasure of God in its prohibition. We will therefore proceed to our second proposition, which is—

Second. That it was incorporated in the only national constitution emanating from the Almighty. By common consent, that portion of time stretching from Noah, until the law was given to Abraham's posterity, at Mount Sinai, is called the patriarchal age; this is the period we have reviewed, in relation to this subject. From the giving of the law until the coming of Christ, is called the Mosaic or legal dispensation. From the coming of Christ to the end of time, is called the Gospel dispensation. The legal dispensation is the period of time we propose now to examine, in reference to the institution of involuntary and hereditary slavery, in order to ascertain, whether, during this period, it existed at all, and if it did exist, whether with the divine Sanction, or in violation of the divine will. This dispensation is called the legal dispensation, because it was the pleasure of God to take Abraham's posterity by miraculous power, then numbering near three millions of souls, and give them a written constitution of government, a country to dwell in and a covenant of special protection and favor, for their obedience to his law until the coming of Christ. The laws which he gave them emanated from his sovereign pleasure, and were designed, in the first place, to make himself known in his essential perfections; second, in his moral character; third, in his relation to man; and fourth, to make known those principles of action by the exercise of which man attains his highest moral elevation, viz: supreme love to God, and love to others as to ourselves.

All the law is nothing but a preceptive exemplification of these two principles; consequently, the existence of a precept in the law, utterly irreconcilable with these principles, would destroy all claims upon us for an acknowledgment of its divine original. Jesus Christ himself has put his finger upon these two principles of human conduct, (Deut. vi. 5–Levit. xix. 18,) revealed in the law of Moses, and decided, that on them hang all the law and the prophets.

The Apostle Paul decides in reference to the relative duties of men, that whether written out in preceptive form in the law or not, they are all comprehended in this saying, viz: "thou shalt love thy neighbor as thyself." With these views to guide us, as to the acknowledged design of the law, viz: that of revealing the eternal principles of moral rectitude, by which human conduct is to be measured, so that sin may abound, or be made apparent, and righteousness be ascertained or known, we may safely conclude, that the institution of slavery, which legalizes the holding one person in bondage as property forever by another, if it be morally wrong, or at war with the principle which requires us to love God supremely, and our neighbor as ourself, will, if noticed at all in the law, be noticed, for the purpose of being condemned as sinful. And if the modern views of abolitionists be correct, we may expect to find the institution marked with such tokens of divine displeasure, as will throw all other sins into the shade, as comparatively small, when laid by the side of this monster. What, then, is true? Has God ingrafted hereditary slavery upon the constitution of government he condescended to give his chosen people—that people among whom he promised to dwell, and that he required to be holy? I answer, he has. It is clear and explicit. He enacts, first, that his chosen people may take their money, go into the slave markets of the surrounding nations, (the seven devoted nations excepted,) and purchase men-servants and women-servants, and give them, and their increase, to their children and their children's children, forever; and worse still for the refined humanity of our age—he guarantees to the foreign slaveholder perfect protection, while he comes in among the Israelites, for the purpose of dwelling, and raising and selling slaves, who should be acclimated and accustomed to the habits and institutions of the country. And worse still for the sublimated humanity of the present age, God passes with the right to buy and possess, the right to govern, by a severity which knows no bounds but the master's discretion. And if worse can be, for the morbid humanity we censure, he enacts that his own people may sell themselves and their families for limited periods, with the privilege of extending the time at the end of the 6th year to the 50th year or jubilee, if they prefer bondage to freedom. Such is the precise character of two institutions, found in the constitution of the Jewish commonwealth, emanating directly from Almighty God. For the 1,500 years, during which these laws were in force, God raised up a succession of prophets to reprove that people for the various sins into which they fell; yet there is not a reproof uttered against the institution of *involuntary slavery*, for any species of abuse that ever grew out of it. A severe judgment is pronounced by Jeremiah, (chapter xxxiv. see from the 8th to the 22d verse,) for an abuse or violation of the law, concerning the *voluntary servitude* of Hebrews; but the prophet pens it with caution, as if to show that it had no reference to any abuse that had taken place under the system of *involuntary slavery*, which existed by law among that people; the sin consisted in making hereditary bond-men and bond-women of Hebrews, which was positively forbidden by the law, and not for buying and holding one of another nation in hereditary bondage, which was as positively allowed by the law. And really, in view of what is passing in our country, and elsewhere, among men who profess to reverence the Bible, it would seem that these must be dreams of a distempered brain, and not the solemn truths of that sacred book. . . .

Having shown from the Scriptures, that slavery existed with Abraham and the patriarchs, with divine approbation, and having shown from the same source, that the Almighty incorporated it in the law, as an institution among Abraham's seed, until the coming of Christ, our precise object now is, to ascertain whether *Jesus Christ has abolished it, or recognized it as a lawful relation*, existing among men, and prescribed duties which belong to it, as he has other *relative duties*; such as those between husband and wife, parent and child, magistrate and subject. . . .

The Scriptures we have adduced from the New Testament, to prove the recognition of hereditary slavery by the Savior, as a lawful relation in the sight of God, lose much of their force from the use of a word by the translators, which by time, has lost much of its original meaning; that is, the word *servant*. Dr. Johnson, in his Dictionary, says: "Servant is one of the few words, which by time has acquired a softer signification than its original, knave, degenerated into cheat. While servant, which signified originally, a person preserved from death by the conqueror, and reserved for slavery, signifies only an obedient attendant." Now, all history will prove that the servants of the New Testament addressed by the Apostles, in their letters to the several churches throughout the Roman Empire, were such as were preserved from death by the conqueror, and taken into slavery. This was their condition, and is a fact well known to all men acquainted with history. Had the word which designates their condition, in our translation, lost none of its original meaning, a common man could not have fallen into a mistake as to the condition indicated. But to waive this fact, we are furnished with all the evidence that can be desired. The Savior appeared in an age of learning—the enslaved condition of half the Roman Empire, at the time, is a fact embodied with all the historical records—the constitution God gave the Jews, was in harmony with the Roman regulation on the subject of slavery. In this state of things, Jesus ordered his Gospel to be preached in all the world, and to every creature. It was done as he directed; and masters and servants, and persons in all conditions, were brought by the Gospel to obey the Savior. Churches were constituted. We have examined the letters written to the churches, composed of these materials. The result is, that each member is furnished with a law to regulate the duties of his civil station—from the highest to the lowest.

Source Note: Thornton Stringfellow, *A Brief Examination of the Scripture Testimony on the Institution of Slavery* (New York, 1841).

Slavery, Its Origin, Nature, and History Considered in the Light of Bible Teachings, Moral Justice, and Political Wisdom
by Thornton Stringfellow

Extract from Address of Prof. S.F.B. Morse.
   It cannot but be obvious to all intelligent minds, that among the complex questions which have so long agitated the whole land, and which have mingled

their discordant elements in producing the present alarming political condition of the country, so deeply distressing to every patriotic mind, the moral and religious question of slavery stands forth most prominent. Indeed, it is the fundamental question, and demands, first of all, a satisfactory settlement; for on the right decision of this moral and religious question depends all the other questions relating to slavery. Whether slavery, or the condition of being held in subjection to the will of another, is a divine institution, sanctioned by laws and commands, and regulated from the earliest times, or is forbidden as a sin—as a violation of the laws of God—is surely a fundamental question. The difference here, at the start, is antipodal. The course of conduct pursued by the believers in these two extremes, must of necessity lead to results as diverse as light from darkness. Until this point is satisfactorily settled we cannot reach the expediency or inexpediency, the advantage or disadvantage, of this system of servitude. If it is a sin, if the Bible shows it to be a sin, the controversy is settled; we can have no compromise with sin; we have nothing to do with it but to forsake it. Hence all whose consciences sustain them in that view of the question are at least consistent in their zealous opposition to slavery, and their determination to uproot it everywhere and at all hazards. On the other hand, if God has shown in his word and by his providence, that servitude or slavery, in its various modifications of form and duration, and of mild or severe character, has, from the beginning of the world, been an essential feature in His government of man; that viewed from a loftier stand-point than is circumscribed by earth or time, there are benevolent ends in part comprehensible even by our short-sightedness, ends only attainable by this system, then they whose consciences sustain them in this view of the question, will be cautious how they rudely and recklessly fight against God and destroy it with violence. A glance at the character of the litigants on this question, show ranged on each side of the two opposing opinions, men of the highest intellectual and moral character. Rash, indeed, would it be to charge either party with hypocrisy. There is no need for such an uncharitable assumption. The humble seeker after truth will not suffer its golden sands to escape him, even if he has to separate them, with labor, from the mire of human weakness and error, and hence he may not neglect the extremist views of the bitterest opponents. Yet mindful of our own weakness and of our need of enlightenment, to what standard, but God's word, shall we appeal as the arbiter in such a controversy? "To the laws and to the testimony."

Slavery and Government

CHAPTER I. There has never been an assertion made and believed, which all might know with so much certainty to be untrue. Man, when born is helplessly dependent, free to do nothing without permission, and entirely under parental control, until he is given up to the control of the State, which holds him under control until death. If this constitutes freedom, then all men are born free, but not otherwise.

The second thing affirmed in this Declaration of Independence, and, which with the above error, has been adopted by a portion of our countrymen as part of the Bible, is, that "all men are born equal." I will only reply in language which all men know to be true, that they are not born intellectually equal; that they are not born morally equal; that they are not born politically equal; that they are not born equal in social position, or advantages; nor are they in any other sense equal, as integral parts of earthly governments, of which I can conceive, from their birth until their death. And yet a belief in these abstractions, these palpable falsehoods, is at the bottom of a crusade against organized society and constitutional liberty in the United States, which aims at the destruction of all the safeguards of life and property, and a universal overthrow of law and order, save that of the "higher law" of every murder's conscience. We have lately had a specimen of the conscience which this "higher law" produces. It was exhibited in the person of John Brown and a few others.

This specimen is much admired by all of the same faith and order—so—who is destined to be as much honored for substituting his own conscience for the Bible, as Jesus Christ has been for giving eternal life to them that love him; and who prove that love, as the Bible directs, by yielding a willing obedience to law and order in all the relations of life. And because of this assumed freedom and equality, with certain assumed unalienable rights, the conclusion is drawn, according to this new political Bible, that all good government must; originate in the consent of the governed. . . .

Family government is a necessity in nature. Every new family instinctively assumes it because it is God's ordinance. It is the best model of a State. Here the principles and objects of governments are first learned. Without this school the idea of government could not be known.

Adam's family were parts of himself; and so of all families. This is the Divine guarantee for a right use of family authority. The impulses of nature constitute the guarantee that the divinely constituted head will rule the family in righteousness, and not abuse his authority in chastizing for disobedience.

Family government cannot be dispensed with; without it, the world would be depopulated. It is the nursery and school-room in which the materials for large families or States, must of necessity be prepared. A well-governed family is the best model for a State which exists among men. It is in the family that every human being learns the nature, the necessity, and the objects of government, and necessity for such modifications as *experience* suggests. Here we learn that government must begin in absolute despotism, instead of absolute freedom. Here we learn that all men are born slaves to parents who have a right to their service; and a right to control them until they are qualified to raise families, and use political freedom. All self-control, which is freedom, is cruelty to the infant man, and utterly inconsistent with doing to others "as we would they should do unto us." (It is here we learn to what extent authority may be relaxed in subordination to the general good, that what would be a good to one would be an evil to another; that the object of government is to prevent the evil, to promote the good, and to educate the body and mind. It is here we learn that the government suited to one individual, or family, would be very unsuitable to another. That the amount of self-control to which some members entitle themselves in a family, can never be safely granted to others. It is in the family we learn to love each other, to sympathize with each other, to do justice, to speak truth, what virtue is, what vice is, what personal and property rights are, what law is, what authority is, and how, and why it should be used in enforcing law.) It is here we learn the qualifications which fit us to raise families, and meet the responsibilities of political freedom. And here we learn that wisdom, experience, and the highest degree of interest in the well-being of those to be governed, are necessary qualifications in those who govern. This government has been sanctioned by the States of the Federal Union for every white family and their slave. . . .

The service or labor of our child is legally our money; we can coerce this labor at home—we can hire out this labor to another—or we can sell it at any price it will command in the market; and by such sale we pass to the purchaser our authority to control our child, by all necessary and proper means for that end, until he is twenty-one years old. This, and no more, is true of the African slave, except as to length of time he serves. The service or labor of our slave, is legally our money for life. The service or labor of our child, is legally our money for twenty-one years. We can hire this service or labor of our slave to another, just as we can that of our child; or we can sell it for life, just as we can that of our child for twenty-one years; and with this service or labor we pass to the purchaser our authority to control our slave, just as we do our child—and by means only for that end which are necessary and proper.

Now for this service or labor and for this subjection and control what does the child receive on the one hand, and what does the African slave receive on the other, that makes this slavery just? Unless they both receive in return "what is due"—or, "what is accommodated to the action," this slavery of our children and of the African is unjust.

What does our child receive as a compensation for his labor and subjection to our control for twenty-one years? He receives a sleepless and untiring watch-care from his birth, night and day, in sickness and in health, in prosperity and adversity, until he is twenty-one years old. He receives also an exemption from all care—food to eat, and raiment to put on; a home to shield him and a hand to defend him, a teacher to instruct and a friend to restrain him; until his mental and physical nature is sufficiently developed, and his character and habits sufficiently formed, to take the responsibilities of life on himself; or in other words, to provide for and govern a family, and meet the demands of political freedom. For all of this, which commences with his first breath, and intermits not for acquisition of habits which will make him a blessing to himself and the world; the parent receives about eight years service and the most of that worth but little, from the fact that skill and strength have first to be acquired for every species of labor which has any value to the parent for the present, or to hereafter.

The Almighty has subjected all of Adam's posterity to a state of slavery as they are born into the world. Instead of giving them at their birth full-grown maturity and freedom, which was easy for infinite wisdom and Almighty power,

He ordained helplessness at their birth,—delegated power to Adam to rule over them—and then by a necessity growing out of this helplessness, compelled him to take charge of them, until their physical and intellectual natures could be educated to take charge of themselves.

The Divine constitution of things on which social happiness and prosperity are made to depend, is adapted to this condition of helpless dependence at our birth, and the want of equality in every individual of the species. In this constitution of things there is a harmonious blending of unequals. Instead of created *equality*, which does not exist among men—and which can be found nowhere, we find created *inequality* everywhere, and this *inequality* among men, is made of God to be the *cohesive element* which binds all together in the social body; so that the head *cannot* say to the feet, I have no need of thee; so that the least honourable make up but one social body without any schism—all the members equally needful, and harmoniously blending in the production of results which can never be reached by the control of any principle, which refuses subordination, subjection, and dependence among the various members.

In the family, which is the oldest and most important social organization, inequality, in every respect, is found to exist among all members. Some have endowments to advance the general welfare; some are so dwarfed as to be incapable of a higher function than that of executing what another contrives; some have powers fitting them for control—others have qualities fitting them for humble submission and grateful dependence. In this most ancient organization, experience unfolds the principles for constructing a social body out of parts unequal, by which each member shall be rendered useful, made a contributor to the general welfare, and a partaker in the general result to the full amount of his due.

It is in the family that the individuals learn *dependence upon each other*—how they can help each other, and how they can injure each other. It is here that our moral nature is trained to "weep with them that weep," and to "rejoice with them that do rejoice." Here we learn to love each other, and to be grateful.

The white child is held to service and control until he is supposed to be qualified to use political and constitutional freedom. This freedom, when it is accorded to him at the age of twenty-one, is accorded on the supposition that he is qualified to use it. If, upon trial, however, this supposition proves to be a mistake in the case of an individual, the State reserves to herself the right to withdraw his constitutional and political freedom, and to subject him to such a system of slavery or servitude, as in her judgment is best adapted to promote his own good, and that of the State; and to continue that state of slavery or servitude for any length of time which the State thinks will best subserve this end. This slavery to the State may consist in rendering service or labor in the penitentiary, in the work-house, or to a domestic master for a price to the State which he shall pay for this service, which belongs of right to the State. All this shows that the reason for which persons should be subjected to slavery in any form, for limited or unlimited periods, is because they are unfit to use freedom as a good to themselves, in subserviency to the good of the community. . . .

We have shown why slavery is just to minors; that they received as much, or more, than they were justly entitled to; and in a form best accommodated to the service and subjection rendered, as an equivalent for it. It remains to be shown that domestic slavery for life is just and proper for the African race—because they are not qualified to use political freedom, and because they receive the full due for this service and labor, and that in a form accommodated to the service they pay for it.

The African race is constitutionally inferior to the white race. Experience proves this in all the conditions and countries they have ever occupied. The African has left no memorial which proves his capacity to improve, unaided by a superior race, or to progress when improvements have been given him. There is a great physical, moral, and intellectual difference between the two races. The tendency upon each race of the same set of circumstances, does not diminish, but increases this difference through life. The age of twenty-one, which gives bodily maturity to both races, develops moral and intellectual manhood in the white race, while the African remains, at the end of that time, a mere child in intellectual and moral development, perfectly incapable of performing the great functions of social life. By nature he is contented everywhere in destitution, until want pinches him. In freedom, he cannot be educated to provide for his present wants—much less to lay by him in store for the future. It is the present only that excites him to action. No wages will secure habitual and continued labor from him, while he is free to consult his own will. He can imitate, but cannot originate any thing. He can execute, but cannot contrive. By nature he is affectionate to his master, and if he has a good one, will separate from wife and children. He intuitively looks up to the superior race for control and protection. In slavery he yields hearty submission to authority, and is as proud of a rich master as if his master's wealth were all his own. He instinctively turns from the poor white man, unless he shows by his manners that he has been well raised. The slave looks with disgust upon the free negro, because of his poverty and rags, and because he lacks those qualities which entitle freedom to respect. As a general rule, he refuses marriage with a free negro, because of his merited degradation in society. The slaves have no aspirations for political freedom, or freedom of any kind, except freedom to do nothing.

A universal tendency is seen in those slaves who have been advanced in civilization, to retrograde under the influence of freedom when it is bestowed on them; and this tendency is seldom arrested until it reaches the lowest level. It would be difficult to find an exception to this general rule, and more so, to find an instance of progressive improvement after freedom is obtained. One trait in their character in the United States corresponds in a remarkable degree with their native character in Africa; that is, an affectionate loyalty to their master. They will stand by him here, and in Africa, to the death against foreign enemies. . . . The same fidelity was shown by them in the late attempt to alienate them at Harpers Ferry. They form an exception in this respect to all other races of men. Their intelligence has regularly progressed since they first landed on this continent. As their intelligence increases, so does their devotion to the white race, and to the relation they sustain to that race. Hence, at the present time, a large per cent. of African intelligence repudiates freedom, and for reasons so sensible, so unanswerable, as to make misguided philanthropy blush for its want of sound, practical commonsense. Their answer to the sophistry of this spurious benevolence is always at hand, and will continue to be so, as long as free negroes are to be found in their present condition everywhere on the globe. They have acquired a pretty correct knowledge of what they cannot see at a distance, and that confirms them in the opinion they have formed from what they do see around them—and that opinion is, that as a race, the protection, control, and social advantages of the white race are a positive necessity to them, and that they are worth more to them as a race, than their service or labor can be to the white race, after abstracting for themselves a full supply for every want during the vicissitudes of an entire life. And with the permission and encouragement of their masters, they would exterminate the agents who come among us to alienate them from their allegiance.

My purpose, thus far, has been to show that African slavery in the United States is a social and political necessity, and to show that it is just to the African, as it accords to him, in a form best adapted to his nature, more than an equivalent for his service, or labor; and that it is in accordance with the obligation to "do good to all men," and to "do to others as we would they should do unto us." . . .

Slavery, or control by the will of another, in some form, and to the extent which varying circumstances make proper, is now, and has been in all ages, an indispensable necessity. Too large a measure or too great an abridgement of liberty is equally fatal to the welfare of a people and to the happiness of individuals.

On this continent, at an early stage of our history, well meant efforts were permitted in the providence of God, the object of which was to bless Ham's race by releasing them from our control, and giving them freedom. These efforts have gone on among well-meaning men for more than two centuries. For the whole of this time, facts have been accumulating, which prove *their freedom to be a curse*, both to them and the white race. Still, additional aids, suggested by benevolence, have been resorted to by good men in the slave States, to make the experiment successful, until the demonstration seems complete, that freedom to them is a curse on this continent, and everywhere else on the globe. These untiring efforts on the part of benevolent individuals, have been in silent progress in the slave States, and are but little known by those at a distance.

Long and anxiously in our country had the highest order of minds, the purest philanthropy, the most disinterested patriotism, and the most self-sacrificing benevolence, sought to do good to this race of people, and to originate and put in operation a practical plan for elevating them to the blessings of a higher civilization, and a more enlarged freedom, self-control. For accomplishing their desires, these great men, so distinguished in the world's history for disinterested goodness, met in the city of Washington in 1816; and, after mature deliberation, adopted a plan for carrying out their wishes by the agency of an organization which they called "The American Colonization Society." Their purpose was, to aid free persons of color to settle a colony or colonies in Africa. In pursuance of this plan, they raised by voluntary contribution a sufficient fund, employed suitable agents to explore the coast, and finally purchased of the natives on the continent a territory large enough for the settlement of every negro, free and bond, in the United States.

So great was the desire of Southern philanthropists to succeed in this experiment, that through their influence indirect aid was obtained from the Federal Government, to sustain the infant colony against the hostile natives. Places of defenses were built by the aid of our sailors, and the presence of war ships afforded security against aggression.

I have said the evidence which proves the unfitness of the African for freedom, stares us in the face as the sun in the heavens—that it amounts to a demonstration. That evidence has been passed in review before my reader. It consists first, in the experiment at the South, of giving freedom to the most promising of the race. We of the South know that it has proved a curse to them. It has involved them in a little more than ten times the amount of crime, and a measure of poverty destructive of all comfort. An unwillingness to labor is almost universal among them.

The North emancipated that portion of the race they held in bondage. From the same unwillingness to labor they are too poor to raise families, are diminishing in numbers, and are degraded by the amount of crime which exceeds more than twelve times that of the white race.

It remains to be shown that domestic slavery for life is just and proper for the African race—because they are not qualified to use political freedom, and because they receive the full due for this service and labor, and that in a form accommodated to the service they pay for it. . . .

CHAPTER II. Having, in the preceding chapter, attempted to show that slavery is nothing more nor less than control by the will of another, and that this control is an indispensable necessity from our birth until our physical, moral, and intellectual faculties are sufficiently developed for the responsibilities of social and political life; and that this development is generally reached by the white race in about twenty-one years, and that it has never as yet been reached by the black race at any age, either on this continent or anywhere else, of which we have knowledge; and having assigned that as a true, proper, and sufficient reason for holding them under the control of the white race, both as a good to that race and themselves,—I will now proceed to examine slavery by the Bible, as a question of morals. It will be of service to those who reverence the Bible, but who do not know what it teaches, or where to look for its teachings on the subject of slavery, to sum up a portion of them on that subject, and refer to the books, chapters, and verses, where they may be found.

Abraham is the first domestic slaveholder mentioned in the Bible, and he is

constantly held up to view as the most distinguished man for piety in the patriarchal age. There is a mistake frequently made by readers of the Bible, in supposing the servants of the patriarchs, and those servants instructed by the Apostles, in the New Testament, to be hired servants, and not hereditary slaves. I ask
my reader to criticize the quotations as they are brought to view, by the references which follow, that he may see for himself that this mistake has no foundation to rest upon.

Abraham intrusted this mission of getting a wife for Isaac, to the most distinguished servant he had. At an earlier period of Abraham's life, and before he
had a child, he thought of making this servant, on account of his high qualities
and sterling integrity, the heir of his whole estate. He now sends him on this
delicate and important mission, under special instruction.

After this marriage of Isaac was consummated, Abraham married again, and
had six sons by Keturah, besides his first-born son Ishmael by Hagar. Before his
death, he sent these seven sons out of the country which God had given his
posterity through Isaac.

Question—Can holding men and women in bondage, giving them to our
children when we die, and sharing the honor they in part give us in the sight of
God and men while we live, be sinful? that is, if the word of God was written to
teach us what sin is.

The lawlessness and malignity of these people were enough to awaken the
fears of this princely slaveholder. We are living under analogous circumstances.
While we may not have for our comfort the direct assurance of this great slaveholder, that God will be with us, and bless us; yet, through patience and comfort of the Scriptures, we may have hope that he will.

For more than five hundred years Abraham's descendants had been domestic
slaveholders; but until this time the Almighty had never given them his sanction
to enslave their own brethren, and to make property of them. But He now
opens a new source of supply for slave labor in several classes of Abraham's
descendants. In the first, He authorized Abraham's poor female children to be
sold into hereditary bondage by their fathers. The proof of this is found in Exo.
Xxi. 7, and Deut. Xv. 17. "If a man sell his daughter to be a maidservant, she
shall not go out, as the men servants do." Again: He authorized the poor male
descendants of Abraham to sell themselves, and their wives, and their children,
into bondage for six years. If they had no wife when they were sold, then the
Almighty allowed their master to give them one of his slave women to be their
wife. If, at the end of six years, the man who came in with a wife and children
chose to re-assume freedom, then he with his wife and children were entitled to
it; and also to a provision made by the same law, for housekeeping again.

But in the case of him who had married his master's slave, she and her
children remained the property of the master. If either of those men, after an
experience of six years in slavery, preferred hereditary bondage to freedom, then
the Almighty allowed them to alienate their freedom, and become slaves forever. Exo. Xxi. 2 to 6. "If thou buy an Hebrew Servant, six years shall he serve,
and in the seventh, he shall go out free for nothing. If he came in by himself, he

shall go out by himself; if he were married, then his wife shall go out with him. If his master have given him a wife, and she have borne him sons or daughters, the wife and her children shall be her master's, and he shall go out by himself"; (and in Deut. Xv. 13, 14, 18, the master is bound to furnish him for housekeeping again). "But if the servant shall plainly say, I love my master, my wife, and my children; I will not go out free; then his master shall bring him into the judges; he shall also bring him to the door, or unto the doorpost; and his master shall bore his ears through with an awl; and he shall serve him forever."

These persons belong to classes, which will be found in all civilized society until time ends. The persons who make up these classes, embody moral purity in the onset of life; but are without the qualifications to contend successfully with the difficulties of securing a comfortable support—and hence they are exposed to the temptations which assail social virtue and moral purity with great severity. For the social comfort and moral security of these classes of his peculiar people, these laws were enacted by the Almighty. . . .

The oppression of the hireling, in not having his wages paid to him, is one of the great sins of the Old Testament. The abolitionists gather up all the passages in which this sin of oppression is spoken of, and apply the sin to Southern slaveholders. They profess to believe that the slave of the South is defrauded of wages for his labor; to which, according to the Bible, he is entitled as a hireling; overlooking, at the same time, the astonishing and remarkable fact, that, as a class, they receive wages in the shape of a comfortable home for life, and supply for their wants that is equaled by no such number of free laborers on the globe.

For the benefit of men who wish to know the truth of the Bible on this subject, I will add a little for their instruction. In the first place, the hireling of the Bible, who is not to be oppressed, and whose oppression is the great sin of the Bible, is the free man of the Bible, or the man whom the Bible declares to be free—and not the hereditary bondman of the Bible, the man who is declared by the Bible to be his master's money. All this will be seen in the legislative protection given by the law of Moses to three classes of laborers. These three different classes of laborers are plainly set forth in that law. Two of these classes were created by that law—the other class by their own free choice. The two classes created by the law were slaves—the other class consisted of free persons, who hired themselves to work for wages. One of these slave classes were Abraham's descendants, who were sold under the sanction of the law into slavery for six years. At the end of this time they were released by the law from this slavery, and restored to their freedom again. The other class of these slaves were heathens, who were bought for money according to the law in Xxv. Leviticus, and were made by that law to be their master's money, and to be hereditary bondmen and bondwomen to him and his children forever.

For the class of free laborers who hired themselves for wages, a law was enacted, (which has been quoted,) that requires their wages to be paid to them promptly. . . .

Nothing is more prominent in the Old Testament than the legal protection given to free labor. God threatened by judgments, that were awful, to avenge the oppressions of the free laborer. There is one law for their benefit, which embodies the divine benevolence in a very conspicuous manner. He gives the free laborer a right to borrow of his brother, (even victuals when hard pressed,) and makes it the duty of that rich brother, under a heavy penalty—that of having God's blessing withheld—to loan him a supply, and that without usury, and to release him from all that was unpaid at the Sabbatic year, or the year of release. Deut. Xv. 7 to 10. The Divine legislation for this class of free laborers suggests to the mind that there is a natural tendency with the rich to oppress free labor—because, in all God's legislation against oppression, there is not a law passed, or a judgement threatened to guard the hereditary slave against want, or oppression of any kind, save that of personal abuse in anger. To prevent this, he freed the slave so treated, as we have seen in Exod. Xx. 26, 27. This remarkable fact of legislative silence for the protection of slaves, can only be accounted for by supposing what we of the South know to be true, that the relation in the nature of things constituted the strongest guarantee that can bind the superior to take care of the inferior man. That it was more effectual than legal enactments enforced by the severest penalties—and therefore no laws were necessary to secure the hereditary slave from oppression and want, as the relation itself would make it the interest of the master to provide well for his slave, and not oppress him. This relation abates "the irrepressible conflict" between free labor and capital, and secures the affection and confidence of the slave to his master and family where he lacks nothing. And hence the remarkable fact, that in all the divine legislation for a slaveholding nation there is not a single law, express or implied, against servile insurrection. The wisdom of this omission is proved by the historical fact, that, in the fifteen hundred years of their national existence, they never had a single fear awakened on the subject.

The subordination of the inferior to the superior stands prominently to view in every thing that comes from the hand of infinite wisdom. Rebellion against this principle peopled the realms of darkness with those who were once the angels of light. The same thing brought upon us "all our woe." The Gospel of the Son of God was designed to re-establish the dominion of this principle. When this object is accomplished, the wilderness and the solitary place of the human heart are seen to bud and blossom as the rose. The rebellion of abolitionism against this principle, as an element in the social structure, is active, and dangerous in the highest degree to regulated liberty and Christian civilization. If the Bible was duly reverenced, and but slightly examined, the evil could be corrected. But when we see men who are eminently intellectual, professing allegiance to Christ, and claiming, at the same time, his authority for doing and teaching what he has in his word denominated blasphemy, it awakens unavoidably the painful foreboding which the inspiring Spirit authorizes in this declaration: "Because they receive not the love of the truth, that they might be saved," "God, for this cause, shall send them strong delusion, that they should believe a lie, that they all might be damned who believe not the truth, but have pleasure in unrighteousness," (2 Thess. 2:9–11) and has given the highest pleasure to abolitionists. They are seeking to overthrow governments whose models have

John Brown (1800–59), opposed to slavery since his youth, is shown here in an artist's version of how he organized African-Americans in a secret league of Gileadites at Springfield in the early 1850s. By 1855 he had moved to Kansas, where he led the Potawatomie Massacre. He would return to Massachusetts to gather money and support before Harpers Ferry, for which raid he was hanged. From: Mason A. Green, *Springfield, 1636–1886, History of Town and City*, 1888. By permission of Ruth Owen Jones and Paul Jones of Amherst, Mass.

the express sanction of the Almighty. The Scriptures I have quoted from the Old Testament, prove that God ordained at Mount Sinai a slave government for his own people; and those quoted from the New Testament prove that Christ, by the Apostles, sanctioned slave governments organized by men, as ordinances of God. . . . One of the ordinances of God is that man shall eat bread in the sweat of his face; that is, that he shall by labor contribute his share to the common stock of human wants. Christ has ordained that, in his kingdom, no man shall eat unless he work. We have sent Ham's descendants to Africa to raise and govern families, and to assume the higher responsibilities of organizing and governing states. From the best authenticated facts we can gain, we are obliged to believe that they are not qualified to do either, because they will not perform voluntary labor. No people can multiply and raise families, unless they have homes and are well fed. In the Northern States, in Jamaica, and in Liberia, the deaths among the free blacks steadily exceed the births. The slaves at the South multiply faster than the white race at the North. . . .

There remains another letter to be noticed, which was written by the Apostle Paul. It is the letter to Philemon. I am often reminded by the existence and contents of this letter, of the character given by the apostle to the word of God. There is a fullness, suitableness, and perfection ascribed to the Scriptures, which, it is said, leave us in ignorance on no subject of which, as Christians, it is essential for us to have knowledge. By the Scriptures the man of God is said to be thoroughly furnished with all the knowledge necessary for guiding him in every good word and work. Little, perhaps, did the apostle think, that in writing this short letter, he was erecting a standard by which not only *men* were to measure and be measured, but a standard by which *States* were to measure and be measured, not only in *moral* and social, but also in *personal* and *national righteousness*. This letter is so full of Divine magic, that more putridity in individuals and States can be unmasked by it, as readily as by the Savior when he exposed the rottenness to view, which lay concealed beneath beautifully whited sepulchres.

Before the writing of this letter, no Scripture furnished the information which is now needed—that is, in a form that cannot be misunderstood. In the progress of human events, this information was not needed until the nineteenth century. But the precise information which this letter furnishes is now wanting. It is wanted to show the sin which men are now committing against God and men—not only in opposing slavery, but in refusing to deliver up fugitive slaves.

Among all the covenants made by nations involving the obligations of morality and good neighborship up to the eighteenth century, there was none to deliver up fugitive slaves to their owners. During Solomon's reign Shimei pursued and recovered two of his slaves who had taken refuge with Achish, son of the king in a neighboring State. There were delivered upon application of the owner—and national comity, as in that case, has frequently been practised in regard to fugitives from labor and fugitives from justice. But no solemn covenant has ever been entered into by nations to deliver them upon application of their owners, until the original sovereign States which formed this Union covenanted to do so. When this compact was entered into, the obligation of an oath was relied on; and by the solemnities of an oath, the parties to this compact, in the person of their agents, bound themselves before heaven and earth to deliver up fugitive slaves.

Paul little thought, when writing this letter by a fugitive slave, and returning him to his Christian master, (who was also a minister of the Gospel,) and most affectionately entreating that Christian master to receive this fugitive again and to forgive him, and binding himself in writing to pay that master for all which this slave had stolen or wrongfully taken from him—that it would prove as leaven hid in three measures of meal, until it produced such a sense of what was just, and proper, and right, and Christian-like, as to induce thirteen sovereign States, seventeen hundred and twenty-nine years after that letter was written, to copy his example, and bind themselves in a solemn covenant to imitate him in their future course of national conduct. How painful it is to see the moral power of this inspired example dying away under the sway of infidelity, which repudiates the Bible, and proclaims "freedom and equality," where God in his word teaches there is none.

Here is an incident in the providence of God, so remarkably surrounded with peculiarities, as to make it on this subject a complete compendium of all that is written in the Bible on the subject of slavery.

If all other institutions given to the Church and the world were blotted out from the Bible, there would still remain in what this little letter contains, all the doctrine, and all the duty, which belong to the whole subject. And a complete and perfect answer would be furnished by it, to all the questions which can suggest themselves to an honest and candid mind, as to the will of God, and the duty of men on the subject of slavery.

The letter presents us with a runaway slave. It informs us that that slave in a distant country from his master, is converted to Christianity through the agency of the Apostle Paul. That the apostle was a prisoner at that time in the city of Rome. This convert lets the apostle know that he is a slave, and that he had fled from his master. There was no law in the Roman empire by which it was made the Apostle's duty to have this slave returned to his master. There was no specific law from Christ or the Holy Spirit through the Apostles, requiring the *Church*—or enjoining any of her members—to do this. This letter informs us that the master of this slave was a Christian; that he was known to the apostle to be not only a Christian, but a preacher of the Gospel; and not only a preacher standing high in the Apostle's esteem for those qualities which adorn the private and official character of a Christian minister. The Apostle, after this slave's conversion, was so delighted with his Christian deportment that he felt a deep interest in him, and cherished a most intense affection to him.

The letter informs us that the apostle was advanced in years, had long been bound with a prisoner's chain, and was daily looking for the sentence of a prejudiced tribunal that would end his life. He was poor, and occupied a position which made his friends quail under the expression of sympathy for him. In this trying condition he found his fugitive convert pre-eminently fitted to minister to him, and that he took great pleasure in doing so. Upon the master of this slave the apostle had the strongest claims for any favor he might ask of him. Any man under like circumstances, who was not the immediate representative of God, in word and deed, would have first written to the master, and begged as a favor that the slave might remain and minister to him. Any man without intense feelings of responsibility to God and men for every word he spoke, and every act he performed, would have allowed his *condition*, under such circumstances, to furnish a sanction for retaining this servant until the master could be heard from. How completely this case is invested with all the circumstances which can give weight and character to the lesson God designed to teach by it! The running away of this slave, his conversion to Christ by the Apostle of the Gentiles, in a distant country, its connection with the apostle's condition at the time, and with his personal acquaintance and high estimate of this slave's master, his high claims upon that master, his assigning the injustice of appropriating to his comfort what belonged to another man as the reason of sending the slave home: putting these things together, can any man on earth read this letter, and allow it to expand in his thoughts to the circumference of its plain import, and then look his fellow-man in the face and say, that slavery is a sin; that to return a fugitive slave to his master is sinful! In the light of this case no man on earth can believe it.

Source Note: Rev. Thornton Stringfellow, D.D. *Slavery, Its Origin, Nature, and History Considered in the Light of Bible Teachings, Moral Justice, and Political Wisdom* (New York, 1861).

Alexander McCaine (1768–1856)

Alexander McCaine was a prominent contributor to the proslavery debate. He was born in Ireland in 1768. Little is known about his youth, but at twenty, he emigrated to the United States, settling at first in Charleston, South Carolina. He became a Methodist clergyman and began to write profusely first on theological matters and then on the contemporary social issue of slavery in the United States. He published *The History and Mystery of Methodist Episcopacy* (1827) and *Letters on the Organization and Early History of the Methodist Episcopal Church* (1850), and with other religious reformers, he organized a treatise called *Mutual Rights* (1824).

McCaine's significance in the slavery movement derives from a single publication but an important and very influential one, *Slavery Defended from the Scripture against the Attacks of the Abolitionists* (1842). As the title suggests, the text specifically addresses problems raised by the abolitionist and antislavery opposition with Scripture references, so that McCaine's position has the authority of a clergyman's interpretation of the Bible to reinforce it. Like Thornton Stringfellow, he layers his argument with contemporary references as well as scriptural ones, so that he provides the reader with a seemingly authoritative, airtight argument in favor of slavery.

McCaine was an eloquent and powerful speaker, which made him an effective clergyman. According to the *Dictionary of American Biography*, "he was a striking figure, with a majestic head and clearly cut features. As a preacher, he was endowed with great native eloquence. He despised shams, was impetuous in his defense of what he thought was the truth, and was bold to bluntness in dealing with personalities, a characteristic which often left him open to criticism" (p. 560). McCaine died just before the Civil War, on June 1, 1856, firmly believing in the Divine Right of slavery as sanctioned by Scripture.

SUGGESTIONS FOR FURTHER READING

Further information about McCaine may be found in the *Dictionary of American Biography* and in numerous histories of the Methodist Church in the United States. He is cited in a book (difficult to find) by William Sumner Jenkins, *Proslavery Thought in the Old South* (Chapel Hill: University of North Carolina Press, 1935).

Slavery Defended from Scripture against the Attacks of the Abolitionists by Alexander McCaine

"Your committee [Methodist Protestant Church Conference, 1842], after prayerful and patient deliberation, have come to the conclusion that the time has arrived when some action should be had by this General Conference, whereby the Northern Conferences should be exonerated from all participation in this great moral evil, as your committee *conceive* it to be, and we can discover no way in which this can be done, short of some rule being laid down by this body, whereby the 9th item of the elementary principles of our Church shall be more.

"1. Resolved, That slavery as it exists in the Methodist Protestant Church in these United States is opposed to the morality of these holy Scriptures, and consequently a great moral evil."

Nor, if we consider the character of those who were possessed of slaves, can we pronounce slavery a "*great moral evil.*" Abraham is the first, of whom we read, who held slaves, and he had 318 who were born in his house. Gen. xiv. 14. With these he pursued the confederate kings, who had captured his nephew Lot; and with them, rescued Lot, "his goods, the women and the people." He had slaves given him by Pharaoh, when he dwelt in Egypt. Compare Gen. xii. 16, with xvi. 1. By Abimeleck, king of Gerar. Gen. xx. 14. And he had slaves "bought with his money." See Gen. xvii. 13 and 27.

Next to Abraham stands Sarah his wife. "Now Sarai, Abram's wife, bare him no children: and she had a handmaid, an Egyptian, whose name was Hagar. Gen. xvi. 1. Dr. Clarke remarks on this passage,—"As Hagar was an Egyptian, St. Chrysostom's conjecture is very probable, that she was one of those female slaves which Pharaoh gave to Abram when he sojourned in Egypt. Gen. xii. 16." . . . "The slave being the absolute property of the mistress, not only her person, but the fruits of her labour, with all her children, were her owner's *property* also. The children, therefore, which were born of the slave, were considered as the children of the mistress. It was on this ground that Sarai gave her slave to Abram."

Now, these few instances may suffice to show, that some of the most eminent of the Old Testament saints were slaveholders; nor is there the least hint by any of the New Testament writers, that they were guilty of *a great moral evil* in holding their fellow beings in bondage. Where do the abolitionists, then, get their authority for anathematising slaveholders, and fixing on them such opprobrious and unchristian epithets as "thieves," "robbers," "pirates," &c? For this they have no authority, neither from the Old Testament nor the New.

"Slavery," says Professor Dew, "was established and sanctioned by Divine Authority, among even the elect of Heaven—the favored children of Israel. Abraham, the founder of this interesting nation, and the chosen servant of the Lord, was the owner of *hundreds* of slaves. That magnificent shrine, the Temple of Solomon, was reared by the hands of slaves. Egypt's venerable and enduring piles were reared by similar hands. Slavery existed in Assyria and Babylon. The ten tribes of Israel were carried off in bondage to the former by Shalmanezar, and the two tribes of Judah were subsequently carried in triumph by Nebuchadnezzar, to beautify and adorn the latter.

"The Hebrews had two sorts of servants or slaves. Lev. Xxv. 44, 45, &c. Some were strangers, bought, or taken in war; and their masters kept them, exchanged them, or sold them as their goods. The others were Hebrew slaves, who being poor, sold themselves, or were sold to pay their debts; or were delivered for slaves by their parents, in cases of necessity. This sort of Hebrew slave continued in slavery, only to the year of Jubilee: when they might return to their liberty, and their masters could not detain them against their wills. If they desired to continue with their masters, they were brought before the judges; here they made a declaration, that for this time they disclaimed the privilege of the law, and had their ears bored with an awl against the door-posts of their master's house, after which they had no longer any power of recovering their liberty." Calmet's Dictionary.—Article, Servant.

Now, from the above accounts, the condition of the slave among the Jews, as well as among the Romans, was far worse than the condition of the slave in these United States. In the former, the life of the slave was in certain cases, at the disposal of the master: not so in these United States. Here the master has no power to put his slave to death, for any offence whatever. And even if the master considers him deserving correction, the law prescribes the instrument and extent of the correction. "The slave is here carefully protected in life, limb, and even in a moderate share of liberty, by the policy of the laws; and his nourishment and subsistence are positively enjoined." (Dew on Slavery.)

But, what is that thing called slavery, which it is said, "exists in the Methodists Protestant Church in these United States," which has been pronounced by the majority of the committee . . . as opposed to the morality of the Holy Scriptures, and consequently a great moral evil? Before it was thus denounced, it ought to have been done: and it is worthy of special notice, that neither the memorials which have been presented—the friends who have brought them up—nor their supporters on the floor of this Conference, have attempted a definition. Nor, in the discussion, has even one argument been offered, nor one single text of Scripture quoted, to prove that slavery is wrong. All is rant. All is declamation. This omission I shall now proceed to supply, but shall first consider the *law* and the *action* itself, which is either right or wrong, as it conforms with, or is contrary to the precept of the law.

And what is *moral law*? Moral law is a rule of moral conduct prescribed by the Supreme Being, commanding what is right, and prohibiting what is wrong. And, "an action is rendered *moral* by two circumstances—that it is *voluntary*—and that it has respect to some *rule* which determines it to be good or evil. Moral good and evil" says Locke, "is the conformity or disagreements of our voluntary actions to some law, whereby good or evil is drawn upon us, from the will or power of the law maker." (Watson Institute, page 9.)

And what is slavery? My brother from Virginia has defined it as being "the condition of an individual, whose will is in complete subjection to the will of another." (Thornton Stringfellow, *A Brief Examination of Slavery*, 1841.) To this definition I will subscribe, as far as it goes: but it does not go far enough for me. I would say—slavery is that condition of a human being, in which neither his time, nor his labor are things of value. I would define slavery, in one word, as that state where the individual is the *property* of another. This, sir, is slavery, whether it exists in the Patriarchal Church, the Jewish Church, or the Christian Church. Yes, I repeat it, the slave is the *property* of his master, whoever that master may be; and to contemplate him in any other point of light, will make all those parts of the Holy Scriptures which treat of slavery, as a jumble of unmeaning and inapplicable directions utterly unworthy of a wise and holy God.

I shall now consider the principal causes or sources of slavery, which I shall class under three heads—conquest, cupidity, and crime; and under each head shall offer an instance or two illustrative of my positions. Conquest, or the laws of war. Although God had promised Canaan to the descendants of Abraham, Gen. xvii. 8, yet, when the children of Israel entered it, under their leader Joshua, they had to war with the several nations which inhabited it. This they did, and were victorious.

The Israelites reduced to a state of slavery in Egypt, may properly be cited also, as falling under the head of cupidity. Their bondage may have had its origin in jealousy and the love of gain. The king of Egypt was jealous of the increasing numbers and growing power of the Israelites; and wished to turn their labor to his own advantage.

I am now come, Mr. President, to the part of my argument which, I am sure, will secure me the attention of this Conference, because, sir, I have laid down a position which contradicts, point blank, the assertion of the majority of the committee in their report on memorials. For me to have denied that "slavery, as it exists in these United States, is opposed to the morality of the gospel," &c., was, in the opinion of the abolitionists, going too far. But to intimate, as I did, a few days ago, that slavery has always had the sanction of Almighty God, was more than they were able to bear. I saw how they were affected by the declaration. It shocked them to a man. And this blasphemous doctrine, as I believe they considered it, affected their delicate sensibilities, as much as a shock of electricity would have affected their nerves.

The numerous cases which I have already brought forward from the Old Testament, will serve as so many irrefragable proofs of the truth of this position.—But as I have much more to offer than what I have already advanced, I shall, for the sake of perspicuity, throw my arguments into the form of a series of propositions. . . .

PROPOSITION II. Slavery has been sanctioned by Almighty God.

In the third month after Moses had safely conducted the children of Israel through the Red Sea, they were encamped before Mount Sinai. From the top of this Mount, God delivered the Ten Commandments first orally, Exod. xx. 1, next in writing, Exod. xxxi. 9, and thirdly on two tables of stone, to replace those which had been broken by Moses, Exod, xxxiv. 1. The last of these commandments reads thus:—"Thou shalt not covet thy neighbour's house, thou shalt not covet thy neighbor's wife, nor his man servant, nor his maid servant, nor his ox, nor his ass, nor any thing that is thy neighbour's." Although this commandment is so perspicuous and plain, yet I shall make a few remarks on it. 1. Slavery is recognised by God: for *manservant and maidservant are slaves*. 2. The slave is *property*, as much so as the house, the ox, or the ass. 3. The right of the master to hold such property is allowed and defended. 4. Coveting this species of property is forbidden. 5. There can be nothing *immoral* in holding slaves, since God has sanctioned and defended slavery.

But say the abolitionists, we do not want your slaves—we would not have them if you were to give them to us. Well, then, according to their own declaration, it is not to enrich themselves, or promote their own interest by slave labour, that they have undertaken this crusade against institutions of the South. This being so, I ask, what then is their object? Is it the freedom of the slave? I think not, for they are decidedly hostile to colonization—they are not for sending one negro out of the country, even if by so doing, he could obtain his liberty. What then can they want? To turn three millions of slaves, with all their ignorance and habits of idleness and vice, loose upon the community? Surely this plan evinces neither *wisdom* nor *goodness*. But if it does will these same tender-hearted and loving souls take these liberated negroes into their fellowship? Will they receive them into their houses and place them at their tables, or take them, in the holy ordinance of matrimony, as partners, to their beds? This, I think, they will not do. This leveling system, then, is intended exclusively for Southern men. But Southern men have as great a right, on gospel principles, to exact the performance of these things from abolitionists, as abolitionists have from them. . . .

PROPOSITION V. The sanction given to slavery, in the Old Testament is renewed and confirmed by the Saviour in the New.

Christ, in his sermon on the Mount, rescued the moral law from those false glosses and interpretations, that were given it by Judaising teachers and in doing this, he uttered this most important declaration, "Think not that I am come to destroy the Law or the Prophets: I am not come to destroy the law or the Prophets: I am not come to destroy, but to fulfil." Mat. V. 17, 18. To show that the Savior meant the moral law, or the ten commandments, I shall quote the language of a few eminent commentators.

'Do not' imagine that I am come to violate the Law—kaialusai, from kai and luo, I loose, violate or dissolve. I am not come to make the Law of no effect—to *dissolve* the connection which subsists between its several parts, or the obligation men are under to have their lives regulated by its *moral precepts.*

PROPOSITION VII. There is but one standard of morals—and that standard is one and indivisible—it is uniform and perpetual.

It is not popular opinion—it is not the law of the land—but it is the word of God that I receive as the standard of morals. It is this, and this alone, which determines what is *great moral evil* and what is not.

PROPOSITION IX. If God communicates his grace and spirit to the slaveholder, he holds communion and fellowship with the *sinner.*—If he does not, the slaveholder is a false witness before God.

Here, again, the doctrine of the abolitionists is at war with the doctrine of the Bible. The abolitionists say, slavery is a "great moral evil," and, of consequence, that the slaveholder is *a great sinner.* If this be true, Abraham was a great sinner, and so were all the slaveholders in the Patriarchal and Jewish Churches.

Again: Thousands and tens of thousands of slaveholders, have made a profession of the religion of Jesus Christ, at the very time they owned slaves. Now, is their testimony to pass for nothing? It must, or the doctrine that I am combating, must be found in error. The slaveholder tells us that God has pardoned his sins—converted his soul—and given him his holy spirit to witness, with his spirit, that he is a child of God. Now, this testimony is true, or it is false.

A very large portion of all the property, in several of the New England States, was earned in the slave trade. It has been estimated, for example, that if every acre of land in Rhode Island were worth a hundred dollars, the aggregate has been twice over earned by the extensive and long continued operations of her citizens in the slave trade. The towns of New Port, Bristol, and Providence, in Rhode Island—Stonington, and Salem, in Massachusetts, were engaged, to a greater or less extent, for a number of years, in the slave trade.

But there is one point of light in which this subject has not been considered—it is this. The Constitution of the Church, like the Constitution of the United States, was framed and adopted in the spirit of compromise. There were, in the Convention, slaveholders, and there were men who were opposed to slavery. These all agreed to offer up their respective peculiarities on one common altar, for the glory of God and for the good of his Church. In this spirit of peace, the constitution was adopted, and the church organized. Now, who are they that would disturb this order? Who are they who are so clamorous for change? Who are they, that wish us to violate our conventional faith, and falsify our vows unto each other, and to the Lord? Men, who had no church existence when the church was organized! Men, who, when they were about to join the Church, knew the regulations on the subject of slavery, as well as they do now. If they did not like the regulations, why did they join? If they were so violently opposed to slavery, they might have staid without, or gone elsewhere.

Source Note: Alexander McCaine. *Slavery Defended from Scripture against the Attacks of the Abolitionists, in a Speech Delivered before the General Conference of the Methodist Protestant Church in Baltimore* (1842).

Biblical Antislavery Arguments

There are four documents in this section, and they share several characteristics in common. First, all four use the Bible as a source for the development of antislavery arguments, often critiquing the same texts used by proslavery advocates to advance the opposite cause. Second, all these documents are relatively free from the exacting scriptural exegetical habits of mind that are found in proslavery sermons on the Bible. While abolitionists and antislavery advocates both used the Bible as an antislavery resource, they were less able to turn to Scripture for precedent and example than the proslavery writers because the Old Testament, and some parts of the New Testament, offer historical precedents for the divine sanction of slavery. Proslavery ministers used the traditional protestant sermon form, very popular among the New England Puritans and the fundamentalists of the antebellum South, whereby the minister would commence his sermon with a text, out of which he would derive a doctrine, and following a lengthy exegesis of this text and doctrine, he would apply the lessons of the doctrine and exegesis to his congregation in a well-delineated third section called the "application." Proslavery sermons tended to follow this format rather exactly because the "doctrine" often derived from the Old Testament text was that God approved of the practice of slavery. The "application" section of the traditional sermon format gave antislavery preachers an opportunity to lead their congregations through moral arguments derived from the New Testament, especially the teachings of Jesus.

Just as the New England Puritans had sought to demonstrate that their "errand into the wilderness" was a recapitulation of the excursion from Egypt to the Promised Land by the Israelites of Old, proslavery advocates, especially in the South, attempted to use the Old Testament as a precedent-setting text for the sanctioned practice of chattel slavery.

Antislavery advocates likewise followed the sermon format of text, doctrine, and application. However, their emphasis was less on the exegesis of text and more on the moral application of the spiritual principles inherent in the text to the social and political issue of slavery in America. For example, in James Freeman Clarke's "Thanksgiving Day Sermon of 1842," a special-occasion sermon that would have been attended by many more listeners than the usual Sunday sermon, one finds very little exegesis but long passages emphasizing the moral wrong of slavery.

> First, the evils to the slave are very great. He is not always treated badly, but he is always *liable* to be so treated. He is entirely at the mercy of his master. If he is liable to be beaten, starved, over-worked, and separated from his family; whoever knows human nature, knows that such cases will not be rare. . . . I could tell you stories of

barbarities which I knew of, which it would sicken you to hear, as it does me to think of them. . . . A worse evil to the slave than the cruelties he sometimes endures, is the moral degradation which results from his condition. Falsehood, theft, licentiousness, are natural consequences of his situation. He steals,—why should he not?—he cannot, except occasionally, earn money; why should not he steal it?

Similarly, Joshua Burt, who also preached in 1843, used anecdotal moral examples rather than Scripture precedents to develop his antislavery argument: "Go to South Carolina and give a single child of oppression a single tract, on which is impressed God's First Commandment, 'Thou shalt have no other Gods before me,' and you are liable to arrest and imprisonment for the deed!!—but I cannot dwell on the detail of slavery's doings. It is a crushing system from beginning to end. Mental, moral and religious light, to a most fearful extent, it puts out. It is claimed, that all this severity, and all this cruelty, are necessarily incident to the system? Be it so. That fact shows what the system is; and is itself one of the most powerful arguments against it."

Of the texts that follow, the most conventional sermon is preached by Alexander McLeod, "Negro Slavery Unjustifiable" (1802 and 1846), in which the minister commences with a text taken from Exodus 21.16, "He that stealeth a man, and selleth him, or if he be found in his hand, he shall surely be put to death." "Manstealing" was indeed a capital crime in ancient Israel, but slaves were often not "stolen" but taken in battle. Nevertheless, McLeod immediately concludes, on the strength of his exegesis, that "the practice of buying, holding, or selling our unoffending fellow-creatures as slaves is immoral." Even here, where the minister has commenced with a textual allusion to the Old Testament, and has followed the conventional format of the exegetical sermon, McLeod almost immediately turns to Enlightenment doctrine to prove his case rather than use the precedents of the Old Testament. "It is intended in this discourse, to confirm the doctrine of the proposition, to answer objections to it, and to make some improvement of it . . . [that] to hold any of our fellow-men in perpetual slavery is sinful. This appears from the inconsistency of the practice of holding slaves with the *natural rights of man*." For scriptural evidence, McLeod turns to the Enlightenment "family of man" argument that he finds supported by New Testament texts. "The Bible is the criterion of doctrine and conduct. It represents the European and the Asiatic, the African and American, as different members of the same great family—the different children of the same benign and universal parent. *God has made one blood of all nations of men for to dwell on all the face of the earth, and hath determined the bounds of their habitation*, Acts xvii. 26." Theodore Dwight Weld also turns to the "manstealing" argument, showing the immorality of the law codes of Southern states, such as Louisiana, in the context of this scriptural prohibition against human bondage. "From the giving of the law at Sinai, immediately proceed the promulgation of that body of laws and institutions called the Mosaic System. Over the gateway of that system, fearful words were written by the finger of God, 'He that stealeth a man and selleth him, or if he be found in his hand, he shall surely be put to death.' Exodus xxi. 16." Robert Dale Owen's *The Wrong of*

Slavery (1864) is a relatively late example of this reasoning process by which the antislavery advocate would commence with a biblical text but depart from it quickly and advance instead a moral or philosophical argument based on the Enlightenment doctrine of universal human value.

These divergent approaches to Scripture were an inevitable result of the prominence of the Bible in the culture of antebellum America. The literacy rate was relatively high, particularly in the North, and among the slaves themselves, the Bible became a text that was heard orally if not always understood through reading, as the training of slaves to read and write was prohibited by law in most of the slaveholding Southern states. In Harriet Beecher Stowe's *Uncle Tom's Cabin*, the Bible is the staple of Tom's literary diet, and he regularly annotates his copy, which he reads to Eva as they share scriptural and moral lessons. Thus the Bible became a pawn, routinely brokered by pro- and antislavery advocates to advance their own sides of the argument, and to defeat the opposition. As it has served throughout its history, the Bible was a resource document for a wide variety of divergent arguments concerning slavery and contemporary human behavior.

It is important to distinguish the various strains of antislavery sentiment in the United States during the first half of the nineteenth century. Most historians acknowledge a religious undercurrent in the antislavery arguments of the seventeenth and eighteenth centuries, especially in those documents authored by Quakers, such as John Woolman's *Some Considerations on the Keeping of Negroes*, excerpted in this volume. The first two decades of the nineteenth century saw important political and social changes concerning slavery, such as the abolition of the slave trade by Parliament in 1807, soon followed by congressional legislation prohibiting the slave trade effective January 1, 1808.

It is coincidental that Johann Friedrich Blumenbach's treatise on race theory, which influenced contemporary racial thinking in Great Britain and in the United States, was published in 1808 (see introduction to chapter 7, "Science in Antebellum America"). Its appearance turned abolitionist thinking away from the moral evils of the slave trade, which had been abruptly halted, at least legally, to a defense of the African's status as a human being. Proslavery advocates justified slavery by insisting on the natural inferiority of the African; abolitionists focused on the natural rights theories developed during the Enlightenment. The followers of Garrison, Wendell Phillips, and Lydia Maria Child argued for a militant form of abolitionist behavior, for immediate and unconditional emancipation of the slaves with no compensation for slaveholders, and for full racial equality. The latter argument caused dissension among the abolitionists, even within the ranks of the Garrisonians, so that after the publication of David Walker's *Appeal* and William Lloyd Garrison's first issue of the *Liberator*, on January 1, 1831, the whole framing of the debate was changed. "Moral suasion" dominated the early arguments against slavery, and even the biblical antislavery rhetoric digressed into moral reasoning rather than biblical exegesis. But after 1831, the terms of the argument of both sides changed dramatically, and the country was engaged continuously in an ideological conflict that eventually erupted on the battlefields of Gettysburg and Atlanta.

THEODORE DWIGHT WELD (1803–1895)

Theodore Dwight Weld was born November 23, 1803, in Connecticut. His youth was spent in revival meetings and reform gatherings, including the Oneida Institute in New York. He was deeply influenced by Lewis and Arthur Tappan and by 1830, while still in his twenties, had become active in the abolitionist movement to which the Tappans also belonged. (See "The New York Abolitionists" in chapter 8.) There were two vigorous antislavery institutions in Ohio in the 1830s: Lane Seminary in Cincinnati and Oberlin College. Both were centers of controversy and debate, and Oberlin College continued to carry the torch of African-American rights long after the passage of the Thirteenth (1865) and Fifteenth (1870) Amendments to the Constitution, one abolishing chattel slavery and the other giving the franchise to emancipated male slaves. Theodore Weld was active in both of them. Lane Seminary became the pulpit for President Lyman Beecher, father of Harriet Beecher Stowe, and it was there that Weld organized a series of antislavery debates between leading ministers and intellectuals. As Robert Abzug has noted, Theodore Weld "masterminded" the Lane Seminary debates and essentially created a platform for voicing his own abolitionist sentiment, which led to a confrontation with the Board of Trustees. "In 1834, the Board curtailed the right of students to engage in such controversial projects. Weld retaliated by leading a walkout of the majority of Lane's students, which crippled the seminary's reputation and infuriated its president, the Reverend Lyman Beecher. . . . Some became the nucleus for the student body of Oberlin College, a new revival-based institution led by Charles Grandison Finney and committed to reform activity" (Abzug, *American National Biography*, p. 928). In 1837, Weld met Angelina Grimké, one of two sisters from a South Carolina slaveholding family who had left the South and slaveholding to join the abolitionist movement. As their contributions to this volume attest, they were reformers for women's rights as well as antislavery advocates, and their temperaments ideally suited Weld's "calling" to the antislavery cause. Angelina Grimké and Theodore Dwight Weld were married in 1838, and the two sisters and Weld continued an antebellum partnership committed to women's rights and the abolition of slavery.

Weld authored two important antislavery works, *The Bible against Slavery* (1838) and *Slavery as It Is: The Testimony of a Thousand Witnesses* (1839). Stowe credited the latter volume in her *Key to Uncle Tom's Cabin* (1853) as having inspired her to write the book, and she borrowed heavily from its "testimonies," or authentic examples clipped from newspapers and other first-hand sources, to create episodes in her novel. Weld became a vocal supporter of the Union cause during the Civil War, and he lived long enough to eulogize Wendell Phillips,

William Lloyd Garrison, and the Grimké sisters. His wife, Angelina Grimké, is represented in this volume in chapter 8, "The Abolitionist Crusade," with her "Letters to Catharine E. Beecher, in reply to an Essay on Slavery and Abolitionism" (1838).

SUGGESTIONS FOR FURTHER READING

Abzug, Robert. *Cosmos Crumbling: American Reform and the Religious Imagination*. New York: Oxford University Press, 1994.

———. *Passionate Liberator: Theodore Dwight Weld and the Dilemma of Reform*. New York: Oxford University Press, 1980.

———, ed. *New Perspectives on Race and Slavery in America: Essays in Honor of Kenneth Stampp*. Lexington: University of Kentucky Press, 1986.

Dumond, Dwight L. *Antislavery Origins of the Civil War in the United States*. Ann Arbor: University of Michigan Press, 1961.

Lowance, Mason, Jr., ed. *Against Slavery: an Abolitionist Reader*. New York: Penguin-Putnam, 2000.

Perry, Lewis Curtis, and Michael Fellman, eds. *Antislavery Reconsidered: New Perspectives on the Abolitionists*. Baton Rouge: Louisiana State University Press, 1979.

Stewart, James B. *Holy Warriors and the Abolitionists and American Slavery*. New York: Hill and Wang, 1976.

"Theodore Weld." In *American National Biography*, ed. John Garraty and Mark Cames (New York, 1999).

Weld, Theodore D. *The Bible against Slavery*. New York, 1838.

———. Manuscripts and Correspondence, William Clements Library of the University of Michigan.

———. *Slavery As It Is: The Testimony of a Thousand Witnesses*. New York, 1839.

The Bible against Slavery
by Theodore Dwight Weld

If we would know whether the Bible is the charter of slavery, we must first determine *just what slavery is*. . . .

That this is American slavery, is shown by the laws of slave states. Judge Stroud, in his *Sketch of the Laws relating to Slavery*, says, The cardinal principles of slavery, that the slave is not to be ranked among sentient beings, but among *things*—as an article of property, a chattel personal, obtains as undoubted law in all of these states, (the slave states.) The law of South Carolina thus lays down the principle, Slaves shall be deemed, held, taken, reputed, and adjudged in law to be chattels *personal* in the hands of their owners and possessors, and their executors, administrators, and assigns, to ALL INTENTS, CONSTRUCTIONS, AND PURPOSES WHATSOEVER (*Brevard's Digest*, 229). In Louisiana, a slave is one who is in the power of a master to whom he *belongs*; the master may sell him, dispose of his *person, his industry, and his labor*; he can do nothing, possess nothing, nor acquire any thing, but what must belong to his master. *Civil Code of Louisiana*, Art. 35. . . .

This is American slavery. The eternal distinction between a person and a thing, trampled under foot—the crowning distinction of all others—their centre and circumference—the source, the test, and the measure of their value—the rational, immortal principle, embalmed by God in everlasting remembrance, consecrated to universal homage in a baptism of glory and honor, by the gift of His Son, His Spirit, His Word, His presence, providence, and power; His protecting shield, upholding staff, and sheltering wing; His opening heavens, and angels ministering, chariots of fire, and songs of morning stars, and a great voice in heaven, proclaiming eternal sanctions, and confirming the word with the signs following. . . .

Having stated the *principle* of American slavery, we ask, DOES THE BIBLE SANCTION SUCH A PRINCIPLE? To the *law* and the *testimony*. First, the moral law, or the ten commandments. Just after the Israelites were emancipated from their bondage in Egypt, while they stood before Sinai to receive the law, as the trumpet waxed louder, and the mount quaked and blazed, God spoke the ten commandments from the midst of clouds and thunderings. *Two* of those shalt not take from another what belongs to him. All man's powers of body and mind are God's gift to *him*. . . .

The eighth commandment *presupposes and assumes the right of every man to his powers, and their product*. Slavery robs him of both. . . .

From the giving of the law at Sinai, immediately proceed the promulgation of that body of laws and institutions, called the Mosaic system. Over the gateway of that system, fearful words were written by the finger of God—HE THAT STEALETH A MAN AND SELLETH HIM, OR IF HE BE FOUND IN HIS HAND, HE SHALL SURELY BE PUT TO DEATH. See Exodus, xxi. 16. . . .

No wonder that God, in a code of laws prepared for such a people at such a time, should light up on its threshold a blazing beacon to flash terror to slaveholders. *He that stealeth a man and selleth him, or if he be found in his hand, he shall surely be put to death.* Ex. xxi. 16. God's cherubim and flaming sword guarding the entrance to the Mosaic system! See also Deut. xxiv. 7. . . .

The crime specified is that of *depriving* SOMEBODY *of the ownership of a man*. Is this somebody a master? And is the crime that of depriving a *master* of his *servant*?

The crime, as stated in the passage, is three-fold—man *stealing, selling*, and *holding*. All are put on a level, and whelmed under one penalty—DEATH. . . .

But in the case of stealing a *man*, the first act drew down the utmost power of punishment; however often repeated, or however aggravated the crime, human penalty could do no more. The fact that the penalty for *man*-stealing was death, and the penalty for *property*-stealing, the mere *restoration of double*, shows that the two cases were adjudicated on totally different principles. . . .

Further, when *property* was stolen, the whole of the legal penalty was a compensation of the person injured. But when a *man* was stolen, no property compensation was offered. . . .

If God permitted man to hold *man* as property, why did he punish for stealing *that* kind of property infinitely more than for stealing any *other* kind of property? Why did he punish with *death* for stealing a very little, perhaps not a sixpence worth, of *that* sort of property, and make a mere *fine*, the penalty for stealing a thousand times as much, of any other sort of property—especially if God did by his own act annihilate the difference between man and *property*, by putting him *on a level with it?* . . .

The incessant pains-taking throughout the Old Testament, in the separation of human beings from brutes and things, shows God's regard for the sacredness of his own distinction. . . .

In the beginning the Lord uttered it in heaven, and proclaimed it to the universe as it rose into being. He arrayed creation at the instant of its birth, to do it reverent homage. Why that dread pause, and that creating arm held back in mid career, and that high conference in that godhead? *Let us make man in* OUR IMAGE, *after* OUR LIKENESS, AND LET HIM HAVE DOMINION *over the fish of the sea, and over the fowl of the air, and over the cattle, and over all the earth, and over every living thing that moveth upon the earth.* . . .

Then while every living thing, with land, and sea, and firmament, and marshaled worlds, waited to catch and swell the shout of morning stars—THEN, GOD CREATED MAN IN HIS OWN IMAGE. IN THE IMAGE OF GOD CREATED HE HIM. This solves the problem, IN THE IMAGE OF GOD CREATED HE HIM. . . .

What an enumeration of particulars, each separating infinitely, MEN, brutes and things!

> 1. *Thou hast made him a little lower than the angels.* Slavery drags him down among *brutes*.
>
> 2. *And hast crowned him with glory and honor.* Slavery tears off his crown, and puts on a *yoke*.
>
> 3. *Thou madest him to have dominion* OVER *the works of thy hands.* Slavery breaks his sceptre, and casts him down *among* those works—yea, *beneath them*.
>
> 4. *Thou hast put all things under his feet.* Slavery puts HIM *under the feet of an owner*, with beasts and creeping things. Who, but an impious scorner, dare thus strive with his Maker, and mutilate HIS IMAGE, and blaspheme the Holy One, who saith to those that grind his poor, *Inasmuch as ye did it unto one of the least of these, ye did it unto me.* . . .

Objections Considered

The advocates of slavery are always at their wits' end when they try to press the Bible into their service. Every movement shows that they are hard-pushed. Their odd conceits and ever varying shifts, their forced constructions, lacking even plausibility, their bold assumptions, and blind guesswork, not only proclaim their *cause* desperate, but themselves. Some of the Bible defences thrown around slavery by ministers of the Gospel, do so torture common sense, Scripture, and historical fact, that it were hard to tell whether absurdity, fatuity, ignorance, or blasphemy, predominates, in the compound. Each strives so lustily for the mastery, it may be set down a drawn battle.

How often has it been set up in type, that the color of the negro is the *Cainmark*, propagated downward. Doubtless Cain's posterity started an opposition to the ark, and rode out the flood with flying streamers! Why should not a miracle be wrought to point such an argument, and fill out for slaveholders a Divine title-deed, vindicating the ways of God to men?

OBJECTION 1. *Cursed be Canaan, a servant of servants shall he be unto his brethren.* Gen. I. 25.

This prophecy of Noah is the *vade mecum* of slaveholders, and they never venture abroad without it. It is a pocket-piece for sudden occasion—a keepsake to dote over—a charm to spell-bind opposition, and a magnet to attract whatsoever worketh abomination, or maketh a lie. But closely as they cling to it, cursed be Canaan is a poor drug to stupefy a throbbing conscience—a mocking lullaby, vainly wooing slumber to unquiet tossings, and crying. Peace, be still, where God wakes war, and breaks his thunders.

Those who plead the curse on Canaan to justify negro slavery, *assume* all the points in debate.

1. That the condition prophesied was slavery, rather than the mere *rendering of service* to others, and that it was the bondage of *individuals* rather than the condition of a *nation tributary* to another, and in *that* sense its *servant*.

2. That the *predication* of crime *justifies* it; that it grants absolution to those whose crimes fulfill it, if it does not transform the crimes into virtues. How piously the Pharaohs might have quoted God's prophecy to Abraham, *Thy seed shall be in bondage, and they shall afflict them for four hundred years.* And then, what *saints* were those that crucified the Lord of glory!

3. That the Africans are descended from Canaan. Whereas Africa was peopled from Egypt and Ethiopia, and Mizraim settled Egypt, and Cush, Ethiopia. See Gen. x. 15–19, for the locations and boundaries of Canaan's posterity. So on the assumption that African slavery fulfills the prophecy, a curse pronounced upon one people, is quoted to justify its infliction upon another. Perhaps it may be argued that Canaan includes all Ham's posterity. Whereas the history of Canaan's descendants, for more than three thousand years, is a record of its fulfillment. First, they were made tributaries by the Israelites. Then Canaan was the servant of Shem. Afterward, by the Medes and Persians. Then Canaan was the servant of Japheth, mainly, and secondarily of the other sons of Ham. Finally, they were subjected by the Ottoman dynasty, where they yet remain. Thus Canaan is *now* the servant of Shem and Japheth and the other sons of Ham.

But it may still be objected, that though Canaan is the only one *named* in the curse, yet the 22d and the 23d verses show that it was pronounced upon the posterity of Ham in general. *And Ham, the father of Canaan, saw the nakedness of his father, and told his two brethren without.*—Verse 22. In verse 23 Shem and

Japheth cover their father with a garment. Verse 24, *And Noah awoke from his wine, and knew what his* YOUNGER *son had done unto him, and said,* &c.

It is argued that this *younger* son cannot be *Canaan*, as he was not the *son*, but the grandson of Noah, and therefore it must be *Ham*. We answer, whoever that *younger son* was, or whatever he did. *Canaan* alone was named in the curse. Besides, the Hebrew word *Ben*, signifies son, grandson, great-grandson, or *any one* of the posterity of an individual. Gen. xxix. 5, *And he said unto them, Know ye Laban the* SON *of Saul, came down to meet the king.* But Mephibosheth was the son of Jonathan, and the *grandson* of Saul. 2 Sam. ix. 6. So Ruth iv. 17. *There is a SON born to Naomi.* This was the son of Ruth, the daughter-in-law of Naomi. Ruth iv. 13,15. So 2 Sam. xxi. 6. *Let seven men of his (Saul's) SONS be delivered unto us,* &c. Seven of Saul's *grandsons* were delivered up. 2 Sam. xxi. 8, 9. So Gen. xxi. 28, *And hast not suffered me to kiss my* SONS *and my daughters; and* in the 55th verse, *And early in the morning Lan rose up and kissed his* SONS, &c. These were his *grandsons.* So 1 Kings ix. 20, *The driving of Jehu, the* SON *of Nimshi.* So 1 Kings xix. 16. But Jehu was the *grandson* of Nimshi. 2 Kings ix. 2,14. Who will forbid the inspired writers to use the *same* word when speaking of *Noah's* grandson?

Further, if Ham were meant, what propriety in calling him the *younger* son? The order in which Noah's sons are always mentioned, make Ham the *second*, and not the *younger* son. If it be said that Bible usage is variable, and that the order of birth is not always preserved in enumerations; the reply is, that, enumeration in the order of birth, is the rule, in any other order the *exception.* Besides, if the younger member of a family, takes precedence of older ones in the family record, it is a mark of pre-eminence, either in original endowments, or providential instrumentality. Abraham, though sixty years younger than his eldest brother, and probably the youngest of Terah's sons, stands first in the family genealogy. Nothing in Ham's history warrants the idea of his pre-eminence; besides, the Hebrew word *Hakkaton*, rendered *younger*, means the *little, small.* The same word is used in Isaiah xl. 22. A LITTLE ONE *shall become a thousand.* Also in Isaiah xxii. 24. *All vessels of* SMALL *quantity.* So Psalms cxv. 13. *He will bless them that fear the Lord, both* SMALL *and great.* Also Exodus xvii. 22. *But every* SMALL *matter they shall judge.* It would be a perfectly literal rendering of Gen. ix. 24, if it were translated thus, when Noah knew what his little son, or grandson (Benno hakkaton) had done unto him, he said, "cursed be Canaan."

Even if the Africans were the descendants of Canaan, the assumption that their enslavement is a fulfillment of this prophecy, lacks even plausibility, for, only a mere *fraction* of the inhabitants of Africa have at any one time been the slaves of other nations. If the objector say in reply, that a large majority of the Africans have always been slaves *at home*, we answer, 1st. *It is false in point of fact*, though zealously bruited often to serve a turn. 2d. *If it were true*, how does it help the argument? The prophecy was, Cursed be Canaan, a servant of servants shall he be *unto his* BRETHREN, not unto himself!

Source Note: Theodore Dwight Weld, *The Bible against Slavery* (Boston, 1838).

James Freeman Clarke (1810–1888)

James Freeman Clarke was born in Hanover, New Hampshire, and graduated from Harvard College (1829) and the Harvard Divinity School (1833). His early education was conducted by his step-grandfather, James Freeman, for whom he was named. Clarke's intense tutoring and excellent tutelage led Clarke to be critical of his subsequent educational experiences, particularly the disciplined classical curriculum at Harvard College. He once wrote that "No attempt was made to interest us in our studies. We were expected to wade through Homer as though the *Iliad* were a bog, and it was out duty to get along at such a rate *per diem*. Nothing was said of the glory and grandeur, the tenderness and charm of this immortal epic" (Hodder, p. 69). At age ten he entered the Boston Latin School, which led to studies at Harvard College and the Harvard Divinity School. At Harvard College he was a classmate of William Ellery Channing, with whom he remained a lifelong friend. Like many contemporary abolitionists, Clarke began his career as a temperance reformer, a path that was also followed by William Lloyd Garrison. Most of his life's work was devoted to theological matters, and his bibliography of published works includes primarily doctrinal discussions of Unitarianism and its relations to Christianity and Transcendentalism. Clarke was clearly influenced by Samuel Taylor Coleridge, as was his friend and mentor, Ralph Waldo Emerson, but he did not share Emerson's challenge to the divinity of Jesus Christ, preferring the more conservative life of a reformer in the Unitarian Church.

Reform work—whether theological in nature or social and moral—ultimately claimed Clarke's attention. He wrote and preached against the abuses of alcohol, and he attacked the United States' involvement in the war with Mexico. As Hodder has noted, Clarke "lobbied hard for social and educational reform, supporting what he called 'constructive socialism,' and in later years, he became an outspoken advocate for women's suffrage and access to higher education" (p. 73).

James Freeman Clarke also wrote and preached eloquently against chattel slavery. Like William Ellery Channing, he was distanced from the more militant Garrisonian abolitionists, who argued for immediate and unconditional emancipation of all slaves, no compensation for slaveholders, and political and social equality for the emancipated Africans. However, Clarke moved slowly from a cautious, "gradualist" perspective to a more morally outraged position as the antislavery struggle continued. In 1836 he took over the editorship of *The Western Messenger*, a monthly magazine dedicated to Unitarian theology, Transcendentalism, and the arts. Under Clarke's editorship it also became a voice for antislavery writing, and both he and Channing contributed antislavery rhetoric to its pages. Two of his most famous antislavery writings are *Slavery in the United States*, preached in 1842 and published in 1843 (excerpted here), and *The Church as It Is, as It Was, and as It Ought to Be*, published in 1848. In May of 1854, an event shocked Boston in general and Clarke in particular: the fugitive slave Anthony Burns was returned to his Southern plantation overseer by a federal court in Boston. Clarke was outraged and began tireless work in the antislavery movement, continuing his activity for the Union cause during the Civil War, primarily in sermons that gave moral strength to his anxious congregation. Although the majority of Clarke's writings were devoted to theological matters, particularly Unitarian and Transcendental philosophy, he is regarded to have been an important and influential antislavery voice in the 1840s and 1850s. No social injustice fired his indignation as slavery did.

> Edward Everett Hale, in his memoir of Clarke, pointed out that his friend had never joined any of the antislavery parties, since he was opposed on principle to some of the abolitionists' more confrontational tactics. But few of the religious or secular leaders of the city [of Boston] spoke out against slavery as effectively as Clarke did. "I learned my antislavery lessons from slavery itself," he noted ruefully in *Anti-Slavery Days, A Sketch of the Struggle Which Ended in the Abolition of Slavery in the United States* (1883), a late-life history of the struggle to end slavery in the United States that includes some recollections of his first encounters with slavery. No sooner had he taken charge of *The Western Messenger* than he began turning it into an organ of protest against slavery. In his first issue he published excerpts from a pamphlet by William Ellery Channing that, while it deplored slavery, nevertheless argued for a peaceful and conciliatory approach to its abolition. From the standpoint of the radical followers of William Lloyd Garrison, Channing's cautious recommendations smacked of moral weakness, but this gradualist approach to abolition seemed judicious to Clarke at the time. With the passage of years, however, Clarke's resentment began to mount. [Hodder, p. 73]

After emancipation Clarke continued his lifelong interest in education reform, self-improvement, and moral development. In 1880, he published a series of lectures entitled *Self-Culture: Physical, Intellectual, Moral, and Spiritual*. This "blueprint for educational reform in the United States" became Clarke's most fully developed statement of concern for educational principles. He was also an editor of the *Monthly Journal of the American Unitarian Association* (connected to *The Western Messenger*) and *The Christian World*, in addition to his public speaking, preaching, and authorship of over one hundred published titles. He died in Boston on June 8, 1888.

SUGGESTIONS FOR FURTHER READING

Albanese, Catherine. *Corresponding Motion: Transcendental Religion and the New America*. Philadelphia: Temple University Press, 1977.

Bolster, Arthur. *James Freeman Clarke: Disciple to Advancing Truth*. Boston: Beacon Press, 1954.

Colville, Derek. "The Transcendental Friends: Clarke and Margaret Fuller." *New England Quarterly* 30 (Sept. 1957): 378–82.

Doudna, Martin. "Thoreau and James Freeman Clarke on 'Doing Good.'" *Thoreau Society Bulletin* 156 (1981): 1.

Frothingham, Octavius Brooks. *Transcendentalism in New England: A History*. New York: Putnam, 1876. Often reprinted and available in paperback.

Hodder, Alan. "James Freeman Clarke." In *Dictionary of Literary Biography*: The American Renaissance in New England, 3rd series, vol. 235 (Ann Arbor: Gale Research, 1994), pp. 63–76.

Hutchinson, William R. *The Transcendentalist Ministers*. New Haven: Yale University Press, 1959.

Myerson, Joel. "James Freeman Clarke." In *The New England Transcendentalists and the Dial: A History of the Magazine and Its Contributors* (Rutherford, NJ: Fairleigh Dickinson University Press, 1980), pp. 127–33.

Neufeldt, Leonard. "James Freeman Clarke." In *The Transcendentalists: A Review of Research and Criticism*, ed. Joel Myerson (New York: Modern Language Association, 1984), pp. 112–16.

———. "James Freeman Clarke: Notes toward a Comprehensive Bibliography." *Studies in the American Renaissance* (1982): 209–26.

Stange, Douglas. *Pattern of Anti-Slavery among American Unitarians, 1831–1860*. Rutherford, NJ: Fairleigh Dickinson University Press, 1977.

Stewart, James B. *Holy Warriors and the Abolitionists and American Slavery*. New York: Hill and Wang, 1976.

Thomas, John Wesley. *James Freeman Clarke: Apostle of German Culture to America*. Boston: J. W. Luce, 1949.

———, ed. *The Letters of James Freeman Clarke to Margaret Fuller*. Hamburg: Cram, de Gruyter, 1957.

Wright, Conrad, ed. *A Stream of Light: A Sesquicentennial History of American Unitarianism*. Boston: Unitarian Universalist Association, 1975.

Slavery in the United States, Sermon Delivered in Armory Hall, Thanksgiving Day, November 24, 1842
by James Freeman Clarke

You may say, "*we can do nothing to remove the evils of slavery*." Will it do no good to look at great moral questions,—questions of right and wrong, toward which the intellect of the World is turning its attention? It will not do, when we stand before the judgment-seat of Christ, to say that two millions of our fellow beings were under a hard yoke, under a system of government which we were supporting, under laws which we were enacting, and that we would not so much as ask whether we could do any thing to abate the evil. . . .

I feel somewhat qualified to speak of it,—if a seven years' residence in a slave-holding community can entitle one to claim some acquaintance with the facts,—if an intimate friendship with many slaveholders, and many obligations and kindnesses received at their hands, can vindicate one from any prejudice against the men,—and if a New England love for freedom, breathed in with her air in childhood, confirmed in youth, and I thank God never relinquished amid other influences in manhood, can prevent me from having imbibed an undue partiality for the system. . . .

I. Let us look, then in the first place, at *the evils* in the system of slavery. . . .

People have imagined that the slaves were being whipped and worked all the time, that they were dripping with blood, that their misery was constant and universal. Yet the *real* evils of slavery never have been, and hardly can be exaggerated. Some circumstances about it may be. There are many very kind masters,—very many. . . .

There are also many pleasing features connected with the system. God has given alleviations and compensations to the worst institutions. There is often a strong attachment between the master and servant, very different from the mercenary relations which exists so much among ourselves between employer and domestic. The white child and black grow up together,—they play together on the floor when children, and as they grow up, the one feels the responsibility of a protector, and the other the affection which comes from respect and reliance. Evils, sufficiently enormous remain, after all such abatements. . . .

1. First, the evils to the slave are very great. He is not always treated badly, but he is always *liable* to be so treated. He is entirely at the mercy of his master. If he is liable to be beaten, starved, over-worked, and separated from his family; whoever knows human nature, knows that such cases will not be rare. . . .

I could tell you stories of barbarities which I knew of, which it would sicken you to hear, as it does me to think of them. But it would give you a false impression. It would be as if I should collect all the accounts of murders and other atrocities committed in this city. It is enough to know, that when men are trusted with irresponsible power they will often abuse it. . . .

A worse evil to the slave than the cruelties he sometimes endures, is the moral degradation which results from his conditions. Falsehood, theft, licentiousness, are natural consequences of his situation. He steals,—why should he not?—he cannot, except occasionally, earn money; why should not he steal it? He lies,—it is the natural weapon of weakness against tyrant strength. He goes to excess in eating and drinking and animal pleasures,—for he has no access to any higher pleasures. And a man cannot be an animal without sinking below an animal,—a brutal man is worse than a brute. An animal cannot be more savage or more greedy than the law of this nature allows. But there seems to be no limit to the degradation of a man. Slavery is the parent of vice; it always has been, and always will be. Cowardice and cruelty, cunning and stupidity, abject submission and deadly vindictiveness are now as they always have been the fruits of slavery. . . . The system of slavery, then, is a soul-destroying system. . . .

I have spoken of a few of the evils of the system of slavery to the slave himself. The evils to his master are, perhaps, nearly as great. This is admitted by intelligent slaveholders. It was admitted by Mr. Clay, when he said at a speech at Lexington, before he became the champion of the institution,—"that he considered the system as a curse to the master as well as a bitter wrong to the slave, and to be justified only by an urgent political necessity." It is an evil to the slaveholder every way. . . .

There is no comfort, no cleanliness, no improvement with slaves in your family. It is perpetual annoyance and vexation. Society is poisoned in its roots by the system. The spirit, tone, and aim of society is incurably bad, wherever slavery is. . . .

The political evils of slavery form a distinct and important part of the argument,—but I cannot stop to dwell on them. I refer you to the speeches of John Quincy Adams, that noble old man who stood up alone in manly opposition to the encouragements of slavery, and bore the tumultuous and furious denunciations of its champion, when no Northern man had the courage to take a stand by his side. "Unshaken, unseduced, unterrified," he stood like the mountain, round which cluster and darken the black clouds and against whose summit they discharge fire and hail, but which emerges from the tumult serene and calm, while there broken, baffled wreathes of mist are driven down the wind. . . .

II. Let us now examine the question of the *sinfulness* of slavery.

There are two theories on this subject which I think extreme,—one, of the Abolitionists who demand immediate emancipation,—the other, of the South Carolina party of slaveholders.

The first theory declares that to hold slaves, or to have anything to do with holding slaves, is always sinful, and to be repented of immediately,—that no slaveholder should be permitted to commune in our churches, and that we should come out and be separate from this unclean thing as far as possible. They support this theory by the inconsistencies of slavery with the rights of man and the spirit of the gospel. . . .

The other party, among who, I am sorry to say, are to be found ministers of the gospel at the South and the North, professors of moral philosophy in Southern colleges, and distinguished cities of the free States, declare slavery to be a system which is sanctioned by the Bible, has existed in all times and is necessary to the progress of the world in freedom and happiness. They speak much of the patriarchs of the Old Testament, and of the fact while slavery, in atrocious forms, existed in the times of Christ and his Apostles, neither Jesus nor his Apostles were abolitionists, or rebuked it, but instead of commanding the masters to emancipate their slaves, or the slaves to run away, told the masters to be just and kind, and the slaves to be obedient and faithful in their relations. . . .

The answer of the Abolitionists to this is not satisfactory, because they wish to prove too much,—they denied that slavery did exist under Mosaic institutions; and they accuse their opponents of "torturing the pages of the blessed Bible." . . .

But what shall we say of those who attempt to justify the system, and would have us believe, that because Jesus did not denounce it had approved of it,—that God ordained that Jesus approved a system that turns man into a brute,—degrades the soul, and makes it almost incapable of progress,—a system, then, which allowed the master to crucify his slave, and throw him into a fish pond to be eaten by carp, for breaking a glass dish,—that Jesus, who taught that we are to love our brethren as ourselves, did not disapprove of this system, or think it sinful? . . .

III. I must now say something on the third point,—*what are our duties in relation to slavery?*

OBJECTION 1. *"We ought to let the whole matter alone; we have nothing to do with it. It is a Southern matter, and should be left exclusively to the South."*

We have a good deal to do with slavery. We support it indirectly throughout the South. It is the strength of the Union which supports slavery, not the strength of the South. It is the power of the free States which upholds this system. If the Union between the free and slave States were dissolved, slavery could not last ten years. . . .

Again, by the clause in the Constitution which declares that the slave, escaping North, shall be given up to his Southern master, Massachusetts becomes a hunting ground for the South. She is not wholly a free State,—not so free as Canada. The soil of Canada cannot tolerate the presence of a slave; the soil of New England can. The Southern bondman, flying North, and entering the limits of New England, is still a bondman. When he has passed through New England and crossed the Canada boundary, he has ceased to be a slave. His chains have fallen off from him. Slavery, then, can and does exist on our soil.

We ought not cease our efforts, wisely and earnestly conducted, for the abolition of slavery, till it can be said of New England as it could long ago be said of Old England, that a slave's foot cannot tread her soil, a slave's breath taint her air. . . .

But we ought to take higher ground. Have we nothing to do with slavery? Are we, then, Christians? Is not our neighbor the suffering man, at the pole or beneath the equator? Ought we not to love him as ourselves? Shall Mason and Dixon's line be an insurmountable barrier to our Christian sympathies? Shall we send missionaries to Africa or India, and help to Poland and Greece, and think nothing of the poor slaves in Georgia and Missouri? Or is political freedom so much more valuable a possession than personal, that it becomes a duty to interfere on behalf of a nation which is taxed without being represented, but criminal to interfere on behalf of a *man*, who is made chattel, and despoiled of all his rights? . . .

OBJECTION 2. *"But you can do nothing. The North cannot do anything for the slave. We cannot approach him. And if we could, the system is too deeply rooted, and too extensive to be overthrown by human efforts. We must leave it to the Providence of God."*

. . . There is every probability that in a few years Kentucky, Maryland and Virginia will emancipate their slaves and secede from the ranks of slavery.

These, and other facts, show that there are natural causes at work, under Providence, which indicate very certainly that slavery in the United States must terminate sooner or later. For there will always be a determined opposition made to every movement towards emancipation in the South, and to resist this, moral convictions are needed, and the influence of a sound public opinion at the North. . . .

However we may differ from some of the sentiments and some parts of the course pursued by abolitionists, they deserve the credit of having been the first effectually of this great subject. . . .

OBJECTION 4. *"But they do not wish to be free; they are an inferior race."*

So they [the slaves] are, sometimes. Undoubtedly they are often satisfied with their lot. But not generally. I have generally found, on conversing with them, a strong desire for freedom deeply seated in their breasts. If they do not desire freedom, why are the southern newspapers constantly filled with advertisements of runaway negroes, and constantly decorated with a series of embellishments representing a black man, with a bundle on his shoulder, running? . . .

OBJECTION 5. *"But they are not intended to be free. They are an inferior race."*

It is a mistake to speak of the African as an inferior race to the Caucasian. It is doubtless *different* from this, just as this is also different from the Malay, the Indian, the Mongolian. There are many varieties in the human family. The Englishman, Welshman, Scotchman and Irishman are organically different—so are the Pawnee, the Mandan and the Winnebago Indians. But it will not do to say *now* that the African is inferior—he never has been tried. In some faculties he probably is inferior—in others probably superior. The colored man has not so much invention as the white, but more of the perceptive powers. The black child will learn to read and write as fast or faster than the white child, having equal advantages. The blacks have not the indomitable perseverance and will, which make the Caucasian, at least the Saxon portion of it, *masters* wherever they go—but they have a native courtesy, a civility like that from which the word "gentleman" has its etymological meaning, and a capacity for the highest refinement of character. More than all, they have almost universally, a strong religious tendency, and that strength of attachment which is capable of any kind of self-denial, and self-sacrifice. If this an inferior race—so inferior as to be only fit for chains? . . .

What then is our duty? We ought to remember the bond as bound with them. In our thoughts and our prayers remember them. . . .

We should make those whom we send to Congress feel that if they suffer the encroachments of slave power, that if they do not manfully uphold the rights of the North we shall hold them faithless and recreant, unworthy to have been born on the hills of New England. We ought to watch them. . . .

What is needed more than anything else now, on this, and many other subjects, is a class of *independent* men—who will not join the abolitionists in their denunciations and their violence, nor join the South in their defence of slavery—who can be temperate without being indifferent—who can be moderate and zealous also—who can make *themselves felt* as a third power, holding the balance between violent parties, and compelling both to greater moderation and justice. . . .

We can rebuke every man who truckles or bows to slavery, or who voluntarily offers himself as its instrument—rebuke him by refusing him our countenance or support as long as he shows this disposition. Finally, feeling that the Lord reigns, and that no evil can triumph forever, we can calmly look to him for aid, and rely on his Providence, yet doing ourselves also, whatever our hand finds to do, working while the day lasts, knowing that the night cometh when no man can work.

Source Note: James Freeman Clarke, "Slavery in the United States, Sermon Delivered in Armory Hall, Thanksgiving Day, November 24, 1842" (Boston, 1843).

ALEXANDER McLEOD (1774–1833)

Alexander McLeod was, like Robert Dale Owen, a Scotsman by birth. He emigrated to the United States at the age of eighteen and entered Union College in 1796 in Schenectady, New York, where he also taught Greek. He was associated with the Reformed Presbyterian Church, and was always pressing his church to defend human rights, particularly with reference to slavery. He was pastor of the First Reformed Presbyterian Church of New York City and soon became a leading orator in the antislavery cause. Highly regarded for his pulpit oratory, McLeod was associated with reform movements within the church, and with a lifetime commitment to human rights. He was very active in promoting causes in New York City, and was a member of the American Society for Meliorating the Condition of the Jews and the New York Society for Instruction of the Deaf and Dumb. He was a vigorous defender of human liberty, whether from governmental tyranny or chattel slavery. He wrote very little concerning the slavery question, but his sermon of 1802 became a classic biblical antislavery argument and was regularly utilized by the abolitionists. An early antislavery advocate, he later became associated with the American Colonization Society. His sermon excerpted here, *Negro Slavery Unjustifiable* (1802), is an early exegesis of Scripture in the cause of emancipation. Here as in his other writings, McLeod offers his readers and congregation a reasoned, logical, methodical response to Bible-based proslavery arguments that makes good moral sense. This text should be compared to Alexander McCaine's *Slavery Defended from Scripture against the Attacks of the Abolitionists* (1842). McLeod was an early "gradualist," and was active in the American Colonization Society.

SUGGESTIONS FOR FURTHER READING

McLeod, Alexander. *Scriptural View of the Character, Causes, and Ends of the Present War*. New York, 1815.

Rowan, Stephen N. *Tribute to the Memory of Alexander McLeod, D.D.* New York, 1833.

Stewart, James B. *Holy Warriors and the Abolitionists and American Slavery*. New York: Hill and Wang, 1976.

Walker, Peter F. *Moral Choices: Memory, Desire, and Imagination in Nineteenth-Century Abolition*. Baton Rouge: Louisiana State University Press, 1978.

Wylie, Samuel B. *Memoir of Alexander McLeod, D.D.* New York, 1855.

Negro Slavery Unjustifiable
by Alexander McLeod

This sermon was preached and published in America in 1802, and published in this country [England] in 1804.

The author was a Scotchman, the son of an eminent clergyman of the Established Church in Mull. He emigrated to America in early life, and, by his talents and character, rose to eminence and influence as a minister of the Gospel.

The principle upon which Dr. McLeod acted in refusing an invitation to the ministry and pastoral charge, till the community calling him was purged of the scandal of slave-holding, he never abandoned nor relaxed. He regarded the country of his adoption with what some, on his side of the water, may consider an overweening partiality; but he was not blind to its evils. In a sermon which was published during the late war, in 1815, he lifted a faithful testimony against the immoralities of the Federal Government of the United States. "By the terms of the national compact," says he, "God is not at all acknowledged, and holding men in slavery is authorised. The constitution of our government recognises the practice of holding *men*, without being convicted of any offence, in *perpetual slavery*. This evil, prohibited by the divine law, Exod. xxi. 16, is equally inconsistent with what is said in the declaration of American independence to be a self-evident truth: "We hold these truths to be self-evident, that all men are created equal, that they are endowed by the Creator with certain unalienable rights, that among these are life, liberty, and the pursuit of happiness, that to secure these rights governments are instituted among men." In direct opposition to these *self-evident* maxims, the Constitution provided for the continuance of the slave trade till the year 1808, and it still provides for the continuance of *slavery* in this free country. It even gives to the slaveholder an influence in legislation, proportioned to the number of his fellowmen he holds in bondage. For these national immoralities, I am bound, as a minister of the Gospel, who derives his politics from the Bible, to pronounce upon the Government the sentence—TEKEL, *thou art weighed in the balances, and art found wanting*. Let me not be understood, however, as conveying the idea, that the other belligerent is not faulty in these respects. Great Britain set the example to her colonies of prosecuting the slave-trade. She still continues, in her numerous provinces, holding thousands in abject bondage. A few good men, after the repeated, the continued exertions of years in the British Parliament, obtained, at last, victory honourable to themselves, and to the cause of humanity, in finally abolishing the African trade; but these injured people, already in durance, have no hope of release for themselves or their offspring. Slavery is a black, a vile inheritance left to America by her royal stepmother.

And we believe that the time is come for a decision, for the trumpet giving a certain sound, and for sending faithful and reiterated remonstrances to American Christians on the sin and danger of implication in the evil of slavery. We have strong views on this necessity, and have pleasure and encouragement in the harmony and decision of sentiment on the subject in the documents appended. How can we read otherwise than with emotions of grief and indignation, as we did the other day in the advertising columns of an American newspaper, of date May 5, 1846? "SLAVES FOR SALE. A likely family of NEGROES, consisting of a MAN, twenty-seven years old, his wife twenty-three, and four children, from eight to two years old, raised in this climate, and fully guaranteed." And this stands among a considerable number of similar advertisements. What! shall families be knocked down to the highest bidder like herds and flocks? Shall the tenderest ties of nature be forcibly—unfeelingly ruptured? Shall husband and wife, in opposition to the strongest affections of the human heart, and in spite of the revealed law of Heaven, be torn asunder from one another? Shall the parents and offspring be cruelly and for ever separated? Shall rational beings be abandoned to ignorance and misery? Shall unoffending fellowmen be doomed to perpetual slavery, and to leave only this inheritance to their children? Shall immortal souls be left to be destroyed for ever for lack of knowledge? Reason, humanity, justice, mercy, interest, lift their indignant voices against all this; and high above them all, while in harmony with them, our holy and benevolent Christianity lifts its loudest protestations! How long shall such enormities be obtruded on the public eye? [*from the preface by Andrew Symington*]

The Practice of Holding Men in Perpetual Slavery Condemned
Exodus. xxi. 16.

He that stealeth a man, and selleth him, or if he be found in his hand, he shall surely be put to death.

The divine law declares this a crime, and prescribes the punishment. *He who stealeth a man, and selleth him, or if he be found in his hand, he shall surely be put to death.*

From the text, I consider myself authorised to lay before you the following proposition:

The practice of buying, holding, or selling our unoffending fellow-creatures as slaves is immoral.

The text will certainly support this proposition. According to the common principles of law, the receiver of stolen goods, if he know them to be such, is esteemed guilty as well as the thief. The slaveholder never had a right to force a man into his service, or to retain him, without an equivalent. To sell him, therefore, is to tempt another to sin, and to dispose of that, for money, to which he never had a right. . . .

It is intended, in this discourse, to *confirm the doctrine of the proposition, to answer objections to it, and make some improvement of it.*

I. To hold any of our fellow-men in perpetual slavery is sinful.

1. This appears from the inconsistency of the practice of holding slaves with the *natural rights of man.* This is a term which has been much abused. It is proper that accurate ideas should be annexed to it, otherwise its force, in the present argument, will not be perceptible. If man were a being, owing his existence to accident, and not a creature of God, his rights would indeed be negative. If he stood in a state of independency of his Maker, and not a subject of law, his rights could be determined only by the will of society. But he is *neither the son of chance nor the possessor of independency.*

2. If one man have a right to the services of another, without an equivalent, right stands opposite and contrary to right. This confounds the distinction be-

tween right and wrong. It destroys morality and justice between man and man, between nation and nation. I have a right to enslave and sell you. You have an equal right to enslave and sell me. The British have a right to enslave the French, and the French the British—the Americans the Africans, and the Africans the Americans. This would be to expel right from the human family—to resolve law into force, and justice into cunning. In the struggle of contending rights, violence would be the only arbiter. The decisions of reason would be perverted, and the sense of morality extirpated from the breast. . . .

3. The practice of enslaving our fellowmen stands equally opposed to the general tenor of sacred scriptures.

The Bible is the criterion of doctrine and conduct. It represents the European and the Asiatic, the African and the American, as different members of the same great family—the different children of the same benign and universal parent. *God has made of one blood all nations of men for to dwell on all the face of the earth, and hath determined the bounds of their habitation*, Acts xvii. 26. In relation to one another, they are equally bound to the exercise of benevolence, and are respected as naturally having no inequality of rights. Every man is bound to respect his fellowman as his neighbour, and is commanded to love him as himself. Our reciprocal duties the divine Jesus summarily comprehends in that direction commonly called the golden rule: *Whatever ye would that men should do to you, do ye even so to them: for this is the law and the prophets*. This is the sum of the duties inculcated in the law of Moses. . . .

4. The practice which I am opposing is a manifest violation of four precepts of the decalogue.

If this can be shown, it will be an additional confirmation of the doctrine of the proposition. Revelation informs us, that whosoever offends in one point is guilty of all, James ii. 10. And the reason is added, because the same authority is wantonly opposed in that one point which gives sanction to the whole divine revelation. By inference, therefore, the whole decalogue is violated, but there is a direct breach of the fifth, the sixth, the eighth, and the tenth commandments.

The *sixth* requires the use of all lawful means to preserve the lives of men. But ah! Slavery, how many hast thou murdered? Thou hast kindled wars among the miserable Africans. Thou hast carried the captive, who escaped death, into a still more miserable state. Thou hast torn from the bosom of the grieved mother her beloved daughter and brought down the grey hairs of an aged parent with sorrow to the grave. Thou hast hurried them on board the floating prisons, and hast chained them in holds, which have soon extinguished the remaining spark of life. The few who have escaped, thou hast deprived of liberty, dearer itself than life. . . .

It debases a part of the human race, and tends to destroy their intellectual and active powers. The slave, from his infancy, is obliged implicitly to obey the will of another. There is no circumstance which can stimulate him to exercise. If he think or plan, his thoughts and plans must give way to those of his master. He must have less depravity of heart than his white brethren, otherwise he must, under this treatment, become thoughtless and sullen. The energies of his mind are left to slumber. Every attempt is made to smother them. It is not surprising that such creatures should appear deficient in intellect. . . .

Their moral principles also suffer. They are never cultivated. They are early suppressed. While young, the little tyrants of their master's family rule over them with rigour. No benevolent tie can exist between them. The slave, as soon as he can exercise his judgment, observes laws to protect the life, the liberty, and the property of his master; but no law to procure these for him. He is private property. His master's will is his rule of duty. We have no right to expect morality or virtue from such an education and such examples.

Another evil consequence is the encouragement of licentiousness and debauchery.

The situation of the blacks is such as to afford every encouragement to a criminal intercourse. This is not confined to the blacks themselves, but frequently and shamefully exists between them and their masters. The lust of the master may be gratified and strengthened by intercourse with the slave, without fear of prosecution for the support of the offspring, or the character of the mother. The situation of these women admits of few guards to their chastity. Their education does not strengthen it. In the Southern States, illicit connection with a negro or mulatto woman is spoken of as quite a common thing. The number of mulattos in the Northern States proves that this evil is also prevalent among their inhabitants. It is usually a concomitant of slavery.

This leads to a fourth lamentable consequence—the destruction of natural affection.

An irregular intercourse renders it difficult for the father to ascertain his proper offspring. Among the slaves themselves marriage is a slender tie. The master sells the husband to a distance from his wife, and the mother is separated from her infant children. This is a common thing. It must destroy, in a great measure, natural affection. Nor is the evil confined to the slaves. Their master, in this instance, exceeds them in hardness of heart. He sees his slave nursing an infant resembling himself in colour and in features. Probably it is his child, his nephew, or his grand-child. He beholds such, however, not as relatives, but as slaves, and rejoices in the same manner that he does in viewing the increase of his cows or his horses.

O'America, what hast thou to account for on the head of slavery! Thou alone of all the nations now on earth, didst commission thy delegates, in peace, and in security from the overawing menaces of a tyrant, or of factions, to form thy Constitution. Thou didst possess, in a peculiar sense, the light of reason, of science, of revelation, of past argumentation, and of past experience. Thou hadst thyself formerly condemned the principle, and, in the most solemn manner, made an appeal to heaven for the justice of thy cause. Heaven heard, and answered agreeably to thy wishes. Yet thou didst contradict a principle so solemnly asserted. Thou has made provision of increasing the number, and continuing the bondage of thy slaves. Thy judgments may tarry, but they will assuredly come. . . .

There is God; and while godliness continues to have *the promise of the life which now is, as well as that which is to come*, those who continue to practise the system of slavery may expect to suffer loss.

I have now finished what I designed to say in confirmation of the doctrine of the proposition and shall proceed.

II. To refute objections offered to the principle I have been defending.

OBJECTION I. "Nature has made a distinction between man and man. One has stronger intellectual powers than another. As physical strength prevails in the subordinate ranks of creation, let superiority of intellect preside among intelligent creatures. The Europeans and their descendants are superior in this respect to the Africans. These latter are, moreover, in their own country, miserable. Their state is not rendered worse by being enslaved. It is just for the more intelligent to rule over the more ignorant, and to make use of their services."

ANSWER. The distinctions which nature makes between man and man are probably not so great as those which owe their existence to adventitious circumstances.

The inferiority of the blacks to the whites has been greatly exaggerated. Let the fact, however, be granted, and the inference which is the principle of the objection will not follow. It is the essence of tyranny. It is founded in false notions concerning the nature of man. You say, "a greater proportion of intellect gives a right to rule over the less intelligent." But you are to observe that man is not only a creature capable of intellectual exertion, but also one who possesses moral sentiments, and is a free agent. He has a right, from the constitution given by the Author of Nature, to dispose of himself and be his own master in all respects, except in violating the will of Heaven. He naturally acts agreeably to the motives presented to him, with a liberty of choice respecting them. He who argues a right to rule from natural endowments must have more than a superior understanding to show. He must evidence a superiority of moral excellence, and an investiture with authority; otherwise he can have no right to set aside the principle of self-government, and act in opposition to that freedom which is necessarily implied in personal responsibility to the Supreme Moral Governor. Consider the consequences which the objection, if granted, would involve. He who could, by cunning contrivance, reduce his innocent and more simple neighbour under his power, would be justifiable in enslaving him and his offspring for ever.

OBJECTION II. "The negroes are a different race of people from us. Their capacities, their shape, their colour, and their smell, indicate their procedure originally from a different pair. They are inferior to the white people in all these respects. This gives a right to the use of the other subordinate ranks of animated being."

ANSWER. This goes upon the footing of discrediting Scripture authority. In a discourse to professed Christians I might reject it without consideration. There may, however, be in my hearing a slaveholder who is an unbeliever of revelations. I would reason even with him, that, if possible, I may serve the cause of justice, of liberty, and of man. The use of sound reason and philosophy Christianity by no means discards.

The principle of your arguments is inadmissible; and if it were not, it would not serve your purpose.

1. It is inadmissible. Among the individuals of every species there is a difference. No more causes than are sufficient to account for any phenomenon are required by the rules of philosophizing. The action of the elements on the human body, the diet and the manners of men, are causes sufficient to account for that change in the organization of bodies which gives them a tendency to absorb the rays of light, to perspire more freely, and to put on that shape which is peculiar to the inhabitants of Guinea and their descendants. A single century will make a forcible distinction between the inhabitants of a northern and a southern climate, when the diet and manners are similar. A difference in this can make a distinction in the latitude. It is impossible to prove that twenty or thirty centuries, during which successive generations did not mingle with a foreign race, could not give to the African negro the peculiarity of bodily appearances which so stubbornly adheres to him when translated into another clime. A few years of a hot sun may produce a swarthiness of complexion which the mildest climate cannot, for years, exchange for a rosy cheek. According to the laws for propagating the species, the offspring resembles the parent. It is not to be expected that a very apparent change should be wrought on the complexion of the offspring of negroes already in this country. Ten times the number of years which have passed over the heads of the successive generations on the coast of Guinea, may be necessary before the negroes can retrace the steps by which they have proceeded from a fair countenance to their present shining black. The causes of bodily variety in the human species which I have stated are known to exist. It is highly unphilosophical to have recourse to others which are only conjectural. Enmity to revelation makes many a one think himself a philosopher. . . .

OBJECTION III. "I firmly believe the scriptures. All the families of the earth are brethren. They are originally descended from Adam and secondarily from Noah. But the blacks are the descendants of Ham. They are under a curse and a right is given to their brethren to rule over them. We have a divine grant, in Gen. ix. 25–27, to enslave the negroes."

ANSWER. This threatening may have extended to all the descendants of Ham. It is, however, to be noticed, that it is direct to Canaan, the son of Ham. In order to justify negro slavery from this prophecy, it will be necessary to prove four things. 1. That all the posterity of Canaan were devoted to suffer slavery. 2. That African negroes are really descended of Canaan. 3. That each of the descendants of Shem and Japheth has a moral right to reduce any of them to servitude. 4. That every slave-holder is really descended from Shem or Japheth. Want of proof in any one of these particulars will invalidate the whole objection. In a practice so contrary to the general principles of the divine law, a very express grant from the Supreme authority is the only sanction to us. But not one of the four facts specified as necessary can be supported with unquestionable documents. On each of them, however, we may spend a thought.

1. The threatening is general. It does not imply particular personal servitude

as much as political inferiority and national degradation. It does not imply that every individual of that race should of right be kept in a state of slavery.

2. It is possible the negroes are descended from Ham. It is even probable. But it is almost certain that they are not the offspring of Canaan. The boundaries of their habitation are defined, Gen. X. 19. The Canaanish territory is generally known from subsequent history.

3. The supposition, however, that the curse fell on the negroes, may be granted with safety to the cause of those who are opposed to the system by which they are enslaved. It will not serve as a warrant for this practice. It is not to be considered as a rule of duty, but as the prediction of a future event. God has, in his providence given many men over to slavery, to hardships, and to death. But this does not justify the tyrant and the murderer. Had it been predicted, in so many words, that the Americans should, in the beginning of the nineteenth century, be in possession of African slaves, we might argue from the fact the truth of the prophecy, but not the propriety of the slave-holder's conduct. It was foretold that Israel should be in bondage in Egypt, Gen. xv. 13. This did not justify the cruelty of Pharaoh. He was a vessel of wrath. Jesus, our God and Redeemer, was the subject of many predictions. According to ancient prophecy, and to satisfy divine justice, he was put to death. The characters who fulfilled this prediction were wicked to an extreme, Acts ii. 23.

4. Slave-holders are probably the descendants of Japheth, although it cannot be legally ascertained. And they may be fulfilling the threatening on Canaan, although they are not innocent. Be not afraid, my friends; prophecy shall be fulfilled, although, you should liberate your slaves. This prediction has had its accomplishment three thousand years ago. The descendants of Shem did, by divine direction, under the conduct of Joshua, subjugate the offspring of Canaan, when they took possession of the promised land.

This naturally leads us to consider another objection—the most plausible argument that can possibly be offered in defence of the unhallowed practice of holding our fellow men in perpetual bondage. . . .

OBJECTION IV. "God permitted the ancient Israelites to hold their fellow creatures in servitude. Men and women were bought and sold among them. The bond servant is called his master's money, Exod. xxi. 21. Had it been wrong in its nature to enslave any human being, God could not have granted the Hebrews a permission to do it. Negro slavery, stripped of some accidental cruelties, is not necessarily wicked."

ANSWER. This objection requires minute attention. The fact is granted Heaven did permit the Hebrews to purchase some of the human race for servitude. The general principle deduced from this fact is also granted. It is, in certain cases, lawful to enslave our fellow creatures. The application of it to justify the practice of modern nations is by no means admissible.

God is the Lord of the Universe. As the SUPREME GOVERNOR, he does what is right. His subjects have violated his law, abused their liberty, and rebelled against the majority of Heaven. They have forfeited to his justice the liberty and the life he gave them. These they must yield. They will, at the time appointed by the Judge, be enclosed in the grave. The sovereign has also a right to the use of whatever instrument he chooses in the execution of the sentence. He may choose the famine or the pestilence, the winds or the waves, wild beast or human beings, to be the executioners.

Civil society has certain laws, to which its members, voluntarily claiming its privileges, have assented. A violation of these is the violation of a contract, and the penalty stipulated must be paid by the offender. When, by a person's licentiousness, justice is violated, or society endangered, it is just and necessary to enslave the criminal, and make his services, if possible, useful to society. This much I cheerfully grant; and shall now proceed to show that the objection does not apply to the doctrine which I have been endeavoring to establish.

You cannot argue conclusively, in defence of negro slavery, from the practice of the ancient Hebrews, unless you can prove, 1st, That the slavery into which they were permitted to reduce their fellow creatures was similar to that in which the negroes are held, and, 2dly, That you have the same permission which they had extended to you. If proof fails in *either* of these, the objection is invalid, and I undertake to show that *both* are without proof. . . .

Source Note: Alexander McLeod, *Negro Slavery Unjustifiable: A Discourse by the Late Alexander McLeod, D.D.* (Edinburgh, 1846), with Preface and Appendix by Andrew Symington, D.D., ed.

ROBERT DALE OWEN (1801–1877)

Robert Dale Owen was a relative latecomer to the abolitionist cause, writing his most important work, *The Wrong of Slavery*, in 1864. However, he was a social reformer from a very early age, and the son of Robert Owen, a Scottish reformer, who developed in his son theories of social reform and labor welfare that easily transferred to the antislavery cause. Robert Owen traveled widely in reform circles in Britain and Europe, and knew William Godwin, Jeremy Bentham, and Mary Wollstonecraft Shelley. In the United States, Owen edited *The Free Enquirer*, a reform publication. He also participated in the development of one of the popular utopian communities in mid-nineteenth-century America, the commune at New Harmony, Indiana. A natural politician and reformer, he served three terms in the Indiana state legislature and was a member of the U.S. House of Representatives 1836–38. He was largely responsible for legislation that founded the Smithsonian Institution in Washington, D.C., and he wrote an important letter to President Abraham Lincoln in 1862 that apparently had some influence on the president's decision to emancipate the slaves one year later. Two of his best-known theological titles are *Footfalls on the Boundary of Another World* (1860) and *The Debatable Land between This World and the Next* (1872). Owen died at Lake George, New York, June 24, 1877.

SUGGESTIONS FOR FURTHER READING

Kolmerten, Carol A. *Women in Utopia: The Ideology of Gender in the American Owenite Communities*. Bloomington: Indiana University Press, 1990.

Owen, Robert. *A New View of Society and Other Writings*. Ed. Gregory Claeys. New York: Penguin, 1991.

The Wrong of Slavery, the Right of Emancipation and the Future of the African Race in the United States
by Robert Dale Owen

Preface

It is little more than three years since the first insurgent gun was fired against Fort Sumter—three years, as we reckon time; a generation, if we calculate by the stirring events and far-reaching upheavals that have been crowded into the eventful months.

Things move fast in days like these. War changes the legal relations of the combatants. War, in its progress, presents unlooked-for aspects of affairs, brings upon us necessities, opens up obligations. The rebellion—creator and teacher as well as scourge and destroyer—confers new rights, discharges from old bonds, imposes bounden duties.

Great questions come to the surface—questions of national policy, demanding solution. In deciding some of these, we find little aid from precedent; for our condition as a nation is, to a certain extent, unprecedented.

We have been trying an experiment that never was tried in the world before. We have been trying to maintain a democratic government over thirty millions of people, of whom twenty millions existed under one system, industrial and social, ten millions under another. The twenty millions, chiefly one race, carried out among themselves a Declaration made eighty-eight years ago touching the equal creation and the inalienable rights of man. The ten millions consisted in nearly equal portions, of two races—one the descendants of voluntary emigrants who came hither seeking freedom and happiness in a foreign land, the other deriving their blood from ancestors against whom was perpetrated a terrible wrong, who came in chains and were sold as chattels. From these forced emigrants and their descendants were taken away almost all human rights, the right of life and of perpetuating a race of bondsmen excepted. Laws denied to them the rights of property, of marriage, of family, of education, of self-defense. The master-race sought to live by their labor.

The experiment we have been trying for more than three-quarters of a century was, whether, over social and industrial elements thus discordant, a republican government, asserting freedom in thought, in speech, in action, can be peacefully maintained.

Grave doubts, gloomy apprehensions, touching the nation's Future, have clouded the hopes of our wisest public men in days past. Even the statesmen of the Revolution saw on the horizon the cloud no bigger than a man's hand. Gradually it rose and spread and darkened. The tempest burst upon us at last.

Then some, faint-hearted and despairing of the Republic, prophesied that the good old days were gone, never to return. Others, stronger in hope and faith, recognized, through the gloom, the correcting and reforming hand of God. They acknowledged that the experiment had failed, but they confessed also that it ought never to have succeeded. In adversity men look into their hearts, there to read lessons which prosperity has failed to teach them.

The experiment ought never to have succeeded, because it involved a grievous offense against Humanity and Civilization. In peace, before the acts of slave-holders made them public enemies, we scrupled to look this offense in the face, seeing no remedy. But war, which has its mission, opened our eyes and released our hands. Times disturbed and revolutionary bring their good as well as their evil. In such times abuses ripen rapidly; their consequences mature, their ultimate results become apparent. We are reminded of their transitory character. We are reminded that, although for the time and in a certain stage of human progress some abuses may have their temporary use, and for this, under God's economy, may have been suffered to continue, yet all abuses have but a limited life: The Right only is eternal. Great, under such circumstances, are our responsibilities; momentous are the issues, for good or for evil, that hang upon our decisions.

. . . In briefly tracing, from its inception in this hemisphere, the rise and progress of the great wrong which still threatens the life of the nation, I have followed the fortunes of a vast multitude, equal in number to the population, loyal and disloyal, black and white, of these United States. I have sketched, by the light of authentic documents, the dismal history of that multitude through three centuries and a half seeking out their representatives, and inquiring into the numbers and the condition of these, at the present day. In so doing, I have arrived at conclusions which, to those who have never looked closely into the subject, may seem too marvelous for belief.

. . . In concluding this branch of the subject, I have spoken of Emancipation as a solemn national duty which, now that the constitutional obstacle has been removed, we cannot, consistently with what we owe to God and man, neglect or postpone. I have shown that our faith is pledged, and cannot be broken without bringing upon us the contempt of the civilized world.

Finally, after having traced the connection of the two races in the past, and set forth the duty of one race towards the other in the present, I have sought to look forward and inquire how they are likely, when both shall be free, to live together in the future; whether we shall have a race among us unwilling or unable to support itself, whether admixture of the races, both being free, is probable or desirable; whether without admixture, the reciprocal social influence of the races on each other promises good or evil, what are the chances that a base prejudice of race shall diminish and disappear; and, lastly, whether, in case the colored man shall outlive that prejudice, disgraceful to us and depressing to

him, and shall be clothed by law with the same rights in search of which we sought this Western World, there will be any thing in connection with his future in these United States to excite regret or inspire apprehension.

Source Note: Robert Dale Owen, *The Wrong of Slavery, the Right of Emancipation and the Future of the African Race in the United States* (Philadelphia: J. B. Lippincott, 1864).

The Economic Arguments Concerning Slavery

From the beginnings of abolitionist sentiment in the eighteenth century to the Civil War and Reconstruction, arguments about slavery centered on the economic necessity of the "peculiar institution" to the survival of the South. It was argued that the way of life on Southern plantations depended entirely on slavery for profit and that to turn the plantation system into the factory system of the North would not only destroy the Southern way of life; it would also emancipate millions of people who would be ill equipped to cope for themselves. Thus there evolved an early abolitionist movement between the American Revolution and the 1830s, when William Lloyd Garrison and Wendell Phillips entered the debates. These abolitionists sought a gradual phasing-in of emancipation, so that attrition of slavery through death or removal would follow a legislative prohibition against the buying and selling of human beings. The "gradualists," as these thinkers were called, embraced a wide variety of adherents, such as the slaveholder Thomas Jefferson, who struggled with slavery in his writings but who did not manumit his slaves until his death (and not all of them even then), through the provisions of his will. William Ellery Channing, another gradualist, was an early-nineteenth-century minister of the Arlington Street Unitarian Church in Boston, whose book *Slavery* (1835) became a classic exposition of the slavery issue from an early abolitionist perspective, though it was published late in the game. This early phase also saw the founding of antislavery societies both North and South, and the establishment of the colonization societies, which sought to end slavery by returning the Africans, both slave and free, to Africa. Liberia was the usual destination sought by the "colonizationists," and from the outset, the economic problems associated with emancipation and colonization became a focus for pro- and antislavery debate.

The economics of colonization are confusing and often contradictory. By one estimation, the basic cost of transporting nearly four million slaves back to Africa in 1860 would have been more than the annual budget for the United States and would have resulted in a national bankruptcy. Then of course there was the essential problem of placement: the colonization schemes were usually worked out without full agreement from the African nations involved, and in fact Liberia was barely consulted in the matter. Nor did the colonizationists consult the slaves who were to be emancipated as they planned the deportation of nearly one-sixth of the population of the United States. Economic arguments accompanied the moral, biblical, political, and race-theory categories of debate; however, their representation took place primarily in the congressional record for those antebellum decades or in treatises devoted to the "science" of the slave economy. The selections that follow fall into the latter category, and they are

limited in scope and number, as a wider representation of the economic argument would have resulted in another volume altogether.

Antislavery rhetoric in the eighteenth century focused on the evils of the slave trade, the transatlantic Middle Passage, and the immoral practices that resulted from this link between Africa and the United States. However, by 1808, the slave trade had been declared illegal both in England and America, so that the slave traders, shipbuilders, and numerous middlemen associated with the trade either were forced into alternative sources of generating income or continued slave trading illegally. The historian Hugh Thomas estimates that even after the 1807 and 1808 decrees prohibiting the slave trade, some 250,000 slaves were illegally imported to the United States.

Another essential force that brought an end to the slave trade, but not to slavery as an institution, was the Industrial Revolution, both in England and in the United States. By all accounts, the slave trade had been a vital source of cheap labor for the plantation owners of the South, where unskilled labor in large quantities was needed for the maintenance of the agricultural economy. However, in the North, slave labor was impractical and unnecessary, because the more skilled laborers needed for factory work were easily imported as wage-slaves under the system of indentured servitude. As the slave narrators Harriet Jacobs and Frederick Douglass both observed, indentured servitude was indeed difficult, but it differed from chattel slavery in that the sharecropper or factory worker was indentured for a temporary period and was not subject to sale or transfer against his will. Both Jacobs and Douglass cite the essential differences between these two forms of labor in their slave narratives, and it is very clear that from an insider's point of view, wage slavery was preferred to chattel slavery. The Industrial Revolution brought many changes in American economic practices, producing everything from the rapid growth of cities in the midst of an agricultural landscape to the development of powerful economic empires by the builders and owners of railroads, lumber mills, textile factories, and manufacturers of goods required by the ever-expanding population of the United States. The historian Richard Abbott notes this change in the economic landscape during the nineteenth century:

> In the quarter-century that followed the War of 1812, the Industrial Revolution transformed the state of Massachusetts. Businessmen who had once invested in commercial and shipping activities [such as the slave trade] redirected their capital into the construction of industrial plants that came to dominate the landscape of the eastern part of the state. . . . By 1860, Massachusetts had become the most thoroughly industrialized portion of the earth outside England. [Abbott, p. 10]

New England became a center for the textile industry, which, in turn, depended almost entirely on cotton grown on Southern plantations employing slave labor. It is well known that Eli Whitney's invention of the cotton gin in the 1790s did not bring an end to the demand for slave labor; rather, it made the growing of cotton pay even better because its production was more efficient and less labor intensive. The first permanent cotton-processing factory in New

England was built in Beverly, Massachusetts, in 1787, by John Cabot and John Fisher. Cabot had formerly been a slave trader and had built a capital base for investment in the cotton industry through his profits in the slave trade. He was typical of the transition that took place after Congress outlawed the slave trade just as the Industrial Revolution made factory ownership even more lucrative than importing slaves had been. Later in the nineteenth century, industrialists such as the Lowells, Appletons, and Lawrences became familiar New England names associated with the Industrial Revolution. Many former slave traders transferred the profits made as traders into new ventures as pioneering industrialists. They had, after all, ready access to capital, which is the primary prerequisite for venture capital investing. And because the Southern plantation system could sustain its labor force through an explosive growth of the slave population already in the United States, and by additional slaves imported illegally, the industrial mills of the North were effectively in league with the cotton growers of the South. Kenneth Stampp observes that "slave labor had several competitive advantages over free white labor. In the first place, it was paid less: the average wage of a free laborer exceeded considerably the investment and maintenance costs of a slave. In the second place, masters exploited women and children more fully than did the employers of free labor. Finally, the average bondsman worked longer hours and was subjected to a more rigid discipline" (Stampp, p. 400).

With the rapid expansion of factories in the North and the importation of inexpensive European immigrant labor, the demand for cotton produced in the South grew exponentially. In 1800, only 500 bales per year of Southern cotton were needed in the mills of New England; by 1810, the number was 10,000, and by 1815, some 15,000 bales were needed to satisfy the demands of the Northern mill owners. It is important to observe that both slaves in the South and wage earners in the North were exploited horribly by the owners of the cotton empire. Kenneth Stampp shows that "the yearly charge for the support of an adult slave seldom exceeded $35, and was often considerably less than this" (Stampp, p. 406). Calculating the thirty-five-dollar figure to be a high average for the annual maintenance of a plantation slave, the figure becomes only sixty-seven cents per week, much less than the approximately three to five dollars per week a free adult male could expect to receive in wages from a Northern mill. Moreover, the mill worker in the North would be entitled to "overtime" for any labor that exceeded ten hours per day, where the slaveowner paid nothing for overtime to his chattel slaves. While the mill owner would incur costs associated with increased productivity, the slaveowner could increase productivity by requiring longer hours of labor from each slave, without incurring additional costs. The price of cotton remained relatively low, compared to that of the manufactured cotton goods in Northern mills, and the differences between wage slavery and chattel slavery helped to keep the price of cotton stable.

The profitability of New England's mills is perhaps best evidenced by the explosive growth in their numbers in the first half of the nineteenth century. In 1815, there

were 99 mills in Rhode Island and 52 in Massachusetts. After scarcely more than a decade, the number of mills in 1828 had grown to 150 in Rhode Island and to 160 in Massachusetts. Such growth is a textbook example of profitability in a perfectly competitive industry such as New England's cotton manufacture. In a perfectly competitive industry, new firms will continue to enter as long as positive profits can be realized. Positive profit—that is, net revenue above and beyond what is necessary to pay dividends to all current investors—attracts new investors to the industry who will support the entrance of new firms, and finance the expansion of existing firms. Moreover, positive profits exist only under the circumstance of substantial rates of profit. The vast and quick multiplication of cotton mills in New England during the industry's first decades thus suggests the presence of positive profits, made possible primarily by cheap Southern cotton produced by slave labor. In considering the Northern textile community's support of slavery, it is also important to note that their interest in a consistent and abundant supply of cotton figured just as prominently as their interest in a cheap supply of cotton. A healthy supply of Southern cotton insured that prices would not be driven skyward by scarcity. More importantly, though, the South's increasing cotton production saved the New England capitalists from having to import their raw materials. In addition to increasing the costs of production, reliance upon a foreign source of cotton would have wrecked the balance of trade for the United States. Thus cotton, and by association, slavery, came to dominate all aspects of economic life in New England. New England shipping, though it had long since stopped its slave traffic, still depended on slavery via the new cotton industry. Northern ships carried the exports of finished cotton manufactures as well as raw cotton from the South. Boston's financial institutions, along with its private citizens, invested heavily in the Southern cotton plantations. [Saulmon, pp. 8–9]

Obviously, such close association between the production of cotton in the South and the manufacture of cotton goods in New England produced political, social, and economic alliances between the two regions that were both extremely dependent on the slave labor of the plantation system. If wage slavery and indentured servitude dominated the economy of the Northern mills, chattel slavery was the primary labor force for the cotton plantation system. The proslavery advocates in Southern legislatures correctly argued that any disruption of this system through the abolition of slavery would jeopardize the economic well-being of the Southern slaveholding states, and it would also negatively impact the economy of the textile industry of the North. The opposing free labor argument stated that the potential market for inexpensive cotton goods, the nearly 3,954,000 slaves living in the Southern states by 1860, was entirely lost because slaves did not possess enough disposable income to impact the economy, even though they accounted for one-eighth of the country's population in that year.

THE TEXTS

The reader will observe that some of these economic debates are not what the modern scholar would label "economic"; rather, they are broad-based political, social, and philosophical arguments that use as the foundation for their reasoning some form of economic argument. For example, Edmund Ruffin, in *The Political Economy of Slavery* (1853), takes up the subject of European socialism and its impact on the culture of the American South, but his examples of economic evidence are largely anecdotal rather than detailed and analytical:

> So far as their facts and reasoning go, and in their main doctrines, the socialists are right. Associated labor can be much more productive, and be conducted more economically, than the labors of individual persons or families. The socialist theorists reasoned correctly, and in their practical experiments they devised good but defective plans. . . . Supply the one supreme head and governing power to the association of labor . . . and the scheme and its operation will become as perfect as can be expected of any human institution. But in supplying this single ruling power, the association is thereby converted to the condition of domestic slavery. And our system of domestic slavery offers in use, and to the greatest profit for all parties in the association, the realization of all that is sound and valuable in the socialists' theories and doctrines, and supplies the great and fatal defect of all their plans for practically associating labor.

David Christy, in an essay excerpted from *Cotton Is King; or, the Culture of Cotton and Its Relation to Agriculture, Manufactures and Commerce* (1855), showed how the economy of the South was strong because of slavery, and that emancipation would wreck the very foundation on which this powerful economy rested.

These economic generalizations were widespread and accompanied the more traditional arguments taken from the Bible or race theory. Two figures who used economic arguments in opposing each other were George Fitzhugh and Hinton Rowan Helper. Helper developed a unique argument that quantified the value of Southern land, which he tried to prove had been degraded by slaveholding, while the value of Northern land, where free labor was practiced, had increased during the same period. The historian George Fredrickson, who edited the John Harvard Library edition of Helper's *The Impending Crisis*, has called Helper's book the most influential work to appear before the Civil War, with the possible exception of Stowe's *Uncle Tom's Cabin*. Helper included tables and graphs in his treatise, attempting to show how the abolition of slavery would become an economic advantage for the South. He was widely opposed by writers like Samuel Wolfe, who immediately retaliated against this North Carolinian whom he regarded to be a turncoat.

George Fitzhugh wrote two important works in favor of slavery, *Sociology for the South* (1854) and *Cannibals All!* (1857). Both documents are excerpted here. Fitzhugh was raised near Alexandria, Virginia. He became a lawyer, wrote for *Debow's Review*, and served in the attorney general's office in Washington during the Buchanan administration. The *Dictionary of American Biography* entry on Fitzhugh notes that he "deserves credit for seeking to convert the slavery debate on the Southern side, from a mere negative rebuttal into an aggressive doctrine of positive benefit. He believed that free capitalist society, animated by the laissez-faire doctrines of Adam Smith, was a gross failure" (*DAB*, p. 438). Fitzhugh based his idea on "economic" observations like these: "The profits of slave labor are that portion of the products of such labor which the power of the master enables him to appropriate. These profits are less, because the master allows the slave to retain a larger share of the results of his own labor than do the [Northern] employers of free labor." Excerpts from Fitzhugh's writing give the reader a sense of how "economic debates" were in essence sociological and philosophical debates rather than exacting economic treatises.

SUGGESTIONS FOR FURTHER READING

Abbott, Richard H. *Cotton and Capital*. Amherst: University of Massachusetts Press, 1991.

Elkins, Stanley. *Slavery: A Problem in American Institutional and Intellectual Life*. Chicago: University of Chicago Press, 1959.

Eno, Arthur L., Jr. "The Civil War: Patriotism vs. King Cotton." In *Cotton Was King* (Keane: New Hampshire Publishing Co., 1976), pp. 127–40.

Foner, Eric. *Free Soil, Free Labor, Free Men: The Ideology of the Republican Party before the Civil War*. London: Oxford University Press, 1970.

Garrison, William Lloyd. *Thoughts on African Colonization; or, an Impartial Exhibition of the Doctrines, Principles, and Purposes of the American Colonization Society*. Boston: Garrison and Knapp, 1832.

Genovese, Eugene. *The Political Economy of Slavery: Studies in the Economy and Society of the Slave South*. New York: Vintage Books, 1965.

Mannix, Daniel P., and Malcolm Cowley. *Black Cargoes*. New York: Viking Press, 1962.

Morgan, Edmund S. *American Slavery, American Freedom: The Ordeal of Colonial Virginia*. New York: W. W. Norton, 1975.

O'Connor, Thomas H. *Lords of the Loom: the Cotton Whigs and the Coming of the Civil War*. New York: Charles Scribner's Sons, 1968.

Saulmon, Gregory. "A Peculiar Relationship: The Rise and Fall of New England's Participation in Slavery." Unpublished essay, University of Massachusetts at Amherst, 2000.

Stampp, Kenneth M. *The Peculiar Institution*. New York: Vintage Books, 1956.

Staudernraus, Philip J. *The African Colonization Movement, 1816–1865*. New York: Columbia University Press, 1961.

Weeden, William. *Economic and Social History of New England*. New York: Hillary House, 1963.

Woodman, Harold D. *Slavery and the Southern Economy*. New York: Harcourt, Brace and World, 1966.

EDMUND RUFFIN (1794–1865)

Edmund Ruffin was born January 5, 1794, in Virginia. His family was a James River plantation family, economically secure, but in poor health. His parents died when he was young, and Ruffin developed studious habits of mind in an atmosphere of personal isolation. He attended but left the College of William and Mary and served briefly during the War of 1812. In 1813, he married Susan Hutchings Travis, and the couple had eleven children. He had inherited a 1,600-acre farm on the James River, and he became a leading expert in agricultural economics and the science of farming, which was in its infancy. For example, William Scarborough notes that when Ruffin's plantation failed to grow crops appropriately, he speculated that soil acidity was the cause, and developed a series of experimental substances made from shells, which are rich in calcium and would act as an antidote to the high acidity in the soil (Scarborough, p. xviii). His grand-scale experiment was very successful, and he subsequently published his discoveries in a large book, *An Essay on Calcareous Manures* (1832). Ruffin was not primarily an economist but an agriculturalist, what today we might even call an environmentalist. However, his proslavery activity and advocacy of secession eclipsed his reputation as an agricultural scientist.

Politically, he was also a staunch defender of states' rights and of the institution of chattel slavery, and he accepted contemporary race theories concerning the inferiority of the Negro to the white. Ruffin was primarily a secessionist, and argued vigorously for the formation of a separate, Southern, Confederate nation. As Scarborough observed:

> He vigorously defended slavery on historical, scientific, and economic—but not Biblical—grounds. Deeming the Liberian experiment a failure of monumental proportions, he became a bitter opponent of the Colonization Society and sought to end both federal and state subsidies to that organization. He regarded the free Negro element as a menace to society and devised a scheme whereby that group would be gradually eliminated. A thoroughgoing white supremacist, Ruffin enthusiastically supported white domination, not only in the South, but throughout the world. He applauded European imperial ventures in Asia and deplored the ascendancy of Negro elements in certain Latin American states, especially Haiti. [p. xviii]

His proslavery feelings were intense. He enlisted for only one day in the Virginia Military Institute cadet corps so that he might witness the execution of John Brown in 1859. He published frequently in the proslavery *Debow's Review* once it became clear to him that his cherished Southern institutions were under assault by the abolitionists. He joined the fledgling Confederate Army, and is mythically credited in having fired the first shot on Fort Sumter on April 12, 1861, although "who fired the first shot at Fort Sumter" is still disputed by historians (*Webster's American Biographies*, p. 902). The surrender of Robert E. Lee at Appomattox courthouse on April 9, 1865, plunged Ruffin into a deep depression. After elaborate planning following the decline of his estate and his depression over the abolition of slavery and the loss of the Confederacy, he "executed the act of self-destruction by shooting himself in the mouth with a silver-mounted musket shortly after noon on Saturday, June 17, 1865" (Scarborough, p. 42). He died on his own plantation, Redmoor, in Amelia County, Virginia (*WAB*, p. 902).

SUGGESTIONS FOR FURTHER READING

Allmendinger, David F. *Ruffin: Family and Reform in the Old South.* New York: Oxford University Press, 1990.

————, ed. *Incidents in My Life: Edmund Ruffin's Autobiographical Essays.* Charlottesville: University Press of Virginia, 1990.

Craven, Avery O. *Edmund Ruffin, Southerner: A Study in Secession.* New York: D. Appleton, 1966.

Genovese, Eugene. *The Political Economy of Slavery: Studies in the Economy and Society of the Slave South.* New York: Vintage Books, 1965.

Mathew, D. *Edmund Ruffin and the Crisis of Slavery in the Old South.* Athens: University of Georgia Press, 1988.

Mitchell, Betty L. *Edmund Ruffin: a Biography.* Bloomington: Indiana University Press, 1981.

"Ruffin, Edmund." In *Webster's American Biographies* (*WAB*), ed. Charles Van Doren (Springfield, MA: G. C. Merriam & Co., 1975), pp. 902–3.

Scarborough, William K., ed. *The Diary of Edmund Ruffin*, "Introduction," from vol. 1: *Toward Independence, October, 1856–April, 1861* (Baton Rouge: Louisiana State University Press, 1972), p. xviii.

Stampp, Kenneth M. *The Peculiar Institution: Slavery in the Antebellum South.* New York: Knopf, 1956.

The Political Economy of Slavery; or, The Institution Considered in Regard to Its Influence on Public Wealth and the General Welfare
by Edmund Ruffin

. . . The socialists of Europe, and of the Northern States of this Union, (there are none existing in our Southern States,) of every sect, and however differing on other points, have all advocated the *association of labor*, in some form or other, as the great means for reforming the evils of society arising from starving competition for labor. The founders and preachers of socialism had all observed and earnestly appreciated these evils. They saw that, in advanced society, labor was the slave of capital, and that the more capital was enriched by the employment of labor, the less was acquired and retained by the individual laborers, and the more their wants and sufferings were increased. They also saw, and correctly, that there was great loss of time and labor in the domestic operations of every poor family, and most in the poorest families—and also, that the productive labors of all, if associated, and thus aiding each other, might be made much more productive. And if by laborers being associated in large numbers, and directed by their combined knowledge to the most profitable purposes and ends, all unnecessary waste (as occurs in isolated families) was prevented, and all the actual efforts of labor utilized—the net profits and economy of such associated labor would be much increased, and thus, the laborers might secure and retain a sufficient subsistence, out of the larger share of the profits of their labors, which now goes to the share of employers and capitalists. Their views and doctrines are true in the main, and are altogether so plausible, and so applicable to the wretched condition of labor in the most advanced conditions of society in Europe, that the teachers have found numerous believers and zealous disciples. Sundry associations have been originated in Europe, and established in America, (as a new country only offered the needed facilities), to carry out, in different modes, the great object of associating and combining labor, for the common and general profit and benefit. But every such attempt has met with signal, and also speedy, failure; except a few of the religious associations, which were under the guidance and direction of a single despotic head.

Yet, so far as their facts and reasoning go, and in their main doctrines, the socialists are right. Associated labor can be much more productive, and be conducted more economically, than the labors of individual persons or families. The socialist theorists reasoned correctly, and in their practical experiments they devised good but defective plans. They constructed admirable and complex machinery to produce certain final results, in which every wheel and other operating agent was well adjusted as a secondary cause, or effect of another preceding cause. But in all these great and complicated works, the artificers had omitted to supply the first and great motive power, which is to be found only in one directing mind, and one controlling will. Supply the one supreme head and governing power to the association of labor, (for the suitable conditions of society,) and the scheme and its operation will become as perfect as can be expected of any human institution. But in supplying this single ruling power, the association is thereby converted to the condition of *domestic slavery*. And our system of domestic slavery offers in use, and to the greatest profit for all parties in the association, the realization of all that is sound and valuable in the socialists' theories and doctrines, and supplies the great and fatal defect of all their plans for practically associating labor. . . .

Source Note: Edmund Ruffin, *The Political Economy of Slavery; or, The Institution Considered in Regard to Its Influence on Public Wealth and the General Welfare* (Washington, DC, 1857).

[*In 1853, Edmund Ruffin published* The Political Economy of Slavery; or, the Institution Considered in Regard to Its Influence on Public Wealth and the General Welfare (*Washington, DC, 1853*). *Like most of Ruffin's writings, this work examined slavery from an economic perspective, grossly distorting facts and figures to make a case for the retention of slavery in the South. But it also included a vigorous defense of slavery based on Ruffin's conviction that the African was intellectually, morally, and essentially inferior to the white. With the economic argument, this became a cornerstone for his defense of slavery, and should be compared to the writings of Josiah Nott and George Gliddon in chapter 7 of this volume.*]

From *The Dogma of the Natural Mental Equality of the Black and White Races Considered*

When the antislavery doctrines were first taught, and for many years after, one of the main positions of the advocates was, the assumption of the natural equality and capacity for mental improvement of the black and white races, or the negro and Caucasian. This bold assumption of the one party was either tacitly admitted, or but rarely and faintly denied by the other. . . . Since, there have been practical trials in practice which have served so fully to prove the contrary, that no unprejudiced mind can now admit the equality of intellect of the two races, or even the capacity of the black race either to become or remain industrious, civilized, when in a state of freedom and under self-government—or, indeed, in any other condition than when held enslaved and directed by white men.

From *The Intellectual Inferiority of the Black Race, Tested by Facts in the United States*

Hundreds of thousands of individual cases of emancipated negro slaves, and their descendants, have existed in this country in the last two centuries. . . . Yet, in all this long time, and among such great numbers of free negroes, everywhere protected in person and property, and in the facilities to acquire property—and in some of the Northern States, endowed with political, as well as civil rights and power, equal with the white citizens—still to this day, and with but few individual exceptions, the free negroes in every State of this Confederacy, are noted for ignorance, indolence, improvidence, and poverty, and, very generally, also, for vicious habits, and numerous violations of the criminal laws. In this plentiful country, where the only great want is for labor, and where every free laborer may easily earn a comfortable support, this free negro class is so little self-sustaining, that it now scarcely increases, by procreation, and would annually decrease throughout the United States, if not continually recruited by new emancipations, and by fugitives from slavery. . . .

In all this long time of freedom, and with great facilities for improvement, there has not appeared among all these free negroes a single individual showing remarkable, or even more than ordinary, power of intellect—or any power of mind that would be deemed worth notice in any individual of the white race. Yet, in the Northern States, free schools are open to the children of the blacks as freely as to the whites—many have received collegiate education—and no other but the immutable decree of God, fixing on them mental inferiority, has prevented high grades of intellect and of learnng, being displayed in numerous cases. Further, the absence of industry is as general as the inferiority of mental powers.

Some new free negroes are laborious, frugal, provident, and thrifty. A very few have acquired considerable amounts of property. But these rare qualities were not hereditary—and the children of these superior individuals would be as like as others to fall back to the ordinary condition of their class. In short, taken throughout, and with but few exceptions, the free negro class, in every part of this country, is a nuisance, and noted for ignorance, laziness, improvidence, and vicious habits.

Source Note: Edmund Ruffin, *The Political Economy of Slavery; or, the Institution Considered in Regard to Its Influence on Public Wealth, and the General Welfare* (Washington,

DC, 1853), in Louis Ruchames, ed., *Racial Thought in America from the Puritans to Abraham Lincoln* (Amherst: University of Massachusetts Press, 1969), pp. 420–23. By permission of Bruce Wilcox, Director.

George Fitzhugh (1806–1881)

George Fitzhugh was born in Virginia on November 4, 1806. At this time, both the slave population and the plantation system for producing cotton were growing rapidly. Between 1790 and 1820, the slave population in the United States grew from just over 750,000 to over one million, although importing slaves became illegal after January 1, 1808. By 1860, the slave population would increase to approximately four and one-half million. Ironically, when Eli Whitney invented the cotton gin in the 1790s, demand for slave labor had been expected to decline. Separating cotton seeds from cotton by hand had been a time-consuming task, and the cotton gin enabled a single operator to process the same quantity of raw cotton in ten hours that had previously required one hundred hours. However, worldwide demand for cotton increased as production capacity increased, and the demand for slaves remained high. The cotton gin, in effect, made slavery pay.

Fitzhugh became a lawyer, a plantation owner, and a staunch defender of slave labor. He fought abolition vigorously, defending slavery and advocating the extension of slavery into new territory. Fitzhugh was a regular contributor to *Debow's Review*, a proslavery periodical, and the Richmond *Enquirer*. He traveled to Northern states to explain his views, and engaged Harriet Beecher Stowe in a discussion of the "rightness" and "wrongness" of slavery. Although he acknowledged that the institution had some problems and needed reform, he believed that plantation slaves should remain enslaved.

Fitzhugh collected his speeches, articles, and editorials into two books. The first, *Sociology for the South; or, the Failure of Free Society* (1854), was a popular proslavery text. The second, *Cannibals All! or, Slaves without Masters* (1857), compared the evils of the Northern factory system with the paternalistic and benevolent system of plantation slavery. In both books, Fitzhugh argued that "Northern capitalism was ultimately doomed and, anticipating Frederick Jackson Turner's 'frontier thesis,' contended that only the open frontier and the opportunity it gave white industrial workers to escape wage slavery and become landholders suppressed class violence north of the Mason-Dixon line. Fitzhugh's writings provoked a storm of protest in the North, and passages were taken from his books out of context to suggest that he favored the enslavement of white industrial workers and the poor" (Phillips, p. 270).

Fitzhugh was well aware of Marxist economic theory, but he was fully engaged in a defense of Southern slavery from racial, economic, social, and political perspectives. As Phillips notes, Fitzhugh anticipated Abraham Lincoln's "House Divided" address of 1858, where the future president decreed that the

Union would not survive "half slave and half free," when he argued (in *Sociology for the South*) that slavery would be "everywhere abolished" or "everywhere reinstituted" (Phillips, p. 270). As an economist, Fitzhugh bitterly opposed the laissez-faire doctrines of Adam Smith (1723–90) and the free trade arguments that had developed out of Smith's treatise, *An Inquiry into the Nature and Causes of the Wealth of Nations* (1776). As a race theorist, he fused his grim view of the Northern factory system with a refutation of the Revolutionary doctrine that "all men are created equal."

Fitzhugh's attitude toward the African slave was that he was incapable of self-government and that he could not even provide for himself. Slavery was the only salvation for the African. In *Sociology for the South*, Fitzhugh wrote: "He [the Negro] is but a grown up child, and must be governed as a child, not as a lunatic or criminal. The master occupies towards him the place of parent or guardian. . . . The negro race is inferior to the white race, and living in their midst, they would be far outstripped or outwitted in the chase of free competition. . . . We presume that the maddest abolitionist does not think the negro's providence of habits and money-making capacity at all to compare to those of the whites. This defect of character would alone justify enslaving him, if he is to remain here. In Africa or the West Indies, he would become idolatrous, savage and cannibal, or be devoured by savages and cannibals. At the North, he would freeze or starve" (pp. 83–84).

Fitzhugh was harshly critical of the factory system of the North because it exploited workers, leaving them without the necessary paternalistic support systems provided by the plantation system of the South. He believed not only in white supremacy but also in a master race descended from English aristocrats who inhabited the Southern states as plantation owners and slave masters. He died in Texas in July of 1881. In the pages that follow, Melba Jensen presents excerpts from both of Fitzhugh's major writings and provides interpretative commentary.

SUGGESTIONS FOR FURTHER READING

Faust, Drew Gilpin, ed. *The Ideology of Slavery: Proslavery Thought in the Antebellum South, 1830–1860*. Baton Rouge: Louisiana State University Press, 1981.

Fredrickson, George, ed. Introduction to *The Impending Crisis of the South: How to Meet It*, by Hinton Rowan Helper (1857). Cambridge: Harvard University Press, 1973.

Gale, Robert. "George Fitzhugh." In *Dictionary of American Biography* (New York: Oxford University Press, 1995).

Genovese, Eugene D. *The World the Slaveholders Made: Two Essays in Interpretation*. New York: Pantheon, 1969.

Hobson, Fred. *Tell About the South: The Southern Rage to Explain*. Baton Rouge: Louisiana State University Press, 1983.

Loewenberg, Robert J. *Freedom's Despots: The Critique of Abolition*. Durham: Carolina Academic Press, 1986.

Phillips, Michael. "George Fitzhugh." In Junius P. Rodriguez, ed., *The Histori-cal Encyclopedia of World Slavery* (Santa Barbara: ABC-CLIO, 1997), vol. 1, pp. 269–72.

Rideout, Victoria Jane. "Strange Relations: The Personal and Intellectual Dia-logue of George Fitzhugh and Gerrit Smith." Thesis, Syracuse University, 1986.

Rubin, Louis D. *The Edge of the Swamp: A Study of the Literature and Society of the Old South.* Baton Rouge: Louisiana State University Press, 1989.

Van Woodward, C., ed. Introduction to *Cannibals All! or, Slaves without Mas-ters,* by George Fitzhugh (1857). Cambridge: Belknap Press of Harvard Uni-versity Press, 1973.

Wish, Harvey, ed. *The Antebellum Writings of George Fitzhugh and Hinton Rowan Helper on Slavery.* New York: Capricorn, 1960. This widely used text is available in paperback.

Wish, Harvey. *George Fitzhugh: Propagandist of the Old South.* Gloucester, MA: Peter Smith, 1962.

GEORGE FITZHUGH AND THE ECONOMIC ANALYSIS OF SLAVERY
edited and introduced by Melba Jensen

George Fitzhugh's defense of slavery marked a new phase in the national de-bate. Members of the revolutionary generation had condemned slavery but al-lowed it to continue. Later generations had maintained that the "peculiar insti-tution" could not be understood by any except Southerners and ought not be discussed. George Fitzhugh condemned the hypocrisy and ambivalence of these positions. He argued that slavery was the "natural and normal" state of a civi-lized society by contrasting the vulnerability of a free-laborer with the protec-tion afforded a slave:

> The duty of protecting the weak involves the necessity of enslaving them—hence, in all countries, women and children, wards and apprentices, have been essentially slaves, controlled, not by law, but by the will of a superior. This is a fatal defect in the poor-house system. Many men become paupers from their own improvidence or misconduct, and masters alone can prevent such misconduct and improvidence.[1]

Fitzhugh contended that the Southern slave had the more desirable situation:

> The negro slaves of the South are the happiest, and in some sense, the freest people in the world. The children and the aged and infirm work not at all, and yet have all the comforts and necessaries of life provided for them. They enjoy liberty, because they are oppressed neither by care nor labor. The women do little hard work, and are protected from the despotism of their husbands by their masters. The negro men and stout boys work, on the average, in good weather, not more than nine hours a day. The balance of their time is spent in perfect abandon.[2]

Fitzhugh's work blended the racism of a Virginia plantation owner with a romantic view of slaveholder benevolence. However, neither of these qualities functioned as the defining feature of his work when it was compared to that of other proslavery writers. Fitzhugh's beliefs about race varied over time. During the 1850s, he rejected the determinism embraced by those like Josiah C. Nott who advanced theories of innate African inequality. In 1861, he changed his mind, but biological determinism was not a necessary feature of his proslavery arguments.[3] Nor did Fitzhugh's romantic belief in slaveholder benevolence distinguish his work. In response to Harriet Beecher Stowe's publication of *Uncle Tom's Cabin*, many Southern writers like Mary Eastman produced fictions about kind slaveowners. What distinguished Fitzhugh's writing—what should be teased out of the more conventional proslavery arguments with which it was entwined—was his economic critique of Northern capitalism and its exploitation of the free-laborer.[4]

If slavery was the mote in the eye of the South, Fitzhugh believed capitalism was the log in the eye of the North, particularly the abolitionist North. Fitzhugh had support for this idea among the laboring classes of the North. Congressman Mike Walsh represented New York City in the U.S. House of Representatives. During the Kansas-Nebraska debates of 1854, he frequently lampooned the small antislavery block in Congress. Abolitionists, Walsh argued, would weep over the slave they had never seen while they watched the local laborers starve.

> I have to say, that the only difference between the Negro slave of the South, and the white wages slave of the North, is, that the one has a master without asking for him, and the other has to beg for the privilege of becoming a slave. . . . I would ask . . . point me to one single solitary degradation heaped on the Negro of the South that a white man at the North is not liable to have imposed on him for the time being through poverty.[5]

Fitzhugh's contention that chattel slavery was a less exploitive alternative to wage slavery appalled Northern abolitionists, but he had identified a problem that they often failed to address. How would the slaves live after emancipation? What economic and social relationships would they have?

Fitzhugh's critique of free-labor was grounded in personal experience. His knowledge of the world and his education had been circumscribed by the sluggish economy of King George County, Virginia, where his father owned a plantation called *Bellmount*. Accessible more easily by river than road, the county had been bypassed by commerce, and its population actually decreased between 1810 and 1820. Young George was educated in the "field school," which probably had a single room and a single teacher. His educational prospects were further circumscribed by his father's death in 1825 when he was nineteen years old. Young Fitzhugh prepared himself for a career by reading law, but he disliked the profession and his practice was not profitable. In 1829, *Bellmount* was sold to pay the family's debts.[6]

Fitzhugh's fortunes improved after his marriage to Mary Brockenbrough.

Through his marriage, he acquired a few slaves and an aging plantation house at Port Royal, Virginia, whose masonry was riddled with cracks that widened every year. Before the Revolutionary War, Port Royal's tobacco trade had linked it directly to England, but all that remained of this prosperity were the exhausted farms and the elegant mansions. In 1829, *Port Royal* had the same problems as *Bellmount*. It was an agricultural port with little to draw commerce or new residents. As the house aged and nine children were born, Fitzhugh's privileges threatened to crush him physically and financially, but *Port Royal* maintained his social position among Virginia's landed gentry.[7]

Fitzhugh employed his leisure to read. He was an avid reader of newspapers and journals, and he educated himself regarding the political economy of Western Europe, particularly England. Historically, England had depended on its colonies to supply both food for its population and raw materials for its manufacturing, and the colonies had depended on slaves.[8] England could emancipate the slaves of the West Indies because it retained the populations of India and Ireland in virtual slavery. He also noticed the precarious economic situation of the English laboring class. Should the stream of raw materials from the colonies cease, the laborers would lose their subsistence wages. Should the factory owners desire more profits, they could simply collude to increase the laborers' workload.[9] From these observations, Fitzhugh concluded that abolishing slavery would further subjugate English laborers to the owners of the factories. The Enlightenment vision of the individual had, in his opinion, not liberated the worker or given him "property in himself." It had handed him over to the capitalists to exploit and discard.

> The bestowing upon men equality of rights, is but giving license to the strong to oppress the weak. It begets the grossest inequalities of condition. Menials and day laborers are and must be as numerous as in a land of slavery. And these menials and laborers are only taken care of while young, strong and healthy. If the laborer gets sick, his wages cease just as his demands are greatest. . . . There is no equality, except in theory, in such society, and there is no liberty.[10]

In 1854, Fitzhugh distilled his mixture of historical, economic, and philosophical observations into a book, *Sociology for the South; or, the Failure of Free Society*. He proposed the Southern plantation as an alternative to the failures of English and Northern society. He rewrote the plantation into an agricultural collective and slavery into a benign condition of dependence. It protected the young, the weak, and the ignorant from harm and neglect, and properly regulated by government, it insured each individual a share of the agricultural produce of the plantation. Slavery should not be eliminated, Fitzhugh argued. It should be expanded to place all the poor under the protection of a master so they could be cared for and employed.

These ideas proved profitable. The book received endorsements from Southern newspapers, and these papers offered him additional venues for his writing. In 1855, he obtained an editorial position with the Richmond *Enquirer*. This confirmed Fitzhugh as something of an anomaly in the South. He was a self-educated man in a world that clung to custom and tradition. He had become an employee in a culture that disparaged work and a professional in a society organized by caste.

Fitzhugh found an audience for his ideas because the South needed proslavery propaganda. Congress had passed the Kansas-Nebraska Act of 1854. The Kansas territory was now open for settlement, but the decision regarding whether it would be a free state or slave state would be made by the residents at some point in the future. This situation created two distinct needs for arguments to defend slavery. One need was political. The Democratic Party had split after the passage of the act, and Northern Democrats were joining new political parties. These parties were electing congressmen who would try to eliminate slavery or at least limit the extension of Southern influence through slavery. The small contingent Mike Walsh had lampooned in 1854 would be larger when the next session of Congress began. Southern Democrats faced the possibility that antislavery legislation would be introduced and that they would have to defend slavery in debate. The other need for proslavery propaganda was military. By 1855, Southern settlers were defending their interests in Kansas by force. They had clashed violently with Northern settlers over Kansas's status as a free state versus a slave state. Fitzhugh's claims that slavery was the natural and rightful social system helped recruit volunteers and arms to defend Kansas against free-state settlers and their free-labor views.

Fitzhugh's goal was to articulate a mode of Southern thought suited to maintain the institution of slavery and an economy based on slave labor, and he succeeded. He also exerted significant influence on the development of antislavery thought and Republican Party rhetoric in the North. During the election season of 1856, Abraham Lincoln used Fitzhugh's ideas to rally the Illinois Republicans. Fitzhugh maintained that slavery was, in the abstract, as good for poor whites as for blacks. Lincoln pointed to these ideas as evidence of a Southern desire to enslave Northerners, and he attacked the Democrats for continuing in a party with Southerners.[11] But Fitzhugh functioned as more than a foil for Republican Party work. Lincoln used Fitzhugh's writing to probe the logic of proslavery arguments and formulate his counter-arguments. In his notes, Lincoln wrote: "If A. can prove, however conclusively, that he may, of right, enslave B.—why may not B. snatch the arguments, and prove equally, that he may enslave A?—."[12] No man could claim skin color, intelligence, or interest as the basis for enslaving another, Lincoln concluded, because he would soon meet someone with lighter skin, more intelligence, or greater interest to make a slave of him. In response to Fitzhugh's writing, Lincoln moved beyond an anti–Democratic Party rhetoric and toward an antislavery stance.

Lincoln's response to Fitzhugh's writing supported Fitzhugh's contention that the Northern system of free-labor and the Southern system of chattel slavery were irreconcilably opposed. This was the only contention of Fitzhugh's that Lincoln could accept. Both agreed: "A house divided against itself cannot stand."

In the 1860s, the house had divided, fallen, and was attempting to reconstruct itself. *Port Royal* had been bombarded by artillery during the Civil War. The roof was damaged and the chimney was threatening to collapse, but Fitzhugh continued to live there. He also continued to write about the South. His racism had exacerbated—he now claimed that blacks were innately inferior to whites—but he occasionally expressed optimism about Southern economic development. More railroads were being built in Virginia, and he found free-labor more productive than slave labor. Despite these observations, his ideas quickly found their old grooves. Free-labor, he concluded, combined with the "monopoly of property, or capital, by the few, and the consequent subjection of the many to the domination, taxation and exploitation of these few," was not an evil. In fact, Fitzhugh wrote, it was a positive "blessing."[13]

1. George Fitzhugh, *Cannibals All! or, Slaves without Masters* (Cambridge, MA: Belknap Press of Harvard University Press, 1960), 28.

2. Ibid.

3. Harvey Wish, *George Fitzhugh: Propagandist of the Old South* (Gloucester, MA: Peter Smith, 1962), 42–43.

4. Eugene D. Genovese, *The World the Slaveholders Made: Two Essays in Interpretation* (New York: Pantheon, 1969), 158. Genovese identifies Fitzhugh's economic critique as defining, but his essays emphasize Fitzhugh's goal to critique the social relations that capitalism enabled.

5. *Congressional Globe*, 33rd Congress (1853–55), 1st Session, vol. 23, pt. 2, 1232.

6. Wish, *Fitzhugh*, 8–13.

7. Ibid., 13–15.

8. George Fitzhugh, *Sociology for the South; or, the Failure of Free Society: Electronic Edition* (Chapel Hill: University of North Carolina Press, 1998), p. 255; http://docsouth.unc.edu/fitzhughsoc/fitzhugh.html.

9. Ibid., 232–33.

10. Ibid., 233.

11. Wish, *Fitzhugh*, 156–57.

12. Stephen B. Oates, *With Malice Toward None: A Life of Abraham Lincoln* (New York: HarperCollins, 1994), 126. Oates notes that the editors of Lincoln's *Collected Works* assign this undated fragment to July 1854, but he assigns it to the period 1856–58.

13. Wish, *Fitzhugh*, 336.

Sociology for the South; or, the Failure of Free Society
by George Fitzhugh

Now, it is clear the Athenian democracy would not suit a negro nation, nor will the government of mere law suffice for the individual negro. He is but a grown up child, and must be governed as a child, not as a lunatic or criminal. The master occupies towards him the place of parent or guardian. We shall not dwell on this view, for no one will differ with us who thinks as we do of the negro's capacity, and we might argue till dooms-day in vain, with those who have a high opinion of the negro's moral and intellectual capacity.

Secondly. The negro is improvident; will not lay up in summer for the wants of winter; will not accumulate in youth for the exigencies of age. He would become an insufferable burden to society. Society has the right to prevent this, and can only do so by subjecting him to domestic slavery. In the last place, the negro race is inferior to the white race, and living in their midst, they would be far outstripped or outwitted in the chase of free competition. . . . We presume the maddest abolitionist does not think the negro's providence of habits and money-making capacity at all to compare to those of the whites. This defect of character would alone justify enslaving him, if he is to remain here. In Africa or the West Indies, he would become idolatrous, savage and cannibal, or be devoured by savages and cannibals. At the North he would freeze or starve.

We would remind those who deprecate and sympathize with negro slavery, that this slavery here relieves him from a far more cruel slavery in Africa, or from idolatry and cannibalism, and every brutal vice and crime that can disgrace humanity; and that it christianizes, protects, supports and civilizes him; that it governs him far better than free laborers at the North are governed.

Abolish negro slavery, and how much of slavery still remains. Soldiers and sailors in Europe enlist for life, here, for five years. Are they not slaves who have not only sold their liberties, but their lives also? And they are worse treated than domestic slaves. No domestic affection and self-interest extend their aegis over them. No kind mistress, like a guardian angel, provides for them in health, tends them in sickness, and soothes their dying pillow. Wellington at Waterloo was a slave. He was bound to obey, or would have been shot for gross misconduct, and might not, like a common laborer, quit his work at any moment. He had sold his liberty, and might not resign without the consent of his master, the king. The common laborer may quit his work at any moment, whatever his contract; declare that liberty is an inalienable right, and leave his employer to redress by a useless suit for damages. The highest and most honourable position on earth was that of the slave Wellington; the lowest, that of the free man who cleaned his boots and fed his hounds. The African cannibal, caught, christianized and enslaved, is as much elevated by slavery as was Wellington. The kind of slavery is adapted to the men enslaved. Wives and apprentices are slaves; not in theory only, but often in fact. Children are slaves to their parents, guardians and teachers. Imprisoned culprits are slaves also. Three-fourths of free society are slaves, no better treated, when their wants and capacities are estimated, than negro slaves.

Negro slavery would be changed immediately to some form of peonage, serfdom or villeinage, if the negroes were sufficiently intelligent and provident to manage a farm. No one would have the labor and trouble of management, if his negroes would pay in hires and rents one-half what free tenants pay in rent in Europe. Every negro in the South would be soon liberated, if he would take liberty on the terms that white tenants hold it. The fact that he cannot enjoy liberty on such terms, seems conclusive that he is only fit to be a slave.

Our negro merchants do not work so hard, have many more privileges and holidays, and are better fed and clothed than field hands, and are yet more valuable to their masters. The slaves of the South are cheated of their rights by the purchase of Northern manufactures which they could produce. Besides, if we would employ our slaves in the coarser processes of the mechanic arts and manufacturers, such as brick making, getting and hewing timber for ships and houses, iron mining and smelting, coal mining, grading railroads and plank roads, in the manufacture of cotton, tobacco, &c., we would find a vent in new employments for their increase, more humane and more profitable than the vent afforded by new states and territories. The nice and finishing processes of manufactures and mechanics should be reserved for the whites, who only are fitted for them, and thus, by diversifying pursuits and cutting off dependence on the North, we might benefit and advance the interests of our whole population.

Would the abolitionists approve of a system of society that set white children free, and remitted them at the age of fourteen, males and females, to all the rights, both as to person and property, which belong to adults? Would it be criminal or praiseworthy to do so? Criminal, of course. Now, are the average of negroes equal in formation, in native intelligence, in prudence or providence, to well-informed white children of fourteen? We who have lived with them for forty years, think not. The competition of the world would be too much for the children. They would be cheated out of their property and debased in their morals.

The negro would be exposed to the same competition and greater temptations, with no greater ability to contend with them, with these additional difficulties. He would be welcome nowhere; meet with thousands of enemies and no friends. If he went North, the white Israelites would kick him and cuff him, and drive him out of employment. If he went to Africa, the savages would cook him and eat him.

Free society has continued long enough to justify the attempt to generalize its phenomenon, and calculate its moral and intellectual influences. It is obvious that, in whatever is purely utilitarian and material, it incites invention and stimulates industry. Benjamin Franklin, as a man and philosopher, is the best exponent of the working system. His sentiments and his philosophy are low, selfish, atheistic and material. They tend directly to make man a mere "featherless biped," well-fed, well-clothed and comfortable, but regardless of his soul as "the beasts that perish."

Human progress consisting in moral and intellectual improvement, and there being no agreed and conventional standard weights or measures of moral and intellectual qualities and quantities, the question of progress can never be accurately decided. We maintain that man has not improved, because in all save the mechanic arts he reverts to the distant past for models to imitate, and he never imitates what he can excel.

We need never have white slaves in the South, because we have black ones. Our citizens, like those of Rome and Athens, are a privileged class. We should train and educate them to deserve the privileges and to perform the duties which society confers on them. Instead of, by a low demagoguism, depressing their self-respect by discourses on the equality of man, we had better excite their pride by reminding them that they do not fulfil the menial offices which white men do in other countries. Society does not feel the burden of providing for the few helpless paupers in the South. And we should recollect that here we have but half the people to educate, for half are negroes; whilst at the North they profess to educate all. It is in our power to spike this last gun of the abolitionists. We should educate all the poor. The abolitionists say that it is one of the necessary consequences of slavery that the poor are neglected. It was not so in Athens, and in Rome, and should not be so in the South. If we had less trade with and less dependence on the North, all our poor might be profitably and honorably employed in trades, professions and manufactures. Then we should have a rich and denser population. Yet we but marshal her in the way that she was going. The South is already aware of the necessity of a new policy, and has begun to act on it. Every day more and more is done for education, the mechanic arts, manufactures and internal improvements. We will soon be independent of the North.

We deem this peculiar question of negro slavery of very little importance. The issue is made throughout the world on the general subject of slavery in the abstract. The argument has commenced. One set of ideas will govern and control, after awhile, the civilized world. Slavery will everywhere be abolished, or everywhere be re-instituted. We think the opponents of practical, existing slavery, are stopped by their own admission; nay, that unconsciously, as socialists, they are the defenders and propagandists of slavery, and have furnished the only sound arguments on which its defence and justification can be rested. We have introduced the subject of negro slavery to afford us a better opportunity to disclaim the purpose of reducing the white man anywhere to the condition of negro slaves here. It would be very unwise and unscientific to govern white men as you would negroes. Every shade and variety of slavery has existed in the world. In some cases there has been much of legal regulation, much restraint of the master's authority; in others, none at all. The character of slavery is necessary to protect the white man, whilst it is more necessary for the government of the negro even than for his protection. But even negro slavery should not be outlawed. We might and should have laws in Virginia, as in Louisiana, to make the master subject to the presentment by the grand jury and to punishment, for any inhuman or improper treatment or neglect of his slave.

We abhor the doctrine of the "Types of Mankind;" first, because it is at war with scripture, which teaches us that the whole human race is descended from a common parentage; and, secondly, because it encourages and incites brutal masters to treat negroes, not as weak, ignorant and dependent brethren, but as wicked beasts, without the pale of humanity. This Southerner is the negro's friend, his only friend. Let no intermeddling abolitionist, no refined philosophy, dissolve this friendship.

Source Note: George Fitzhugh, *Sociology for the South; or, the Failure of Free Society: Electronic Edition* (Chapel Hill: University of North Carolina Press, 1998), p. 255; http://docsouth.unc.edu/fitzhughsoc/fitzhugh.html.

Cannibals All! or, Slaves without Masters
by George Fitzhugh

Chapter I. The Universal Trade

. . . We are all, North and South, engaged in the White Slave Trade, and he who succeeds best is esteemed most respectable. It is far more cruel than the Black Slave Trade, because it exacts more of its slaves, and neither protects nor governs them. We boast that it exacts more when we say, "that the *profits* made from employing free labor are greater than those from slave labor." The profits, made from free labor, are the amount of the products of such labor, which the employer, by means of the command which capital or skill gives him, takes away, extracts, or "exploitates" from the free laborer. The profits of slave labor are that portion of the products of such labor which the power of the master enables him to appropriate. These profits are less, because the master allows the slave to retain a larger share of the results of his own labor than do the employers of free labor. But we not only boast that the White Slave Trade is more exacting and fraudulent (in fact, though not in intention) than Black Slavery; but we also boast that it is more cruel, in leaving the laborer to take care of himself and family out of the pittance which skill or capital have allowed him to retain. When the day's labor is ended, he is free, but is overburdened with the cares of family and household, which make his freedom an empty and delusive mockery. But his employer is really free, and may enjoy the profits made by others' labor, without a care, or a trouble, as to their well-being. The negro slave is free, too, when the labors of the day are over, and free in mind as well as body; for the master provides food, raiment, house, fuel, and everything else necessary to the physical well-being of himself and family. The master's labors commence just when the slave's end. No wonder men should prefer white slavery to capital, to negro slavery, since it is more profitable, and is free from all the cares and labors of black slave-holding.

. . . But mark! [Do] not spend your capital. That would be to do as common working men do; for they take the pittance which their employers leave them to live on. They live by labor; for they exchange the results of their own labor for the products of other people's labor. It is, no doubt, an honest, vulgar way of living, but not at all a respectable way. The respectable way of living is to make other people work for you, and to pay them nothing for so doing—and to have no concern about them after their work is done. Hence, white slave-holding is much more respectable than negro slavery—for the master works nearly as hard for the negro as he for the master. But you, my virtuous, respectable reader, exact three thousand dollars per annum from white labor (for your income is the product of white labor) and make not one cent of return in any form. You retain your capital, and never labor, and yet live in luxury on the labor of others. Capital commands labor, as the master does the slave. Neither pays for labor; but the master permits the slave to retain a larger allowance from the proceeds of his own labor, and hence "free labor is cheaper than slave labor." You, with the command over labor which your capital gives you, are a slave owner—a master, without the obligations of a master. They who work for you, who create your income, are slaves, without the rights of slaves. Slaves without a master! Whilst you were engaged in amassing your capital, in seeking to become independent, you were in the White Slave Trade. . . .

The negro slaves of the South are the happiest, and, in some sense, the freest people in the world. The children and the aged and infirm work not at all, and yet have all the comforts and necessaries of life provided for them. They enjoy liberty, because they are oppressed neither by care nor labor. The women do little hard work, and are protected from the despotism of their husbands by their masters. The negro men and stout boys work, on the average, in good weather, not more than nine hours a day. The balance of their time is spent in perfect abandon. Besides, they have their Sabbaths and holidays. White men, with so much of license and liberty, would die of ennui; but negroes luxuriate in corporeal and mental repose. With their faces upturned to the sun, they can sleep at any hour; and quiet sleep is the greatest of human enjoyments. "Blessed be the man who invented sleep." 'Tis happiness in itself—and results from contentment with the present, and confident assurance of the future. We do not know whether free laborers ever sleep. They are fools to do so; for, whilst they sleep, the wily and watchful capitalist is devising a means to ensnare and exploite them. The free laborer must work or starve. He is more of a slave than the negro, because he works longer and harder for less allowance than the slave, and has no holiday, because the cares of life with him begin when its labors end. He has no liberty, and not a single right. We know, 'tis often said, air and water are common property, which all have equal right to participate and enjoy; but this is utterly false.

Free laborers have not a thousandth part of the rights and liberties of negro slaves. Indeed, they have not a single liberty, unless it be the right or liberty to die. But the reader may think that he and other capitalists and employers are freer than negro slaves. Your capital would soon vanish, if you dared indulge in the liberty and abandon of negroes. You hold your wealth and position by the tenure of constant watchfulness, care, and circumspection. You never labor; but you are never free. . . .

Chapter II. Labor, Skill, and Capital

. . . Nothing written on the subject of slavery from the time of Aristotle is worth reading until the days of the modern Socialists. Nobody, treating of it, thought it worth while to inquire from history and statistics whether the physical and moral condition of emancipated serfs or slaves had been improved or rendered worse by emancipation. None would condescend to compare the evils of domestic slavery with the evils of liberty without property. It entered into no one's head to conceive a doubt as to the actual freedom of the emancipated. The relations of capital and labor, of the property-holders to the non-property-holders were things about which no one had thought or written. After the French and other revolutions in Western Europe in 1830, all men suddenly discovered that the social relations of men were false, and that social, not political, revolutions were needed. Since that period, almost the whole literature of free society is but a voice proclaiming its absolute and total failure. Hence the works of the socialists contain the true defence of slavery. . . .

It is impossible to place labor and capital in harmonious or friendly relations, except by the means of slavery, which identifies their interests. Would that gentleman lay his capital out in land and negroes, he might be sure, in whatever hands it came, that it would be employed to protect laborers, not to oppress them; for when slaves are worth near a thousand dollars a head, they will be carefully and well provided for. In any other investment he may make of it, it will be used as an engine to squeeze the largest amount of labor from the poor for the least amount of allowance. We say allowance, not wages; for neither slaves nor free laborers get wages, in the popular sense of the term: that is, the employer or capitalist pays them from nothing of his own, but allows them a part, generally a very small part, of the proceeds of their own labor. Free laborers pay one another, for labor creates values, and capital, after taking the lion's share by its taxing power, but pays the so-called wages of one laborer from the proceeds of the labor of another. Capital does not breed, yet remains undiminished. Its profits are but its taxing power. Men seek to become independent in order to cease to pay labor, in order to become masters, without the cares, duties, and responsibilities, of masters. Capital exercises a more perfect compulsion over free laborers than human masters over slaves; for free laborers must at all times work or starve, and slaves are supported whether they work or not. Free laborers have less liberty than slaves, are worse paid and provided for, and have no valuable rights. Slaves, with more of actual practical liberty, with ampler allowance, and constant protection, are secure in the enjoyment of all the rights which provide for their physical comfort at all times and under all circumstances. The free laborer must be employed or starve, yet no one is obliged to employ him. The slave is taken care of, whether employed or not. Though each free laborer has no particular master, his wants and other men's capital make him a slave without a master, or with too many masters, which is as bad as none. It were often better that he had an ascertained master, instead of an irresponsible and unascertained one. . . .

Chapter VIII. Liberty and Slavery

. . . It seems to us that the vain attempts to define liberty in theory, or to secure its enjoyment in practice, proceed from the fact that man is naturally a social and gregarious animal, subject, not by contract or agreement, as Locke and his followers assume, but by birth and nature, to those restrictions of liberty which are expedient or necessary to secure the good of the human hive, to which he may belong. There is no such thing as *natural human* liberty, because it is unnatural of man to live alone and without the pale and government of society. Birds and beasts of prey, who are not gregarious, are naturally free. Bees and herds are naturally subjects or slaves of society. Such is the theory of Aristotle promulgated more than two thousand years ago, generally considered true for two thousand years, and destined, we hope, soon again to be accepted as the only true theory of government and society. . . .

What is falsely called Free Society is a very recent invention. It proposes to make the weak, ignorant, and poor, free, by turning them loose in a world owned exclusively by the few (whom nature and education have made strong, and whom property has made stronger) to get a living. In the fanciful state of nature, where property is unappropriated, the strong have no weapons but superior physical and mental power with which to oppress the weak. Their power of oppression is increased a thousand fold when they become the exclusive owners of the earth and all the things thereon. They are masters without the obligations of masters, and the poor are slaves without the rights of slaves.

It is generally conceded, even by abolitionists, that the serfs in Europe were liberated because the multitude of laborers and their competition as freemen to get employment, had rendered free labor cheaper than slave labor. But, strange to say, few seem to have seen that this is in fact asserting that they were less free after emancipation than before. Their obligation to labor was increased; for they were compelled to labor more than before to obtain a livelihood, else their free labor would not have been cheaper than their labor was. . . .

Chapter XVII. The *Edinburgh Review* on Southern Slavery

. . . The *Edinburgh Review* well knows that the white laborers of England receive more blows than are inflicted on Southern slaves. In the Navy, the Army, and the Merchant Service of England, there is more cruelty, more physical discomfort than on all the farms of the South. This *Review*, for twenty years, has been a grand repository of the ignorance, the crimes, and sufferings of the workers in mines and factories, of the agricultural laborers, of the apprentices, and, in fine, of the whole laboring class of England. We might appeal to its pages almost *passim* to establish these facts. Half the time of Parliament is consumed in vain efforts to alleviate the condition of the cruelly treated and starving poor; and much of this *Review* is taken up in chronicling the humane but fruitless action of Parliament. No man in the South, we are sure, ever bred slaves for sale. They are always sold reluctantly, and generally from necessity, or as a punishment for misconduct. The Southwest has been settled in great part by farmers from the older slave States, removing to them with their negroes. The breaking up of families of whites and of blacks keeps equal pace. But we have no law of impressment in the South to sever the family ties of either blacks or whites. Nor have we any slavery half so cruel as that to which the impressed English seaman is subjected. The soldiers torn from their wives and children, to suffer and to perish in every clime and on every sea, excite not the sympathies of the Reviewer; they are all reserved for imaginary cases of distress occasioned by the breaking up of families of Southern negroes. The so-called slave trade of the South is no evil, because the instances of the improper severing of family ties are rare. . . .

From the *Edinburgh Review*, 1846.

The moral and domestic feelings of the slave are sacrificed, and his intellect is stunted; but in respect of his physical condition he may be a gainer. "It is necessary," says Aristotle, in his celebrated justification of slavery, "that those who cannot exist separately should live together. He who is capable of foreseeing by his intellect, is naturally a master; he who is able to execute with his body what another contrives, is naturally a slave: wherefore the interest of the master and slave is one." There is a certain degree of force in this argument, if it is limited to the economical relations of the two parties. It is the interest of the master to maintain his slave in good working order. In general, therefore, he is comparatively well fed, clothed, and lodged; his physical wants are provided for; he is clothed like the lilies of the field, he has no thought or care for the morrow. . . .

Slavery excludes the principle of competition, which reduces the wages of the free laborer, increases his hours of work, and sometimes deprives him of means of subsistence. The maintenance of slaves as one household, or *familia*, likewise conduces to thrift; their supply on a large scale is, or ought to be, less expensive than when each laborer, as in a state of freedom, has a separate cottage and a family of his own. With slaves thus supported, there is no more waste than with horses or cattle. There is none of the loss or damage which arises from the drunkenness and improvidence of the free laborer expending his own wages. . . .

Chapter XXI. Negro Slavery

. . . The world at large looks on negro slavery as much the worst form of slavery; because it is only acquainted with West India slavery. Abolition never arose till negro slavery was instituted; and now abolition is only directed against negro slavery. There is no philanthropic crusade attempting to set free the white slaves of Eastern Europe and of Asia. The world, then, is prepared for the defense of slavery in the abstract—it is prejudiced only against negro slavery. These prejudices were in their origin well founded. The Slave Trade, the horrors of the Middle Passage, and West India slavery were enough to rouse the most torpid philanthropy.

But our Southern slavery has become a benign and protective institution, and our negroes are confessedly better off than any free laboring population in the world.

How can we contend that white slavery is wrong, whilst all the great body of free laborers are starving; and slaves, white or black, throughout the world, are enjoying comfort?

We write in the cause of Truth and Humanity, and will not play the advocate for master or for slave.

The aversion to negroes, the antipathy of race, is much greater at the North than at the South; and it is very probable that this antipathy to the person of the negro, is confounded with or generates hatred of the institution with which he is usually connected. Hatred of slavery is very generally little more than hatred of negroes.

There is one strong argument in favor of negro slavery over all other slavery:

that he, being unfitted for the mechanic arts, for trade, and all skillful pursuits, leaves those pursuits to be carried on by the whites; and does not bring all industry into disrepute, as in Greece and Rome, where the slaves were not only the artists and mechanics, but also the merchants.

Whilst, as a general and abstract question, negro slavery has no other claim over other forms of slavery, except that from inferiority, or rather peculiarity, of race, almost all negroes require masters, whilst only the children, the women, the very weak, poor, and ignorant, &c., among the whites, need some protective and governing relation of this kind; yet as a subject of temporary, but worldwide importance, negro slavery has become the most necessary of all human institutions.

Source Note: George Fitzhugh, *Cannibals All! or, Slaves without Masters* (Richmond, VA, 1857).

DAVID CHRISTY (1802–N.D.) AND E. N. ELLIOTT (N.D.)

In 1860, E. N. Elliott compiled important and influential proslavery documents into a single volume called *Cotton Is King, and Pro-slavery Arguments; Comprising the Writings of [James H.] Hammond, Harper, [David] Christy, [Thornton] Stringfellow, Hodge, [Albert T.] Bledsoe, and Cartwright, on this Important Subject*. Elliot took the title of his volume from David Christy's 1855 essay *Cotton Is King: or, The Culture of Cotton, and Its Relation to Agriculture, Manufactures and Commerce*. Elliott's and Christy's titles allude to "King Cotton," a political jibe at the imperious influence that cotton producers exercised on the U.S. Congress. They also refer to James H. Hammond's 1858 prediction that, if the South were prevented by war or chose not to produce a cotton crop for three years, the economy of both England and the North would be destroyed. "You dare not make war on cotton," said Hammond. "No power on earth dares to make war upon it. Cotton is king."[1]

Elliott designed his volume to reply to the antislavery arguments of the abolitionists, including Stowe's novel *Uncle Tom's Cabin*. He included a variety of essays, most concerned with the economy of slavery and the survival of the Southern plantation. Elliott did not emphasize biblical, moral, or historical justifications for slavery, though he did include an essay by Thornton Stringfellow (who is represented in chapter 3 of this volume). Rather, he emphasized pragmatic ones, and *Cotton Is King* is focused on economic arguments. Though the arguments would be considered superficial by modern standards of economic analysis, the essays illustrate the present state of affairs in the slave states, and some of the essays prophesy the economic future of the plantation system if slavery were abolished. Most of the authors concluded that the Southern plantation economy was the backbone of the national economy, and they argued that without it, the national economy would deteriorate rapidly.

There is a reference in Christy's essay to Benjamin Franklin. Franklin voiced his opposition to chattel slavery (not to indentured servitude), and he published

John Woolman's *Some Considerations on the Keeping of Negroes* (1762), excerpted in chapter 1.

While *Cotton Is King* did not have the national impact of George Fitzhugh's *Sociology for the South* (1854) and *Cannibals All!* (1857), it was reprinted several times, and it garnered support for the proslavery advocates who sought an economic justification for the continuation and extension of slavery.

1. James Henry Hammond, "On the Admission of Kansas, Under the Lecompton Constitution," speech given in the U.S. Senate, March 4, 1858. *Congressional Globe*, 35th Congress, 1st Session, vol. 27, pt. 1, p. 961.

Introduction to Cotton Is King, *and Proslavery Arguments*
by E. N. Elliott

In the following pages, the words *slave* and *slavery* are not used in the sense commonly understood by the abolitionists. With them, these terms are contradistinguished from *servants* and *servitude*. According to their definition, a slave is merely a "chattel" in human form; a *thing* to be bought and sold, and treated worse than a brute; a being without rights, privileges or duties. Now, if this is a correct definition of the word, we totally object to the term, and deny that we have any such institution as *slavery* among us. We recognize among us no class, which, as the abolitionists falsely assert that the Supreme Court decided, "had no rights which a white man was bound to respect." The words *slave* and *servant* are perfectly synonymous, and differ only in being derived from different languages; the one from Slavonic, the other from the Latin, just as feminine and womanly are respectively of Latin and Saxon origin. . . .

The word *slavery* is used in the following discussions, to express the condition of the *African race* in our Southern States, as also in the other parts of the world, and in other times. This word, as defined by most writers, does not truly express the relation which the African race in our country *now* bears to the white race. . . .

The true definition of the term, as applicable to the domestic institution in the Southern States is as follows: Slavery is the duty and obligation of the slave to labor for the mutual benefit of both master and slave, under a warrant to the slave of protection, and a comfortable subsistence, under all circumstances. The person of the slave is not property, no matter what the fictions of the law may say, but the right to his property, or as the right to the services of a minor or an apprentice may be transferred. Nor is the labor of the slave concerned; for himself, to repay the advances made for this support in childhood, for present subsistence, and for guardianship and protection, and to accumulate a fund for sickness, disability, and old age. The master, as the head of the system, has a right to the obedience and labor of the slave, but the slave has also his mutual rights in the master: the right of protection, the right of counsel and guidance, the right of subsistence, the right of care and attention in sickness and old age. He has also a right in his master as the sole arbiter in all his wrongs and difficulties, and as a merciful judge and dispenser of law. . . . Such is American slavery. . . .

Source Note: E. N. Elliott, "Introduction," *Cotton Is King, and Proslavery Arguments: Comprising the Writings of Hammond, Harper, Christy, Stringfellow, Hodge, Bledsoe, and Cartwright, on this Important Subject* (Augusta, GA, 1860).

Cotton Is King
by David Christy

. . . The issue taken, that slavery is *malum in se*—a sin in itself—was prosecuted with all the zeal and eloquence they [the abolitionists] could command. Churches, adopting the *per se* doctrine, inquired of their converts, not whether they supported slavery, by the use of its products, but whether they believed the institution itself sinful. Could public sentiment be brought to assume the proper ground; could the slaveholder be convinced that the world denounced him as equally criminal with the robber and murderer; then, it was believed, he would abandon the system. Political parties, subsequently organized, taught, that to vote for a slaveholder, or a pro-slavery man, was sinful, and could not be done without violence to conscience; while, at the same time, they made no scruples of using the products of slave labor—the exorbitant demand for which was the great bulwark of the institution. This was a radical error. . . . As long as all used their products, so long the slaveholders found the *per se* doctrine working them no harm; as long as no provision was made for supplying the demand for tropical products, by free labor, so long there was no risk in extending the field of their operations. Thus, the very things necessary to the overthrow of American slavery were left undone, while those essential to its prosperity were continued in the most active operation; so that, now, after nearly a "thirty-years' war," we may say, emphatically, COTTON IS KING, and his enemies are vanquished.

. . . We propose, therefore, to examine this subject, as it stands connected with the history of our country; and especially to afford some light to the free colored man, on the true relations he sustains to African slavery, and to the redemption of his race.

. . . The work of emancipation, begun by the four States named [Massachusetts, Connecticut, Ohio, and Rhode Island], continued to progress, so that, in seventeen years from the adoption of the Constitution, New Hampshire, Vermont, New York, and New Jersey had also enacted laws to free themselves from the burden of slavery.

. . . When the four States first named liberated their slaves, no regular exports of cotton to Europe had yet commenced; and the year New Hampshire set hers free, only 138,328 pounds of that article shipped from the country. Simultaneously with the action of Vermont, in the year following, the *Cotton Gin* was invented, and an unparalleled impulse given to the cultivation of cotton. At the same time, Louisiana, with her immense territory, was added to the Union and room for the extension of slavery vastly increased. New York lagged behind

Vermont for six years before taking her first step to free her slaves, when she found the exports of cotton to England had reached 9,500,500. . . .

Four years after the emancipations by states had ceased, the slave trade was prohibited; but, as if each movement for freedom must have its counter-movement to stimulate slavery, that same year the manufacture of cotton goods was commenced in Boston. . . . But the year 1817, memorable in this connection, from its being the date of the organization of the Colonization Society, found our exports augmented to 95,660,000 lbs., and her consumption enlarged to 126,240,000 lbs. Carding and spinning machinery had now reached a good degree of perfection, and the power-loom was brought into general use in England, and was also introduced into the United States. Steamboats, too, were coming into use, in both countries; and great activity prevailed in commerce, manufactures, and the cultivation of cotton.

. . . With freedom to the slaves came anxieties among the whites as to the results. Nine years after Pennsylvania and Massachusetts had taken the lead in the trial of Emancipation, [Benjamin] Franklin issued an Appeal for aid to enable his Society to form a plan for the promotion of industry, intelligence, and morality among the free blacks. . . . He expressed his belief, that such is the debasing influence of slavery on human nature that its very extirpation, if not performed with care, may sometimes open a source of serious evils; and that so far as emancipation should be promoted by the Society, it was a duty incumbent on its members to instruct, to advise, to qualify those restored to freedom, for the exercise and enjoyment of civil liberty.

How far Franklin's influence failed to promote the humane object he had in view, may be inferred from the fact, that forty-seven years after Pennsylvania struck off the shackles from her slaves, and thirty-eight years after he issued his Appeal, one-third of the convicts in her penitentiary were colored men. . . .

. . . The failure of Franklin's plan for their elevation confirmed the popular belief that such an undertaking was impractical; and the whole African race, freedmen as well as slaves, were viewed as an intolerable burden—such as the imports of foreign paupers are now considered. Thus, the free colored people themselves, ruthlessly threw the car of emancipation from its track, and tore up the rails on which, alone, it could move.

. . . The slow progress made by the great body of the free blacks in the North, or the absence, rather, of any evidences of improvement in industry, intelligence, and morality, gave rise to the notion that, before they could be elevated to an equality with whites, slavery must be wholly abolished throughout the Union. . . . Those who adopted this view, seem to have overlooked the fact that the Africans, of savage origin, could not be elevated at once to an equality with the American people, by the mere force of legal enactments. More than this was needed for their elevation, as all are now reluctantly compelled to acknowledge.

. . . The improvement of the free colored people, in the presence of the slave, was considered impracticable. Slave labor had become so profitable as to leave little ground to expect general emancipation, even though all other objections had been removed. The slave trade had increased twenty-five percent during the preceding ten years. Slavery was rapidly extending itself in the tropics, and could not be arrested but by the suppression of the slave trade. The foothold of the Christian missionary was yet so precarious in Africa as to leave it doubtful whether he could sustain his position.

. . . When the statistics on the subject be examined, it appears that nearly all the cotton consumed in the Christian world is the product of the slave labor of the United States. This is the monopoly that has given slavery its commercial value; and, while this monopoly is retained, the institution will continue to extend itself wherever it can find room to spread.

This is not all. The economical value of slavery, as an agency for supplying the means of extending manufactures and commerce, has long been understood by statesmen. The discovery of the power of steam, and the inventions in machinery, for preparing and manufacturing cotton, revealed the important fact that a single Island, having the monopoly secured to itself, could supply the world with clothing. *Great Britain attempted to gain this monopoly*; and to prevent other countries from rivaling her, she long prohibited all emigration of skillful mechanics from the kingdom as well as all exports of machinery.

. . . In speaking of the economical connections of slavery, with the other material interests of the world, we have called it a *tri-partite alliance*. It is more than this. It is *quadruple*. Its structure includes four parties, arranged thus: The Western Agriculturists; the Southern Planters; the English Manufacturers; and the American Abolitionists! By this arrangement, the abolitionists do not stand in direct contact with slavery; they imagine, therefore, that they have clean hands and pure hearts, so far as sustaining the system is concerned. But they, no less than their allies, aid in promoting the interests of slavery. Their sympathies are with England on the slavery questions, and they very naturally incline to agree with her on other points. She advocates *Free Trade* as essential to her manufactures and commerce; and they do the damage, not willing to inquire into its bearings upon *American Slavery*. We refer now to the people, not to their leaders, whose integrity we choose not to endorse. The free trade and protective systems, in their bearings upon slavery, are so well understood, that no man of general reading, especially an editor, or member of Congress, who professes anti-slavery sentiments, at the same time advocating free trade, will ever convince men of intelligence, pretend what he may, that he is not either woefully perverted in his judgment, or emphatically a "dough face" in disguise! England, we were about to say, is in alliance with the cotton planter, to whose prosperity free trade is indispensable. Abolitionism is in alliance with England. All three of these parties, then, agree in their support of the free trade policy. It needed but the aid of the Western farmer, therefore, to give permanency to this principle. His adhesion has been given, the *quadruple alliance* has been perfected, and slavery and free trade *nationalized*!

Source Note: David Christy, *Cotton Is King: Of the Culture of Cotton, and Its Relation to Agriculture, Manufactures and Commerce; to the Free Colored People; and to Those Who Hold That Slavery Is in Itself Sinful, by an American* (Cincinnati: 1855).

Hinton Rowan Helper (1829–1909)

Hinton Rowan Helper wrote one of the most important antislavery documents published in the heated decade before the Civil War. *The Impending Crisis of the South and How to Meet It* (1857) was even more significant because Helper was a North Carolinian, making him a Southern abolitionist at a period when the antebellum slavery debates had heated to explosive temperatures. Helper was unable to find a publisher anywhere in the South because the book advised the forcible overthrow of slavery by organized efforts of nonslaveholding white laborers, and Southern slaveholders lived in increasing fear of another insurrection such as the Nat Turner rebellion of 1831. Helper's book was eventually published by a Northern press, and he dedicated the volume to the "non-slaveholding Whites of the South." While George Fredrickson rightly calls Helper's book, together with Stowe's *Uncle Tom's Cabin*, one of the most significant antislavery publications to appear before the Civil War, Wallace Hettle argues that

> Helper's contempt for aristocratic slaveholders resonated throughout the book, and he posited that slavery did not produce profits because it exhausted the soil and impoverished nonslaveholders by degrading manual labor. Having little hope that the master class would change its way of life, and wishing instead for a political revolt of nonslaveholding whites against an economic system that denied job opportunities readily available to Northern workers, Helper demanded that nonslaveholding whites must be organized for independent political action. Although he asked for immediate abolition of slavery, Helper hated slaves even more than their owners. He saw abolition as a historic opportunity to remove African Americans from the South, and advocated removing African Americans to Central America or to Africa. [Hettle, p. 338]

An abridged edition of 100,000 copies was published in 1858, and the book became central to the congressional debates about slavery that occupied Congress in 1859. "Helperism" was a derisive term that arose to characterize those who supported Helper's brand of abolitionism, and his book was rejoined by numerous opposing views, one of which is excerpted here, Samuel Wolfe's *Impending Crisis Dissected* (1860). The reader will find that Helper's argument depended on an economic analysis of the institution of slavery, using some of the same statistics that proslavery advocates were using to endorse its continuation and perpetuation. Helper succeeded not only in dividing Northerners and Southerners over the issue of slavery; he also succeeded in dividing the aristocratic Southern planter, or plantation owner, from the white Southern farmer who worked for low wages and often without slave labor. *The Impending Crisis* was, in every sense of the word, an extremely important and divisive work. George Fredrickson's edition of the book is excerpted here, including some of his introduction.

SUGGESTIONS FOR FURTHER READING

Bailey, Hugh C. *Hinton Rowan Helper: Abolitionist Racist.* Tuscaloosa: University of Alabama Press, 1965.

Fredrickson, George, ed. *Hinton Rowan Helper's "The Impending Crisis of the South and How to Meet It."* Cambridge: Harvard University Press, 1968.

Hettle, Wallace. "Hinton Rowan Helper." In *Encyclopedia of World Slavery*, ed. Junius Rodriguez (Oxford: ABC-CLIO, 1997), pp. 337–39.

Introduction to The Impending Crisis of the South
by George Fredrickson

The Impending Crisis of the South by Hinton Rowan Helper is one of those rare works which not only gave direct and vivid expression to an historical situation, but also had a dramatic influence in shaping events. Indeed, it would not be difficult to make a case for *The Impending Crisis* as the most important single book, in terms of its political impact, that has ever been published in the United States. Even more perhaps than *Uncle Tom's Cabin*, it fed the fires of sectional controversy leading up to the Civil War; for it had the distinction of being the only book in American History to become the center of bitter and prolonged Congressional debate.

The work of an obscure North Carolinian who had migrated to the North, *The Impending Crisis* was published in New York in 1857 at the author's own risk. As an attack on slavery, it said very little that had not been said before. But two things about the book drew the interest of Horace Greeley, influential antislavery editor of the *New York Tribune*. One was the potential effectiveness of the book as an antislavery polemic. It combined, as Greeley put it in a full-page review on the day the book was published, the "heavy artillery of statistics" with "rolling volleys and dashing charges of argument and rhetoric." Secondly, it was written by a Southerner and attacked slavery by appealing to the interests of the non-slaveholding Whites of the South. . . .

After its initial publication, the book was promoted by Greeley, praised by the antislavery press, and attacked violently in the South. On March 20, 1858, it was cited in Senate debate by Senator Henry Wilson of Massachusetts as an accurate picture of Southern society and the harmful effects of slavery. . . . In July of 1859, a new version, the *Compendium of the Impending Crisis of the South*, was published, with the endorsement of a number of Republican leaders, and plans were quickly developed to distribute this version as a Republican document during the election campaign of 1860. The *Compendium* was a somewhat watered down version of the original, with some of the inflammatory passages and personal attacks deleted. But the substance of the argument was untouched: slavery was totally incompatible with economic progress and individual opportunity, and should be abolished in the interest of the oppressed non-slaveholding majority of the South. By December 1859, the demand for the *Compendium* was enormous; the *New York Tribune*, as the main source of distribution, was sending out five hundred copies a day and hoped to increase the number to one thousand. . . .

Source Note: George Fredrickson, "Introduction," *The Impending Crisis of the South and How to Meet It*, by Hinton Rowan Helper (Cambridge: Harvard University Press, 1968).

The Impending Crisis of the South and How to Meet It
by Hinton Rowan Helper

Here are truths. "Southern men expect to get talent without paying for it." A very natural expectation, considering that they have been accustomed to have all their material wants supplied by the uncompensated toil of their slaves. In this instance it may seem an absurd one, but it results legitimately from the system of slavery. That system, in fact, operates in a two-fold way against the Southern publisher; first, by its practical repudiation of the scriptural axiom that the laborer is worthy of his hire; and secondly, by restricting the circle of readers through the ignorance which it inevitably engenders. How is it that the people of the North build up their literature?—Two words reveal the secret: *intelligence—compensation*. They are *a reading people*—the poorest artisan or day-laborer has his shelf of books, or his daily or weekly paper, whose contents he seldom fails to master before retiring at night; and *they are accustomed to pay for all the books and papers which they peruse*. Readers and payers—these are the men who insure the prosperity of publishers. Where a system of enforced servitude prevails, it is very apt to beget loose notions about the obligation of paying for anything; and many minds fail to see the distinction, morally, between compelling Sambo to pick cotton without paying him wages, or compelling Lippincott & Co. to manufacture books for the planter's pleasure or edification upon the same liberal terms. . . .

WHAT HAS PRODUCED THIS LITERARY PAUPERISM OF THE SOUTH?

One single word, most pregnant in its terrible meanings, answers the question. That word is—SLAVERY! But we have been so long accustomed to the ugly thing itself, and have become so familiar with its no less ugly fruits, that the common mind fails to apprehend the connection between the one, as cause, and the other as effect; and it therefore becomes necessary to give a more detailed answer to our interrogatory. . . .

The truth is, there is a vast inert mass of stupidity and ignorance, too dense for individual effort to enlighten or remove, in all communities cursed with the institution of slavery. Disguise the unwelcome truth as we may, slavery is the parent of ignorance, and ignorance begets a whole brood of follies and of vices, and every one of these is inevitably hostile to literary culture. The masses, if they think of literature at all, think of it only as a costly luxury, to be monopolized by the few. . . .

Our limits, not our materials, are exhausted. We would gladly say more, but can only, in conclusion, add as the result of our investigations in this department of our subject, that *Literature and Liberty are inseparable; the one can never have a vigorous existence without being wedded to the other*.

Our work is done. It is the voice of the non-slaveholding whites of the South, through one identified with them by interest, by feeling, by position. That voice, by whomsoever spoken, must yet be heard and heeded. The time hastens—the doom of slavery is written—the redemption of the South draws nigh. . . .

Chapter II. How Slavery Can Be Abolished

. . . The oligarchs say we cannot abolish slavery without infringing on the right of property. Again we tell them we do not recognize property in man; but even if we did, and if we were to inventory the negroes at quadruple the value of the last assessment, still, impelled by a sense of duty to others, and as a matter of simple justice to ourselves, we, the non-slaveholders of the South, would be fully warranted in emancipating all the slaves at once, and that, too, without any compensation whatever to those who claim to be their absolute masters and owners. . . .

This claim we bring against you, because slavery, which has inured exclusively to your own benefit, if, indeed, it has been beneficial at all, has shed a blighting influence over our lands, thereby keeping them out of market, and damaging every acre to the amount specified. Sirs! are you ready to settle the account? Let us see how much it is. There are in fifteen slave States, 346,048 slaveholders, and 544,926,720 acres of land. Now the object is to ascertain how many acres are owned by slaveholders, and how many by non-slaveholders. Suppose we estimate five hundred acres as the average landed property of each slaveholder, will that be fair? We think it will, taking into consideration the fact that 174,503 of the whole number of slaveholders hold less than five slaves each— 68,820 holding only one each. According to this hypothesis, the slaveholders own 173,024,000 acres, and the non-slaveholders the balance, with the exception of about 40,000 of acres, which belong to the General Government. The case may be stated thus:

	Area of the Slave States	544,926,720 acres
Estimates	Acres owned by slaveholders	173,024,000
Estimates	Acres owned by the government	40,000,000–213,024,000
Estimates	Acres owned by non-slaveholders	331,902,720

Now, *chevaliers* of lash, and worshipers of slavery, the total value of three hundred and thirty-one million nine hundred and two thousand seven hundred and twenty acres, at twenty-two dollars and twenty-three cents per acre, is *seven billion five hundred and forty-four million one hundred and forty-eight thousand eight hundred and twenty-five dollars*; and this is our account against you on a single score. Considering how your villainous institution has retarded the development of our commercial and manufacturing interests, how it has stifled the aspiration of the inventive genius; and, above all, how it has barred from us the heaven-born sweets of literature and religion—concernments too sacred to be estimated in a pecuniary point of view—might we not, with perfect justice and propriety, duplicate the amount, and still be accounted modest in our demands? Fully advised, however, of your indigent circumstances we feel it would be utterly useless to call on you for the whole amount that is due us; we shall, therefore, in your behalf, make another draft on the fund of non-slaveholding generosity, and let the account, meager as it is, stand as above. . . .

. . . The amount of that damage is $7,544,148,825; and now, Sirs, we are ready to receive the money, and if it is perfectly convenient to you, we would be glad to have you pay it in specie! It will not avail you, sirs, to parley or prevaricate. We must have a settlement. Our claim is just and overdue. We have already indulged you too long. Your criminal extravagance has almost ruined us. We are determined that you shall no longer play the profligate, and fare sumptuously every day at our expense. How do you propose to settle? Do you offer us your negroes in part payment? We do not want your negroes. We would not have all of them, nor any number of them, even as a gift. We hold ourselves above the disreputation and iniquitous practices of buying, selling, and owning slaves. What we demand is damages in money, or other absolute property, as an equivalent for the pecuniary losses we have suffered at your hands. You value your negroes at sixteen hundred millions of dollars, and propose to sell them to us for that sum; we should consider ourselves badly cheated, and disgraced for all time, here and hereafter, if we were to take them off your hands at sixteen farthings! We tell you emphatically, we are firmly resolved never to degrade ourselves by becoming the mercenary purchasers or proprietors of human beings. Except for the purpose of liberating them, we would not give a handkerchief or a tooth-pick for all the slaves in the world. But, in order to show how brazenly absurd are the howls and groans which you invariably set up for compensation, whenever we speak of the abolition of slavery, we will suppose your negroes are worth all you ask for them, and that we are bound to secure to you every cent of the sum before they can become free—in which case, our accounts would stand thus:

Non-slaveholder's account against slaveholders	$7,544,148,825
Slaveholders' account against non-slaveholders	$1,600,000,000
Balance due non-slaveholders	$5,944,148,825

Now, Sirs, we ask you in all seriousness, It is not true that you have filched from us nearly five times the amount of the assessed value of your slaves? Why, then, do you still clamor for more?

Out of our effects your have long since over paid yourselves for your negroes; and now, Sirs, you *must* emancipate them—speedily emancipate them, or we will emancipate them for you! Every non-slave holder in the south is, or ought to join us at once in our laudable crusade against "the mother of harlots." Slavery has polluted and impoverished your lands; freedom will restore them to their virgin purity, and add from twenty to thirty dollars to the value of every acre. Correctly speaking, emancipation will cost you nothing; the moment you abolish slavery, that very moment will putative value of the slave become actual value in soil. . . .

What is the import of these figures? They are full of meaning. They proclaim themselves the financial intercessors for freedom, and, with that open-hearted liberality which is so characteristic of the sacred cause in whose behalf they plead, they propose to pay you upward of three thousand nine hundred millions of dollars for the very "property" which you, in all the reckless extravagance of your inhuman avarice, could not find a heart to price at more than one thousand six hundred millions. In other words, your own lands, groaning and anguishing under the monstrous burden of slavery, announce their willingness to pay you all you ask for the negroes, and offer you, besides, a bonus of more than twenty-three hundred millions of dollars, if you will but convert those lands into free soil! *Our* lands, also, cry aloud to be spared from the further pollutions and desolations of slavery; and now, Sirs, we want to know explicitly, whether or not, it is your intention to heed these lamentations of the ground? We want to know whether you are men or devils—whether you are entirely selfish and cru-elly dishonest, or whether you have any respect for the rights of others. We, the non-slaveholders of the South, have many very important interests at stake—interests which, heretofore, you have steadily despised and trampled under foot, but which henceforth, we shall foster and defend in utter defiance of all the unhallowed influences which it is possible for you, or any other class of slave-holders or slavebreeders to bring against us. Not the least among these interests is our landed property, which, to command a decent price, only needs to be disencumbered of slavery. . . .

Some few years ago, when certain ethnographical oligarchs proved to their own satisfaction that the negro was an inferior "type of mankind," they chuckled wonderfully, and avowed, in substance, that it was right for the stronger race to kidnap and enslave the weaker—that because Nature had been pleased to do a trifle more for the Caucasian race than for the African, the former, by virtue of its superiority, was perfectly justifiable in holding the latter in absolute and perpetual bondage! No system of logic could be more antagonistic to the spirit of true democracy. It is probable that the world does not contain two persons who are exactly alike in all respects; yet "*all* men are endowed by their Creator with certain *inalienable* rights, among which are life, *liberty*, and the pursuit of happiness." All mankind may or may not be the descendants of Adam and Eve. In our own humble way of thinking, we are frank to confess, we do not believe in the unity of the races. This is a matter, however, which has little or nothing to do with the great question at issue. Aside from any theory concerning the original parentage of the different races of men, facts, material and immaterial, palpable and impalpable—facts of the eyes and facts of the conscience—crowd around us on every hand, heaping proof upon proof, that slavery is a shame, a crime, and a curse—a great moral, social, civil, and political evil—an oppressive burden to the blacks, and an incalculable injury to the whites—a stumbling block to the nation, an impediment to progress, a damper on all the nobler instincts, principles, aspirations and enterprises of man, and a dire enemy to every true interest.

Waiving all other counts, we have, we think, shown to the satisfaction of every impartial reader, that as elsewhere stated, on the single score of damages to lands, the slave holders, are, at this moment, indebted to us, the non-slave-holding whites, in the enormous sum of nearly seventy-six hundred millions of dollars. What shall be done with this amount? It is just; shall payment be demanded? No; all the slaveholders in the country could not pay it; nor shall we ever ask them for even a moiety of the amount—no, not even for a dime, nor yet for a cent; we are willing to forfeit every farthing for the sake of freedom; for ourselves we ask no indemnification for the past: we only demand justice for the future.

Source Note: Hinton Rowan Helper, *The Impending Crisis of the South and How to Meet It*, ed. George Fredrickson (Cambridge: Harvard University Press, 1968), and Harvey Wish, ed., *The Antebellum Writings of Hinton Rowan Helper and George Fitzhugh* (New York: Capricorn Books, 1960).

Impending Crisis Dissected
by Samuel M. Wolfe

I could not insult that gentleman [Hinton Rowan Helper] more grossly than to ask him if he is willing to throw open the sacred precincts of his family and allow the negro to come in as an equal member. No, sir; but he is for *freeing his labor*, and, possibly, for giving him the right of voting, and by that means bringing him in contact and equality, *not with himself*, but with *the laboring white freemen of the North*; and why such a proposition does not kindle a consuming flame of indignation among those laboring freemen of the North, is one of those political phenomena for which I will not undertake to account.

Sir, the only cause of the difference between the legislation of the Northern and Southern States upon the subject of slavery is, that the negroes are not sufficient in numbers at the North to make it necessary to reduce them to the conditions of domestic servitude, while with us that condition is indispensable to the good order and welfare of the whole society. And it is demonstrable—and I will make it so appear, if I have time—that the negro in the Southern States has reached a moral and intellectual development. That he contributes more, in his present condition, to the good of mankind, and that their moral and intellectual development is superior to his race in any other position in which he has been placed. What was his condition when he was first brought here? Look at him upon his native continent. The most humane explorers of the African continent tell us that they exist there without social or political order, without modesty or shame,—some of the tribes not even reaching the civilization of the fig-leaf.

"The negro, as already observed, exhibits the natural man in his completely wild and untamed state." Free as the wild bird of his native forest, bold as the stream which dashed down his mountain gorges, generous as the bounteous nature around him, the American Indian goes into history the poetic embodiment of savage life. What has been his fate, compared with that of the African?

What has become of the Narragansetts, Pequots, Senecas, Oneidas, and Delawares? Driven back by the advancing wave of European civilization to continually contracting circles, with diminished means of subsistence, into degradation, wretchedness, and extinction.

The African, with all its foulness, with all its prosaic vulgarities, domesticated and disciplined, has been by the same wave borne up higher and higher, until now it furnishes inspiration for Northern song, heroes and heroines for Northern romances, and is invited by Northern statesmen into their charmed circle of political and social equality. Not just yet, gentlemen, if you please. He is not your equal; and history proves that even when he has reached this point of civilization, if you take from under him the institution which has borne him up to it, he relapses into his pristine barbarism.

How do the interests of the white race require the restriction of slavery? They say that free labor is dishonored by its contact with slave labor. How? The two systems co-exist under our Republic. Look at labor as it exists at the North—the mighty North—the seat of commerce, manufacturers, mechanic arts, accumulated wealth, and common schools. Look at the mighty population that fills that vast territory with the hum of its free industry. . . .

Mr. Helper quotes the Bible as condemning slavery. Man will, when his mind becomes prejudiced, pervert the Holy Scriptures to evil,—his ideas thus giving it a meaning that was never intended by the inspired writers, viz: a contradiction of itself.

In Rome. "For slaves the lash was the common punishment; but for certain crimes, they used to be branded on the forehead, and sometimes were forced to carry a piece of wood round their necks wherever they went. When slaves were beaten, they used to be suspended with a weight tied to their feet, that they might not move them. When punished capitally, they were commonly crucified. If a master of a family was slain in his own house, and the murderer not discovered, all his domestic slaves were liable to be put to death. There was a continual market for slaves at Rome. The seller was bound to promise for the soundness of his slaves, and not to conceal their faults. Hence they were commonly exposed to sale naked; and they carried a scroll hanging at their necks, on which their good and bad qualities were specified."—Adam's Rom. Ant. pp. 48, 51.

In Greece. The condition of slaves in Greece appears to have been much the same as at Rome.—Potter's Gr. Ant. 1, 10.

If it be answered to this, that the race is one condemned by heaven, and the authority of the Old Testament (which is not recognized as applicable by modern science) is cited to explain the reasons for that state of degradation which has ever been the lot of the African;

But, perhaps, the Northern philanthropist to whom these arguments were supposed to be addressed, having been fortunate enough to be born in Boston, and therefore, by divine right, knowing rather more than other people, might have answered the questions, though he could not have denied the facts.

"Jefferson, in his *Notes* [*on the State of Virginia*], says slavery is an evil," (vehemently assert the gentlemen from the North). And Jefferson was a slaveholder, and a Virginian, too. Certainly, he was more than this: he was a patriot—the author of the Declaration of Independence. He was a scholar, and a philosopher in his way also. But then Jefferson was, after all, a man, and "*humanum est errare*" was as true when he lived as at this day.

Unfortunately for his authority upon this point, most of that knowledge which can really render this question of slavery or abolition a rational one, was then unknown, or had, rather, no regular or scientific form. History, it is true, taught its lessons then as now. . . .

Yet slavery in the nations of antiquity, and also of the middle ages, was far more reprehensible than that of the United States: for it was the bondage of the white man to the white man—of equal to equal—as the event has in all these instances shown.

To sum up: We know that, in the scale of humanity, the negro holds the lowest place; that no system of jurisprudence, no principle of science, no rule of art, has ever originated from the brain of an African.

That he has not the capacity for becoming, under any circumstances, an enlightened man; that the nearest approach to that state which he has made has not been permanent; and that, deprived of his teacher, he again degenerates into the condition of a barbarian.

If the hypothesis before stated be true to the extent to which some persons interpret it, the assertion of the "*equality*" of the races is neither more nor less than a contradiction of the manifest will, and an endeavor to change the evident intention of the creator, and the attempted demonstration by the Scriptures of the enormity of slaveholding becomes an absurdity.

It is a fact well authenticated, that certain differences exist between the four great types of mankind, which have been permanent since the earliest period to which our knowledge extends. Whether the examination and analysis of these idiosyncrasies are sufficient to prove that the Caucasian, American, Mongol, and Negro were aborigine, distinct and different races, is not our intention to inquire. All that we shall attempt is a demonstration of the physical inferiority of the African to the white man, and a brief review of the reasons which these afford us for placing this species of the "*genus homo*" in the rank which nature appears to have designed them to occupy.

The culminating point in the scale of created beings (physically considered) is man,—and of men, the Caucasian. The nearer the approach to this type, the greater the capacity has been, the more powerful the influence upon the history of humanity, and the more enlightened the individual and nation. This type, moreover, presents besides the physical conformation most in accordance with the ideal in art, peculiarities of temperament and intellect which have, under all circumstances, urged them onward; they are the masters of the world,—the investigators, the inventors.

Between the first mentioned race (the Caucasian) and the Negro, two great types intervene, the Mongol and the American; the first, capable of civilization but not enlightenment; the second, in his pure and unmixed blood, incapable of either.

Without asserting the identity of the spiritual and material, it is an indisputable fact that intellectual superiority generally depends upon and is coincident with organic. Though the quality, rather than the quantity, of the brain, is considered the sign of mind, yet it is as impossible to suppose the power of an engine residing in its miniature paten, as the intelligence for the cranium whose facial angle is 85 degrees existing in one of little more than half the capacity. The lower orders of animated nature, are ranked according to their approach to the anatomical structure of man. The same holds good in the classification for the races themselves. The negro is the further removed from the perfect type, and the nearest to the anthropoid simian of any.

Nature has, for three thousand years, made no change in this conformation, and as the law of hybridity applies as well to men as other animals, is not likely to do so now. The profession of friendship and brotherly kindness on the part of the Abolition Party, can scarcely make a difference in the shape of the bones of the cranium and body. And while these do exist, if there can be any judgment of the future, formed from the events of the past, the African will still be a slave, if not to one master, at least to another.

Source Note: Samuel M. Wolfe, *Impending Crisis Dissected* (Philadelphia: J. T. Lloyd, 1860).

Writers and Essayists in Conflict over Slavery

Nineteenth-century American writers are perhaps the best-known literary ambassadors ever to represent the United States. Names like Nathaniel Hawthorne, Herman Melville, Washington Irving, Ralph Waldo Emerson, Henry David Thoreau, Emily Dickinson, Frederick Douglass, Walt Whitman, Mark Twain, Henry James, Stephen Crane, Harriet Beecher Stowe, Kate Chopin, and Edith Wharton are now so well recognized that we often forget how obscure some of these figures were in their own time. For example, after the Harper's fire in 1852, when most of the first edition of *Moby-Dick* was burned, the now-classic American epic was never reprinted during Melville's lifetime. Stowe's role as an abolitionist author is well remembered; but the sections of *Leaves of Grass* in which Walt Whitman voices similar antislavery sentiments are less well recognized, as are Emerson's antislavery writings, except perhaps for his "Lecture on Slavery." In this section we have brought together a number of writers who express antislavery points of view in their literature, and we have juxtaposed these voices against one significant proslavery writer who represents the other side of the debate. This apparent imbalance is justified because, first, proslavery writers like William Gilmore Simms and George Washington Cable basically echo the viewpoints provided here by James Kirke Paulding, whose 1836 treatise, *Slavery in the United States*, stood for decades as a literary pronouncement concerning the issue of slavery. Similarly, Mary Eastman's "Preface" to *Aunt Phillis's Cabin* (1853) was written as a direct response to Harriet Beecher Stowe's *Uncle Tom's Cabin* (1852) and we have included the "Preface" with Stowe's "Concluding Remarks" as a point-counterpoint representation of pro- and antislavery opinion in fictional representation.

The chapter examines John Greenleaf Whittier's "The Slave Ships," a graphic depiction of the cruelty of the Middle Passage aboard a slaver, which first appeared in *The Liberator* on October 11, 1834. William Lloyd Garrison, the founding editor of the antislavery newspaper, had begun publication on January 1, 1831, and he called for immediate and unconditional emancipation of all chattel slaves held in the United States, regardless of region. He had also recruited to his progressive antislavery cause Whittier, who not only composed antislavery poetry, but also wrote articles for *The Liberator*. James Russell Lowell is another prominent abolitionist literary figure who devoted much writing skill to the composition of antislavery essays, which were collected at the end of the nineteenth century as *The Antislavery Writings of James Russell Lowell*. Lowell's essays are very important because they engage the proslavery advocates by name, as in his response to "Mr. Calhoun's Report" or his essay on Daniel Webster, whom Lowell regarded to be a failure as a thinker and politician because he argued in support of the 1850 Fugitive Slave Law. Walt Whitman is here represented not only by his 1846 essay "Slavers and the Slave Trade" but also by his entry into the free-soil controversy in 1847, with "New States: Shall They Be Slave or Free?" His poem "The House of Friends" (1850) and those sections of *Leaves of Grass* (1855) where antislavery sentiment appears, are accompanied by a new analytical essay by William Pannapacker, who has also edited the selections by Whitman and Emerson.

Emerson is here represented by his famous 1855 "Lecture on Slavery," which is often excerpted but rarely fully reprinted. Thoreau's "A Plea for Captain John Brown" (1858) is not included and is readily available elsewhere, but *Slavery in Massachusetts* is provided. Generally, the Transcendentalists of Concord, Massachusetts, were antislavery in sentiment; though few actively participated in the operation of the Underground Railroad, most spoke against slavery in Lyceum lectures or wrote essays for antislavery publications. None were as determined abolitionists as William Lloyd Garrison and Wendell Phillips, who essentially gave over their entire careers to the antislavery cause, which, we must remember, was never a guaranteed success. In fact, proslavery sentiment was so powerful both North and South that these abolitionist voices appear to us to be far more prominent in the public press than they actually were in antebellum America.

It is significant that Herman Melville entered into the slavery controversy in a veiled manner, through the writing of *Benito Cereno* (1856), a relatively late entry into the fray but one which treats the subject of mutiny aboard a slave ship. While based on actual sources taken from the trial of the mutineers, and the account of Captain Amasa Delano in *Narrative of Voyages and Travels* (1817), the story is a fictional account in which the social and moral issue of slavery is shrouded in an allegory about good and evil, so that Melville's position on the national crisis, just five years before the Civil War, is elusive and unclear. Similarly, while Nathaniel Hawthorne left an unambiguous critique of contemporary utopian socialist movements in *The Blithedale Romance*, and while he spent part of one year in residence at Brook Farm, a Massachusetts utopian commune, he ignored the slavery issue in his writings, although he regularly addressed the parallel issue of women's rights in works such as *The Scarlet Letter* (1850) and *The Blithedale Romance* (1852).

Emerson's "Lecture on Slavery" was edited for this volume by William Pannapacker, who also wrote the accompanying introductory essay. Professor Len Gougeon has contributed an essay on the roles of Emerson and Thoreau as antislavery writers and thinkers in which he clarifies their positions and their contributions to the slavery debates. The Concord Transcendentalists to which they both belonged were not militant abolitionists like their neighbor in Boston, William Lloyd Garrison, Wendell Phillips, and Lydia Maria Child. Nor were their antislavery essays as gripping or immediate as the antebellum slave narratives of Frederick Douglass, Josiah Henson, and Harriet Jacobs. But they contributed their voices and their reputations as writers to the antislavery cause. Each writer's primary material is introduced by headnotes that provide a brief biographical sketch; most also have interpretative commentary that should clarify for the reader each writer's place in the spectrum of antislavery discourse.

One nineteenth-century author must be treated briefly and separately for several reasons. First, Emily Dickinson contributed no essay or poems to the antebellum slavery debates that are the subject of this book. Second, her poems on the slavery issue, and the relations of whites and blacks in the United States, came late in the final decade before the Civil War. Third, her public exposure was severely limited, precisely because she published fewer than ten poems during her entire lifetime, out of the 1,776 belonging to her. Nevertheless, Emily Dickinson deserves mention in this volume, if not full treatment, because she voiced the human dignity of all people in terse, powerful verses like the one that follows this introduction. Moreover, she experienced the Civil War and its harsh consequences through association with men from Amherst who fought in the war, including Thomas Wentworth Higginson, her mentor, friend, and advisor. "Color, Caste, Denomination" is characteristic of her humanistic view of political and social problems, especially slavery and race. While it does not take a political position on slavery, it is clear that Dickinson regarded discrimination based on color to be anathema to her simple humanism. It could easily be argued that she entirely ignored the impact of slavery and the mounting opposition to its perceived immorality because there are so few references to the slavery controversy in Dickinson's verse, and equally few references in her letters. However, the few allusions to slavery that are known are expressions of opposition not only to the inhumanity of the peculiar institution, but also to the injustices and horrors of the Civil War. Dickinson represents writers and citizens who were not active participants in either side of the conflict but whose lives were deeply affected by slavery, racial discrimination, and the war itself.

For example, Dickinson's relationship to her mentor and editor, Thomas Wentworth Higginson, is well known. Not so well known is that Higginson was wounded during the Civil War in South Carolina, where he was the commanding officer of an African-American Union regiment. "Dickinson never questions the specifics of his assignment, or the political implications of [Higginson's] command over a group of African-American soldiers [33rd U.S. Colored Troops, the First South Carolina Regiment]. Instead, she is interested only in the way the war will impact her life, as it affects her close friends and family. She writes in a fearful tone, 'I did not know that you were hurt. Will you tell me more? Mr. Hawthorne died. . . . Will you tell me of your health? I am surprised and anxious since receiving your note'" (Leyda, vol. 2, p. 90). Dickinson internalizes the news concerning Higginson, and converts its message into a brief verse that expresses anxiety about the war in purely personal terms:

> The Only News I know,
> Is bulletins all day
> From Immortality.

"These verses are a sort of playful ways to deal with the news of death she receives on a regular basis—the bulletins from the war, telegrams and letters notifying her of death and injury, even Hawthorne's death seems a 'bulletin from immortality.' Of course she is also punning on her relationship to her own poetry, in that her poems themselves could be construed as 'bulletins' channeled from her muse, immortality" (Tiffany, p. 12).

A more revealing allusion to the Civil War is found in a letter from Dickinson to her Norcross cousins about the death of a soldier from Amherst:

> Mrs. Adams had news of the death of her boy today, from a wound at Annapolis. Telegram signed by Frazar Stearns. You remember him. Another one died in October—from fever caught in the camp. Mrs. Adams has not risen from bed since then. "Happy New Year." Step softly over such doors as these. . . . Frazar Stearns is just leaving Annapolis. I hope that ruddy face won't be brought back frozen. [Leyda, p. 42]

This passage appears to be concerned with the deaths of friends; however, Frazar Stearns, the son of the president of Amherst College, had not yet died, although he would two months after this letter was composed, suggesting that Emily Dickinson had an eerie premonition about casualties in the Civil War based on her preoccupation with immortality and death. Indeed, tragedy in Emily Dickinson's immediate family was averted, in part, because Austin Dickinson, her brother, who lived in the Evergreens next door to the family "Homestead," paid five hundred dollars for a substitute at the time he was drafted (see Tiffany, pp. 12–16).

A valuable insight into Dickinson's awareness of the antebellum slavery debates is found in her father's inconsistent position regarding slavery. Edward Dickinson was elected to Congress in 1852, the year Harriet Beecher Stowe's *Uncle Tom's Cabin* was first published in book form. Dickinson had supported the Missouri Compromise of 1820, at the time regarded to be a liberal, if not antislavery, "compromise" with slaveholding because it prohibited slavery in the territories west of the Mississippi. But Edward Dickinson was also a politician and lawyer, and he understood the importance of the voters' support. In 1861, he wrote to the Massachusetts Republican Party the following words: "Let us denounce, as subversive of all Constitutional guarantees . . . the heretical dogma that immediate and universal emancipation of slaves should be proclaimed by the government, as the means of putting an end to the war" (Leyda, vol. 2, p. 34). This denunciation of William Lloyd Garrison's militant abolitionism and of the Civil War as a way of ending slavery ran counter to all antislavery sentiment of the time. However, by 1863, Dickinson had altered his position and expressed his views this way: "I shall be glad to have this war ended—when the rebellion is crushed between the upper and the nether millstone—and not before—*when slavery has made its last squeak and when traitors have all gone to their own place*" (Leyda, p. 77, as cited by Tiffany p. 14). Edward Dickinson's vengeance is heaped not on the immoral slaveholders of the South, but on Southerners as secessionists. It seems clear that the antebellum slavery debates had little impact on the Dickinson household, and that Emily Dickinson had to find ways of expressing her deeply felt human compassion through verses that celebrated humanity and the horror of war without specifically championing the antislavery cause.

This chapter is concluded with a direct confrontation between Harriet Beecher Stowe's *Uncle Tom's Cabin* (1852) and Mary Eastman's *Aunt Phillis's Cabin* (1853). While few modern readers are familiar with Eastman's account, it was published alongside other proslavery plantation narratives, including John Pendleton Kennedy's *Swallow Barn* (1832), fantasy tales of Southern plantation life that romanticize the antebellum South, while Stowe more realistically depicts the cruelties and barbarities of American slavery. While it may be commonly assumed that fictional writers have little impact in the arena of politics and practical affairs, Stowe's work sold more than four million copies in the United States by the outbreak of the Civil War in 1861, so that when she met Abraham Lincoln in the White House in November 1862, he allegedly greeted her by saying, "So this is the little lady who started this great big war." The introductory essay for Stowe and Eastman shows the vital importance of Stowe's *Uncle Tom's Cabin* to the antebellum slavery debates. In a total population of only thirty-one million and a literate reading population of fewer than twenty million, mostly in the Northern states, where the book was not prohibited from circulation, *Uncle Tom's Cabin* had sold several million copies by 1861, and it had been translated into sixteen languages. (Today, that figure is over one hundred languages, including Welsh and Bengali). *Uncle Tom's Cabin* and Margaret Mitchell's *Gone with the Wind* (1936) have done much to popularize the stereotypes of Southern plantation life, particularly the stereotypes of African slaves. However, Stowe's book's fundamental antislavery argument aroused more than a sentimental response to the slave experience; it was instrumental in developing strong antislavery feeling among its readers and it has been credited as being one of the most powerful arguments against the institution of chattel slavery developed during the antebellum slavery debates. The "Concluding Remarks" of *Uncle Tom's Cabin* contain a prophecy of apocalyptic dimensions, that either the United States will rid itself of the cancerous growth spreading throughout its Southern states and new territories, or the Union will end sadly at Judgment Day when slaveholders and sympathizers alike will be judged. Stowe's rhetorical power has been recently analyzed in books and articles concerned primarily with the strategies she conceived to deliver her antislavery message. Several are listed below.

The writers of the American Renaissance, 1820–65, gave the nation a literature of protest and reform that touched on all of the great issues of the day, including slavery, and it is the purpose of this chapter to represent some of the more prominent voices in the debates that took place within the literary community.

SUGGESTIONS FOR FURTHER READING

Andrews, William. *To Tell a Free Story: The First Century of African-American Autobiography, 1760–1865*. Urbana: University of Illinois Press, 1986.

Bell, Bernard. *The Tradition of the Afro-American Novel*. Amherst: University of Massachusetts Press, 1985.

Buell, Lawrence. *Literary Transcendentalism*. Ithaca, NY: Cornell University Press, 1973.

———. *New England Literary Culture: From Revolution through Renaissance*. New York: Cambridge University Press, 1986.

Elliott, Emory, ed. *The Columbia Literary History of the United States*. New York: Columbia University Press, 1988.

Emerson, Everett. *The Authentic Mark Twain*. Philadelphia: University of Pennsylvania Press, 1984.

Foner, Phillip. *The Life and Writings of Frederick Douglass*. 5 vols. New Haven: Yale University Press, 1970–75.

Gougeon, Len. *Emerson's Antislavery Writings*. New Haven: Yale University Press, 1995.

Jackson, Blyden. *A History of Afro-American Literature: The Long Beginnings, 1746–1895*. Baton Rouge: Louisiana State University Press, 1989.

Leyda, Jay. *The Years and Hours of Emily Dickinson*, vol. 2. New Haven: Yale University Press, 1960.

Lowance, Mason, Jr. "The Slave Narrative in American Literature." In *African-American Writers*, ed. Lea Baechler and A. Walton Litz (New York: Charles Scribner's Sons, 1991, 2001).

———, et al., eds. *The Stowe Debate: Rhetorical Strategies in "Uncle Tom's Cabin."* Amherst: University of Massachusetts Press, 1994.

Lowell, James Russell. *The Antislavery Writings of James Russell Lowell*. Reprint. New York: Negro University Press, 1973.

———. *The Biglow Papers, First Series*. Ed. Thomas Worthington. DeKalb: Northern Illinois University Press, 1977.

Matthiessen, F. O. *American Renaissance: Art and Expression in the Age of Emerson and Whitman*. New York: Oxford University Press, 1941.

McFeely, William. *Frederick Douglass*. New York: Norton, 1991.

Myerson, Joel, ed. *The American Renaissance in New England*. Detroit: Gale Research, 1978.

———, ed. *Antebellum Writers in New York and the South*. Detroit: Gale Research, 1979.

———, ed. *The Transcendentalists: A Review of Research and Criticism*. New York: Modern Language Association, 1984.

Porte, Joel. *Representative Man: Ralph Waldo Emerson in His Time*. New York: Oxford University Press, 1979.

Rees, Robert, and Earl Halbert. *Fifteen American Authors before 1900: Bibliographic Essays on Research and Criticism*. Madison: University of Wisconsin Press, 1971, 1984.

Reynolds, David. *Beneath the American Renaissance*. Cambridge: Harvard University Press, 1988.

———. *Walt Whitman's America*. New York: Knopf, 1994.

Rubin, Louis D., et al. *The History of Southern Literature*. Baton Rouge: Louisiana State University Press, 1985, 1990.

Tiffany, Lisa. "Emily Dickinson: Slavery and the Civil War." Unpublished ms., Amherst, MA, 2000.

Color, Caste, Denomination
by Emily Dickinson

Color—Caste—Denomination—
These—are Time's Affair—
Death's diviner Classifying
Does not know they are—

As in sleep—All Hue forgotten
Tenets—put behind—
Death's large—Democratic fingers
Rub away the Brand—

If Circassian—He is careless—
If He put away
Chrysalis of Blonde—or Umber
Equal Butterfly—

They emerge from His Obscuring—
What Death—knows so well—
Our minuter intuitions—
Deem implausible—

Emily Dickinson, 1864
Amherst, Massachusetts

PHILLIS WHEATLEY (1753–1784)
"ON BEING BROUGHT FROM AFRICA TO AMERICA"

The story of Phillis Wheatley is a remarkable one. She was born sometime in 1753 in Africa and was transported across the Atlantic on the Middle Passage in the slaveship, *Phillis*, arriving in Boston in 1761. Only eight or nine years old, she was fortunately purchased by John Wheatley, a Boston tailor, and his wife Susannah. Typically, she was given their surname; in addition, she was given the Christian name of the vessel on which she had crossed. The Wheatleys treated her as a child of their own, and she was given an exceptional education for a woman of her time, let alone a slave-woman. John Milton and Alexander Pope were her most admired English poets, and she also learned Latin and was well versed in the Bible. In 1773, she traveled to England and presented for publication her *Poems on Various Subjects, Religious and Moral*, which was published later that year. These verses made Phillis Wheatley an instant celebrity, particularly in Boston, where the Wheatleys and other prominent Bostonians gave much recognition to this slave-girl turned poet who brought to their attention some of the feelings of African-Americans concerning the inconsistencies between the condition of American slaves and the Enlightenment principles of the American Revolution. In dedicating her verses to William Lege, the Earl of Dartmouth, for example, she argues:

> Should you, my lord, while you peruse my song,
> Wonder from whence my love of Freedom sprung,
> Whence flow these wishes for the common good,
> By feeling hearts best understood,
> I, young in life, by seeming cruel fate
> Was snatched from Afric's fancied happy seat:
> What pangs excruciating must molest,
> What sorrows labor in my parent's breast?
> Steeled was that soul and by no misery moved
> That from a father seized his babe beloved:
> Such, such my case. And can I then but pray
> Others may never feel tyrannic sway?

This suggested correlation between abduction from Africa for the slave and the tyranny of Britain over the colonies was one of Phillis Wheatley's most prominent themes. However, much of her verse is neo-classical celebratory poetry, such as "To the University, in New England," "On the Death of the Rev. Mr. George Whitefield, 1770," and "To His Excellency, General Washington." Wheatley was deeply religious and not only wrote the eulogy to George Whitefield, an evangelical minister who toured New England with Jonathan Edwards and conducted the revival movement now known as the Great Awakening, but she also wrote the celebratory poem "Thoughts on the Works of Providence," which betrays her persistent voice of protest against slavery and the oppression of the colonies by Great Britain. "Almighty, in these wond'rous works of Thine, / What Power, what Wisdom, and what Goodness shine! / And are Thy wonders, Lord, by men explored, / And yet creating glory unadored!" is a passage that contains none of the irony and even the bitterness of her expression of anguish over the condition of herself and her fellow Africans who have been made slaves in America. One brief poem represents her many views on this subject, and it is one of her best known, "On Being Brought from Africa to America":

> Twas mercy brought me from my pagan land,
> Taught my benighted soul to understand
> That there's a god, that there's a Savior too:
> Once, I redemption neither sought nor knew.
> Some view our sable race with scornful eye.
> "Their color is a diabolic dye."
> Remember, Christians, Negroes, black as Cain,
> May be refined, and join the angelic train.

Here, Wheatley ironically expresses one of the most prominent antebellum proslavery arguments, that Christianizing the barbarous pagans of Africa justified the institution of chattel slavery, without which the African would never have known Christian redemption. The final couplet here makes clear Wheatley's rejection of this doctrine, and her assertion of the equality of the races socially, culturally, biologically, and certainly theologically. Throughout her short life, she presented these veiled views of the condition of her people, and the tragedy of her marriages and the death of two of her three children. At the time of her death in 1784, her third child was also dying and passed away soon after Wheatley.

Source Note: Julian D. Mason, ed., *The Poems of Phillis Wheatley* (1989), as cited in Louis Ruchames, *Racial Thought in America from the Puritans to Abraham Lincoln* (Amherst: University of Massachusetts Press, 1955), with permission of Bruce Wilcox, Director.

SUGGESTIONS FOR FURTHER READING

Kendrick, Robert. "Re-membering America: Phillis Wheatley's Intertextual Epic." *African American Review* 30:1 (1996): 71–88.

Richard, M. A. *Bid the Vassal Soar: Interpretive Essays on the Life and Poetry of Phillis Wheatley (1753–1784) and George Moses Horton (1797–1883)*. Washington, DC: Howard University Press, 1974, pp. 3–78.

Robinson, William H. *Phillis Wheatley and Her Writings*. Garland Reference Library of the Humanities 402. New York: Garland, 1984.

JOHN GREENLEAF WHITTIER (1807–1892)

John Greenleaf Whittier was born into a Quaker family on December 17, 1807, in Haverhill, Massachusetts. His education was limited and he spent most of his youth among Quaker farmers, from whom he developed a strong sense of social responsibility and a social conscience. As a young adult, he formed a close friendship with William Lloyd Garrison, who in 1826 published Whittier's first poem in his antislavery newspaper. Garrison recruited Whittier for the social reform work of abolitionism, and together they produced many essays and poems for *The Liberator*, which Garrison edited from 1831 to 1865, when the paper and the abolitionist movement had achieved many of their objectives in the ratification of the Thirteenth Amendment to the Constitution, by which slavery was abolished in the United States. (On December 6, 1865, Georgia was the twenty-seventh state to ratify the amendment, providing the necessary two-thirds for passage.) Whittier's Quaker upbringing would inspire him to abolitionist sentiments throughout his career, and his poems, such as "The Slave Ships," reflect a highly sensitive perspective on the horrors of the Middle Passage and chattel slavery. Like Garrison, he lived in relative poverty, and he never married. He entered the political arena through election to the Massachusetts legislature in 1835 and by joining the Liberty Party, an abolitionist splinter group, in 1839. His long poem, "Massachusetts to Virginia," reprinted here, sentimentalizes the spirit of 1776 with its emphasis on natural rights and human liberty contrasted with the horrors of chattel slavery as it was practiced in Virginia and other Southern states.

Whittier also wrote essays and treatises, some for Garrison's *Liberator*. *Justice and Expediency* articulates Whittier's antislavery principles that are also found in the poetry. He called for the "immediate abolition of slavery; an immediate acknowledgment of the great truth, that man cannot hold property in man; an immediate surrender of baneful prejudice to Christian love; an immediate practical obedience to the command of Jesus Christ: 'Whatsoever ye would that men should do unto you, do you even so to them.'" Whittier died on September 7, 1892.

SUGGESTIONS FOR FURTHER READING

Pickard, John B. *The Life and Letters of John Greenleaf Whittier*, 2 vols. Boston: Houghton-Riverside, 1894.

Woodwell, Rolad H. *John Greenleaf Whittier: A Biography*. Amesbury, MA: Whittier Homestead, 1985.

The Slave Ships
by John Greenleaf Whittier

"In addition to recruiting women, the abolitionists sought the support of philanthropists, humanitarians, and literary figures in the North. The Quaker poet John Greenleaf Whittier, first discovered by Garrison in 1826, joined the New England Anti-Slavery Society in 1831 and two years later helped Garrison write the Declaration of Sentiments of the national society. Vigorous and unyielding in his hatred of slavery, Whittier proved an invaluable ally. His early poem "The Slave Ships" (1834) appeared in numerous antislavery publications, among them the October 11, 1834, issue of The Liberator." [Louis Ruchames, *The Abolitionists* (New York: Putnam, 1960), p. 136.]

"The French ship *Le Rodeur*, with a crew of twenty-two men, and with one hundred and sixty negro slaves, sailed from Bonny in Africa, April. 1819. On approaching the line, a terrible malady broke out, an obstinate disease of the eyes, contagious, and altogether beyond the resources of medicine. It was aggravated by the scarcity of water among the slaves (*only half a wine glass per day* being allowed to an individual) and by the extreme impurity of the air which they breathed. By the advice of the physician, they were brought up on deck occasionally, but some of the poor wretches, locking themselves in each other's arms, leaped overboard, in the hope which so universally prevails among them, of being swiftly transported to their own homes in Africa. To check this, the captain ordered several who were stopped in the attempt, to be shot, or hanged, before their companions. The disease extended to the crew and one after another were smitten with it, until only one remained unaffected. Yet even this dreadful condition did not preclude calculation: to save the expense of supporting slaves rendered unsaleable, and to obtain grounds for a claim against the underwriters, thirty-six of the negroes, having become blind, were thrown into the sea and drowned! (Speech of M. Benjamin Constant in the French Chamber of Deputies, June 17, 1820.)

In the midst of their dreadful fears, lest the solitary individual, whose sight remained unaffected, should also be seized with the malady, a sail was discovered. It was the Spanish Slaver, *Leon*. The same disease had been there; and, horrible to tell, all the crew had become blind! Unable to assist each other, the vessels parted. The Spanish ship has never since been heard of. The *Rodeur* reached Guadeloupe on the twenty-first of June; the only man who had escaped the disease, and had thus been enabled to steer the slaver into port, caught it three days after its arrival. (*Bibliotheque Opthamologique, for November, 1819.*)" [*Ruchames, p. 137.*]

"All ready?" cried the Captain;
"Ay, Ay!" the seamen said—
"Heave up the worthless lubbers,
The dying and the dead."
Up from the slave-ship's prison
Fierce, bearded heads were thrust—
"Now let the sharks look to it—
Toss up the dead ones first!"

Corpse after corpse came up—
Death had been busy there.
Where every blow is mercy,
Why should the spoiler spare?
Corpse after corpse they cast
Sullenly from the ship,
Yet bloody with the traces
Of fetter-link and whip.

Gloomily stood the captain,
With his arms upon his breast,
With his cold brow sternly knotted,
And his iron lip compress'd.
"Are the dead dogs all over?"
Growl'd through that matted lip—
"The blind ones are no better.
Let's lighten the good ship!"

Hark! From the ship's dark bosom,
The very sounds of hell!—
The ringing clank of iron—
The maniac's short, sharp yell!
The hoarse, low curse, throat-stifled—
The starving infant's moan—
The horror of a breaking heart
Pour'd through a mother's groan!

Up from that loathsome prison
The stricken blind ones came—
Below, had all been darkness
Above, was still the same.

Yet the holy breath of heaven
Was sweetly breathing there,
And the heated brow of fever
Cool'd in the soft sea-air.

"Overboard with them, shipmates!"
Cutlass and dirk were plied:
Fetterd and blind, one after one,
Plunged down the vessel's side.
The sabre smote above—
Beneath the lean shark lay,
Waiting with wide and bloody jaw
His quick and human prey.

God of the earth! What cries
Rang upward unto Thee?
Voices of agony and blood,
From ship-deck and from sea.
The last dull plunge was heard—
The last wave caught its stain—
And the unsated sharks look'd up
For human hearts in vain.

•

Red glow'd the western waters—
The setting sun was there,
Scattering alike on wave and cloud
His fiery mesh of hair.
Amidst a group in blindness,
A solitary eye
Gazed, from the burden'd slaver's deck,
Into that burning sky.

"A storm," spoke out the gazer,
"Is gathering and at hand—
Curse on't—I'd give my other eye
For one firm rood of land."
And then he laugh'd—but only
His echoed laugh replied—
For the blinded and the suffering
Alone were at his side.

Night settled on the waters,
And on a stormy heaven,
While fiercely on that lone ship's track
The thunder-gust was driven.

"A sail—thank God! A sail!"
And, as the helmsman spoke,
Up through the stormy murmur
A shout of gladness broke.

Down came the stranger vessel
Unheeding, on her way.
So near, that on the slaver's deck
Fell off her driven spray—
"Ho! For the love of mercy—
We're perishing and blind!"
A wail of utter agony
Came back upon the wind.

"Help us! for we are stricken
With one blindness every one—
Ten days we've floated fearfully.
Unnoting star or sun.
Our ship's the slave Leon—
We've but a score on board—
Our slaves are all gone over—
Help—for the love of God!"

On livid brows of agony
The broad-red lightning shone—
But the roar of wind and thunder
Stifled the answering groan.
Wail'd from the broken waters
A last despairing cry,
As kindling in the stormy light,
The stranger ship went by.

•

In the sunny Guadeloupe
A dark hull's vessel lay—
With a crew who noted never
The night-fall or the day.
The blossom of the orange
Waved white by every stream
And tropic leaf, and flower, and bird,
Were in the warm sun-beam.

And the sky was bright as ever,
And the moonlight slept as well,
On the palm-trees by the hill-side,
And the streamlet of the deli.
And the glances of the Creole

Were still as archly deep,
And her smiles as full as ever
Of passion and of sleep.

But vain were bird and blossom,
The green earth and the sky,
And the smile of human faces,
To the ever-darken'd eye—
For, amidst a world of beauty,
The slaver went abroad,
With his ghastly visage written
By the awful curse of God!

Source Note: John Greenleaf Whittier, "The Slave Ships," in *The Complete Poetical Works of John Greenleaf Whittier* (Cambridge, MA: Houghton-Mifflin, 1894).

Massachusetts to Virginia
by John Greenleaf Whittier

The blast from Freedom's Northern hills, upon its Southern way,
Bears greeting to Virginia from Massachusetts Bay:
No word of haughty challenging, nor battle bugle's peal,
Nor steady tread of marching files, nor clang of horsemen's steel,

No trains of deep-mouthed cannon along our highways go;
Around our silent arsenals untrodden lies the snow;
And to the land-breeze of our ports, upon their errands far,
A thousand sails of commerce swell, but none are spread for war.

We hear thy threats, Virginia! thy stormy words and high
Swell harshly on the Southern winds which melt along our sky;
Yet not one brown, hard hand foregoes its honest labor here,
No hewer of our mountain oaks suspends his axe in fear.

Wild are the waves which lash the reefs along St. George's bank;
Cold on the shores of Labrador the fog lies white and dank;
Through storm, and wave, and blinding mist, stout are the hearts which man
The fishing-smacks of Marblehead, the sea-boats of Cape Ann.

The cold north light and wintry sun glare on their icy forms,
Bent grimly o'er their straining lines or wrestling with the storms;
Free as the winds they drive before, rough as the waves they roam,
They laugh to scorn the slaver's threat against their rocky home.

What means the Old Dominion? Hath she forgot the day
When o'er her conquered valleys swept the Briton's steel array?
How, side by side with sons of hers, the Massachusetts men
Encountered Tarleton's charge of fire, and stout Cornwallis, then?

Forgets she how the Bay State, in answer to the call
Of her old House of Burgesses, spoke out from Faneuil Hall?
When, echoing back her Henry's cry, came pulsing on each breath
Of Northern winds the thrilling sounds of "Liberty or Death!"

What asks the Old Dominion? If now her sons have proved
False to their fathers' memory, false to the faith they loved;
If she can scoff at Freedom, and its great charter spurn,
Must we of Massachusetts from truth and duty turn?

We hunt your bondmen, flying from Slavery's hateful hell;
Our voices, at your bidding, take up the bloodhound's yell;
We gather, at your summons, above our fathers' graves,
From Freedom's holy altar-horns to tear your wretched slaves!

Thank God! not yet so vilely can Massachusetts bow;
The spirit of her early time is with her even now;
Dream not because her Pilgrim blood moves slow and calm and cool,
She thus can stoop her chainless neck, a sister's slave and tool!

All that a sister State should do, all that a free State may,
Heart, hand, and purse we proffer, as in our early day;
But that one dark loathsome burden ye must stagger with alone,
And reap the bitter harvest which ye yourselves have sown!

Hold, while ye may, your struggling slaves, and burden God's free air
With woman's shriek beneath the lash, and manhood's wild despair;
Cling closer to the "cleaving curse" that writes upon your plains
The blasting of Almighty wrath against a land of chains.

Still shame your gallant ancestry, the cavaliers of old,
By watching round the shambles where human flesh is sold;
Gloat o'er the new-born child, and count his market value, when
The maddened mother's cry of woe shall pierce the slaver's den!

Lower than plummet soundeth, sink the Virginia name;
Plant, if ye will, your fathers' graves with rankest weeds of shame;
Be, if ye will, the scandal of God's fair universe;
We wash our hands forever of your sin and shame and curse.

A voice from lips whereon the coal from Freedom's shrine hath been,
Thrilled, as but yesterday, the hearts of Berkshire's mountain men:
The echoes of that solemn voice are sadly lingering still
In all our sunny valleys, on every wind-swept hill.

And when the prowling man-thief came hunting for his prey
Beneath the very shadow of Bunker's shaft of gray,
How, through the free lips of the son, the father's warning spoke;
How, from its bonds of trade and sect, the Pilgrim city broke!

A hundred thousand right arms were lifted up on high,
A hundred thousand voices sent back their loud reply;
Through the thronged towns of Essex the startling summons rang,
And up from bench and loom and wheel her young mechanics sprang!

The voice of free, broad Middlesex, of thousands as of one,
The shaft of Bunker calling to that of Lexington;
From Norfolk's ancient villages, from Plymouth's rocky bound
To where Nantucket feels the arms of ocean close her round;

From rich and rural Worcester, where through the calm repose
Of cultured vales and fringing woods the gentle Nashua flows,
To where Wachuset's wintry blasts the mountain larches stir,
Swelled up to Heaven the thrilling cry of "God save Latimer!"

And sandy Barnstable rose up, wet with the salt sea spray;
And Bristol sent her answering shout down Narragansett Bay!
Along the broad Connecticut old Hampden felt the thrill,
And the cheer of Hampshire's woodmen swept down from Holyoke Hill.

The voice of Massachusetts! Of her free sons and daughters,
Deep calling unto deep aloud, the sound of many waters!
Against the burden of that voice what tyrant power shall stand?
No fetters in the Bay State! No slave upon her land!

Look to it well, Virginians! In calmness we have borne,
In answer to our faith and trust, your insult and your scorn;
You've spurned our kindest counsels; you've hunted for our lives;
And shaken round our hearths and homes your manacles and gyves!

We wage no war, we lift no arm, we fling no torch within
The fire-damps of the quaking mine beneath your soil of sin;
We leave ye with your bondmen, to wrestle, while ye can,
With the strong upward tendencies and God-like soul of man!

But for us and for our children, the vow which we have given
For freedom and humanity is registered in heaven;
No slave-hunt in our borders,—no pirate on our strand!
No fetters in the Bay State,—no slave upon our land!

Source Note: John Greenleaf Whittier, *The Complete Poetical Works of John Greenleaf Whittier* (Cambridge, MA: Houghton-Mifflin, 1894).

Our Political Responsibility
by John Greenleaf Whittier

The season of our annual election is at hand: and it is a question of deep
interest, whether the cause of Freedom is to be honored by the faithfulness of its

professed friends, or dishonored and disgraced by their treachery and apostasy, at the ballot-box. It should not be forgotten by any of us, that we live in a land where the acknowledged source of all authority is with the people themselves—that if there be evil in our government, in its primary constitution, or its occasional legislation, WE are responsible for it. Is the public functionary unworthy, corrupt, oppressive? His is our own choice. Is the Indian hunted from his home? Are the chains of the slave strengthened by pro-slavery legislation? The evil is our own—its instrumentality is the work of our hands. God is not mocked. "The wheels of His providence are not moved onward by blind chance—they are full of eyes round about." We will demand an account of our stewardship, as the sovereigns and rulers of this republic. . . .

How serious, in this point of view, is the reflection that every American citizen is a ruler—a monarch! No one set over him whom he may not remove—the temporary lawgiver only his representative—the power wielded by the magistrate his own—the highest functionary the work of his own hands, the manifestation and embodiment of his own will! Do abolitionists fully realize this? That so far as they are instrumental in electing a bad man to office, in sustaining corrupt and unprincipled parties—nay more, so far as they neglect to use their regal prerogative in behalf of just men and just laws, they are verily guilty of all those national crimes which provoke the judgments of heaven. How has this truth been overlooked and disregarded! . . . We must cease to look upon election day as a sort of carnival season—a release from conscience and moral obligation. In a government like ours, the decision of the ballot-box is the voice of the supreme power. *Each ballot, as it falls from the hand of the elector, is a declaration of freedom to the slave, or a warrant for his further oppression.*

. . . The right of suffrage in our hands should be regarded as a sacred trust, to be used only for the promotion of truth and the establishment of justice—a power silent but mighty, peaceful yet effectual, clothing its possessor with the tremendous responsibility of lawgiver and judge. Government, in its legitimate sense—the authority of just and equal laws—seems to us as necessary in society as in physical nature. To establish and maintain such a government, clothed with sanctions of justice and the attractions of benevolence, is our high duty and privilege. This is the POLITICAL ACTION to which we are now summoned. . . .

We are aware that, at this time, there exists an honest difference of opinion among abolitionists as to the best means of making our influence felt at the ballot-box. Our own mind is fixed in this respect—but we have no controversy with those who, agreeing with us in the fundamental point, that the franchise of the abolitionists should be held sacred to Freedom, differ with us as to the mode of its application. What we ask is, that no abolitionists may vote, under any conceivable circumstances, for any other than a decided and hearty advocate of immediate emancipation. Whether the candidates of our choice succeed or not is comparatively of little consequence. What is wanted—what is indeed indispensible to the success of our cause, is a SOLEMN PROTEST OF ALL THE ABOLITIONISM OF THE LAND, UTTERED THROUGH THE BAL-

LOT-BOX AT EVERY ELECTION, AGAINST THE PRO-SLAVERY LEGISLATION OF A PRO-SLAVERY GOVERNMENT. Our prayer—our agony of solicitude—is for the preservation of anti-slavery integrity. So long as our professed friends vote as they have heretofore, to a great extent, for mere party candidates, with the collar of political servitude upon them, they undo on the day of election all that they can possibly do for the slave in the other three hundred and sixty-four days of the year. . . . The slaveholder sees the inconsistency and insincerity of such reprovers of his sin. He feels justified in imputing low and base motives to abolitionists generally—he classes the innocent with the guilty—the honest advocate of freedom with the canting professor praying one way and voting another. Thus the unfaithfulness of so many of our number neutralized even the moral influence of the honest and upright.

Friends of the slave! Brethren of the holy cause of humanity—how long shall these things be? . . . will you longer continue to yield to the seductions or threats of political partisans, and on the very day when of all others the wrongs of the slave and the rights of humanity should be held in special remembrance, suffer yourselves to be yoked and collared and led up to the pools to vote for slavery? Shall not "the time past suffice?" . . . Are you not now prepared to say with Gerrit Smith, when, in 1838, he consecrated his citizenship to Liberty— "Under a solemn sense of my responsibilities at the judgment, my heart is fixed: I pledge myself that I will not aid in electing an anti-abolitionist to office: come what may, I will not vote for a pro-slavery man for a law-maker."

J.G.W.

Source Note: The American and Foreign Anti-Slavery Reporter, October 1, 1841. Reproduced from the original in the Library of Congress, Washington, DC.

Justice and Expediency; or, Slavery Considered with a View to Its Rightful and Effectual Remedy, Abolition
by John Greenleaf Whittier

John Greenleaf Whittier was an early member of the abolitionist societies that Garrison founded. He was, with Garrison, a prominent founder of the American Anti-Slavery Society. His treatise, Justice and Expediency, *demands immediate and unconditional emancipation of the slaves, and this commitment places him squarely within the Garrison camp of reformers and abolitionists. According to Ruchames, the pamphlet was first published in a run of only five hundred copies; however, it was soon reprinted in a much larger edition of 5,000 copies by the abolitionist Arthur Tappan. (Ruchames, p. 131)*

. . . And what is this system which we are thus protecting and upholding? A system which holds two millions of God's creatures in bondage, which leaves one million females without any protection save their own feeble strength, and which makes the exercise of that strength in resistance to outrage punishable with death! which considers rational, immortal beings as articles of traffic, vendible commodities, merchantable property—which recognizes no social obligations, no natural relations—which tears without scruple the infant child from the mother, the wife from the husband, the parent from the child. . . .

I come now to the only practicable, the only just scheme of emancipation: Immediate abolition of slavery; an immediate acknowledgment of the great truth, that man cannot hold property in man; an immediate surrender of baneful prejudice to Christian love; an immediate practical obedience to the command of Jesus Christ: "Whatsoever ye would that men should do unto you, do ye even so to them." . . . The term immediate is used in contrast with that of gradual. Earnestly as I wish it, I do not expect, no one expects, that the tremendous system of oppression can be instantaneously overthrown. The terrible and unrebukable indignation of a free people has not yet been sufficiently concentrated against it. . . .

Let them [the slave-holders] at once strike off the grievous fetters. Let them declare that man shall no longer hold his fellow-man in bondage, a beast of burden, an article of traffic, within the governmental domain. . . . If our fathers intended that slavery should be perpetual, that our practice should forever give the lie to our professions, why is the great constitutional compact so guardedly silent on the subject of human servitude? . . .

What, then, is our duty?

To give effect to the spirit of our Constitution; to plant ourselves upon the great declaration and declare in the face of all the world that political, religious, and legal hypocrisy shall no longer cover as with loathsome leprosy the features of American freedom; to loose at once the bands of wickedness; and to undo the heavy burdens, and let the oppressed go free. . . .

I deny the right of the slave-holder to impose silence on his brother of the North in reference to slavery. What! Compelled to maintain the system, to keep up the standing army which protects it, and yet be denied the poor privilege of remonstrance! Ready, at the summons of the master to put down the insurrections of his slaves, the outbreaking of that revenge which is now, and has been, in all nations, and all times, the inevitable consequence of oppression and wrong, and yet like automata to act but not to speak! Are we to be denied even the right of a slave, the right to murmur? . . .

The slave-holding states are not free. The name of liberty is not there, and the spirit is wanting. They do not partake of its invaluable blessings. Wherever slavery exists to any considerable extent, with the exception of some recently settled portions of the country and which have not yet felt in a great degree the baneful and deteriorating influences of slave labor, we hear at this moment the cry of suffering. . . . A moral mildew mingles with and blasts the economy of nature. It is as if the finger of the everlasting God had written upon the soil of the slave-holder the language of His displeasure. Let, then, the slave-holding states consult their present interest by beginning without delay the work of emancipation. . . . Let the cause of insurrection be removed, then, as speedily as possible. Cease to oppress. "Let him that stole steal no more." Let the laborer have his hire. Bind him no longer by the cords of slavery, but with those of kindness and brotherly love. Watch over him for his good. Pray for him; instruct him; pour light into the darkness of his mind. Let this be done and the horrible fears which now haunt the slumbers of the slave-holder will depart. Conscience will take down its racks and gibbets, and his soul will be at peace. His lands will no longer disappoint his hopes. Free labor will renovate them.

Historical facts; the nature of the human mind; the demonstrated truths of political economy; the analysis of cause and effect, all concur in establishing:

1. That immediate abolition is a safe and just and peaceful remedy for the evils of the slave system.
2. That free labor, its necessary consequence, is more productive, and more advantageous to the planter than slave labor.

In proof of the first proposition it is only necessary to state the undeniable fact that immediate emancipation, whether by an individual or a community, has in no instance been attended with violence and disorder on the part of the emancipated; but that on the contrary, it has promoted cheerfulness, industry, and laudable ambition in the place of sullen discontent, indolence, and despair. . . . Because slave labor is the labor of mere machines; a mechanical impulse of body and limb, with which the mind of the laborer has no sympathy, and from which it constantly and loathingly revolts. Because slave labor deprives the master altogether of the incalculable benefit of the negro's will. That [the will] does not cooperate with the forced toil of the body. This is but the necessary consequence of all labor which does not benefit the laborer. It is a just remark of that profound political economist, Adam Smith, that "a slave can have no other interest than to eat and waste as much, and work as little, as he can." . . .

The conflicting interests of free and slave labor furnish the only ground for fear in relation to the permanency of the Union. The line of separation between them is day by day growing broader, and deeper; geographically and politically united, we are already, in a moral point of view, a divided people. But a few months ago we were on the very verge of civil war, a war of brothers, a war between the North and the South, between the slave-holder and the free laborer. The danger has been delayed for a time; this bolt has fallen without mortal injury to the Union, but the cloud from whence it came still hangs above us, reddening with the elements of destruction. . . .

To counteract the dangers resulting from a state of society so utterly at variance with the great Declaration of American freedom should be the earnest endeavor of every patriotic statesman. Nothing unconstitutional, nothing violent, should be attempted; but the true doctrine of the rights of man should be steadily kept in view; and the opposition to slavery should be inflexible and constantly maintained. The almost daily violations of the Constitution in consequence of the laws of some of the slave states, subjecting free colored citizens of New England and elsewhere, who may happen to be on board one of our coasting vessels, to imprisonment immediately on their arrival in a Southern port, should be provided against. Nor should the immediate imprisonment of the free colored citizens of the Northern and Middle states, on suspicion of being runaways, subjecting them, even after being pronounced free, to the costs of their confinement and trial, be longer tolerated; for if we continue to yield to innovations like these upon the Constitution of our fathers, we shall erelong have the name only of a free government left us.

Dissemble as we may, it is impossible for us to believe, after fully considering the nature of slavery, that it can much longer maintain a peaceable existence among us. A day of revolution must come, and it is our duty to prepare for it. Its threatened evil may be changed into a national blessing. The establishment of schools for the instruction of the slave children, a general diffusion of the lights of Christianity, and the introduction of a sacred respect for the social obligations of marriage and for the relations between parents and children, among our black population, would render emancipation not only perfectly safe, but also of the highest advantage to the country. Two millions of freemen would be added to our population, upon whom in the hour of danger we could safely depend; "the domestic foe" would be changed into a firm friend, faithful, generous, and ready to encounter all dangers in our defence. It is well known that during the last war with Great Britain, wherever the enemy touched upon our Southern coast, the slaves in multitudes hastened to join them. On the other hand, the free blacks were highly serviceable in repelling them. So warm was the zeal of the latter, so manifest their courage in the defense of Louisiana, that the present Chief Magistrate of the United States publicly bestowed upon them one of the highest eulogiums ever offered by a commander to his soldiers. . . .

An intense and powerful feeling is working in the mighty heart of England; it is speaking through the lips of Brougham and Buxton and O'Connell [British abolitionists], and demanding justice in the name of humanity according to the righteous law of God. The immediate emancipation of eight hundred thousand slaves is demanded with an authority which cannot much longer be trifled with. That demand will be obeyed; justice will be done; the heavy burdens will be unloosed; the oppressed set free. It shall go well for England.

And when the stain on our own escutcheon shall be seen no more; when the Declaration of Independence and the practice of our people shall agree; when truth shall be exalted among us; when love shall take the place of wrong; when all the baneful pride and prejudice of caste and color shall fall forever; when under one common sun of political liberty the slave-holding portions of our republic shall no longer sit, like the Egyptians of old, themselves mantled in thick darkness, while all around them is glowing with the blessed light of freedom and equality, then, and not till then, shall it go well for America!

Source Note: The Prose Works of John Greenleaf Whittier (Boston, 1892), vol. III, pp. 9–57.

JAMES KIRKE PAULDING (1778–1860)

The "Writers and Essayists in Conflict over Slavery" chapter contains many antislavery writings because most of the nineteenth-century authors widely recognized today as contributors to the American Renaissance, that flourishing period of literary excellence that roughly corresponds to the era of the antebellum slavery debates, were either abolitionists or antislavery sympathizers, or both. There were, however, Southern apologists for slavery like John Pendleton Kennedy (*Swallow Burn*), William Gilmore Simms (*The Yemassee*), and Mary Eastman (*Aunt Phillis's Cabin*) who were closely identified with proslavery sentiment and whose fictional depictions of plantation life left no doubts concerning their romantic views of Southern aristocracy. James Kirke Paulding was unusual among proslavery writers because he was a Northerner, born in Putnam County, New York, and because he began his long, successful writing career composing satirical narratives such as *The Diverting History of John Bull and Brother Jonathan (1812)*, which placed him clearly in the mainstream of emerging early national literary efforts, including those of his friend, Washington Irving. Like Irving, Paulding sought to establish a pantheon of American national heroes, and in 1835 he composed a *Life of Washington*. In 1836, he contributed a long book to the antebellum slavery debates titled *Slavery in the United States*. This work is essentially a Northerner's defense of segregation and slavery, just as Hinton Rowan Helper's *The Impending Crisis* (1857) would be a North Carolinian's attack on the institution of slavery. The text here provides a representative if incomplete account of this document, which is difficult to find because it has not been recently reprinted in readily available form. Other Paulding titles include *The United States and England* (1812), *The Dutchman's Fireside* (1831), *Westward Ho!* (1832), *The Old Continental* (1846), and *The Puritan and His Daughter* (1849).

Paulding's defense of slavery is exemplified by *Slavery in the United States*. He did not believe slavery to be inherently evil or morally wrong, and he consistently argued that anarchy would result from the emancipation of the African slaves. Like his contemporary, Samuel F. B. Morse, inventor of the Morse code and the telegraph, Paulding opposed the fanaticism of the abolitionists and argued for a balanced social order that privileged harmony and civilization over justice. "The Bible and religion upheld slavery. The Constitution and laws of property protected slaveholding. Englishmen, not Americans, were responsible for the introduction of slavery in America. The laws of slavery protected slaves from harsh masters. He devoted nearly one-third of the whole [text] to the political economy of slavery, attempting to prove that American slavery was as mild and as beneficial as any other form of labor in the world. After comparing the condition of the slave to that of native Africans, English factory workers, European peasantry and common laborers in the North, Paulding found that 'the bondman of the United States is free from all obligation or anxiety' and that his lot in life was 'decidedly preferable' to that of his fellows elsewhere" (Tise, p. 247).

Perhaps Paulding's most widely accepted argument is the view that the African was inherently inferior to the white. As chapter 7 ("Science in Antebellum America") in this volume shows clearly, even among abolitionists acceptance of contemporary race theory views was widespread, and Paulding's text addresses these concerns directly. "Negroes bear the burden of a natural and incurable inferiority," and they therefore posed threats of amalgamation and racial warfare against white superiors and oppressors. Paulding argued vigorously against "universal emancipation" and claimed that it would lead to a "mongrel race" or an "inferior mixture" of mulattos, thereby destroying America's "natural aristocracy of virtue and talent." He claimed that the African was incapable of "enjoying the privileges and responsibilities of liberty. Nor could a Negro be educated in the abstract principles of freedom, since such instruction would make him 'a libertine in morals and an anarchist in politics.' The 'wooly-headed race' had never demonstrated any ability to live in freedom under a rule of law. Hence, it was not surprising that 'anatomists and physiologists have classed the negro as the lowest in the scale of rational beings'" (Tise, pp. 247–48).

These harsh judgments were conventional arguments for perpetuating slavery and for keeping the African in bondage. As chapter 3 illustrates, the proslavery advocates used the Bible and ancient precedent to bolster their arguments, but contemporary Americans were most alarmed by the fear of African insurrection, such as the Nat Turner rebellion or the *Amistad* mutiny. These retaliatory uprisings were brutal, but in the context of what had been done to the African in the Middle Passage or in the Southern plantation system of chattel slavery, these "all or nothing" responses and the atrocities associated with them seem a logical result. The proslavery arguments included an alarmist fear of such uprisings, which would result in mass killings of whites and a total overthrow of the cherished republican form of government protected by the Constitution. Such alarmist arguments may also be found in the South African defense of apartheid, which is examined sensitively in Alan Paton's *Cry, the Beloved Country*. The fear of miscegenation is also a prominent theme in the novels of William Faulkner, especially *Absalom, Absalom!* Paulding's *Slavery in the United States* was a full-scale attack on the tactics, methods, and arguments of the abolitionists, and Paulding reserved all the privileges of "natural rights" for white republicans. "Abolitionism is a 'holy alliance' of the enemies of liberty in Europe with misguided fanatics in America to destroy American Republicanism. Under the guise of philanthropy, fanatical abolitionists would 'overturn the whole fabric of human rights, and destroy all personal liberty'" (Tise, p. 248).

SUGGESTIONS FOR FURTHER READING

Ratner, Lorman. *James Kirke Paulding: The Last Republican*. Contributions in American History 146. Westport, CT: Greenwood, 1992.

Tise, Larry. *Proslavery: A History of the Defense of Slavery in America, 1701–1840*. Athens: University of Georgia Press, 1987.

Slavery in the United States
by James Kirke Paulding

Introduction

. . . The subject of slavery, at all times one of extreme delicacy in the United States, has lately assumed a vast and alarming importance, in consequence of the proceedings of the advocates of immediate emancipation, who have denounced it as utterly at war with the law of God and the rights of nature. It has become the fruitful theme of calumny, declamation, and contention; the stalking horse of political parties and fanatical reformers. It has produced lamentable violations of the laws, and disturbed the peace of communities and states. It menaces the disruption of our social system, and tends directly to a separation of the Union. The institution has been assailed on one hand with violence and obloquy; on the other defended with invincible determination. The obligations of truth have been sacrificed to unmitigated reproach, and the laws and constitution of the country attempted to be trampled under foot, in hot pursuit of the rights of humanity. . . . In asserting the natural rights of one class of men, the constitutional rights of another have been denounced as violations of the law of God, and, as if it were impossible to be sincere without becoming mad, a ferocious, unrelenting, unbrotherly warfare has been, still is, waging against a large portion of the good citizens of the United States, which, if continued, must inevitably separate this prosperous and happy Union into discordant and conflicting elements, that, instead of co-operating in the one great end of human happiness, will be productive only of contention and ruin.

In this state of things it is thought that a calm, dispassionate consideration of the subject, on the broad general ground of its influence on the happiness of all parties concerned might not be without its uses at the present moment. . . . It is a question concerning rights and duties of the greatest magnitude, the decision on which must vitally affect the present age, as well as long ages to come. In short, it is a case in which nations are called to the bar, and the two great races of mankind are parties to the issue.

. . . It is to decide whether THE UNION SHALL LAST ANY LONGER; that union which all good citizens believe to be the great palladium of their present happiness, and that of their posterity. . . . *That no beneficial consequences to any class of mankind or to the whole universe, can counterbalance the evils that will result to the people of the United States from the dissolution of the Union, and that, therefore, no project ought ever to be tolerated by them which places it in jeopardy.* Whether this principle accords with the nice metaphysical subtleties or abstract dogmas of fanaticism, he neither knows or cares.

Hitherto, almost all that has appeared on the subject has been on one side. The horrors of slavery have been depicted in such glowing colours as to blind us to the consequences that may, and assuredly will result from attempting to get rid of it in the summary manner *demanded* by the advocates of immediate abolition, who, one might almost be tempted to believe, consider it the only evil existing in the world. . . .

It will be perceived, in the course of the following discussion, that the writer does not consider slavery, as it exists in the United States, an evil of such surpassing enormity as to demand the sacrifice of the harmony and consequent union of the states, followed by civil contention and servile war, to its removal. If the question were now for the first time to be decided, whether it should be permitted to ingraft itself on the institutions of the country, he would assuredly oppose it with a zeal at least equal to that with which he is about to combat the unlawful interference of the abolitionists. But inasmuch as it is now deeply rooted in our land, and intertwined with the interests, the habits, the domestic policy, and social relations of a large portion of the people of this Union; inasmuch as it is identified with the constitutional rights, and the value of the property of millions of free citizens who will not be persuaded, and cannot be controlled; and, above all, inasmuch as the treatment it may receive must and will deeply affect their peace, safety, and happiness, he is for leaving it to the humanity and discretion of those whom alone it concerns. If it be an evil, let those who cherish it bear it. It is their business, not ours, since no duty renders it obligatory on us to go crusading about the world redressing wrongs, real or imaginary, which we had no hand in inflicting. If it reflects dishonour, none of it can fall to our share, since the institution of slavery is guarded by constitutional barriers which cannot be overleaped or broken down, and we have done our part by abolishing it wherever it was within our jurisdiction. If it be a crime to have inherited the property of slaves; if it be a crime to decline divesting themselves of it in a manner which all rational reflecting men believe will be equally pernicious to the master and the slave; if it be a crime to resent, resist, or counteract by every means in their power, any interference with a subject involving all that is dear to men, then let them meet the consequences; but let not us, their kindred, neighbours, and countrymen, become instruments to scatter the firebrands of fanaticism among them, and lend a helping hand to insurrection and massacre.

Let us not forget that in our furious zeal to give freedom to the blacks, we are laying the axe to the root of the fairest plant of freedom that adorns the New or the Old World; that in our ardour to bring about a questionable good, we are provoking vast and alarming evils; and that there is no precept of religion or morality more inflexible in its application than that which forbids doing evil that good may ensue. Where the evil is immediate and morally certain, on every ground of reason and experience, and the good remote, contingent, and hypothetical, it is the part of a wise and good man to shrink from thus arrogating to himself the attributes of Omniscience, and pretending to look into futurity. When mankind are gifted with a prophetic inspiration directly derived from Heaven; or when they acquire the prerogative of planning and controlling the economy of the universe, then, and not till then, should they dare to do evil in the presumptuous anticipation that the miseries they may inflict on the living, will be repaid by the happiness of those yet unborn.

New York,
November 1835.

Chapter I. *Of the Opposition of Slavery to the Law of God.*

SLAVERY. A reference to the Old Testament will show that the abolitionists can derive from it no authority to sustain their position, that slavery is contrary to the Law of God. The only text they have been able to bring to bear directly upon the subject, is that which denounces the penalty of death to the "man-stealer," while, on the contrary, slavery is made the subject of express regulation in the social institutions of the Jews, and this without a single expression of disapprobation on the part of the divine Lawgiver. It is evident, therefore, that the denunciation of death to the man-stealer is not applicable to those who hold slaves. A declaration in any other manner, would be to pervert its principles into a warrant for the violation of all human statutes, under the sanction of the inalienable rights of nature. It [the Law of God as revealed in the Bible] was not an elaborate metaphysical discussion of human rights, but a mere assertion of great general principles; and to have enumerated all the exceptions would have been giving the world a volume in folio, instead of a simple declaration of rights. The charge of inconsistency between our principles and practice, is therefore entirely unfounded. . . .

Chapter III. *Of Emancipation and its Consequences, admitting its practicability.*

It is not among the least revolting consequences of the proceedings of the abolitionists, that they involve the necessity of inquiring into a subject so fraught with everything that can render it aggravating to the feelings of humanity. That the slaves may, at some not very distant period of time, be excited by the goadings of the abolitionists to the most desperate atrocities, is more than sufficiently probable, but that they will succeed in attaining their freedom by force, is beyond the reach of all rational anticipation. It is scarcely possible that a general conspiracy throughout all, or in any one of the southern states, could be formed and brought to maturity without discovery. It is scarcely possible, that if it were, any considerable number of them could provide themselves with arms; or that if they did, they could assemble in sufficient force to cope with their masters. They might consume their houses, desolate their fields, lay waste the country in various sections, and sacrifice by midnight assassinations hundreds of innocent women and children, as at the late insurrection in Lower Virginia, but they could go no further. The white men would soon assemble, and the sense of inferiority, which makes every slave a coward in the presence of his master, would come in aid of his superiority in all other respects. The most terrible retribution would be exacted of the incendiaries and murderers. No abstract dogma would protect them from utter annihilation. There would be no safety but in destroying them. The race of the black, like that of the red men, who once hunted within our borders, would become extinct, and modern philanthropy be compelled to seek new victims.

. . . Would the sum of human happiness be increased by such a result? Would the pangs of murdered white men, women, and infants; the agonies of the exiled and impoverished survivors, and the destruction of all the landmarks of social improvement, be replaced by the refreshing spectacle of an enlightened, industrious, and happy nation of blacks, living in the enjoyment of rational freedom, sharing the comforts of salutary labor, and the high gratification of moral and intellectual improvement? Look at the following picture of the island of Jamaica, as it presents itself at this moment.

"Every day the negroes are becoming more licentious and corrupt. Singing psalms at the chapels is made an excuse and a cloak by the apprentices for laziness. They do not many of them work over two hours a day. The streets of Kingston, once famed for their orderly quiet, are now nightly the scenes of drunken debauchery, negro drumming, and dancing, much of it under the mask of preaching and singing at the evening conventicles. Jamaica promises soon to become as pestiferous a sink of vice and corruption as the most libertine enthusiast can desire." . . .

Chapter IV. *Of Amalgamation, and a Community of Social and Political Rights.*

. . . The project of intermarrying with the blacks, is a project for debasing the whites by a mixture of that blood which wherever it flows *carries* with it the seed of deterioration. It is a scheme for lowering the standard of our nature, by approximating the highest grade of human beings to the lowest, and is equivalent to enhancing the happiness of mankind by a process of debasement. That the negro should relish the idea of thus improving his breed at the expense of the white race is quite natural; that there should be bound among the latter, men who recommend and enforce such a plan, even from the pulpit, appears somewhat remarkable, as an example of extraordinary disinterestedness. But that there should be white women, well educated and respectable females, supporting it by their money and their influence, their presence and co-operation; apparently willing, nay, anxious to barter their superiority for the badges of degradation; to become the mothers of mulattos; voluntarily to entail upon their posterity a curse that seems coeval with the first existence of the negro, and cast away a portion of the divinity within them at the shrine of a mere abstract dogma, is one of the wonders which fanaticism alone can achieve.

. . . The idea of educating the children of the free white citizens of the United States to consider the blacks their equals, is founded on a total ignorance of nature, its affinities and antipathies. These antipathies may be for a moment overcome or forgotten in the madness of sensuality, but they return again with the greater force from their temporary suspension. White and black children never associate together on terms of perfect equality, from the moment the former begin to reason. There exist physical incongruities which cannot be permanently reconciled and let us add, that we have a right to conclude, from all history and experience, that there is an equal disparity of mental organization.

The difference seems more than skin-deep. The experience of thousands of years arrayed against the principle of equality between the white men and the blacks. Thousands, tens of thousands of the former. In all ages and nations, we have triumphed over every barrier of despotism and slavery. . . . Has the black man ever exhibited similar energies, or achieved such triumphs in his native land or anywhere else? All that he has ever done is to approach to the lowest scale of intellectual eminence; and the world has demonstrated its settled opinion of his inferiority, by pronouncing even this a wonder. . . .

And what has been the result, ninety-nine times in a hundred? Idleness, insolence, and profligacy. Instead of striving to approach the sphere of the white man by becoming expert in some trade or business—some liberal pursuit or daring adventure—his ambition is limited to aping his dress, imitating his follies, caricaturing his manners. . . . What prevents them from acquiring property? They have precisely the same incentives as the white man, like him they have wants to supply and families to maintain; they have civil rights like him to exercise their ambition, and though they may not successfully aspire to high offices of state, there is no obstacle to their becoming of consequence by acquiring an influence over their own colour, which is assuredly a noble object of ambition.

There is nothing under heaven to prevent an industrious, honest, prudent free negro from acquiring property here. . . .

It may be urged, in reply to this, that the negroes labour under the consciousness of being looked upon as an inferior race, and that their genius is repressed by the sense of degradation; that their minds are fettered, their intellects deadened and paralyzed by a conviction that, do what they will, they cannot overcome the disadvantages of their peculiar state, or rise to the level of the white man. But has not the latter, in every age and nation, been some time or other fettered by similar disadvantages? The time has been when the people of Europe were subjected to a state of hereditary vassalage, carrying with it all the attributes of slavery. They possessed no property—they enjoyed no political rights; and the distance between them and the feudal lords was as broad, and apparently as impassable, as that between the slave of the United States and his master. The distinction of colour alone was wanting to render the similitude complete. Yet the mind of the white man, gradually, by mighty efforts, rose superior to all the disadvantages of his situation, and achieved victory after victory over what seemed invincible to human efforts. He never sunk to the level of the negro; his mind was not subjugated; he possessed within himself the principle of regeneration, and to this day continues marching steadily, resolutely, irresistibly forward to his destiny, which is to be free.

The mind of the African, not only in his native country, but through every change, and in all circumstances, seems in a great degree divested of this divine attribute of progressive improvement. In his own country he has, for a long series of ages, remained in the same state of barbarism. For aught we can gather from history, the woolly-headed race of Africans had the same opportunities for improvement that have fallen to the lot of inhabitants of Asia and Europe. . . . Yet they have never awakened from their long sleep of barbarism. They remained, and still remain, savages and pagans, destitute of the rudiments of civilization; three-fourths of them hereditary slaves, and the remainder subject to the will of little arbitrary despots, whose tyranny is proportioned to the insignificance of their dominions. Without the virtues of barbarians, they possess the vices of a corrupted race. . . .

They seem, indeed, like their own native deserts, to be incapable of cultivation, destitute of the capacity of improvement. The dews that would seem desirous to bless them produce no verdure; the rains only descend to sink into the barren insatiable soil that gives back nothing in return. . . . It may be said, indeed, with emphatic truth, that Africa is the region of desert sterility, of savage beasts and savage men, that cannot compare with the white race of Europe, or their descendants in the New World, who, under every disadvantage of situation, have attained to an elevated superiority which they now seem anxious to sacrifice in the desperate hope, that instead of sinking to the dead level of the African, they will be able to lift him to their own. Admitting, however, the theory, that the inferiority of the negro in the United States, and every other country in which he has been held in bondage, may be traced to that gradual debasement which is the natural result of successive generations of slavery, and that will bring them up to the level of equality with ourselves, it seems somewhat unreasonable to call upon the South to pay the penalty, and bear all the consequences of the experiment.

Chapter V. *On the Social and Political Relations that would subsist between Whites and the Blacks, in case of the Emancipation of the latter.*

. . . Separated as are the two races by impassable barriers, carrying in their very faces the badge of that separation, and animated as they must necessarily be by conflicting interests, there can be no doubt that the first struggle would be for ascendancy in political power, and that it would be one of far greater excitement than the ordinary contests of parties in the United States. The master with all his ancient *prejudices*, if you please, all his accustomed ideas and habits of superiority, would be obliged to enter into a struggle for power with his quondam slave; the latter, flushed with all the insolence of newly acquired freedom and glowing not only with the recollections of the past but the hopes of the future. Would such a contest be a peaceable one? Would it approximate to our ordinary elections, in which the struggle is between two parties recognizing in each other equals and associates, while here it will be whether the master shall be governed by his former slave? Impossible. Elections would become battles; and blood, not ballots, would decide the mastery. The body politic would be rent asunder by eternal and inveterate struggles; civil strife would ensue, and a deadly war of extermination be the end of this woeful experiment of philanthropy, where the numbers of the two races were in any way equal. Where the blacks outnumbered the whites, the latter would pass under the yoke of the negro, and become the victims of a legislation of ignorant slaves, unacquainted with every principle of civil liberty or the rights of property, and prepared by the doctrines of the abolitionists to believe that it would be in accordance with the law of God and the rights of nature to claim an equal share of the wealth of the United States. The white race would either become victims or exiles, for it is impossible to conceive they could live under a government so constituted.

Let us now inquire what would be the social relations between the white and the black races, in the event of universal emancipation. . . .

The blacks, though enjoying equal political rights, would be forever excluded from all social equality, and that in a much greater degree than the distinction of ranks now occasions in Europe. This, without doubt, would prove a fruitful source of gnawing irritation and jealous malignity, far more venomous than the feeling with which the starving Irish pauper contemplates the splendid nobleman rioting in luxury, because the pauper sighs only for bread, not equality; whereas the emancipated negro receives at the same time the boon of equal rights and an equal voice in the state. . . .

. . . Without property, yet with equal rights and superior numbers, the blacks would wrest from their ancient masters the power of the state, and beyond doubt exercise it for the purpose of oppressing them. Without those habits and that experience, which are always indispensable to self-government, they would endeavour to modify the state to suit their own wayward purposes; and without any other religion than fanaticism, the piety of ignorance, they would become the dictators of the public faith. Their ascendancy would be a despotism over white men, and the fabric of civilization and liberty, which consumed ages in its construction, would be demolished in a few years by the relentless fury of ignorant barbarians. A new Africa would spring up in the place of free and enlightened states, and the race of the white men be either forced to abandon their homes, or to level themselves with the degradation around. . . .

It is suggested that the emancipated slaves would find their way to the North. But how are they to get here? Who is to support them by the way? Or are they to travel like clouds of locusts, laying waste, and devouring the fruits of the earth? What is to become of their bedrid parents, and helpless children? Such numbers could not work their way for hundreds of miles, and such an army of paupers would exhaust the charity of the abolitionists themselves. . . .

Chapter X. *Of the Fanaticism of the Abolitionists, and its hostility to Religion, Morals, Liberty, Patriotism, and the Social Virtues.*

. . . Thus, fanaticism is the leading influence actuating the proceedings of the abolitionists directly at war with the Scriptures as well as with the progress of religion among the slaves in the South. But this is not all. It takes a wider range of mischief. It is the most fatal enemy of the great and true principles of religion everywhere and at all times. The excesses committed by its votaries, and the mischief which in every age they have brought down on the heads of mankind, under the sanction of religion, are such, that nothing but its being upheld by an Almighty arm, could have prevented the human race from repudiating a faith coming, not in the semblance of a bright celestial influence descending like a dove from heaven with the olive in its grasp and peace nestling under its wings, but rising from the impenetrable darkness of error and delusion like a destroying fiend, smiting the blessings of the earth with blight and mildew, tracking its course with blood and fire, and offering up thousands of hecatombs to the God of mercy and forgiveness. It is this perversion of the most mild, forgiving, and merciful code ever pronounced to mankind, that has driven more sheep from the fold of the divine Shepherd, and made more infidels, than the mission of

Mohammed, or the progress of free principles, which the supporters of monarchy are pleased to represent as the most dangerous enemies to true religion.

Happily for us, the fanatics cannot as yet resort to the stake and the fagot in this country. It is boasted that the mild and tolerant spirit of this wonderful age has banished those persecutions which disgraced the earlier periods of Christianity. But, like much of the vapourings of the times, the vaunt is rather unsubstantial. It is true that it is no longer the fashion to pass laws preventing a diversity in religious opinions, nor bring about a conformity, as Procrustes did in the length of his victims by stretching them on a bed of torture. But the fanatical zealots can and do little, in the spirit of bitter persecution and in the shade of slanderous libels, by denouncing whole communities, states, and sections of the country, containing millions of people, as "man-stealers and murderers," living in the daily violation of the precepts of humanity and the laws of God. They can and do undermine their happiness; destroy the security of their domestic fireside; stimulate their dependents to insurrection and murder; pervert the precepts of religion to the purposes of defamation, and under the sanction of its name rush into direct opposition to its spirit. Such a course can be called by no other name than persecution, and that of the bitterest kind, equally at war with the attributes of the Supreme Being, as the welfare of his creatures.

. . . It is thus with the sect of fanatics which has rallied under pretense of vindicating the rights of the slave. Their whole proceedings are in direct hostility to all freedom of person and property; for if they can find one text of Scripture which renders it imperative on the master "instantly"—as they maintain in their great manifesto—to manumit his slaves, there is no knowing but that in good time they may detect in the dream of Isaiah or the Song of Solomon, another, which commands us to restore to the Indians the lands which they once held within the limits of the United States. There is no mischievous absurdity that may not be imposed upon us, where the code is a text, and its interpreters madmen or impostors.

Fanaticism, when assuming the garb of universal philanthropy, is equally opposed to all patriotism, and all the social relations of life. It has no fireside, no home, no centre. The equal lover of "the entire human race," such as Mr. Garrison and his associates, is in effect a traitor to his country, a bad citizen, a cold-hearted friend, a worthless husband, and an unnatural father if he acts up to his principles. He is false to his native land and to the nearest and dearest ties and duties, moral, social, and political, for he stands ready to sacrifice them all for the benefit of strangers, aliens, and enemies.

Source Note: James Kirke Paulding, *Slavery in the United States*, New York, 1836.

JAMES RUSSELL LOWELL (1819–1891)

The death of James Russell Lowell in 1891 was one of three significant losses within one year for American literature. Herman Melville, who was Lowell's exact contemporary, also died in 1891, and Walt Whitman died in 1892. Lowell had enjoyed a secure position as professor of poetry at Harvard University, while Melville worked as a customs inspector and Whitman held various positions in journalism, usually until he was dismissed. Lowell came from a distinguished New England family with deep connections to Boston and Harvard, and as a graduating senior, he was selected to compose the class poem in 1838. At age nineteen, he had already discovered a poetic voice. His poem was a clever satire of contemporary culture, including in its targets Transcendentalism, abolition, women's rights, and even temperance reform. Later, in the *Biglow Papers* (1848 and 1867), a similar satirical persona would appear; and throughout his career, Lowell employed the "Yankee voice of political reason" to critique contemporary culture, including the humorous persona of Hosea Biglow.

Following his undergraduate career at Harvard, Lowell took a degree in law, also at Harvard, and very briefly set up a practice in Boston. Self-awareness led him to abandon the law at the very time when "literary nationalism," the desire of some Americans to focus on American culture and to abandon dependence on European and especially British culture, was expressing itself in new journals and periodicals such as *The Atlantic Monthly*. Naturally drawn to these enterprises because of his instinct for reform and cultural criticism, Lowell eventually became editor of *The Atlantic Monthly* in 1857. In 1856, he was appointed to full the post of professor of poetry at Harvard, a position just vacated by Henry Wadsworth Longfellow. Throughout his life, Lowell traveled widely, and he spent two years in Europe, 1872 to 1874. He also cultivated friendships with literary luminaries in New England, such as Ralph Waldo Emerson. In 1864, he commenced a relationship with Charles Eliot Norton, who would edit Lowell's collected works after his death. Together, they coedited the *North American Review* from 1864 to 1868.

If Lowell's literary life was immensely successful, his personal life was tragic. Lowell's first wife, Maria, had extremely poor health and they traveled to Europe in 1851 and 1852 to seek a milder climate; in 1853, Maria died. Three of the four Lowell children that had been born between 1845 and 1850 did not live beyond two years of age. These events parallel the dates on all of the Lowell pieces included in this volume. In the 1840s, Lowell became an editor for two journals that were dedicated to the abolition of slavery in the United States: *The Pennsylvania Freeman* and *The National Anti-Slavery Standard*. Some of the titles of this chapter's selections indicate the content of these journals: "The Abolitionists and Emancipation" and "The Moral Argument against Slavery" are both from *The National Anti-Slavery Standard*. Readers should also note that one of Lowell's essays, "Ethnology," is included in chapter 7, "Science in Antebellum America." In this piece, Lowell discusses contemporary race theory and the science of ethnology. He is joined there by Frederick Douglass's two essays on the subject of ethnology and race theory, "The Color Line" and "The Claims of the Negro Ethnologically Considered" (1854).

Lowell effectively applied his Yankee satirical voice to contemporary social and political subjects, and, like the Quaker poet John Greenleaf Whittier, was a frequent contributor and essayist in newspapers and journals that condemned the institution of chattel slavery. Lowell was ideologically allied with William Lloyd Garrison and the more militant wing of the abolitionist group. The selections here show clearly his criticism of the institutional church's role in the slavery controversy, his intense dislike of slavery as an institution, and his view that the government had not done enough to oppose such an immoral practice. (See "Politics and the Pulpit," where these concerns are merged, *National Anti-Slavery Standard*, January 25, 1849.)

Modern readers know very little of Lowell, because his satirical style, which had been modeled on precedents such as Washington Irving's Jonathan Oldstyle and Jeffrey Crayon, Gent., was eclipsed by the more powerful satirical voice of Mark Twain by the end of the nineteenth century. Twain's *Huckleberry Finn* (1885) and *Puddn'head Wilson* (1894) were both popular and effective critiques of the antebellum South and slavery, and both books were widely circulated to a much larger audience than Lowell had enjoyed. Still, Lowell's cultural and social criticism came during the decades of antebellum slavery, while Twain's works addressed the legacy of slavery and issues of race relations by pairing Jim and Huck, Tom Driscoll and "Chambers" during the crucial years of Jim Crow legislation and the Supreme Court case of *Plessy v Ferguson* (1896), by which "separate but equal" became the law of the land from the highest federal bench.

Lowell was slugging it out in the trenches in the 1840s while the slavery debates were still a critical antebellum social issue, and his voice was a most important one in spreading the gospel of antislavery and abolitionist sentiment. According to Thomas Wortham, a leading contemporary scholar of Lowell, the neglect of Lowell's writings in the twentieth century does not invalidate his importance to his own time; and no understanding of the cultural life of America in the nineteenth century can be complete without recognition of Lowell's centrality and versatility (Wortham, p. 43). Lowell and Whittier were two antebellum poets who devoted much time and energy to writing verses and essays against slavery, even though their voices today are not as well recognized as those of Emerson, Thoreau, and Whitman.

SUGGESTIONS FOR FURTHER READING

Duberman, Martin. *James Russell Lowell*. Boston: Houghton Mifflin, 1966.

Fletcher, Angus. "James Russell Lowell." In *Encyclopedia of American Poetry: The Nineteenth Century*, ed. Eric L. Haralson (Chicago: Dearborn, 1998), pp. 271–77.

Howard, Leon. *Victorian Knight-Errant: A Study of the Early Literary Career of James Russell Lowell*. Berkeley: University of California Press, 1952.

Lowell, James Russell. *The Complete Writings of James Russell Lowell*. Elmwood edition, ed. Charles Eliot Norton, 16 vols. Boston and New York: Houghton Mifflin, 1904. Many university libraries house this collected edition.

"Lowell, James Russell." In *The Transcendentalists: A Review of Research and Criticism*, ed. Joel Myerson (New York: Modern Language Association, 1984), pp. 336–42.

Rees, Robert A. "James Russell Lowell." In *Fifteen American Authors before 1900: Bibliographic Essays on Research and Criticism*, ed. Rees and Earl Herbert (Madison: University of Wisconsin Press, 1971).

Rourke, Constance. *American Humor: A Study in National Character*. New York: Harcourt, Brace, 1931. Often reprinted and available in paperback.

Scudder, Horace E. *James Russell Lowell: Biography*. New York: Houghton, 2001.

Wortham, Thomas. "James Russell Lowell." In *Dictionary of Literary Biography*, vol. 1, *The American Renaissance in New England* (Ann Arbor: Gale Research, 1999), pp. 126–31. An excellent brief overview.

The Abolitionists and Emancipation
by James Russell Lowell

Next to the charge of being possessed of only a single idea, the accusation most often brought against Abolitionists has been that they have retarded the progress of emancipation and made more galling the fetters of the slave. If emancipation at all hazards be the one idea of the Abolitionists, this is the one idea of their opponents. . . .

In the first place has there really been a change of public opinion for the worse, either at the North or the South, since the Liberator came into existence eighteen years ago? We select this period as the point of departure, and not because we have forgotten Woolman, Benezet, and Lundy, but because these stand in the same relation to the Anti-slavery movement in America that Dante, the Lollards and Huss hold in respect to Luther.

. . . Moreover, at the time when the movement began, Slavery was regarded as a distant and detached object. The immense spread of its roots, and how they had forced themselves into every crevice in the foundations of Church and State, was not even suspected. . . .

Any one who has read Clarkson's "History of the Abolition of the Slave Trade" cannot fail to be struck with the similarity of the objections brought against the advocate of that measure in England and those which are constantly thrown in the way of American Anti-slavery. . . .

. . . The simple fact undoubtedly is that were the Abolitionists now to go back to the position from which they started, they would find themselves less fanatical than a very respectable minority of the people. . . . The Garrison of 1831 might be a popular man and a member of Congress now. But it is part of the order of Providence that there should be always Garrisons as well as popular men and members of Congress.

. . . So much for the retarding effect of the Anti-slavery agitation at the North. At the South, if violent opposition has been excited, it has been a mere offset to equal violence on the other side. It has arisen from the fact that the defenders of slavery instinctively felt that their weakness was in their own camp. How could what is in its own nature the most unreasonable of institutions, be reasonably defended? How could that which is founded on force and fraud be gently and honestly supported? . . . The efforts of the Abolitionists have drawn so much attention toward slavery, and their sentiments have found so much sympathy even in some of the Slave States themselves, that every evil, cruelty and misery belonging to the system has become painfully conspicuous. The slaveholder in the remotest rice swamp of Florida feels that the walls have eyes and ears.

The fanaticism of the Abolitionists has retarded emancipation, just in the same way that Luther retarded the Reformation. Considering the immense odds against which they have had to struggle, they have brought about a revolution in a wonderfully short space of time. It does not matter that the advocates of emancipation in the Slave States shrink from accepting the abolition doctrine in all its length and breadth. . . . Along the slender wire of Northern Anti-slavery the Southern Abolitionist receives the inspiring influx of the religious senti-ment, the love of freedom, and the humanity of entire Christendom. Slavery has nothing behind it but the sheer precipice, nothing before it but the inevitable retributive Doom.

Source Note: James Russell Lowell, "The Abolitionists and Emancipation," *The Na-tional Anti-Slavery Standard*, March 1, 1849.

Politics and the Pulpit
by James Russell Lowell

There can be no fallacy greater or more dangerous than is contained in the popular axiom that politics and religion should be kept carefully disjoined. It is an axiom which had its origin in the unprincipled self-interest of politicians. It *is* of a piece with the system which would shut God out from the secular part of the week and imprison Him in a particular day and in certain buildings. With equal propriety the merchant might banish religion from business, and the tradesman keep it carefully away from his shop. Indeed it is too often true that, as the clergyman leaves his robes hanging in the vestry, the congregation doff their religion to be locked up in the church where it will be kept safely till they need it to put on again when the seventh day, appropriate to that ceremony, shall have come *round* again.

Next to having no religion at all, this kind, which can be put on and off at will, is certainly the most convenient. . . .

The great hardship of the Christian revelation lies in the exact closeness with which it will fit you and me. Embodying a universal truth, it possesses within itself a principle of development which renders it a test for the church, the state and the individual in every possible phase of society. It is a standard which cannot warp or shrink, and which indicates with impartial indifference every deviation from the immutable line of right and duty. It cannot well be a very comfortable instrument in the hands of a faithful minister.

. . . Abolitionists have no quarrel with the Church as a Church, but only with the Church as it is. This is the reason why they are odious to sect-wrights and divinity-mongers. They do not deny the great services which the Church and the Clergy have rendered to truth and progress as the instruments of order and organization. But they affirm that a Church, to be of any benefit, must be in advance of the social ideas of the age, and demand of the Clergy that they no longer organize sects, but society. It is not politics which they ask them to preach, but Christianity itself.

To state the matter more strictly, it is not the Abolitionist who makes the demands. They are the requisitions of our present social condition. Nor is the Church so much called upon to be a Reformer, as to be truly a Church. The clergy, at least in America, are no longer a privileged order. They do not and cannot any longer occupy the position which they held when the mouth and the pen were the only vehicles and disseminators of truth. They are no longer the only priests, and there are other pulpits than those on churches. . . .

Nevertheless a certain amount of prestige still attaches itself to the clergy. They are still looked upon as guardians specially set apart to watch over religion and spiritual things. A seventh part of the year is reserved for them, and their obligations to truth are larger in proportion to the opportunity afforded them to disseminate and enforce it. . . .

Source Note: James Russell Lowell, "Politics and the Pulpit," *The National Anti-Slavery Standard*, January 25, 1849. Reprinted in *The Anti-Slavery Papers of James Russell Lowell* (Boston: Houghton Mifflin and Co., 1902; reprinted 1969 by Negro Universities Press, New York).

The Church and the Clergy
by James Russell Lowell

. . . There is no such short and easy way to popularity among the thoughtless and uneducated portion of the people as that of assuming to be the defender of their religious prejudices, however absurd and monstrous they may be. When a system has become corrupt, an indifferent skepticism gradually pervades the more refined and intellectual classes of society, while the zeal of the brutal and unintelligent in its defence becomes proportioned always to the nearness of its approach to their sympathies and tastes, and the indulgences it allows to their appetites. . . .

Every true abolitionist is thoroughly persuaded that the most terrible weapon which they can bring to bear, not only against slavery, but against all other social vices, is the religious sentiment of the country. But it is the *true* religious sentiment, and not that of which the churches and clergy of the land are the present exponents, which they are striving to reach; and the religious system of the country, as now existing, is the greatest obstacle in their way. . . . The political and religious principles of a nation must, in order to have any useful vitality, be in advance of that nation's civilization. When they have brought the civilization of that nation up to their own higher level, they must move forward another step. In this country the civilization of the people has not yet come nearly up to the political principles set forth in the Declaration of Independence, but it has already gone beyond the religious principle as now represented by the church. It is time, then, for the church to re-form itself so as to be the emblem of something higher and purer—of something which shall satisfy the demand of the foremost spirits of the age—and no longer be content, by remaining fixed in a traditionary and retrospective excellence, to be the time-serving cloak and excuse for the indolent or interested who lag behind. . . .

Source Note: James Russell Lowell, "The Church and the Clergy," *The National Anti-Slavery Standard*, February 27, 1845.

The Church and the Clergy Again
by James Russell Lowell

. . . If the church carry this divine authority with it, it should be always in advance of public opinion. It should not wait till the Washingtonians, by acting the part which, in virtue of the station it arrogates to itself, should have been its own, had driven it to sign the pledge and hold fellowship with the degraded and fallen. It should not wait until the abolitionists, by working a change in the public sentiment of the people, have convinced it that it is more politic to sympathize with the slave than with the slave-owner, before it ventures to lisp the alphabet of anti-slavery. The glorious privilege of leading the forlorn hope of truth, of facing the desperate waves of prejudice, of making itself vile in the eyes of men by choosing the humblest means of serving the despised cause of the Master it professes to worship, all these belong to it in right of the position it has assumed.

Instead of timidly yielding to, and in many instances encouraging, the prejudices or the ignorant rage of the mob, it is the clergy themselves who should have been the victims (if any there must be) of the first wrath of assaulted sin. It is they who should have been mobbed, who should have endured insult and contumely. . . .

The church is, in its true sense, merely the outward symbol of the religious sentiment as that sentiment ought to be. When it becomes merely the symbol of that sentiment as it is, there is no longer any use or fitness in it, and it degrades the moral sense of the nation which it was its duty to elevate. Then it is time for all those who have some innate principle of religion, and who are therefore competent to reform it, to begin an attack upon it which shall compel it to move forward in reality to that lofty stand which it has duped men into believing that it occupies already. . . .

Source Note: James Russell Lowell, "The Church and the Clergy Again," *The National Anti-Slavery Standard*, March 27, 1845.

The Moral Argument against Slavery
by James Russell Lowell

. . . The American Anti-Slavery Society advocates disunion on anti-slavery grounds that it draws up to itself odium and denunciation. . . .

Whatever opinion the editor of an anti-slavery paper may entertain as to the evils or benefits which would result from a dissolution of the union, he should never himself (nor let his readers) lose sight of the fact that those who urge that measure do so from an intense appreciation of the horrors of slavery. They are men and women who keep the popular mind alive to an example of self-devotion in behalf of a purely moral object and charge it with a portion of the magnetism of their self-sacrifice, who attack fearlessly and without question of odds every institution, however venerable with time or hallowed with associations, which affords shelter or vantage ground to the forces of the evil principle they are at war with. . . .

Meanwhile, a pure Ethical Idea can never be defeated. It cannot, indeed, be brought into conflict with material organizations, but only applied to them as an impartial test. It cannot attract to itself the rancorous animosity, nor the imputation of motives of personal aggrandizement, to which a political association, however pure, is liable. It does not present to the gross and undiscriminating popular eye a divided object. Its activity is not sensible of any seasons of peculiar intensity or depression. It is not restricted to time and place—the year long caucuses are held in the family and the workshop. It knows no distinction of age or sex, but draws to itself the yet undissipate sympathies of youth and contracts indissoluble alliance with the finer instinct and more persistent enthusiasm of woman.

Two things especially absorb the admiration and sympathy of men—practical success and that weariless devotion which does not need the stimulus of success. The former is the key to the popularity of Taylor, the latter to the power of Garrison. People without ideas laugh at the man of one. But these men are not so common as is generally imagined. That mind is of no ordinary strain which, through long years of obloquy and derision, can still keep its single object as fresh and attractive as at first. It is the man of one idea who attains his end. Narrowness does not always imply bigotry, but sometimes concentration.

. . . But the necessity of renewed and continuous exertion on the part of non-political abolitionists is enforced by all the signs of the times. It is they who keep alive the scattered sparks which are fanned into flame during the gusty days of electioneering excitement. Nay, at what altar was the firebrand lighted which the Fox of Kinderhook carried into the standing corn of the Philistines?

Source Note: James Russell Lowell, "The Moral Argument against Slavery," *The National Anti-Slavery Standard*, February 22, 1849.

Daniel Webster
by James Russell Lowell

Mr. Edward Webster *has* arrived in town for the purposes of recruiting a company of volunteers for the Mexican War. He *has* taken this step, we understand with the full approval of his distinguished father.
—(*Boston Papers*)

. . . Among the thousand and one so-called great men of this so-called democracy, Daniel Webster always excites in us the most painful feeling of regret. A man who might have done so much, and who will die without having disburthened the weary heart of Humanity of one of its devouring griefs! What has freedom to thank Daniel Webster for? What has Peace? What has Civilization? What has that true Conservatism, which consists in bringing the earth forward and upward to the idea of its benign Maker? In one word, how is God the better served, how are heaven and earth more at one for His having bestowed upon this man that large utterance, that divine faculty of eloquent speech? How was man made in the image of God, save that the capacity was given him of being an adequate representative on earth of some one of the attributes of the Great Father, and His loyal ambassador to man?

Who that has ever witnessed the wonderful magnetism which Webster exerts over masses of men can doubt that his great powers have been staked against the chances of the presidential chair and lost, gambled, thrown away by the fortune of the dice? The influence of his physical presence is prodigious. He owes half his fame to it. . . .

It is said that great occasions summon forth great minds to be their servants and to do their work. Rather, we should say, the world is full of great occasions, but only great minds can see them, and surrender themselves unreservedly to their dictation. Such men as Washington are called providential men. And so they are; yet there were men of far greater intellectual capacity than Washington in the day of the Revolution. Washington had a great *character*, and it is in proportion as they possess this mysterious faculty (*we* may call it) that men make their mark upon their age, and are valued by posterity. Herein consists the great strength of such men as Garrison, and it is precisely here that Webster is wanting. . . .

Will God decide that the occasion has been wanting to Daniel Webster? How far might not that trumpet voice have reached, in behalf of the oppressed, from the commanding position conceded to his powerful intellect! How far might it not have aroused who now sleep, forgetful of their duty to their fellow-man! God has given him eminent faculties, and what is the harvest? Will they who from among the crowding tares of the world glean the sparse wheat ears for God's hungry poor, be forced to pull down their barns and build greater because Daniel Webster has lived? . . . He has won the title "Defender of the Constitution" by his zeal in fostering the corrupt public sentiment which sets the political shifts of men above the law of nature and of God. . . . And finally, he has sent his youngest son (a youth who has just about brains enough to be conveniently come at by a cannon ball) to Boston to recruit company for the Mexican War, as if his subserviency to the slave power had not already amply atoned for his federalism in the last war, and richly earned for him the title of *patriot* as it is understood in America.

. . . Verily, we say again, there is no sadder sentence than "*might have been.*"

Source Note: James Russell Lowell, "Daniel Webster," *National Anti-Slavery Standard*, July 2, 1846. Reprinted in *The Anti-Slavery Papers of James Russell Lowell* (Boston: Houghton Mifflin and Co., 1902; reprinted 1969 by Negro Universities Press, New York).

WALT WHITMAN (1819–1892)
edited and introduced by William Pannapacker

"I was anti-slavery," Whitman said in 1888, "from the first: and not only anti-slavery: a friend, indeed, all around of the progressist [*sic*] fellows: that's where, why, how, I finally cut off from the Democratic party."[1] In 1846 Whitman supported the terms of the Wilmot Proviso in one of the first articles he wrote for the Brooklyn *Daily Eagle*, "Slavers—and the Slave Trade." Slavery, he writes, "is a disgrace and blot on the character of our Republic, and on our boasted humanity!" He describes the horrors of the Middle Passage and advocates the end of slave trafficking by military force. Nevertheless, Whitman was alienated by the fiery rhetoric of both sides of the slavery debate. In "New States: Shall They Be Slave or Free?" Whitman attacks "the unquestionable folly, the wicked wrong, of 'abolitionist' interference with slavery in the Southern States," but he expresses a belief that all new states should be free, and that free soil for American workers is part of the national destiny.

Whitman became a Free-Soil Democrat who opposed the extension of slavery into the western territories but was willing to permit slavery in states where it already existed. Slavery was never Whitman's primary interest as a reformer: "I saw other evils that cried to me in perhaps even a louder voice: the labor evil . . . to speak of only one."[2] Above all, he was concerned with the interests of the "common people" against the interests of "aristocratic" slaveholders. In "American Workingmen, Versus Slavery" he hoped that the new territories provided by the Mexican War would become available for tradesmen and manual laborers. Whitman believed that white workers could not compete economically with slavery, and that the institution degraded the nobility of labor in general. Whitman was outraged by the Compromise of 1850 and wrote four poems for the New York papers, including the "The House of Friends," which attacks Northern politicians for betraying the ideals of the nation for personal gain, holding them more responsible than Southern leaders. During the Civil War Whitman's paramount concern—like Lincoln's—was the preservation of the Union; the end of slavery was only a "strange and marvelous" side effect. "The negro was not the chief thing: the chief thing was to stick together," he later said.[3]

As Whitman moved from political journalism to poetry from 1847 through the early 1850s, he fell increasingly under the influence of Emerson and Transcendentalism. *Leaves of Grass* (1855) seems a radical departure from Whitman's earlier Free Soil stance; while it echoes the populist celebration of labor found in editorials such as "American Workingmen, Versus Slavery," it also expresses support for violent abolitionism, admiration for African-Americans, and sympathetic identification with slaves. It is this Whitman who eventually attained public prominence and attracted the praise of Sojourner Truth and Langston Hughes. Whitman remained more concerned with white labor than the plight of African-Americans, but he increasingly saw the centrality of their experience to the Civil War and the unfolding of the American mission he celebrated.

SUGGESTIONS FOR FURTHER READING

Scholarly editions of Whitman's varied writings have been issued by New York University Press and include: *The Correspondence*, six vols., ed. Edwin Haviland Miller (1961–77); *The Early Poems and the Fiction*, ed. Thomas L. Brasher (1963); *Prose Works 1892*, 2 vols., ed. Floyd Stovall (1963–64); *Leaves of Grass, Comprehensive Reader's Edition*, ed. Sculley Bradley and Harold W. Blodgett (1965); *Daybooks and Notebooks*, 3 vols., ed. William White (1978); *Leaves of Grass: A Textual Variorum of the Printed Poems*, 3 vols., ed. Sculley Bradley et al. (1980); *Notebooks and Unpublished Prose Manuscripts*, 6 vols., ed. Edward F. Grier (1984). Whitman's journalism is partly collected in *The Journalism, 1834–1846*, ed. Herbert Bergman, Douglass A. Noverr, and Edward J. Recchia (1998); additional writings are reprinted in a variety of sources: *The Gathering of the Forces*, 2 vols., ed. Cleveland Rodgers and John Black (1920); *I Sit and Look Out: Editorials from the Brooklyn Daily Times*, ed. Emory Holloway and Vernolian Schwartz (1966); *Walt Whitman of the New York Aurora*, ed. Joseph Jay Rubin and Charles H. Brown (1950); and *New York Dissected*, ed. Emory Holloway and Ralph Adimari (1936). *Walt Whitman's Workshop*, ed. Clifton Joseph Furness (1928), remains a valuable source of Whitman's unpublished writings, including a chapter of "Anti-Slavery Notes." Whitman's conversations from 1888 to 1892 were recorded by Horace Traubel in nine volumes by various publishers under the title, *With Walt Whitman in Camden* (1906–96). Whitman's critical reception may be traced in *Walt Whitman: The Contemporary Reviews*, ed. Kenneth M. Price (1996).

The standard biography of Whitman is Gay Wilson Allen's *The Solitary Singer* (1967); David Reynolds's *Walt Whitman's America: A Cultural Biography* (1995) provides substantial commentary on Whitman's relationship with abolitionism and African-Americans. Other works containing examinations of this relationship include Eric Foner, *The Inner Civil War* (1980); Martin Klammer, *Whitman, Slavery, and the Emergence of Leaves of Grass* (1995); and M. Wynn Thomas, *The Lunar Light of Whitman's Poetry* (1987). Indispensable references are Scott Giantvalley's *Walt Whitman, 1838–1939: A Reference Guide* (1981); Donald D. Kummings's *Walt Whitman, 1947–1975: A Reference Guide* (1982); Joel Myerson's *Walt Whitman: A Descriptive Bibliography* (1993); and *The Walt Whitman Encyclopedia*, ed. Donald Kummings and J. R. Le Master (1998).

1. Horace Traubel, *With Walt Whitman in Camden* (New York: Rowman and Littlefield, 1961), 3:91.
2. Ibid., 1:454.
3. Ibid.

Slavery and the Slave Trade
by Walt Whitman

Public attention, within the last few days, has been naturally turned to the slave trade—that most abominable of all man's schemes for making money, without regard to the character of the means used for the purpose. Four vessels have in about as many days, been brought to the American territory, for being engaged in this monstrous business! It is a disgrace and blot on the character of our Republic, and on our boasted humanity!

Though we hear less now-a-days of this trade—of the atrocious slave hunt—of the crowding of a mass of compact human flesh into little more than its equal of space—we are not to suppose that such horrors have ceased to exist. The great nations of the earth—our own first of all—have passed stringent laws against the slave traffic. But Brazil openly encourages it still. And many citizens of Europe and America pursue it notwithstanding its illegality. Still the negro is torn from his simple hut—from his children, his brethren, his parents, and friends—to be carried far away and made the bondman of a stranger. Still the black-hearted traitors who ply this work, go forth with their armed bands and swoop down on the defenseless villages, and bring their loads of human trophy, chained and gagged, and sell them as so much merchandise!

The slave ship! How few of our readers know the beginning of the horrors involved in that term! Imagine a vessel of the fourth or fifth class, built more for speed than space, and therefore with narrow accommodations even for a few passengers; a space between decks divided into two compartments three feet three inches from floor to ceiling—one of these compartments sixteen feet by eighteen, the other forty by twenty-one—the first holding two hundred and twenty-six children and youths of both sexes—the second, *three hundred and thirty-six men and women*—and all this in a latitude where the thermometer is at eighty degrees in the shade! Are you sick of the description? O, this is not all, by a good sight. Imagine neither food nor water given these hapless prisoners—except a little of the latter, at long intervals, which they spill in their mad eagerness to get it; many of the women advanced in pregnancy—the motion of the sea sickening those who have never before felt it—dozens of the poor wretches dying, and others already dead, (and they are most to be envied!)—the very air so thick that the lungs cannot perform their office—and all this for filthy lucre! Pah! we are almost a misanthrope to our kind when we think they will do such things!

Of the nine hundred negroes (there were doubtless more,) originally on board the *Pons*, not six hundred and fifty remained when she arrived back, and landed her inmates at Monrovia! It is enough to make the heart pause its pulsations to read the scene presented at the liberation of these sons of misery.—Most of them were boys, of from twelve to twenty years. What woe must have spread through many a negro mother's heart, from this wicked business!

It is not ours to find an excuse for slaving, in the benighted condition of the African. Has not God seen fit to make him, and leave him so? Nor is it any less our fault because the chiefs of that barbarous land fight with each other, and take slave prisoners. The whites encourage them, and afford them a market. Were that market destroyed, there would soon be no supply.

We would hardly so insult our countrymen as to suppose that any among them yet countenance a system—only a little portion of whose horrors we have been describing—did not facts prove the contrary. The "middle passage" is yet going on with all its deadly crime and cruelty. The slave-trade yet exists. *Why?* The laws are sharp enough—too sharp. But who ever hears of their being put in force, further than to confiscate the vessel, and perhaps imprison the crews a few days? But the laws should pry out every man who helps the slave-trade— not merely the sailor on the sea, but *the cowardly rich villain, and speculator on the land*—and punish *him*. It cannot be effectually stopped until that is done— and Brazil, forced by the black muzzles of American and European men-of-war's cannon, to stop her part of the business, too!

Source Note: First published in the Brooklyn *Daily Eagle*, March 18, 1846. Reprinted in *The Gathering of the Forces*, 2 vols., ed. Cleveland Rodgers and John Black (New York: G. P. Putnam's Sons, 1920), 1:187–91.

New States: Shall They Be Slave or Free?
by Walt Whitman

It is of not so much importance, the difference in the idea of a proper time to discuss, if we are only united in the *principle* that whatever new territory may be annexed to the United States shall be free territory, and not for slaves. With the present slave States, of course, no human being any where out from themselves has the least shadow of a right to interfere; but in new land, added to our surface by the national arms, and by the action of our government, and where slavery does not exist, it is certainly of momentous importance one way or the other, whether that land shall be slave land or not. All ordinary "weighty issues" are insignificant before this: it swallows them up as Aaron's rod swallowed the other rods. It involves the question whether the mighty power of this Republic, put forth in its greatest strength, shall be used to root deeper and spread wider an institution which Washington, Jefferson, Madison, and all the old fathers of our freedom, anxiously, and avowedly from the bottom of their hearts, sought the extinction of, and considered inconsistent with the other institutions of the land. And if those true and brave old men were now among us, can any candid person doubt which "side" they would espouse in this argument? Would the great apostle of Democracy—in his clear views of right and wrong, and their linked profit and loss—would he *now*, seeing the stalwart giants of the free young West, contrasted with the meager leanness of the South—meagre with all her noble traits—would *he* hesitate in bending his divine energies to the side of freedom?

The man who accustoms himself to *think*, when such matters are put before him, and does not whiff his opinion rapidly out, from mere heedlessness, or from a more degrading motive, will see the wide and radical difference between the unquestionable folly, and wicked wrong, of "abolitionist" interference with slavery in the Southern States—and this point of establishing slavery in a fresh land. With the former we have nothing to do; but with the latter, we should all be derelict to our highest duties as Christians, as men, and as Democrats, if we did not throw ourselves into the field of discussion, using the utmost display of every energy wherewith God has endowed us, in behalf of the side which reason and religion proclaim as the right one. Is *this* the country, and *this* the age, where and when we are to be told that slavery must be propped up and extended? And shall any respectable portion of our citizens be deluded either by the sophisms of Mr. Calhoun, or those far, very far, lower influences of the darkest and meanest phases of demagogism, which are rife more in the North than the South, to act in a matter which asks consideration purely on points of high justice, human rights, national advantage, and the safety of the Union in the future?

Source Note: First published in the Brooklyn *Daily Eagle*, April 22, 1847. Reprinted in *The Gathering of the Forces*, 1:200–2.

American Workingmen, Versus Slavery
by Walt Whitman

The question whether or no there shall be slavery in the new territories which it seems conceded on all hands we are largely to get through this Mexican war, is a question between *the grand body of white workingmen, the millions of mechanics, farmers, and operatives of our country*, with their interests on the one side—and the interests of the few thousand rich, "polished," and aristocratic owners of slaves at the South, on the other side. Experience has proved, (and the evidence is to be seen now by any one who will look at it) that a stalwart mass of respectable workingmen, cannot exist, much less flourish, in a thorough slave State. Let any one think for a moment what a different appearance New York, Pennsylvania, or Ohio, would present—how much less sturdy independence and family happiness there would be—were slaves the workmen there, instead of each man as a general thing being his own workman. We wish not at all to sneer at the South; but leaving out of view the educated and refined gentry, and coming to the "common people" of the whites, everybody knows what a miserable, ignorant, and shiftless set of beings they are. Slavery is a good thing enough, (viewed partially,) to the rich—the one out of thousands; but it is destructive to the dignity and independence of all who work, and to labor itself. An honest poor mechanic, in a slave State, is put on a par with the negro slave mechanic—there being many of the latter, who are hired out by their owners. It is of no use to reason abstractly on this fact—farther than to say that the pride of a Northern American freeman, poor though he be, will not comfortably stand such degradation.

The influence of the slavery institution is to bring the dignity of labor down to the level of slavery, which, God knows! is low enough. And this it is which must induce *the workingmen of the North, East, and West, to come up, to a man, in defense of their rights, their honor, and that heritage of getting bread by the sweat of the brow, which we must leave to our children*. Let them utter forth, then, in tones as massive as becomes their stupendous cause, that their calling shall *not* be sunk to the miserable level of what is little above brutishness—sunk to be like owned goods, and driven cattle!—We call upon every mechanic of the North, East, and West—upon the carpenter, in his rolled up sleeves, the mason with his trowel, the stonecutter with his brawny chest, the blacksmith with his sooty face, the brown fisted shipbuilder, whose clinking strokes rattle so merrily in our dock yards—upon shoemakers, and cartmen, and drivers, and pavers, and porters, and millwrights, and furriers, and ropemakers, and butchers, and machinists, and tinmen, and tailors, and hatters, and coach and cabinet makers— upon the honest sawyer and mortarmixer too, whose sinews are their own—and every hard-working man—to speak in a voice whose great reverberations shall tell to all quarters that the *workingmen* of the free United States, and their business, are not willing to be put on the level of negro slaves, in territory which, if got at all, must be got by taxes sifted eventually through upon them, and by their hard work and blood. But most of all we call upon *the farmers*, the workers of the land—that prolific brood of brown faced fathers and sons who swarm over the free States, and form the bulwark of our Republic, mightier than walls or armies—upon them we call to say whether *they* too will exist "free and independent" not only in name but also by those social customs and laws that are greater than constitutions—or only so by statute, while in reality they are put down to an equality with slaves!

There can be no half way work in the matter of slavery in new territory: we must either have it there, or have it not. Now if either the slaves themselves, or their owners, had fought or paid for or gained this new territory, there would be some reason in the pro-slavery claims. But every body knows that the cost and work come, forty-nine fiftieths of it, upon the free men, the middling classes and working-men, who do their own work and own no slaves. Shall *these* give up all to the aristocratic owners of the South? Will even the poor white freemen of the South be willing to do this? It is monstrous to ask such a thing!

Not the least curious part of the present position of this subject is, the fact of *who* advances the claims of slavery, and the singular manner in which those claims are half-allowed by men at the North who ought to know better. The truth is that all practice and theory—the real interest of the planters themselves—and the potential weight of the opinions of all our great statesmen, Southern as well as Northern, from Washington to Silas Wright [*Wright (1795–1847) was a congressman and governor of New York who helped create the Barnburners, a faction of the Democratic Party violently opposed to the extension of slavery.*]—are strongly arrayed in favor of limiting slavery to where it already exists. For this the clear eye of Washington looked longingly; for this the great voice of Jefferson plead, and his sacred fingers wrote; for this were uttered the prayers of Franklin and Madison and Monroe. But now, in the South, stands a little band, strong in chivalry, refinement and genius—headed by a sort of intellectual Saladin—assuming to speak in behalf of sovereign States, while in reality they utter their own idle theories; and disdainfully crying out against the rest of the Republic, for whom their contempt is but illy concealed. The courage and high tone of these men are points in their favor, it must be confessed. With dexterous but brazen logic they profess to stand on the Constitution against a principle whose very existence dates from some of the revered framers of that Constitution! And these—this band, really little in numbers, and which could be annihilated by one pulsation of the stout free heart of the North—these are the men who are making such insolent demands, in the face of the working farmers and mechanics of the free States—the nine-tenths of the population of the Republic. We admire the chivalric bearing (sometimes a sort of impudence) of these men. So we admire, as it is told in history, the dauntless conduct of kings and nobles when arraigned for punishment before an outraged and too long-suffering people. . . . But the course of moral light and human freedom, (and their consequent happiness,) is not to be stayed by such men as they. Thousands of noble hearts at the North—the entire East—the uprousing giant of the free East—will surely, when the time comes, sweep over them and their doctrines as the advancing ocean tide obliterates the channel of some little brook that erewhile ran down the sands of its shore. Already the roar of the waters is heard; and if few short-sighted ones seek to withstand it, the surge, terrible in its fury, will sweep them too in the ruin.

Source Note: First published in the Brooklyn *Daily Eagle*, September 1, 1847. Reprinted in *The Gathering of the Forces*, 1:208–14.

Prohibition of Colored Persons
by Walt Whitman

The new Constitution of Oregon prohibits colored persons, either slave or free, from entering the State—making an exclusively white population. This is objected to by several of the abolition Senators in the U. S. Senate—Mr. Hale and others. Mr. Seward, however, is going to vote in favor of the Constitution.

We shouldn't wonder if this sort of total prohibition of colored persons became quite a common thing in New Western, Northwestern, and even Southwestern States. If so, the whole matter of slavery agitation will assume another phase, different from any phase as yet. It will be a conflict between the totality of White Labor, on the one side, and on the other, the interference and competition of Black Labor, or of bringing in colored persons on any terms.

Who believes that the Whites and Blacks can ever amalgamate in America? Or who wishes it to happen? Nature has set an impassable seal against it. Besides, is not America for the Whites? And is it not better so? As long as the Blacks remain here how can they become anything like an independent and heroic race? There is no chance for it.

Yet we believe there is enough material in the colored race, if they were in some secure and ample part of the earth, where they would have a chance to develop themselves, to gradually form a race, a nation that would take no mean rank among the peoples of the world. They would have the good will of all the civilized powers, and they would be compelled to look upon themselves as freemen, capable, self-reliant—mighty. Of course all this, or anything toward it, can never be attained by the Blacks here in America.

So that prohibitions like that in the new Constitution of Oregon, are not to be dismissed at first sight as arbitrary and unjust. We think the subject will bear much further examination. We even think it not unlikely but it would, when thus examined, meet the approval of the best friends of the Blacks, and the farthest-sighted opponents of Slavery. For, we repeat it, once get the slavery question to be argued on, as a question of White Workingmen's Labor against the Servile Labor of Blacks, and how many years would slavery stand in two-thirds of the present Slave-States?

Source Note: First published in the Brooklyn, *Daily Times*, May 6, 1858. Reprinted in *I Sit and Look Out: Editorials from the Brooklyn Daily Times*, Ed. Emory Holloway and Vernolian Schwarz (New York: Columbia University Press, 1932), 89–90.

The House of Friends
by Walt Whitman

"And one shall say unto him, What are those wounds in thy hands? Then
he shall answer, Those with which I was wounded in the house of my
friends."—*Zechariah*, xiii.6

If thou art balked, O Freedom,
The victory is not to thy manlier foes;
From the house of friends comes the death stab.

Vaunters of the Free,
Why do you strain your lungs off southward?
Why be going to Alabama?
Sweep first before your own door;
Stop this squalling and this scorn
Over the mote there in the distance;
Look well to your own eye, Massachusetts—
Yours, New-York and Pennsylvania;
—I would say yours too, Michigan,
But all the salve, all the surgery
Of the great wide world were powerless there.

Virginia, mother of greatness,
Blush not for being also mother of slaves.
You might have borne deeper slaves—
Doughfaces, Crawlers, Lice of Humanity—
Terrific screamers of Freedom,
Who roar and bawl, and get hot i' the face,
But, were they not incapable of august crime,
Would quench the hopes of ages for a drink—
Muck-worms, creeping flat to the ground,

A dollar dearer to them than Christ's blessing;
All loves, all hopes, less than the thought of gain;
In life walking in that as in a shroud:
Men whom the throes of heroes,
Great deeds at which the gods might stand appalled
The shriek of a drowned world, the appeal of women,
The exulting laugh of untied empires,
Would touch them never in the heart,
But only in the pocket.

Hot-headed Carolina,
Well may you curl your lip;
With all your bondsmen, bless the destiny
Which brings you no such breed as this.

Arise, young North!
Our elder blood flows in the veins of cowards—
The gray-haired sneak, the blanched poltroon,
The feigned or real shiverer at tongues
That nursing babes need hardly cry the less for—
Are they to be our tokens always?
Fight on, band braver than warriors,
Faithful and few as Spartans;
But fear not most the angriest, loudest malice—
Fear most the still and forked fang
That starts from the grass at your feet.

Source Note: Originally published in the New York *Tribune*, June 14, 1850. The poem protests the support given by leading Democrats to the compromise movement in Congress.

EMERSON, THOREAU, AND ANTISLAVERY
by Len Gougeon

Opinions of Ralph Waldo Emerson (1803–82) and Henry David Thoreau (1817–62) as social reformers have varied greatly over the years. Largely because they are universally recognized as leaders in the Transcendental movement, a movement which emphasized the divinity of man and the self-sufficiency of the individual in establishing the means to live a virtuous and meaningful life, both have been criticized by some as encouraging withdrawal from society and its distractions and disparaging organized efforts at social reform, especially the antislavery movement.[1] According to this school of thought, Emerson withdrew to the comfort of his Concord study and, like the proverbial coach who was never a player, philosophized about reform without practicing it himself. Similarly, Thoreau was drawn to his hermitage at Walden Pond, where he contemplated the beauty and solitude of nature while grumbling about the self-centered "do gooders" of the world.[2] There is a modicum of truth to this position. In the 1830s and early 1840s Transcendentalists in general, and Emerson and Thoreau in particular, did emphasize self-culture and individual moral reform as the preferred means of achieving a comprehensive social reform. However, historical events, especially the continued expansion of the slave power in the same period, would lead to dramatic changes in their social reform philosophies. As the following discussion will demonstrate, from the mid-1840s on, Emerson and Thoreau would become increasingly active in supporting various abolition organizations and their efforts; they would speak out with increasing frequency and ire on the slavery issue, and both would eventually support and promote civil disobedience and even the use of violence in protecting and/or seeking the freedom of those threatened by the slave power whether in Massachusetts, Kansas, or Virginia. It should also be noted, however, that, while Emerson and Thoreau followed similar trajectories in their antislavery careers, there were differences in their approaches as various national events unfolded. Sometimes these differences led to misunderstandings between the two which would test their friendship. Ultimately, however, both remained totally and enthusiastically committed to the antislavery movement and consistently lent their energy to the cause of human equality and freedom. This is their story.

Emerson gave his first antislavery speech in his hometown of Concord, Massachusetts, in November 1837, the year Thoreau graduated from Harvard. He was prompted to give his address by the recent murder of Elijah Lovejoy, an abolitionist publisher, by an anti-abolition mob at Alton, Illinois. The emphasis of Emerson's address was mainly on the importance of free speech, which was just then being threatened by mob violence against abolitionists throughout the country.[3] In speaking of slavery, he noted, "when we have distinctly settled for ourselves the right and wrong of this question, and have covenanted with ourselves to keep the channels of opinion open . . . . I think we have done all that is incumbent on most of us to do."[4] Emerson's belief at this time was that each individual should focus on reforming himself, completely and fully, and that through this means the reform of the entire society would be accomplished. Obviously, moral suasion was the key element in the process, and, hence, Emerson's concern with defending freedom of speech.

Except for publishing an open "Letter to Martin Van Buren" (April 23, 1838), expressing opposition to the forced removal of the Cherokees from their homeland, Emerson would not speak out again on a specific social reform issue until August 1, 1844.[5] In the interim, he occasionally gave presentations where he touched upon the topic of social reform generally. In these he sometimes criticized various self-centered reformers and their causes. Thus, in his famous essay, "Self-Reliance" (1841), Emerson offers a fairly harsh criticism of the "angry bigot [who] assumes this bountiful cause of Abolition" but who has not yet reformed himself.[6]

In the spring of 1844 Emerson and Thoreau both addressed a gathering of reformers at Amory Hall in Boston, where they expressed similar views. While

Emerson appreciated his audience's concern with promoting reform, he criticized them for taking a piecemeal approach to the problems of society, as if
moral reform could be accomplished by attacking only one evil. Also, he criticized their reliance on association, which he felt diminished individualism and
self-reliance, the keys to true personal and, hence, social reform. Thus, in his
address, titled "New England Reformers," he noted, "if partiality was one fault
of the movement party, the other defect was their reliance on Association" (*CW*
3:155). Thoreau, who was just beginning to develop his public voice at this
time, took a similar tack in his address, "Reform and the Reformers." In his
presentation he noted, "It is not the worst reason why the reform should be a
private and individual enterprise, that perchance the evil may be private also."[7]
Thoreau felt, as Emerson did at this time, that the reform of society would be
accomplished when every private citizen confronted and conquered his own evil,
and he encouraged them to do so. In recognizing this emphasis, one scholar has
noted, "Where the other lecturers at Amory Hall were speaking to the already
converted . . . Emerson and Thoreau sought to convert the congregation of
reformers yet again, turning their attention from society's ills to the resources of
the self, the only realm where true liberation might be gained."[8]

Because of this emphasis on personal reform, Emerson and, less directly,
Thoreau, were sometimes criticized by organized pro-active social reformers,
especially the abolitionists. Thus, Maria Weston Chapman, one of the leading
female abolitionists in Boston, noted in a draft article on Emerson in 1844 that
his "character being rather contemplative than active . . . he has been a philosophical speculator rather than a reformer." She goes on to note, with obvious
disappointment, that "Hundreds of young persons have made him their excuse
for avoiding the Anti Slavery battle & talking about the clear light."[9] All of that,
however, was about to change dramatically.

After winning its independence from Mexico, Texas first petitioned for annexation to the United States on August 4, 1837. The petition was immediately
controversial. Southerners favored the proposition as a way of increasing the
power and influence of the slave states, and Northerners opposed it for the same
reason. Emerson felt that Massachusetts should "resist the annexation with
tooth & nail," and that "the great & governing sentiment of the State is antislavery & anti-Texas."[10] Thoreau undoubtedly felt the same way. Despite such
Northern opposition, however, the momentum for annexation, abetted by a
surge of nationalistic feeling which would soon be known as "manifest destiny,"
continued to grow. With President Tyler urging Congressional authorization of
the measure in the spring of 1844, approval appeared inevitable.

Emerson and Thoreau now recognized that their earlier faith in the power of
moral suasion and personal reform had not resulted in the diminution of America's most egregious social evil. In fact, the slave power was not only not mendi-
cant, but aggressive. It was not contracting, but expanding. Clearly, a new tack
was called for. Emerson's response was not long in coming. Despite his earlier
reservations about one-issue reforms, about reform associations, and about efforts to impose reform from the outside rather than evoking it from the inside,

when asked to address a gathering of abolitionists in Concord at their annual celebration of Emancipation in the British West Indies, he agreed to do so.[11] It was an extraordinary turnabout in his philosophy of social reform, and one that he was not completely comfortable with, but desperate times required desperate measures. Thoreau agreed and was prepared to offer assistance.

The gathering in Concord was not without controversy. When various authorities refused the use of Concord's churches, the group decided to use the courthouse, but the sexton of the First Parish Church refused to ring the town bell in the church steeple to announce the meeting. When no one would order him to do it, Thoreau boldly rang the bell himself and the meeting was joined.[12]

Emerson's presentation was passionate and marks a significant turning point in his social reform career.[13] In his speech, "An Address on the Emancipation of the Negroes in the British West Indies," the preparation of which he labored over for some time, he presented a detailed history of the reform movement that brought about the end of slavery in the British Empire. Clearly, he hoped this would serve as a model here. He also struck a somewhat militant note, praising Negro revolutionaries like "Touissant and the Haytian heroes, . . . [and] the leaders of their race in Barbados and Jamaica" who fought successfully for their freedom. For Emerson, "the anti-slavery of the whole world is dust in the balance before this . . . the might and the right are here: here is the anti-slave: here is man; and if you have man, black or white is an insignificance" (*AW*, p. 31). The speech was enthusiastically received by abolitionists everywhere. It was reported on extensively in virtually all of the antislavery journals, and Thoreau arranged for the publication of the speech in pamphlet form. A British edition soon followed. Now that the ice had been broken, Emerson would address antislavery audiences several more times before the end of the decade as his association with the abolitionists grew into a virtual alliance.[14]

In the spring of 1845 Thoreau began his famous experiment in simple living at Walden Pond, on property owned by Emerson. Both of them would join in a successful effort at this time to force the Concord Lyceum to allow Wendell Phillips, one of the most articulate and controversial of the abolitionist orators, to speak in Concord. When conservative curators resigned in protest, Thoreau and Emerson replaced them. The next day Thoreau wrote his first and only "letter to the editor" to William Lloyd Garrison's *Liberator*, detailing the incident and their eventual triumph. Garrison gladly published the lengthy document in its entirety.[15] This was but one more indication that Emerson and Thoreau were moving ever closer to the very abolitionists whom they had only recently criticized.

Texas was admitted to the Union in December 1845, a development which Mexico refused to accept. Tensions between the two countries escalated quickly and the United States declared war on Mexico in May of 1846. As noted earlier, many Northerners were opposed to annexation, which they saw as an effort to extend the slave power. War with Mexico made the situation even more unpalatable. This led to Thoreau's famous protest against the war and slavery. He refused to pay his state poll tax, since the revenue was being used, in part, to support the war. As a result, he was arrested in July 1846 and spent one night in jail. (An unknown party, probably a family member, quietly paid the tax the next day.) The experience made a deep impression on Thoreau and from it came his classic essay, "Resistance to Civil Government," more popularly known as "Civil Disobedience." Thoreau's action also precipitated the first rupture between himself and Emerson on the issue of social reform.

Thoreau's action was predicated on the principle, stated in "Resistance to Civil Government," that "under a government which imprisons any unjustly, the true place for a just man is also a prison" (*RP*, p. 76). He also insisted that "the only obligation which I have a right to assume, is to do at any time what I think right" (*RP*, p. 65). Hence his protest. For his part, Emerson felt that it was the wrong action at the wrong time. He was deeply concerned with the growth of the "no Union with slaveholders" movement which was growing in popularity among abolitionists at this time.[16] He felt that simply separating the North from the South was not going to improve the moral status of either society, and that such a measure was tantamount to giving up the struggle against slavery and its attendant evils, which, in turn, was tantamount to giving up on the effort to reform and redeem mankind. In his 1841 address "Man the Reformer," he expressed his belief that "The power, which is at once spring and regulator in all efforts of reform, is faith in Man, the conviction that there is an infinite worthiness in him which will appear at the call of worth, and that all particular reforms are the removing of some impediment" (*CW* 1:156). Emerson's journal comments show clearly that he feared Thoreau's actions suggest a loss of this faith in mankind, generally. He notes, "But you, nothing will content. . . . Your objection then to the state of Massachusetts is deceptive. Your true quarrel is with the state of Man" (*JMN* 9:447).

Emerson also felt that the particular issue at hand could not justify Thoreau's extreme action. "The State," he noted, "is a poor good beast who means the best" and he warns against following those who "run amuck against the world" in a dispute over trivia. Rather they should "have a good case to try the question on." He then goes on to note, "It is the part of a fanatic to fight out a revolution on the shape of a hat or surplice. . . . You can not fight heartily for a fraction. But wait until you have a good difference to join issue upon." He concludes his reflection with the prophetic comment, "You will get one by & by. But now I have no sympathy" (*JMN* 9:446).

Whether Emerson ever shared these concerns with Thoreau is not clear. They remained close friends for the time. Emerson would travel to England and lecture from October 1847 to July 1848. During this time Thoreau took up residence in the Emerson household as handyman and family friend. For his part, Thoreau remained committed to the principles of passive resistance suggested by his act of civil disobedience. In January 1848, he spoke on "the relation of the individual to the State" in the Concord Lyceum. In May of 1849, Elizabeth Peabody published the lecture, with the title, "Resistance to Civil Government," in her journal, *Aesthetic Papers*.

As noted earlier, Emerson spoke out several more times on the slavery issue after 1844. In November of 1845 he boycotted the New Bedford Lyceum because of their racist membership policy, and his letter to the Lyceum was published in the *Liberator* and elsewhere.[17] While in England, Emerson was impressed and encouraged by the efforts of the Chartist reformers to expand the rights of citizens there. When invited by Garrison to speak yet again at a celebration of Emancipation in the British West Indies in August 1849, he accepted. In his short speech, he expressed a general optimism that slavery would eventually be abolished, and he praised the abolitionists for their efforts in the cause. "It is the glory of these preachers of freedom," he said, "that they have strengthened the moral sense, that they have anticipated this triumph which I look upon as inevitable, and which it is not in man to retard" (*AW*, p. 49).

It is generally agreed that there was a cooling in the personal relationship between Emerson and Thoreau beginning around 1849.[18] In this year Thoreau published his first book, *A Week on the Concord and Merrimack Rivers*. The work contained a wide range of social, political, and religious commentary, much of which was recorded in his journals in the period following his arrest in 1846, but the book was not a commercial success.[19] In many ways *A Week* signaled the growing intellectual maturity and independence of Thoreau, but he and Emerson would remain generally like-minded as their antislavery campaigns accelerated throughout the turbulent decade of the 1850s.

The optimism that Emerson felt upon his return from England in 1849 was soon shattered by the passage of the Fugitive Slave Law in September of 1850. This law, which was one element of a multipart legislative effort which came to be known as the "Compromise of 1850," in effect, made every free citizen of Massachusetts a slave catcher. This dramatic development led Emerson to actively promote civil disobedience. In his journal he questioned how this "filthy enactment" could have been "made in the 19th Century, by people who could read & write," and he angrily vowed, "I will not obey it, by God" (*JMN* 11:412). In an open letter to the abolitionists, he urged a pro-active response. "At this moment, it seems imperative that every lover of human rights should, in every manner, singly or socially, in private and in public, by voice and by pen—and, first of all, by substantial help and hospitality to the slave, *and defending him against his hunters*,—enter his protest for humanity against the detestable statute of the last Congress" (*AW*, p. 51, emphasis mine). With his insistence on active, rather than passive, resistance to the state, Emerson both met and exceeded Thoreau's earlier standard of resistance. Soon, however, they would both be on the same page once again.

The passage of the Fugitive Slave Law affected Emerson and Thoreau like few other events. Emerson, despite his longstanding reservations about politics, now, for the first time, threw himself, body and soul, into a political campaign. At the urging of Charles Sumner, the soon-to-be abolitionist senator from Massachusetts, Emerson waged a stump campaign to elect John Gorham Palfrey to Congress on the Free Soil ticket. His campaign speech, which he repeated at several locations in his Middlesex district, was his "'Address to the Citizens of Concord' on the Fugitive Slave Law," undoubtedly his most acerbic presentation ever. Emerson was especially outraged by the recent rendition of Thomas Sims, a teenage fugitive slave who was seized in Boston on April 3, 1851, and, after a legal proceeding where he was represented by Richard Henry Dana, Jr., and others, returned to Savannah, Georgia, on April 19, where he was brutally whipped. In his speech Emerson stated, "I thought none, that was not ready to go on all fours, would back this law," and yet the good citizens of Boston did. Thomas Sims, on arriving in Boston seeking sanctuary and freedom, discovered, said Emerson, that "The famous town of Boston is his master's hound." The moral fiber of Massachusetts had apparently worn thin, its culture degraded, and the young runaway discovered that "the learning of the Universities, the culture of elegant society, the acumen of lawyers, the majesty of the Bench, the eloquence of the Christian pulpit, the stoutness of Democracy, the respectability of the Whig party, are all combined to kidnap him" (*AW*, p. 56).

Emerson was especially critical of Massachusetts senator Daniel Webster in his speech because of the senator's crucial support of the Compromise in the U.S. Senate. He stated that it was clear Webster was "irresistibly taking the bit in his mouth and the collar on his neck, and harnessed himself to the chariot of the planters. The fairest American frame ends in this filthy law" (*AW*, p. 66). For Emerson, Webster is, unfortunately, a person who "obeys his powerful animal nature;—and his finely developed understanding only works truly and with all its force, when it stands for animal good; that is for property" (*AW*, p. 66).

Thoreau had made a similar criticism of Webster's conservatism in "Resistance to Civil Government," where he noted that "Webster never goes behind government, and so cannot speak with authority about it." He always supported the status quo, no matter how immoral, and hence, he said of slavery, "Because it was a part of the original compact,—let it stand" (*RP*, pp. 87–88).

Thoreau took no part in Emerson's political campaign because he had no faith in politics and the voting process, which he described in "Resistance to Civil Government" as "a sort of gaming, like chequers or backgammon." "Even voting *for the right,*" he noted there, "is *doing* nothing for it" (*RP*, p. 69). For his part, Emerson always voted, and always encouraged others to do so. Undoubtedly, this is because he believed, as he stated in his first West Indian Emancipation address, that "What great masses of men wish done, will be done," and in a democracy those wishes are expressed as votes (*AW*, p. 28).

Like Emerson, Thoreau was appalled at the fate of Thomas Sims. For days following the boy's return to slavery, he filled the pages of his journal with diatribes against the South and slavery.[20] On the twenty-third of April he began his lecture, "The Wild," before the Concord Lyceum with the statement, "I feel that I owe my audience an apology for speaking to them tonight on any other subject than the Fugitive Slave Law on which everyman is bound to express a distinct opinion."[21] Perhaps because Thoreau felt satisfied that Emerson's forceful expression would suffice for the two of them, for the time, he would work privately, even clandestinely, to subvert the law. Thus, while Emerson was addressing the subject publicly throughout Middlesex County, Thoreau served as a conductor on the Underground Railroad, which was especially active in Concord.[22] Thoreau's biographer relays the following commentary about his contributions in this regard, as reported by one of his contemporaries. "Henry Thoreau more often than any other man in Concord looked after them [fugitive slaves] . . . caring for them for the night, purchasing their tickets, escorting them to the station . . . or for further protection accompanying them on the trains for awhile."[23] For their part, Waldo and Lidian Emerson were among a small group of Concordians who promised aid and shelter to any fugitive slave who "should appear at their door."[24] Very soon the rendition of another famous fugitive slave would cause both Emerson and Thoreau to speak out with fiery rhetoric against the growing aggression of the slave power. For Thoreau, it would signal the end of his philosophy of "passive resistance" as, once again, he and Emerson would share nearly identical positions on this increasingly disturbing issue.

The year 1854 brought two major crises for abolitionists. In early May, the fugitive slave Anthony Burns, who had been living in Boston, was seized by Southern slave catchers. Like Sims, after a hearing where he was represented by Richard Henry Dana, Jr., and others, Burns was ordered by the courts to be returned to his Southern master. Again, abolitionists were outraged, and this time, under the leadership of Thomas Wentworth Higginson and Theodore Parker (two Transcendental reformers), and others, an effort was made to free him through the use of force.[25] The effort failed. A guard was killed in the scuffle, and Higginson, who was wounded in the effort, was later arrested, along with Parker and Wendell Phillips, and charged with treason. (All were later acquitted.)

In addition to these disturbing events, on May 30 the Kansas-Nebraska Act was passed. This measure effectively nullified the Missouri Compromise of 1820, which specifically excluded slavery from the territories of the Louisiana Purchase north of the line 36° 30′, thus making vast new areas available for the creation of additional slave states. In anticipation of this development, in April, the Massachusetts Emigrant Aid Society (later the New England Emigrant Aid Company) was established to promote the settlement and protection of New England farmers in Kansas, with the ultimate objective of making it a free state under the principle of "popular sovereignty." These settlers were opposed by proslavery "Border Ruffians" from Missouri. The situation would soon result in open warfare between the two parties. Emerson and Thoreau both would contribute funds to purchase Sharpe's rifles for the protection of the New Englanders.

Such developments appalled and outraged Emerson and Thoreau, and they felt compelled to take to the platform with fiery orations condemning the evil of the times. Emerson would deliver his second "Fugitive Slave Law Address" on numerous occasions, beginning in New York City on March 7, the anniversary of Webster's perfidy. Once again, he relentlessly attacked Webster, who had passed away the year before, as a symbol of the evil of the time. When the crisis of the moment arose, said Emerson, and the question to be decided was "Are you for man and for the good of man; or are you for the hurt of man? . . . Mr.

Webster and the country went for the quadruped law. Immense mischief was done" (*AW*, p. 79).

Thoreau expressed himself on the issues of the day at a large abolitionist gathering in Framingham, Massachusetts, on the Fourth of July. In what is undoubtedly his most vitriolic address, "Slavery in Massachusetts," Thoreau, like Emerson, evinced a clearly militant attitude. Also like Emerson, he complained in his address about the generally low level of morality in American society, particularly in his own state. In "Resistance to Civil Government" Thoreau had noted that government was "an expedient by which men would fain succeed in letting one another alone" (*RP*, p. 64). It was thus, properly, an instrument for insuring individual freedom. Unfortunately, it was now clear that the governor of Massachusetts had failed to use his power for this purpose and so he was, in Thoreau's opinion, "useless, or worse, . . . [because he] permits the laws of the state to go unexecuted" (*RP*, p. 94). The laws to which Thoreau refers are the Personal Liberty Laws, which Massachusetts had passed in the 1840s precisely to protect fugitive slaves in the state. Because of the passage of the Federal Fugitive Slave Law in 1850, however, these state statutes were effectively abrogated as Massachusetts bowed to the growing influence of the slave power. The result, as Thoreau observes bitterly, is that "The whole military force of the State is at the service of a Mr. Suttle, a slaveholder from Virginia, to enable him to catch a man whom he calls his property; but not a soldier is offered to save a citizen of Massachusetts from being kidnapped!" (*RP*, p. 94). Thoreau himself was determined, like Emerson, to defy the Fugitive Slave Law, which he suggested trampling underfoot and "Webster, its maker, with it, like the dirt-bug and its ball" (*RP*, p. 97). He also attacked the timidity and materialism of his fellow citizens for refusing to oppose the state, even when they knew its actions were unjust, and judges who were more concerned with the technical constitutionality of a law, rather than its morality. A further indication of Thoreau's new militancy in the matter is his praise for those citizens who participated in the recent "heroic attack on the Boston Court-House," men like Higginson, Parker, and Phillips, whom he refers to as "the champions of liberty" (*RP*, p. 105). For Thoreau, as for Emerson and other Transcendentalists, there was clearly a "higher law than the Constitution" and it was that law which must be followed (*RP*, p. 104).

Finally, Thoreau offered in his speech some reflections on his earlier reform philosophy, where he, like Emerson, had once sought to practice a virtuous and private self-culture as a means of reforming society, a philosophy which now seemed inadequate in addressing the national crisis at hand. "I have lived for the last month," he said, "with the sense of having suffered a vast and indefinite loss," and what he had lost, he said, was "a country." Previously he had "foolishly thought" that he "might manage to live here, minding my private affairs, and forget it," but that was no longer possible "since Massachusetts last deliberately sent back an innocent man, Anthony Burns, to slavery." "I dwelt before," he said, "in the illusion that my life passed somewhere only *between* heaven and hell, but now I cannot persuade myself that I do not dwell *wholly within* hell"

(*RP*, p. 106). It was now clear to Thoreau that "If we would save our lives, we must fight for them" (*RP*, p. 108). Until victory over the corrupting influence of slavery was assured, no peace was possible. Even a walk in the woods, that former place of refuge and peace, brought no relief, because "The remembrance of my country spoils my walk. My thoughts are murder to the State, and involuntarily go plotting against her" (*RP*, p. 108).

Thoreau would follow up this jeremiad with another outspoken attack on the moral deficiencies and material self-interest of his society in December 1854. "Life without Principle" offers an indictment of the clergy and moral leaders generally, as well as politicians for their failure to speak out against the gross moral abuses of the time. The latter, in particular, instead of seeking the improvement of society, concerned themselves with "legislating to *regulate* the breeding of slaves" (*RP*, p. 176).

Ironically, just ten years earlier, on another Fourth of July, Thoreau celebrated his independence from such turmoil by moving into his cabin at Walden Pond. This year would see the publication of the results of that noble experiment, *Walden, or Life in the Woods* (1854). Interestingly, while that work has emerged as a classic of American literature, and an articulate statement of Thoreau's philosophy of life, it does not reflect the evolution of his philosophy of social reform, especially the militant activism and open hostility to the state expressed so vividly above. His two years at Walden in the mid-1840s appear placid when compared to the social turbulence of the 1850s.

The tensions between North and South, free states and slave states, grew steadily throughout the 1850s. Emerson spoke with increasing frequency against slavery and in support of the abolitionists, with whom he grew closer with each new crisis. In stark contrast to his warnings in the early 1840s regarding the dangers of association, in his 1855 "American Slavery" address he stated, "Whilst I insist on the doctrine of independence and the inspiration of the individual, I do not cripple but exalt the social action," and he added, with obvious enthusiasm, "A wise man delights in the powers of many people" (*AW*, p. 103).

The situation in Kansas continued to grow worse following the passage of the Kansas-Nebraska Act in 1854. Violent clashes between pro- and antislavery parties became more frequent, and soon the phrase "Bleeding Kansas" was common currency. Violence was not limited to Kansas, however. On May 22, 1856, Emerson's friend and Massachusetts senator, Charles Sumner, was nearly beaten to death at his Senate desk by Preston Brooks, a representative from South Carolina who was offended by the senator's "Crime Against Kansas" speech in which he bitterly denounced the "slave oligarchy," namely, those who supported the proslavery partisans in Kansas. The event sent shock waves throughout the North. Emerson, in his address, "Assault on Charles Sumner," delivered at a protest meeting in Concord, observed ominously, "I do not see how a barbarous community and a civilized community can constitute one state. I think we must get rid of slavery, or we must get rid of freedom" (*AW*, p. 107). In September he would speak at a Kansas relief meeting in Cambridge, Massachusetts. There he pleaded for contributions. "The People of Kansas," he said, "ask for bread, clothes, arms, and men, to save them alive, and enable them to stand against these enemies of the human race. They have a right to be helped, because they have helped themselves" (*AS*, p. 112). Clearly, the time had come to meet force with force.

The most famous of the freedom fighters in Kansas was John Brown. Brown was a dynamic and charismatic individual who visited Concord in 1857 to raise money for his cause. Thoreau met Brown at his mother's boarding house, where he was introduced by Franklin Sanborn. Emerson dropped by later. All were fascinated by Brown's tales of Kansas warfare, and all contributed to his cause, following his dramatic lecture that evening. Brown returned to Concord in May of 1859, again to speak and raise money. Not long after, in October, Brown staged his famous raid on the Federal Arsenal in Harpers Ferry, Virginia, in a failed effort to incite a general insurrection of the slaves throughout the South. The event was like a lightning bolt striking along the Mason-Dixon line. Virtually all Southerners, and most Northerners, condemned the raid as insane and incendiary, an act that could lead to civil war. Emerson and Thoreau, however, while they questioned the appropriateness of the attack, were electrified by Brown's daring gesture. Emerson called him a "saint," and both of them saw Brown as a true Transcendental hero, a man who was willing to sacrifice everything, even his life, for his principles. Thoreau's biographer observes that, after hearing news of the attack, "For days Thoreau could think of nothing else. Even nature temporarily lost its appeal and he confessed, 'I was so absorbed in him as to be surprised whenever I detected the routine of the natural world surviving still.' He breathed a fire into his journals even greater than at the time of the Burns incident."[26]

Brown, who was wounded in the raid, was later tried and convicted of treason and was executed on December 2, 1859. Despite local opposition, Emerson and Thoreau both spoke at multiple events memorializing Brown, and raising money to support his family. Both saw Brown as a martyr to the antislavery cause and both were adamant in approving his use of force. Thoreau noted in his "Plea for Captain John Brown" that "It was his peculiar doctrine that a man has a perfect right to interfere by force with the slaveholder, in order to rescue the slave. I agree with him" (*RP*, p. 132). He went on to note, "I speak for the slave when I say, that I prefer the philanthropy of Captain Brown to that philanthropy which neither shoots nor liberates me. . . . I do not wish to kill nor to be killed, but I can foresee circumstances in which both these things would be by me unavoidable" (*RP*, p. 133).

Militancy now became a fact of life, even in Concord. When federal agents appeared in town in April 1860 to arrest Emerson's friend and neighbor, Franklin Sanborn, for possible implication in the Harpers Ferry raid, the citizens, including Emerson and Thoreau, joined forces and drove them off. Later, they formed a vigilance committee which would protect the citizens of Concord from further abuses by the slave power. Such conflict was a foreshadowing of a national eruption. When Fort Sumter was fired upon on April 12, 1861, signal-

ing the outbreak of the Civil War, both Emerson and Thoreau welcomed the
event as an opportunity to rid the nation, once and for all, of the moral and
social plague of slavery. Emerson would go on to play an important role in
defending and supporting the Union cause in wartime addresses like "Civilization at a Pinch" (1861), "Emancipation Proclamation" (1862), and "Fortune of
the Republic" (1863), as well as enlistment speeches for the Massachusetts 54th,
the Union's first regular Negro regiment, and occasional poems to celebrate the
heroism of that regiment and other major events in the war. He would live to
see his abolitionist goals realized with the passage of the Thirteenth Amendment to the Constitution in 1865, eliminating slavery forever. Thoreau, unfortunately, died from consumption (tuberculosis) on May 6, 1862. Although he
did not live to see his dream of emancipation come true, he no doubt took
comfort in the realization that, like his friend, mentor, and neighbor, Ralph
Waldo Emerson, he made a significant and, in the end, lasting contribution to
the cause of freedom in America and in the world.

1. For an informative discussion of the Transcendental movement, see David Robin-
son's "Transcendentalism in its Time," in *The Cambridge Companion to Ralph Waldo
Emerson*, ed. Joel Porte (Cambridge: Cambridge University Press, 1999), pp. 13–29. For
Emerson and the tension between individualism and social reform, see Wesley Mott's
"The Age of the First Person Singular: Emerson and Individualism," in *A Historical
Guide to Ralph Waldo Emerson*, ed. Joel Myerson (New York: Oxford University Press,
2000), pp. 61–100.

2. For an interesting overview of the critical debate on Emerson and social reform,
see T. Gregory Garvey, "Two Faces of Emerson: A Review of Recent Books," *College
Literature* 25:1 (winter 1998): 261–76. On Thoreau and Transcendental reform, see my
"Thoreau and Reform," in *The Cambridge Companion to Henry David Thoreau*, ed. Joel
Myerson (Cambridge: Cambridge University Press, 1998), pp. 194–214.

3. For a discussion of this phenomenon, see Leonard Richards, *Gentlemen of Property
and Standing: Anti-Abolition Mobs in Jacksonian America* (New York: Oxford University
Press, 1970).

4. Quoted in James Elliott Cabot, *A Memoir of Ralph Waldo Emerson* (Boston:
Houghton Mifflin and Co., 1887), 2:426.

5. The Cherokee letter can be found in *Emerson's Antislavery Writings*, ed. Len
Gougeon and Joel Myerson (New Haven: Yale University Press, 1995), pp. 1–5. All
subsequent references to Emerson's antislavery writings are to this edition and will appear
parenthetically in the text as *AW*.

6. *The Collected Works of Ralph Waldo Emerson*, 5 vols. to date, ed. Alfred R. Ferguson
et al. (Cambridge: Harvard University Press, 1971–), 2:30. All subsequent references
to Emerson's works are to this edition and will appear parenthetically in the text as
CW.

7. Henry David Thoreau, *Reform Papers*, ed. Wendell Glick (Princeton: Princeton
University Press, 1972), p. 183. All subsequent references to Thoreau's reform writings
are to this edition and will appear parenthetically in the text as *RP*.

8. Linck Johnson, "Reforming the Reformers: Emerson, Thoreau, and the Sunday
Lectures at Amory Hall, Boston," *ESQ* 37 (1991): 265.

9. Quoted in my *Virtue's Hero: Emerson, Antislavery, and Reform* (Athens: University of Georgia Press, 1990), p. 49.

10. *The Journals and Miscellaneous Notebooks of Ralph Waldo Emerson*, 16 vols., ed. William Gilman et al. (Cambridge: Harvard University Press, 1960–82), 9:74, 180. All subsequent references to Emerson's journals are to this edition and will appear in the text parenthetically as *JMN*.

11. The British outlawed slavery in the British West Indies, and throughout their empire, in 1834. American abolitionists celebrated this event every August 1 as a way of promoting American abolition efforts.

12. Walter Harding, *The Days of Henry Thoreau* (New York: Alfred A. Knopf, 1965), p. 175.

13. For a detailed discussion of this important turning point, see my "Emerson's Abolition Conversion," forthcoming in *The Emerson Dilemma: Essays on Emerson and Social Reform*, ed. T. Gregory Garvey (Athens: University of Georgia Press).

14. The addresses which Emerson delivered in the balance of the decade, as well as other antislavery utterances from this period, can be found in *Emerson's Antislavery Writings*.

15. The letter can be found in *RP*, pp. 59–62.

16. For a discussion of this phenomenon and Emerson's reaction to it, see my *Virtue's Hero*, pp. 114 ff.

17. Emerson's protest letter can be found in *AW*, pp. 39–40.

18. Harding, *Days of Thoreau*, pp. 298 ff. See also Robert D. Richardson, Jr., *Emerson: The Mind on Fire* (Berkeley: University of California Press, 1995), pp. 459 ff., and Robert Sattelmeyer, "When He Became My Enemy: Emerson and Thoreau 1848–49," *NEQ* 62 (June 1989): 187–204.

19. Linck Johnson, *Thoreau's Complex Weave: The Writing of "A Week on the Concord and Merrimack Rivers," with the Text of the First Draft* (Charlottesville: University of Virginia Press, 1986).

20. Harding, p. 315.

21. Harding, *Days of Thoreau*, pp. 316–17.

22. Gougeon, *Virtue's Hero*, p. 152.

23. Harding, *Days of Thoreau*, p. 317.

24. Richardson, *Emerson*, p. 496.

25. For a comprehensive discussion of this dramatic event, see Albert von Frank, *The Trials of Anthony Burns: Slavery and Freedom in Emerson's Boston* (Cambridge: Harvard University Press, 1998).

26. Harding, *Days of Thoreau*, p. 416.

HENRY DAVID THOREAU (1817–1862)

Henry David Thoreau is usually remembered as the author of *Walden* (1854), a remarkable book that demonstrates humanity's relationship to the cycles of nature while providing the reader with detailed biological and scientific information about this most famous of the Massachusetts "kettle ponds." *Walden* is mistakenly regarded to be Thoreau's record of his residence next to the pond between the summer of 1845 and his removal from Walden Pond in

September of 1847. In fact, his residence there is best recorded in Thoreau's journals, a very complete and detailed account of his life experience. Thoreau is less well remembered as the author of *A Week on the Concord and Merrimack Rivers* (1849), his only other full-length book published during his lifetime. While *Walden* is today one of the most popular works in American literature, both on and off the college campus, it was not highly regarded during Thoreau's lifetime, and *A Week* also suffered horrible neglect. Unable to secure a commercial publisher, Thoreau financed the publication of *A Week* himself, and was left with over seven hundred of the one thousand copies printed, most of which remained in storage in his attic. Several other book-length works were not completed and published during his lifetime, including *Cape Cod* and *The Maine Woods*.

As Len Gougeon's essay makes clear, Thoreau was one of the most outspoken antislavery speakers and writers among the Concord Transcendentalists. A popular lecturer for the abolitionists, though not formally a member of any abolitionist society, Thoreau was once called upon to replace Frederick Douglass (who was indisposed) at an antislavery convention in Boston. He passionately supported the work of the militant and aggressive abolitionist John Brown, whose Harpers Ferry raid in 1859 led to his conviction and hanging, but not before Thoreau had penned "A Plea for Captain John Brown," in which he compared the martyr Brown to Jesus Christ. Thoreau's essay "Slavery in Massachusetts," included here, is a damning attack not only on the institution of chattel slavery, but also on the governments that tolerate it while pretending that "all men are created equal." As such, "Slavery in Massachusetts" goes right to the center of the antebellum slavery debates in America: that the charter documents were inconsistent with the practices of the new democracy. Among the antislavery advocates, Thoreau was respected and well known. His contemporary reputation was that of an antislavery activist and a critic of government, as seen in his essay, "Civil Disobedience." This classic work is usually taught with *Walden*, and it was admired by Gandhi, who used its arguments in his struggle for Indian independence from England, and by Martin Luther King, Jr., who adopted its principles of "non-violence" and "passive resistance."

Although he is remembered for living an ascetic, spartan life in a small cabin in the Massachusetts woods outside Concord, Thoreau was in fact a very learned, accomplished intellectual. He completed the work for a degree at Harvard University, but refused to come to the ceremony to take the degree and graduate with his class. He was a harsh critic of rote learning, and advocated learning through life experience, through an association with nature. But he was skilled in Latin and Greek, and knew the English classics, admiring the work of Thomas Carlyle. He was a close friend of Ralph Waldo Emerson, over a decade his senior, and shared many intellectual qualities with his mentor. Thoreau was not a "social" participant in the life of the Concord Transcendentalists, although he knew Bronson Alcott and Nathaniel Hawthorne well. Hawthorne described Thoreau as the "most disagreeable man I know." He was also highly regarded as a scientist by Louis Agassiz and other contemporary naturalists.

Henry David Thoreau was born in Concord in 1817 and lived there most of his life, except for his residence in Cambridge at Harvard and his brief excursions away from home, which are fully recorded in his travel narratives such as *The Maine Woods* and *Cape Cod*. All of his writing contains elements of his basic philosophy that humanity's most complete self-expression will come through an intimate association with nature rather than human society. Thoreau never married. He may have lived a celibate life; and, unlike Hawthorne, he never celebrated women either in his journals or his published works. On May 6, 1862, with many of his works still in progress or incomplete, Thoreau died in Concord where he had always lived, which over the next century would become legendary because of its association with Walden and the American Revolution.

SUGGESTIONS FOR FURTHER READING

Fink, Stephen. *Prophet in the Marketplace: Thoreau's Development as a Professional Writer*. Princeton: Princeton University Press, 1992.

Harding, Walter. *The Days of Henry David Thoreau: a Biography*. New York: Knopf, 1965.

Meyerson, Joel, ed. *The Cambridge Companion to Henry David Thoreau*. New York: Cambridge University Press, 1995.

Richardson, Robert. *Henry Thoreau: a Life of the Mind*. Berkeley: University of California Press, 1986.

Slavery in Massachusetts
by Henry David Thoreau

I lately attended a meeting of the citizens of Concord, expecting, as one among many, to speak on the subject of slavery in Massachusetts; but I was surprised and disappointed to find that what had called my townsmen together was the destiny of Nebraska, and not of Massachusetts, and that what I had to say would be entirely out of order. I had thought that the house was on fire, and not the prairie; but though several of the citizens of Massachusetts are now in prison for attempting to rescue a slave from her own clutches, not one of the speakers at that meeting expressed regret for it, not one even referred to it. It was only the disposition of some wild lands a thousand miles off, which appeared to concern them. The inhabitants of Concord are not prepared to stand by one of their own bridges, but talk only of taking up a position on the highlands beyond the Yellowstone river. Our Buttricks, and Davises, and Hosmers are retreating thither, and I fear that they will have no Lexington Common between them and the enemy. There is not one slave in Nebraska; there are perhaps a million slaves in Massachusetts.

They who have been bred in the school of politics fail now and always to face the facts. Their measures are half measures and make-shifts, merely. They put off the day of settlement indefinitely, and meanwhile, the debt accumulates. Though the Fugitive Slave Law had not been the subject of discussion on that occasion, it was at length faintly resolved by my townsmen, at an adjourned meeting, as I learn, that the compromise compact of 1820 having been repudiated by one of the parties, "Therefore, . . . the Fugitive Slave Law must be repealed." But this is not the reason why an iniquitous law should be repealed. The fact which the politician faces is merely, that there is less honor among thieves than was supposed, and not the fact that they are thieves.

As I had no opportunity to express my thoughts at that meeting, will you allow me to do so here?

•

I listen to hear the voice of a Governor, Commander-in-Chief of the forces of Massachusetts. I hear only the creaking of crickets and the hum of insects which now fill the summer air. The Governor's exploit is to review the troops on muster days. I have seen him on horseback, with his hat off, listening to a chaplain's prayer. It chances that is all I have ever seen of a Governor. I think that I could manage to get along without one. If *he* is not of the least use to prevent my being kidnapped, pray of what important use is he likely to be to me? When freedom is most endangered, he dwells in the deepest obscurity. A distinguished clergyman told me that he chose the profession of a clergyman, because it afforded the most leisure for literary pursuits. I would recommend to him the profession of a Governor.

Three years ago, also when the Sim's tragedy was acted, I said to myself, there is such an officer, if not such a man, as the Governor of Massachusetts,—what has he been about the last fortnight? Has he had as much as he could do to keep on the fence during this moral earthquake? It seemed to me that no keener satire could have been aimed at, no more cutting insult have been offered to that man, than just what happened—the absence of all inquiry after him in that crisis. The worst and the most I chance to know of him is, that he did not improve that opportunity to make himself known, and worthily known. He could at least have *resigned* himself into fame. It appeared to be forgotten that there was such a man, or such an office. Yet no doubt he was endeavoring to fill the gubernatorial chair all the while. He was no Governor of mine. He did not govern me.

But at last, in the present case, the Governor was heard from. After he and the United States Government had perfectly succeeded in robbing a poor innocent black man of his liberty for life, and, as far as they could, of his Creator's likeness in his breast, he made a speech to his accomplices, at a congratulatory supper!

I have read a recent law of this State, making it penal for any officer of the "Commonwealth" to "detain, or aid in the . . . detention," anywhere within its limits "of any person, for the reason that he is claimed as a fugitive slave." Also, it was a matter of notoriety that a writ of replevin to take the fugitive out of the custody of the United States Marshal could not be served, for want of sufficient force to aid the officer.

I had thought that the Governor was in some sense the executive officer of the State; that it was his business, as a Governor, to see that the laws of the State were executed; while, as a man, he took care that he did not, by so doing, break the laws of humanity; but when there is any special important use for him, he is useless, or worse than useless, and permits the laws of the State to go unexecuted. Perhaps I do not know what are the duties of a Governor; but if to be a Governor requires to subject one's self to so much ignominy without remedy, if it is to put a restraint upon my manhood, I shall take care never to be Governor of Massachusetts. I have not read far in the statutes of this Commonwealth. It is not profitable reading. They do not always say what is true; and they do not always mean what they say. What I am concerned to know is, that the man's influence and authority were on the side of the slaveholder, and not of the slave—of the guilty, and not of the innocent—of injustice, and not of justice. I never saw him of whom I speak; indeed, I did not know that he was Governor until this event occurred. I heard of him and Anthony Burns at the same time, and thus, undoubtedly, most will hear of him. So far am I from being governed by him. I do not mean that it was any thing to his discredit that I had not heard of him, only that I heard what I did. The worst I shall say of him is, that he proved no better than the majority of his constituents would be likely to prove. In my opinion, he was not equal to the occasion.

•

These very nights, I heard the sound of a drum in our streets. There were men *training* still; and for what? I could with an effort pardon the cockerels of Concord for crowing still, for they, perchance, had not been beaten that morning; but I could not excuse this rub-a-dub of the "trainers." The slave was carried back by exactly such as these, i.e., by the soldier, for whom the best you can say in this connection is, that he is a fool made conspicuous by a painted coat.

Three years ago, also, just a week after the authorities of Boston assembled to carry back a perfectly innocent man, and one whom they knew to be innocent, into slavery, the inhabitants of Concord caused the bells to be rung and the cannons to be fired, to celebrate their liberty—and the courage and love of liberty of their ancestors who fought at the bridge. As if *those* three millions had fought for the right to be free themselves, but to hold in slavery three millions others. Now-a-days, men wear a fool's cap, and call it a liberty cap. I do not know but there are some, who, if they were tied to a whipping-post, and could get but one hand free, would use it to ring the bells and fire the cannons, to celebrate *their* liberty. So some of my townsmen took the liberty to ring and fire; that was the extent of their freedom; and when the sound of the bells died away, their liberty died away also; when the powder was all expended, their liberty went off with the smoke.

The joke could be no broader, if the inmates of the prisons were to subscribe for all the powder to be used in such salutes, and hire the jailers to do the firing and ringing for them, while they enjoyed it through the grating.

This is what I thought about my neighbors.

Every humane and intelligent inhabitant of Concord, when he or she heard those bells and those cannons, thought not with pride of the events of the 19th of April, 1775, but with shame of the events of the 12th of April, 1851. But now we have half buried that old shame under a new one.

Massachusetts sat waiting Mr. Loring's decision, as if it could in any way affect her own criminality. Her crime, the most conspicuous and fatal crime of all, was permitting him to be the umpire in such a case. It was really the trial of Massachusetts. Every moment that she hesitated to set this man free—every moment that she now hesitates to atone for her crime, she is convicted. The Commissioner on her case is God; not Edward G. God, but simply God.

I wish my countrymen to consider, that whatever the human law may be, neither an individual nor a nation can ever commit the least act of injustice against the obscurest individual, without having to pay the penalty for it. A government which deliberately enacts injustice, and persists in it, will at length ever become the laughing-stock of the world.

Much has been said about American slavery, but I think that we do not even yet realize what slavery is. If I were seriously to propose to Congress to make mankind into sausages, I have no doubt that most of the members would smile at my proposition, and if any believed me to be in earnest, they would think that I proposed something much worse than Congress had ever done. But if any of them will tell me that to make a man into a sausage would be much worse,—would be any worse, than to make him into a slave,—than it was to enact the Fugitive Slave Law, I will accuse him of foolishness, of intellectual incapacity, of making a distinction without a difference. The one is just as reasonable a proposition as the other.

I hear a good deal said about trampling this law under foot. Why, one need not go out of his way to do that. This law rises not to the level of the head or the reason; its natural habitat is in the dirt. It was born and bred, and has its life only in the dust and mire, on a level with the feet, and he who walks with freedom, and does not with Hindoo mercy avoid treading on every venomous reptile, will inevitably tread on it, and so trample it under foot,—and Webster, its maker, with it, like the dirt-bug and its ball.

Recent events will be valuable as a criticism on the administration of justice in our midst, or, rather, as showing what are the true resources of justice in any community. It has come to this, that the friends of liberty, the friends of the slave, have shuddered when they have understood that his fate was left to the legal tribunals of the country to be decided. Free men have no faith that justice will be awarded in such a case; the judge may decide this way or that; it is a kind of accident, at best. It is evident that he is not a competent authority in so important a case. It is not time, then, to be judging according to his precedents, but to establish a precedent for the future. I would much rather trust to the sentiment of the people. In their vote, you would get something of some value, at least, however small; but, in the other case, only the trammeled judgment of an individual, of no significance, be it which way it might.

It is to some extent fatal to the courts, when the people are compelled to go behind them. I do not wish to believe that the courts were made for fair weather, and for very civil cases merely,—but think of leaving it to any court in the land to decide whether more than three millions of people, in this case, a sixth part of a nation, have a right to be freemen or not! But it has been left to the courts of *justice*, so-called—to the Supreme Court of the land—and, as you all know, recognizing no authority but the Constitution, it has decided that the three millions are, and shall continue to be, slaves. Such judges as these are merely the inspectors of a pick-lock and murderer's tools, to tell him whether they are in working order or not, and there they think that their responsibility ends. There was a prior case on the docket, which they, as judges appointed by God, had no right to skip; which having been justly settled, they would have been saved from this humiliation. It was the case of the murderer himself.

The law will never make men free; it is men who have got to make the law free. They are the lovers of law and order, who observe the law when the government breaks it.

Among human beings, the judge whose words seal the fate of a man furthest into eternity, is not he who merely pronounces the verdict of the law, but he, whoever he may be, who, from a love of truth, and unprejudiced by any custom or enactment of men, utters a true opinion or *sentence* concerning him. He it is that *sentences* him. Whoever has discerned truth, has received his commission from a higher source than the chiefest justice in the world, who can discern only law. He finds himself constituted judge of the judge.—Strange that it should be necessary to state such simple truths.

●

It is evident that there are, in this Commonwealth, at least, two parties, becoming more and more distinct—the party of the city, and the party of the country. I know that the country is mean enough, but I am glad to believe that there is a slight difference in her favor. But as yet, she has few, if any organs, through which to express herself. The editorials which she reads, like the news, come from the sea-board. Let us, the inhabitants of the country, cultivate self-respect. Let us not send to the city for aught more essential than our broadcloths and groceries, or, if we read the opinions of the city, let us entertain opinions of our own.

Among measures to be adopted, I would suggest to make as earnest and vigorous an assault on the Press as has already been made, and with effect, on the Church. The Church has much improved within a few years; but the Press is almost, without exception, corrupt. I believe that, in this country, the press exerts a greater and a more pernicious influence than the Church did in its worst period. We are not a religious people, but we are a nation of politicians. We do not care for the Bible, but we do care for the newspaper. At any meeting of politicians,—like that at Concord the other evening, for instance,—how impertinent it would be to quote from the Bible! how pertinent to quote from a newspaper or from the Constitution! The newspaper is a Bible which we read every morning and every afternoon, standing and sitting, riding and walking. It is a Bible which every man carries in his pocket, which lies on every table and counter, and which the mail, and thousands of missionaries, are continually dispensing. It is, in short, the only book which America has printed, and which America reads. So wide is its influence. The editor is a preacher whom you voluntarily support. Your tax is commonly one cent daily, and it costs nothing for pew hire. But how many of these preachers preach the truth? I repeat the testimony of many an intelligent foreigner, as well as my own convictions, when I say, that probably no country was ever ruled by so mean a class of tyrants as, with a few noble exceptions, are the editors of the periodical press in *this* country. And as they live and rule only by their servility, and appealing to the worst, and not the better nature of man, the people who read them are in the condition of the dog that returns to his vomit.

The *Liberator* and the *Commonwealth* were the only papers in Boston, as far as I know, which made themselves heard in condemnation of the cowardice and meanness of the authorities of that city, as exhibited in '51. The other journals, almost without exception, by their manner of referring to and speaking of the Fugitive Slave Law, and the carrying back of the slave Sims, insulted the common sense of the country, at least. And, for the most part, they did this, one would say, because they thought so to secure the approbation of their patrons, not being aware that a sounder sentiment prevailed to any extent in the heart of the Commonwealth. I am told that some of them have improved of late; but they are still eminently time-serving. Such is the character they have won.

But, thank fortune, this preacher can be even more easily reached by the weapons of the reformer than could the recreant priest. The free men of New England have only to withhold their cents, to kill a score of them at once. One whom I respect told me that he purchased Mitchell's *Citizen* in the cars, and then threw it out the window. But would not his contempt have been more fatally expressed, if he had not bought it?

•

The majority of the men of the North, and of the South, and East, and West, are not men of principle. If they vote, they do not send men to Congress on errands of humanity, but while their brothers and sisters are being scourged and hung for loving liberty, while—I might here insert all that slavery implies and is,—it is the mismanagement of wood and iron and stone and gold which concerns them. Do what you will, O Government! with my wife and children, my mother and brother, my father and sister, I will obey your commands to the letter. It will indeed grieve me if you hurt them, if you deliver them to overseers to be hunted by hounds or to be whipped to death; but nevertheless, I will peaceably pursue my chosen calling on this fair earth, until perchance, one.day, when I have put on mourning for them dead, I shall have persuaded you to relent. Such is the attitude, such are the words of Massachusetts.

Rather than do thus, I need not say what match I would touch, what system endeavor to blow up,—but as I love my life, I would side with the light, and let the dark earth roll from under me, calling my mother and my brother to follow.

I would remind my countrymen, that they are to be men first, and Americans only at a late and convenient hour. No matter how valuable law may be to protect your property, even to keep soul and body together, if it do not keep you and humanity together.

I am sorry to say, that I doubt if there is a judge in Massachusetts who is prepared to resign his office, and get his living innocently, whenever it is required of him to pass sentence under a law which is merely contrary to the law of God. I am compelled to see that they put themselves, or rather, are by character, in this respect, exactly on a level with the marine who discharges his musket in any direction he is ordered to. They are just as much tools and as little men. Certainly, they are not the more to be respected, because their master enslaves their understandings and consciences, instead of their bodies.

The judges and lawyers,—simply as such, I mean,—and all men of expediency, try this case by a very low and incompetent standard. They consider, not whether the Fugitive Slave Law is right, but whether it is what they call *constitutional*. Is virtue constitutional, or vice? Is equity constitutional, or iniquity? In important moral and vital questions like this, it is just as impertinent to ask whether a law is constitutional or not, as to ask whether it is profitable or not. They persist in being the servants of the worst of men, and not the servants of humanity. The question is not whether you or your grandfather, seventy years ago, did not enter into an agreement to serve the devil, and that service is not accordingly now due; but whether you will not now, for once and at last, serve God,—in spite of your own past recreancy, or that of your ancestor,—by obeying that eternal and only just CONSTITUTION, which He, and not any Jefferson or Adams, has written into your being.

The amount of it is, if the majority vote the devil to be God, the minority will live and behave accordingly, and obey the successful candidate, trusting that some time or other, by some Speaker's casting vote, perhaps, they may reinstate God. This is the highest principle I can get out of or invent for my neighbors. These men act as if they believed that they could safely slide down hill a little way—or a good way—and would surely come to a place, by and by, where they could begin to slide up again. This is expediency, or choosing that course which offers the slightest obstacles to the feet, that is, a down-hill one. But there is no such thing as accomplishing a righteous reform by the use of "expediency." There is no such thing as sliding up hill. In morals, the only sliders are backsliders.

Thus, we steadily worship Mammon, both School, and State, and Church, and the Seventh Day curse God with a tintamar from one end of the union to the other.

Will mankind never learn that policy is not morality—that it never secures any moral right, but considers merely what is expedient? chooses the available candidate, who is invariably the devil,—and what right have his constituents to be surprised, because the devil does not behave like an angel of light? What is wanted is men, not of policy, but of probity—who recognize a higher law than the Constitution, or the decision of the majority. The fate of the country does not depend on how you vote at the polls—the worst man is as strong as the best at that game; it does not depend on what kind of paper you drop into the ballot-box once a year, but on what kind of man you drop from your chamber into the street every morning.

What should concern Massachusetts is not the Nebraska Bill, nor the Fugitive Slave Bill, but her own slaveholding and servility. Let the State dissolve her union with the slaveholder. She may wriggle and hesitate, and ask leave to read the Constitution once more; but she can find no respectable law or precedent which sanctions the continuance of such a Union for an instant.

Let each inhabitant of the State dissolve his union with her, as long as she delays to do her duty.

•

The effect of a good government is to make life more valuable,—of a bad one, to make it less valuable. We can afford that railroad, and all other merely material stock, should lose some of its value, for that only compels us to lie more simply and economically; but suppose that the value of life itself should be diminished! How can we make a less demand on man and nature, how live more economically in respect to virtue and all noble qualities, than we do? I have lived for the last month, and I think that every man in Massachusetts capable of the sentiment of patriotism must have had a similar experience,—with the sense of having suffered a vast and indefinite loss. I did not know at first what ailed me. At last it occurred to me that what I had lost was a country. I had never respected the Government near to which I had lived, but I had foolishly thought that I might manage to live here, minding my private affairs, and forget it. For my part, my old and worthiest pursuits have lost I cannot say how much of their attraction, and I feel that my investment in life here is worth many per cent. Less since Massachusetts last deliberately sent back an innocent man, Anthony Burns, to slavery. I dwelt before, perhaps, in the illusion that my life passed somewhere only *between* heaven and hell, but now I cannot persuade myself that I do not dwell *wholly within* hell. The site of that political organization called Massachusetts is to me morally covered with volcanic *scoriae* and cinders, such as Milton describes in the infernal regions. If there is any hell more unprincipled than our rules, and we, the ruled, I feel curious to see if Life itself being worth less, all things with it, which minister to it, are worth less. Suppose you have a small library, with pictures to adorn the walls—a garden laid out around—and contemplate scientific and literary pursuits, &c., and discover all at once that your villa, with all its contents, is located in hell, and that the justice of the peace has a cloven foot and a forked tail—do not these things suddenly lose their value in your eyes?

I feel that, to some extent, the State has fatally interfered in my lawful business. It has not only interrupted me in my passage through Court Street on errands of trade, but it has interrupted me and every man on his onward and upward path, on which he had trusted soon to leave Court Street far behind. What right had it to remind me of Court Street? I have found that hollow which even I had relied on for solid.

•

Slavery and servility have produced no sweet-scented flower annually, to charm the senses of men, for they have no real life; they are merely a decaying and a death, offensive to all healthy nostrils. We do not complain that they *live*, but that they do not get *buried*. Let the living bury them; even they are good for manure.

Source Note: Henry David Thoreau, *Slavery in Massachusetts. An Address, Delivered at the Anti-Slavery Celebration at Framingham, July 4th, 1854.*

Ralph Waldo Emerson (1803–1882)
edited and introduced by William Pannapacker

Ralph Waldo Emerson was always a deeply committed social reformer, but he was often ambivalent about the means to achieve his ends. Born in Boston, Emerson studied theology at Harvard and was ordained a Unitarian minister in 1829. Plagued by spiritual doubts, he resigned his ministry in 1832, traveled abroad, and settled in Concord, Massachusetts, in 1834. After the publication of his short treatise *Nature* (1836), Emerson became the central figure of the Transcendentalist movement in the United States and a guiding intellect for numerous American writers including Henry David Thoreau and Walt Whitman.

Although Emerson resided near the geographic and social center of abolitionism, he initially resisted an open alliance with the more militant leaders of the movement whom he regarded, at first, as lawless, unkempt, and self-righteous. Emerson was suspicious of organizations and a reluctant leader, viewing himself as a scholar and poet rather than as a political agitator. Much as he hoped for the abolition of slavery, he thought this could best be achieved by reforming the nature of the individual rather than through collective action. Emerson resisted the notion that society could be improved by single-issue reform movements aimed at the passage of legislation; morality had to come from the consonance of individual hearts, each independently perceiving the same ideal truths. In "Self-Reliance," Emerson actually chides abolitionists for being overly concerned with the sins of far-away neighbors while neglecting their own shortcomings.

Nevertheless, Emerson's journals show that he was concerned with the evil of slavery from his youth forward, and he even dreamed that he might somehow deliver slaves from bondage. As a minister, Emerson frequently used slavery as an example of a human injustice. But it was not until 1837 that Emerson was provoked by the murder of an abolitionist publisher, Elijah P. Lovejoy, into delivering a moderate antislavery address. At this point, Emerson still maintained that reform was best achieved by the moral suasion of individuals rather than by the militant action of groups. Over the next seven years Emerson read more deeply into the horrors of slavery, his fears concerning its expansion grew, and he acquired a deep admiration for the abolitionist movement, which he expressed in a moving speech in Concord on August 1, 1844. He stated, "we are indebted mainly to this movement, and to the continuers of it, for the popular discussion of every point of practical ethics." Thereafter, he was welcomed by the abolitionists with enthusiasm.

Emerson shared the outrage of abolitionists at the Compromise of 1850 and the Fugitive Slave Law, which required states to return escaped slaves to their owners. Denouncing what he believed to be an unjust law, Emerson finally became willing to advocate open resistance to civil government. Conventional political means were incapable of redressing an immoral law; the "higher law" of the individual conscience was of more importance than a corrupted Constitution. Emerson's outrage escalated in 1854 when Massachusetts Chief Justice Lemuel Shaw returned the fugitive slave Anthony Burns to bondage and Congress passed the Kansas-Nebraska Act, effectively nullifying the Compromise of 1820 by permitting the expansion of slavery into the territories. It was shortly after these events that Emerson wrote the "Lecture on Slavery," which is reprinted here. He first delivered the lecture in Boston on January 25, 1855, before the Massachusetts Anti-Slavery Society, and he delivered it four more times over the next month. It was received warmly by abolitionists, but it earned Emerson a great deal of criticism from those who supported the paternalistic doctrines of George Fitzhugh.

Rather than emphasizing individual reflection, Emerson's "Lecture on Slavery" assumes a more activist posture: "I do not cripple but exalt the social action," he writes. He asserts unequivocally that slavery is a moral evil, a violation of America's sacred mission, and a threat to the integrity of the entire nation. The Fugitive Slave Law is unjust, he argues, and honest men are not obliged to uphold it. Most specifically, Emerson proposes that a negotiated settlement should be reached with the slaveholders, offering them compensation for emancipating their slaves without acknowledging their right to ownership. Although Emerson continued to resist the inflexibility of the Garrisonians, the crisis of the mid-1850s provoked him out of his intellectual malaise into a specific—if moderate—plan to end the "peculiar institution."

SUGGESTIONS FOR FURTHER READING

The Complete Works of Ralph Waldo Emerson, edited in twelve volumes by Edward Waldo Emerson (1903–4), has long been the standard edition. It will be superseded by the *Collected Works of Ralph Waldo Emerson*, ed. Alfred R. Ferguson et al., which remains under production by Harvard University Press; five volumes have appeared as of 1998. Other useful primary sources are *The Journals and Miscellaneous Notebooks of Ralph Waldo Emerson*, ed. William H. Gilman et al. (1960–82); *The Letters of Ralph Waldo Emerson*, vols. 1–6 ed.

Ralph L. Rusk (1939), and volumes 7–8 ed. Eleanor Tilton (1990–91); *The Correspondence of Emerson and Carlyle*, ed. Joseph Slater (1964); *The Complete Sermons of Ralph Waldo Emerson*, 4 vols., ed. Albert J. Von Frank et al. (1989–92); and *The Early Lectures of Ralph Waldo Emerson*, ed. Robert E. Spiller et al. (1966–72). Widely available anthologies of Emerson's writings are published by the Library of America: *Essays and Lectures*, ed. Joel Porte (1983), and *Collected Poems and Translations*, ed. Harold Bloom and Paul Kane (1994). Joel Myerson has edited the authoritative *Ralph Waldo Emerson: A Descriptive Bibliography* (1982).

The most comprehensive general biography is Ralph Leslie Rusk's *The Life of Ralph Waldo Emerson* (1949). It is well-complemented by the intellectual biographies of Stephen Whicher, *Freedom and Fate: An Inner Life of Ralph Waldo Emerson* (1953), and Robert Richardson, *Emerson: The Mind on Fire* (1995). Particularly useful essay collections are *Ralph Waldo Emerson: A Collection of Critical Essays*, ed. Lawrence Buell (1993), and *On Emerson: The Best from American Literature*, ed. Edwin H. Cady and Louis J. Budd (1988). The reception of Emerson's works may be traced in *Emerson and Thoreau: The Contemporary Reviews*, ed. Joel Myerson (1992). Examinations of Emerson's relationship with abolitionism may be found in *Virtue's Hero: Emerson, Antislavery, and Reform*, by Len Gougeon (1990); *Emerson's Antislavery Writings*, ed. Len Gougeon and Joel Myerson (1995); and *The Trials of Anthony Burns: Freedom and Slavery in Emerson's Boston*, by Albert J. Von Frank (1998).

Lecture on Slavery
by Ralph Waldo Emerson

Gentlemen,

I approach the grave and bitter subject of American slavery with diffidence and pain. . . .

The subject seems exhausted. An honest man is soon weary of crying "Thief!" Who can long continue to feel an interest in condemning homicide, or counterfeiting, or wife-beating? 'Tis said, endless negation is a flat affair. . . .

We have to consider that, however strongly the tides of public sentiment have set or are setting towards freedom, the code of slavery in this country is at this hour more malignant than ever before. The recent action of Congress has brought it home to New England, and made it impossible to avoid complicity.

The crying facts are these, that, in a Republic professing to base its laws on liberty, and on the doctrines of Christianity, slavery is suffered to subsist: and, when the poor people who are the victims of this crime, disliking the stripping and peeling process, run away into states where this practice is not permitted,—a law has been passed requiring us who sit here to seize these poor people, tell them they have not been plundered enough, and must go back to be stripped and peeled again, and as long as they live.

But this was not yet the present grief. It was shocking to hear of the sufferings of these men: But the district was three hundred, five hundred, and a thousand miles off, and, however leagued with ours, was yet independent. And, for the national law which enacted this complicity, and threw us into conspiracy with the thief, it was an old dead law, which had been made in an hour of weakness and fear, and which we guarded ourselves from executing,—now revived and made stringent. But there was no fear that it would be valid.

But the destruction was here. We found well-born, well-bred, well-grown men among ourselves, not outcasts, not foreigners, not beggars, not convicts, but baptised, vaccinated, schooled, high-placed, official men, who abetted this law. "O by all means, catch the slave, and drag him back." And when we went to the courts, the interpreters of God's right between man and man said, "catch the slave, and force him back."

Now this was disheartening. Slavery is an evil, as cholera or typhus is, that will be purged out by the health of the system. Being unnatural and violent, I know that it will yield at last, and go with cannibalism, tattooing, inquisition, dueling, burking; and as we cannot refuse to ride in the same planet with the New Zealander, so we must be content to go with the southern planter, and say, you are you, and I am I, and God send you an early conversion.

But to find it here in our sunlight, here in the heart of Puritan traditions in an intellectual country, in the land of schools, of sabbaths and sermons, under the shadow of the White Hills, of Katahdin, and Hoosac;[1] under the eye of the most ingenious, industrious, and self-helping men in the world,—staggers our faith in progress. . . .

Look at our politics. The great parties coeval with the origin of the government,—do they inspire us with any exalted hope? Does the Democracy stand really for the good of the many? of the poor? for the elevation of entire humanity? Have they ever addressed themselves to the enterprise of relieving this country of the pest of slavery?

The Party of Property, of education, has resisted every progressive step. Did Free Trade come from them? Have they urged the abolition of Capital Punishment? Have they urged any of the prophetic action of the time? No. They would nail the stars to the sky. With their eyes over their shoulders, they adore their ancestors, the framers of the Constitution. Nolumus mutari.[2] We do not wish to touch the Constitution. They wish their age should be absolutely like the last. There is no confession of destitution like this fierce conservatism. Can any thing proclaim so loudly the absence of all aim or principle? What means this desperate grasp on the past, if not that they find no principle, no hope, no future in their own mind? Some foundation we must have, and, if we can see nothing, we cling desperately to those whom we believe can see.

Our politics have run very low, and men of character will not willingly touch them. This is fast becoming, if it has not already become, discreditable work. Those who have gone to Congress were honest well-meaning men. I heard congratulations from good men, their friends, in relation to certain recent members, that "these were honest and thoroughly trustworthy, obstinately honest." Yet they voted on the late criminal measures with the basest of the populace. They ate dirt, and saw not the sneer of the bullies who duped them with an alleged state-necessity: and all because they had no burning splendor of law in their own minds. Well, what refuge for them? They had honor enough left to feel degraded: they could have a place in which they could not preserve appearances. They become apathized and indifferentists. We leave them in their retreats. They represented the property of their constituency. Our merchants do not believe in anything but their trade. They loll in republican chairs, they eat and drink in republican Astor, Tremont, and Girard Houses.[3] They roll in easy and swift trains, telegraphing their wishes before them. And the power of money is so obtrusive as to exclude the view of the larger powers that control it.

I am sorry to say, that, even our political reforms show the same desperation. What shall we think of the new movement? We are clear that the old parties could not lead us. They were plainly bankrupt, their machineries and politicians discredited. We will have none of them. Yes, but shall we therefore abdicate our common sense? I employed false guides and they misled me; shall I therefore put my head in a bag?

The late revolution in Massachusetts no man will wonder at who sees how far our politics had departed from the path of simple right. The reigning parties had forfeited the awe and reverence which always attaches to a wise and honest government. And as they inspired no respect, they were turned out by an immense frolic. But to persist in a joke;—I don't like joking with edge-tools, and there is no knife so sharp as legislation. . . .

There are periods of occulation when the light of mind seems to be partially withdrawn from nations as well as from individuals. This devastation reached its crisis in the acquiescence to slavery in this country,—in the political servitude of Europe, during the same age. And there are moments of greatest darkness, and of total eclipse. In the French Revolution, there was a day when the Parisians took a strumpet from the street, seated her in a chariot, and led her in procession, saying, "This is the Goddess of Reason." And, in 1850, the American Congress passed a statute which ordained that justice and mercy should be subject to fine and imprisonment, and that there existed no higher law in the universe than the Constitution and this paper statute which uprooted the foundations of rectitude and denied the existence of God.

Thus in society, in education, in political parties, in trade, and in labor, in expenditure, or the direction of surplus capital, you may see the credence of men; how deeply they live, how much water the ship draws. In all these, it is the thought of men, what they think, which is the helm that turns them all about. When thus explored, instead of rich belief, of minds great and wise sounding the secrets of nature, announcing the laws of science, and glowing with zeal to act and serve, and life too short to read the revelations inscribed on earth and heaven, I fear you will find non-credence, which produces nothing, but leaves sterility and littleness.

This skepticism assails a vital part when it climbs into the Courts, which are the brain of the state. The idea of abstract right exists in the human mind, and lays itself out in the equilibrium of nature, in the equalities and periods of our system, in the level of seas, in the action and reaction of forces, that nothing is allowed to exceed or absorb the rest; if it do, it is disease, and is quickly destroyed.

Among men, this limitation of my liberty by yours,—allowing the largest liberty to each compatible with the liberty of all,—protection in seeking my benefit, as long as it does not interfere with your benefit,—is justice,—which satisfies everybody. . . .

The fathers, in July 1787, consented to adopt population as the basis of representation, and to count only three-fifths of the slaves, and to concede the reclamation of fugitive slaves;—for the consideration, that there should be no slavery in the Northwest Territory. They agreed to this false basis of representation and to this criminal complicity of restoring fugitives: and the splendor of the bribe, namely, the magnificent prosperity of America from 1787, is their excuse for the crime. It was a fatal blunder. They should have refused it at the risk of making no Union. Many ways could have been taken. If the southern section had made a separate alliance with England, or gone back into colonies, the slaves would have been emancipated with the West Indians, and then the colonies could have been annexed to us. The bribe, if they foresaw the prosperity we have seen, was one to dazzle common men, and I do not wonder that common men excuse and applaud it. But always so much crime brings so much ruin. A little crime, a minor penalty; a great crime, a great disaster.

If the south country thinks itself enriched by slavery, read the census, read the valuation tables, or weigh the men. I think it impoverished. Young men are born in that country, I suppose, of as much ability as elsewhere, and yet some blight is on their education: in the present generation is there one living son to make good the reputation of the Past? If the north think it a benefit, I find the north saddled with a load which has all the effect of a partnership in a crime, on a virtuous and prosperous youth. It stops his mouth, ties his hands, forces him to submit to every sort of humiliation, and now it is a fountain of poison which is felt in every transaction and every conversation in this country.

Well, certain men were glad perceivers of this Right, with more clearness and steadiness than others, and labored to establish the application of it to human affairs. They were Lawgivers or Judges. And all men hailed the Laws of Menu, the Laws of Lycurgus, laws of Moses, laws of Confucius, laws of Jesus, the laws of Alfred, and of men of less fame, who in their place, believing in an ideal right, strove to make it practical,—the Code of Justinian, the famous jurists, Grotius, Vattel, Daguesseau, Blackstone, and Mansfield.[4] These were original judges, perceivers that this is no child's play, no egotistic opinion, but stands on the original law of the world. And the reputation of all the judges on earth stands on the real perception of these few natural or God-anointed judges. All these men held that law was not an opinion, not an egotism of any king or the will of any mob, but a transcript of natural right. The judge was there as its organ and expounder, and his first duty was to read the law in accordance with equity. And, if it jarred with equity, to disown the law. All the great lawgivers and jurists of the world have agreed in this, that an immoral law is void. So held Cicero, Selden, Hooker; and Coke, Hobart, Holt, and Mansfield, chief justices of England.⁵ Even the Canon law says, "Neither allegiance nor oath can bind to obey that which is unlawful." Grotius, Vattel, Daguesseau, and Blackstone teach the same. Of course they do. What else could they? You cannot enact a falsehood to be true, nor a wrong act to be right.

And I name their names, not of course to add authority to a self-evident proposition, but only to show that black-letter lawyers supposed to be more than others tied to precedent and statute, saw the exquisite absurdity of enacting a crime.

And yet in America justice was poisoned at its fountain. In our northern states, no judge appeared of sufficient character and intellect to ask not whether it was constitutional, but whether it was right.

This outrage of giving back a stolen and plundered man to his thieves was ordained and under circumstances the most painful. There was enough law of the State of Massachusetts to resist the dishonor and the crime, but no judge had the heart to invoke, no governor was found to execute it. The judges feared collision of the State and Federal Courts. The Governor⁶ was a most estimable man—we all knew his sterling virtues, but he fell in an era when governors do not govern, when judges do not judge, when Presidents do not preside, and when representatives do not represent.

The judges were skeptics too and shared the sickness of the time. The open secret of the world was hid from their eyes, the art of subliming a private soul with inspirations from the great and public and divine soul from which we live. A man is a little thing whilst he works by and for himself. A judge who gives voice as a judge should, to the rules of love and justice, is godlike; his word is current in all countries. But a man sitting on the Bench servile to precedent, or a windy politician, or a dangler trying to give authority to the notions of his superiors or of his set, pipes and squeaks and cheeps ridiculously. . . .

Now what is the effect of this evil government? To discredit government. When the public fails in its duty, private men take its place. When the British ministry is weak, the Times' editor governs the realm. When the American government and courts are false to their trust, men disobey the government, put it in the wrong; the government is forced into all manner of false and ridiculous attitudes. Men hear reason and truth from private men who have brave hearts and great minds. This is the compensation of bad governments,—the field it affords for illustrious men. And we have a great debt to the brave and faithful men who in the very hour and place of the evil act, made their protest for themselves and their countrymen by word and deed. They are justified and the law is condemned.

It is not to societies that the secrets of nature are revealed, but to private persons, to each man in his organization, in his thoughts. A serious man who has used his opportunities will early discover that he only works and thinks securely when he is acting on his own experience. All forcible men will agree that books and learned societies could not supply what their own good sense taught them. . . .

But whilst I insist on the doctrine of the independence and the inspiration of the individual, I do not cripple but exalt the social action. Patriotism, public opinion, have a real meaning, though there is so much counterfeit rag money abroad under it, that the name is apt to disgust. . . .

And as the state is a reality, so it is certain that societies of men, a race, a people have a public function, a part to play in the history of humanity. Thus, the theory of our government is Liberty. The thought and experience of Europe had got thus far, a century ago, to believe, that, as soon as favorable circumstances permitted, the experiment of self-government should be made. America afforded the circumstances, and the new order began. All the mind in America was possessed by that idea. The Declaration of Independence, the Constitution of the States, the Parties; the newspapers, the songs, star-spangled banner, land of the brave and home of the free, the very manners of the Americans, all showed them as the receivers and propagandists of this lesson to the world. Liberty; to each man the largest liberty compatible with the liberty of every other man. It was not a sect, it was not a private opinion, but a gradual and irresistible growth of the human mind. That is the meaning of our national pride. It is a noble office. For liberty is a very serious thing. It is the severest test by which a government can be tried. All history goes to show, that it is the measure of all national success. Religion, arts, science, material production are as is the degree of liberty. Montesquieu said, "Countries are not cultivated in proportion to their population, but in proportion to their freedom."

Most unhappily, this universally accepted duty and feeling has been antagonized by the calamity of southern slavery. And that institution in its perpetual encroachment has had through the stronger personality, shall I say, of the southern people, and through their systematic devotion to politics, the art so to league itself with the government, as to check and pervert the natural sentiment of the people by their respect for law and statute.

And this country exhibits an abject regard to the forms, whilst we are swindled out of the liberty. . . .

Men inspire each other. The affections are the Muses. Hope is a muse, Love is, Despair is not, and selfishness drives away the angels. It is so delicious to act with great masses to great aims. For instance the summary or gradual abolition of slavery. Why in the name of common sense and the peace of mankind is not this made the subject of instant negotiation and settlement? Why do not the men of administrative ability in whose brain the prosperity of Philadelphia is rooted;—the multitude of able men who lead each enterprize in the City of New York; in Boston, in Baltimore; why not the strong courageous leaders of the south; join their heads and hearts to form some basis of negotiation to settle this dangerous dispute on some ground of fair compensation, on one side, and of satisfaction, on the other, to the conscience of the Free States. Is it impossible to speak of it with reason and good nature? Why? Because it is property? Why, then it has a price. Because it is political? Well then, it ultimately concerns us, threatens us, and there will never be a better time than the present time. It is really the great task fit for this country to accomplish, to buy that property of the planters, as the British nation bought the West Indian slaves. I say buy,—

never conceding the right of the planter to own, but that we may acknowledge the calamity of his position, and bear a countryman's share in relieving him, and because it is the only practicable course, and is innocent.

Well, here is right social or public function which one man cannot do, which all men must do. We shall one day bring the states shoulder to shoulder, and the citizens man to man, to exterminate slavery. It is said, it will cost two thousand millions of dollars. Was there ever any contribution levied that was so enthusiastically paid as this will be? The United States shall give every inch of the public lands. The states shall give their surplus revenues, their unsold lands. The citizen his private contribution. We will have a chimney tax. We will give up our coaches, and wine, and watches. The churches will melt their plate. The Father of his country shall wait well-pleased a little longer for his monument:[7] Franklin for his; the Pilgrim Fathers for theirs. We will call on those rich benefactors who found Asylums, Hospitals, Athenaeums, Lowell Institutes, Peabody Institutions, Bates and Astor City Libraries.[8] On wealthy bachelors and wealthy maidens to make the State their heir as they were wont in Rome. The merchant will give his best voyage. The mechanic will give his fabric. The needlewoman will give. Children will have cent societies. If really the matter could come to negotiation and a price were named, I do not think any price founded on an estimate that figures could tell would be quite unmanageable. Every man in the land would give a week's work to dig away this accursed mountain of sorrow once and forever out of the world.

Source Note: Emerson first delivered this lecture before the Massachusetts Anti-Slavery Society in Boston on January 25, 1855. He repeated the lecture in New York on February 6, in Philadelphia on February 8, in Rochester on February 21, and in Syracuse on February 25. This reprinting is derived from *Emerson's Antislavery Writings*, ed. Len Gougeon and Joel Myerson (New Haven and London: Yale University Press, 1995), pp. 91–106.

1. The White Mountains are in New Hampshire; Mount Katahdin is in Maine; and Mount Hoosac is part of the Berkshires in western Massachusetts.

2. "We are unwilling to be changed."

3. Elite hotels in New York, Boston, and Philadelphia, respectively.

4. The Laws of Menu (or Manu) are commentaries on Indian law compiled between 200 B.C. and A.D. 200. Lycurgus was a Spartan statesperson; Alfred "the Great" (840–99), an English king who drew up a legal code; Justinian I (483–565), known as "the Great," a Byzantine emperor who codified Roman law; Hugo Grotius (1583–1645), a Dutch scholar who wrote the first treatise on international law; Daguesseau is Henri-François d'Aguesseau (1668–1751), a French magistrate and legal scholar; William Blackstone (1723–80), a famous British jurist whose four-volume *Commentaries* (1765–69) was the standard treatment of English law; and William Murray, Lord Mansfield (1704–93), an English jurist.

5. John Selden (1584–1654) was an English jurist; Richard Hooker (1554?–1600), an English theologian. Edward Coke (1552–1634), Henry Hobart, John Holt (1642–1710), and William Murray, Lord Mansfield (1704–93), were all eminent English magistrates.

6. Emerson is probably referring to one of four governors of Massachusetts during this period: George N. Briggs (1796–1861), governor 1844–51; George S. Boutell (1818–1905), governor 1851–53; John H. Clifford (1809–76), governor 1853–54; or Emory Washburn (1800–77), governor 1854–55.

7. The Washington Monument was started in 1848 but not completed until 1885.

8. John Lowell, Jr. (1799–1836) established the Lowell Institute in Boston; George Peabody (1795–1869) established the Peabody Institute in Baltimore; Joshua Bates (1788–1864) funded the Boston Public Library; and John Jacob Astor (1763–1848) helped to form the New York Public Library.

HARRIET BEECHER STOWE (1811–1896) AND MARY EASTMAN (1818–1880)

Harriet Beecher Stowe was divinely inspired to write *Uncle Tom's Cabin*. While attending a church service, she had a vision of an old slave being flogged to death by an unscrupulous slave master. She had already composed several pieces of fiction and other writings, so her sister, on learning of this vision, suggested that she write something against slavery. The Fugitive Slave Law of 1850, incorporated into the Compromise of 1850, had incensed the antislavery forces and militant Garrisonian abolitionists throughout the nation, and had effectively galvanized opposition to slavery as never before. The wife of a minister, the daughter of Lyman Beecher, President of Lane Seminary in Cincinnati, Ohio, and the sister of five ministers, Stowe was well prepared to compose a jeremiad against the institution of chattel slavery, which she viewed as being the Antichrist in an eternal struggle of good versus evil. Slave narratives, such as *The Narrative of the Life of Frederick Douglass, an American Slave* (1845), had already given the nation an insider's view of the cruelties of American slavery, such as brutal floggings and family-destroying slave auctions. But Stowe's work captured the national imagination in ways that even the nonfictional accounts by ex-slaves had been unable to do. Stowe's masterpiece was first published serially, in *The National Era*, the year before it appeared as a finished volume. This periodic publication accounts in part for its episodic character and loose structural design, which were criticized by Charles Dickens.

Stowe's novel became an instant best-seller. Published in the spring of 1852, in its first week it sold 10,000 copies. By the year's end, 150,000 copies had been sold in the United States alone and over 300,000 worldwide, and by 1861, the book was being read in sixteen languages and had sold four and one-half million copies. This is a remarkable statistic even today; *Uncle Tom's Cabin* would have been on the *New York Times* best-seller list all of those years, had the *Times* list existed. In 1861, however, the population of the United States was only 32 million, and some 4 million of that number were slaves living in the South, where the book was effectively banned by most state legislatures. (Only 5 to 8 percent of the slave population in the South was sufficiently literate to read Stowe's novel.) Thus the population remaining among whom the book circulated was only 22 million, of whom only 18 million were sufficiently literate to

"Good Times on the Old Plantation," by Currier and Ives, by permission of Georgia Barnhill, Mellon Curator of Graphic Arts, American Antiquarian Society, Worcester, Mass.

read the book through. As a percentage of the literate, reading population in the years between 1852 and 1861, the outbreak of the Civil War, *Uncle Tom's Cabin* was a media success comparable to cablevision or CNN today.

In addition, the dramatic force of the novel was suitable for stage presentation, and in 1859–60, there were no fewer than nine separate stage companies in New York City offering adaptations of scenes from *Uncle Tom's Cabin*. Many of these shows employed minstrel versions of characters from the novel, such as Topsy as "pickaninny," and the nation was captivated by both the story line and the dramatic scenes from Stowe's novel. Death scenes sold books in nineteenth-century Britain and America, and the lengthy death scene of little Eva was a popular episode adapted for the stage. It would later appear in *Dimples*, the 1936 Shirley Temple film about these stage adaptations of *Uncle Tom's Cabin*. Some of these adaptations were musical versions; few people today realize that Stephen Foster's "My Old Kentucky Home," now a classic in the repertoire of American folk music, was originally composed in 1852 to accompany stage presentations of the novel. The song, a lamentation, was scored for Tom's character, as he longed for his wife, Chloe, and his children who were still in Kentucky after he had been sold to the slave trader, Haley, who took him South, away from his family.

The impact of *Uncle Tom's Cabin* was enormous. Queen Victoria was allegedly given a copy one morning and she read it throughout the day and into the night, sobbing at the sentimental and dramatic tale. It is also alleged that when Abraham Lincoln invited Stowe to the White House in 1863, he greeted her with these words: "So this is the little lady who started this great big war." Lincoln would not have been far off the mark. Together with Hinton Rowan Helper's 1857 publication, *The Impending Crisis of the South: How to Meet It*, Stowe's book stirred up antislavery sentiment everywhere, and anti-Southern sentiment in the North, as it highlighted the moral arguments concerning American slavery. The book's very popularity aroused deep resentment in the South, where feeling ran strong that Stowe had misrepresented Southern slavery by emphasizing the cruelty of owners like Simon Legree and barbarous practices like the separation of families at slave auctions. Slave narratives like Frederick Douglass's, and Harriet Jacobs's *Incidents in the Life of a Slave Girl* (1861), corroborated Stowe's fictional version with detailed accounts of cruelty, and one of Stowe's sources, Theodore Dwight Weld's *American Slavery As It Is: the Testimony of a Thousand Witnesses* (1839), provided actual newspaper accounts of mistreatment and cruelty. Still, Southern writers responded immediately to Stowe, openly condemning her inexperience with slavery; although Stowe had wintered near Jacksonville, Florida (Stowe lived in Mandarin, Florida, after the Civil War), she had little direct experience of the plantation system, and her critics were swift to remind her of the inauthenticity of her work. She responded in kind. In 1853, Stowe published *A Key to Uncle Tom's Cabin*, a nonfiction compilation of sources she used in writing the novel, including Josiah Henson's slave narrative of 1842, ostensibly the source for Uncle Tom's character. She had also lived at Lane Seminary in Cincinnati on the Ohio River, where she had ready access to accounts of slavery through the Underground Railroad, where she would interview escaped slaves as they made their way to freedom in the North. This experience would appear in Eliza's dramatic escape over the ice floes from Kentucky to Ohio.

The Southern congressmen railed against Stowe's popular depiction of the degrading effects that slavery has on everyone, from Simon Legree's alcoholism to Tom's untimely sacrifice and Cassy's concubinage to Legree's lust. Viewing Southern slavery as a paternalistic institution that provided opportunities for "Christianizing" and "civilizing" the heathen and barbarous African slaves, Southern writers portrayed slavery as a beneficial institution that made salvation available to pagans and family life in the secure, monogamous western mode available to the polygamous tribal members fortunate enough to be sold into American slavery. The Currier and Ives lithograph reproduced in this volume, "The Happy Slaves, or Good Times on the Plantation," is a misrepresentation of plantation society that paralleled these Southern responses to Stowe.

One genre of writing that evolved to offset Stowe's influence on public opinion was the proslavery novel, here represented by Mary Eastman's *Aunt Phillis's Cabin; or, Southern Life as It Is* (1852), composed as a direct response to Stowe's alleged misrepresentation of plantation life. Eastman's account is a romantic fantasy of life on the plantation, showing how paternalistic slavery is a necessary institution for the African "children" who are essentially inferior to the whites and are unable to govern or care for themselves. A view of slavery embraced by early colonial slaveowners such as George Washington and even Thomas Jefferson, this paternalistic image of the extended slave family is easily seen in another Currier and Ives lithograph, and it is precisely the image of slavery that Eastman and her proslavery novelist contemporaries sought to portray. Here, happy slaves dance and frolic around a well-tended slave cabin, which has curtains in the windows and flower boxes decorating the house. All of this joy is viewed, at a distance, by the Lord of the Manor, the plantation owner, who sits in the background in the "big house," high on the hill, supervising the play of his dependent children. Similar to Eastman's account was that of John Pendleton Kennedy, who wrote *Swallow Barn* (1832), a highly romanticized vision of plantation life that eulogizes the Virginia planter and his treatment of his extended slave family. Both Douglass's *Narrative* (1845) and Jacobs's *Incidents in the Life of a Slave Girl* (1861) dramatically reveal how inaccurate the proslavery novel's version of plantation life was, but this view of antebellum slavery was extremely popular. While Stowe's version had enormous impact in antebellum America, the romantic description of slavery reappeared in 1936 in Margaret Mitchell's *Gone with the Wind*, an antebellum (and postbellum) romance that sanitized slavery and provided the reading and moviegoing world with characters such as Mammy, portrayed in the 1939 film version by Hattie McDaniel, who won the first Oscar ever by an African-American.

This benign view of the "peculiar institution" corroborated early twentieth-century views of antebellum America as a pastoral world in which Southern planters presided over large extended families at "Tara" and "Twelve Oaks" while the Africans, whose total dependence on the slave master after emancipation was demonstrated by the book, never evolved beyond the status they had enjoyed in the antebellum world. Not only is Mitchell's world devoid of flogging and slave auction scenes—two staples of insider slave narratives—it represents the antebellum and postbellum South as a place of harmony and mutual dependence among whites and blacks, ignoring the slave uprisings, such as the Nat Turner rebellion, and the more unpleasant aspects of plantation life.

Mary Eastman's *Aunt Phillis's Cabin* never achieved the status of Stowe's novel in the decade before the Civil War, but the antebellum world it depicted held fast in the popular imagination until the mid-twentieth century, when college courses in Reconstruction, African-American history, and race relations began to provide less romantic and more realistic accounts of slavery before the Civil War. Stowe's powerful visionary novel was indeed prophetic. The "Concluding Remarks," excerpted here, articulate a vision of doom for American society if slavery is allowed to continue, and in this brief chapter, Stowe resorts to her ministerial background to deliver an extremely effective sermonic jeremiad against the "peculiar institution," which she views as a Northern as well as a Southern problem, because of the Fugitive Slave Law. Calling Northern support of this law a "common capital of sin," she shows clearly that the day of doom awaits any society that continues to support the barbarous inhumanity of slavery, which degrades everything in its path, not just the victimized slaves. Indeed, Stowe views all Americans as victims of slavery, and argues effectively that redemption for such a long history of immersion in sin can only come through legislative action and prayer. *Uncle Tom's Cabin* is structured as a sentimental novel, but its rhetorical strategies include recuperation of slave narrative techniques, the voice overlays of direct address and omniscient narration, and the employment of sermon strategies, all of which would have been very familiar to her reading audience. This novel was no accident, as some critics have claimed, citing the relative obscurity of much of Stowe's other work. It is, rather, a unique historical moment, one where a work of fiction so inspired moral indignation against its adversary, the institution of slavery, that a nation rose up to embrace abolition.

Reaction to Stowe's novel was swift and uncompromising. Early critical reviews included numerous attacks on the artless invective of the novel, treating it more as propaganda and polemic than serious fiction. But the primary thrust of the objections to *Uncle Tom's Cabin* were ideological, criticizing her inexperience with plantation slavery and the exaggerated, often wooden and stereotyped characters through whom she dramatized the plight of the Southern slave. Character stereotyping has remained a serious objection to the novel over the years, and in 1949, James Baldwin wrote the most vehement of these attacks in "Everybody's Protest Novel," which appeared in the *Paris Review*. Reprinted in 1954 in Baldwin's *Nobody Knows My Name*, it has remained one of the most prominent modern essays objecting to continued study of Stowe's work. Arguing that *Uncle Tom's Cabin* is more than an historical artifact, Baldwin effectively showed that the character stereotypes in the novel have entered the mainstream of American popular culture in ways that negatively represent the African-American. Topsy, for example, is not simply the childhood friend of Little Eva; she is also part of a modern vocabulary drawn from minstrel characterizations of her as a "pickaninny" child, one whose unruly behavior confirms the antebellum conviction that the African was incapable of self-government and that emancipation would lead to social anarchy. As Eva attempts to "Christianize" and "civilize" her African friend, the characters are polarized in a manner that is virtually fixed and immutable. Like many ideological critics of Stowe's work, Baldwin cites the crucial passage where Stowe summarized the difference between the two children:

> There stood the two children, representatives of the two extremes of society. The fair, high-bred child, with her golden head, her deep eyes, her spiritual, noble brow, and the prince-like movements; and her black, keen, subtle, cringing, yet acute neighbor. They stood the representatives of their races. The Saxon, born of ages of cultivation, command, education, physical and moral eminence; the Afric, born of ages of oppression, submission, ignorance, toil, and vice! [Chapter 20]

There is no question that this passage taken out of context would offend African-American readers and any modern sensibility. The context is the scene where Miss Ophelia, that Vermont do-gooder who came South to set things right, is given Topsy as her personal slave by Augustine St. Clare "for you to educate." The scene provides Stowe an opportunity to dramatize the extreme differences between ideological commitment to racial equality and action that will benefit the African slaves. Miss Ophelia, who represents the reformer ideology, is initially offended by everything Topsy represents—filth, human degradation, illiteracy, and paganism. St. Clare takes the opportunity to chastise Ophelia for her hypocrisy, broadening his critique to include the Christian church, a target of Stowe's criticism throughout the novel, as she states, in "Concluding Remarks:"

> O, Church of Christ, read the signs of the times! . . . Christians! Every time that you pray that the kingdom of Christ may come, can you forget that prophecy associates, in dread fellowship, the day of vengeance with the year of his redeemed? A Day of Grace is yet held out to us. Both North and South have been guilty before God; and the Christian Church has a heavy account to answer. Not by combining together, to protect injustice and cruelty, and making a common capital of sin, is this Union to be saved,—but by repentance, justice and mercy; for, not surer is the eternal law by which the millstone sinks in the ocean, than that stronger law, by which injustice and cruelty shall bring on nations the wrath of Almighty God!

Just over nine years later, the firing on Fort Sumter, South Carolina, initiated the Civil War, a conflict that destroyed more American lives than all the combined wars in which the United States has engaged since the American Revolution. Stowe's prophetic voice predicted these events, and her ability to write a novel that forced readers to examine their positions on slavery and racial equality held a mirror up to society that has been unequaled in American literary history.

Uncle Tom's Cabin
by Harriet Beecher Stowe

Concluding Remarks

To fill up Liberia with an ignorant, inexperienced, half-barbarized race, just escaped from the chains of slavery, would be only to prolong, for ages, the period of struggle and conflict which attends the inception of new enterprises. Let the church of the north receive these poor sufferers in the spirit of Christ; receive them to the educating advantages of Christian republican society and schools, until they have attained to somewhat of a moral and intellectual maturity, and then assist them in their passage to those shores, where they may put in practice the lessons they have learned in America.

There is a body of men at the north, comparatively small, who have been doing this; and, as the result, this country has already seen examples of men, formerly slaves, who have rapidly acquired property, reputation, and education. Talent has been developed, which, considering the circumstances is remarkable;

and, for moral traits of honesty, kindness, tenderness of feeling—for heroic efforts and self-denials, endured for the ransom of brethren and friends yet in slavery—they have been remarkable to a degree that, considering the influence under which they were born, is surprising.

The writer has lived, for many years, on the frontier-line of slave states, and has had great opportunities of observation among those who formerly were slaves. They have been in her family as servants; and, in default of any other school to receive them, she has, in many cases, had them instructed in a family school, with her own children. She has also the testimony of missionaries among the fugitives in Canada, in coincidence with her own experience; and her deductions with regard to the capabilities of the race, are encouraging to the highest degree.

The first desire of the emancipated slave, generally, is for *education*. There is nothing that they are not willing to give or do to have their children instructed; insofar as the writer has observed herself, or taken the testimony of teachers, they are remarkably intelligent and quick to learn.

This is an age of the world when nations are trembling and convulsed. A mighty influence is abroad, surging and heaving the world, as with an earth-quake. And is America safe? Every nation that carries in its bosom great and unrepressed injustice has in it the elements of this last convulsion.

For what is this mighty influence thus rousing in all nations and languages those groanings that cannot be uttered, for man's freedom and equality?

O, Church of Christ, read the signs of the times! Is not this power the spirit of HIM whose kingdom is yet to come, and whose will to be done on earth as it is in heaven?

But who may abide the day of his appearing? "For that day shall burn as an oven: and he shall appear as a swift witness against those that oppress the hirelings in his wages, the widow and the fatherless, and that *turn aside the stranger in his right*: and he shall break in pieces the oppressor."

Are not these dread words for a nation bearing in her bosom so mighty an injustice? Christians! every time that you pray that the kingdom of Christ may come, can you forget that prophecy associates, in the dread fellowship, the *day of vengeance* with the year of his redeemed?

A day of grace is yet held out to us. Both North and South have been guilty before God; and the *Christian church* has a heavy account to answer. Not by combining together, to protect injustice and cruelty, and making a common capital of sin, is this Union to be saved—but by repentance, justice and mercy; for, not surer is the eternal law by which the millstone sinks in the ocean, than that stronger law, by which injustice and cruelty shall bring on nations the wrath of Almighty God!

Source Note: Harriet Beecher Stowe, *Uncle Tom's Cabin* (Boston, 1852; New York: Penguin, 1986).

BLACK STEREOTYPES IN *UNCLE TOM'S CABIN*
by Sandra C. Duvivier

STEREOTYPICAL PRESENTATION OF MAJOR BLACK CHARACTERS (IN ORDER OF APPEARANCE):

Harry "Jim Crow," Eliza, and George Harris: The first black characters we meet are of mixed origin. Harry, son of Eliza and George Harris, is described as a "small quadroon boy, between four and five years of age. . . . There was something in his appearance remarkably beautiful and engaging" (43). Eliza is a quadroon slave with a "peculiar air of refinement, that softness of voice and manner, which seems in many cases to be a particular gift to the quadroon and mulatto women" (54); in other words, the "unmixed" slaves are not bestowed with these "gifts." Eliza's husband, George Harris, is "a bright and talented young mulatto man," who is naturally attractive from his description. George's talents are reflected in his invention, a machine for cleaning hemp, which makes his master jealous. In fact, mulattos, quadroons, and so on are depicted as beautiful human beings who possess a sense of intelligence and superiority that the "darkies"—the unmixed characters that all seem to be a shade of midnight black—lack. It is also interesting to note that these characters have a surname, while other black characters do not. The Harrises represent the stereotype of mulatto superiority (over African-Americans), since they appear to be more delicate and refined because of "white" blood.

Aunt Chloe: Aunt Chloe, Uncle Tom's wife, is a stereotypical mammy—a desexualized, happy-go-lucky, heavyset black woman: she's an excellent cook, possessing a "round, black, shining face," and a "plump countenance" (66–67). Whenever her cooking was complimented, "she would shake her fat sides with honest pride and merriment" (67). Regarding attire, mammy is depicted as wearing a head rag, which can be paralleled with Aunt Chloe's "well-starched checked turban."

Aunt Chloe also lacks the refinement and eloquence attributed to the mulatto and quadroon slaves, as evidenced by her speech: "Here you, Mose and Pete! Get out de way, you niggers! Get away, Mericky, honey, mammy'll give her baby some fin, by and by" (69).

Uncle Tom: Uncle Tom, the central black character of the text, embodies the "good nigger" stereotype: he's a Sambo, a passive, complacent, non-threatening slave, who, although he yearns for freedom, fails to challenge slavery because of his God-fearing Christian humility. He only acts out of Christian love, showing no other emotion—not even anger. Regarding appearance, Uncle Tom is a "large, broad-chested, powerfully-made man, of a full glossy black, and a face whose truly African features were characterized by an expression of grave and steady good sense, united with much kindliness and benevolence" (68). Similar to his wife, Uncle Tom's speech is also unrefined. Tom's "inarticulacy" and Christian humility can be seen with his following remark to Aunt Chloe when they learn of his impending trade: "Chloe! now, if ye love me, ye won't talk so, when perhaps jest the last time we'll ever have together! And I'll tell ye, Chloe, it goes agin me to hear one word agin Mas'r" (164).

Topsy: Topsy, the black imp, is the stereotypical heathen, the barbaric African possessing no civilization, who, through guidance and Christian nurturing from the superior white being, becomes more human, though still inferior. Black Topsy is a counterpart to pure white Eva, the angelic creature whom Tom saves from drowning. While Eva acts out of loving-kindness, Topsy acts out of sheer mischief. Not only does she steal, but she also declares her wickedness: "Cause I's wicked,—I is. I's mighty wicked, anyhow. I can't help it" (360). (Note the unrefined nature of her speech.) As for her appearance, she resembles a minstrel show character, which is seen in contemporary American culture with buffoonish cartoon portrayals of African-Americans and in Spike Lee's modern-day minstrel show satire, *Bamboozled*. Regarding Topsy's origins, she has as confused roots as her name suggests: when asked her age, she replies "Dun no, Miss"; when asked of her parentage, she says, "Never had none"; in fact, she declares that she "Never was born" (355). Similar to topsoil, this creature obviously grew from the ground, from dirt, which explains her heathenish, nonhuman ways.

STEREOTYPES TREATED IN AFRICAN-AMERICAN LITERATURE

These stereotypes not only continue to appear in American literature and culture, but they have also caused a backlash among African-American writers, expressed in essays, short stories, and novels of the nineteenth and twentieth centuries. A few—but definitely not all—examples of this backlash:

Essays—James Baldwin's "Everybody's Protest Novel": In "Everybody's Protest Novel" (1949), author, activist, and critic James Baldwin lambastes *Uncle Tom's Cabin* for its overt sentimentality and stereotypical portrayal of African-Americans, including the color hierarchy Stowe presents among the slaves: "Apart from her lively procession of field hands, house niggers, Chloe, Topsy, etc. . . . she has only three other Negroes in the book. These are the important ones, and two of them may be dismissed immediately, since we have only the author's word that they are Negro and they are, in all other respects, as white as she can make them" (13). (Baldwin excludes Harry as one of the major black characters.)

Baldwin also notes how Tom is racialized and desexualized:

Uncle Tom, who is a figure of controversy yet, is jet-black, wooly haired, illiterate; and he is phenomenally forbearing. He has to be; he is black; only through this forbearance can he survive or triumph. . . . His triumph is metaphysical, unearthly; since he is black, born without the light, it is only through humility, the incessant

mortification of the flesh, that he can enter into communion with God or man. . . .
Here, black equates with evil and white with grace. [14]

(Although Uncle Tom is not illiterate, his rudimentary "education" cannot be paralleled or equated with George Harris's literacy.) Uncle Tom is also an old character, one devoid of sexuality, rather than a "'carnal man, the man of the flesh.' Tom, therefore, [Stowe's] only black man, has been robbed of his humanity and divested of his sex. It is the price for that darkness with which he has been branded."

Short Stories—Richard Wright's Uncle Tom's Children: Richard Wright, one of the major black "protest" writers and one-time mentor to James Baldwin, published *Uncle Tom's Children* (1938), a collection of short stories about African-Americans living in Jim Crow Mississippi, who, unlike Uncle Tom, react to their racist environment with anything but God-fearing humility. These characters retaliate against their white oppressors, and (some of them) are racially conscious activists who resist white racial hegemony. In the introduction to *Uncle Tom's Children*, Richard Yarborough declares that "with *Uncle Tom's Children*, Richard Wright, anticipating countless black authors who followed his wake, could indeed proclaim, 'Uncle Tom is dead!'" (p. xxix).

Novels—Martin R. Delany's Blake; or, the Huts of America, *Frances E. W. Harper's* Iola Leroy; or, Shadows Uplifted, *Zora Neal Hurston's* Their Eyes Were Watching God, *and Richard Wright's* Native Son.
Blake; or, the Huts of America: Martin R. Delany, a nineteenth-century politician, doctor, and writer, whose father was a slave, authored *Blake* (originally published in serial form 1861–62), a novel that responds to Stowe's Uncle Tom with a racially conscious protagonist, a fugitive slave—Henry Blake— who agitates for change, and attempts to lead an insurrection. Delany criticizes Christian humility in *Blake* because this reliance on the Lord to "take care of everything" does not bring the slave to take necessary actions to (attempt to) escape from bondage.
Iola Leroy; or, Shadows Uplifted: Frances E. W. Harper's *Iola Leroy* (1892) features an octoroon protagonist who learns of her black identity after her white father's death, and briefly becomes a slave. This black identity, however, serves as a source of pride for Iola Leroy and her brother, Harry, who develop into racially conscious people who feel equal, and not superior, to the darker members of their race, eliminating the color hierarchy depicted in Stowe's novel. When Harry proposes to Lucille Delany, a "phenotypical" black, he informs her that despite the feelings of superiority that mulattos internalized from white society toward darker African-Americans, his family is "too noble to indulge in such sentiments" (278).
Their Eyes Were Watching God: Zora Neale Hurston's *Their Eyes Were Watching God* (1937) also challenges the stereotype of mulatto superiority. Janie,

the protagonist, is of mixed origin, but she sees no distinction between herself and darker African-Americans, nor does she feel superior to them: "all of us got black kinfolks as well as yaller kinfolks," she argues (141). To her, dark-skinned African-Americans and mulattos, quadroons, and octoroons are all part of the same family or race.

Native Son: Richard Wright's *Native Son* (1940), the quintessential work of black protest, is a direct response to *Uncle Tom's Cabin*. In fact, Bigger Thomas, the protagonist—whose name intentionally resembles his predecessor—is Uncle Tom's alter ego: while Uncle Tom's actions are based on his Christian humility, Bigger reacts to his racist, economically exploitative environment with fear, and its facets, hatred and rage. Uncle Tom is the non-threatening "good nigger" of protest literature and his descendant, Bigger Thomas, is the "bad nigger."

SUGGESTIONS FOR FURTHER READING

Baldwin, James. "Everybody's Protest Novel." *James Baldwin: Collected Essays*, ed. Toni Morrison (New York: Penguin, 1998), pp. 11–18.

Harper, Frances E. W. *Iola Leroy; or, Shadows Uplifted*. Oxford ed. New York: Oxford University Press, 1988.

Hurston, Zora Neale. *Their Eyes Were Watching God*. First Perennial Classics ed. New York: Harper Perennial, 1998.

Stowe, Harriet Beecher. *Uncle Tom's Cabin*. Penguin Classics ed. New York: Penguin, 1981.

Yarborough, Richard. "Introduction to the Harper Perennial Edition." In *Uncle Tom's Children*, by Richard Wright (First Harper Perennial ed., New York: Harper Perennial, 1993), pp. ix–xxix.

Aunt Phillis's Cabin; or, Southern Life As It Is
by Mary Eastman

Preface

A writer on Slavery has no difficulty in tracing back its origin. There is also the advantage of finding *it*, with its continued history, and the laws given by God to govern his own institution, in the Holy Bible. Neither profane history, tradition, nor philosophical research are required to prove its origin or existence; though they, as all things must, come forward to substantiate the truth of the Scriptures. God, who created the human race, willed they should be holy like himself. Sin was committed, and the curse of sin, death, was induced: other punishments were denounced for the perpetration of particular crimes—the shedding of man's blood for murder, and the curse of slavery. The mysterious reasons that here influenced the mind of the Creator it is not ours to declare. Yet may we learn enough from his revealed word on this and every other subject to confirm his power, truth and justice. There is no Christian duty more insisted upon in Scripture than reverence and obedience to parents. "Honor thy father and thy mother, that thy days may be long in the land which the Lord thy God giveth thee." The relation of child to parent resembles closely that of man to his Creator. He who loves and honors his God will assuredly love and honor his parents. Though it is evidently the duty of every parent so to live as to secure the respect and affection of his child, yet there is nothing in the Scriptures to authorize a child treating with disrespect a parent, though he be unworthy in the greatest degree.

We are told in Gen. Ix. 22, "And Ham, the father of Canaan, saw the nakedness of his father, and told his two brethren without;" and in the 24th, 25th, 26th, and 27th verses we read, "And Noah awoke from his wine, and knew what his younger son had done unto him; and he said, Cursed be Canaan, a servant of servants shall he be unto his brethren. And he said, Blessed be the Lord God of Shem, and Canaan shall be his servant. God shall enlarge Japheth, and he shall dwell in the tents of Shem, and Canaan shall be his servant." Is it not preposterous that any man, any Christian, should read these verses and say slavery was not instituted by God as curse on Ham and Canaan and their posterity?

And who can read the history of the world and say this curse has not existed ever since it was uttered?

"The whole continent of Africa," says Bishop Newton, "was peopled principally by the descendants of Ham; and for how many ages have the better parts of that country lain under the dominion of the Romans, then of the Saracens, and now of the Turks! In what wickedness, ignorance, barbarity, slavery, misery, live most of the inhabitants! And of the poor negroes, how many hundreds every year are sold and bought like beasts in the market, and conveyed from one quarter of the world to do the work of beasts in another!"

But does this curse authorize the slave-trade? God forbid. He commanded the Jews to enslave the heathen around them, saying, "they should be their bondmen forever;" but he has given no such command to other nations. The threatenings and reproofs uttered against Israel, throughout the Old Testament, on the subject of slavery, refer to their oppressing and keeping in slavery their own countrymen. Never is the slightest imputation of sin, as far as I can see, conveyed against them for holding in bondage the children of heathen nations.

Yet do the Scriptures evidently permit slavery, even to the present time. The curse on the serpent, ("And the Lord God said unto the serpent, Because thou hast done this, thou art cursed above all cattle and above every beast of the field.") uttered more than sixteen hundred years before the curse of Noah upon Ham and his race, has lost nothing of its force and true meaning. "Cursed is the ground for thy sake: in sorrow shalt thou eat of it, all the days of thy life," said the Supreme Being. Has this curse failed or been removed?

Remember the threatened curses of God upon the whole Jewish tribe if they forsook his worship. Have not they been fulfilled?

But it has been contended that the people of God sinned in holding their fellow creatures in bondage! Open your Bible, Christian, and read the commands of God as regards slavery—the laws that he made to govern the conduct of the master and the slave!

But *again-we* live under the glorious and new dispensation of Christ; and He came to establish God's will, and to confirm such laws as were to continue in existence, to destroy such rules as were not to govern our lives!

When there was but one family upon the earth, a portion of the family was devoted to be slaves to others. God made a covenant with Abraham: he included in it his slaves. "He that is born in thy house, and he that is bought with thy money," are words of Scripture. A servant of Abraham says, "And the Lord has blessed my master greatly, and he is become great, and he hath given him flocks and herds, and silver and gold, and men-servants and maid-servants, and camels and asses." The Lord has called himself the God of Abraham and Isaac and Jacob. These holy men were slaveholders!

The existence of slavery then, and the sanction of God on his own institution, is palpable from the time of the pronouncing of the curse, until the glorious advent of the Son of God. When he came, slavery existed in every part of the world.

Jesus Christ, the Son of God, came from the heaven and dwelt upon the earth: his mission to proclaim the will of God to a world sunk in the lowest depths in iniquity.

Look at his miracles—the cleansing of the leper, the healing of the sick, the casting out of unclean spirits, the raising of the dead, the rebuking of the winds and seas, the control of those possessed with devils—and say, was he not the Son of God—yea, was he not God?

He came on an errand of mercy to the world, and he was all powerful to accomplish the Divine intent; but, did he emancipate the slave? The happiness of the human race was the object of his coming; and is it possible that the large portion of them then slaves could have escaped his all-seeing eye! Did he condemn the institution which he had made? Did he establish universal freedom? Oh! No; he came to redeem the world from the power of sin; his was no earthly mission; he did not interfere with the organization of society.

The application made by the Abolitionists of the golden rule is absurd: it might then apply to the child, who *would have* his father no longer control him; to the apprentice, who *would* no longer that the man to whom he is bound should have a right to direct him. Thus the foundations of society would be shaken, nay, destroyed. Christ would have us deal with others, not as they desire, but as the law of God demands: in the condition of life in which we have been placed, we must do what we conscientiously believe to be our duty to our fellow-men.

Christ alludes to slavery, but does not forbid it. "And the servant abideth not in the house forever, but the son abideth ever. If the Son therefore shall make you free, you are free indeed."

Show me in the history of the Old Testament, or in the life of Christ, authority to proclaim *as a sin* the holding of the race of Ham and Canaan in bondage.

In the times of the apostles, what do we see? Slaves are still in bondage, the children of Ham are menials as they were before. Christ had come, had died, had ascended to heaven, and slavery still existed. Had the apostles authority to do it away? Had Christ left it to them to carry out, in this instance, his revealed will?

It is well known and often quoted that the holy apostle did all he could to restore a slave to his master—one whom he had been the means of making free in a spiritual sense. Yet he knew that God had made Onesimus a slave, and, when he had fled from his master, Paul persuaded him to return and to do his duty toward him. Open your Bible, Christian, and carefully read the letter of Paul to Philemon, and contrast its spirit with the incendiary publications of the Abolitionists of the present day. St. Paul was not a fanatic, and therefore *could not* be an Abolitionist. The Christian age advanced and slavery continued, and we approach the time when our fathers fled from persecution to the soil we now call our own, when they fought for the liberty to which they felt they had a right. Our fathers fought for it, and our mothers did, more when they urged forth their husbands and sons, not knowing whether the life-blood that was glowing with religion and patriotism would not soon be dyeing the land that had been their refuge, and where they fondly hoped they should find a happy home. Oh, glorious parentage! Children of America, trace no farther back—say not the crest of nobility once adorned thy father's breast, the gemmed coronet thy mother's brow—stop here! It is enough that they earned for thee a home— a free, a happy home. And what did they say to the slavery that existed then and had been entailed upon them by the English government?

In the North, slavery was useless; nay, more, it was a drawback to the prosperity of that section of the union—it was dispensed with. In other sections, gradually, our people have seen their condition would be more prosperous without slaves—they have emancipated them. In the South, they are necessary: though an evil, it is one that cannot be dispensed with; and here they have been retained, and will be retained, unless God should manifest his will to the contrary.

The whole nation sanctioned slavery by adopting the Constitution which provides for them, and for their restoration (when fugitive) to their owners. Our country was then like one family—their souls had been tried and made pure by a united struggle.

The subject of slavery was agitated among them; many difficulties occurred, but they were all settled—and, they thought, effectually. They agreed then, on the propriety of giving up runaway slaves, unanimously.

As long as England needed sons and daughters of Africa to do her bidding, she trafficked in the flesh and blood of her fellow-creatures; but our immortal fathers put an end to the disgraceful trade. They saw its heinous sin, for they had no command to emancipate the slave; therefore they wisely forbore farther to interfere. They drew the nice line of distinction between an unavoidable evil and a sin.

Slavery was acknowledged, and slaves considered as property all over our country, at the North as well as the South—in Pennsylvania, New York, and New Jersey. Now, has there been any law reversing this, except in the States that have become free? Out of the limits of these States, slaves are property, according to the Constitution.

Let the people of the North take care of their own poor.

Let the people of the South take care of theirs.

Let each remember the great and awful day when they must render a final account to their Creator, their Redeemer, and their Judge.

Source Note: Mrs. Mary H. Eastman, *Aunt Phillis's Cabin; or, Southern Life As It Is* (Philadelphia, 1852).

Science in Antebellum America

> I agree with you that there is a natural aristocracy among men. The
> grounds of this are virtue and talents. . . . The natural aristocracy I
> consider as the most precious gift of nature for the instruction, the trusts
> and the government of society. . . . May we not even say that the form of
> government is the best which provides the most effectually for a pure
> selection of these *natural aristoi* into the offices of government?
> Thomas Jefferson, writing to John Adams in 1813[1]

In the nineteenth century, scientific inquiry challenged the biblical account of creation, which argued a monogenic evolution from the original parents, Adam and Eve; scientists developed polygenic theories of the multiple origins of humanity. Obviously, the monogenic, biblical account was best suited to antislavery arguments, while polygenic theories often supported proslavery advocates. There were many shades of grey between these two opposed camps, however, and occasionally the theories would be distorted to suit the purposes of a pro- or antislavery author.

In 1859, Charles Darwin published *On the Origin of Species*, in which he advanced the theory of evolution, which forever altered the terms of the scientific debate and opened new arguments between the biblical fundamentalists and scientists that continued well into the twentieth century in the infamous Scopes "Monkey" trial in Tennessee. The debates concerning race and racial characteristics continue today, and the popularity of *The Bell Curve* in the mid-1990s indicates how opinion concerning race in America is still vigorously divided. *The Bell Curve*, a study which argues the intellectual differences between whites and blacks based on a limited sample of Oakland, California, students and I.Q. tests, remained on the *New York Times* best-seller list for over a year, suggesting either that the conclusions were extremely controversial in an atmosphere of liberal rejection of the theory, or that the study reinforced prejudices for which the American public was seeking hard evidence. Numerous studies of racial attitudes among Americans from the seventeenth to the twentieth centuries are listed in the "Suggestions for Further Reading," which follows the introduction to this volume.

Race theory has ancient biblical and classical origins and requires too long a history to review extensively here. However, an overview would suggest that the "demonizing of the other" which occurs frequently in the Old Testament, as when the Canaanites are regularly cited as the enemies of God because they oppose the invasion of God's chosen people, is a rhetorical strategy that invokes racial attitudes and values. Tribalism and group identity run throughout the Old Testament, as the Hebrew people are defined as being essentially different and religiously monotheistic, while being surrounded by worshippers of pagan gods such as Baal.

The ancient Greek democracies and the Roman republic, which provided political inspiration during the era of the American Revolution, practiced and accepted slavery, although in Greece the slaves and masters were often from the same racial group, suggesting a class rather than a racial differentiation. Aristotle's *Politics* defined the slave as "merely the possession and property . . . of that master" (see Thomas, pp. 20–21). But it was the biological concept of man, with its emphasis on physical and essential characteristics, unchangeable through education or cultivation, that was used to support the idea that "Blacks were inherently inferior. . . . and therefore not entitled to the same rights [as whites]" (Fredrickson, *Black Image*, pp. 71–74).

Race theory developed first as theories of racial difference, but in the seventeenth century, scientific schemes of race classification evolved that gave the strength of evidence to these assumptions concerning superiority and inferiority. In 1684, for example, François Bernier introduced classification schemes which were expanded by Carl von Linnaeus with a revolutionary classification of plant and animal life, and a fourfold division of humanity in which *Homo Europeaus* was at the pinnacle of development, and *Homo Afer* near the bottom of the scale (Joshi, p. 51). In his *Documents of American Prejudice*, S. T. Joshi argues that "the single most important work in the history of racism" was Joseph Arthur, Compte de Gobineau's *Inequality of the Human Races* (1853–55). Compte de Gobineau proposed that "The negroid variety is the lowest, and stands at the foot of the ladder. . . . [His] mental faculties are dull, or even non-existent. . . . The very strength of his sensations is the most striking proof of his inferiority" (Joshi, pp. 64–65). American race theory throughout the antebellum nineteenth century, moreover, drew heavily upon the work of biologists, anthropologists, and political theorists who were writing and publishing well before 1800 (Schnakenberg, "Proslavery and Antebellum Race Theory Arguments," p. 3).[2]

During the eighteenth century, for example, when western European, British, and American thinkers followed the discoveries of reason and argued theories of the perfectibility of man, the African slave trade enjoyed enormous prosperity, paradoxically suggesting that the African was to be excluded from all Enlightenment discourse. While antislavery sentiment was focused on the evils and immorality of the slave trade itself, and secondarily on the inhumanity of the institution of chattel slavery, race theorists were developing arguments that would hinder the progress of the African toward full racial equality well into the twentieth century. Gordon Turnbull, drawing heavily on Hume and Montesquieu, argued that slavery was "one of those indispensable and necessary links, in the great chain of causes and events, which cannot be broken" (David Brion Davis, *The Problem of Slavery in Western Culture*, p. 392). On the nature of Africans, Baron Montesquieu declared that "it would be impossible for us to suppose that these beings should be men" (Davis, p. 392). Edward Tyson, after surveying the Hottentot tribe of Africa, published *Orang-Outang, sive Homo*

Sylvestris, attempting to prove anatomical similarities between man and ape. This led to repeated cultural association of the African with animals (Davis, p. 454).

As Schnakenberg observes, this hierarchical classification of *homo sapiens* into racial groups was refined by Linnaeus and others during the eighteenth century. These biological arguments, or essentialist theories, suggest that all other characteristics of racial difference are genetically linked to biology which is signified by race itself. For example, the Enlightenment emphasis on reason and human progress was challenged by many kinds of evidence that white society had progressed well beyond that of the imported African slaves, at least by the measurements of western culture. David Brion Davis has shown that one result of these anthropological investigations was the conclusion that "the white man was the human norm, the Negro was the deviation" (Davis, p. 456). The association of African inferiority with race became an argument, in the nineteenth century, after the slave trade had ended, for extending slavery and denying the rights of citizenship to the slave.

Hierarchical classifications of race led to conclusions of superiority and inferiority based on relative cultural standards such as literary genius, religious practices, and long traditions of civilized behavior. For example, since the fifteenth century, after the spread of literacy and the dissemination of print culture that followed the publication with movable type of Gutenberg's Bible, the ability to read and to analyze complex texts became the mark of civilization, and orders of civilization were ranked according to the literate powers of their people. If Francis Bacon declared that the arts, including literature, could determine the place of *homo sapiens* in the natural scheme of things, Peter Heylyn argued, in his *Little Description of the Great World* (1621), that the African lacked the "use of Reason which is peculiar unto man; . . . [he is] of little wit, and destitute of all arts and sciences" (Gates and Davis, p. xxiv). Davis and Gates also note that Immanuel Kant, in his *Observations on the Beautiful and the Sublime*, conflated color with intellectual capacity. Karla Zelaya notes that "Correlating blackness and ignorance as a self evident association, Kant proposed that 'so fundamental is the difference between the black and white races of man, that it appears to be as great in regard to mental capacities as in color'" (Zelaya, p. 5).

Thus the racial inferiority of blacks, an essentialist argument, was correlated with a perceived absence of literacy and culture. As Frederick Douglass would later discover that his "pathway to freedom" lay in the gaining of literacy, these Enlightenment thinkers were building the foundation for later proslavery arguments by suggesting that indeed the "leopard could not change his spots," and that the absence of Western civilization and learning in African culture was clear evidence of biological, essential inferiority. This tautology was difficult to refute, especially in a society where the majority of the white, European descendants were inclined to accept it. Indeed, in the antebellum decades, 1820–60, there were very few proponents of full racial and biological equality, even among the abolitionists.

As Zelaya notes, the absence of literary, and indeed linguistic, mastery signified the African's absence of reason and culture. Notable American thinkers of the eighteenth and nineteenth centuries, influenced by Enlightenment philosophy and science of race, contributed to the discourse concerning the racial inferiority of the slave population. George Bancroft, echoing the sentiments of most nineteenth-century white Americans, expressed that blacks were "gross and stupid . . . undisciplined in the exercise of reason and imagination" (Walker, *De-romanticizing Black History*, p. 5). And Thomas Jefferson's *Notes on the State of Virginia* (1785–87) followed Immanuel Kant in conflating color with intellectual capacity, although Jefferson claimed that his observations were inductive rather than deductive, based on his careful annotations and observations of the slave population at Monticello. Jefferson contributed to the evolving argument that the intellectual inferiority of Africans was inherently attributed to blackness:

> Comparing them by their faculties of memory, reason, and imagination, it appears to me that in memory they are equal to whites; in reason much inferior . . . and that in imagination they are dull, tasteless, and anomalous. . . . never yet could I find that a black had uttered a thought above the level of plain narration. . . . This unfortunate difference of color, and perhaps of faculty is a powerful obstacle to the emancipation of these people. [Ruchames, p. 64]

A Jefferson contemporary, Dr. Benjamin Rush, who was one of early America's leading medical authorities, went so far as to attribute "blackness" to a specific disease, leprosy. In his *Medical Inquiries and Observations Upon the Diseases of the Mind*, we find:

> The skin becomes black, thick, and greasy. . . . It may perhaps be ascribed to disease, and that of the leprous kind. . . . The leprosy induces a morbid insensibility in the nerves. . . . It is common to say that the person is devoid of sensibility. . . . The big lip, the flat nose . . . are symptoms of leprosy. [pp. 265–67]

The essentialist observations of Jefferson and Rush were echoed throughout the nineteenth century by proslavery advocates as well as social and anthropological scientists. It is very tempting to denigrate all these investigations as pseudoscience, but in antebellum America, the discourse about race centered on the essential characteristics and qualities of racial groups, so that a vast majority of the population would have embraced at least some portion of these observations as being essentially true and based on observable evidence.

For example, in 1836, William Drayton published *The South Vindicated from the Treason and Fanaticism of the Northern Abolitionists*, in which he charged that "the Negro [was] constitutionally indolent . . . his mind [is] heavy, dull, and unambitious." Slavery was thus the "natural consequence of the inferiority of his character" (Fredrickson, *Arrogance*, p. 203). This was the year after William Ellery Channing had penned his important work called *Slavery*, a study which opposed the institution of chattel slavery but skirted the issue of full racial equality for Africans. An opposing view was voiced by Alexis de Tocqueville, whose *Democracy in America* (1835) argued that the characteristics of African behavior were not essential or biological but were the result of environmental influences over centuries of degradation and oppression. (Tocqueville's observations are excerpted in chapter 9, "Concluding Remarks," and his opinion was echoed in Mark Twain's *Pudd'nhead Wilson*, discussed in the introduction to this volume.) "Having been told from infancy that his race is naturally inferior to that of whites, he assents to the proposition and is ashamed of his own nature."

This juxtaposition of the essentialist "Nature" argument against the environmental "Nurture" argument dominated the race theory discourse for nearly two centuries. It also framed the proslavery and antislavery debates in antebellum America. As Karla Zelaya notes, "Slavery engendered a cultural and psychosocial racism that created a powerful, irrational basis for qualifications of races as either superior or inferior. An attempt to counter racist theories of black inferiority, and, subsequently, enslavement, came from those imbued with the revolutionary ideals of equality and freedom, as well as antislavery advocates and militant abolitionists. In an attempt to politicize the abolition of slavery, antislavery proponents and militant abolitionists had first to prove the essential humanity of their manacled brethren" (Zelaya, p. 7).

If the natural rights arguments of the Enlightenment had caused antislavery advocates to focus attention on the evils and immorality of the slave trade, until it was abolished in 1808, the antebellum arguments centered on the essential humanity of the African. Proslavery advocates argued the rightness of slavery because the African was naturally, essentially, and biologically inferior. Antislavery advocates continued to argue the moral wrong of the institution of chattel slavery, quite independent of the abuses of the slave trade, but they had difficulty reconciling their antislavery positions with widely held beliefs in the essential inferiority of the African.

Even where the environment was blamed rather than nature, the inferiority argument managed to surface. In John Wesley's *Thoughts on Slavery* (1774), the founder of Methodism directly addressed the alleged mental inferiority of slaves, both in the British colonies and in what would later be the United States: "Allowing them to be stupid, as you say, to whom is that stupidity owing? . . . Their stupidity in our plantations is not natural; otherwise than it is the natural effect of their condition. Consequently, it is not their fault, but yours, inhuman masters, you must answer for it, before God and man" (see Aptheker, p. 21).

These early antislavery arguments were religious in nature, and they relied heavily on the teachings of the New Testament, rather than the examples of the Old Testament, for their moral authority. In the eighteenth century, Judge Samuel Sewall opposed slavery but noted that the African would always be a kind of "extravasat blood" in the body politic. (See chapter 1 of this volume, "The Historical Background.") John Woolman continued and expanded the debate between Sewall and Saffin. The debate heated up further late in the century, at the time of the American Revolution, when principles of liberty and equality were being tested politically and militarily. Thomas Paine devoted his first published essay in the *Pennsylvania Journal and Weekly Advocate* to "African Slavery in America." He helped to draft an act to abolish slavery which was passed by the Pennsylvania Assembly on March 1, 1780. Paine, who became an American hero for his "Rights of Man" and "Common Sense" essays, called for the restoration of "the common blessings that they [Africans] were by nature entitled to" (Aptheker, pp. 88–89). And Samuel Hopkins, minister of the First Congregational Church in Newport, Connecticut, issued, in 1776, *A Dialogue Concerning the Slavery of Africans*, in which he told the Continental Congress that slavery had "no just cause" and that it should be abolished (Aptheker, pp. 89–90). But the arguments about the "rightness" or "wrongness" of slavery continued for almost another century, both sides honing their rhetorical skills as they framed the debate about racial equality and the justification for slavery.

One feature of these debates should be clearly noted. From the beginning to the "literacy tests" and "voting rights tests" of the Reconstruction and Jim Crow eras, which, in some areas, extended into the 1960s, the association of citizenship with literacy and intelligence was prominent. As Henry Louis Gates makes clear, the United States is a nation that "formed itself through one written document, the Declaration of Independence, and negotiated the terms of its existence through another, the Constitution, [which] caused writing to become associated with legitimacy" (Gates, "Literature of African-Americans," p. 1172). The principles articulated in these early national documents intensified the debates about slavery. A republic whose revolution against the tyranny of Great Britain had been established in beliefs about the fundamental equality of man and the natural rights arguments of the Enlightenment could hardly embrace the institution of chattel slavery without controversy and intellectual debate about this inconsistency. Political decisions such as the Naturalization Act of 1793, which restricted citizenship to whites only, made these debates central arguments of the new legislative bodies, and the nineteenth century became a battleground for establishing not only the beginnings of the new nation, but the place of Africans in that multiracial society. The new society was, after all, a "melting pot" of races and ethnic backgrounds, divorced by choice from the monarchial history of Europe and its inherited privileges. In theory, at least, all inhabitants of the new democracy could enjoy equal rights and privileges, as "all men are created equal" became a rallying cry for antislavery advocates, even though this phrase appears in the Declaration of Independence and not in the Constitution by which the nation was to be governed.

The Frenchman Hector St. John de Crèvecoeur had articulated the character of the United States in his *Letters from an American Farmer*, based on observations made while traveling in the very new nation and published in 1782. Crèvecoeur asked, rhetorically,

> What then is the American, this new man? He is either a European, or the descendant of a European, hence that strange mixture of blood, which you will find in no other country. I could point out to you a family whose grandfather was an Englishman, whose wife was Dutch, whose son married a French woman, and whose present four sons have now four wives of different nations. He is an American who, leaving behind him all his ancient prejudices and manners, receives new ones from

the new mode of life he has embraced, the new government he obeys, and the new rank he holds. He becomes an American by being received in the broad lap of our great Alma Mater. Here individuals of all nations are melted into a new race of men, whose labors and posterity will one day cause great changes in the world.[3]

This impression of the egalitarian society of the very new United States clearly suggests ethnic intermingling and intermarriage, a breakdown of the "tribalism" that often characterized European monarchies and is so tragically represented in Henry James's novel, *The American.* The United States had been separated politically from Great Britain, which was figured as a tyrannical oppressor in the political rhetoric of the era of the American Revolution. The individual reigned supreme and had rights and privileges enjoyed by the very few in Europe. Tragically, the African was excluded from these privileges, and the elaborate race theories that evolved over the next century to justify the exclusion of African slaves and freedmen from the American dream are represented in the selections excerpted here.

What was especially problematic about the antebellum scientific debates concerning slavery was that the conclusions reached often determined whether or not the institution of slavery itself could be justified by the "new science," as well as by the more historically grounded biblical arguments. Recent controversy over Herrnstein and Murray's book, *The Bell Curve* (1993), shows how a type of science continues to be used to argue that there are natural differences between blacks and whites. *The Bell Curve* has been reviewed to show how inattention to environmental influences on I.Q. test performance can grievously distort the interpretation of test results. Nevertheless, its popularity indicates the attitudes and values of the society that has so enthusiastically welcomed and supported it. It seems clear that because American society is still deeply divided in its views of race, the debates that were begun among the scientists of the antebellum United States continue today.

As this is an extremely complex subject area and because attitudes concerning race and "race theory" are by definition inflammatory, it is extremely important to observe that the early national period, from 1776 through the Civil War, was a battleground of competing ideas, not only concerning slavery as a national institution but also biblical fundamentalism, women's rights, the nature and destiny of man, and the role of individualism in a democratic society. It is too easy a solution to view this period as "racist," socially retarded, and barbaric based on the texts that follow. These readings, many of which will appear offensive to modern sensibilities, were the science of the time, and as such, they belong to an historical context that may be generally described as follows.

The United States' experiment in democracy was derived from the Enlightenment's belief in natural rights and the dignity of the individual. These radical views were diametrically opposed to the European and English theories of monarchy and "divine right," and they also challenged the biblically grounded notion of a "chosen people," and a hierarchy of the saved and the damned. But these radical Enlightenment doctrines fueled a progressive ideology that was secular in nature and centered on Thomas Jefferson's phrasing that "all men are created equal." While many Americans have challenged this declaration, it has remained the cornerstone of our national ideology; and it also undergirds the legal system of the United States, with its large immigrant population.

A second secular impulse governed cultural and social developments in early-nineteenth-century America. The democratic experiment was part of a larger belief in social progress, in the ultimate perfectibility of a social order that could be self-governing, even self-determining. Theories of "manifest destiny" justified the claiming and settling of the western territories, and a fundamental belief in human progress was being manifested in the successful expansion of the new nation through the Louisiana Purchase from France by President Thomas Jefferson (1803) and the annexation of Texas following the war with Mexico in the 1840s. In addition, writers and cultural historians like the poet Joel Barlow saw in the rise of science and commerce a fulfillment of the destiny of the new nation, and they phrased these secular beliefs in the language of biblical prophecy and fulfillment. In his prose notes to the epic poem *The Columbiad* (1807), Barlow cites science and commerce as reasons why the United States will succeed. "The future progress will probably be more rapid than the past. Since the invention of printing, the application of the properties of the magnet, and the knowledge of the structure of the solar system, it is *difficult to conceive of a cause that can produce a new state of barbarism*; unless it be some great convulsion in the physical world, so extensive as to change the face of the earth or a considerable part of it" (emphasis added). For Barlow and many of his contemporaries, it is the spirit of scientific inquiry and commerce that generates millennial prosperity and progress. Society would advance through commercial enterprise and the advancement of science through education. "The spirit of commerce is happily calculated to open an amicable intercourse between all countries, to soften the horrors of war, to enlarge the field of science, and to assimilate the manners, feelings, and languages of all nations. This leading principle, in its remoter consequences, will produce advantages in favor of free government, give patriotism the character of philanthropy, induce all men to regard each other as brethren and friends, and teach them the benefits of peace and harmony among nations." This utopian vision of the "Peaceable Kingdom" was widespread, and Edward Hick's emblematic painting was widely reproduced to signify the fusion of America's past with its future.

But omitted from this vision and from the charter documents of the United States that articulated it, including the Declaration of Independence and the Constitution, were notions of how African slaves were to participate in the progressive development of the new nation. Political debates about equality and inequality were joined to scientific theory about race to produce a definition of citizenship that excluded Africans (see the Constitutional controversy between Wendell Phillips and Lysander Spooner in chapter 8 of this volume). As the previous chapters have shown, the arenas of debate centered on biblical, moral, philosophical, economic, and finally, scientific evidence to support pro- or anti-slavery positions. In the Lane Seminary debates political opinion and biblical arguments were dominant; another venue for discourse about slavery and race was the series in Richmond, Virginia, that occurred in 1831 and 1832, immediately following the Nat Turner slave rebellion of 1831. Turner's revolutionaries slaughtered over fifty white people, resulting in his capture and execution. The insurrection fueled anxiety about emancipation, especially in the South, where the African population was large. It momentarily retarded the influence of the abolitionist societies, particularly in the South, but it also fueled debate about the essential nature of the African and his future role in American society.

The Richmond debates centered on these issues of race theory. Africans were often compared with animals, and their savage barbarism stressed. William Roane said, "I do not believe that all men are by nature equal, or, that it was the power of human art to make them so. I no more believe that the flat-nosed, wooly headed black native of the deserts of Africa, is equal to the straight-haired, white man of Europe, than I believe that the stupid, scentless greyhound is equal to the noble generous dog of Newfoundland." Following Nat Turner and the Richmond debates, Southerners produced voluminous treatises on the "natural inequality of man." The scientific inquiries of the time became useful supports for these arguments. Thomas R. Dew's *Review of the Debate* (1832) argued that emancipation would be catastrophic, even apocalyptic, because Africans were "utterly unfit for a state of freedom among the whites . . . the emancipated black carries a mark which no time can erase; he forever wears the symbol of his inferior condition; the Ethiopian cannot change his skin, nor the leopard his spots." As Reginald Horsman put it, in *Race and Manifest Destiny*, "Blackness, not slavery, was the essential cause of the Negro condition," according to Dew, who avoided the more scientific species question, but "his general theme was clear; blacks could not be free to participate in white society, for all men and all races were not created equal" (p. 123).

As the introduction to this volume has shown, numerous publications were generated from these scientists, who advanced the belief that there were multiple origins in creation, called polygenesis. The differences, whether physical, moral, intellectual, or character distinctions among the races, constituted a classification system that could not be altered through advancement or through education. There were "essential" or "natural" qualities in race theory that were irrevocable; individuals might excel or achieve greatness, but one's racial and ethnic grouping had a determining influence on ability. By the end of the 1840s, some contended that there had been various creations of human beings in different parts of the world. Samuel George Morton's research, published in his *Crania Americana* (1839), though controversial, was regarded as basic to an understanding of human racial origins. Morton had collected a wide variety of human skulls, which for him represented the gradations of human intelligence. By comparing cranial size, capacity, and structure, Morton emphasized the basic physical differences between the races. Morton and his contemporaries then deduced that cranial capacity would be a significant determinant of intellectual ability and native intelligence. This primitive scientific argument remained prominent in antebellum America, until Charles Darwin challenged the work of the American scientists with his publication of *On the Origin of Species* in 1859 and *The Descent of Man* in 1871 (Horsman, pp. 124–25).

The texts that follow include Thomas Jefferson's defamatory remarks about the African character in general and the poet Phillis Wheatley in particular, found in Jefferson's *Notes on the State of Virginia*. It is widely known that Jefferson sired children with his slave mistress, Sally Hemings. It is also well known that despite his abhorrence for the institution of slavery, he manumitted some of his own slaves only in his will, and that he accepted the principal tenets of contemporary race theory, as it was transmitted to him through European, British, and American scientific scholarship. Like many early scientists, Jefferson commenced his remarks with theorems which he then sought to prove with evidence gathered from history and some anecdotal experience.

The rise of the European university as a center for scientific inquiry, particularly in Germany, provided these early researchers with support and a platform for developing theories of heredity well before Darwin advanced his theory of natural selection in 1859. The British anthropologist James Pritchard articulated widely influential views on race classification, by which a hierarchy of races was established, and in Germany, Johann Friedrich Blumenbach (1742–1840) argued that there were five basic racial types, placing the Anglo-Saxon at the pinnacle of the polygenic chain, and the African at the bottom.

This development was, in retrospect, extremely important in establishing the European conception of the African. The eighteenth century, or Age of Enlightenment, had embraced theories of race that stressed the unity of humanity. It was recognized that there were vast differences between specific persons, including racial differences, but these differences were perceived to be, in Cassirer's words, "'varieties' of a common breed that were all considered capable of 'progress.'" (Grégoire, p. xxxviii). Jean-Jacques Rousseau's "noble savage" celebrated the primitive state of man's development, and the "savage" was not regarded with the same measure of contempt with which the nineteenth century later regarded him. Jonathan Edwards, the leading minister of the Great Awakening in New England (1730–50) and a devout believer in the Calvinist doctrine of the "innate depravity of man," joined his contemporary Benjamin Franklin in accepting the Enlightenment doctrine of the perfectibility of man, without regard to race. Until the nineteenth century, it was not difficult to establish the "humanity" of Africans even if it was problematic to establish their equality with Europeans.

However, with the increasing authority of science, researchers like Samuel Morton, J. B. Turner, Josiah Nott, George R. Gliddon, J. H. Van Evrie, and O. S. Fowler argued particularly strong challenges to the notion that "all men are created equal," challenges that were persuasively advanced. They sought to establish the "hierarchy of races" not only in the scientific literature, but also in the popular cultural assumptions about race. As an ally of the proslavery advocates, the scientific community posited theories of the inferiority of the African to the European that became widely accepted, appearing in political discourse, in the racial stereotyping of minstrel entertainment, and in fictional representations such as Harriet Beecher Stowe's *Uncle Tom's Cabin* (1852). Even abolitionists like Theodore Parker articulated contemporary race theory, and it was not unusual for the most vocal abolitionists to accept the inferiority of Africans to whites as part of their emancipation argument. As Abraham Lincoln put it in the letter to the Reverend Frederick Ross (which appears in the introduction to this volume), assuming that the African is inferior to the white, the doctrines of Christianity obligate followers to reach out to the subjugated race, rather than enslave him. The moral argument advanced by Lincoln represents much abolitionist thinking on race. Only a few of the abolitionists argued for full racial equality: William Lloyd Garrison, Wendell Phillips, Gerrit Smith, and Lydia Maria Child, who were among the most vocal abolitionists, seemed to hold firm to a guiding belief in full, unconditional emancipation *and* full racial equality.

The essentialist argument dominated European and American thinking concerning the African for over one hundred years, as many of the texts excerpted here illustrate. Because an assumption of the essential inferiority of the African was so widely accepted by both proslavery proponents and some abolitionists, there were very few voices opposing these arguments, and William Lloyd Garrison contributed no counterbalancing treatise on race theory to those of his opposition, although he regularly voiced the opinion that racial equality should accompany emancipation.

In the texts that follow, James Russell Lowell offers opposition in his essay of February 1, 1849, called "Ethnology," which appeared in the *National Antislavery Standard*. Similarly, the former slave Frederick Douglass delivered an opposing viewpoint in a commencement address at Western Reserve College on July 12, 1854. The African-American John Rock (1825–66) vigorously opposed the essentialist arguments of abolitionist Theodore Parker in his "Speech to the Boston Massacre Commemorative Festival," in March 1858. Like many abolitionists, Parker crusaded against the *institution* of slavery but accepted the racial hierarchy theory. Both Rock and Parker are excerpted in this section. The widespread popularity, if not the logic of these essentialist arguments, overwhelmed and muted opposition voices. Indeed, even the most powerful political opponent of slavery in the Civil War era, Abraham Lincoln, publicly argued the inferiority of the African when debating Stephen Douglas in 1858.

One of the most important voices opposing racial essentialism was that of the Frenchman Henri Grégoire, who, in 1808, published *On the Cultural Achievements of Negroes* (Paris, 1808). This extremely controversial volume was a response to Jefferson's criticism of the African in his *Notes on the State of Virginia*. Jefferson promptly responded to Grégoire's critique in a letter he wrote to the poet Joel Barlow that year:

I believe him a very good man, with imagination enough to declaim eloquently, but without judgement to decide. He wrote to me also on the doubts I had expressed five or six and twenty years ago, in *Notes on the State of Virginia*, as to the grade of understanding of the Negroes, and he sent me his book on the literature of the Negroes. His credulity has made him gather up every story he could find of men of color, without distinguishing whether black, or of what degree or mixture, however slight the mention, or light the authority on which they are quoted." [Jefferson to Barlow, as quoted by Cassirer and Brière in Grégoire, p. xliv]

Jefferson's patronizing treatment of Grégoire was caused by Grégoire's attacks on Jefferson's reasoning in *On the Cultural Achievements of Negroes*, and this dialogue is a classic example of the "slavery debates" and their connection with the essentialist race theory arguments of antebellum Europe and America. In chapter 2, "Opinions Concerning the Moral Inferiority of Negroes," Grégoire opposed essentialism by stating that "The opinion that the Negroes are inferior is not new. The claims of white superiority are defended only by whites speaking in their own interest. Before attacking their opinion we should question whether they are qualified to make such a judgement" (Grégoire, p. 20). Grégoire was particularly incensed against Jefferson for his lack of historical perspective:

> Jefferson furnishes arms against himself in his answer to Raynal, who reproached Americans for not having produced, so far, any famous men. Once we have been in existence as a nation, says this learned American, as long as the Greeks before they had a Homer, the Romans a Virgil, or the French a Racine, observers will have a right to be astonished. In like manner we can say that once Negroes have lived in a state of civilization as long as the inhabitants of the United States, there will be some justification for believing that the Negroes are totally lacking in genius, if they have not produced men like Franklin, Rittenhouse, Jefferson, Madison, Washington, Monroe, Warren, Rush, Barlow, Mitchell, Rumford, and Barton. . . . In most parts of Africa, civilization and the arts are in their infancy. If you believe this is because the inhabitants are Negroes, explain to us why white or copper-colored men of other countries have remained savages and even cannibals? [Grégoire, pp. 21–22]

As Theodore Dwight Weld would do in *American Slavery As It Is* (1839), Grégoire offered a catalog of incidents to dramatize his burning sense of injustice caused by slavery. In this early document, he outlined the brutality of slavery not only to the slave's body but also to his mind and soul. "This torturing system has been pursued so far as to prevent all development of the mental faculties. By a regulation adopted in the State of Virginia, slaves are not allowed to learn to read. To have been able to read cost one of those black men his life. He demanded that the Africans should share the benefits promised by American liberty, and he supported his demand by the first Article of the Bill of Rights. This argument was unanswerable. In such cases, where refutation is impossible, the Inquisition incarcerates those whom formerly it would have burned. All tyrannies have similar features. The Negro was hanged" (Grégoire, p. 31).

The abolitionist's courageous opposition voice attacked the brutalities of slavery by providing precise examples reinforced by sermonic preaching. "When the truth about the tormenting of the slaves and the barbarity of the masters was substantiated thousands of times, the masters denied that the Negro is capable of morality or of intelligence, and on the scale of all living beings, they placed him between man and the animals" (Grégoire, p. 32). He also attacked the proslavery biblical advocates, who used the Christian religion to extend and continue the institution of chattel slavery. Invoking the voice of one morally outraged, Grégoire thundered, "the Negroes have been slandered, first in order to establish the right to enslave them, then to justify keeping them in slavery, and also out of a feeling of guilt toward them. The accusers are both judges and executioners, and yet they call themselves Christians! They have tried many times to distort the sense of the Holy Scriptures, in order to find therein an apology for colonial slavery, although the Scriptures declare that all mortals are children of the Heavenly Father and spring from the same family. Religion admits of no distinction. . . . the Heavenly Oracle proclaims that we ought to do to others what we wish to be done to us" (Grégoire, p. 35). This fusion of moral, biblical, and hereditarian theories often characterized early scientific inquiry. Toward mid-century, race and hereditarian theory were more scientifically presented, as in the works of Nott, Gliddon, and Morton. But the biblical proslavery advocates, like Thornton Stringfellow of Virginia, were able to fuse their scriptural arguments with these scientific theories to make a formidable statement of African inferiority.

Many of the texts that follow, including Grégoire's, are not often reprinted or anthologized because of their inflammatory nature. It is likely that this section of *A House Divided* will be the most controversial one because so much of this material is provocative and requires a detached, historical perspective for accurate interpretation. For example, the readings included here by Theodore Parker, particularly his "The Present Aspect of Slavery in America," and "Some Thoughts on the Progress of America, and the Influence of Her Diverse Institutions," which is Parker's statement of race theory, will seem hypocritical and inconsistent to the modern reader, coming, as they do, from one of the leading abolitionists of antebellum America. As Dean Grodzins argues in his introduction to Parker, it was very common for abolitionists to embrace contemporary race theories and to hold essentialist views of African inferiority. Disapproval of slavery as an institution of human government did not necessarily exonerate one from essentialist attitudes toward Africans concerning their character, nature, and origin.

Together with Morton's *Crania Americana*, an extremely influential nineteenth-century American text excerpted in this section, is Josiah Clark Nott and George R. Gliddon's *Indigenous Races of the Earth, or, New Chapters of Ethnological Inquiry* (1857). Nott and Gliddon were widely known thinkers in the antebellum scientific community, and they espoused the polygenic theory of multiple human origins. Though Darwin's later thinking challenged the notion of polygenesis by suggesting the possibility of an evolutionary development from multiple or single originals, the polygenesis of Nott and Gliddon joined Darwin in providing a serious, scientifically based challenge to the monogenic version of Creation found in the Book of Genesis. These versions, in turn, gave proslavery advocates new perspectives from which to establish the inferiority of the African and the "rightness" of slavery.

Nott's *Types of Mankind* is an excellent example of the spurious reasoning that resulted from a distortion of evolution and polygenesis. By contrast, the mono-genic theory of Creation argued the opposite, that while Adam and Eve may not have been the true, literal parents of all humankind, there was nevertheless a single creation from which all human beings derive. Thus cultural differences and environmental adaptations constitute the major mutations in the development of a diverse contemporary population, not essential, natural, or hereditary differences. Nott and Gliddon, like Morton, used cranial measurements—which they graphed and charted carefully—taken from skull collections, adding to the scientific appearance of their influential texts. In his 1971 study, cultural historian George Fredrickson surveyed a host of responses that refute the essentialist positions of Nott and Gliddon. (See George Fredrickson's *The Black Image in the White Mind*.)

This science chapter also contains selections from O. S. Fowler, whose *Hereditary Descent* (New York, 1848) became a foundational document for the new science of phrenology. Phrenology was basically an offspring of the polygenic theory of creation, but it focused on the ability of a researcher to determine the moral integrity, character, intelligence, and other essential characteristics of a person by an intensive examination of the skull shape and head formation, suggesting that the brain power could be determined by external physical examination and from this, features of character and intellect could be inferred, as though the skull could be read as a text and as a language. In the materials that follow, Christopher Hanlon of the University of Massachusetts at Amherst introduces Fowler's work and the science of phrenology, a practice that straddled the border between science and popular culture in the antebellum United States.

All of the scientific arguments that appear here continued to have influence long after the Civil War and the emancipation of the slaves. During Reconstruction and the Jim Crow years that followed, these texts continued to be cited as Southerners and Northerners argued about segregation and Jim Crow laws, both above and below the Mason-Dixon line. The assumption of African inferiority would lie behind many social and political arguments defending segregation, such as the *Plessy v Ferguson* case that was heard by the United States Supreme Court in 1896. A fictional representation of the debate is found in Mark Twain's *Pudd'nhead Wilson* (1894), and an analysis of Twain's judgment of antebellum race theory may be found in the introduction to this volume. Although a fictional narrative, the story of two babies switched in their cribs at birth—one a mulatto and the other the white plantation owner's son—shows by narrative example the impact of the environment, in this case the institution of slavery, on one's personality, intelligence, and character, without regard to race. It is a fitting response to the antebellum race theorists whose works are contained in this chapter.

What is important to note is that this "scientific endeavor" was not isolated theory, nor was it important only to some fringe minority of academics. The scientists who developed and propagated antebellum race theory were some of the most respected and well known in the world, and their views were perceived as true and their research as correct. Ultimately, Linnaeus, Blumenbach, Knox,

Pritchard, Broca, and Gobineau all proclaimed Aryan superiority over the African (and other people of color). The German anthropologist Blumenbach identified color categories that were associated with a declining scale of intelligence and intellect: white, yellow, red, brown, and black. The well-established British anthropologist Pritchard argued for race classification as did Robert Knox, who claimed that the Africans were simply subhuman. Broca, a respected authority on the human brain, developed an early form of the cranial index, which used the relationship between the length and width of the skull as an indication of intelligence within the racial group. Gobineau would assert that the Aryan racial group was the primary creative and culture-bearing force of humankind. (See Schnakenberg, "Proslavery and Antebellum Race Theory Arguments," pp. 3–6.)

American scientists, who were well versed in European race theory, also disseminated the race classification index, and the phrenologists, led by O. S. Fowler, made the study of the human skull a widely popular American pastime. In 1833 Richard H. Colfax brought the idea of separate origins into his proslavery argument, and in the early 1840s, the "American School of Ethnology" affirmed the separate creation of distinct and unequal species of humans. Samuel George Morton of Philadelphia published *Crania Americana* in 1839, popularizing the cranial capacity doctrine for the measurement of human intelligence. Morton would eventually reach the conclusion that only Caucasians were the true descendants of the biblical Adam. Dr. Josiah Nott of Mobile, Alabama, argued that "the mulatto was a hybrid and characteristically less fertile and weaker than either pure white or pure black individuals." The Swiss biologist Louis Agassiz argued, in 1846, for the plural or polygenic origins of humankind.

William Lloyd Garrison observed that race theory, or the belief in the superiority of one racial group over another, was essential to the maintenance of chattel slavery in the United States. His *Liberator* regularly argued for full racial equality as it thundered against the institution of chattel slavery. Garrison clearly believed that race theory ideology made possible the widespread support of chattel slavery. Even where the "condition" of the African, both as a slave and as a legally uneducated group in America, was admitted to be the *cause* of inferiority, proslavery advocates would insist on "essential" differences between the races. Thomas Cobb and E. N. Elliot, whose *Cotton Is King* is excerpted in chapter 5, "The Economic Arguments Concerning Slavery," were accepted proslavery historians who emphasized that the well-established institution of chattel slavery was appropriate because the "Negro species" had indeed "become an inferior species."

While Morton, Nott, and Agassiz were usually read in the academic and scientific communities, popularizers such as John H. Van Evrie, George Sawyer, and Samuel Cartright played a significant role in the dissemination of race theory to the general population. Together, the popularizers, scientists, and biblical proslavery advocates constituted a formidable adversary for the militant abolitionists like Garrison, Phillips, and Child, who called not only for immediate and unconditional emancipation of the slaves with no compensation for the slaveholders, but also for full racial equality of blacks and whites. The debate has continued well into the present. Scientific inquiry for the past three hundred years has given both sides of the slavery debates much theoretical discourse on which the opposing arguments have been based.

SUGGESTIONS FOR FURTHER READING

Agassiz, Louis (1807–73). "The Diversity of Origin of the Human Races." *The Christian Examiner*, July 1850.

Aptheker, Herbert. *Antiracism in United States History*. Westport, CT: Greenwood Press, 1992.

Bachman, John (1790–1874). *The Doctrine of the Unity of the Human Race Examined on the Principles of Science*. Charleston, SC: C. Canning, 1850.

Blumenbach, Johann Friedrich (1752–1840). *Collectio Craniorium Diversarum Gentium*. 1790–1828. Blumenbach's discussion and description of his organization of human skulls into a classification system.

———. *De Generis Humani Varietate Nativa*. 1775. This text provides the five divisions of mankind which have been the basis of all subsequent race theory racial classifications.

———. *Handbuch der Vergleichenden Anatomie*. 1805.

Caldwell, Charles (1772–1853). *Thoughts on the Original Unity of the Human Race*. New York, 1830.

Colfax, Richard H. *Evidence against the Views of the Abolitionists, Consisting of Physical and Moral Proofs, of the Natural Inferiority of the Negroes*. New York, 1833.

Crèvecoeur, J. Hector St. John de (1735–1813). *Letters from an American Farmer, by J. Hector St. John de Crèvecoeur*. London: J. M. Dent, 1982.

Davis, Charles T., and Henry Louis Gates, Jr., eds. *The Slave's Narrative*. New York: Oxford University Press, 1985.

Davis, David Brion. *The Problem of Slavery in Western Culture*. New York: Oxford University Press, 1966.

Dew, Thomas R. (1802–46). *Review of the Debate in the Virginia Legislature of 1831 and 1832*. Richmond, 1832.

Emerson, Everett. *The Authentic Mark Twain: A Literary Biography of Samuel L. Clemens*. Philadelphia: University of Pennsylvania Press, 1984. See especially the discussion of *Pudd'nhead Wilson*, pp. 180–90.

Fowler, Orson S. (1809–87). *Phrenological Chart*. Baltimore, 1836.

——— and Lorenzo N. Fowler (1811–96). *Phrenology Proved, Illustrated, and Applied*. 35th edition. New York, 1846.

Fredrickson, George. *The Arrogance of Race: Historical Perspectives on Slavery, Racism, and Social Inequality*. Middletown: Wesleyan University Press, 1988.

———. *The Black Image in the White Mind: The Debate on Afro-American Character and Destiny, 1817–1914*. Middletown: Wesleyan University Press, 1971.

———. *Racism: A Short History*. Princeton: Princeton University Press, 2002.

Gates, Henry Louis, Jr. "Literature of African-Americans." In *Africana: the Encyclopedia of the African and African American Experience* (New York: Basis Books, 1999).

Grégoire, Henri. *On the Cultural Achievements of Negroes.* Ed. Thomas Cassirer and Jean-François Brière. Amherst: University of Massachusetts Press, 1996.

Horsman, Reginald. *Race and Manifest Destiny.* Cambridge: Harvard University Press, 1981.

Jordan, Winthrop. *White over Black: American Attitudes toward the Negro, 1550–1812.* Chapel Hill: University of North Carolina Press, 1968.

Joshi, S. T., ed. *Documents of American Prejudice.* New York: Basic Books, 1999.

Kevles, Daniel. *In the Name of Eugenics: Genetics and the Uses of Human Heredity.* Cambridge: Harvard University Press, 1995.

Ruchames, Louis. *Racial Thought in America: from the Puritans to the Civil War.* Amherst: University of Massachusetts Press, 1963.

Schnakenberg, David. "The Origins of American Race Theory: Proslavery and Antebellum Race Theory Arguments." Unpublished typescript, University of Massachusetts "Race and Slavery" course, Amherst, MA, 2000.

Smith, Samuel Stanhope. *An Essay on the Causes of the Variety of Complexion and Figure in the Human Species.* Ed. Winthrop Jordan. Cambridge: Harvard University Press, 1965.

Stanton, William R. *The Leopard's Spots: Scientific Attitudes Toward Race in America, 1815–1859.* Chicago: University of Chicago Press, 1960.

Thomas, John, ed. *Slavery Attacked: The Abolitionist Crusade.* Englewood Cliffs, NJ: Prentice-Hall, 1963.

Walker, Clarence. *De-romanticizing Black History.* Knoxville: University of Tennessee Press, 1991.

Zelaya, Karla. "Race Theory in Nineteenth-Century America." Unpublished typescript, University of Massachusetts "Race and Slavery" course, Amherst, MA, 2000.

1. From *The Adams-Jefferson Letters: The Complete Correspondence between Thomas Jefferson and Abigail and John Adams,* ed. Lester Cappon (Chapel Hill: University of North Carolina Press, 1988), p. 273.

2. See David Schnakenberg's "The Origins of American Race Theory: Proslavery and Antebellum Race Theory Arguments," p. 3. This informative essay includes two important citations. One is from the American anthropologist Robert Knox's *The Races of Men: a Fragment.* "The fate of nations cannot always be regulated by chance; its literature science, art, wealth, language, laws, and morals, cannot surely be the result of merely accidental circumstances. . . . With me, race, or hereditary descent, is everything; it stamps the man. . . . I have endeavored to view mankind as they now exist, divided as they are, and seem always to have been, into distinct races." Schnakenberg observes: "Broca is the most respected authority on the brain of his time. He developed the concept of the cranial index, which exploited the relationship between length and width of the skull (which translated into brain size) as an indication of intelligence within race. Gobineau is accredited with being the father of modern racism, a French diplomat who believed the Aryan race was the creative and culture-bearing force of mankind. He claimed that because of racial impurity and inbreeding with Blacks, Slavic peoples, Asians, Latinos, and Jews, the human race was doomed to be reduced to unthinking cattle before their ultimate demise." Gobineau speaks of the races of man as such:

Races are naturally divided into three, and three only—the white, the black, and the yellow. . . . We have shown that races differ physically from each other: we must now ask if they are also unequal in beauty and muscular strength. The answer cannot be long doubtful . . . the human groups to which the European nations and their descendants belong are the most beautiful. One has only to compare the various types of men scattered over the earth's surface to be convinced of this . . . the peoples who are now of white blood approach beauty, but do not attain it. . . . Those who are most akin to us come nearest to beauty; such are the degenerate Aryan stocks of India and Persia, and those Semitic people who are least infected by contact with the black race. As these races recede from the white type, their features and limbs become incorrect in form . . . thus the human groups are unequal in beauty; and this inequality is rational, logical, permanent, and indestructible. . . . Is there also an inequality in physical strength? . . . If we take the peoples as a whole, and judge them by the amount of labor they can go through without flinching, we shall give the palm to those belonging to the white race. [Gobineau, as cited by Schnakenberg, pp. 3–5]

See Fredrickson, *The Black Image in the White Mind*, introduction and chaps. 1–3.

3. Crèvecoeur, Letter III, "What is an American?" in *Norton Anthology of American Literature*, ed. Nina Baym (New York: Norton, 1998), vol. 1, p. 643.

NOTES ON STEPHEN JAY GOULD'S CRITIQUE OF GEORGE MORTON'S RACE THEORIES
by Adam Linker

Stephen Jay Gould's *Mismeasure of Man* is the leading history and critique of nineteenth-century racist, or racialist, thought. Among the pantheon of racist thinkers in antebellum America, Samuel George Morton was the most respected and lauded. Gould sketches Morton's rise to international acclaim and then carefully analyzes Morton's "objective" scientific work. Morton kept company with Louis Agassiz and Josiah Nott as theorists of polygeny, otherwise known as the "American school" of anthropologists. Morton, Agassiz, and Nott all argued that "races" constituted different species with separate and distinct origins. Although none of these scientists were atheists, their theory of origins was profoundly at odds with theologians who insisted that all people descended from Adam and Eve. Within a broad overview of this American school of polygeny theorists, Gould examines the thought of Morton in microscopic detail.

Morton's fame, Gould tells us, stemmed primarily from his enormous collection of human skulls (approximately 1,000 by the time of his death in 1851). The goal of Morton's research was simple: measure skulls belonging to different human groups and rank the intelligence of human populations according to brain size. Gould's purpose, on the other hand, is to reexamine Morton's data and debunk his racist theories. At face value Gould's task is not difficult. After all, as he points out, Morton's initial premises were deeply flawed. For example, intelligence cannot be inferred from brain size. Elephants have larger brains than humans but few would argue that elephants are therefore smarter. Additionally, Morton's scholarship assumes (incorrectly) that race has some basis in biology. Therefore, his writings are filled with superstitious language about "pure Negroes" and "perfect Caucasians." Dismissing Morton would not prove difficult; however, Gould's argument is more informative and complex than a simple write-off. Gould accepts Morton's classifications and instead reanalyzes Morton's data to make broader claims about scientific observation.

For his landmark books, *Crania Americana* and *Crania Aegyptiaca*, Morton methodically filled each member of his skull collection with mustard seed or lead shot and recorded the cranial capacity in cubic inches. In both studies, Caucasians are the highest ranked among their less fortunate, smaller brained, fellow humans. Also in Morton's research, Africans perpetually bring up the rear in cranial capacity and intellectual endowment. For measurements in *Crania Americana*, Gould notes, Morton used mustard seed to determine skull size. However, by the time he published *Crania Aegyptiaca* he preferred lead shot. His results had been too erratic with seed, as results varied according to how well the grains were packed. To be sure, Morton's research was skewed by how hard he packed the skulls and, consciously or unconsciously, Caucasian skulls were more tightly packed than were Indian skulls. However, with the change to lead shot, blacks and Indians did not fare any better. Despite the reliability of "lead BBs," biases crept into Morton's research in more subtle ways.

Gould shows that preconceived notions of a racial hierarchy affected every step of Morton's observations. For example, when mean skull size was calculated for a given race, the Caucasian numbers were rounded up, whereas the black numbers were rounded down. This statistical sleight of hand brought the evidence closer to Morton's hypothesis of racial rankings. Also, larger Indian and black skulls and smaller Caucasian skulls were all removed from their respective samples. Therefore, the racial gap between mean skull sizes increased even more drastically. Another important problem was Morton's failure to calculate the skull sizes of men and women separately. Because men are larger, they tend to have larger brains. Without making gender distinctions, Morton's Indian samples could easily have included more women than men, thus biasing their mean cranial capacity downward. In fact, once Gould corrects for sex, those skulls designated "negroid male" have a higher average skull size than those deemed "caucasian male." Overall, Gould concludes, "My correction of Morton's conventional ranking reveals *no* significant differences among races for Morton's own data."

Gould deftly illustrates that social context powerfully affects scientific observation. After reviewing the data, Gould does not accuse Morton of outright forgery. Rather, Morton wanted so badly to prove that intelligence could be ranked according to race that he fudged his statistics in small yet important ways. Few at the time questioned Morton's conclusions. Some Southerners, such as Josiah Nott, heralded Morton's books as revelations. Others did not disagree with ranking intellectual capacity but rejected the blasphemous theories of polygeny advanced by Morton and Nott. However, despite detractors, Morton attracted an enormous international following and was hailed as an objective man of empirical observation. To be sure, his popular books tightened the chains of black Southerners and provided a foundation for countless works of racism that would follow.

SUGGESTIONS FOR FURTHER READING

Gould, Stephen Jay. *The Mismeasure of Man.* New York: Norton, 1996.

White Supremacy and Negro Subordination
by J. H. Van Evrie

This work, if carefully and generally read, will dispel that terrible delusion which plunged us into Civil War, whereby nearly a million of lives have been sacrificed, the prosperity of our country destroyed, and enmity and ill-will engendered between two sections of our common country, which formerly had been, and always should be, cemented together in true brotherly love.

It presents in language that can be easily understood, even by the commonest reader, the true relation of the races to each other, proving even beyond question or cavil, that when the two races are in juxta-position, the negro should hold an inferior or subordinate position to the white race, and that in such condition only can the negro race be prosperous and happy.

It will show that the normal condition of the negro when in contact with the white man, is to be guided and controlled socially and politically by the white race.

It will show that the *normal* or natural condition of all living beings is the only condition in which they can enjoy freedom, for the reason that if you attempt to make an animal or person act contrary to its nature, you thereby make it a slave, and, as the census shows, destroy its life.

It will show you that there are six distinct races of Men, five of which are below the White or Caucasian Race in the scale of the human creation, and that the negro is the lowest of all, and inferior to all.

It will prove to you that the four millions of negroes in their so-called slavery in the South were happier and more improved, intellectually, than the same number of the same class in any other portion of the world.

Source Note: J. H. Van Evrie, M.D., *White Supremacy and Negro Subordination, or, Negroes a Subordinate Race, and, Slavery Its Normal Condition*, 2nd ed. (New York: Van Evrie, Horton, & Co., 1870), Preface.

THOMAS JEFFERSON (1743–1826)

Abraham Lincoln once remarked that "The United States were founded on a proposition, and Thomas Jefferson authored that proposition." The "proposition" was, of course, the Declaration of Independence, in which Jefferson declared emphatically the belief that "all men are created equal," a rallying cry for

racial, social, and political equality that has fomented the debate about constitutional principles since 1787, when this phrasing was omitted from the Constitution. Jefferson was the third president of the United States, and he has dominated the study of early American history and culture. The bibliography of
book-length studies about Jefferson runs to some two volumes, second in number only to those treating Abraham Lincoln.

Jefferson was born a Virginia aristocrat on April 13, 1743. He is the most
illustrious graduate of the College of William and Mary, although he is usually
associated with the University of Virginia at Charlottesville, an institution
which he founded, and whose central quadrangle he designed with elaborate
architectural plans. More than a physical design, Jefferson's "academical village"
was a model of the modern American college or university, where faculty and
students shared common grounds and participated in the adventure of learning
throughout the day and night. Jefferson was trained as a lawyer, and was admitted to the Virginia Bar in 1767. But politics were his passion, and he served
in the Virginia House of Burgesses from 1769 to 1775. He was very active in
the formation of Virginia's representative government, and later not only authored and signed the Declaration of Independence, but also served as Washington's first secretary of state. He was vice-president under John Adams and
was elected president of the United States (serving two terms) in 1801. Jefferson
possessed a brilliant intellect and he authored books in numerous areas, including politics, philosophy, and natural science. His *Notes on the State of Virginia*,
excerpted here, was first published in France in 1784–85, and went through
many editions, in France, England, and the United States. It was long in the
making; Jefferson had worked on a study of the natural environment of Virginia—both a cultural and biological study—since the early 1780s. However,
the death of his wife Martha, after the birth of their sixth child in 1782, delayed
his work on the book and left him in despair. Politics and the founding of the
United States occupied him fully throughout the 1780s and 1790s. He served as
president for the first decade of the nineteenth century; his work on the University of Virginia commenced in 1815. Jefferson's long and extremely productive
life ended on July 4, 1826, fifty years to the day after the signing of the Declaration of Independence, and on the same day that his colleague, friend, and sometimes adversary, John Adams, also died. Jefferson is buried at his beloved *Monticello*, in Charlottesville, another remarkable neoclassical architectural monument
he personally designed.

It is easy to forget that *Monticello* was the "big house" of a large plantation
that often held over three hundred slaves. In *Notes on the State of Virginia*,
Jefferson established his reputation as a scientist and scholar. Here, he also expressed his opposition to slavery, even while holding slaves himself, and his
ambivalent attitude toward the "peculiar institution" is seen on the one hand in
his desire to emancipate the slaves for purposes of colonization, or the return to
Africa, and on the other, his clear articulation of beliefs in the inferiority of the
African and his acceptance of the arguments of contemporary race theory. This
seeming inconsistency of Jefferson's belief in Negro inferiority and his affair

with Sally Hemings has plagued Jefferson scholars from 1800 to the present, particularly since it has now been established, with DNA evidence, that Jefferson sired children by his African slave concubine.

Thomas Jefferson's clearly articulated principles of race theory established a popular and credible foundation for assumptions about the "essential" differences between blacks and whites that reappeared in the stereotypes of Africans throughout the nineteenth and twentieth centuries. These stereotypes were widely circulated, for example, in Harriet Beecher Stowe's *Uncle Tom's Cabin* (1852), a work which, while vigorously antislavery in sentiment, popularized the racial stereotypes reflected in Jefferson's *Notes on the State of Virginia*. Although Jefferson argued against the "institution" of slavery as a political structure, and saw in it destructive power for the newly formed democratic nation, he nevertheless embraced contemporary race theory views that were shared by many white Americans, including some of the abolitionists.

SUGGESTIONS FOR FURTHER READING

Two studies that should be consulted concerning Jefferson are *The American Sphinx: the Character of Thomas Jefferson* (New York: Knopf, 1997), by Joseph Ellis, and *Jefferson and His Times* (Boston: Little, Brown, 1948–81), the standard biography, a six-volume study by Dumas Malone. Both are magisterial studies, and are only two of literally hundreds of biographical works on Thomas Jefferson.

Notes on the State of Virginia
by Thomas Jefferson

First printed in France in 1784–85, Jefferson's Notes on the State of Virginia *went through many editions and helped create the author's reputation as a scholar and pioneer American scientist. In this book, Jefferson expressed his opposition to slavery, but suggested the desirability of joining colonization to African emancipation. He based his opinion upon what he believed to be the inherent antagonism of the races and the inferiority of the African.*

To declare them a free and independent people, and extend to them our alliance protection, till they have acquired strength; and to send vessels at the same time to other parts of the world for an equal number of white inhabitants; to induce them to migrate hither, proper encouragements were to be proposed. . . .

The first difference which strikes us is that of color. Whether the black of the negro resides in the reticular membrane between the skin and scarf-skin, or in the scarf-skin itself; whether it proceeds from the color of the blood, the color of the bile, or from that of some other secretion, the difference is fixed in nature, and is as real as if its seat and cause were better known to us. And is this difference of no importance? Is it not the foundation of a greater or less shade of beauty in the two races? . . . Are not the fine mixtures of red and white, the expression of every passion by greater or less suffusions of color in the one, preferable to that eternal monotony, which reigns in the countenances, that immovable veil of black which covers the emotions of the other race? Add to these, flowing hair, a more elegant symmetry of form, their own judgement in favor of the whites, declared by their preference of them, as uniformly as is the preference of the Oranootan [*sic*] for the black woman over those of his own species. The circumstance of superior beauty, is thought worthy attention in the propagation of our horses, dogs, and other domestic animals; why not in that of man? Besides those of color, figure, and hair, there are other physical distinctions proving a difference of race. They have less on the face and body. They secrete less by the kidneys, and more by the glands of the skin, which gives them a very strong and disagreeable odor. This greater degree of transpiration, renders them more tolerant of heat, and less so of cold than the whites. Perhaps, too, a difference of a structure in the pulmonary apparatus, which a late ingenious experimentalist has discovered to be the principal regulator of animal heat, may have disabled them from extricating, in the act of inspiration, so much of that fluid from the outer air, or obliged them in expiration, to part with more of it. They seem to require less sleep. A black after hard labor through the day, will be induced by the slightest amusements to sit up till midnight, or later, though knowing he must be out with the first dawn of the morning. They are at least as brave, and more adventuresome. But this may perhaps proceed from a want of forethought, which prevents their seeing a danger till it be present. When present, they do not go through it with more coolness or steadiness that the whites. They are more ardent after their female; but love seems with them to be more an eager desire, than tender delicate mixture of sentiment and sensation. Their griefs are transient. Those numberless afflictions, which render it doubtful whether heaven has given life to us in mercy or in wrath, are less felt, and sooner forgotten with them. In general, their existence appears to participate more of sensation than reflection. To this must be ascribed their disposition to sleep when abstracted from their diversions, and unemployed in labor. An animal whose body is at rest, and who does not reflect, must be disposed to sleep of course. Comparing them by their faculties of memory, reason, and imagination, it appears to me that in memory they are equal to the whites; in reason much inferior, as I think one could scarcely be found capable of tracing and comprehending the investigation of Euclid; and that in imagination they are dull, tasteless, and anomalous. It would be unfair to follow them to Africa for this investigation. We will consider them here, on the same stage with the whites, and where the facts are not apocryphal on which a judgment is to be formed. It will be right to make great allowances for the difference of conditions, of education, of conversation, of the sphere in which they move. Many millions of them have been brought to, and born in America. Most of them, indeed, have been confined to tillage, to their own homes, and their own society. . . .

They astonish you with strokes of the most sublime oratory; such as prove their reason and sentiment strong, their imagination glowing and elevated. But never yet could I find that a black had uttered a thought above the level of plain narration; never see even an elementary trait of painting or sculpture. In music they are more generally gifted than the whites with accurate ears for tune and time, and they have been found capable of imagining a small catch. Whether they will be equal to the composition of a more extensive run of melody, or of complicated harmony, is yet to be proved. Misery is often the parent of the most affecting touches in poetry. Among the blacks is misery enough, God knows, but no poetry. Love is the peculiar oestrum of the poet. Their love is ardent, but it kindles the senses only, not the imagination. Religion, indeed, has produced a Phillis Wheatly; but it could not produce a poet. The compositions published under her name are below the dignity of criticism. Ignatius Sancho has approached nearer to merit in composition; yet his letters do more honor to the heart than the head. . . .

Upon the whole, thought we admit him to the first place among those of his own color who have presented themselves to the public judgment, yet when we compare him with the writers of the race among whom he lived and particularly with the epistolary class in which he has taken his own stand, we are compelled to enroll him at the bottom of the column. This criticism supposes the letter published under his name to be genuine, and to have received amendment from no other hand; points which would not be of easy investigation. The improvement of the blacks in body and mind, in the first instance of their mixture with the whites, has been observed by every one, and proves that inferiority is not the effect merely of their condition of life. . . .

Yet notwithstanding these and other discouraging circumstances among the Romans, their slaves were often their rarest artists. They excelled too in science, inasmuch as to be usually employed as tutors to their master's children. Epictetus, Terence, and Phaedrus were slaves. But they were of the race of whites. It is not their condition then, but nature, which has produced the distinction. . . .

But the slaves of which Homer speaks were whites. Notwithstanding these considerations which must weaken their respect for the laws of property, we find among them numerous instances of the most rigid integrity, and as many as among their better instructed masters' of benevolence, gratitude, and unshaken fidelity. The opinion that they are inferior in the faculties of reason and imagination must be hazarded with great diffidence. . . .

I advance it, therefore, as a suspicion only, that the blacks, whether originally a distinct race, or made distinct by time and circumstances, are inferior to the whites in the endowments both of body and mind. . . .

This unfortunate difference of color, and perhaps of faculty, is a powerful obstacle to the emancipation of these people. Many of their advocates, while they wish to vindicate the liberty of human nature, are anxious also to preserve its dignity and beauty. . . .

Source Note: Thomas Jefferson, *Notes on the State of Virginia*, ed. Frank Shuffleton (New York: Penguin-Putnam, 1999), pp. 266–67.

Henri Grégoire (1750–1831)

Although Henri Grégoire was not an American, his work *On the Cultural Achievements of Negroes*, published in Paris in 1808, became an important text in the antebellum slavery debates that were concerned with race theory. Grégoire's response to Josiah Friedrich Blumenbach's racial classification theory, also published in 1808, provided antislavery advocates with a philosophical argument to refute the widely popular classification race theory. It was translated into German in 1809 and into English by Bailie Warden in 1810, and was widely read on both sides of the Atlantic.

Grégoire was born in 1750 in Veho, a village in the duchy of Lorraine, and he later became a Catholic priest. Throughout his life, he was an advocate of human rights and liberties, and his first book, *Essai sur la regeneration physique, morale, et politique des Juifs* (1788) argued for the assimilation of French Jews into the general population instead of their treatment as foreigners. He was appointed to the political body of France, the Estates General, and later, to the French National Assembly. Thomas Cassirer notes that "Grégoire's interest in 'men of all colors' and colonial matters began in September, 1789, after he had been appointed to the Credential Committee of the National Assembly. Among other issues, this Committee had to examine a most volatile question: Do free mulattoes of the French West Indies . . . have a right to be represented along with the white colonists in the colonial deputation to the Assembly." Grégoire fought vigorously for rights of all men, slave or free, and his ultimate objective was the worldwide abolition of slavery. His important treatise was re-edited by Thomas Cassirer and Jean-François Brière, and published by the University of Massachusetts Press in Amherst, in 1996.

SUGGESTIONS FOR FURTHER READING

Bender, Thomas ed. *The Antislavery Debate: Capitalism and Abolitionism as a Problem of Historical Interpretation*. Berkeley: University of California Press, 1992.

Cassirer, Thomas and Jean-François Brière introduction to *On the Cultural Achievements of Negroes*, by Henri Grégoire (1750–1831), Amherst: University of Massachusetts Press, 1996, p. xix.

On the Cultural Achievements of Negroes
by Henri Grégoire

Chapter 2. *Opinions Concerning the Moral Inferiority of Negroes. Discussion of This Topic. Of the Obstacles which Slavery Places in the Way of the Development of Their Faculties. These Obstacles Combated by the Christian Religion. Of Negro Bishops and Priests.*

The opinion that the Negroes are inferior is not new. The claims of white superiority are defended only by whites speaking in their own interest. Before attacking their opinion we should question whether they are qualified to make such a judgment. This reminds us of the fable of the lion who sees a picture representing one of his species brought down by a man, and merely comments that lions have no painters.

In his essay on national character Hume distinguishes four or five races but maintains that only the white race possesses culture and that no black has ever distinguished himself by his actions or by his knowledge. . . .

Barre-Saint-Venant thinks that while nature has endowed Negroes with a certain ability to combine ideas, which raises them above other animals, nature has also made them incapable of deep feelings and sustained activity of the intellect, creative genius, and reason.

To our regret we find the same prejudice in a man whose name is always mentioned amongst us with the most profound esteem and with a respect he deserves. Jefferson, in his *Notes on Virginia*. To support his opinion he did not merely disparage the talent of two Negro writers; he also found it necessary to establish by argument and by a multitude of facts, that even if blacks and whites lived under the same circumstances, the blacks could never compete with the whites.

Jefferson was attacked by Beattie, and since then with considerable heat by Imlay, his compatriot, especially concerning Phillis Wheatley. Imlay transcribes moving passages from her work. But he is also in error when he says to Jefferson that to cite Terence is awkward, since Terence was an African and in fact a Numidian, and thus a Negro. . . .

Moreover, Jefferson furnishes arms against himself in his answer to Raynal, who reproached America for not having produced, so far, any famous men. Once we have been in existence as a nation, says this learned American, as long as the Greeks before they had Homer, the Romans a Virgil, or the French a Racine, observers will have a right to be astonished. In like manner we can say that once Negroes have lived in a state of civilization as long as the inhabitants of the United States, there will be some justification for believing that the Negroes are totally lacking in genius, if they have not produced men like Franklin, Rittenhouse, Jefferson, Madison, Washington, Monroe, Warren, Rush, Barlow, Mitchell, Rumford, Barton. . . . Then we might say with Gentry, "How could one ever expect genius to spring up in the midst of infamy and deprivation, when there is not a glimpse of recompense and no hope of relief!" Now that I have argued against an error in Jefferson's mind, I must not leave this topic without rendering homage to his heart. By his speeches and his actions, both as president and as a citizen, he has unceasingly called for the liberty and education of the slaves, and for all other measures to better their existence.

In most parts of Africa, civilization and the arts are still in their infancy. If you believe this is because the inhabitants are Negroes, explain to us why white or copper-colored men of other countries have remained savages and even cannibals? Why did the nomadic hunters of North America not even become pastoral tribes before the arrival of the Europeans? Yet no one contests their capacity for improvement. It would be contested, for sure, if there were ever a design to subject them to the slave trade. It can be taken for granted that greed would discover pretexts to justify their slavery.

The arts originate from natural or from artificial needs. Artificial needs are almost unknown in Africa, and as to the natural needs for food, clothing, and shelter, they are minimal on account of the heat of the climate. The first of these needs is quite limited and easily satisfied, because in that region nature is prodigal of her riches. The recent reports by travelers have greatly modified the opinion that the African countries are little more than unfruitful deserts. In that respect James Field Stanfield echoes these travelers in his fine poem *Guinea*.

The Christian religion is an infallible means of extending and securing civilization. Such has been, and will always be its effect. It was by its influence that our ancestors, the Gauls and the Franks, ceased to be barbarians, and that the sacred woods were no longer stained with the blood of human sacrifices. It was this faith that enlightened the African Church, formerly one of the most splendid regions of Catholicity. When Christianity forsook these regions, they were again plunged in darkness. The historian Long reproaches the Negroes for eating wild cats, as if this were a crime, and a circumstance unknown in Europe. This from a man who tries to persuade us that Negroes are incapable of attaining the highest achievements of the human mind, while he himself refutes his own assertions in many passages of his work, as we intend to point out; for instance, in the section concerning Francis Williams. Long also states that Negroes are given to superstition, as though Europe were free of this infection, and particularly the country of that historian. We can find in Grose a long and ridiculous enumeration of the superstitious observances of English Protestants.

While the superstitions are to be pitied, they are at least not inaccessible to sound notions. False glimmering may be dispelled by the splendor of light. Those who are superstitious may be compared to fertile land that produces poisonous or wholesome plants, depending on whether the soil is neglected or cultivated. A completely sterile soil, on the other hand, could be a symbol for anyone who denies all religious principles. Only the belief in a God who rewards and punishes, can assure the probity of a man who is hidden from the eyes of his fellow men, and who could steal or commit any other crime with impunity, since he does not need to fear public vengeance. These reflections enable us to resolve a problem that is so often discussed: namely, Which is worse, superstition or atheism? Even though in many individuals the passions stifle every sentiment of justice and probity, yet as a general principle we cannot hesitate on the choice between an individual who to be virtuous merely needs to act in conformity with his beliefs, and another who must be inconsistent with his general principles if he wishes to avoid becoming dishonest.

. . . One could fill thick volumes with the recital of the crimes by which the slaves have been victimized. When the partisans of slavery find they cannot deny this, they fall back on the argument that this was the past but that nothing of this kind has recently sullied the records of the colonies. To be sure, there are planters who are worthy in every respect and cannot be accused of cruelty. If anyone should protest as though he was being attacked individually, we would answer, with Erasmus, that by protesting he reveals his bad conscience. However, the story is quite recent of the captain of a slave ship, who when he was short of water and saw his cargo ravaged by death, threw the blacks by hundreds into the sea. Not long ago another captain of a slave ship was annoyed by the cries of the child of a Negro woman, dragged it from its mother's bosom, and threw it into the water. Then he was bothered by the groans of the unfortunate mother, and the only reason why she did not experience a similar fate was that this trader hoped to profit by her sale. I am persuaded, says John Newton, that all mothers worthy of the name, will lament for her fate. The same author mentions another captain who put down an insurrection and then devoted himself for a long time to devising the most refined tortures in order to punish what he called a revolt.

In 1789, we received the following account from Kingston, in Jamaica: "Besides tearing the flesh of the Negroes with the lash of the whip, they muzzle them to prevent them from sucking the sugarcane which is watered with their sweat, and the instrument of iron with which the mouth is compressed, stifles their cries when they suffer under the lash." . . .

Oh! that it had pleased God to cause the waves to swallow up these devourers of human flesh, trained and directed by man against his fellow man. I have heard it asserted that on the arrival of the dogs at Saint Domingue, by way of experiment they were let loose on the first Negro who happened along. The promptitude with which they devoured their prey delighted those white tigers with a human face.

. . . These pamphleteers speak incessantly of unhappy planters, and never of unhappy Negroes. The planters keep repeating that the soil of the colonies has been watered by their sweat, and never utter a word concerning the sweat of their slaves. The colonial settlers are right to describe as monsters those Negroes of Saint Domingue who had recourse to criminal repression and butchered the whites; but they never say that the whites provoked this vengeance by drowning Negroes, or letting dogs devour them. . . .

. . . Slaves are almost entirely delivered over to the discretion of their masters. The laws have done everything for the latter, and everything against the former. Condemned to legal incapacity, they cannot even be admitted as witnesses against whites. If a Negro endeavors to escape, the Black Code of Jamaica gives the tribunal power to condemn him to death.

. . . While the lives of the slaves enjoy at best minimal protection, their sense of modesty is totally defenseless against brutish lewdness. John Newton, who was employed for nine years in the slave trade, and then became an Anglican clergyman, makes upright souls shudder as he laments the outrages committed against Negro women, "even though we often admire traits of modesty and delicacy among them of which a virtuous Englishwoman might be proud."

In the French, English, and Dutch colonies, the laws, or public opinion, rejected mixed marriages to such a degree, that those who entered into them were considered to have constituted an honorable exception. In their colonies a Catholic marriage sets the slave free. It is not surprising that Barre-Saint-Venant inveighs against this religious regulation, since he dares to censure the ever-celebrated decree by which Constantine facilitated the freeing of the slaves. What has resulted from these legal prohibitions, more particularly those that relate to marriage? Libertinism has eluded the law or has broken through the prejudice. This will always take place when men try to act in contradiction to nature.

. . . The Negroes are accused of a vindictive disposition. What other temper can men possess, who are vexed and deceived continually, and by this treatment are provoked into being vengeful? Of this we could cite a thousand proof; we shall, however, confine ourselves to a single fact. The Negro Baron, in Surinam, is skilled, educated, and faithful. He is taken to Holland by his master, who promises him his freedom on their return. Notwithstanding this promise, when they arrive back in Surinam, Baron is sold. He obstinately refuses to work and receives a lashing at the foot of a gibbet; he escapes, joins the Maroons, and becomes the implacable enemy of the whites.

This torturing system has been pursued so far as to prevent all development of the mental facilities. By a regulation adopted in the state of Virginia, slaves are not allowed to learn to read. To have been able to read cost one of those black men his life. He demanded, that the Africans should share the benefits promised by American liberty, and he supported this demand by the first article of the Bill of Rights. The argument was unanswerable. In such cases, where refutation is impossible, the inquisition incarcerates those whom formerly it would have burned. All tyrannies have similar features. The Negro was hanged.

. . . It has always been the custom of tormentors to slander the victims. The slave traders and the planters have denied or attenuated the facts of which they are accused. They even tried to make a pretense of being humanitarian by maintaining that all the slaves brought from Africa were prisoners of war, or criminals destined for execution who ought to congratulate themselves that their lives were saved, and that they are permitted to cultivate the soil of the Antilles. They have been refuted by many eyewitnesses. . . .

When the truth about the tormenting of the slaves and the barbarity of the masters was substantiated thousands of times, the master denied that the Negro is capable of morality or intelligence, and on the scale of all living beings they placed him between man and the animals.

. . . This discussion is pertinent to my subject; if the principles of morality cover even the relations that man has with animals, then the Negroes, even if they were lacking in intelligence, would still have grounds for protesting against their condition. But the most thorough research proves that there is only one human constitution, notwithstanding the different shades of skin color, whether yellow, copper, black, or white. If the presence of virtues and talents among Negroes offers incontrovertible proof that they have the potential for all combinations of intelligence and morality and that, under a differently colored skin, they belong to the same species as we, then how much more guilty do those Europeans appear who scorn enlightened knowledge and the sentiments propagated by Christianity and then by civilization, as they throw themselves on the bodies of the unfortunate Negroes and suck their blood to extract gold out of it.

Twenty years of experience have taught me what arguments are used by the merchants of human flesh. If they are to be believed, one needs to have lived in the colonies in order to have the right to an opinion on the legitimacy of slavery.

Even if it were true that these countries cannot flourish without the assistance of Negroes, we would have to come to a conclusion that is very different from what the colonial settlers advocate. They constantly have recourse to the past in order to justify the present, as if abuses were legitimate because they were long established. If we speak about justice they answer by talking about sugar, indigo, and the balance of trade.

. . . The Negroes have been slandered, first in order to establish the right to enslave them, then to justify keeping them in slavery, and also out of a feeling of guilt toward them. The accusers are both judges and executioners, and yet they call themselves Christians! They have tried many times to distort the sense of the Holy Scriptures, in order to find therein an apology for colonial slavery, although the Scriptures declare that all mortals are children of the Heavenly Father and spring from the same family. Religion admits of no distinction. If we sometimes see blacks and mulattos relegated, in the churches of the colonies, to seats separate from those of the whites, and even admitted separately to participation in the Eucharist, it is criminal of the pastors to tolerate a custom that is so contrary to the spirit of religion. In the words of Paley, it is particularly in the church that the poor man raises his humiliated head and the rich man regards him with respect. It is there that, in the name of Heaven, the minister at the altar reminds his listeners that by their origin they are all equal before a God who declares that for Him there is no respect of persons. There the Heavenly oracle proclaims that we ought to do to others what we wish to be done to us.

It is the glory of the Christian religion alone to have sheltered the weak from the strong. It is this religion that, in the fourth century, established the first hospital in the West. It has constantly labored to console the unfortunate, whatever be their country, their color, or religion. The parable of the Samaritan marks persecutors with the seal of censure. It is a curse laid for all times on anyone who would exclude a single member of the human race from the circle of charity.

Chapter 3. *Moral Qualities of the Negroes; Their Love of Industry, Their Courage, Bravery, Affection between Parents and Children, Generosity &c.*

. . . The Negroes are accused of laziness. Bosman, to prove it, says that they are in the habit of asking, not "How are you?" but "How have you rested?" They have a maxim that it is better to be lying than seated: better to be seated than to stand, and better to stand than to walk. Since we made them so wretched, they have added the India proverb, that death is preferable to all this.

The accusation of indolence, which is not without some degree of truth, is often exaggerated. It is exaggerated in the mouths of those who are in the habit of employing a bloody whip to conduct the slaves to forced labor; it is true in the sense that men cannot have a great inclination to industry when they own nothing, not even their own person, and when the fruits of their sweat feed the luxury or avarice of a merciless master. Nor are men inclined to be industrious in regions favored by nature, where her spontaneous products, or work that requires no great effort, provide abundantly for man's natural needs. But whether they are black or white, all men are hardworking when stimulated by the spirit of property, by utility, or by pleasure. . . .

Source Note: Henry Grégoire, On the Cultural Achievements of Negroes (1808), translated and edited by Thomas Cassirer and Jean-François Brière (Amherst: University of Massachusetts Press, 1996), by permission of Bruce Wilcox, director.

The Claims of the Negro Ethnologically Considered
by Frederick Douglass

[When it was announced that Douglass would address the prestigious Philozetian and Phi Delta literary societies of Western Reserve College in Hudson, Ohio, during commencement week in 1854, the news was greeted with incredulity, praise, and disapproval. Never before had a black person been the keynote speaker at the graduation exercises of a major American university. Western Reserve, one of the first colleges established in the West, had an antislavery tradition dating back to the early 1830s. Douglass labored "many days and nights" on the speech—"Written orations had not been in my line"—and this first effort, he felt later, "was a very defective production." Yet the nearly three thousand people who filled the spacious tent on the campus at 1:00 P.M. on July 12, 1854, did not think so, even though some of them had come hoping to see the quondam slave fall on his face. "Douglass commanded the most fixed attention of two hours, on a hot summer afternoon," reported the Hudson (Ohio) Observer. His eloquence brought "many glistening tears" to the eyes of the audience, said the Chronicle and Transcript. See also the headnote for Frederick Douglass in chapter 2 of this volume.]

The relation subsisting between the white and black people of this country is the vital question of the age. In the solution of this question, the scholars of America will have to take an important and controlling part. This is the moral battle field to which their country and their God now call them. . . .

The first general claim which may here be set up, respects the manhood of the negro. This is an elementary claim, simple enough, but not without question. It is fiercely opposed. A respectable public journal, published in Richmond, Va., bases its whole defense of the slave system upon a denial of the negro's manhood.

"The white peasant is free, and if he is a man of will and intellect, can rise in the scale of society; or at least his offspring may. He is not deprived by law of those 'inalienable rights,' 'liberty and the pursuit of happiness,' by the use of it. But here is the essence of slavery—that we do declare the negro destitute of these powers. We bind him by law to the condition of the laboring peasant for ever, without his consent, and we bind his posterity after him. Now, the true question is, have we a right to do this? If we have not, all discussions about his comfortable situation and the actual condition of free laborers elsewhere, are

"The Fugitive's Song," the title page of sheet music celebrating Frederick Douglass as an escaped slave, by permission of Georgia Barnhill, Mellon Curator of Graphic Arts, American Antiquarian Society, Worcester, Mass.

quite beside the point. If the negro has the same right to his liberty and the pursuit of his own happiness that the white man has, then we commit the greatest wrong and robbery to hold him a slave—an act at which the sentiment of justice must revolt in every heart—and negro slavery is an institution which that sentiment must sooner or later blot from the face of the earth."—*Richmond Examiner*

After stating the question thus, the *Examiner* boldly asserts that the negro has no such right—BECAUSE HE IS NOT A MAN!

There are three ways to answer this denial. One is by ridicule; a second is by denunciation; and a third is by argument. . . .

Man is distinguished from all other animals, by the possession of certain definite faculties and powers, as well as by physical organization and proportions. He is the only two-handed animal on the earth—the only one that laughs, and nearly the only one that weeps. Men instinctively distinguish between men and brutes. Common sense itself is scarcely needed to detect the absence of manhood in a monkey, or to recognize its presence in a negro. His speech, his reason, his power to acquire and to retain knowledge, his heaven-erected face, his habitudes, his hopes, his fears, his aspirations, his prophecies, plant between him and the brute creation, a distinction as eternal as palpable. . . . Tried by all the usual, and all unusual tests, whether mental, moral, physical, or psychological, the negro is a MAN—considering him as possessing knowledge, or needing knowledge, his elevation, or his degradation, his virtues, or his vices—whichever road you take, you reach the same conclusion, the negro is a MAN. . . .

Dr. Samuel George Morton may be referred to as a fair sample of American Ethnologists. His very able work *Crania Americana*, published in Philadelphia in 1839, is widely read in this country.[1] In this great work his contempt for negroes is ever conspicuous. I take him as an illustration of what had been alleged as true of his class.

. . . It is the province of prejudice to blind; and scientific writers, not less than others, write to please, as well as to instruct, and even unconsciously to themselves (sometimes), sacrifice what is true to what is popular. Fashion is not confined to dress; but extends to philosophy as well—and it is fashionable now, in our land, to exaggerate the differences between the negro and the European. If, for instance, a phrenologist or naturalist undertakes to represent in portraits, the differences between the two races—the negro and the European—he will invariably present the *highest* type of European, and the *lowest* type of the negro.

The European face is drawn in harmony with the highest ideas of beauty, dignity and intellect. Features regular and brow after the Websterian mold. The negro, on the other hand, appears with features distorted, lips exaggerated, forehead depressed—and the whole expression of the countenance made to harmonize with the popular idea of negro imbecility and degradation. I have seen many pictures of negroes and Europeans, in phrenological and ethnological works; and all, or nearly all, excepting the work of Dr. Prichard, and that other great work, Combs' *Constitution of Man*,[2] have been more or less open to this objection. I think I have never seen a single picture in an American work, designed to give an idea of the mental endowments of the negro, which did any thing like justice to the subject; nay, that was not infamously distorted. . . .

A powerful argument in favor of the oneness of the human family, is afforded in the fact that nations, however dissimilar, may be united in one social state, not only without detriment to each other, but, most clearly, to the advancement of human welfare, happiness, and perfection. While it is clearly proved, on the other hand, that those nations freest from foreign elements, present the most evident marks of deterioration. Dr. James McCune Smith, himself a colored man, a gentleman and scholar, alleges—and not without excellent reason—that this, our own great nation, so distinguished for industry and enterprise, is largely indebted to its composite character. We all know, at any rate, that now, what constitutes the very heart of the civilized world—(I allude to England)— has only risen from barbarism to its present lofty eminence, through successive invasions and alliances with her people. . . .

. . . I sincerely believe, that the weight of the argument is in favor of the unity of origin of the human race, or species—that the arguments on the other side are partial, superficial, utterly subversive of the happiness of man, and insulting to the wisdom of God. Yet, what if we grant they are not so? What, if we grant that the case, on our part, is not made out? Does it follow, that the negro should be held in contempt? Does it follow, that to enslave and imbrute him is either *just* or *wise*? I think not. Human rights stand upon a common basis; and by all the reasons that they are supported, maintained and defended, for one variety of the human family, they are supported, maintained and defended for *all* the human family; because all mankind have the same wants, arising out of a common nature. A diverse origin does not disprove a common nature, nor does it disprove a united destiny. The essential characteristics of humanity are everywhere the same. . . .

. . . The history of the negro race proves them to be wonderfully adapted to all countries, all climates, and all conditions. Their tenacity of life, their powers of endurance, their malleable toughness, would almost imply especial interposition on their behalf. The ten thousand horrors of slavery, striking hard upon the sensitive soul, have bruised, and battered, and stung, but have not killed. The poor bondman lifts a smiling face above the surface of a sea of agonies, *hoping on, hoping ever*. His tawny brother, the Indian, dies, under the flashing glances of the Anglo-Saxon. *Not* so the negro, civilization cannot kill him. He accepts it—becomes a part of it. In the Church, he is an Uncle Tom; in the State, he is the most abused and least offensive. All the facts in his history mark out for him a destiny, united to America and Americans. Now, whether this population shall, by FREEDOM, INDUSTRY, VIRTUE, and INTELLIGENCE, be made a blessing to the country and the world, or whether their multiplied wrongs shall kindle the vengeance of an offended God, will depend upon the conduct of no class of men so much as upon the Scholars of the country. . . .

Source Note: Frederick Douglass, *The Claims of the Negro Ethnologically Considered: An Address, before the Literary Societies of Western Reserve College, at Commencement, July 12,*

1854, from *The Frederick Douglass Papers*, edited by John W. Blassingame (New Haven: Yale University Press, 1982).

1. Douglass refers to Samuel G. Morton, *Crania Americana; or, A Comparative View of the Skulls of Various Aboriginal Nations of North and South America* (Philadelphia, 1839). Published by subscription, *Crania Americana* became the most famous of Morton's works. A compendium of essays and lithographs on the relationship between the crania and customs of the American Indians, the work argues that different races were created to adapt to their original environments and that external causes do not affect physical characteristics. Josiah G. Nott and George R Gliddon, *Types of Mankind; or, Ethnological Researches* (Philadelphia, 1854), pp. xxii–xvii; William R. Stanton, *The Leopard's Spots: Scientific Attitudes toward Race in America, 1815–59* (Chicago: University of Chicago Press, 1960), pp. 30, 40.

2. Douglass probably refers to James Cowles Prichard, *Researches into the Physical History of Mankind* (5 vols., 1813; London, 1841), and George Combe, *The Constitution of Man Considered in Relation to External Objects* (3d American ed., Boston, 1834).

O. S. FOWLER (1809–1887)

Orson Squire Fowler was a phrenologist and science writer. He is best known for his writing and lecturing on phrenology, a science that emerged in the early nineteenth century which argued that there was a direct correlation between the brain, which was defined as an organ of the mind, and the shape and size of the human skull. Thus human attributes, such as intelligence, character, moral judgment, disposition, and talents or skills, could be inferred by a careful and thorough examination of each individual's skull shape and size. It is not difficult to see how phrenology was immediately applied to race theory arguments and how these scientists, such as George Morton, who authored *Crania Americana* in 1839, would use phrenology to provide evidence for their theories on the origins and classification of races throughout the world. As the introduction to chapter 7 shows, phrenology was one facet of a much wider argument concerning the historical and geographical classification of the races of the world. Skull collections like Morton's were used to prove the evolution of race from a lower to a higher form, or to demonstrate that one racial group was superior to another because of skull shape and brain size.

Phrenology became a very popular form of the science of race classification. Human heads were reproduced by the hundreds, with the supposed location of various characteristics indicated on the corresponding part of the skull surface. Phrenology was "popular culture" in the best sense of the term; a phenomenon that had originated in the science lab was very quickly disseminated to many households throughout the United States in this elementary and inaccurate pseudoscience. Chris Hanlon has here not only provided an edited text of O. S. Fowler's classic treatise, *Phrenology*; he has also written an illuminating essay on the science itself and Fowler's contributions to its advancement.

It is important to remember that phrenology was initially regarded to be a very legitimate scientific enterprise, and that the theory of human brain development was closely allied with the discoveries of phrenologists before mid-century. The educator Horace Mann (1796–1859) embraced phrenology as a way of determining the intellectual capacities of children, and Henry Ward Beecher (1813–87), religious leader and prominent social reformer, also was attracted to phrenology. As the antebellum slavery debates intensified, phrenology was exploited by proslavery advocates to support their theories of racial classification and the spectrum of human intellectual abilities.

Fowler had many interests beyond phrenology. He was an architect, and like Horatio Greenough, his contemporary, argued that "form follows function"; and he became a devotee of the octagonal house shape, several of which he designed and built. He was thus a precursor of Frank Lloyd Wright, according to Madeleine Stern (*Dictionary of American Biography*, p. 330). In the 1870s, Fowler turned his attention to the science of human sexuality and behavior, publishing *Sexual Science* (1870); *Creative and Sexual Science* (1870); *Life: Its Science, Laws, Faculties* (1871); and *The Practical Phrenologist* (1876).

SUGGESTIONS FOR FURTHER READING

Stern, Madeleine B. "Bibliographical Essay." In *A Phrenological Dictionary of Nineteenth-Century Americans* (Westport, CT: Greenwood, 1982), pp. 421–24.

O. S. FOWLER AND *HEREDITARY DESCENT*
edited and introduced by Christopher Hanlon

One of the strangest and most fascinating footnotes in the history of science in America, phrenology appears to modern students of American culture as a mixture of superstition and charlatanism, a form of fortune-telling dignified by practitioners who regarded themselves as scientists. But for most Americans living during the middle and later decades of the nineteenth century, phrenology was a scientific achievement on par with the invention of telegraphy or daguerreotypy; in some ways, the popular attitude toward phrenology from the 1820s to the '70s in America is comparable to the attitude present-day Americans entertain toward the science of genetics. At its most fundamental level, phrenology was a system for the measurement of such "positive" human qualities as intelligence, honesty, and industriousness—as well as such "negative" propensities as enviousness, violence, and greed—a system that treated the curvature of the human skull as the index of these attributes. The creation of the Viennese physician Franz Josef Gall in the first decade of the nineteenth century, phrenology taught that particular personality traits corresponded to particular "organs" or convolutions of the brain, so that a person given to lust, for example, could be expected to possess a large "philoprogenitive" or "amative" organ, which was determined to lie near the very back of the head. The dimensions of the human cranium, phrenologists believed, almost precisely matched the curves, bulges, and depressions of the brain within, so that a well-trained "craniologist," equipped with the appropriate tools for measuring the contours of a subject's head, could produce a "phrenological chart" illustrating this same subject's intellectual and moral strengths or deficiencies. As the New York phrenologist Samuel Wells expressed in 1899,

> Now, as is the soul which is incarnate in it, so is the brain in texture, size, and configuration; and as is the brain, so is its bony encasement, the cranium, on which may be read, in general forms and special elevations and depressions, and with unerring certainty, a correct outline of the intellectual and moral character of the man.[1]

Inasmuch as it emphasized the idea that "the soul" could no longer effectively hide within the body but rather must be regarded as constantly speaking through it—betraying and articulating its own presence through a vocabulary of telltale bumps, depressions, and marks—the field of phrenology was an outgrowth of the older field of physiognomy, which treated the human body as a kind of "text" to be read by the trained professional. As the physiognomist John Caspar Lavater wrote in the 1770s, the "original language of Nature, written on the face of man" could be translated to the language of a plain and usable science.[2]

Phrenology was a "popular" science in the truest sense; from the 1830s onward, masses of Americans reported to the offices and studios of phrenologists in nearly every major American city in order to "have their chart drawn." And for those who could not actually make the trip to place their head between the phrenologist's calipers, another of the century's scientific wonders could be made to assist. In an advertisement placed at the back of a phrenological handbook published for the layperson,

> We always recommend a personal examination where possible. If you cannot come to us perhaps there is a graduate of the American Institute of Phrenology in your neighborhood. If, however, for any reason personal examination is impossible, delineations from photographs by our method will be found very satisfactory. . . . Have two photographs, profile and full front, taken especially for the purpose. Have the hair *smoothed* (not frizzy or curly) to show the contours of the head. Send these to us with the following measurements: Distance between the openings of the ears over crown of the head. Distance between root of nose and the projection at base of back head (occipital spine), also the circumference of the head.[3]

But it was probably through books and magazine articles that most Americans came into contact with phrenology. The writers of these books and articles (even when they were not themselves practicing phrenologists) presented phrenology and physiognomy as a sort of miracle cure for—or at least a dependable method of diagnosing—society's ailments. The emphases of these books usually fell on human deficiencies of some sort (criminal propensities, insanity, idiocy) and these deficiencies were often tied to ethnicity through a line of thinking filled with generalizations and clichés. In his discussion on the hereditary nature of mental characteristics, for example, Orson Fowler attributed to Jews an innate, immutable tendency toward "acquisitiveness":

One can hardly walk Chatham-street, New York, without being asked to purchase, or else taken by the arm, and half-coaxed, forced into one of their shops to make a purchase. . . . Look again at their pawnbrokers' frauds, their usury, and those innumerable devices to which they resort for extraordinary purposes, and say whether they have not inherited Abraham's love of riches, together with Jacob's craft, and Rachel's and Rebekah's deception. And what still confirms our argument, that their extraordinary acquisitiveness has been transmitted from Abraham's father throughout all their generations to the present day, is, that they now hoard the same KINDS of property laid up by Abraham, Isaac, and Jacob. . . . [139]

As it lent itself to this way of elaborating ethnic difference as a matter of "character" difference (difference which, it implied, was the legacy of the separate "origins" or "blood-lines" of separate races), phrenology became extremely useful to proslavery ethnologists such as Josiah Nott, whose investment in the notion of polygenesis, the proslavery answer to the monogenetic model which espoused the shared origin and kinship of all races, caused him to gravitate toward phrenological and physiological theories of essential difference. Turning his attention elsewhere, for instance, Fowler sketches a similarly deterministic view of the "African personality." The African race, Fowler asserts, is endowed with a weak sense of "causality," or logic, but Africans are "proverbially polite" and "excellent as waiters." "And this African mentality," Fowler reminds his audience, "will undoubtedly descend from sire to son, throughout all their generations, till this race, like the Indian, yields its place to those naturally superior" (135).

[The African race] has a form of head peculiar to itself, as much as the Indian. It is long and narrow, while that of the copper-colored race is the reverse. It is also high at the crown, and so is that of mulattoes, in proportion to their African origin. . . . And this form of head appertains to colored infants equally with adults, which shows it to be innate, not educational. Their predominant individual organs are Self-Esteem, Secretiveness, Tune, Language, Individuality, and Philoprogenitiveness, with less Combativeness and Destructiveness. Hence their proverbial politeness, urbanity, excellence as waiters, love of ornament, swelling and swaggering propensities, timidity, eye-service, fondness for and patience with children . . . garrulity, and sometimes eloquence, and superior musical passions and talents. . . . Their perceptives are usually strong, Causality less,[4] and temperament neither fine nor active. In short, they have a distinct mental character of their own, which is more or less apparent in mulattos, in proportion to the amount of colored blood flowing in their veins, and which is as much INNATE as are their physical peculiarities.[5]

Such analogies between enslaved Africans and vanquished Native Americans were common enough in phrenological books. Fowler's partner Samuel Wells, for instance, urges his readers to

see what a contrast between the Caucasian skull and those of the North American Indian and the negro here represented! One of the most distinctive features of the aboriginal American skull is roundness. This quality is very manifest in every aspect, but still more so in the vertical and back views than in the one here presented [through lithographic figures]. Great breadth immediately above the ears and in the region of Cautiousness and Secretiveness, and a lofty coronal region, are also prominent characteristics. The forehead is broad and very prominent at the lower part, but retreating, and not very high. The back-head in the region of the affections is, in general, only moderately developed, but there is almost always a large and sharply defined occipital protuberance [Amativeness, the organ of sexual excitement].

The negro cranium is long and narrow. Compared with that of the Caucasian, the difference is seen to be striking. In the side view of the former the frontal region is less capacious than in the latter, the forehead more retreating, and the occiput comparatively more full. The facial angle is about 70°, the jaws being large and projecting, and forming what is called the prognathous type. Here the animal feelings dominate over both the intellect and the moral sentiments.[6]

It is no coincidence that American phrenologists were also preoccupied with the heads of criminals, since both incarcerated whites and enslaved blacks represented a class of Americans whose imprisonment seemed to require some sort of "scientific" justification and/or explanation. That is, both the criminal and the slave were treated by phrenology as genetic "types" whose natural dispositions were at odds with the values of an upwardly mobile, civil society; in Eliza Farnham's "Appendix" to Marmaduke Sampson's 1846 *Rationale of Crime*, for example, "B. F.," a white inmate of a Long Island facility, is "charted" as temperamentally unfit for life outside of a prison:

[B. F.] is partially idiotic, and the very imperfect development of the superior portion of the brain, with the small size of the whole, clearly indicates the character of his mental capacities. . . . B. F. is vicious, cruel, and apparently incapable of any elevated or humane sentiments.[7]

This tendency to delineate criminality as something not nearly as learned as grafted onto the human mind at birth was an extenuation of the physiognomist's argument that certain "temperaments" were naturally disposed to physical labor, while others were best suited for more privileged mental pursuits such as legislating or philosophizing. Just as race and class became entangled (even if ostensibly treated separately) within the phrenological world, so was gender configured as a determining factor in the development of the individual's personality. As one contemporary scholar points out, the female skull was often charted in terms that resembled the phrenological description of the skulls of the "lower races."

Women's low brain weights and deficient brain structures were analogous to those of the lower races . . . [women] shared with Negroes a narrow, childlike, and delicate skull, so different from the more robust and rounded heads characteristic of males of "superior" races. Similarly, women of higher races tended to have slightly protruding jaws, analogous to, if not as exaggerated as, the apelike jutting jaws of lower races. . . . In short, lower races represented the "female" type of the human species, and females the "lower race" of gender.[8]

Even as phrenology evolved into a technique of justifying various forms of subordination as reasonable social responses to unalterable biological facts, the field also came to stress another side of the practical application of its principles. If the growing body of phrenological "knowledge" allowed practitioners to recognize the inner gifts and depravities of any given individual—if, in other words, phrenology was able to make "visible" what had always been "invisible" about any human subject—then it seemed prudent (even necessary) for phrenologists to disseminate as much information as possible to the layperson, who could then use the principles of science to avoid entering into marital union with a flawed partner—to avoid, in other words, producing morally or intellectually deficient offspring. As Orson Fowler urged in 1848:

> We investigate and apply [scientific] principles to the improvement of stock, yet its far higher application to the improvement of humanity is almost wholly neglected. But has not the time fully come for collecting and disseminating that knowledge on this vitally important subject, which shall enable parents to bestow on offspring personal beauty, physical stamina, muscular strength, and, above all, high intellectual and moral endowments?[9]

So while phrenology had begun as a theoretical "science" in the 1820s, it had blossomed into an activist project by the 1870s. With the publication of books such as *The Parent's Guide* (Hester Pendelton, 1871), phrenology became a source of personal guidance for its followers; even isolated sections from Fowler's earlier work prefigured this role for phrenology, urging prospective couples and parents to "anxiously inquire,"

> "What qualities, mental and physical, in a companion, united with mine, will endow my prospective offspring with good bodies, strong minds, and exalted morals? My physiological and phrenological developments being such as they are, what qualities, in a companion, will prevent our offspring from being diseased and vicious, on the one hand, and, on the other, impart to them the most favorable physical, intellectual, and moral constitution?" Momentous, yet difficult, questions these; because, here as elsewhere, "what is one's meat is another's poison." Those who, united with given individuals, would parent superior offspring, if married to others, would, of necessity, produce a sickly, or precocious, or stupid, or animal issue.[10]

Henceforward, phrenology's coordinates became firmly grounded in what we might term "family values" for the late 1800s. What was now at stake in the dissemination of phrenological theory was not only the happiness, health, and stability of the family unit, but more importantly the stability of society itself and civilization's potential to evolve to something greater, increasingly refined, more pedigreed. The phrenological project became an urgent one, for if the essential differences between human beings of disparate races were in fact available for recognition (if only one knew how to correctly discern the corporeal signifiers, as it were, of these differences), then the racial body needed to be plotted carefully in the hopes that the "data" yielded by such examination could be used by prospective husbands and wives worldwide. "What is one's meat is another's poison," Fowler had written. In its simplest terms, phrenology was now happily in the service of the notion of racial purity.

There was another dimension to the battle phrenology now waged. For all phrenologists could do to educate its followers on the evils of "cross-breeding" or "miscegenation," interracial sex was by this time a two-hundred-year-old fact in America. The mulatto presented a special problem for the proponent of polygenic models of sexual reproduction: if there were people among the Caucasian population who appeared Caucasian, "acted" Caucasian, even had apparently "Caucasian" parents, but were in fact "not" Caucasian, how could the ethnologically conscientious prospective parent avoid committing miscegenation inadvertently? Phrenologists and physiognomists fervently turned their attention to mulattos, looking for some physical marker that could signify true "non-Caucasian" status, some defining feature that could be recognized by the rest of the Caucasian population.

> Another mark of African descent is this. All pure-blooded Caucasians have a division or furrow in the gristle of the nose, plainly discerned by touch, while both Africans and all mulattos have no such separation. (25)

The idea of a system of clues written on the body, clues that could lead the informed observer to a dependable conclusion about any given individual's true racial background, resonated deeply with a public nearly consumed with the fear of becoming genetically—that is, racially—tainted. The polygenicist obsession with the mulatto threat to racial purity was enacted much later in Kate Chopin's "Désirée's Baby," in which the wife of a southern plantation owner finds herself "reading" the physiognomy of her newborn son, discovering, to her horror, that her child bears a more distinct resemblance to the African slaves who surround him than to the Caucasians who are his parents. Unable to cope with her conclusion, that she herself is the carrier of "colored blood" and is therefore unable to provide her husband with a fit, "pure," Caucasian heir, Désirée drowns herself and her baby. Chopin's story thus focuses on the tragic power of polygenetic thought to turn inward on itself, causing the "Caucasian" individual to embark on a process of self-scrutinization and, eventually, self-loathing and self-destruction.[11]

Though there is often a tendency to view the "major" writers of the American nineteenth century as figures whose thinking was much more of a revolt against the popular culture of the day than it was overtly informed by it, we can begin to understand phrenology's enormous currency within the social climate of the 1800s by observing that many of the writers now considered canonical by literary historians were in fact greatly impressed with the "science" of phrenology—and that, in fact, much of this impression was registered in their writing. When Walt Whitman wrote, in "By Blue Ontario's Shore,"

Who are you indeed who would talk or sing to America?
Have you studied out the land, its idioms and men?
Have you learn'd the physiognomy, phrenology . . . of
the land?

he was speaking as a true believer in phrenology who, in 1849, reported to Orson Fowler's New York examination studio to have his phrenological chart drawn.[12] To many antebellum writers, like Whitman, phrenology was no "pseudoscience" at all but rather one of the many marvelous human developments the nineteenth century had produced and refined. Though his own allusion to the field appears more cautious than Whitman's, Ralph Waldo Emerson acknowledged the pervasive influence of phrenological theory when he wrote, in the essay on "Fate" (1860): "The gross lines are visible to the dull; the cabman is phrenologist so far, he looks in your face to see if his shilling is sure." Edgar Allan Poe described the wonders of phrenology with almost unbridled enthusiasm; in the midst of a review of one 1836 phrenological text, he wrote that "phrenology is no longer to be laughed at. . . . It has assumed the majesty of a science; and, as a science, ranks among the most important which can engage the attention of thinking human beings."[13]

Perhaps an even greater testament to the "science's" appeal, however, is that its overtly racist agenda did not prevent it from being embraced by abolitionist writers. Harriet Beecher Stowe, for instance, whose *Uncle Tom's Cabin* was both the most popular book of the century and one of the most stridently abolitionist texts of the antebellum period, ranks right alongside of Whitman and Poe in terms of the "phrenological accuracy" of her writing. *Uncle Tom's Cabin* contains several examples of what we might call "phrenological types," the most clear example of which emerges in the novel's description of the sadistic Simon Legree, whom Stowe introduces with conspicuous attentiveness to the contours of his head, which she describes as "round" and shaped like a "bullet" with large eye sockets and an equally "large, coarse mouth" (411). As late as 1891, an abnormally round head was thought to be an indicator of murderous tendencies,[14] and exaggerated or extended Malar bones (those cradling the eye socket) indicated a forcefulness of character;[15] such a combination of tendencies describes Legree's personality well, and so we see that Stowe's rendition of Legree's character is carried out with sound phrenological insight. Equally telling is Legree's body type. Stout and broad, Legree's body would denote, to a physiognomist, a "bilious" temperament, or a personality disposed to "warlike inclinations.[16] Usually "arrogant and domineering," the bilious character often shows "sanguine" or aggressively ambitious traits as well, these traits being marked by a lightness of skin and hair, as well as gray or light blue eyes. All of these traits mark Simon Legree, and at the same time, would have provided the nineteenth-century reader with an index to his dangerous character.

Fascinatingly, the reader of *Uncle Tom's Cabin* is introduced to Legree at the most public and official examination of bodies and heads that mid-nineteenth-century America had to offer: the slave auction. The irony here is profound and contingent on the fact that while slave-purchasers such as Legree attend the auction in order examine fully the black bodies they will then purchase, the reader of *Uncle Tom's Cabin* is invited to examine the body of Legree with equal deliberation, confident that this inspection will yield insight into the man's demonic nature.

Uncle Tom's Cabin is in fact filled with such phrenological types as Legree, as if a detailed knowledge of any particular character's skull should forewarn readers of that character's inner qualities. The character who represents Legree's moral opposite, the virtuous Eva, is described in terms that might have come out of George Combe's *Essays on Phrenology*: "The shape of her head . . . [was] peculiarly noble," Stowe writes, and of Miss Ophelia, Eva's abolitionist second cousin, we are told that "Her face was thin, and rather sharp in its outlines; the lips compressed, like those of a person who is in the habit of making up her mind definitely on all subjects. . . ." John Caspar Lavater was one early physiognomist who would have approved of Stowe's rendition of Ophelia; as he wrote in his *Essays*: "Firm lips, firm character; weak lips . . . weak and wavering character."[17]

What follows is a selection from Orson Fowler's 1848 *Hereditary Descent*, one of the several phrenological handbooks Orson and Lorenz Fowler produced and distributed for the general public. In order to relay as closely as possible the manner in which phrenological theory was disseminated and consumed by its American proponents and readers, the original format of Fowler's text has been reproduced here, along with the text's lithographic figures.

Hereditary Descent
by O. S. Fowler

The Laws which Entail the Physiology, Also Transmit the Mentality

That progeny inherit the PHYSICAL conditions of parentage is thus conclusively demonstrated. To the ACCUMULATIVE force of our proof, attention is once more invited. Proving that likeness and shape are transmitted, helps to prove that statue and shape are also entailed; and these positions once established, confirm every preceding, every succeeding position, and prove that marks, longevity, beauty, and all other physical peculiarities are descended from parents to offspring.

Establishing this great principle of hereditary entailment, goes far toward proving that diseases in like manner come under this general law of entailment, and, besides rendering a far lower order and amount of evidence sufficient to establish this point, greatly increases the force of such proof. So, also, proving that consumption or scrofula is inherited, not only confirms every preceding hereditary law, but also redoubles the proof that every other disease is equally handed down from generation to generation. Nor would strictly logical argumentation require that more than one physical quality or disease be proved to be transmitted; because analogy then shows that all others are governed by the same hereditary laws which govern these—that since one is entailed, all are therefore equally so.

Yet we have done more. Every position, thus far taken, has been demonstrated by an order and array of FACTS abundantly sufficient, considered independently, to prove, beyond all reasonable evasion or doubt, each one IN AND OF ITSELF. How overwhelming the evidence, how absolutely impregnable, then, this inductive reasoning considered COLLECTIVELY?

Nor does it end with showing that physiology is transmitted. It applies with increased momentum to the entailment of the mentality, to which our subject now brings us. Indeed, the preceding has been penned mainly in reference to the succeeding. Though the facts of the entailment of all the physical conditions, and especially all the diseases, are of vast moment in and of themselves, and intrinsically entitled to the practical consideration of every matrimonial candidate, yet they are mainly important by way of proving the far more momentous law, that the MENTAL faculties and characteristics are also transmitted. They have been proved thus conclusively, mainly as laying a solid foundation in the nature of man upon which to build our superstructure, that MIND as well as body is transmitted. And we have been thus minute and particular in noting these facts which are "known and read of all men," because they furnish such conclusive proof that the WHOLE man is governed by the same laws of entailment. The descent of physical qualities has been proved thus incontestably to be an ordinance of nature chiefly as BASE LINES AND ANGLES to be applied to the transmissibility of the MENTAL powers and characteristics. What relation, then, does the hereditary entailment of the physiology bear to that of the mentality?

Man is an INTELLECTUAL and MORAL no less than a physical being. Nor are these two departments of his nature strangers to each other; but are inter-related in the most perfectly reciprocal manner conceivable. Indeed, the physical was created to serve the mental. The MIND constitutes the man—the great object of human creation—while flesh and blood are only its habitation and servant. Since, therefore, the physiology is transmitted, and since the reciprocity between it and the mentality is PERFECT—since as is either so is also the other, and since those laws which govern either govern both, the descent from parents to offspring of the body, and all its multifarious conditions, necessarily implies and conclusively proves that of the mind and all its powers and characteristics.

Character as Shape, and Both Equally Transmissible

Moreover, CHARACTER IS AS SHAPE. Given forms of body always accompany certain instincts and mental predilections. Thus, the tiger has a fixed physiognomy of form of body, and also corresponding mental characteristics; and the leopard, lynx, panther, tiger-cat, catamount, and cat, partake of the general shape of the tiger, and all the animals which thus resemble the tiger type of configuration—the entire feline genus and species—also resemble his type of

MENTALITY. And the more nearly or remotely in either, proportionally closely or distantly in the other. Indeed, the cereal, pomological, and entire vegetable kingdom conform to this law. All fish, all ruminating animals resemble all others of their species, and as far as animals approximate toward man in shape do they resemble him in character; of which the monkey, baboon, and ourang-outang tribes furnish pertinent proofs and examples. Do not African, Indian, and Circassian character always accompany their respective physical conformations? Indeed, are not all who are human in shape, also human in mentality, and all which is animal or vegetable in conformation, equally so in character?

Besides, can we not predicate character from shape? Are not idiocy and superior talents, sincerity and cunning, goodness and selfishness, nobleness and meanness, and most other mental characteristics, indicated in the form, features, and physiognomical expressions of their respective possessors? And what is this—what all kindred indices of character*—but fixed coincidences between various shapes and their corresponding states of mind? That shape is as structure, and structure is as character, and therefore shape as character, is attested by universal observation throughout all departments of nature.

That certain forms of the HEAD always accompany corresponding powers and peculiarities of the mind, constitutes and is established by the science of PHRENOLOGY. In its appropriate place the author has PROVED this doctrine to be founded in the nature of things—to embody those laws in harmony with which God created all animated nature. Assuming its truth—and this work is founded in such assumption—by proving that family likenesses are transmitted, and of course the forms of the FOREHEAD as well as the face, we virtually proved that the FOREHEADS of parents, as well as of the other parts of their faces, are transmitted to their descendants, and, by parity of reasoning, that the various forms of parental heads, as a whole, and of course the relative size of their phrenological faculties, are equally transmitted. And since given forms of the forehead and head are both transmitted, and also accompany certain mental characteristics, of course the latter are transmitted by those same laws which entail the former. In short, the fact already conclusively established, that family likenesses and forms are transmitted, taken in connection with the truth of Phrenology, necessarily presupposes and proves that the relative size of those various intellectual organs which give the forehead its form, descend from parents to children, and of course those intellectual powers and predilections which Phrenology shows to accompany these forms. And since the relative size of a PART of the phrenological organs, and, of course, relative energy of some of the mental faculties, is thus transmitted, of course ALL the phrenological organs and faculties, in all their various degrees of development, are equally transmitted. Since one is hereditary, of course all are. That same law which entails any part, equally, and for the same reason, hands down all. Indeed, those very laws, in all their respective applications, already shown to transmit the various physical conditions of parents to offspring, equally transmit their mental likeness, their intellectual capabilities, and their moral character.

•

Universality of All the Mental Faculties

But the converging principles, that since the mental depends upon the physiology, and since the latter is hereditary, therefore the former must be equally so, are by no means the main or even the strongest proof of the transmissibility of the mental powers and characteristics. Facts, the most extensive in range and varied in kind, prove the hereditary descent of the mental qualities to be fixed ordinance of nature. Thus, the entire human family have always evinced the same primary elements as now—the same propensities, moral sentiments, and intellectual capabilities; the same domestic affections, appetite for food, spirit of resistance, love of money, power and glory, and fear of danger; the same sentiments of justice, kindness, and religious devotion; the same primary faculties of observation, memory of persons, places, colors, and events, as well as reasoning and communicating disposition and capability. This, who questions? As far back as history, sacred or profane, furnishes any record of man, and his desires and pursuits, it shows that they have been from the beginning just what they are now. It shows that in spite of all those ever-diversified modes of government and education, opposite climate and circumstances, and the like, which have been perpetually modifying human character for so many ages, all races, nations, and individuals have alike bowed submissive at the shrine of beauty, been led willing captives by the all-conquering power of love, relished food and drink, defended rights and life, scrambled after property, loved honor and courted fame, fed and sheltered the benighted stranger, loved their children and friends, hated enemies, worshipped a Supreme Being of some sort, adapted ways and means to ends, and manifested every primitive mental faculty now possessed. In short, so synonymous is human nature, that whoever has learned, or can operate on it at one time or place, can read or move it in all others. And since it has thus far remained fundamentally the same, will it not continue so while the race exists? But how can this oneness be secured or accounted for except by hereditary influences? Without that inflexible adherence to its original constitution thus secured, different circumstances, climates, educations, etc., would soon warp it, as they have language, so that various masses and nations would differ GENERICALLY from each other, instead of, as now, being substantially alike.

The Mental Peculiarities of the Indian Race Transmitted

Though this hereditary argument, drawn from the unity of human nature, is perfectly conclusive, yet the characteristics of the five races both furnish additional illustrations, and render assurance doubly sure. Though man's primitive mental faculties are alike, yet different races, masses, nations, and individuals, possess in them different DEGREES OF DEVELOPMENT, and hence, while all mankind are alike in all that is fundamental, yet they differ in details of character and capability.

Thus, the Indian is always cunning, revengeful, wild, and free. Enslave an

Indian! Nothing can subdue him. Who ever saw his proud spirit subdued? Torture him with your utmost ingenuity, and he laughs in your face, and taunts and defies you—his proud spirit absolutely indomitable. If it had been possible to subdue him, would not Caucasian cupidity long ago have pursued him throughout his native forests, as it chases the South American horse, and even now been scourging him with the lash of slavery? You may kill his body, but his lofty soul never surrenders. This love of liberty is INNATE, as is also his gratitude for favors and revenge for wrongs. He is always eloquent, but never forgiving. By nature he loves the chase, but hates to work, observes the stars and predicts the weather, but dislikes books, and, though beaten "in a mortar with a pestle," yet he is an Indian still—so by BIRTH and mental constitution, as well as physical, and unalterable by any concatenation of circumstances.

That these characteristics are innate rather than educational, is proved by his phrenology—always peculiar to himself. The developments of the infant papoose—and the author speaks from the personal inspection of hundreds from among various tribes—are essentially Indian, and partake of the same shortness from occiput to forehead, low and short coronal region, and breadth in the region of propensity, especially Destructiveness and Secretiveness, as seen in the accompanying drawings of the Indian chiefs Big Thunder and Meche-kele-a-tah.

An Indian is one at birth, and by NATURE, before rendered so by education, because papooses are as much Indian in character before education has had time to fully mould their characters as they ever are, whereas if this difference were the result of their education, their phrenology would resemble that of Caucasian infants, and become more and more Indian the longer they live. Their having Indian heads in infancy proves that they are Indian by nature, and not by training.

•

Mental Characteristics of the African Race

This race has a form of head peculiar to itself, as much the Indian. It is long and narrow, while that of the copper-colored race is the reverse. It is also high at the crown, and so is that of mulattoes, in proportion to their African origin. The accompanying engraving of Hewlitt, a mulatto actor, will serve as a good general profile of the African head.

And this form of head appertains to colored infants equally with adults, which show it to be innate, not educational. Their predominate individual organs are Self-Esteem, Approbativeness, Cautiousness, Secretiveness, Tune, Language, Individuality, and Philoprogenitiveness, with less Combativeness and Destructiveness. Hence their proverbial politeness, urbanity, excellence as waiters, love of ornament, swelling and swaggering propensities, timidity, eye-service, fondness for and patience with children, and consequent excellence as nurses, garrulity, and sometimes eloquence, and superior musical passion and talents. And their STYLE of music is so peculiar, that a practiced ear can generally select their songs from those of all other nations. The structure of their sentences, and their modes of expression, are also peculiar to themselves. Their perceptives are usually strong, Causality less[†], and temperament neither fine nor active. In short, they have a distinct mental character of their own, which is more or less apparent in mulattoes, in proportion to the amount of colored blood flowing in their veins, and which is as much INNATE as are their physical peculiarities. And this African mentality will undoubtedly descend from sire to son, throughout all their generations, till this race, like the Indian, yields its place to those naturally superior.

Source Note: O. S. Fowler, *Hereditary Descent: Its Laws and Facts Applied to Human Improvement* (New York, 1848; New York, Garland, 1984), pp. 125–34.

* See a series of articles on this most interesting subject, entitled "Signs of Character," in the *American Phrenological Journal*, vols. VII., VIII., and IX., by the author, who hopes ultimately to prepare a work in elucidation of this law of things, and show what mental characteristics accompany given forms of body and face. [Fowler's note]

[†] This organ, and also the intellectual organs in general, are somewhat larger, comparatively, in African children than in adults; so that their intellectual inferiority is owing, in part, to want of culture. Yet this difference is not sufficient to modify our hereditary argument, but it shows that we owe a great moral duty to this down-trodden race. The native African head is also superior to those born in this country, especially in the south, so that our republican institutions, every way calculated to improve humanity, actually tend to depreciate one important portion of it. The heads of heathen Africa superior to those of Christian and republican America! [Fowler's note]

1. Samuel R. Wells, *How to Read Character* (New York: Fowler & Wells, 1899), p. vi.

2. John Caspar Lavater, preface to *Essays on Physiognomy Designed to Promote the Knowledge and the Love of Mankind*, vol. 1, trans. Henry Hunter (London: J. Murray, 1792).

3. Wells, *Character* (unnumbered page at the end of the book).

4. [Fowler's note:] "This organ, and also the intellectual organs in general, are somewhat larger, comparatively, in African children than in adults; so that their intellectual inferiority is owing in part, to want of culture."

5. Orson Fowler, *Hereditary Descent* (1848; reprint, New York: Garland, 1984), pp. 134–35.

6. Wells, *Character*, p. viii.

7. Marmaduke Sampson, *Rationale of Crime and Its Appropriate Treatment, Being a Treatise on Criminal Jurisprudence Considered in Relation to Cerebral Organization* (New York: Appleton, 1846), p. 174. It is interesting to note that phrenologically inclined thinkers such as Farnham and Sampson viewed criminality as a form of "moral insanity," beyond the control of the criminals themselves, and thus attempted to translate phrenological theory into an argument against the death penalty.

8. Nancy Stepan, "Race and Gender: The Role of Analogy in Science," in *The Anatomy of Racism*, ed. David Theo Goldberg (Minneapolis: University of Minnesota Press, 1990), pp. 39–40.

9. Fowler, *Hereditary Decent*, p. 5.

10. Ibid., p. 261.

11. See Kate Chopin, *The Complete Works of Kate Chopin*, ed. Per Seyersted, 2 vols. (Baton Rouge: Louisiana State University Press, 1982), vol. 1, pp. 241–45.

12. Also see Madeleine Stern, *Heads and Headlines: The Phrenological Fowlers* (Norman: University of Oklahoma Press, 1971), pp. 99–123. For more on Whitman's intimate relationship with phrenology—and a close reading of the ways in which the field helped to shape and to qualify Whitman's poetry—see David Reynolds, *Beneath the American Renaissance* (Cambridge, MA, and London: Harvard University Press, 1989), pp. 325–28. Reynolds notes, for instance, that "So close was [Whitman] in spirit to the Fowlers . . . that they distributed the first edition of *Leaves of Grass* and published the second edition" (p. 326).

13. See Reynolds, *Beneath the American Renaissance*, pp. 244–46, for a "phrenological" reading of Poe's habits of character description.

14. Nelson Sizer and H. S. Drayton, *Heads and Faces and How to Study Them* (New York: Fowler & Wells, 1891), p. 11.

15. Lavater, *Essays*, pp. 392–93.

16. Sizer and Drayton, *Heads and Faces*, p. 23.

17. Lavater, *Essays*, p. 394.

Ethnology
by James Russell Lowell

[*See the headnote for James Russell Lowell in chapter 6.*]

We have just seen the hopes of the friends of liberalism and progress in central Europe thwarted in a great measure by foolish disputes about races and nationalities. . . .

Almost all races, in proportion as they have become powerful and distinguished, have endeavored to justify their preeminence, as it were, by attributing to themselves a divine or at least a noble origin. Nations, like individuals, when they have risen in the social scale, go immediately to the herald's office for a coat of arms and a pedigree. Had the Pilgrims landed at Plymouth a thousand years earlier, their exodus from the land of bondage and their sojourn in the Promised Land would have been forerun and accompanied by an abundance of signs and wonders. As it were, we are obliged to content ourselves with vague assertions of our Anglo-Saxon descent, the truth being that only the settlers of New England, and of those only a very few, can lay any probable claim to such an origin.

We have no especial interest in these assertions of national nobility, except in as far as they have been the cause or the apology of national oppressions. Men are very willing to excuse any unnatural feature in their social system by tracing it up to some inscrutable divine arrangement. Whatever revolts from the natural religion of the human heart they shore up with the props of their artificial and traditional religion. . . .

When the descent of the negro races from the Scriptural Ham had been pretty clearly disproved, and the application of the curse entailed upon his progeny transferred to another race, pro-slavery was necessarily reduced to another line of defense. A divine origin was attributed to slavery by tracing its natural cause to an innate inferiority, both mental and physical, of the negro family of man. It is here that the researches of ethnologists become particularly interesting to Abolitionists, and furnish them with arguments more generally appreciable by the mass of mankind than those appealing exclusively to the principles of abstract justice and right. . . .

Ethnology, or the science of races, is of very recent origin, and, dependent as it necessarily must be on glottology (the science of languages), which is also in its infancy, it must generally make its appeals to inferences and probabilities rather than to actual demonstration. Its conclusions may in fact be assumed as incapable of experimental proof since periods of time quite beyond our ordinary conceptions of duration, as derived from human history, might be required to produce any foretold result. And yet a sufficient number of examples may be found in various kinds, in localities widely separated, and wholly independent of each other, where certain causes have produced certain effects, to establish a firm basis for reasonable induction.

The most comprehensive work on the science of races is that of Dr. Prichard, "The Natural History of Man."[1] It is necessarily somewhat deficient in arrangement, because ethnology is as yet less an exact system than an agglomeration of detached facts, all, however, tending to one result, so that it is not difficult for the reader to generalize for himself. . . .

The instances hitherto collected by ethnological students seem to put beyond question the fact that difference of physical structure, and of the color of the skin, may all be referred to climatic causes, and do not in the least countenance the theory of essential diversity of race. The examples by which this proposition is supported are very numerous, are found among all races and in all quarters of the globe, and are to our mind perfectly convincing.

These natural causes are to be found in difference of climate, habits, and food. Of the influence of climate a remarkable example is afforded by the Berbers inhabiting a mountainous region of Africa. Their language, their habits, their history, and their traditions all prove them to be of one unmixed descent, and yet they differ in complexion and some other characteristics in proportion as the particular tribes occupy a position farther from the plain, ranging from hair, fair complexion and blue eyes, to black skins and wooly hair.

We have seen the influence of climate upon complexion and the color and texture of the hair. Changes equally remarkable in the shape of the skull, in the length and general characteristics of the limbs, and in the development and tissue of the muscular system are brought about by the habits and diet of a race, dependent upon the climate or some other circumstances of local condition. . . .

The most important general conclusion to be drawn from the study of ethnology is that the difference in type exhibited by different races of men is not greater than may be found existing in individuals of the same race subjected for a long period of time to the action of climatic or other physical causes. We may say further that the conclusion to which many inquirers have been led is that the white skin, and not the black, is a divergence from the original type, effected either by climate or by the propagation of an accidental variety, such as we still find to be produced among races naturally black.

Source Note: James Russell Lowell, "Ethnology," *The National Anti-Slavery Standard*, February 1, 1849.

1. James Cowles Prichard, a British scientist, advocated the classification of races and the inferiority of the Negro to the white. He was author of *The Natural History of Man: Comprising Inquiries into the Modifying Influence of Physical and Moral Agencies on the Different Tribes of the Human Family* (3rd ed., London: H: Bailliere, 1848).

THEODORE PARKER (1810–1860) VS. JOHN S. ROCK (1825–1866) ON THE
ANGLO-SAXON AND THE AFRICAN
edited and introduced by Dean Grodzins

In March 1858, Boston abolitionists assembled to commemorate the death, nearly eighty years earlier, of a black patriot, Crispus Attucks, in the Boston Massacre. William C. Nell, author of *The Colored Patriots of the American Revolution*, had organized the memorial event. By celebrating black participation in the Revolution, he wanted to counter the claim of the Supreme Court, made a year earlier in the Dred Scott decision, that blacks had never been citizens of the United States. No doubt to Nell's surprise, this occasion honoring equal rights became the scene of an almost unique public exchange between a white abolitionist and a black one on the ethnological characteristics of African-Americans.[1]

The white abolitionist was Theodore Parker. A famous preacher and scholar, he was also among the most prominent and militant antislavery ministers.[2] He advocated the destruction of the Southern "slave power" by any means necessary, legal or illegal, peaceful or violent. He led resistance to the efforts of the federal government to capture fugitive slaves in Boston, and once harbored a famous fugitive, Ellen Craft, in his home. He championed equal legal rights for blacks, favoring, for example, the end to legal segregation in the Boston public schools (achieved in 1855). He welcomed blacks into his Boston church: the antislavery lecturer Charles Lenox Remond worshiped there, as did the prominent lawyer Lewis Hayden, and William C. Nell himself served for many years as the church sexton.[3] Yet Parker, despite his radical abolitionism, believed Americans of African descent, due to innate racial characteristics, were less capable of civilization and progress than "Anglo-Saxons." Blacks, he thought, would always hold an "ignoble" relation to whites, and in 1857 he privately predicted that even after twenty generations of freedom blacks would never rise above the level of waiter.[4]

Parker's views on race were strongly colored by contemporary ethnology, the supposedly scientific study of racial characteristics.[5] He became fascinated by the subject in the late 1840s, and references to it appear in almost all his major political and historical writings from the 1850s. He accepted the common ethnological concept, first proposed by the German naturalist Johann Friedrich Blumenbach, that there were five human "races": the "African" (black), the "American" (Native American), the "Malay" (Pacific Islander), the "Mongolian"

CAUTION!!

COLORED PEOPLE

OF BOSTON, ONE & ALL,

You are hereby respectfully CAUTIONED and advised, to avoid conversing with the

Watchmen and Police Officers of Boston,

For since the recent ORDER OF THE MAYOR & ALDERMEN, they are empowered to act as

KIDNAPPERS

AND

Slave Catchers,

And they have already been actually employed in KIDNAPPING, CATCHING, AND KEEPING SLAVES. Therefore, if you value your LIBERTY, and the *Welfare of the Fugitives* among you, *Shun* them in every possible manner, as so many *HOUNDS* on the track of the most unfortunate of your race.

Keep a Sharp Look Out for KIDNAPPERS, and have TOP EYE open.

APRIL 24, 1851.

THEODORE PARKER'S PLACARD

Placard written by Theodore Parker and printed and posted by the Vigilance Committee of Boston after the rendition of Thomas Sims to slavery in April, 1851.

"Caution!! Colored People of Boston," a broadside printed in 1854 by Theodore Parker, abolitionist, by permission of Georgia Barnhill, Mellon Curator of Graphic Arts, American Antiquarian Society, Worcester, Mass.

(East Asian), and the "Caucasian" (white). Parker followed ethnological convention by further dividing the Caucasian "race" into "families," such as "Shemetic" (Jewish), "Sclavonic" (Slavs), "Celtic" (Irish and French), and "Teutonic" (Germanic). The Teutonic family he split into "tribes," such as the "Scandinavian" and "Anglo-Saxon." Each division and subdivision of humanity, he believed, was marked by distinct physical, linguistic, and spiritual characteristics.

This idea, and some version of these classifications, gained wide acceptance in the mid-nineteenth century. Usually, they were combined with a belief that Africans were inferior to Caucasians, and sometimes with "polygenesis," the theory that Africans were a distinct *species* from Caucasians. The "American School" of ethnology (whose work is represented by the works of Samuel Morton, Josiah Nott, and George R. Gliddon) promoted both polygenesis and African inferiority. Yet not all ethnologists promoted both or either. The Swedenborgian Alexander Kinmont, who agreed that Africans were a distinct species, argued that they were religiously superior to Caucasians and so would lead the world into the Christian millennium.[6] Again, Martin Delany, called the "father of black nationalism," thought Africans and Caucasians belonged to the same species, but insisted that Africans were a superior variety of human.[7] Parker, for his part, despite his belief in African inferiority, rejected polygenesis.

Most abolitionists seemed to have accepted that innate racial differences existed, but many also held blacks and whites to be, if not exactly equal, then at least *equivalent* in ability (i.e., that each was inferior in some respects but superior in others). For instance, white abolitionists generally accepted the idea that Africans were less aggressive yet more religious than Anglo-Saxons. This view served both to counter the proslavery argument that blacks, if freed from the "discipline" of bondage, would revert to brutal savagery, and to critique materialism and violence in contemporary white society. As such, the stereotype of the innately pious, gentle African won wide white acceptance. Only a few white abolitionists (among them Wendell Phillips and John Brown) rejected it outright; meanwhile, it was accepted even by such strong white opponents of the idea of African inferiority as Lydia Maria Child, Charles Sumner, Theodore Tilton, and Moncure Conway, and even by a few black thinkers, among them the minister Henry Highland Garnet.[8]

Abolitionists like these disagreed with Parker's ranking of Africans below Anglo-Saxons, but did not dissent when he pronounced Anglo-Saxons to be singularly aggressive and Africans singularly unwarlike. They found Parker's ideas palatable in part because he did not glorify Anglo-Saxon aggression. For example, in an 1854 speech, "Some Thoughts on the Progress of America," excerpted below, he dwells on the Anglo-Saxon tendency to "exterminate" other peoples. Yet Parker clearly indicates that, in his opinion, Anglo-Saxons lead the march of modern civilization.

As for Africans, Parker saw their supposed lack of aggression as a failing. In a speech delivered in January 1858, "The Present Aspect of Slavery in America," also excerpted below, he tells the true story of a slave he calls "John" (his real name was Josiah Henson)[9] who refuses to kill his owners to free himself, even when he had them in his power. Parker criticizes John's restraint, which he says is typical of all Africans. Had they been more willing to use violence, Parker insists, they would never have been enslaved or kept in slavery; he contrasts John's scruples unfavorably with the martial bravery of white New England soldiers at the Battle of Bunker Hill (he could see the Bunker Hill monument from the Massachusetts State House, where he was speaking).

Several weeks after delivering this speech, when Parker went to address the Boston Massacre commemoration, his remarks on black aggression were challenged by Dr. John Rock. Rock, a physician and lawyer, is remembered as the first African-American to be admitted to practice law before the United States Supreme Court (1865); but he was also a popular lecturer on ethnology.[10] The speech excerpted below is the only one of his many ethnological addresses to survive. Rock here criticizes and satirizes Parker's racial outlook and ethnological terminology, especially as expressed in "The Present Aspect of Slavery in America." American slaves have not revolted, he argues (and here contemporary historians agree with him), only because the odds are overwhelmingly against them. He points out that Caucasians, despite their supposed aggressiveness, in fact are oppressed all over the world. Citing the example of the Haitian Revolution and of heroic slave escapes, Rock dismisses the idea that Africans are inherently unwilling to fight for freedom. He predicts (accurately) that thousands of black troops would fight in the next war. He concludes with a stirring call for black self-sufficiency and pride.

After Rock finished speaking, Parker responded, not angrily but almost apologetically. As the excerpt below indicates, he retracts none of his earlier statements about the docility of Africans, but he does suggest that *in future* they would take up arms against slavery. His statement, so far as it went, was sincere. Within a few days of making it, he had agreed to help finance the abolitionist militiaman John Brown's secret plan to organize an interracial army that would fight a guerrilla war against slavery in Virginia. This effort resulted more than a year later in Brown's famous "raid" on the federal arsenal at Harpers Ferry, Virginia, which helped precipitate the Civil War.

SUGGESTIONS FOR FURTHER READING

Grodzins, Dean, and Joel Myerson. "The Preaching Record of Theodore Parker." *Studies in the American Renaissance* (1994): 55–122.

Some Thoughts on the Progress of America, and the Influence of Her Diverse Institutions
by Theodore Parker

[Address prepared for Anti-Slavery Convention in Boston, May 31, 1854]

The Anglo-Saxon tribe is composite, and the mingling so recent, that we can still easily distinguish the main ingredients of the mixture. There are, first, the Saxons and Angles from North Germany; next, the Scandinavians from Denmark and Sweden; and, finally, the Normans, or Romanized Scandinavians, from France.

This tribe is now divided into two great political branches, namely, the Anglo-Saxon Briton, and the Anglo-Saxon American; but both are substantially the same people, though with different antecedents and surroundings. The same fundamental characteristics belong to the Briton and the American. . . .

I must say a word of the leading peculiarities of this tribe.

1. There is a strong Love of Individual Freedom. This belongs to the Anglo-Saxons in common with all the Teutonic family. But with them it seems eminently powerful. Circumstances have favored its development. They care much for freedom, little for equality.

2. Connected with this, is a Love of Law and Order, which continually shows itself on both sides of the ocean. Fast as we gain freedom, we secure it by law and constitution, trusting little to the caprice of magistrates.

3. Then there is a great Federative Power—a tendency to form combinations of persons, or of communities and States—special partnerships on a small scale for mercantile business; on a large scale, like the American Union, or the Hanse towns,[11] for the political business of a nation.

4. The Anglo-Saxons have eminent Practical Power to organize things into a mill, or men into a State, and then to administer the organization. This power is one which contributes greatly to both their commercial and political success. But this tribe is also most eminently material in its aims and means; it loves riches, works for riches, fights for riches. It is not warlike, as some other nations, who love war for its own sake, though a hard fighter when put to it.

5. We are the most Aggressive, Invasive, and Exclusive People on the earth. The history of the Anglo-Saxon, for the last three hundred years, has been one of continual aggression, invasion, and extermination.

I cannot now stop to dwell on these traits of our tribal anthropology, but must yet say a word touching this national exclusiveness and tendency to exterminate. . . .

In America, the Frenchman and the Spaniard came in contact with the red man . . . and . . . associated with him on equal terms. The pale-face and the red-skin hunted in company; they fished from the same canoe in the Bay of Fundy and Lake Superior; they lodged in the same tent, slept on the same bear-skin; nay, they knelt together before the same God, who was "no respecter of persons,"[12] and had made of one blood all nations of men! The white man married the Indian's daughter; the red man wooed and won the pale child of the Caucasian. . . . But the Anglo-Saxon disdains to mingle his proud blood in wedlock with the "inferior races of men."[13] He puts away the savage—black, yellow, red. . . . The Anglo-Saxon has carefully sought to exterminate the savages from his territory. . . .

Yet the Anglo-Saxons are not cruel; they are simply destructive. . . . The Spaniard put men to death with refinements of cruelty, luxuriating in destructiveness. The Anglo-Saxon simply shot down his foe, offered a reward for homicide, so much for a scalp, but tolerated no needless cruelty. If the problem is to destroy a race of men with the least expenditure of destructive force on one side, and least suffering on the other, the Anglo-Saxon, Briton, or American, is the fittest instrument to be found on the whole globe.

Source Note: The text is taken from Parker's *Additional Speeches, Addresses and Occasional Sermons* (Boston, 1855), 2:1–70; the excerpts are taken from pp. 3, 4, 6–8, 10–12. Parker was unable to deliver the speech he had prepared for the convention because the week the convention met, in May 1854, he was too busy trying to prevent the return to bondage of the fugitive slave and preacher Anthony Burns (see Albert Von Frank, *The Trials of Anthony Burns: Freedom and Slavery in Emerson's Boston* [Cambridge: Harvard University Press, 1998]).

The Present Aspect of Slavery in America
by Theodore Parker

[*Speech at the State House to the Massachusetts Anti-Slavery Convention, January 29, 1858*]

The African is the most docile and pliant of all the races of men; none has so little ferocity: vengeance, instantial with the Caucasian, is exceptional in his history. . . . In his barbarous, savage, or even wild state,[14] he is not much addicted to revenge; always prone to mercy. No race is so strong in the affectional instinct which attaches man to man by tender ties; none so easy, indolent, confiding, so little warlike. Hence is it that the white men have kidnapped the black, and made him their prey.

This piece of individual biography tells us the sad history of the African race. Not long since, a fugitive slave told me his adventures. I will call him John—it is not his name. He is an entire Negro—his grandfather was brought direct from the Congo coast to America. A stout man, thick-set, able-bodied, with great legs and mighty arms, he could take any man from this platform, and hurl him thrice his length. He was a slave—active, intelligent, and much confided in. He had a wife and children. One day his master, in a fit of rage, struck at him with a huge club, which broke both his arms; they were awkwardly set, and grew out deformed. The master promised to sell the man to himself for a large sum, and take the money by installments, a little at a time. But, when more than half of it was paid, he actually sold him to a trader, to be taken further South, and there disposed of. The appeals of the wife, the tears of the children, moved not the master whom justice had also failed to touch. As the boat which contained poor John shot by the point of land where he had lived, his wife stood upon the shore, and held her babies up for him to look upon for the last time. Descending the Mississippi, the captain of the boat had the river fever, lost his sight for the time, and John took the command. One night, far down the Mississippi, he found himself on board a boat with the three kidnappers[15] who had him in their power, and intended to sell him. They were asleep below—the captain still blind with the disease—he watchful on deck. "I crept down barefoot," said John. "There they lay in their bunks, all fast asleep. They had money and I none. I had done them no harm, but they had torn me from my wife, from my children, from my liberty. I stole up noiselessly, and came back again, the boat's ax in my hand. I lifted it up, and grit my teeth together, and was about to strike: and it came into my mind, 'No murderer hath eternal life.'[16] I put the ax back in its place, and was sold into slavery. What would you have done in such a case?" I told him that I thought I should have sent the kidnappers to their own place first, and then trusted that the act would be imputed to me for righteousness by an all-righteous God. . . .

John's story is also the story of Africa: The stroke of the ax would have settled the matter long ago. But the black man would not strike. One day, perhaps, he will do what yonder monument commends.

Source Note: Text taken from Parker's *Works*, vol. 14, *Saint Bernard and Other Papers* (Boston: Centennial Edition, 1912), pp. 271–316; the excerpts are taken from pp. 273–75.

Speech to the Boston Massacre Commemorative Festival
by John S. Rock

White Americans have taken great pains to try to prove that we are cowards. We are often insulted with the assertion, that if we had had the courage of the Indians or the white man, we would never have submitted to be slaves. I ask if Indians and white men have never been slaves? The white man tested the Indian's courage here when he had his organized armies, his battle grounds, his places of retreat, with everything to hope for and everything to lose. The position of the African slave has been very different. Seized a prisoner of war, unarmed, bound hand and foot, and conveyed to a distant country among what to him were worse than cannibals; brutally beaten, half-starved, closely watched by armed men, with no means of knowing their own strength or the strength of their enemies, with no weapons, and without a probability of success. But if the white man will take the trouble to fight the black man in Africa or in Hayti,[17] and fight him as fair as the black man will fight him there—if the black man does not come off the victor, I am deceived in his prowess. But take a man, armed or unarmed, from his home, his country, or his friends, and place him among the savages, and who is he that would not make good his retreat? "Discretion is the better part of valor,"[18] but for a man to resist where he knows it will destroy him, shows more fool-hardiness than courage. There have been many Anglo-Saxons and Anglo-Americans enslaved in Africa, but I have never heard that they successfully resisted any government. . . .

The courage of the Anglo-Saxon is best illustrated in his treatment of the negro. A score or two of them can pounce upon a poor negro, tie and beat him, and then call him a coward because he submits. Many of their most brilliant victories have been achieved in the same manner. . . . A little more than half a century ago, this race, in connection with their Celtic neighbors,[19] who have long been considered (by themselves, of course) as the bravest soldiers in the world, so far forget themselves as to attack a few cowardly, stupid negro slaves. . . . And what was the result? Why, sir, the negroes drove them out of the island like so many sheep, and they have never dared to show their faces, except hat in hand.[20]

Our true and tried friend, Rev. Theodore Parker, said in his speech at the State House, a few weeks since,[21] that "the stroke of the axe would have settled the question long ago, but the black man would not strike." Mr. Parker makes a very low estimate of the courage of his race, if he means that one, two or three millions of these ignorant and cowardly black slaves could, without means, have brought to knees five, ten, or twenty millions of intelligent brave white men, backed up by a rich oligarchy. But I know no one who is more familiar with the true character of the Anglo-Saxon race than Mr. Parker.[22] I will not dispute this point with him, but I will thank him or any one else to tell us how it could have been done. His remark calls to my mind the day which is to come, when one shall chase a thousand, and two put ten thousand to flight. But when he says the "the black man *would not* strike," I am prepared to say that he does us a great injustice. The black man is not a coward. The history of the bloody struggles for freedom in Hayti, in which the blacks whipped the French and the English, and gained their independence, in spite of the perfidy of that villainous First Consul,[23] will be a lasting refutation of the malicious aspersions of our enemies. . . .

The white man contradicts himself who says, that if he were in our situation, he would throw off the yoke. Thirty millions of white men of this proud Caucasian race are at this moment held as slaves, and bought and sold with horses and cattle.[24] The iron heel of oppression grinds the masses of all the European races to the dust. They suffer every kind of oppression, and no one dares to open his mouth to protest against it. Even in the Southern portion of this boasted land of liberty, no white man dares advocate so much of the Declaration of Independence as declares that "all men are created free and equal, and an inalienable right to life, liberty," &c.

White men have no room to taunt us with tamely submitting. If they were black men, they would work wonders; but, as white men, they can do nothing. "O Consistency, thou art a jewel!"

Now it would not be surprising if the brutal treatment which we have received for the past two centuries should have crushed our spirits. But this is not the case. Nothing but a superior force keeps us down. And when I see the slaves rising up by the hundreds annually, in the majesty of human nature, bidding defiance to every slave code and its penalties, making the issue Canada or death,[25] and that too while they are closely watched by paid men armed with pistols, clubs and bowie knives, with the army and navy of this great Model Republic arrayed against them, I am disposed to ask if the charge of cowardice does not come with an ill-grace.

But some men are so steeped in folly and imbecility; so lost to all feelings of their own littleness; so destitute of principle, and so regardless of humanity, that they dare attempt to destroy everything which exists in opposition to their interests or opinions which their comprehension's cannot grasp.

We ought not to come here simply to honor those brave men who shed their blood for freedom,[26] or to protest against the Dred Scott Decision,[27] but to take counsel of each other, and to enter into new vows of duty. Our fathers fought nobly for freedom, but they were not victorious. They fought for liberty, but they got slavery. The white man was benefited but the black man was injured. I do not envy the white American the little liberty which he enjoys. It is his right, and he ought to have it. I wish him success, though I do not think he deserves it. But 1 would have all men free. We have had much sad experience in this country and it would be strange indeed if we do not profit by some of the lessons which we have so dearly paid for. Sooner or later, the clashing of arms will be heard in this country, and the black man's services will be needed: 150,000 freeman capable of bearing arms, and not all cowards and fools, and three quarters of a million of slaves, wild with the enthusiasm caused by the dawn of the glorious opportunity of being able to strike a genuine blow for freedom, will be a power which white men will be "bound to respect." Will the blacks fight? Of course they will. . . .

The prejudice which some white men have, or affect to have, against my color gives me no pain. If any man does not fancy my color, that is his business, and I shall not meddle with it. I shall give myself no trouble because he lacks good taste. If he judges my intellectual capacity by my color, he certainly cannot expect much profundity, for it is only skin deep, and is really of no very great importance to anyone but myself. I will not deny that I admire the talents and noble characters of many white men. But I cannot say that I am particularly pleased with their physical appearance. If old mother nature had held out as well as she commenced, we should probably have had fewer varieties in the races. When I contrast the fine tough muscular system, the beautiful, rich color, the full broad features, and the gracefully frizzled hair of the negro, with the delicate physical organization, wan color, sharp features and lank hair of the Caucasian, I am inclined to believe that when the white man was created, nature was pretty much exhausted—but determined to keep up appearances, she pinched his features, and did the best she could under the circumstances.

I would have you understand, that I not only love my race, but am pleased with my color; and while many colored persons may feel degraded by being called negroes, and wish to be classed among other races more favored, I shall feel it my duty, my pleasure and my pride, to concentrate my feeble efforts in elevating to a fair position a race to which I am especially identified by feelings and blood.

My friends, we can never become elevated until we are true to ourselves. We can come here and make brilliant speeches, but our field of duty lies elsewhere. Let us go to work—each man in his place, determined to do what he can for himself and his race. . . . Whenever the colored man is elevated, it must be by his own exertions. Our [white] friends can do what many of them are nobly doing, assist us to remove the obstacles which prevent our elevation, and stimulate the worthy to persevere. The colored man who by dint of perseverance and industry, educates and elevates himself, prepares the way for others, gives character to the race, and hastens the day of general emancipation. While the negro who hangs around the corners of the streets, or lives in the grog-shops or by gambling, or who has no higher ambition than to serve, is by his vocation forging fetters for the slave, and is "to all intents and purposes a curse to his race. It is true, considering the circumstances under which we have been placed by our white neighbors, we have a right to ask them not only to cease to oppress us, but to give us encouragement which our talents and industry may merit. . . . When the avenues of wealth are opened to us, we will then become educated and wealthy . . . and black will be a very pretty color. It will make our jargon, wit—our words, oracles. . . . Then, and not till then, will the tongue of slander be silenced, and the lip of prejudice sealed. Then, and not till then, will we be able to enjoy true equality, which can exist only among peers."

Source Note: Text taken from the *Liberator*, March 12, 1858. Rock's speech is reprinted in Thomas R. Frazier, ed., *Afro-American History: Primary Sources* (New York: Harcourt, Brace and World, 1970), pp. 120–24.

Remarks to the Boston Massacre Commemorative Festival
by Theodore Parker

My friend Dr. Rock said a great many good things of the African race, of which he himself is so fair and fine a representative. I assent most heartily to almost all he said, and if I cannot agree with the strictures he was pleased to make on some remarks that fell from my lips the other day, I am only sorry. I was not speaking of the African's future—only of his past. I have said a hundred times, that his was the most pacific race of men on the face of the earth; the least revengeful, the most merciful, the slowest to strike, and readiest to forgive. I think it would be rather incompatible with that long list of virtues to say that he was likewise the most warlike, or equal in his warlike propensities, to the Caucasian, who would rather enslave twenty men, and kill twenty more, than be a slave himself. I spoke of the past, not of the future. I make no doubt he will fight; I do not care how soon he has the opportunity. Slavery will not be exterminated with one blow; it will take a great many blows, and I hope the black man will do his part.

I heartily sympathize with my friend in his admiration for the vigor, the force and the color of the black man. If I had been born black, I hope I should have had sense enough to have been proud of my color. I do not think the Almighty was a less perfect artificer when he made the black man, "the image of God in ebony," than when he made the white man, with the carnation and pink in his cheeks. "Every man to his taste." I was glad to hear my friend say he was proud of his color, as I am when I hear an Englishman say he is proud to be a Briton. I agree, therefore, most heartily with most of the things which Dr. Rock said, and if I cannot agree with all, perhaps he will think it is my misfortune; I am sure he will not think it is my fault. . . .

Source Note: Text taken from the *Liberator*, March 12, 1858.

1. For another account of this incident, see Paul Teed, "Racial Nationalism and its Challengers: Theodore Parker, John Rock, and the Anti-Slavery Movement," *Civil War History*, 41:2 (1995): 142–60.

2. For a sketch of Parker's life, with a bibliography of his writings, see Dean Grodzins, "Theodore Parker," in Wesley Mott, ed., *The Dictionary of Literary Biography: American Renaissance in New England* (Detroit: Bruccoli Clarke Layman/Gale Research, 2001).

3. This information I have gleaned from the records of Parker's church, the 28th Congregational Society of Boston. For a complete account of these records, see Dean Grodzins, "Theodore Parker and the 28th Congregational Society: The Reform Church and the Spirituality of Reformers in Boston," in Charles Capper and Conrad E. Wright, eds., *Transient and Permanent: The Transcendentalist Movement and its Contexts* (Boston: Massachusetts Historical Society; Distributed by Northeastern University Press, 1999), pp. 104–5.

4. Parker to Sarah Hunt, November 16, 1857, quoted in Octavius Brooks Frothingham, *Theodore Parker. A Biography* (Boston, 1874), p. 461. Note that Parker made his most derogatory assessment of black abilities and characteristics in his journal, notebooks, or (like here) in letters to white correspondents, rather than in his public writings.

5. The standard account of pre–Civil War ethnology remains William Stanton, *The Leopard's Spots: Scientific Attitudes towards Race in America, 1815–1859* (Chicago: University of Chicago Press, 1960).

6. George Fredrickson, *The Black Image in the White Mind: The Debate on Afro-American Character and Destiny, 1817–1914* (First printing, 1971; Middletown, CT: Wesleyan, 1987), pp. 103–5.

7. Mia Bey, *The White Image in the Black Mind: African-American Ideas about White People, 1830–1925* (New York: Oxford, 2000), pp. 63–66.

8. Fredrickson, *Black Image*, 107–9, 121, 126; Bey, *White Image*, pp. 52–54.

9. Henson relates this story with slight differences of detail in *The Life of Josiah Henson, formerly a Slave, now an Inhabitant of Canada, as narrated by Himself* (Boston, 1849).

10. Bey, *White Image*, pp. 56–58.

11. A mercantile league of northern German towns in the Middle Ages.

12. Bible, Acts 10:34: "God is no respecter of persons."

13. Note that Parker is not saying Anglo-Saxons do not "mingle their blood" with other "races," but only that they do not do so in *wedlock*.

14. In Parker's day, these were technical terms used to designate specific stages of human civilization. From "lowest" to "highest," these stages were: wild; savage; barbarous; half-civilized; civilized.

15. Parker, like other abolitionists, called "kidnappers" all who engaged in the slave trade or who tried to recapture fugitive slaves.

16. Bible, 1 John 3:15: "Whosoever hateth his brother is a murderer: and ye know that no murderer hath eternal life abiding in him."

17. Hayti (or Haiti), a black-controlled independent state in the Caribbean Sea.

18. Shakespeare *Henry IV*, Part 1, V, iv, 120: "The better part of valor is discretion."

19. Rock is here using ethnological language to refer to the French, classified as a "Celtic" people.

20. Rock is making reference to the Haitian Revolution, in which slaves revolted and took over the island of Haiti (or "Hayti") in the Caribbean. Haitian troops successfully

resisted attempts to take the island by English forces (1798–99) and French ("Celtic") ones (1802).

21. "The Present Aspect of Slavery in America" above.

22. Rock seems to be referring to Parker's depiction of Anglo-Saxon destructiveness, as in the "Some Thoughts on the Progress of America," above.

23. Rock is referring to Napoleon Bonaparte. In 1802, Bonaparte, First Consul of France (later Emperor), was widely believed to have brought about the death of Toussaint L'Ouverture, the captured leader of the Haitian Revolution, by having him starved him to death in a French prison.

24. Rock is apparently referring to serfdom in Russia.

25. Fugitive slaves had to leave the United States for Canada in order to escape federal and state slave catchers.

26. In the Boston Massacre and the American Revolution.

27. The Supreme Court ruled in the Dred Scott decision (1857) that Congress had no power to exclude slavery from the territories and that blacks were not and had never been citizens of the United States. The purpose behind the Boston Massacre Commemoration at which Rock was speaking was to demonstrate that blacks had fought in the American Revolution, that therefore they had been citizens, and thus that the Supreme Court was wrong.

JOSIAH NOTT AND THE AMERICAN SCHOOL OF ETHNOLOGY

Not only did the antebellum United States hotly debate the political institutions of the emerging republic; it also engaged in transatlantic discourse concerning the nature and origin of man. As this volume's introduction and the introduction to this chapter have shown, a distinctly American school of ethnology developed ways of justifying the continuation of slavery and the subordination of the African. "Race theory" was not uniquely American, as these introductory essays have already demonstrated; however, the American variant emphasized polygenesis, or the multiple origins of mankind, rather than monogenesis, the development of man from a single pair of parents, which was an argument widely used by the abolitionists to show the common brotherhood of all mankind. George Morton's *Crania Americana* (1839) correlated skull shape and size to intelligence and moral character; Josiah Nott and George R. Gliddon's *Types of Mankind; or, Ethnological Researches* (Philadelphia, 1854) also illustrated the inferiority of the African and the superiority of the Caucasian. These polygenic views are summarized in Morton's *Distinctive Characteristics of the Aboriginal Race of America* (Philadelphia, 1844), where we find:

In fine, our own conclusion, long ago deduced from a patient examination of facts thus briefly and inadequately stated, is, that the American Race is essentially separate and peculiar, whether we regard it in its physical, its moral, or its intellectual relations. To us there are no direct or obvious links between the people of the old world and the new; for, even admitting the seeming analogies to which we have alluded, these are so few in number and evidently so casual as not to invalidate the main position; and even should it be hereafter shown, that the arts, sciences, and religion of America can be traced to an exotic source, I maintain that the organic characters of the people themselves, through all their endless ramifications of tribes and nations, prove them to belong to one and the same race, and this race is distinct from all others. [Morton, *Distinctive Characteristics of the Aboriginal Race of America*, 35–36]

Morton and Nott were highly regarded scientists in antebellum America, and as outrageous as some of the positions that follow may seem to modern readers, they were based on common scientific assumptions of the 1840s. The famed biologist Louis Agassiz praised Morton's *Crania Americana* as a work of scientific excellence, and allegedly thought that Morton's collection of human skulls was worth a trip from Europe to the United States to study. Ultimately, race theory dominated antebellum scientific discourse right up until the time of the Civil War, when political and military events had already determined the course of slavery and its relationship to the Union. As the texts that follow show, even many abolitionists were race theorists and embraced the fundamental tenets of white superiority. Nott, Gliddon, and Morton were three of the most prominent American school race theorists, and the texts that follow from Nott and Gliddon were among the most popular of this type of literature in the years before the Civil War. It is significant that many of these race theory texts were published in Philadelphia, New York, and even Boston. The ideology on which many of the social and political justifications for the continuation of slavery were based was widely shared both north and south of the Mason-Dixon line.

JOSIAH CLARK NOTT (1804–1873)

One of the most influential and important American race theorists in antebellum America was Josiah Clark Nott, who has been variously described as a physician, ethnologist, educator, and "influential nineteenth-century racist whose writings provided much of the scientific justification for the establishment of strict racial segregation in the United States" (Simonelli, p. 476). Born on March 31, 1804, in Columbia, South Carolina, Nott belonged to a socially prominent and wealthy family of the antebellum South, whose sympathies were naturally inclined toward the proslavery arguments of Thornton Stringfellow and George Fitzhugh. He was descended from New Englanders on his father's side, including abolitionists, and his father, Abraham Nott, was a distinguished judge in South Carolina who served on the Board of Trustees of South Carolina College and who provided his son with the best possible education and social exposure. Nott was well educated, being a graduate of South Carolina College (now the University of South Carolina) and the College of Physicians and Surgeons at Columbia University in New York City, where he received his medical degree in 1827. He taught medicine at the University of Pennsylvania Medical College for several years, worked a few years in Europe, and returned to the American South to practice medicine in Mobile, Alabama. Nott's personal life was tragic, following his spectacular rise in the medical profession. Four of his eight children died in a yellow fever epidemic that ravaged Mobile in 1853, and "two of his remaining sons died in the service of the Confederacy, one at the Battle of Shiloh and the other at the Battle of Chickamauga. At the outbreak of the Civil War, Nott joined the Confederate army and served as a field surgeon throughout the conflict" (Simonelli, p. 476).

These blessings were not lost on Josiah Nott, who later became one of the antebellum South's most distinguished surgeons and medical lecturers. However significant his medical career as a practitioner and author of medical texts, his lasting legacy was as an ethnologist or race theorist. Not only were his contributions widely read and circulated, but whose fundamental belief in the natural inferiority of the African to the Caucasian became one of the most prominent justifications for the continuation of chattel slavery in the antebellum South.

> Although Nott was a productive and well-respected contributor to the medical literature of his day, including innovative work on yellow fever and surgical techniques, his most lasting impact on society in the United States was through his published works on ethnology, which helped lay the foundation for nineteenth-century American racism. Nott believed that humankind was divided, ever since the Creation, into several "fixed types," that these fixed types corresponded to what he identified as the five "races" of mankind, and that these five races could be distinguished by a clear and immutable hierarchy of physical, mental, and moral characteristics. In Nott's hierarchy, Caucasians occupied the highest position and Ethiopians the lowest. Nott concluded that Ethiopians, meaning Africans and African Americans, had little potential for roles in modern society beyond those of slaves and menial laborers. [Simonelli, p. 476]

Nott introduced his theories on immutable racial characteristics in a widely read book, *Connection between the Biblical and Physical History of Man* (1849), and his theories became fixed in the popular consciousness with the publication of *Types of Mankind; or, Ethnological Researches* (1854), which he wrote with a colleague, George R. Gliddon. This text is excerpted here.

Some of Nott's widely popular views include a belief in polygenesis, the argument that there were multiple creations of different types of the human species. This polygenic argument, which had been advanced in Europe before it reached America, was first articulated in the United States by Charles Caldwell in 1830 in *Thoughts on the Original Unity of the Human Race*. Caldwell argued that there were four distinct human species (Nott would embrace the German anthropologist Blumenbach's five race divisions), and that they were arranged by Nature in a hierarchical pattern: Caucasian, Mongolian, Indian, and African: "that the Indian and the African were inferiorly organized and endowed" (Horsman, p. 84). Nott was also strongly influenced by George Morton's book, *Crania Americana*, published in 1839, and by Richard Colfax's *Evidence against the Views of the Abolitionists, Consisting of Physical and Moral Proofs, of the Natural Inferiority of the Negroes* (1833). These two volumes, discussed in the introduction to *A House Divided*, not only were popular in academic circles but were also widely circulated in the general population. Josiah Nott's views and contributions to antebellum race theory had much in common with the development of phrenology, a contemporary "science" which posited a correlation between the physical characteristics of the human skull and the moral and intellectual qualities of the human mind and the character of the individual. (See Christopher Hanlon's essay on O. S. Fowler and Phrenology also in this chapter of *A House Divided*.) "History, wrote Nott, gave positive proof that there was no way to enlarge the brain of a race and expand its intellect through education. Caucasian heads had always been as they were in the nineteenth century—the head was ready formed, and 'when the spark is applied the intellect blazes forth.' Black heads and brains were still as they were in ancient Egypt—inferior in intellectual capacity. This condition could not be changed. The species, argued Nott, was irrevocably fixed in its inferiority. Similarly, the Indian, though 'untamable, carnivorous,' and unlike the 'mild and docile' Negro, was incapable of change. The Indian race 'must soon be extinct—even the pure blood Mexicans, who I have no question are a different race from the aboriginal savage, are going down in darkness to their long home'" (Horsman, p. 107). There are several recent studies of Josiah Nott, most notably Reginald Horsman's *Josiah Nott of Mobile: Southerner, Physician, and Racial Theorist*. The texts by Josiah Nott excerpted here include *Types of Mankind, or, Ethnological Researches* (1854); *Indigenous Races of the Earth, or, New Chapters of Ethnological Inquiry* (1857); and *The Negro Race: Its Ethnology and History, by the Author of Types of Mankind* (1857).

If southern slaveholders had needed a scientific justification for the continuation of chattel slavery in the plantation system, other than the economic and biblical arguments advanced much earlier, Josiah Nott provided that justification. "Most of his writing on ethnology attempted to prove that there was not one but many races, and that blacks were inherently inferior to whites. He believed passionately in the Southern cause, brought up his sons to die for the Confederacy, and thought that the future of republican democracy was as much tied up in the Southern ability to retain its institutions as scientific truth was tied up in proving that Genesis was not a true account of the origin of the human races. Nott was an impassioned racist who firmly believed in the integrity of what he was doing, and he both influenced and was influenced by some of the best minds of his time throughout the United States and Europe. To the end of his life, when all he had defended had collapsed, he still believed that he had devoted himself to the passionate pursuit of scientific truth" (Horsman, p. 3). Nott's publications were often done with the collaboration of George R. Gliddon, sometime consul general in Cairo, Egypt, who was a colleague and friend with whom he both cooperated and had intellectual and professional disagreements. Gliddon was a frequent lecturer on ethnology both in Europe and the United States. The two produced ethnological studies that not only reflected contemporary race theory, but which articulated a strong American argument for polygenesis, until their work was successfully challenged by Charles Darwin's *On the Origin of Species* (1859) and *The Descent of Man* (1871). The "American School" of ethnological research had long advanced the polygenic origins of mankind, and Darwin's theory of evolution challenged the fundamental principles of polygenesis by showing how all species of humans were evolved from lower forms of animal life.

SUGGESTIONS FOR FURTHER READING

Berlin, Ira. *Slaves without Masters: The Free Negro in the Antebellum South*. New York: Pantheon, 1975.

Caldwell, Charles. *Thoughts on the Original Unity of the Human Race*. New York, 1830.

Colfax, Richard. *Evidence against the Views of the Abolitionists, Consisting of Physical and Moral Proofs, of the Natural Inferiority of the Negroes*. New York, 1833.

Dew, Thomas R. *Review of the Debate in the Virginia Legislature of 1831 and 1832*. Richmond, VA, 1832.

Gould, Stephen Jay. *The Mismeasure of Man*. New York: Norton, 1981.

Horsman, Reginald. *Josiah Nott of Mobile: Southerner, Physician, and Racial Theorist*. Baton Rouge: Louisiana State University Press, 1987.

Morton, George. *Distinctive Characteristics of the Aboriginal Race of America*. Philadelphia, 1844.

Simonelli, F. "Josiah Nott." In *The Historical Encyclopedia of World Slavery*, ed. Junius Rodriguez (Santa Barbara: ABC-CLIO, 1997), pp. 476–77.

Types of Mankind; or, Ethnological Researches Based upon the Ancient Monuments, Paintings, Sculptures, and Crania of Races and upon Their Natural Geographical, Philological, and Biblical History
by Josiah Clark Nott and George Gliddon

General Remarks on Types of Mankind

TYPE. "Typical characters are those which belong only to the majority of natural bodies comprised in any group, or to those which occupy the centre of this group, and in some sort serve as the *type* of it, but presenting exceptions when it approaches its extremities, on account of the relations and natural affinities which do not admit well-defined limits between species."

In speaking of Mankind, we regard as *Types* those primitive or original forms which are independent of Climatic or other Physical influences. All men are more or less influenced by external causes, but these can never act with sufficient force to transform one type into another. . . .

GROUP.—Under this term we include all those proximate races, or species which resemble each other most closely in type, and whose geographical distribution belongs to certain zoological provinces; for example, the aboriginal *American*, the *Mongol*, the *Malay*, the *Negro*, the *Polynesian groups*, and so forth. . . .

It will be seen, by comparison of our definitions, that we recognize no substantial differences between the terms *types* and *species*—permanence of characteristics belonging equally to both. . . .

The *Negro* species comprehends the Ethiopian, Hottentot, Oceanic-Negro, and Australian. The *Ethiopian* race comprises those Negroes inhabiting the greater part of Africa, having black skins, wooly heads, &c. Hottentots and Bushmen exhibiting light-brown complexions. . . .

Though many other classifications might be added, the above suffice to testify how *arbitrary* all classifications inevitably must be; because no reason has yet been assigned why, if two original pairs of human beings be admitted, we should not accept an indefinite number. . . .

But many of our readers will doubtless be startled at being told that Ethnology was no new science even before the time of Moses. Our divisions, such as the *Caucasian, Mongol, Negro*, &c., each include many sub-types; and if different painters of the present day were called upon to select a pictorial type to represent a man of these arbitrary divisions, they would doubtless select different human heads. Thus with Egyptians: although the *Red*, or Egyptian, type was represented with considerable uniformity, the White, Yellow, and Black, are often depicted, in their hieroglyphed drawings, with different physiognomies; thus proving, that the same endless variety of races existed at the ancient day that we observe in the same localities at the present hour. So far from there being a stronger similarity among the most ancient races, the dissimilarity actually augments as we ascend the stream of time; and this is naturally explained by the obvious fact that existing remains of primitive types are becoming more and more amalgamated every day. . . .

We have asserted, that all classifications of the races of men heretofore proposed are entirely arbitrary; and that, unfortunately, no data yet exist by which these arrangements can materially be improved. It is proper that we should submit our reasons for this assertion. The field we here enter upon is so wide as to embrace the whole physical history of mankind; but, neither our limits nor plan permitting such a comprehensive range, we shall illustrate our views by an examination of one or two groups of races; premising the remark that, whatever may be true of one human division—call it Caucasian, Mongol, Negro, Indian, or other name—applies with equal force to all divisions. . . .

Our preceding chapters have established that so-called *Caucasian* types may be traced upwards from the present day, in an infinite variety of primitive forms, through every historical record, and yet farther back through the petroglyphs of Egypt (where we lose them, in the medieval darkness of the earliest recorded people, some 3,500 years before Christ), not as a few stray individuals, but as populous nations, possessing distinct physical features and separate national characteristics. We now turn to the African types, not simply because they present an opposite extreme from the Caucasian, but mainly because, from their early communication with Egypt, much detail, in respect to their physical characters, has been preserved in the catacombs and on the monuments. . . .

We have shown that no classification of races yet put forth has any foundation whatever in nature; and that, after several thousands of years of migrations of races and comminglings of types, all attempts at following them up to their original birth-place must, from the absence of historic annals of those primordial times, and in the present state of knowledge, be utterly hopeless. This remark applies with quite as much force to Negroes as the Caucasians. . . .

In order to develop our ideas more clearly, we propose to take a rapid glance at the population of Africa. We shall show, that not only is that vast continent inhabited by types quite as varied as those of Europe or Asia, but that there exists a regular *gradation*, from Cape of Good Hope to the Isthmus of Suez, of which the Hottentot and Bushman form the lowest, and the Egyptian and Berber types the highest links; we can but follow M. Agassiz. . . .

"*Unity of races*" seems to be an idea introduced in comparatively modern times, and never to have been conceived by any primitive nations, such as Egypt or China. Neither does the idea appear to have occurred to the author of *Genesis*. . . .

We shall show, in another place, that history affords no evidence that education, or any influence of civilization that may be brought to bear on races of inferior organization, can radically change their physical, nor, consequently, their moral characters. That the Brain, altered in form, is unchanged, is now admitted by every anatomist; and Prichard, in recapitulating his results as to the races of Central Africa, makes the following important admission:—

"On reviewing the descriptions of all the races enumerated, we may observe a relation between their physical character and moral condition. *Tribes having what is called the Negro character in the most striking degree are the least civilized.* . . . In general, the tribes inhabiting elevated countries, in the interior, are very superior to those who dwell on low tracts on the seacoast, and this superiority is manifest both in mental and bodily question. . . ."

Unless there were really some facts in history, something beyond bare hypotheses, to teach us how these deficient inches could be artificially added, it would seem that the Negroes in Africa must remain substantially in that same benighted state wherein nature has placed them, and in which they have stood, according to Egyptian monuments, for at least 5000 years. . . .

"The distinguishing peculiarities of the African races may be summed up into four heads; viz. the characters of complexion, hair, feature, and figure. We have to remark—

"1. That some races, with woolly hair and complexions of a deep black color, have fine forms, regular and beautiful feature, and are, in their figure and countenances, scarcely different from Europeans. Such are the Iolofs, near the Senegal, and the race of Guber, or of Hausa, in the interior of Sudan. Some tribes of the South African race, as the darkest of the Kafirs, are nearly of this description, as well as some families or tribes in the empire of Congo, while others have more of the Negro character in their countenance and form.

"2. Other tribes have the form and feature similar to those above described: their complexion is black or a deep olive, or a copper color approaching to black. . . .

"3. Other instances have been mentioned in which the complexion is black and the features have the Negro type, while the nature of the hair deviates considerably, and is even said to be rather long and in flowing ringlets. Some of the tribes near the Sambezi are of this class.

"4. Among nations whose color deviates towards a lighter hue, we find some with wooly hair, with a figure and features approaching the European. Such are the Bechuanan Kafirs, of a light brown complexion. . . ."

Pritchard himself tells us, "there are no authentic instances, either in Africa or elsewhere, of the transmutation of other varieties of mankind into Negroes. . . ."

The whole of the countries now described are sometimes called Nigrits, or the Land of Negroes—they have likewise been termed *Ethiopia*. The former of these names is more frequently given to the Western, and the latter to the Eastern parts; but there is no exact limitation between the countries so termed. The names are taken from the races of men inhabiting different countries, and these are interspersed, and not separated by a particular line. Black and wooly-haired races, to which the term Negro is applied, are more predominant in Western Africa;

The Negroes are distinguished by their well-known traits, of which the most strongly marked is their woolly hair; but it is difficult to point out any common property characteristics of the races termed Ethiopians.

The Ethiopian races have generally something in their physical character which is *peculiarly African*, though not reaching the degree in which it is displayed by the black people of Soudan. Their hair, though not woolly, is commonly frizzled, or strongly curled or crisp. . . .

The universal characteristics of all the tribes of this great nation consist in an external form and figure, varying exceedingly from the other nations of Africa: they are much taller, stronger, and their limbs better proportioned. Their color is *brown*; their hair black and woolly. Their countenances have a character peculiar to themselves, and which does not permit their being included in any of the races of mankind above enumerated. They have the high forehead and prominent nose of the Europeans, the thick lips of the Negroes, and the big cheekbones of the Hottentots. Their beards are black, and much fuller than those of the Hottentots. . . .

When we compare the continent of Africa with the other great divisions of the world, it is apparent that it forms a striking contrast in every particular. Here stand obstructions, fixed by nature, which man in early times had no means of overcoming. . . .

Source Note: Josiah Clark Nott and George Gliddon, *Types of Mankind; or Ethnological Researches Based Upon the Ancient Monuments, Sculptures, and Crania of Races and upon Their Natural, Geographical, Philological, and Biblical History* (Philadelphia, 1854).

Indigenous Races of the Earth; or, New Chapters of Ethnological Inquiry
by Josiah Clark Nott and George R. Gliddon

I have already shown, in the "Sketch of the natural provinces of the animal world, and their relation to the different types of man," which you have inserted in the "Types of Mankind," that, so far as their geographical distribution upon the surface of the globe is concerned, the races of man follow the same laws which obtain in the circumscription of the natural provinces of the animal kingdom. . . .

The general typical and for self-evident, reasons, the following description [of an African skull] by LAWRENCE:

The front of the head, including the forehead and the face, is compressed laterally, and considerably elongated towards the front; hence the length of the whole skull, from the teeth to the occiput, is considerable. It forms, in this respect, the strongest contrast to that globular shape which some of the Caucasian races present, and which is very remarkable in the Turk.—The capacity of the cranium is reduced, particularly in its front part. . . . The face, on the contrary, is enlarged. The frontal bone is shorter, and, as well as the parietal, less excavated and less capacious than in the European; the temporal ridge mounts higher, and the space which it includes is much more considerable. The front of the skull seems compressed into a narrow keel-like form between the two powerful temporal muscles, which rise nearly to the highest part of the head; and has a compressed figure, which is not equally marked in the entire head, on account of the thickness of the muscles. Instead of the ample swell of the forehead and vertex, which rises between and completely surmounts the comparatively weak temporal muscles of the European, we often see only a small space left between the two temporal ridges in the Ethiopian.—The foramen magnum is larger, and lies farther back in the head; the other openings for the passage of the nerves are larger.—The bony substance is denser and harder; the sides of the skull thicker, and the whole weight consequently more considerable.—The bony apparatus employed in the mastication, and in forming receptacles for the organs of sense, is larger, stronger, and more advantageously constructed for powerful effect, than in the races where more extensive use of experience and reason, and greater civilization, supply the place of animal strength.—If the bones of the face in the Negro were taken as a basis, and a cranium were added to them for the same relative magnitude which it possesses in the European, a receptacle for the brain would be required much larger than in the latter case. However, we find it considerably smaller. Thus the intellectual part is lessened, the animal organs are enlarged: proportions are produced just opposite to those which are found in the Grecian ideal model. . . . The narrow, low, and slanting forehead, and the elongation of the jaws into a kind of muzzle, give to this head an animal character, which cannot escape the most cursory examination. . . . It is sufficiently obvious, that on a vertical antero-posterior section of the head, the area of the face will be more considerable in proportion to that of the cranium, in such a skull than in the fine European forms.—The larger and stronger jaws require more powerful muscles. The temporal fossa is much larger; the ridge which bonds it rises higher on the skull, and is more strongly marked, than in the European. The thickness of the muscular mass may be estimated from the bony arch, within which it descends to the lower jaw. The zygoma is larger, stronger, and more capacious in the Negro; the cheek-bones project remarkably, and are very strong, broad, and thick: hence these afford space for the attachment of powerful masseters.—The orbits, in particularly external apertures, capacious, the plates windings of ethmoid bone more complicated, the cribriform lamella more extensive, than in the European. The *ossa nasi* are flat and short, instead of forming a bridge-like convexity which we see in the European. They run together above into an acute angle, which makes them considerably resemble the single triangular nasal bone of the monkey. . . . The superior maxillary bone is remarkably prolonged in front; its alveolar portion in the included incisor teeth is oblique, instead of being perpendicular, as in the European. The nasal spine at the entrance of the nose is either inconsiderable, or entirely deficient. The palatine arch is longer and more elliptical. The alveolar edge of the lower jaw stands forward, like that of the upper; and this part in both is narrow, elongated, and elliptical. The chin, instead of projecting equally with the teeth, as it does in the European, recedes considerably like that of the monkey.—The characters of the Ethiopian variety, as observed in the genuine Negro tribes, may be thus summed up: 1. Narrow and depressed forehead; the entire cranium contracted in anteriorly: the cavity less, both in its circumference and transverse measurements. 2. Occipital foramen and condyles placed farther back. 3. Large space for the temporal muscles. 4. Great development of the face. 5. Prominence of the jaws altogether, and particularly of their alveolar margins and teeth: consequent obliquity of the facial line. 6. Superior incisor slanting. 7. Chin receding. 8. Very large and strong zygomatic arch projecting towards the front. 9. Large nasal cavity. 10. Small and flattened ossa nasi, sometimes consolidated, and running into a point above.—In all the particulars just enumerated, the Negro structure approximates unequivocally to that of the monkey. It not only differs from the Caucasian model, but is distinguished from it in two respects; the intellectual characters are reduced, the animal features enlarged, and exaggerated. In such a skull as that represented in the eighth plate, *which, indeed, has been particularly selected, because it is strongly characterized*, no person, however little conversant with natural history or physiology, could fail to recognize a decided approach to the animal form. This inferiority of organization is attended with corresponding inferiority of faculties; which may be proved, not so much by the unfortunate beings who are degraded by slavery, as by every fact in the past history and present condition of Africa.

Thus much for the cranial *physique* of the genuine tropical Negro. The tribes of Western Africa present us with higher forms of the skull, and less degraded physical and intellectual traits. . . . Ethnology, in its etymological and narrowest sense, is . . . the science of nations. It investigates the characteristics and history of the various tribes of man. The time seems to be already come when we may venture to define it more comprehensively as the science of the Human Race. From the investigation of the peculiarities and histories of particular tribes it rises to the conception of mankind as one race, and combining the truth which it gathers from every tribe, presents the whole as the science of the ethnic development of man. Those who may consider it premature to unite all nations in the idea of one race, can still accept the definition as indicating the science that results from a comparison of nations and their developments. Whether all men are descended from one stock or not, may be placed apart as an enquiry by itself, for those who think it worthwhile to pursue it in the present state of our knowledge. All are agreed that man is one of a kind. If the millions who now people the earth had some hundreds of progenitors instead of a single pair, the science which the definition comprises will remain unaffected. . . .

Source Note: Josiah Clark Nott and George R. Gliddon. *Indigenous Races of the Earth; or, New Chapters of Ethnological Inquiry* (Philadelphia: J. B. Lippincott, 1857).

The Negro Race: Its Ethnology and History
by Josiah Clark Nott

Slavery has existed in all ages, and even negro slavery was common in Egypt 5,000 years ago, and has existed there ever since; but in the United States for the first time has *negro* slavery formed the basis of the institutions of a great nation and the groundwork of a peculiar civilization. Negro slaves in Egypt, both ancient and modern, were the fellahs, or native Egyptian population, that *never were black*. This, then, is not a mere abstract question of *liberty or slavery*—an entirely new question comes before you, viz.: that of *races*, and it remains to be seen whether your party has not raised a storm that will leave nothing but devastation behind it.

In my professional round every day I hear complaints that negroes will not work at any price. They are huddled together in shanties around the town, stealing, burning fences for fuel, dying of diseases and want, and yet you cannot get a cook or washer-woman at twenty dollars a month. The trouble is only beginning, and to a great extent it is the work of your [Freedman's] Bureau, to whom the negroes have looked for protection and support.

History proves, indisputably, that a superior and inferior race cannot live together practically on any other terms than that of master and slave, and that the inferior race, like the Indians, must be expelled or exterminated. In every climate where the white man can live and prosper, he drives all others before him. The history of the Chinese in California is adding another melancholy example to many which have gone before of the inequality of races.

To my mind, every people have a right to freedom who know how to use it, and I have never hesitated to say, and to print the declaration, that I was at heart an emancipationist, but have opposed the emancipation of the blacks in the United States upon the ground that all experiments of abolitionists heretofore had utterly failed to improve to condition of the blacks, and resulted in their gradual extermination.

The first question, them, to be settled is, *the capacity of the negro for self-government*. Is he capable of taking any part in the march of civilization beyond that of a mere "hewer of wood and drawer of water?" Does his history afford proof that his intellect is susceptible of any really useful development? These are questions which his past record certainly answers in the negative.

We have abundant material for following up the dark history of the negro through the stream of time for several thousand years, unillumined as it is by a single ray of light from his own records, and we shall show that the same physical and intellectual characteristics have marked him from the earliest antiquity to the present day. No naturalist can now be found to contend that through this long period of time any causes have existed to transform one type of man into another—the white man into a negro, or *vice versa*.

The reader has only to turn to the great works of Champollion, Rosellini, and Lepsius (to say nothing of many others) on the Ancient Monuments of Egypt, published by the French, Tuscan, and Prussian governments, to be satisfied of the truth of these assertions. There you behold, copied from the tombs, temples, and other monuments, the life-like portraits of all the races that lived around the Mediterranean four thousand years ago, and antedating the epochs of Moses, Abraham, and Joseph, and even, Archbishop Usher's date of the deluge.—There are depicted of portraits of negroes literally by thousands as laborers, slaves, traders, &c., with their black skins, woolly heads, peculiar features, &c., as distinctly as if they were drawn from life but yesterday. Not only have we on monuments the faithful portraits, but we have the mummied bodies from the catacombs, contemporary with the drawings. Side by side with the negroes we have equally well depicted the native Egyptians, Abyssinians, the Nubians, the Berbers, the Arabs, the Jews, Assyrians, Persians, and Mongols, that still inhabit surrounding countries, thus proving the permanency of all human types, when not disturbed by miracles or intermixtures. Of the antiquity, then, of the negro race there can be no doubt—nor can there be a doubt with regard to the permanence of his type; for more than a century past the blacks have been torn from their native lands and scattered in America through a wide range of latitude, and still no change has been produced in the color of their skins, the form of their heads, or their grade of intellect, although there is a law well known to naturalists that very few generations produce all the changes of any importance that change of climate can produce.

The permanence of his intellectual peculiarities is not less certain than that of the physical. For many thousand years he has had the greater part of an immense continent to himself, with fertile soil, congenial climate, and all the facilities that other races have had for civilizing himself, and why has he remained stationary? From the Great Desert to the Cape of Good Hope, (the land of the true negro,) not a vestige of civilization is to be found—no remains of art—no ruined temples and cities—no relic of science or literature; and no negro has ever invented even a rude alphabet! His intellect for four thousand years has been as dark as his skin, and all attempts in and out of Africa have failed to enlighten or develop it beyond the grade for which the Creator intended it. The little show of progress made by Mandingos, Joloffs, and other black tribes of the North is attributable to the Mahometan religion, and the infiltration of Arab and other foreign blood and arts.

As before stated, all the races that lived around the Mediterranean 4,000 years ago live there still, in the same localities: Egyptians, Nubians, Berbers, Arabs, Jews, Assyrians, Abyssinians, and Negroes are all clearly portrayed on the early monuments, and have preserved their respective types to the present day.

When the white and black races are bred together a stock is produced, intermediate between the two, both physically and intellectually; they are more intelligent than the blacks, and less so than the whites. It may well be doubted whether intellect enough is added to the negro by admixture to improve him to any useful degree, while on the other hand it is certain that the white race is deteriorated by every drop of black blood infiltrated into it—just as surely as the blood of the cart horse destroys the beauty and speed of the Arabian racer, or that of the greyhound or pointer is polluted by that of a cur. These are not mere idle assertions made for a special object, but they are stubborn facts that any man may verify who will, and which have incalculable practical bearings on the great questions at issue. Fred. Douglass is unquestionably the most brilliant mulatto intellect now before the public; and he is nothing more than what St. Paul calls a "pestilent fellow." He has just brains enough to talk fluently about matters he does not comprehend, and to spit out the venom of a blackguard— witness his attack on President Johnson.

Can there be found in history anything more positive than the utter failure of the negro race in Haiti? There the negro race on Haiti was left in full possession of one of the finest islands in the world, having a tropical climate well suited to his nature. At the time the whites were expelled, their successors were left with everything a people could ask for attaining a position among civilized nations of the earth. A large portion of the population were educated; the system of agriculture was well developed; they possessed a large import and export trade; many of them had been drilled to commercial avocations, to the mechanic and other useful arts; and what has been the result? If a sick man wants a little sugar in this island, which once produced more of the article than any equal territory in Christendom, he now is obliged to send to a druggist's to purchase it as he would medicine! Agriculture, commerce, literature, arts, law and order—all are gone, and I was assured, a few years ago, by Admiral David Porter, that he, on two occasions, saw negroes roasting and eating Dominican prisoners by the wayside, in Haiti! For a time the white blood of the mulatto caste ruled in the island, and with some semblance of semi-civilization; but the blacks, becoming jealous, exterminated them, and swept every remnant of civilization from the country, which soon relapsed into savagism. History affords no example where the white race has had such an opportunity and failed, while it affords many where it has advanced in spite of impediments.

In the face of all these difficulties, Peter the Great, though a coarse, illiterate brute himself, following the promptings of ambition and the instincts of his race, conceived the idea of civilizing his people—of making himself and nation great—and had the sagacity to see how his objects were to be attained. He traveled in foreign countries, observed everything he beheld, noted what was wanting, labored with his own hands in common workshops to learn the mechanic arts, and carried back to his native land the knowledge necessary for the commencement of his grand enterprise. One of his early works was the building of the city of St. Petersburg, in the face of difficulties that would have appalled others, knowing that commerce was one of the leading elements of civilization. He also established schools, colleges, and other public institutions, and the great work thus begun by Peter has been steadily carried on to the present day by a succession of rulers wiser than any other nation in Europe can boast.

Russia, then, with a *white population*, ruled by wise heads of their own race, now stands out as one of the foremost nations, wielding a power that keeps all Europe in awe.

The following table, copied from page 454 of "*Nott & Gliddon's Types of Mankind,*" is based on Dr. Morton's measurements, and shows at a glance the relative size of brains of races in cubic inches:

TABLE—SIZE OF BRAINS IN CUBIC INCHES.

Races Modern White Races	Mean. Cubic In.
Teutonic Group	**92**
Pelasgic	84
Celtic	87
Semetic	89
Ancient Pelasgic	88
Malays	85
Chinese	82
Negroes, African	83
Hindostances	80
Fellahs, (Modern Egyptians)	80
Egyptians, (Ancient)	80
Taltecan Family	**77**
Barbarous Tribes	84
Hottentots	75
Australians	**75**

The critic might here object to an apparent contradiction, viz.: The fact that the negro, in these measurements, presents a brain about the size of those of the Chinese and Malay, and larger than that of the Hindoo; although greatly inferior to all in intellect. But the discrepancy is easily explained. The negro, it is true, *in the aggregate*, has a brain as capacious as that of the Chinese and Malay, and larger than that of the Hindoo; but in the negro the posterior or animal part of the brain greatly preponderates over the anterior or intellectual lobes. In the other races named the anterior or intellectual lobes of the brain greatly preponderate over the posterior or animal portion. The same facts apply to the semi-civilized and barbarous tribes of Indians.

Now, I am no convert to the details of phrenology; but that certain grand divisions of the brain have opposite functions cannot be denied. All agree that the intellectual faculties are grouped together in front; but whether they can be mapped out, as phrenologists pretend, I will not affirm or deny.

But push the arguments to wall, if you please, and call all this speculation;

who will deny the broad historical fact, that the white, which are the large-brained, races have governed the world from time immemorial, and have been the only depositories of true civilization.

The foregoing table affords much food for reflection; it shows a sliding scale of seventeen cubic inches between the Hottentot and Australian at one extreme, and the Teutonic races at the other! The former giving an average mean measurement of but seventy-five cubic inches and the latter ninety-two. The negro races, those from the part of the coast *from which slaves are brought* to America, give an intermediate measurement of eighty-three cubic inches, or *nine inches less than the average of the whites*! These are facts well established among naturalists, though I presume not accepted by the Freedmen's Bureau, as its whole action seems based on an opposite assumption.

It is a well known fact too, even among slave-traders, that only certain tribes of negroes, those of a middle grade of intelligence, will answer for slaves—those from what is called the "slave coast;" and none others have been brought to America, except in the earliest times.

History proves that the negro makes his nearest approach to civilization in slavery, or some subordinate position among whites. Whenever, as in St. Domingo and Jamaica, he is removed from the controlling influence of the superior race, and is left to his own instincts, he soon sinks into savagism. Even now, while I am writing, we are receiving appalling accounts of an insurrection in Jamaica, characterized by all the barbarities that always attend negro wars. Fortunately the race is so wanting in intellect that this outbreak must soon be put down by a handful of white British troops.

The inferiority of the negro is practically admitted in our Northern and Western States by the inferior social position in which he is held, and no legislation or arbitrary rules can change it. In the first place, there is a natural antipathy of race which no human power can efface. Then there is a jealousy of the white towards black labor, which it will not tolerate in competition. The whites will not associate with the blacks as equals and intermarry with them. Some of the States have actually passed laws against the immigration of blacks, and in the face of all this the "so-called" Republican party are stirring the powers of earth to force upon the South what they will not tolerate at home.

What, then, must be the fate of this unfortunate race? I was born among negroes at the South, have spent many years in the study of their natural and civil history, and feel confident in the prediction that they are doomed to extermination—an extermination which is being cruelly hastened by the unwise action of a party that will not study and comprehend the subject it is dealing with. The negro has an instinctive and unconquerable antipathy to steady agricultural labor, and must therefore be gradually supplanted by the whites, whose energy, industry, and intelligence will rule in this and all other important pursuits. Negroes are peculiarly gregarious and social by nature, and have an ungovernable propensity to congregate in villages and towns. It is mainly for these reasons that negro population, out of slavery, can never become dense. No necessity can drive them to the kind of industry which is necessary to develop such crowded communities as those of China and India, or even those of New England. The whole black population of the immense continent of Africa is not more than double that of the British Isles.

There is another striking peculiarity among the negroes, which must play an important part in the gradual extermination of the race in America. I allude to the want of care for each other in sickness, and the mortality among their children from neglect of their parents. Every experienced physician at the South will bear me witness in this assertion. Whether slaves or free, as a general rule, they will not attend to each other in this time of need. I have a thousand times been compelled to call the attention of owners of slaves to the fact, and to insist that the master should look to the wants of the sick. They will often see a fellow-laborer, and even a near relative die for want of a cup of gruel, or of water rather than lose a few hours sleep in watching. What may seem still more remarkable to those not familiar with negro character, is the fact that they are untiring in their kindness and attentions to the members of their master's family in sickness. They watch night after night by the bedside of the whites, as if prompted by an instinct like the canine species. Their devotion in this respect is incredible to those who have not witnessed it; and their history shows that the race is a dependent one.

1st. The intellectual and physical characters of the different races of men were the same as now five thousand years ago, and no causes have existed or now exist that can transform one type of man into another.

2nd. The physical laws which have governed the races of men during this period of time are precisely the same as those which govern the species, varieties, or types of inferior animals.

3rd. Without going back to the mooted question of *original unity or diversity of species*, the diversity of races as it exists can only be regarded as the work of the Almighty.

4th. The negro and other inferior races have never, under the most favored circumstances, shown any capacity for self-government or civilization.

5th. The negro attains his nearest approach to civilization among the whites, in a subordinate capacity; and when separated from them relapses into barbarism, as in Haiti and Jamaica.

6th. The brain of the negro is nine cubic inches less than that of the white man, and the large-headed races have always ruled the earth, and been the only repository of true civilization.

7th. The idea that the brain of the negro or any other race can be enlarged and the intellect developed by education, continued through successive generations, has no foundation in truth, or any semblance of support from history.

8th. The races of men, like those of the canines and other animals, though modified by climates, are never transformed into each other. The white man, the negro, the Jew, the greyhound, the foxhound, the pointer, preserve their types and instincts in all climates.

9th. The blacks, like the American Indians, Tartars, and other nomadic races, are instinctively opposed to agricultural labor, and no necessity can drive them to it.

10th. Slavery is the normal condition of the negro, the most advantageous to him, and the most ruinous, in the end to a white nation.

The white people of the South are of the same blood and flesh as those of the North—profess the same religion, and are actuated by the same feelings, impulses, and interests—they, too, are a proud people, jealous of dictation and foreign interference. In due time the negroes will be educated, their poor will be provided for and they will in every respect be as well cared for by us as by you—but never "on compulsion."

The negroes now refuse to make contracts for the coming year, and when asked for reasons, say they have been informed that the lands are to be divided among them, and that they will be branded and returned to slavery if they make contracts with the old slave-owners!

J. C. NOTT, M. D.
MOBILE, ALA., 25TH November, 1865.

Source Note: Josiah Clark Nott, *The Negro Race, Its Ethnology and History*, Mobile, AL, 1866.

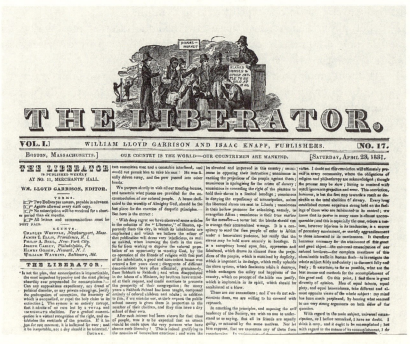

Masthead of William Lloyd Garrison's *The Liberator*, by permission of Ruth Owen Jones, Amherst, Mass.

The Abolitionist Crusade

William Lloyd Garrison and the Abolitionist Crusade

THE NEW VOICE, 1830–1865

William Lloyd Garrison, possibly the most important of the antebellum abolitionists, certainly the most influential of the American antislavery advocates, was born in Newburyport, Massachusetts, on December 10, 1805. When Garrison was only three years old, his father left home and his mother was forced into wage-slavery servitude as a domestic servant. The family was divided when William was only seven. He worked as a printer's apprentice and learned the newspaper trade so that by 1826, when he was only twenty-one, he purchased the *Essex Courant* and renamed it the *Newburyport Free Press*. Thus began one of the most politically and socially important journalistic careers in American history; for a few years later (1829), Garrison became associated with antislavery and abolitionism through his position as coeditor, with Benjamin Lundy, of *The Genius of Universal Emancipation*.

In that same year, Garrison made one of the most important antislavery speeches of his career, speaking in an "Address to the American Colonization Society." In it he tentatively embraced the principles of colonization but rejected the gradualist notion that progress in emancipation would come at a relatively slow pace, if moral suasion was used rather than political upheaval and social discord. When Garrison delivered the address, he was only twenty-four years old. This is a remarkable achievement for anyone that age, but it was especially important given Garrison's limited formal education. Largely self-educated, he read much in American history and especially American political history, and he was thoroughly familiar with the American Revolution and the founding documents, such as the Declaration of Independence and the U.S. Constitution.

Although Garrison would later repudiate the concept of colonization, by which African-Americans, free and slave, would be returned to Africa gradually, thus insuring freedom for all and removing the issue of slavery from the United States, he does temporarily embrace colonization in this early speech. However, the address is important in the canon of his writings not so much for its immediate political stance, as for Garrison's articulation of several principles which would remain constants of his abolitionist arguments throughout his career. Never far away in a Garrison document is the contrast between what is and what ought to be in the American experiment known as democracy. Here, Garrison points out the hypocrisy of the presence of slavery in a new nation dedicated to the fundamental principle that "all men are created equal," as Thomas

Jefferson had put it. Also present here is Garrison's vehement attack on specific institutions of American civilization, such as the churches for their failure to address the slavery problem directly, and the federal Government, for its willingness to allow slavery, under the evasive language of the Constitution, as part of the fabric of American life. Finally, Garrison's directness, his style of immediate and direct confrontation, would also hallmark his speeches and tracts for his career. In this speech, excerpted below, Garrison announced a principle that he would embrace throughout his entire career, namely, that the North as well as the South was implicated in the custom of chattel slavery, and that it was basically illogical to argue that slavery was exclusively a "Southern problem." He wrote: "I assume as distinct and defensible propositions: . . . That, as the free States—by which I mean non-slave-holding States—are constitutionally involved in the guilt of slavery, by adhering to a national compact that sanctions it; and in the danger, by liability to be called upon for aid in case of insurrection; they have the right to remonstrate against its continuance, and it is their duty to assist in its overthrow."

Two related Garrisonian principles are contained in this assertion, principles which again would reappear throughout his career as a leading abolitionist. First, Garrison was very outspoken in his criticism of the United States Constitution, which he perceived to be a "proslavery compact," an agreement with Satan, and a violation of the very principles for which the American Revolution had been fought. Constitutional arguments concerning slavery are regularly contrasted with the principles of the Declaration of Independence in Garrison editorials. Second, Garrison actually became an early "secessionist," arguing that the North should break away from the South and purify itself of the sin of slavery rather than enter into further complicity in the propagation of slavery.

The first editorial he wrote for *The Liberator*, also excerpted here, ends with a verse that states the central themes of the abolitionist movement, 1830–65.

> Oppression! I have seen thee, face to face,
> And met thy cruel eye and cloudy brow,
> But thy soul-withering glance I fear not now—
> For dread to prouder feelings doth give place
> Of deep abhorrence! Scorning the disgrace
> Of slavish knees that at thy footstool bow
> I also kneel—but with far other vow,
> Do hail thee and thy hord of hirelings base:—
> I sweat, while life-blood warms thy throbbing veins,
> Still to oppose and thwart, with heart and hand,
> Thy brutalising sway—till Afric's chains
> Are burst, and Freedom rules the rescued land,—
> Trampling Oppression and his iron rod:
> *Such is the vow I take*—SO HELP ME GOD!

GARRISON AND THE CONSTITUTION

Garrison was, from the beginning of his career, an opponent of the U.S. Constitution, primarily because he believed it to be a proslavery document. He was very consistent in his opposition to the Constitution, and his outspoken critique led him to recommend secession, the North from the South, the free states from the slave states. One of his favorite rhetorical strategies was to contrast the struggle for liberty in the American Revolution with the oppression of Africans who were engaged in their own struggle for liberty, even in the context of the United States's attempt to reconcile its charter documents concerning freedom with the "peculiar institution" that blighted its democracy. In a speech on March 5, 1858, Garrison attacked the hypocrisy of the United States in allowing slavery while celebrating such events as the Boston Massacre, which had occurred on March 5, 1770. Here, at Faneuil Hall, just a few yards from the site of the Boston Massacre, Garrison abused the Constitution and once again called for disunion. "We shall be told that this is equivalent to a dissolution of the Union. Be it so! Give us Disunion with liberty and a good conscience, rather than Union with slavery and moral degradation. What! shall we shake hands with those who buy, sell, torture, and horribly inbrute their fellow-creatures, and trade in human flesh! God forbid! Every man should respect himself too much to keep such company. We must break this wicked alliance with men-stealers, or all is lost. By all the sacred memories of the past—by all that was persistent, courageous, unconquerable in the great struggle for American Independence . . . let us here renew our solemn pledge, that, come what may, we will not lay down our arms until liberty is proclaimed throughout all the land, to all the inhabitants thereof."

This kind of anti-constitutional rhetoric alienated Garrison from many of his white countrymen, and from some fellow abolitionists, including the escaped slave, Frederick Douglass, who came to view the Constitution as an antislavery document. Both Wendell Phillips and Garrison criticized the Constitution as a hypocritical charter for white freedom, and this firm stand, coupled with the ambition of Frederick Douglass to break off from Garrison and to begin his own antislavery newspaper, led to a severe breach between the two abolitionists in 1851. As William Cain put it, "Garrison wished Douglass well when *The North Star* became *Frederick Douglass's Paper* in 1851. But by then he was emphasizing his disagreement with Douglass's new, antislavery interpretation of the Constitution (*Liberator*, July 4, 1851). And to hammer home his point, he published a letter from Reverend Samuel May . . . that slammed Douglass's alliance 'with slaveholders and slave-traders as voluntary supporters of one Constitution and Government.' It was not the rival paper as much as the shift in Douglass's thinking about the Constitution that thrust him and Garrison apart. The final break came at the meeting of the American Anti-Slavery Society in May, 1851, when Douglass repudiated Garrison's proslavery interpretation of the Constitution" (Cain, p. 47).

Garrison's vituperative critique of American hypocrisy over the issue of individual freedom appears throughout his writing, particularly when he was incensed over injustice, as he viewed, for example, the Dred Scott decision of 1857. When the Supreme Court of the United States ruled that Dred Scott, a slave from Missouri who had lived for years with his former master in two free states, Illinois and Wisconsin, would forever remain a slave even on the death of his former master, abolitionists and antislavery advocates voiced vigorous opposition. Garrison engaged in direct, confrontational attack, leaving nothing to the reader's imagination.

"We are here to enter our indignant protest against the Dred Scott decision—against the infamous Fugitive Slave Law—against all unjust and oppressive enactments, with reference to complexional distinctions—against the alarming aggressions of the Slave Power upon the rights of the people of the North—and especially against the existence of the slave system at the South, from which all these have naturally sprung, as streams of lava from a volcano. We are here to reiterate the self-evident truths of the Declaration of Independence, and to call for their practical enforcement throughout our land. We are here to declare that the men who, like Crispus Attucks [an African-American who was killed March 5, 1770, during the Boston Massacre] were ready to lay down their lives to secure American Independence, and the blessings of liberty—who, in every period of our history, at all times, and in all parts of the country, on the land and on the sea, have ever been prompt in the hour of peril to fill the deadly imminent breach, pour out their blood like water, and repel the minions of foreign tyranny from our shores—are not the men to be denied the claims of human nature, or the rights of citizenship. Alas! what have they reaped for all their patriotic toils and sufferings, but contumely, proscription, ostracism? O, shame on this cruelly unjust and most guilty nation! I trust in God that no colored men will ever again be found ready to fight under its banner, however great the danger that may menace it from abroad, until their rights are first secured, and every slave be set free" (Cain, p. 149).

GARRISON AND FREDERICK DOUGLASS

There is no simple explanation for the shifting relationship between William Lloyd Garrison and Frederick Douglass. At the most elementary level, one could conclude that a mentor became disgruntled with an upstart mentee, but this psychological approach to their troubled friendship would be reductive and simplistic. It is clearly an extremely complex issue. As Henry Mayer put it, "Two self-made men as determined and as proud as these would likely have clashed in any setting, but in the crucible of movement politics and the charged atmosphere of American race relations, their ability to forge a decade-long working relationship is as noteworthy as their inability to sustain it for a lifetime. Douglass, of course, had come into the movement under Garrison's aegis, and he had eloquently defended Garrisonian principles, including disunion—which resonated with his own profound alienation—and nonresistance—which perhaps fit less well with his self-assertive temperament and the insurgent rhetoric of new black spokesmen personified by the fiery minister Henry Highland Garnet" (Mayer, p. 372). But when Douglass allowed his British followers to purchase his freedom to the astonishment of the abolitionist establishment in the United States, Garrison came to his defense. "Garrison alone among the AAS leadership defended the 'ransom' as a practical choice that enabled Douglass to return home safely. The editor emphatically disagreed with critics who shrugged off the danger that Douglass might be re-enslaved and who charged that the transaction amounted to an endorsement of compensated emancipation" (Mayer, 372).

Another aspect of the relationship may have resulted from Garrison's own resentment of Douglass's perceived easy success compared to his financial and moral struggle in the 1830s. On the other hand, it may also have been the result of Douglass's resentment of his mentor.

> Much of the ensuing trouble can be traced to a protégé's inevitable resentment of a mentor. Garrison had started a newspaper on a shoestring with nary a subscriber in sight; Garrison had managed to combine editing and lecturing and parlayed his success in each field into enhanced prestige for both; Garrison exercised a moral and inspirational leadership which Douglass rightfully felt himself both capable of and suited for; Garrison, in short, had made himself a success by exactly the route that Douglass now proposed to follow, though it might be pointed out that Garrison did not have the sponsors and backers that Douglass enjoyed and had taken the lion's share in creating the institutional framework that supported Douglass's ascent. Inescapably, however, the younger man felt stifled and believed that his preceptor was trying to suppress a potential competitor. Perhaps he was. (Mayer, p. 373)

Garrison's anti-constitutional arguments may have isolated him from more moderate abolitionists and from many Northern whites, but his claims for African equality, politically, socially, and biologically, placed him in an extreme position even among militant abolitionists. Gerritt Smith, Wendell Phillips, Frederick Douglass, and Lydia Maria Child may have shared some of his views on racial equality, but his outspoken positions on race had the double effect of alienating some of his supporters while clearly defining the racism even among the abolitionists. When defending an attack on Frederick Douglass for his friendship with a white woman, Garrison argued:

> There is nothing which excites more unfeigned astonishment in the old world, than the prejudice which dogs the footsteps of the man of color in this pseudo republic. True, there are many absurd, criminal, aristocratic distinctions abroad, which ought to cease; but these are also found, to a great extent, in the United States, and have been common to all countries, and in every age. They originate in the pride of wealth, in successful enterprise, in educational superiority, in official rank, in civil, military, and ecclesiastical rule. For these, there may be framed some plausible excuses. But to enslave, brutalize, scorn, and insult human beings solely on account of the hue of the skin which it has pleased God to bestow on them; to pronounce them accursed, for no crime on their part; to treat them substantially alike, whether they

are virtuous or vicious, refined or vulgar, rich or poor, aspiring or groveling; to be inflamed with madness against them in proportion as they rise in self-respect, and improve in their manners and morals; this is an act so unnatural, a crime so monstrous, a sin so God-defying, that it throws into the shade all other distinctions known among mankind. Thank God, it is confined to a very small portion of the Globe; though, strange to tell, it is perpetrated the most grossly, and in a spirit the most ferocious and inexorable, in a land claiming to be the pattern-land of the world—the most enlightened, the most democratic, the most Christian. Complexional caste is tolerated nowhere excepting the immediate vicinage of slavery. It has no foundation in nature, reason, or universal custom. But as the origin of it is to be traced to the existence of slavery, so its utter eradication is not to be expected until that hideous system be overthrown. Nothing but the removal of the cause can destroy the effect. (Cain, p. 117)

Here, Garrison sounds the argument that slavery is the inevitable offspring of racial prejudice, a view he would often voice. Always critical of American values and especially of the hypocrisy embodied in the Constitution of the United States, he set forth positive principles of belief and action in several statements drafted for antislavery societies.

Garrison's youthful self-assurance in his *Liberator* editorials was born of genuine determination and religious commitment. He had begun as a temperance crusader. If Frederick Douglass was to become the more politically sensitive of the two abolitionists, enjoying the favor of four U.S. presidents and becoming the confidant of Lincoln as he struggled to preserve the Union and abolish slavery at the same time, Garrison persevered in his beliefs that there should be "no union with slaveholders," no compensation for lost property when the slaves were emancipated, that there should be immediate and unconditional emancipation, and that the U.S. Constitution was essentially a proslavery document because it did not condemn the institution and because it permitted the very existence of slavery in the land of the free and home of the brave. In part because these two leaders edited separate if not rival newspapers, both concerned with the abolition of slavery, and in part because Douglass pressed for constitutional amendments that would abolish slavery while Garrison vigorously fought the Constitution as a proslavery document, the two men drifted apart and eventually became rivals in the antislavery movement. There is no question that both men were significant in the war on slavery that effectively ended in 1865 with the passage of the Thirteenth Amendment to the Constitution, which outlawed slavery in the United States.

Finally, it is important to note that both Frederick Douglass and Garrison were strong supporters of the rights of women as well as fighters for the emancipation of the slaves. Douglass was a speaker at the Seneca Falls Convention of 1848, where the Declaration of Sentiments, an expression of the rights of women, was drafted. Although Garrison is best remembered for his vigorous, lifelong crusade against the "peculiar institution" of chattel slavery, he was also committed to emancipating women from the oppressive conditions forced upon them by a society that denied them voting rights, educational opportunity, and property ownership privileges. Garrison's attacks on the Constitution, on Southern politicians like John C. Calhoun and Henry Clay, on legislation such as the Compromise of 1850, have long been recognized; however, his editorials in favor of women's rights are less heralded. Garrison also spoke at meetings where women's rights held center stage, like the Fourth Annual National Woman's Rights Convention held in Cleveland, Ohio, in October, 1853.

THE GARRISON LEGACY

Garrison regularly preached the immediate, unconditional, uncompensated abolition of slavery from the commencement of his public career at the age of twenty-five through the Civil War and the signing of the Emancipation Proclamation. His tenacity and determined efforts to end the "peculiar institution" were rewarded after thirty-five long years of extremely hard work as an editor and a public speaker, public disapprobation, and a lawsuit for libel in 1829 for which he was jailed for forty-nine days. In 1831, the Georgia Legislature placed a $5,000 bounty on Garrison's head, offering a reward for his capture and imprisonment. Like his contemporary and colleague in the abolitionist movement, Lydia Maria Child, Garrison suffered enormous social discrimination in Boston; neither of these abolitionist leaders was accepted by Boston society after their outspoken criticism of the Constitution and their demand for immediate and unconditional emancipation. Child's *An Appeal in Favor of that Class of Americans Called Africans* (Boston, 1833) followed closely the arguments of the black abolitionist David Walker, whose own *Appeal* (1830) was treated to a hostile reception both North and South. These pioneering attempts to change the system through reasoned discourse ultimately influenced the divisions between proslavery and antislavery advocates in both regions of the United States, setting up the ideological origins of the Civil War. Meanwhile, their proponents, Child, Garrison, and Walker, suffered a wide range of opposition, including disapproval from family members. Thus the youthful but thoughtful protest of Garrison in 1831 is all the more meaningful; with extremely limited social reinforcement and with a determination and conviction about the "sin of slavery," he set out the principles of abolitionism in ideological and in personal terms by articulating, in the opening editorial of the *Liberator*, January 1, 1831, the urgency of his message. These words have now become permanently associated with Garrison's career and beliefs; they are inscribed, in marble, on the base of his larger-than-life monument that resides on the Commonwealth Avenue Mall in Boston's Back Bay.

At twenty-six, Garrison had the courage to stand against the majority of his countrymen and declare:

> I am in earnest, I will not equivocate, I will not excuse, I will not retreat a single inch, and *I will be heard*.

For these stirring words, perhaps his most memorable utterance ever, Garrison will forever be remembered. But it was his persistence, his perseverance, and his determination to eradicate slavery from the United States in his own lifetime and his successful achievement of this goal that he should be eulogized. Few reformers in history have lived to see the fulfillment of their visions and dreams; Garrison was fortunate in agitating for emancipation when the country was engaged in a fierce debate about the "rightness" and "wrongness" of slavery. "In the long struggle to achieve equality in the United States, William Lloyd Garrison occupies a place as central in the history of the nineteenth century as that of Dr. Martin Luther King, Jr., in the history of the twentieth. Both men willingly understood themselves as radicals and used the integrity of their spiritual vision as an independent political force. Both men epitomized the power of a social movement built upon thousands of individual acts of moral witness. Both men exemplified the courage necessary to expose the injustice of established institutions and illuminate the darkness with the beacon of irrefutable truth. Garrison and King both faced, as did their companion in spiritual agitation, M. K. Gandhi, the agony of seeing the strategy of soul-force lost in a spiraling violence that would, in course, claim the lives of the latter two" (Mayer, p. 631). Both men fused the politics of radical reform with the rhetoric of moral discourse and biblical conviction. Although Garrison was never invited into the White House "inner circle," a position which Frederick Douglass enjoyed in several administrations, Garrison, with Lincoln and Douglass, established the moral center of the antebellum slavery debate and paved the way for their twentieth-century successor, Martin Luther King, Jr., and the civil rights movement of the 1960s. Although Garrison was not as powerful a speaker as either Douglass or King, his eloquence in print, in the editorials he composed for *The Liberator*, testify to his place in the tradition of Old Testament prophets, like Jeremiah and Isaiah, whom King admired and whom he quoted frequently. King's famous Lincoln Memorial speech, "I have a dream," is not only configured with the parallelism of Hebrew phrasing; it is also an expressive vision of hope that is based on the moral "rightness" of the promise of America's democracy. This moral "rightness" is sustained in all of Garrison's speeches and editorials for *The Liberator*; like Jeremiah and Isaiah, Garrison saw America for what it was and argued vigorously for what it ought to be. He did not seek public approval or recognition; it seems that at times, he was possessed of an intensity of purpose that was almost destructive. He did not have the political instincts of many of his contemporaries, including some abolitionists. But he too "had a dream," and was fortunate to live long enough to see the realization of that dream. As Abraham Lincoln would phrase it, "I have been only an instrument. The logic and moral power of Garrison and the anti-slavery people of the country and Army have done it all."

SUGGESTIONS FOR FURTHER READING

Cain, William, ed. *William Lloyd Garrison and the Fight against Slavery: Selections from the Liberator*. Boston: Bedford Books, 1995.

Mayer, Henry. *All on Fire*. New York: St. Martin's Press, 1998.

WILLIAM LLOYD GARRISON (1805–1879)

I hate slavery as I hate nothing else in this world. It is not only a
crime, but the sum of all criminality. (1865)
I am in earnest, I will not equivocate, I will not excuse, I will not
retreat a single inch, and *I will be heard*. (1831)

These two pronouncements characterize the rhetorical strategies of William
Lloyd Garrison, one of the most powerful and significant abolitionists of antebellum America. The second declaration, perhaps Garrison's most famous antislavery pronouncement, is engraved on the marble base of a larger-than-life
bronze statue of Garrison which resides on the Commonwealth Avenue Mall in
Boston's Back Bay. Garrison was indeed "larger than life," and he wrote those
famous words at the age of twenty-six, in 1831, as part of his editorial launch-
ing the publication of *The Liberator*, the abolitionist weekly newspaper founded
and edited by Garrison throughout those crucial decades leading up to the Civil
War. If the antebellum antislavery and abolitionist movements have heroes, they
have to be William Lloyd Garrison and Lydia Maria Child among the white,
Northern abolitionists, and Frederick Douglass, David Walker, and Harriet
Jacobs among the leading black abolitionist writers.

Born in Newburyport, Massachusetts, December 10, 1805, the son of a sea
captain, Garrison received almost no formal education but was active in printing
and publishing all of his adult life. In 1826, at the age of twenty-one, he became
editor of *The Free Press*, a journal in which he published the early poems of
John Greenleaf Whittier, a Quaker with whom Garrison maintained a close
friendship throughout his life. Garrison's opposition to slavery was foremost in
his reform activities, but he also opposed other injustices, including the oppression of women, which would later splinter his abolitionist following because
many conservative abolitionists did not favor women's suffrage. Garrison and
Wendell Phillips, another powerful orator and writer, were the mainstays of the
New England abolitionist movement, and they exerted a continuous pressure on
the Congress for "immediate and unconditional emancipation of the slaves."
Garrison's rhetorical flourishes won him enemies as well as adherents. An early
protest demonstrator, on July 4, 1854, in Framingham, Massachusetts, at an
antislavery gathering, Garrison publicly burned the Constitution of the United
States, declaring, "So perish all compromises with tyranny!" (*DAB*, p. 170).
These outbursts were accompanied by his call for disunion, a Northern version
of secession which would sever the Union ties with the slaveholding South. The
Constitution had made no specific provisions concerning slavery and thus was
viewed by the more militant abolitionists to be a charter document that permitted and tolerated slavery. Garrison and Wendell Phillips, who authored *The
Constitution a Proslavery Compact* (1845), viewed it as "a covenant with death
and an agreement with hell." Garrison attacked Daniel Webster, a United States
senator from Massachusetts who had supported the Compromise of 1850 with

Daguerreotype of William Lloyd Garrison, by permission of Ruth Owen
Jones, Amherst, Mass.

Garrison statue on Commonwealth
Mall, Boston, author photo.

its Fugitive Slave Law because he believed that disunion was even worse than
the evil of slavery, and his assault on Webster's politics of compromise was
accompanied by James Russell Lowell's essay, "Daniel Webster," which is excerpted in this volume. Occasionally, he was assaulted by mob violence, and in
1835, he was seized by a mob at a Boston Female Antislavery Society meeting
and dragged through the streets with a rope tied around his neck.

Garrison stands as one of the most important opponents of slavery in antebellum America; his antislavery writings reached more people than anyone except for Harriet Beecher Stowe's *Uncle Tom's Cabin.* His abolitionist principles
were uncompromising, and he was regularly opposed by proslavery Southerners.
The State of Georgia placed a ransom on his head: $5,000 for his arrest and
conviction. In 1830, his newspaper *The Genius of Universal Emancipation* published a libelous article, and Garrison was sued and found guilty. He was imprisoned for seven weeks in a Baltimore jail, until his fine was paid by sympathetic abolitionists from Boston. Like his successor in the Civil Rights
movement, Dr. Martin Luther King, Jr., Garrison was unrelenting and uncompromising. Unlike King, he was inflammatory and anything but passive, advocating secession, disunion, the overthrow of the Constitution, and an immediate, unconditional termination of chattel slavery to bring about emancipation.
His personal life was no less easy. Two of his seven children predeceased him,
and his wife suffered an illness, possibly a stroke, which left her a permanent
invalid. Garrison suffered various forms of illness, and his health was usually
precarious. He endured respiratory infections and kidney disease, and he appar-

ently was attracted to "phrenology, clairvoyance, and spiritualism" (*DAB*, p. 171).

Nevertheless, William Lloyd Garrison led the antebellum abolitionist movement through its several phases of growth, from the gradualist principles of colonization, which he briefly embraced when very young, to his denunciation of colonization in his disagreement with Edward Everett, to his consistent opposition to the Constitution and the Compromise of 1850, with its abhorrent Fugitive Slave Law. Garrison was indeed "larger than life," and his enduring principles of emancipation *and* the equality of the races are almost unique in antebellum America, where even powerful abolitionist voices like Harriet Beecher Stowe and Abraham Lincoln could also embrace elements of contemporary race theory. He was extremely controversial, leading historians to view him as an extremist who voiced unpopular opinions concerning slavery but who was unable to attract a sufficiently large following to form an effective political alliance for emancipation. This perspective on Garrison was particularly widespread among historians for nearly fifty years following his death in May 1879. He is now being reassessed as a necessary and crucial voice in the entire antislavery enterprise, whose vituperation was needed to prompt a reluctant nation to do the right thing and to confront the essential contradiction of the Constitution and the Declaration of Independence when slavery was still tolerated by both state and federal governments. A visit to the Boston Athenaeum (10 Beacon Street, Boston) and to the Boston Public Library, where Garrison's papers are held and where there is a complete collection of his newspaper, *The Liberator*, begun on January 1, 1831, with an editorial against slavery that is excerpted below, will reveal his courage. He was twenty-five years old at the time, and he defied not only the social forces of his own Boston community, but also the law of the land at both state and federal levels.

SUGGESTIONS FOR FURTHER READING

Aptheker, Herbert. *Abolitionism: A Revolutionary Movement*. Boston: Twayne, 1989.

Cain, William, ed. *William Lloyd Garrison and the Fight against Slavery: Selections from the Liberator*. Boston: Bedford Books, 1995.

Filler, Louis. *The Crusade against Slavery, 1830–1860*. New York: Harper and Brothers, 1960.

Fredrickson, George. *William Lloyd Garrison* (Englewood Cliffs: Prentice-Hall, 1968).

Garrison, Wendell Phillips. *William Lloyd Garrison, 1805–1879: the Story of His Life as Told by His Children* (4 vols., 1885–1889).

Kraditor, Aileen S. *Means and Ends in American Abolitionism: Garrison and His Critics on Strategy and Tactics, 1834–1850*. New York: Pantheon, 1969.

Gougeon, Len. "William Lloyd Garrison." In *Dictionary of Literary Biography* (Ann Arbor: Gale Research, 1999).

Lowance, Mason, ed. *Against Slavery: an Abolitionist Reader*. New York: Penguin-Putnam, 2000.

Mayer, Henry. *All on Fire: William Lloyd Garrison and the Abolition of Slavery* (New York: St. Martin's Press, 1998).

Nye, Russel B. *Fettered Freedom: Civil Liberties and the Slavery Controversy, 1830–1860*. Urbana: University of Illinois Press, 1972; originally published 1963.

Pease, Jane H., and William H. Pease. *Bound with Them in Chains: A Biographical History of the Antislavery Movement*. Westport, CT: Greenwood Press, 1972.

Perry, Lewis, and Michael Fellman, eds. *Antislavery Reconsidered: New Perspectives on the Abolitionists*. Baton Rouge: Louisiana State University Press, 1979.

Stewart, James Brewer. *Holy Warriors: The Abolitionists and American Slavery*. New York: Hill and Wang, 1976.

Walters, Ronald G. *The Antislavery Appeal: American Abolitionism after 1830*. Baltimore: Johns Hopkins University Press, 1976.

"William Lloyd Garrison." In *Dictionary of American Biography* (New York: Scribner, 1946–58), pp. 168–75.

An Address to the American Colonization Society, July 4, 1829
by William Lloyd Garrison

Fifty-three years ago, the Fourth of July was a proud day for our country. It clearly and accurately defined the rights of man; it made no vulgar alterations in the established usages of society; it presented a revelation adapted to the common sense of mankind; it vindicated the omnipotence of public opinion over the machinery of kingly government; it shook, as with the voice of a great earthquake, thrones which were seemingly propped up with Atlantean pillars; it gave an impulse to the heart of the world, which yet thrills to its extremities. . . . Sirs, I am not come to tell you that slavery is a curse, debasing in its effect, cruel in its operation, fatal in its continuance. The day and the occasion require no such revelation. I do not claim the discovery as my own, that "all men are born equal," and that among their inalienable rights are "life, liberty, and the pursuit of happiness." Were I addressing any other than a free and Christian assembly, the enforcement of this truth might be pertinent. Neither do I intend to analyze the horrors of slavery for your inspection, nor to freeze your blood with authentic recitals of savage cruelty. Nor will time allow me to explore even a furlong of that immense wilderness of suffering which remains unsubdued in our land. I take it for granted that the existence of these evils is acknowledged, if not rightly understood. My object is to define and enforce our duty, as Christians and Philanthropists.

On a subject so exhaustless, it will be impossible, in the moiety of an address, to unfold all the facts that are necessary to its full development. In view of it, my heart swells up like a living fountain, which time cannot exhaust, for it is perpetual. Let this be considered as the preface of a noble work, which your inventive sympathies must elaborate and complete.

I assume as distinct and defensible propositions:

I. That the slaves of this country, whether we consider their moral, intellectual, or social conditions, are preeminently entitled to the prayers, and sympathies, and charities, of the American people; and their claims for redress are as strong as those of any American could be in a similar condition.

II. That, as the free States—by which I mean non-slave-holding States—are constitutionally involved in the guilt of slavery, by adhering to a national compact that sanctions it; and in the danger, by liability to be called upon for aid in case of insurrection; they have the right to remonstrate against its continuance, and it is their duty to assist in its overthrow.

III. That no justificative plea for the perpetuity of slavery can be found in condition of its victims; and no barrier against our righteous interference, in the laws authorizing the buying, selling, and possessing of slaves, nor in the hazard of a collision with slaveholders.

IV. That education and freedom will elevate our colored population to a rank with the white—making them useful, intelligent and peaceable citizens. . . .

Let me not be misunderstood. My benevolence is neither contracted nor selfish. I pity that man whose heart is not larger than a whole continent. I despise the littleness of that patriotism which blusters only for its own rights, and, stretched to its utmost dimensions, scarcely covers its native territory; which adopts as its creed the right to act independently, even to the verge of licentiousness, without restraint, and to tyrannize wherever it can with impunity. This sort of patriotism is common. . . . But I mean to say, that, while we are aiding and instructing foreigners, we ought not to forget our own degraded countrymen; that neither duty nor honesty requires us to defraud ourselves that we may enrich others.

The condition of the slaves, in a religious point of view, is deplorable, entitling them to a higher consideration, on our part, than any other race; higher than the Turks or Chinese, for they have the privileges of instruction; higher than the Pagans, for they are not dwellers in a gospel land; higher than our red men of the forest, for we do not bind them with gyves [chains], nor treat them as chattels.

And here let me ask, What has Christianity done, by direct effort, for our slave population? Comparatively nothing. She has explored the isles of the ocean for objects of commiseration; but, amazing stupidity! she can gaze without emotion on a multitude of miserable beings at home, large enough to constitute a nation of freemen, whom tyranny has heathenized by law. In her public services they are seldom remembered, and in her private donations they are forgotten. From one end of the country to the other, her charitable societies form golden links of benevolence, and scatter their contributions like raindrops over a parched heath; but they bring no sustenance to the perishing slave. The blood of souls is upon her garments, yet she heeds not the stain. The clankings of the prisoner's chains strike upon her ear, but they cannot penetrate her heart.

I have said that the claims of slaves for redress are as strong as those of any Americans could be, in a similar condition. Does any man deny the position?

The proof, then, is found in the fact that a very large proportion of our colored population were born on our soil, and are therefore entitled to all the privileges of American citizens. This is their country by birth, not by adoption. Their children possess the same inherent and unalienable rights as ours, and it is a crime of the blackest dye to load them with fetters.

Every Fourth of July, our Declaration of Independence is produced, with a sublime indignation, to set forth the tyranny of the mother country, and to challenge the admiration of the world. But what a pitiful detail of grievances does this document present, in comparison with the wrongs which our slaves endure! In the one case, it is hardly the plucking of a hair from the head; in the other, it is the crushing of a live body on the wheel—the stings of the wasp contrasted to the tortures of the Inquisition. Before God, I must say, that such a *glaring contradiction as exists between our creed and practice* the annals of six thousand years cannot parallel. In view of it, I am ashamed of my country. I am sick of our unmeaning declamation in praise of liberty and equality; of our hypocritical cant about the unalienable rights of man. I could not, for my right hand, stand up before a European assembly, and exult that I am an American citizen and denounce the usurpations of a kingly government as wicked and unjust; or, should I make the attempt, the recollection of my country's barbarity and despotism would blister my lips, and cover my cheeks with burning blushes of shame.

I come to my second proposition: the right of the free States to remonstrate against the continuance, and to assist in the overthrow of slavery. . . . On this question, I ask no support from the injunction of Holy Writ, which says: "therefore all things whatsoever ye would that men should do to you, do ye even so to them: for this is the law and the prophets" [Matthew 7:12].

I throw aside the common dictates of humanity. I assert the right of the free States to demand a gradual abolition of slavery, because, by its continuance, they participate in the guilt thereof, and are threatened with ultimate destruction; because they are bound to watch over the interests of the whole country, without reference to territorial divisions; because their white population is nearly double that of the Slave states, and the voice of this overwhelming majority should be potential; . . . Now I say that, on the broad system of equal rights, this monstrous inequality should no longer be tolerated. If it cannot be speedily put down, not by force, but by fair persuasion; if we are always to remain shackled by unjust Constitutional provisions, when the emergency that imposed them has long since passed away; if we must share in the guilt and danger of destroying the bodies and souls of men, as the price of our Union; if the slave States will haughtily spurn our assistance, and refuse to consult the general welfare; then the fault is not ours if a separation eventually take place. . . .

It may be objected, that the laws of the slave States form insurmountable barriers to any interference on our part.

Answer: I grant that we have not the right, and I trust not the disposition, to use coercive measures. But do these laws hinder our prayers, or obstruct the flow of our sympathies?

Cannot our charities alleviate the condition of the slave, and perhaps break his fetters? Can we not operate upon public sentiment . . . by way of remonstrance, advice, or entreaty? Is Christianity so powerful that she can tame the red men of our forests, and abolish the Burman cast, and overthrow the Gods of Paganism, and liberate lands over which the darkness of Superstition has lain for ages; and yet so weak, in her own dwelling place, that she can make no impression upon her civil code? Can she contend successfully with cannibals, and yet be conquered by her own children?

Suppose that, by a miracle, the slaves should suddenly become white. Would you shut your eyes upon their sufferings, and calmly talk of Constitutional limitations? No; your voice would peal in the ears of the taskmasters like deep thunder; you would carry the Constitution by force, if it could not be taken by treaty; patriotic assemblies would congregate at the corners of every street; the old Cradle of Liberty would rock to a deeper tone than ever echoed therein at British aggression; the pulpit would acquire new and unusual eloquence from our holy religion. The argument, that these white slaves are degraded, would not then obtain. You would say, it is enough that they are white, and in bondage, and they ought immediately to be set free. You would multiply your schools of instruction and your temples of worship and rely on them for security. . . .

Sirs, the prejudices of the North are stronger than the South; they bristle, like so many bayonets, around the slaves they forge and rivet the chains of the nation. Conquer them, and the victory is won. The enemies of emancipation take courage from our criminal timidity. . . . It is often said, that the evil of slavery is beyond our control. Dreadful conclusion, that puts the seal of death upon our country's existence! If we cannot conquer the monster in its infancy, while his cartilages are tender and his limbs powerless, how shall we escape his wrath when he goes forth a gigantic cannibal, seeking whom he may devour? If we cannot safely unloose two millions of slaves now, how shall we bind upwards of twenty millions at the close of the present century? But there is no cause for despair. We have seen how readily, and with what ease, that horrid gorgon, Intemperance, has been checked in his ravages. Let us take courage. Moral influence, when in vigorous exercise, is irresistible. It has an immortal essence. . . .

If it be still objected, that it would be dangerous to liberate the present race of blacks; I answer:—the emancipation of all the slaves of this generation is most assuredly out of the question. The fabric, which now towers above the Alps, must be taken away brick by brick, and foot by foot, till it is reduced so low that it may be overturned without burying the nation in its ruins. Years may elapse before the completion of the achievement; generations of blacks may go down to the grave, manacled and lacerated, without a hope for their children; the philanthropists who are now pleading in behalf of the oppressed, may not live to witness the dawn which will precede the glorious day of universal emancipation; but the work will go on—laborers in the cause will multiply—new resources will be discovered—the victory will be obtained, worth the desperate struggle of a thousand years. Or, if defeat follow, woe to the safety of this people! The nation will be shaken as if by a mighty earthquake. A cry of horror, a cry of revenge, will go up to heaven in the darkness of midnight, and re-echo from every cloud. Blood will flow like water—the blood of guilty men, and of innocent women and children. Then will be heard lamentations and weeping, such as will blot out the remembrance of the horrors of St. Domingo. The terrible judgments of an incensed God will complete the catastrophe of Republican America.

And since so much is to be done for our country; since so many prejudices are to be dispelled, obstacles vanquished, interests secured, blessings obtained; since the cause of emancipation must progress heavily, and meet with much un-hallowed opposition,—why delay the work? There must be a beginning, and now is a propitious time, perhaps the last opportunity that will be granted us by a long-suffering God. No temporizing, lukewarm measures will avail ought. We must put our shoulders to the wheel, and heave with our united strength. Let us not look coldly and see our Southern brethren contending single-handed against an all powerful foe—faint, weary, borne down to the earth. *We are all alike guilty. Slavery is strictly a national sin.* New-England money has been expended in buying human flesh; New-England ships have been freighted with sable victims; New-England men have assisted in forging the fetters of those who groan in bondage. . . .

I call upon the ambassadors of Christ everywhere to make known this proclamation: "Thus saith the Lord God of the Africans, Let this people go, that they may serve me." I ask them to "proclaim liberty to the captives, and the opening of the prison to them that are bound."—to light up a flame of philanthropy that shall burn till all Africa be redeemed from the night of moral death, and the song of deliverance be heard throughout her borders.

I call upon the churches of the living God to lead in this great enterprise. If the soul be immortal, priceless, save it from remediless woe. Let them combine their energies and systematize their plans, for the rescue of suffering humanity. Let them pour out their supplications to heaven in behalf of the slave. Prayer is omnipotent; its breath can melt adamantine rocks—its touch can break the stoutest chains. Let anti-slavery charity-boxes stand uppermost among those for missionary, tract, and educational purposes. On this subject, Christians have been asleep; let them shake off their slumbers, and arm for the holy contest.

I call upon our New-England women to form charitable associations to relieve the degraded of their sex. As yet, an appeal to their sympathies was never made in vain. They outstrip us in every benevolent race. Females are doing much for the cause at the South; let their example be imitated, and their exertions surpassed, at the North.

I call upon the great body of newspaper editors to keep this subject constantly before their readers; to sound the trumpet of alarm, and to plead eloquently for the rights of man. They must give the tone to public sentiment. One press may ignite twenty; a city may warm a State; a State may impart a generous heat to a whole country. . . .

I will say finally that I despair of the republic while slavery exists therein. If I look up to God for success, no smile of mercy or forgiveness dispels the gloom of futurity; if to our own resources, they are daily diminishing; if to all history, our destruction is not only possible, but almost certain. Why should we slumber at this momentous crisis? If our hearts were to dread every throb of humanity; if it were lawful to oppress where power is ample; still, if we had any regard for our safety and happiness, we should strive to crush the Vampire which is feeding upon our life-blood. All the selfishness of our nature cries aloud for a better security. Our own vices are too strong for us, and keep us in perpetual alarm; how, in addition to these, shall we be able to contend successfully with millions of armed and desperate men, as we must eventually, if slavery does not cease?

Source note: Selections from the Writings and Speeches of William L. Garrison (Boston: R. F. Walcut, 1852), pp. 45–61. See also Wendell Phillips Garrison and Francis Jackson Garrison, *William Lloyd Garrison, 1805–1879: The Story of His Life Told by His Children*, 4 vols. (Boston: Houghton Mifflin, 1885–89), I: 127–37. As cited in William E. Cain, ed., *William Lloyd Garrison and the Fight Against Slavery* (Boston and New York: Bedford Books of St. Martin's Press, 1995), pp. 61–70.

Truisms
by William Lloyd Garrison

1. All men are born equal, and entitled to protection, excepting those whose skins are black and hair wooly; or, to prevent mistake, excepting Africans, and their descendants.

2. If white men are ignorant and depraved, they ought freely to receive the benefits of education; but if black men are in this condition, common sense dictates that they should be held in bondage, and never instructed.

3. He who steals a sheep, or buys one of a thief, deserves severe punishment. He who steals a Negro, or buys him of a kidnapper, is blameless. Why? Because a sheep can be eaten, and a negro cannot; because he has a black fleece, and it a white one; because the law asserts that this distinction is just, and law, we all know, is founded in equity. . . .

4. The color of the skin determines whether a man has a soul or not. If white, he has an immortal essence; if black, he is altogether beastly. Mulattoes, however, derive no benefit from this rule.

5. The blacks ought to be held in fetters, because they are too stupid to take care of themselves; at least, we are not so stupid as to suffer them to make the experiment.

6. To kidnap children on the coast of Africa is a horrid crime, deservedly punishable with death; but he who steals them, in this country, as soon as they are born, performs not merely an innocent but a praiseworthy act.

7. In Africa, a man who buys or sells another, is a monster of hell. In America, he is an heir of heaven.

8. A man has a right to heap unbounded execration upon the foreign slave trade and the abettors thereof; but if he utter a sentiment derogatory to the domestic traffic, or to those who assist in the transportation of victims, he is to

be imprisoned for publishing a libel, and sentenced to pay a fine of not less than one thousand dollars. [*Garrison was sued for libel by Francis Todd, a slave-trader whom* The Liberator *had attacked in 1830, and he was found guilty of libel and imprisoned for nearly two months. This entry is a clear allusion to that event in his career.*]

9. He who calls American slaveholders tyrants is a fool, a fanatic, or a madman; but if he apologize for monarchial governments, or an hereditary aristocracy, set him down as a tory, and a traitor to his country. . . .

10. There is not the least danger of a rebellion among the slaves; and even if they should revolt *en masse*, what would they do? Their united physical force would be utterly contemptible.

11. None but fanatics or idiots desire immediate abolition. If the slaves were liberated at once, our throats would be cut, and our houses pillaged and burnt.

12. Our slaves must be educated for freedom. Our slaves must never learn the alphabet, because knowledge would teach them to throw off their yoke.

13. People at the north have no right to alleviate physical suffering, or illumine spiritual darkness, at the South. But they have a right to assist the Greeks, or the Hindoos, or any foreign nation. . . .

15. A white man, who kills a tyrant, is a hero, and deserves a monument. If a slave kills his master, he is a murderer, and deserves to be burnt.

16. The slaves are kept in bondage for their own good. Liberty is a curse to the free people of color—their condition is worse than that of their slaves! . . .

17. The slaves are contented and happy. If sometimes they are so ungrateful or deluded as to abscond, it is pure philanthropy that induces their masters to offer a handsome reward for their detection.

18. Blacks have no intellect. The laws, at the South, which forbid their instruction, were not enacted because it was supposed these brutes had brains, or for the sake of compliment, but are owning simply to an itch for superfluous legislation.

19. Slaves are held as property. It is the acme of humanity and justice, therefore, in the laws, to recognize them also as moral agents, and punish them in the most aggravated manner, if they perpetrate a crime; though they cannot read, and have neither seen or known the laws!

20. It is foolish and cruel for an individual to denounce slavery; because the more he disturbs the security of the masters, the more vindictive will be their conduct toward the slaves. For the same reason, we ought to prefer the products of slave labor to those of free; as the more wealthy masters become, the better they will be enabled to feed and clothe their menials.

21. To deny that a man is a Christian or republican, who holds slaves and dooms their children to bondage, is most uncharitable and inconsistent. . . .

23. To doubt the religious vitality of a church, which is composed of slaveholders, is the worst species of infidelity.

24. The Africans are our slaves—not because we like to oppress, or to make money unjustly, but because Noah's curse must be fulfilled, and the Scriptures obeyed.

Source Note: "Truisms" from *The Liberator*, January 8, 1831, Boston Public Library and Neilson Library, Smith College, Northampton, Massachusetts.

The Constitution and the Union
by William Lloyd Garrison

There is much declamation about the sacredness of the compact which was formed between the free and slave states, on the adoption of the Constitution. A sacred compact, forsooth! We pronounce it the most bloody and heaven-daring arrangement ever made by men for the continuance and protection of a system of the most atrocious villainy ever exhibited on earth. Yes—we recognize the compact, but with feelings of shame and indignation; and it will be held in everlasting infamy by the friends of justice and humanity throughout the world. It was a compact formed at the sacrifice of the bodies and souls of millions of our race, for the sake of achieving a political object—an unblushing and monstrous coalition to do evil that good might come. Such a compact was, in the nature of things and according to the law of God, null and void from the beginning. No body of men ever had the right to guarantee the holding of human beings in bondage. . . . By the infamous bargain which they made between themselves, they virtually dethroned the Most High God, and trampled beneath their feet their own solemn and heaven-attested Declaration, that all men are created equal, and endowed by their Creator with certain inalienable rights—among which are life, liberty and the pursuit of happiness. They had no lawful power to bind themselves, or their posterity, for one hour—for one moment,—by such an unholy alliance. It was not valid then—it is not valid now. Still they persisted in maintaining it—and still do their successors, the people of Massachusetts, of New-England, and of the twelve free States, persist in maintaining it. A sacred compact! a sacred compact! What, then, is wicked and ignominious? This, then, is the relation in which we of New-England stand to the holders of slaves at the south, and this is virtually our language toward them:

"Go on, most worthy associates, from day to day, from month to month, from year to year, from generation to generation, plundering two millions of human beings of their liberty and the fruits of their toil—driving them into the fields like cattle—starving and lacerating their bodies—selling the husband from his wife, the wife from her husband, and children from their parents—spilling their blood—withholding the Bible from their hands and all knowledge from their minds —and kidnapping annually sixty thousand infants, the offspring of pollution and shame! Go on, in these practices,—we do not wish nor mean to interfere, . . . although we know that by every principle of law which does not utterly disgrace us by assimilating us to pirates, that they have as good and as true a right to the equal protection of the law as we have. . . . We pledge to you our physical strength, by the sacredness of the national compact—a compact by which we have enabled you already to plunder, persecute, and destroy two millions of slaves, who now lie beneath the sod; and by which we now give you the same piratical license to prey upon a much larger number of victims and all their posterity. Go on—and by this sacred instrument, the Constitution of the United States, dripping as it is with human blood, we solemnly pledge you our lives, our fortunes, and our sacred honor, that we will stand by you to the last."

People of New-England, and of the free States! is it true that slavery is no concern of yours? Have you no right even to protest against it, or to seek its removal? Are you not the main pillars of its support? How long do you mean to be answerable to God and the world, for spilling the blood of the poor innocents? Be not afraid to look the monster Slavery boldly in the face. He is your implacable foe—the vampire who is sucking your life-blood—the ravager of a large portion of your country, and the enemy of God and man. Never hope to be a united, or happy, or prosperous people while he exists. . . . Be assured that slavery will very speedily destroy this Union, if it be let alone; but even if the Union can be preserved by treading upon the necks and spilling the blood, and destroying the souls of millions of your race, we say it is not worth a price like this, and that it is in the highest degree criminal for you to continue the present compact. Let the pillars thereof fall—let the superstructure crumble into dust— if it must be upheld by robbery and oppression."

Source Note: "The Constitution and the Union," *The Liberator*, December 29, 1832, ed. William Lloyd Garrison, in Neilson Library, Smith College, Northampton, Massachusetts.

American Colorphobia
by William Lloyd Garrison

Therefore we believe and affirm—

That there is no difference, in principle, between the African slave trade and American slavery;

That every American citizen, who retains a human being in involuntary bondage, is, according to Scripture, a man-stealer;

That the slaves ought instantly to be set free, and brought under the protection of the law;

That if they had lived from the time of Pharaoh down to the present period, and had been entailed through successive generations, their right to be free could never have been alienated, but their claims would have constantly risen in solemnity. . . .

We further believe and affirm—

That all persons of color who possess the qualifications which are demanded of others, ought to be admitted forthwith to the enjoyment of the same privileges, and the exercise of the same prerogatives, as others; and that the paths of preferment, of wealth, and of intelligence, should be opened as widely to them as to persons of a white complexion.

We maintain that no compensation should be given to the planters emancipating their slaves—

Because it would be a surrender of the great fundamental principle that man cannot hold property in man;

Because slavery is a crime, and therefore it is not an article to be sold;

Because the holders of slaves are not the just proprietors of what they claim; freeing the slaves is not depriving them of property, but restoring it to the right owner; it is not wronging the master but righting the slave, restoring him to himself. . . .

We shall aim at a purification of the churches from all participation in the guilt of slavery.

We shall encourage the labor of freemen over that of the slaves, by giving a preference to their productions; and

We shall spare no exertions nor means to bring the whole nation to speedy repentance.

Source Note: William Cain, ed., *William Lloyd Garrison and the Fight against Slavery: Selections from The Liberator,* (Boston: Bedford/St. Martin's, 1995), pp. 92–93.

Speech to the Fourth Annual National Woman's Rights Convention
by William Lloyd Garrison

1. *Resolved.* That the natural rights of one human being are those of every other; in all cases equally sacred and inalienable; hence, the boasted "Rights of Man," about which we hear so much, are simply the "Rights of Woman," about which we hear so little; or, in other words, they are the Rights of Humankind, neither affected by or dependent upon sex or condition.

2. *Resolved.* That those who deride the claims of woman to a full recognition of her civil rights and political equality, exhibit the spirit which tyrants and usurpers have displayed in all ages towards the mass of mankind—strike at the foundation of all truly free and equitable government—contend for a sexual aristocracy, which is as irrational and unjust in principle, as that of wealth or hereditary descent—and show their appreciation of liberty to be wholly one-sided and supremely selfish.

3. *Resolved.* That for the men of this land to claim for themselves the elective franchise, and the right to choose their own rulers, and to enact their own laws, as essential to their freedom, safety and welfare, and then to deprive all the women of all those safeguards, solely on the ground of a difference of sex, is to evince the pride of self-esteem, the meanness of usurpation, and the folly of a self-assumed superiority.

4. *Resolved.* That woman, as well as man, has a right to the highest mental and physical development—to the most ample educational advantages, to the occupancy of whatever position she can reach in Church and State, in science and art, in poetry and music, in painting and sculpture, in civil jurisprudence and political economy, and in the varied departments of human industry, enterprise and skill, to the elective franchise, and to a voice in the administration of justice and the passage of laws for the general welfare.

5. *Resolved.* That to pretend that the granting of these claims would tend to make woman less amiable and attractive, less regardful of her peculiar duties and obligations as wife and mother, a wanderer from her proper sphere, bringing confusion into domestic life, and strife into the public assembly, is the cant of Papal Rome, as to the discordant and infidel tendencies of the right of private judgment in matters of faith . . . is the false allegation which selfish and timid conservatism is ever making against every new measure of Reform—and has no foundation in reason, experience, practice, or philosophy.

6. *Resolved.* That the consequences arising from the exclusion of woman from the possession and exercise of her natural rights and the cultivation of her mental faculties have been calamitous to the whole human race—making her servile, dependent, unwomanly—the victim of a false gallantry on the one hand, and of tyrannic subjection on the other—obstructing her mental growth, crippling her physical development, and incapacitating her for general usefulness, and thus inflicting an injury upon all born of woman; and cultivating in man a lordly and arrogant spirit; a love of dominion, a disposition to lightly disregard her comfort and happiness, all of which have been indulged in to a fearful extent, to the curse of his own soul, and the desecration of her nature.

7. *Resolved.* That so long as the most ignorant, degraded, and worthless men are freely admitted to the ballot-box, and practically acknowledged to be competent to determine who shall be in office, and how the government shall be administered, it is preposterous to pretend that women are not qualified to use the elective franchise, and that they are fit only to be recognized, politically speaking, as *non compos mentis* [not of sound mind].

Source Note: William L. Garrison, "Fourth Annual National Woman's Rights Convention held in Cleveland, Ohio, in October, 1853," *The Liberator*, October 28, 1853, in the collections of the Neilson Library, Smith College, Northampton, Massachusetts.

Editorial, The Liberator
by William Lloyd Garrison

[*On January 1, 1831, William Lloyd Garrison published a recantation of his position in the "Address to the American Colonization Society" given July 4, 1829. Garrison repudiated his previous support for gradual abolition.*]

Assenting to the self evident truth maintained in the Declaration of Independence, that "all men are created equal, and endowed by their Creator with certain inalienable rights"—I shall strenuously contend for the immediate enfranchisement of our slave population. In Part-Street Church, on the Fourth of July, 1829, in an address on slavery, I unreflectingly assented to the popular but pernicious doctrine of gradual abolition. I seize this opportunity to make a full and unequivocal recantation, and thus publicly to ask pardon of my God, of my country, and of my brethren the poor slaves, for having uttered a sentiment so full of timidity, injustice, and absurdity.

No Compromise with Slavery
by William Lloyd Garrison

. . . Of necessity, as well as of choice, I am a "Garrisonian" Abolitionist—the most unpopular appellation that any man can have applied to him, in the present state of public sentiment; yet, I am more than confident, destined ultimately to be honorably regarded by the wise and good. . . . Representing then, that phase of Abolitionism which is the most condemned—to the suppression of which, the means and forces of the Church and the State are most actively directed—I am here to defend it against all its assailants as the highest expediency, the soundest philosophy, the noblest patriotism, the broadest philanthropy, and the best religion extant. To denounce it as fanatical, disorganizing, reckless of consequences, bitter and irreverent in spirit, infidel in heart, deaf alike to the suggestions of reason and the warnings of history, is to call good evil, and evil good. . . . Let me define my positions, and at the same time challenge anyone to show wherein they are untenable.

I. I am a believer in that portion of the Declaration of Independence in which it is set forth, as among self-evident truths, "that all men are created equal; that they are endowed by their Creator with certain inalienable rights; that among these are life, liberty, and the pursuit of happiness." Hence, I am an Abolitionist. Hence, I cannot but regard oppression in every form—and most of all, that which turns a man into a thing—with indignation and abhorrence. Not to cherish these feelings would be recreancy to principle. They who desire me to be dumb on the subject of Slavery, unless I will open my mouth in its defense, ask me to give the lie to my professions, to degrade my manhood, and to stain my soul. I will not be a liar, a poltroon, or a hypocrite, to accommodate any party, to gratify any sect, to escape any odium or peril, to save any interest, to preserve any institution, or to promote any object. Convince me that one man may rightfully make another man his slave, and I will no longer subscribe to the Declaration of Independence. Convince me that liberty is not the inalienable birthright of every human being, of whatever complexion or clime, and I will give that instrument to the consuming fire. I do not know how to espouse freedom and slavery together. I do not know how to worship God and Mammon at the same time. . . . My crime is, that I will not go with the multitude to do evil. My singularity is, that when I say that Freedom is of God, and Slavery is of the devil, I mean just what I say. My fanaticism is, that I insist on the American people abolishing Slavery, or ceasing to prate of the rights of man. . . .

II. Notwithstanding the lessons taught us by Pilgrim Fathers and Revolutionary Sires, by Plymouth Rock, on Bunker Hill, at Lexington, Concord, and Yorktown; notwithstanding our Fourth of July celebrations, and ostentatious displays of patriotism; in what European nation is personal liberty held in such contempt as in our own? Where are there such unbelievers in the natural equality and freedom of mankind? *Our slaves outnumber the entire population of the country at the time of our revolutionary struggle*. In vain do they clank their chains, and fill the air with their shrieks, and make their supplications for mercy. In vain are their sufferings portrayed, their wrongs rehearsed, their rights defended. . . . For one rebuke of the man-stealer, a thousand denunciations of the Abolitionists are heard. For one press that bears a faithful testimony against Slavery, a score are ready to be prostituted to its service. For one pulpit that is not "recreant to its trust," there are ten that openly defend slaveholding as compatible with Christianity, and scores that are dumb. For one church that excludes the human enslaver from its communion table, multitudes extend to him the right hand of religious fellowship. . . . I have expressed the belief that, so lost to all self-respect and all ideas of justice have we become by the corrupting presence of Slavery, in no European nation is personal liberty held at such a discount, as a matter of principle, as in our own. See how clearly this is demonstrated. The reasons adduced among us in justification of slaveholding, and therefore against personal liberty, are multitudinous. I will enumerate only a dozen of these.

1. "The victims are black."
2. "The slaves belong to an inferior race."
3. "Many of them have been fairly purchased."
4. "Others have been honestly inherited."
5. "Their emancipation would impoverish their owners."
6. "They are better off as slaves than they would be as freemen."
7. "They could not take care of themselves if set free."
8. "Their simultaneous liberation would be attended with great danger."
9. "Any interference in their behalf will excite the ill-will of the South, and thus seriously affect Northern trade and commerce."
10. "The Union can be preserved only by letting Slavery alone, and that is of paramount importance."
11. "Slavery is a lawful and constitutional system, and therefore not a crime."
12. "Slavery is sanctioned by the Bible; the Bible is the word of God; therefore God sanctions Slavery, and the Abolitionists are wise above what is written."

Here then, are twelve reasons which are popularly urged in all parts of the country, as conclusive against the right of a man to himself. If they are valid, in any instance, what becomes of the Declaration of Independence?

III. The Abolitionism which I advocate is as absolute as the Law of God, and as unyielding as His throne. It admits of no compromise. Every slave is a stolen man; every slaveholder is a man-stealer. By no precedent, no example, no law, no compact, no purchase, no bequest, no inheritance, no combination of circumstances, is slaveholding right or justifiable. While a slave remains in fetters, the land must have no rest. Whatever sanctions his doom must be pronounced accursed. The law that makes him a chattel is to be trampled under foot; the compact that is formed at his expense, and cemented with his blood, is null and void; the church that consents to his enslavement is horribly atheistical; the religion that receives to its communion the enslaver is the embodiment of all criminality. Such, at least, is the verdict of my own soul, on the supposition that I am to be the slave; that my wife is to be sold from me for the vilest purposes; that my children are to be torn from my arms, and disposed of to the highest bidder, like sheep in the market. And who am I but a man? What right have I to be free, that another man cannot prove himself to possess by nature? . . . No man is to be injured in his person, mind, or estate. He cannot be, with benefit to any other man, or to any state of society. Whoever would sacrifice him for any purpose is both morally and politically insane. Every man is equivalent to every other man. Destroy the equivalent, and what is left? "So God created man in his own image—male and female created he them." This is a death-blow to all claims of superiority, to all charges of inferiority, to all usurpation, and to all oppressive dominion. . . . No man can show that I have taken one step beyond the line of justice, or forgotten the welfare of the master, in my anxiety to free the slave. . . . But, then, if they are men; if they are to run the same career of immortality with ourselves; if the same law of God is over them as over all others; if they have souls to be saved or lost; if Jesus included them among those for whom he laid down his life; if Christ is within many of them "the hope of glory," then, when I claim for them all that we claim for ourselves, because we are creatures in the image of God, I am guilty of no extravagance, but am bound, by every principle of honor, by all the claims of human nature, by obedience to the Almighty God, to remember them that are in bonds as bound with them, and *to demand their immediate and unconditional emancipation.*

How has the slave system grown to its present enormous dimensions? Through compromise. How is it to be exterminated? Only by an uncompromising spirit. This is to be carried out in all the relations of life—social, political, religious. . . . Whatever may be the guide of the South, the North is still more responsible for the existence, growth, and extension of Slavery. In her hand has been the destiny of the Republic from the beginning. She could have emancipated every slave, long ere this, had she been upright in heart and free in spirit. She has given respectability, security, and the means of sustenance and attack to her deadliest foe. She has educated the whole country, and particularly the Southern portion of it, secularly, theologically, religiously; and the result is, three millions and a half of slaves, increasing at the appalling rate of one hundred thousand a year, three hundred a day, and one every five minutes, the utter corruption of public sentiment, and general skepticism as to the rights of man . . . the pulpits, with rare exceptions, filled with men as careful to consult the popular will as though there were no higher law . . . and now, the repeal of the Missouri Compromise, and the consecration of five hundred thousand square miles of free territory forever to the service of the Slave Power!

And what does all this demonstrate? That the sin of this nation is not geographical—is not specially Southern—but deep seated and Universal. "The whole head is sick, and the whole heart faint." . . . *If it would be a damning sin for us to admit another Slave State into the Union, why is it not a damning sin to permit a Slave State to remain in the Union? . . . Not a single slaveholder will I allow to enjoy repose on any other condition than instantly ceasing to be one. Not a single slave will I leave in his chains, on any conditions, or under any circumstances. . . . The Scriptural injunction is to be obeyed: "Resist the devil, and he will flee from you." My motto is, "No union with slaveholders, religiously or politically." Their motto is, "Slavery forever."*

While the present union exists, I pronounce it hopeless to expect any repose, or that any barrier can be effectually raised, against the extension of Slavery. With two-thousand million dollars' worth of property in human flesh in its hands, to be watched and wielded as one vast interest for all the South, with forces never divided, and purposes never conflictive, with a spurious, Negro hating religion universally diffused, and everywhere ready to shield it from harm, with a selfish, sordid, divided North, long since bereft of its manhood, to cajole, bribe and intimidate, with its foot planted on two-thirds of our vast national domains, and there unquestioned, absolute and bloody in its sway, with the terrible strength and boundless resources of the whole country at its command, it cannot be otherwise than that the Slave Power will consummate its diabolical purposes to the uttermost. . . . In itself, Slavery has no resources and no strength. Isolated and alone, it could not stand an hour; and, therefore, further aggression and conquest would be impossible. . . .

What then, is to be done? Friends of the slave, the question is not whether by our efforts we can abolish Slavery, speedily or remotely, for duty is ours, the result with God; but whether we will go with the multitude to do evil, sell our birthright for a mess of pottage, cease to cry aloud and spare not, and remain in Babylon when the command of God is, "Come out of here, my people. . . . "

Source Note: William Lloyd Garrison, *No Compromise with Slavery: An Address, Delivered in the Broadway Tabernacle*, New York, February 14, 1854 (New York: American Antislavery Society, 1854).

DAVID WALKER (1785–1830)

Garrison was an early militant voice of protest against chattel slavery in the United States, but he was quickly joined by other abolitionist voices, including those of a rising tide of black abolitionist writers. One of the most influential of these black writers was David Walker, who in 1829 authored a pamphlet of some seventy pages which attacked the hypocrisy of the United States vigorously. According to Garrison's biographer, Henry Mayer, Walker attributed the slaves' misery to four basic causes, and he demanded immediate redress. "The barbarity of slavery, a cringing and servile attitude—even among free blacks— that perpetuated ignorance, the indifference of the Christian clergy, and the colonization scheme that insulted black citizenship and aspirations. Walker explicitly attacked Thomas Jefferson's racist assertions about black inferiority and he urged black men to give *Notes on the State of Virginia* to their sons to inspire

CHARLESTOWN, *April* 27, 1769.

TO BE SOLD,

On WEDNESDAY *the Tenth Day of*
MAY *next*,

A CHOICE CARGO OF

Two Hundred & Fifty

NEGROES:

ARRIVED in the Ship
COUNTESS of SUSSEX, THOMAS DAVIES,
Mafter, directly from GAMBIA, by

JOHN CHAPMAN, & Co.

** *THIS is the Veffel that had the Small-Pox
on Board at the Time of her Arrival the* 31*ft of
March laft: Every necefary Precaution hath fince
been taken to cleanfe both Ship and Cargo thoroughly,
fo that thofe who may be inclined to purchafe need not
be under the leaft Apprehenfion of Danger from Infection.*
The NEGROES *are allowed to be the likelieft Parcel
that have been imported this Seafon.*

1769

Slave auction broadside, by permission of Georgia Barnhill, Mellon Curator of Graphic
Arts, American Antiquarian Society, Worcester, Mass.

their anger. He deplored submissiveness among blacks, contended for their right
of self-defense, and raised a prophetic voice for a rebellion in the name of the
Lord's justice. . . . the pamphlet was published in September, 1829, and went
through two more editions over the next six months" (Mayer, p. 83). David
Walker's *Appeal* would have significant influence on the abolitionist writer Lydia
Maria Child, whose 1833 treatise, *An Appeal in Favor of that Class of Americans
Called Africans*, would acknowledge a large debt to David Walker's inspiration.
Walker and Henry Highland Garnet were early African abolitionists whose
works broadened the spectrum of abolitionist sentiment during the first decade
of militant abolitionism, 1830–40. No longer the province of New England
evangelical Christians and Quaker antislavery rhetoricians, the "movement" was
enlarged to embrace black writers and escaped slaves themselves, like Frederick
Douglass, who not only became one of the leading speakers for the abolitionist
cause through New England, but also carried the message to England in person
and argued his case throughout the world by way of his autobiographical *A
Narrative of the Life of Frederick Douglass: an American Slave* (1845), the first of
three such autobiographical documents he would write.

Very little is known about David Walker. He was born in Wilmington, North
Carolina, September 28, 1785. His mother was a free woman, and according to
Stroud's Compendium of the Laws of Slavery (1843), the condition of the mother
determined the condition of the child, whether slave or free. Thus Walker grew
up surrounded by African slaves in the slaveholding South. But at a very early
age, Walker developed a hatred of slavery and the "peculiar institution" that
would inform his rhetoric throughout his short life. He argued, while still living
in North Carolina, "If I remain in this bloody land, I will not live long. As true
as God reigns, I will be avenged for the sorrow which my people have suffered.
This is not the place for me—no, no. I must leave this part of the country. It
will be a great trial for me to live on the same soil where so many men are in
slavery; certainly I cannot remain where I must hear their chains continually,
and where I must encounter the insults of their hypocritical enslavers. Go, I
must." And go he did. Walker made his way to New England and settled permanently in Boston, Massachusetts, where he opened a second-hand clothing
store and became an abolitionist reformer. His major work, the *Appeal*, was
published in 1829, and it went through several printings during the following
two years. Southern slaveholders were unsuccessful in their attempts to suppress
it, so they responded by enacting harsher laws and penalties designed to prevent
Negro slaves from learning to read, to prevent seditious literature like Walker's
Appeal from having any impact on the very group it was designed to inspire.
The book is divided into four sections, or "articles," and the essential elements
are summarized in the first sections of each article. Throughout the work,
Walker, who was entirely self-educated, alludes to the Bible, citing many references to slavery in Egypt and to the emancipation of the Israelites through
Moses' leadership. He used his Bible effectively, for his readership, both black
and white, would have been steeped in biblical folklore and the Judeo-Christian
tradition, a tradition that David Walker and William Lloyd Garrison would use

as rhetorical strategies for their inspirational and motivational appeals to moral conscience.

David Walker's *Appeal* is an angry document. Its author had witnessed the brutal mistreatment of his "brethren" in the South and the race prejudices against Negroes in the North. Like Frederick Douglass and Garrison, he understood the link between race theory and slavery, the connection between a belief in the inferiority of one race and the superiority of another and the institution of chattel slavery. But he also believed that these views were learned, that they were social and political, and not "essential," and certainly not biological in origin. At the conclusion of the *Appeal*, an olive branch is held out to white America, coupled with an implicit threat, which is one of the reasons the book was so inflammatory.

> Remember Americans, that . . . we must and shall be free, and enlightened as you are, will you wait until we shall, under God, obtain our liberty by the crushing arm of power? Will it not be dreadful for you? I speak Americans for your good. We must and shall be free I say, in spite of you. . . . Throw away your fears and prejudices then, and enlighten us and treat us like men, and we will like you more than we do now hate you, and tell us no more about colonization, for America is as much our country, as it is yours. Treat us like men, and there is no danger but we will all live in peace and happiness together. For we are not like you, hard hearted, unmerciful and unforgiving. What a happy country this will be, if the whites will listen. What nation under heaven, will be able to do anything with us, unless God gives us up into his hand? But Americans, I declare to you, while you keep us in bondage, and treat us like brutes, to make us support you and your families, we cannot be your friends. You do not look for it, do you? Treat us then like men, and we will be your friends.

Walker was threatened for his seditious writing, and a reward was offered for him: one thousand dollars for the return of his body, but ten thousand if he were captured and delivered alive—one can only speculate why. The *Appeal* was Walker's most important work, partly because he lived only to the age of forty-five. He died at his home, and at the time there was speculation, now discounted, that he had been murdered (see Mayer, p. 121).

Source Note: David Walker's Appeal: With a Brief Sketch of His Life, by Henry Highland Garnet, and also Garnet's Address to the Slaves of the United States of America (New York: J. H. Tobitt, 1848; reprinted for the *New York Times* by the Arno Press, New York, 1969).

SUGGESTIONS FOR FURTHER READING:

Hinks, Peter P. *To Awaken My Afflicted Brethren: David Walker and the Problem of Antebellum Slave Resistance.* University Park: Pennsylvania State University Press, 1997.

Mayer, Henry. *All on Fire: William Lloyd Garrison and the Abolition of Slavery.* New York: St. Martin's Press, 1998.

Appeal
by David Walker

Preamble.

I am fully aware, in making this appeal to my much afflicted and suffering brethren, that I shall . . . be assailed by those whose greatest earthly desires are, to keep us in abject ignorance and wretchedness, and who are of the firm conviction that heaven has designed us and our children to be slaves and beasts of burden to them and their children. . . . Can our condition be any worse? Can it be more mean and abject? If there are any changes, will they not be for the better, though they may appear for the worse at first? Can they get us any lower? Where can they get us? They are afraid to treat us worse, for they know well, the day they do it they are gone. . . . I appeal to heaven for my motive in writing, who knows that my object is, if possible, to awaken in the breasts of my afflicted, degraded and slumbering brethren, a spirit of enquiry and investigation respecting our miseries and wretchedness in this *Republican Land of Liberty*!!!! . . .

And as the inhuman system of slavery is the source from which most of our miseries proceed, I shall begin with that curse to nations; which has spread terror and devastation through so many nations of antiquity, and which is raging to such a pitch at the present day in Spain and in Portugal. . . . The fact is, the labor of slaves comes so cheap to the avaricious usurpers, and is, as they think, of such great utility to the country where it exists, that those who are actuated by sordid avarice only, overlook the evils, which will as sure as the Lord lives, follow after the good. In fact, they are so happy to keep in ignorance and degradation, and to receive the homage and the labor of the slaves, they forget that God rules in the armies of heaven and among the inhabitants of the earth, having his ears continually open to the cries, tears, and groans of his oppressed people; and being a just and holy Being will at one day appear fully in behalf of the oppressed, and arrest the progress of the avaricious oppressors; for although the destruction of the oppressors God may not effect by the oppressed, yet the Lord our God will bring other destructions upon them—for not infrequently will he cause them to rise up one against another, to be split and divided, and to oppress each other; and sometimes to open hostilities with sword in hand. . . . Their destruction may indeed be procrastinated a while, but can it continue long while they are oppressing the Lord's people? Has He not the hearts of all men in His hand? Will he suffer one part of his creatures to go on oppressing another like brutes always, with impunity? And yet those avaricious wretches are calling for Peace!!! I declare it does appear to me, as though some nations think God is asleep, or that he made the Africans for nothing else but to dig their mines and work their farms, or they cannot believe history, sacred or profane. I ask every man who has a heart and is blessed with the privilege of believing—Is not God a God of justice to all his creatures? Do you say he is? Then if he gives peace and tranquility to tyrants, and permits them to keep our fathers, our mothers, ourselves, and our children in eternal ignorance and wretchedness to support them and their families, would he be to us a God of Justice?? I ask, O ye Christians!! who hold us and our children, in the most abject ignorance and degradation, that ever a people were afflicted with since the world began—I say, if God gives you peace and tranquility, and suffers you thus to go on afflicting us and our children, who have never given you the least provocation, would he be to us a God of Justice? If you will allow that we are men, who feel for each other, does not the blood of our fathers and of us their children, cry aloud to the Lord of Sabbath against you, for the cruelties and murders with which you have, and do continue to afflict us. . . .

Article I.

I promised to demonstrate to the satisfaction of the most incredulous, that we, the colored people of these United States of America, are the most wretched, degraded, and abject set of beings that ever lived since the world began, and that the white Americans having reduced us to the wretched state of slavery, treat us in that condition more cruelly (they being an enlightened and Christian people) than any heathen nation did any people whom it had reduced to our condition. . . . To prove farther that the condition of the Israelites was better under the Egyptians than ours is under the whites, I call upon the professing Christians, I call upon the philanthropist, I call upon the very tyrant himself, to show me a page of history, either sacred or profane, on which a verse can be found, which maintains, that the Egyptians heaped the insupportable insult upon the children of Israel by telling them that they were not of the human family. Can the whites deny this charge?

Have they not, after having reduced us to the deplorable condition of slaves under their feet, held us up as descending originally from the tribes of Monkeys and Orang–Outangs? O! My God! I appeal to every man of feeling—is not this unsupportable? Is it not heaping the most gross insult upon our miseries, because they have got us under their feet and we cannot help ourselves? . . . Has not Mr. Jefferson declared to the world, that we are inferior to the whites, both in the endowments of our bodies and of minds? It is indeed surprising, that a man of such great learning, combined with such excellent natural parts, should speak so of a set of men in chains. . . . Here, let me ask Mr. Jefferson (but he is gone, to answer at the bar of God, for the deeds done in his body while living), therefore I ask the whole American people, had I not rather die, or be put to death than to be a slave to any tyrant, who takes not only my own, but my wife and children's lives by inches? Yea, I would meet death with avidity far in preference to such servile submission to the murderous hands of tyrants. Mr. Jefferson's very severe remarks on us have been so extensively argued upon by men whose attainments in literature, I shall never be able to reach, that I would not have meddled with it, were it not to solicit each of my brethren, who has the spirit of a man, to buy of copy of Mr. Jefferson's "Notes on Virginia," and put it in the hand of his son. For let no one of us suppose that the refutations which have been written by our white friends are enough—they are *whites*—we are *blacks.* . . . The whites have always been an unjust, jealous, unmerciful, avaricious and blood thirsty set of beings, always seeking after power and authority. . . . In fact, take them as a body, they are ten times more cruel, avaricious and unmerciful than ever [the heathens] were; for while they were heathens they were bad enough it is true, but it is positively a fact that they were not quite so audacious as to go and take vessel loads of men, women, and children, and in cold blood and through devilishness, throw them into the sea and murder them in all kinds of ways. While they were heathens, they were too ignorant for such barbarity. But being Christians, enlightened and sensible, they are now completely prepared for such hellish cruelties. . . . The whites have had the essence of the gospel as it was preached by my master and his apostles—the Ethiopians have not . . . the Lord will give it to them to their satisfaction. . . .

Article II. Our Wretchedness in Consequence of Ignorance.

Ignorance, my brethren, is a mist, low down into the very dark and almost impenetrable abyss of which, our fathers for many centuries have been plunged. The Christians, and enlightened of Europe, and some of Asia, seeing the ignorance and consequent degradation of our fathers, instead of trying to enlighten them, by teaching them that religion and light with which God had blessed them, they have plunged them into wretchedness ten thousand times more intolerable, than if they had left them entirely to the Lord, and to add to their miseries, deep down into which they have plunged them, tell them, that they are an inferior and distinct race of beings. . . . The whites want slaves, and want us for their slaves, but some of them will curse the day they ever saw us. As true as the sun ever shone in its meridian splendor, my color will root some of them out of the very face of the earth. They shall have enough of making slaves of, and butchering, and murdering us in the manner which they have. No doubt some may say that I write with a bad spirit, and that I being a black, wish these things to occur. Whether I write with a bad or good spirit, I say if these things do not occur in their proper time, it is because the world in which we live does not exist, and we are deceived with regard to its existence. . . . I should like to see the whites repent peradventure God may have mercy on them, some however, have gone so far that their cup must be filled.

Ignorance and treachery, one against the other—a groveling servility and abject submission to the lash of tyrants, we see plainly, my brethren, are not the natural elements of the blacks, as the Americans try to make us believe; but these are misfortunes which God has suffered our fathers to be enveloped in for so many ages, no doubt in consequence of their disobedience to their Maker and which do, indeed, reign at this time among us, almost to the destruction of all other principles, for I must truly say, that ignorance, the mother of treachery and deceit, gnaws into our very vitals. Ignorance, as it now exists among us, produces a state of things, O my Lord! too horrible to present to the world. Any man who is curious to see the full force of ignorance developed among the colored people of the United States of America, has only to go into the southern and western states of this confederacy, where, if he is not a tyrant, but has the feelings of a human being, who can feel for a fellow creature, he may see enough to make his very heart bleed! He may see there, a son take his mother, who bore almost the pains of death to give him birth, and by the command of a tyrant, strip her as naked as she came into the world, and apply the cow-hide to her, until she falls a victim to death in the road! He may see a husband take his dear wife, not infrequently in a pregnant state, and perhaps far advanced, and beat her for an unmerciful wretch, until his infant falls a lifeless lump at her feet! Can the Americans escape God Almighty? If they do, can he be to us a God of Justice? . . .

How can, Oh! how can those enemies but say that we and our children are not of the Human Family, but were made by our creator to be an inheritance to them and theirs forever? How can the slave-holders but say that they can bribe the best colored person in the country, to sell his brethren for a trifling sum of money, and take that atrocity to confirm them in their avaricious opinion, that we were made to be the slaves of them and their children?

How could Mr. Jefferson but say, "I advance it therefore as a suspicion only, that the blacks, whether originally a distinct race, or made distinct by time and circumstances, are *inferior to the whites in the endowments both of body and mind?* It is not against experience to suppose that different species of the same genus, or varieties of the same species, may possess different qualifications [Here, my brethren, listen to him]. Will not a lover of natural history then, one who views the gradations in all the races of animals with the eye of philosophy, excuse an effort to keep those in the department of man as distinct as nature has formed them? . . .

["]This unfortunate difference of color, and perhaps of faculty, is a powerful obstacle to the emancipation of these people. Many of their advocates, while they wish to vindicate the liberty of human nature are anxious also to preserve its dignity and beauty. Some of these, embarrassed by the question, 'What further is to be done with them?' join themselves in opposition with those who are actuated by sordid avarice only." . . . For my part, I am glad that Mr. Jefferson has advanced his position for your sake; for you will either have to contradict or confirm him by your own actions and not by what our friends have said or done for us; for those things are other men's labors and do not satisfy the Americans who are waiting for us to prove to them ourselves that we are men before they will be willing to admit the fact. . . .

Men of color, who are also of sense, for you particularly is my appeal designed. Our more ignorant brethren are not liable to penetrate its value. I call upon you therefore to cast your eyes upon the wretchedness of your brethren and to do your utmost to enlighten them—*go to work and enlighten your brethren*—Let the Lord see you doing what you can to rescue them and yourselves from degradation. . . . There is a great work for you to do, as trifling as some of you may think of it. You have to prove to the Americans and the world, that we are men, and not brutes as we have been represented, and by millions treated. *Remember, to let the aim of your labors among your brethren, and particularly the youths, be the dissemination of education and religion.* It is lamentable, that many

of our children go to school, from four until they are eight or ten, and sometimes fifteen years of age, and leave school knowing but a little more about the
grammar of their language than a horse does about handling a musket, and not
a few of them are really so ignorant, that they are unable to answer a person
correctly, general questions in geography, and to hear them read would only be
to disgust a man who has a taste for reading. . . . Some few of them, may make
out to scribble tolerably well, over half a sheet of paper, which I believe has
hitherto been a powerful obstacle in our way, to keep us from acquiring knowledge. . . . The cause of this almost universal ignorance amongst us, I appeal to
our school-masters to declare. Here is a fact, which I take from the mouth of a
young colored man, who has been in Massachusetts nearly nine years, and who
knows grammar this day, nearly as well as he did the day he first entered the
school-house, under a white master. This young man says—"my master would
never allow me to study grammar." I asked him why? "The school committee
forbid the colored children learning grammar, they would not allow any but the
white children to study grammar." It is a notorious fact that the major part of
the white Americans have, ever since we have been among them, tried to keep
us ignorant and make us believe that God made us and our children to be the
slaves to them and theirs. *Oh! My God, have mercy on Christian Americans!*

Article III. Our Wretchedness in Consequence of the Preachers of the Religion of Jesus Christ.

Religion, my brethren, is a substance of deep consideration among all nations of
the earth. . . . But pure, and undefiled religion, such as was preached by Jesus
Christ and his apostles, is hard to be found in all the earth. . . . Indeed, the way
in which religion was and is conducted by the Europeans and their descendants,
one might believe it was a plan fabricated by themselves and the devils to oppress us! . . .

> [*Walker turned his critical eye to the hypocrisy he saw in the Christian church
> throughout history, with particular emphasis on contemporary nineteenth-cen-
> tury evangelical Christianity, which had all but abandoned the cause of emanci-
> pation both North and South. There were, of course, exceptions to these general-
> izations, and several are cited in the* Biblical Antislavery Arguments *section of
> this volume. However, Walker was correct in his indictment of the church for its
> hypocrisy. See also introduction to chapter 3, "Biblical Proslavery Arguments."*]

The wicked and ungodly, seeing their preachers treat us with so much cruelty,
they say: our preachers, who must be right, if any body are, treat them like
brutes, and why cannot we?—They think it is no harm to keep them in slavery
and put the whip to them, and why cannot we do the same!—They being
preachers of the gospel of Jesus Christ, if it were any harm, they would surely
preach against their oppression and do their utmost to erase it from the country;
not only in one or two cities, but one continual cry would be raised in all parts
of this confederacy and would cease only with the complete overthrow of the
system of slavery, in every part of the country. But how far the American

preachers are from preaching against slavery and oppression, which have carried their country to the brink of a precipice. . . . Can the American preachers appeal unto God, the Maker and Searcher of hearts, and tell him, with the Bible in their hands, that they make no distinction on account of men's color? Can they say, O God! thou knowest all things—thou knowest that we make no distinction between thy creatures to whom we have to preach thy Word? . . . I believe you cannot be so wicked as to tell him that his Gospel was that of *distinction.* . . . What right, then, has one of us, to despise another and to treat him cruelly, on account of his color, which none but the God who made it can alter? Can there be a greater absurdity in nature, and particularly in a free republican country? But the Americans, having introduced slavery among them, their hearts having become almost seared, as with an hot iron, and God has nearly given them up to believe a lie in preference to the truth!!! and I am awfully afraid that this pride, prejudice, avarice and blood, will, before long, prove the final ruin of this happy republic, or land of liberty!!! Can anything be a greater mockery of religion than the way in which it is conducted by the Americans?

Article IV. Our Wretchedness in Consequence of the Colonization Plan.

[*Walker here summarizes Henry Clay's colonization scheme, which he ironically critiques as he quotes from it, and uses it to further illustrate the cruelty of white Americans to the Africans they have enslaved.*]

That class of the mixt population of our country (colored people) was peculiarly situated; they neither enjoyed the immunities of freemen, nor were they subjected to the incapacities of slaves, but partook, in some degree, of the qualities of both. From their condition, and the unconquerable prejudices resulting from their color, they never could amalgamate with the free whites of this country. It was desirable, therefore, as it respected them, and the residue of the population of the country, to drain them off. Various schemes of colonization had been thought of, and a part of our continent, it was supposed by some, might furnish a suitable establishment for them. But, for his part, Mr. Clay said, he had a decided preference for some part of the coast of Africa. There, ample provision might be made for the colony itself, and it might be rendered instrumental in the introduction into that extensive quarter of the globe, of the arts, civilization, and Christianity. [Here, I ask Mr. Clay, what kind of Christianity? Did he mean such as they have among the Americans—distinction, whip, blood, and oppression? I pray the Lord, Jesus Christ, to forbid it.]

[*Colonization was indeed proposed in various forms, from Thomas Jefferson's time through the middle of the century. It was temporarily embraced by a variety of antislavery and abolitionist thinkers, including William Lloyd Garrison and Abraham Lincoln. However, its association with "gradualism"—the slow removal of slavery as an institution from American soil, the popular form of emancipation theory before the emergence of Garrison, Walker, Child, Phillips, and the militant abolitionist advocates who called for immediate and uncondi-*]

tional emancipation of all slaves in the United States—led to its decline. Even Harriet Beecher Stowe shows how George Harris, a character modeled on the fugitive slave and abolitionist Frederick Douglass, eventually makes his way from the South to the North through Canada to Liberia. Walker's contempt for any form of colonization theory results from his understanding that colonizationists usually embraced contemporary race theory, by which blacks were perceived to be inferior to whites.]

Man, in all ages, and all nations of the earth, is the same. Man is a peculiar creature —he is the image of his God, though he may be subjected to the most wretched condition upon earth, yet that spirit and feeling which constitute the creature man, can never be entirely erased from his breast, because the God who made him after his own image, planted it in his heart; he cannot get rid of it. The whites knowing this, they do not know what to do; they are afraid that we, being men, and not brutes, will retaliate, and woe will be to them; therefore, that dreadful fear, together with an avaricious spirit, and the natural love in them to be called masters, bring them to the resolve that they will keep us in ignorance and wretchedness, as long as they possibly can. . . . Do the colonizationists think to send us off without first being reconciled to us? . . . Methinks colonizationists think they have a set of brutes to deal with, sure enough. Do they think to drive us from our country and homes, after having enriched it with our blood and tears, and keep back millions of our dear brethren, sunk in the most barbarous wretchedness, to dig up gold and silver for them and their children?

Now Americans, I ask you candidly, was your suffering under Great Britain one hundredth part as cruel and tyrannical as you have rendered ours under you? Some of you, no doubt, believe that we will never throw off your murderous government, and "provide new guards for our future security." . . . Some of the whites are ignorant enough to tell us, that we ought to be submissive to them, that they may keep their feet on our throats. And if we do not submit to be beaten to death by them, we are bad creatures and of course must be damned. If any man wishes to hear this doctrine openly preached to us by the American preachers, let him go into the Southern and Western sections of this country. I do not speak from hearsay, what I have written, is what I have seen and heard myself. No man may think that my book is made up of conjecture, I have traveled and observed nearly the whole of those things myself, and what little I did not get by my own observation, I received from those among the whites and blacks, in whom the greatest confidence may be placed. The Americans may be as vigilant as they please, but they cannot be vigilant enough for the Lord, neither can they hide themselves, where he will not find and bring them out.

. . . Remember Americans, that we must and shall be free and enlightened as you are, will you wait until we shall under God obtain our liberty by the crushing arm of power? Will it not be dreadful for you? I speak, Americans, for your own good. We must and shall be free, and enlightened as you are, will you wait until we shall be free I say, in spite of you. . . . Throw away your fears and prejudices then, and enlighten us and treat us like men, and we will like you more than we do now hate you, and tell us no more about colonization, for America is as much our country, as it is yours. Treat us like men, and there is no danger but we will all live in peace and happiness together. For we are not like you, hard hearted, unmerciful and unforgiving. What a happy country this will be, if the whites will listen. What nation under heaven, will be able to do anything with us, unless God gives us up into his hand? But Americans, I declare to you, while you keep us in bondage, and treat us like brutes, to make us support you and your families, we cannot be your friends. You do not look for it, do you? Treat us then like men, and we will be your friends.

Source Note: David Walker's Appeal: with a Brief Sketch of His Life, by Henry Highland Garnet, and also Garnet's Address to the Slaves of the United States of America (New York: J. H. Tobitt, 1848; reprinted for the *New York Times* by the Arno Press, New York, 1969).

LYDIA MARIA CHILD (1802–1880)

One of the most important of the Boston abolitionists, Lydia Maria Child joins William Lloyd Garrison and Frederick Douglass in a triumvirate of leaders whose influence among New England abolitionists was unusually powerful. With her husband, David Child, they formed a strong coalition against slavery and in support of full racial equality when both attitudes were extremely unpopular. Unlike Douglass and Garrison, both had much to lose by their actions. Lydia Child's family was prominent and wealthy in Boston; her marriage to David Child and her radical activities in the abolitionist movement effectively severed her ties to family and many friends, and her publisher removed many of her earlier, popular works from the shelves and terminated her contract. Modern readers are not always aware of the sacrifices that reformers make to achieve their goals; Lydia Child is a good example of one who lost everything for publishing a radical work and for defending its views with integrity and strength of will.

Lydia Maria Child was a prominent early feminist as well as abolitionist. Like her contemporary Frederick Douglass, she linked the issues of antislavery and women's suffrage, and throughout her adult life promoted both causes. The poet John Greenleaf Whittier once said that "she was wise in counsel; and men like Charles Sumner, [William Ellery] Channing, [Thomas Wentworth] Higginson, Salmon Chase, Henry Wilson, and Governor Andrew availed themselves of her foresight and sound judgment of men and measures" (*Dictionary of American Biography*, p. 68). Although she wrote poetry and novels for much of her life, she is best remembered for her antislavery work, especially for the text excerpted here, *An Appeal in Favor of That Class of Americans Called Africans* (1833), and for her practical works designed for women, *The Frugal Housewife*

(1829) and *The Mother's Book* (1831). Her early novels, *Hobomok* (1824) and *The Rebels; or, Boston Before the Revolution* (1825), are currently enjoying a revival as important contributions to American literary history; however, it is her reform works that place her centrally in the antebellum abolitionist camp.

Born February 11, 1802, she received little formal education but enjoyed the stimulation of her brother, a professor at Harvard Divinity School, and later, the partnership in antislavery work with her husband, David L. Child, a Boston attorney and her partner in their lifetime dedication to the abolitionist crusade. Lydia Maria Child's *An Appeal in Favor of That Class of Americans Called Africans* is an extremely radical declaration for its time in that it called not only for immediate rather than gradual emancipation of the slaves, but also argued for full racial equality. The *Appeal* caused a sensation everywhere it was read. It argued the moral urgency of emancipation and the cruel inhumanity of slavery, winning her "converts" among the abolitionists like Channing and Sumner, but alienating more conservative Bostonians and Southern proslavery advocates. The *Appeal*'s radical miscegenation argument recapitulates the plot of her novel *Hobomok*, in which a Puritan woman marries an Indian man, and it anticipates the plot of her 1867 novel, A *Romance of the Republic*, which presents interracial marriage as a solution to America's race problem.

Reaction to the *Appeal*'s argument for biological equality and interracial relationships was extreme and punitive, eclipsing the successes of her two earlier and extremely popular domestic manuals and her numerous children's pieces published in *The Juvenile Miscellany*. Because the *Appeal* indicted both Northern and Southern racial prejudice, the Childs were instantly ostracized by Boston society, and friends and family members abandoned the revolutionary couple, who continued their dedicated work in the abolitionist movement. According to her biographer, Carolyn Karcher, [Lydia's] elder brother "James, who had named his daughters Lydia Maria and Mary Conant (after the heroine of Child's *Hobomok*), turned hostile; a Jacksonian Democrat, he could not stomach either 'niggers' or 'nigger-lovers'. Her father, though he sympathized warmly with her abolitionist principles, did not extend the same sympathy toward David, but instead blamed his son-in-law for the heavy financial price of the couple's antislavery activism" (Karcher, *First Woman*, p. 191). Although Garrison and Phillips and the more militant abolitionists, some of whom also argued for full racial equality, continued to support Lydia Child's *Appeal*, she lost the friendship of many and was ostracized by Harvard professors and contemporary novelists like Catharine Maria Sedgwick, with whom she broke off a friendship because of abolitionism and racial views. "In addition to the pain of broken friendships, Child bore the cost of professional blacklisting as her erstwhile patrons among the Boston aristocracy mobilized against her. Former admirers like Harvard professor George Ticknor slammed their doors in her face, cut her dead in the street, and enforced a policy of ostracism toward anyone who violated the ban against her" (Karcher, *First Woman*, p. 221). While she was engaged in research for her book *The History of the Condition of Women*, the Boston Athenaeum withdrew her free library privileges (Karcher, *First Woman*,

p. 220). "Most damagingly, readers boycotted her writings and parents cancelled their subscriptions to the *Juvenile Miscellany*. *The Mother's Book*, which had been reissued five times in two years, promptly went out of print; the *Miscellany*, though beloved by its broad juvenile audience, folded; even sales of her most commercially successful work, *The Frugal Housewife*, then in its thirteenth printing, plummeted, reducing Child's already meager income to a pittance" (Karcher, *First Woman*, pp. xlv and 148–49). Her literary popularity and social position in Boston were swiftly destroyed. But she joined Garrison and Phillips in moving forward the abolitionist cause and in provoking reactions among both Northern and Southern readers.

Although her text, excerpted here, does little to provide sources for her examples of slave cruelty, in contrast to Theodore Dwight Weld's *American Slavery as It Is* (1839), which details the newspapers and journals from which its evidence was taken, the moral force of her argument was so powerful that the book immediately set the terms of antislavery discourse for the next decade. Biblical examples would now be used in the service of a moral argument against slavery, and the Constitution and Declaration of Independence, so critical to Wendell Phillips and Lysander Spooner, who examined in minute detail the legal foundation for slavery, were muted voices compared to her irrefutable declarations that slavery was morally wrong and opposed to all conceptions of natural rights. As the Canadian historian Margaret Kellow put it,

> Her *Appeal* mounted a searching critique of American slavery and race relations and articulated Child's growing concern about the threat slavery posed to the well-being of the Republic. Recognizing that slavery and race prejudice were grounded in a presumption of the inherent inferiority of African Americans, Child argued that the perceived inferiority of Black Americans was a consequence of enslavement. Only Emancipation would permit a fair assessment of the capacities of African Americans, a test in which Child was convinced African Americans would acquit themselves well. To subjugate an entire race on categorical grounds flew in the face of Child's beliefs about individualism and opportunity. Thus Child's views on racism and sexism flowed from the same source, her commitment to individual liberty. [Kellow, p. 4]

Perhaps her most lasting contribution to reform activities in antebellum America was this fusion of antislavery sentiment with concern for women's rights. Although Child contributed little oratory or essay writing to the specific cause of women's suffrage—which, as early as 1848 with the Seneca Falls Convention and the "Declaration of Sentiments," had charted a course for equality for women—she managed in her antislavery writing to link the two causes together so that the moral force of one arena supported the other. Child did not argue for "identical exactness" between men and women, or indeed between blacks and whites; rather, "like Sarah Grimke and Lucretia Mott, Child grounded her commitment to women's rights solidly in the same commitment to egalitarianism which underwrote her commitment to antislavery. Child did not believe men and women were identical, but such differences as existed be-

tween them did not justify the subordination of women in antislavery or anywhere else" (Kellow, p. 5). Lydia Maria Child edited the text and authored the
introduction for Harriet Jacobs's *Incidents in the Life of a Slave Girl* (1861),
recently edited by Jean Fagan Yellin for the Harvard University Press. This
introduction shows clearly the fusion of antislavery and women's rights, as does
the Jacobs document itself.

Ironically, Child's arguments for immediate emancipation had already been
prominently advanced by William Lloyd Garrison through *The Liberator* and
her views of racial equality were also known, especially in Europe. "The distinctiveness of the *Appeal* lies not in the particular arguments it advances, but in
its all-encompassing synthesis of facts and arguments from an unprecedented
array of sources. Among Child's precursors, the British abolitionist Thomas
Clarkson had detailed the horrors of the slave trade. The American legal scholar
George Stroud had exhaustively studied southern slave laws and demonstrated
their harshness. David Walker and Garrison had dissected colonizationist ideology and exposed its racism and illogicality. The Abbe Grégoire of the French
Amis des Noirs had vindicated blacks against charges of inferiority by amassing
examples of their achievements in science, art, and literature" (Karcher, *First
Woman*, p. 187). But the power of her book is in its capacity to focus the dual
arguments of immediate emancipation and racial equality on a particular contemporary political problem, namely, the colonization movement.

According to Carolyn Karcher, the colonizationists, who argued for gradual
emancipation and the eventual removal of all Africans from the United States to
Africa, expressed the most visible form of resistance to David and Lydia Child's
form of abolitionism. The *Appeal* focused on these issues:

In her pivotal chapter, "Colonization Society, and Anti-Slavery Society," placed at
the center of the book, Child examines the two parties' opposing solutions to the
problem of slavery: gradual emancipation accompanied by repatriation to Africa
versus immediate emancipation followed by the bestowal of "equal civil and political
rights and privileges with the whites." . . . Since the principal point at issue between
Colonizationists and abolitionists is whether prejudice against blacks can and should
be overcome, she devotes the rest of the book to answering that question. Chapters
6 and 7, "Intellect of Negroes," and "Moral Character of Negroes," demolish the
rationale for prejudice—the myth of the Negro's biological inferiority and savage
past—by resurrecting accounts of Africa's ancient civilizations and recalling numerous modern instances of blacks who have distinguished themselves by their talents. The final chapter, "Prejudices against People of Color, and Our Duties in
Relation to This Subject," condemns racial discrimination and urges Americans to
repudiate attitudes and practices inconsistent with the republican creed. Although
the *Appeal* violates the prevailing norms of feminine discourse by its very engagement in political controversy, as well as by its authoritative display of erudition and
its preoccupation with such matters as law, economics, and congressional apportionment, it simultaneously presents a woman's perspective on slavery. Repeatedly, Child
focuses on the special ways in which slavery victimizes women and makes a mockery

of the domestic ideology glorifying "true womanhood." In the process, she pointedly reveals the limitations on her own freedom as a woman that links her to her sisters in bonds. [Karcher, *First Woman*, p. 185]

Lydia Maria Child thus advanced an argument for the fusion of women's rights and the emancipation of the slaves, which, in 1833, was an extremely radical position to take. By 1848, the escaped slave Frederick Douglass, who has won respect as an abolitionist thinker and writer, was invited to speak at the Seneca Falls Convention, where the major issues of women's rights were addressed, and where the charter document of the women's movement in the United States, the "Declaration of Sentiments," was ratified by fewer than the one thousand women who attended. But in 1833, the abolitionists like Garrison and Phillips were primarily focused on the harshness of chattel slavery, making Child's argument in the *Appeal* an important fusion of goals for these important reform movements. Child died on October 20, 1880, at her home in Wayland, Massachusetts.

SUGGESTIONS FOR FURTHER READING

Child, Lydia Maria. *An Appeal in Favor of that Class of Americans Called Africans*, ed. Carolyn Karcher. Amherst: University of Massachusetts Press, 1997.

———. *Correspondence between Lydia Maria Child and Gov. Wise and Mrs. Mason of Virginia*. New York, 1860.

———. *The Duty of Disobedience to the Fugitive Slave Act: An Appeal to the Legislators of Massachusetts*. Boston: American Anti-Slavery Society, 1860.

———. *The Freedmen's Book*. Boston, 1865.

———. "Introduction." *Incidents in the Life of a Slave Girl* (1861). Ed. Jean Fagin Yellin. Cambridge: Harvard University Press, 1987.

———. *Lydia Maria Child: Selected Letters, 1817–1880*. Ed. Milton Meltzer, Patricia G. Holland, and Francine Krasno. Amherst: University of Massachusetts Press, 1982.

———. *The Patriarchal Institution, As Described by Members of Its Own Family*. New York: American Anti-Slavery Society, 1860.

———. *A Romance of the Republic*. Boston: Ticknor and Fields, 1867.

———, ed. *The Antislavery Standard* (1841–49). A weekly antislavery newspaper published in New York.

Clifford, Deborah Pickman. *Crusader for Freedom: A Life of Lydia Maria Child*. Boston: Beacon Press, 1992.

Dubois, Ellen Carol. *Feminism and Suffrage: The Emergence of an Independent Women's Movement in America, 1848–1869*. Ithaca: Cornell University Press, 1978.

Ginzberg, Lori. *Women and the Work of Benevolence: Morality, Politics and Class in the Nineteenth-Century United States*. New Haven: Yale University Press, 1990.

Karcher, Carolyn L. *The First Woman in the Republic: a Cultural Biography of Lydia Maria Child*. Durham, NC: Duke University Press, 1994.

Kellow, Margaret. "Lydia Maria Child and Garrisonian Abolitionism." Unpublished ms. National Endowment for the Humanities Seminar for College Teachers, Newberry Library, Chicago, 1995.

———, ed. *The Lydia Maria Child Reader*. Durham, NC: Duke University Press, 1995.

Matthews, Glenna. *The Rise of Public Woman: Woman's Power and Woman's Place in the United States, 1630–1970*. New York: Oxford University Press, 1992.

Mills, Bruce. *Cultural Reformations: Lydia Maria Child and the Literature of Reform*. Athens: University of Georgia Press, 1994.

Osborne, William S. *Lydia Maria Child*. Boston: Twayne, 1980.

Smith-Rosenbert, Carroll. *Disorderly Conduct: Visions of Gender in Victorian America*. New York: Oxford University Press, 1985.

Tracy, Susan J. *In the Master's Eye: Representations of Women, Blacks, and Poor Whites in Antebellum Southern Literature*. Amherst: University of Massachusetts Press, 1995.

White, Deborah Gray. *Ar'n't I a Woman? Female Slaves in the Plantation South*. New York: Norton, 1985.

Yellin, Jean Fagan. *Women and Sisters: the Antislavery Feminists in American Culture*. New Haven: Yale University Press, 1989.

An Appeal in Favor of That Class of Americans Called Africans
by Lydia Maria Child

I beseech you not to throw down this volume as soon as you have glanced at the title. . . .

I am fully aware of the unpopularity of the task I have undertaken; but though I *expect* ridicule and censure, it is not in my nature to *fear* them. . . .

In almost all great evils there is some redeeming feature—*some* good results, even where it is not intended: pride and vanity, utterly selfish and wrong in themselves, often throw money into the hands of the poor, and thus tend to excite industry and ingenuity, while they produce comfort. But slavery is *all* evil—within and without—root and branch,—bud, blossom and fruit!

In order to show how dark it is in every aspect—how invariably injurious both to nations and individuals,—I will select a few facts from the mass of evidence now before me. . . .

In the first place, its effects upon *Africa* have been most disastrous. . . .

There are green and sheltered valleys in Africa,—broad and beautiful rivers,—and vegetation in its loveliest and most magnificent forms.—But no comfortable houses, no thriving farms, no cultivated gardens;—for it is not safe to possess permanent property, where each little state is surrounded by warlike neighbors, continually sending out their armed bands in search of slaves. The white man offers his most tempting articles of merchandise to the negro, as a price for the flesh and blood of his enemy; and if we, with all our boasted knowledge and religion, are seduced by money to do such grievous wrong to those who have never offended us, what can we expect of men just emerging from the limited wants of savage life, too uncivilized to have formed any habits of steady industry, yet earnestly coveting the productions they know not how to earn! . . .

Villages are set on fire, and those who fly from the flames, rush upon the spears of the enemy. Private kidnapping is likewise carried on to a great extent for he who can catch a neighbor's child is sure to find a ready purchaser; and it sometimes happens that the captor and his living merchandise are both seized by the white slave-trader. Houses are broken open in the night, and defenceless women and children carried away into captivity. If boys, in the unsuspecting innocence of youth, come near the white man's ships, to sell vegetables or fruit, they are ruthlessly seized and carried to slavery in a distant land. . . .

In African legislation, almost all crimes are punished with slavery; and thanks to the white man's rapacity, there is always a very powerful motive for finding the culprit guilty. . . .

When the slave-ships are lying on the coast of Africa, canoes well armed are sent into the inland country, and after a few weeks they return with hundreds of negroes, tied fast with ropes. Sometimes the white men lurk among the bushes, and seize the wretched beings who incautiously venture from their homes; sometimes they paint their skins as black as their hearts, and by this deception suddenly surprise the unsuspecting natives; at other times the victims are decoyed on board the vessel, under some kind pretence or other, and then lashed to the mast, or chained in the hold. Is it not very natural for the Africans to say "devilish white?"

Treachery, fraud and violence desolate the country, rend asunder the dearest relations, and pollute the very fountains of justice. The history of the negro, whether national or domestic, is written in blood. . . .

Having thus glanced at the miserable effects of this system on the condition of Africa, we will now follow the poor *slave* through his wretched wanderings, in order to give some idea of his physical suffering, his mental and moral degradation. . . .

The following account is given by Dr. Walsh, who accompanied Viscount Strangford, as chaplain, on his embassy to Brazil. The vessel in which he sailed chased a slave ship. . . .

Doctor Walsh was an eyewitness of the scene he describes; and the evidence given, at various times, before the British House of Commons, proves that the frightful picture is by no means exaggerated. . . .

The vessel had taken in, on the coast of Africa, three hundred and thirty-six males, and two hundred and twenty-six females, making in all five hundred and sixty-two: she had been out seventeen days, during which she had thrown overboard fifty-five. They were all enclosed under grated hatchways, between decks. The space was so low, and they were stowed so close together, that there was no possibility of lying down, or changing their position, night or day. The greater part of them were shut out from light and air; and this when the thermometer, exposed to the open sky, was standing, in the shade on our deck, at eighty-nine degrees. . . .

The space between decks was divided into two compartments, three feet three inches high. Two hundred and twenty-six women and girls were thrust into one space two hundred and eighty-eight feet square; and three hundred and thirty-six men and boys were crammed into another space eight hundred feet square; giving the whole an average of twenty-three inches; and to each of the women not more than thirteen inches; though several of them were in a state of health, which peculiarly demanded pity.—As they were shipped on account of different individuals, the were branded like sheep, with the owner's marks of different forms; which, as the mate informed me with perfect indifference, had been burnt in with red-hot iron. Over the hatch way stood a ferocious looking fellow, the slave-driver of the ship, with a scourge of many-twisted thongs in his hand; whenever he heard the slightest noise from below, he shook it over them, and seemed eager to exercise it. . . .

The heat of these horrid places was so great, and the odor so offensive, that it was quite impossible to enter them, even had there been room. . . .

The officers insisted that the poor, suffering creatures, should be admitted on deck to get air and water. This was opposed by the mate of the slaver. . . .

The officers, however, persisted and the poor beings were all turned out together. It is impossible to conceive the effect of this eruption—five hundred and seventeen fellow-creatures, of all ages and sexes, some children, some adults, some old men and women, all entirely destitute of clothing, scrambling out together to taste the luxury of a little fresh air and water. They came swarming up, like bees from a hive, till the whole deck was crowded to suffocation from stem to stern; so that it was impossible to imagine where they could all have come from, or how they could have stowed away. . . .

After enjoying for a short time the unusual luxury of air, some water was brought; it was then that the extent of their sufferings was exposed in a fearful manner. They all rushed like maniacs towards it. . . .

There is nothing from which slaves in the mid-passage suffer so much as want of water. . . .

When the poor creatures were ordered down again, several of them came, and pressed their heads against our knees, with looks of the greatest anguish, with the prospect of returning to the horrid place of suffering below. . . .

It was dark when we separated, and the last parting sounds we heard from the unhallowed ship, were the cries and shrieks of the slaves, suffering under some bodily infliction. . . .

Arrived at the place of destination, the condition of the slave is scarcely less deplorable. They are advertised with cattle; chained in droves, and driven to market with a whip; and sold at auction, with the beasts of the field. They are treated like brutes, and all the influences around them conspire to make them brutes. . . .

Some are employed as domestic slaves, when and how the owner pleases; by day or by night, on Sunday or other days, in any measure or degree, with any remuneration or with none, with what kind or quantity of food the owner of the human best may choose. Male or female, young or old, weak or strong, may be punished with or without reason, as caprice or passion may prompt. . . .

From the moment the slave is kidnapped, to the last hour he draws his miserable breath, the white man's influence directly cherishes ignorance, fraud, treachery, theft, licentiousness, revenge, hatred, and murder. It cannot be denied that human nature thus operated upon, *must* necessarily yield, more or less, to all these evils.—And thus do we dare to treat beings, who, like ourselves, are heirs of immortality!

And now let us briefly inquire into the influences of slavery on the *white man's character*, for in this evil there is a mighty re-action. . . .

The effect produced upon *slave-captains* is absolutely frightful. Those who wish to realize it in all its awful extent, may find abundant information in *Clarkson's History of Slavery*. . . .

Of cruelties on board slave-ships, I will mention but a few instances; though a large volume might be filled with such detestable anecdotes perfectly well authenticated. . . .

A child on board a slave-ship, of about ten months old took sulk and would not eat; the captain flogged it with a cat-o'-nine-tails; swearing that he would make it eat, or kill it. From this, and other ill-treatment, the limbs swelled. He then ordered some water to be made hot to abate the swelling. But even his tender mercies were cruel. The cook, on putting his hand into the water, said it was too hot. Upon this the captain swore at him, and ordered the feet to be put in. This was done. The nails and skin came off. Oiled cloths were then put around them. The child was at length tied to a heavy log. Two or three days afterwards, the captain caught it up again, and repeated that he would make it eat, or kill it. He immediately flogged it again, and in a quarter of an hour it died. And after the babe was dead whom should the barbarian select to throw it over-board, but the wretched mother! In vain she tried to avoid the office. He beat her, till he made her take up the child and carry it to the side of the vessel. She then dropped it into the sea, turning her head the other way, that she might not see it. . . .

It may seem incredible to some that human nature is capable of so much depravity. But the confessions of pirates show how habitual scenes of blood and violence harden the heart of man; and history abundantly proves that despotic power produces a fearful species of moral insanity. . . .

Even in the slaveholding states it is deemed disreputable to associate with a professed slave-trader, though few perhaps would think it any harm to bargain with him. . . .

Some of the advocates of this traffic maintained that the voyage from Africa to the slave-market, called the Middle Passage, was an exceedingly comfortable portion of existence. One went so far as to declare it "the happiest part of a negro's life." They aver that the Africans, on their way to slavery, are so merry, that they dance and sing. But upon a careful examination of witnesses, it was found that their singing consisted of dirge-like lamentations for the native land.

After meals they jumped up in their irons for exercise. This was considered so necessary for their health, that they were whipped, if they refused to do it. And this was their dancing. . . .

According to Clarkson's estimate, about two and a half of a hundred of human beings die annually, in the ordinary course of nature, including infants and the aged; but in an African voyage, where few babes and no old people are admitted, so that those shipped are at the firmest period of life, the annual mortality is forty-three in a hundred. . . .

We next come to the influence of this diabolical system on the *slave-owner*, and here I shall be cautioned that I am treading on delicate ground, because our own country-men are slaveholders. . . .

The following is the testimony of Jefferson, who had good opportunities for observation, and who certainly had no New-England prejudices: "There must, doubtless, be an unhappy influence on the manners of the people, produced by the existence of slavery among us. The whole commerce between master and slave is a perpetual exercise of the most boisterous passions; the most unremitting despotism on the one part, and degrading submission on the other. Our children see this and learn to imitate it; for man is an imitative animal. The parent storms; the child looks on, catches the lineaments of wrath, puts on the same airs in a circle of smaller slaves, gives loose to the worst of passions; and thus nursed, educated, and daily exercised in tyranny, cannot but be stamped by it with odious peculiarities. The man must be a prodigy, who can retain his morals and manners undepraved in such circumstances. . . ."

In a community where all the labor is done by one class there must of course be another class who live in indolence; and we all know how much people that have nothing to do are tempted by what the world calls pleasures; the result is, that slaveholding states and colonies are proverbial for dissipation. . . .

The following account was originally written by the Rev. William Dickey, of Bloomingsburg, to the Rev. John Rankin of Ripley, Ohio. It was published in 1826, in a little volume of letters, on the subject of slavery, by the Rev. Mr. Rankin, who assures us that Mr. Dickey was well acquainted with the circumstances he describes. . . .

In the county of Livingston, Kentucky, near the mouth of Cumberland river, lived Lilburn Lewis, the son of Jefferson's sister. He was the wealthy owner of a considerable number of slaves, whom he drove constantly, fed sparingly, and lashed severely. The consequence was, they would run away. Among the rest was an ill-grown boy, about seventeen, who having just returned from a skulking spell, was sent to the spring for water, and, in returning, let fall an elegant pitcher, which dashed to shivers on the rocks. It was night, and the slaves were all at home. The master had them collected into the most roomy negro-house, and a rousing fire made. (Reader, what follows is very shocking; but I have already said we must not allow our nerves to be more sensitive than our consciences. If such things are done in our country, it is important that we should know of them, and seriously reflect upon them.) The door was fastened, that none of the negroes, either through fear or sympathy, should attempt to escape; he then told them that the design of this meeting was to teach them to remain at home and obey his orders. All things being now in train, George was called up, and by the assistance of his younger brother, laid on a broad bench or block. The master then cut off his ankles with a broad axe. In vain the unhappy victim screamed. Not a hand among so many dared to interfere. Having cast the feet into the fire, he lectured the negroes at some length. He then proceeded to cut off his limbs below the knees. The sufferer besought him to begin with his head. It was in vain—the master went on thus, until trunk, arms, and head, were all in the fire. Still protracting the intervals with lectures, and threatenings of like punishment, in case any of them were disobedient, or ran way, or disclosed the tragedy they were compelled to witness. In order to consume the bones, the fire was briskly stirred until midnight. . . .

The negroes were allowed to disperse, with charges to keep the secret, under the penalty of like punishment. When his wife asked the cause of the dreadful screams she had heard, he said that had never enjoyed himself so well at a ball as he had enjoyed himself that evening. . . .

N.B. This happened in 1811; if I be correct, it was on the 16th of December. It was on the Sabbath. . . .

In order to show the true aspect of slavery among us, I will state distinct propositions, each supported by the evidence of actually existing laws.

1. Slavery is hereditary and perpetual, to the last moment of the slave's earthly existence, and to all his descendants, to the latest posterity.

2. The labor of the slave is compulsory and uncompensated; while the kind of labor, the amount of toil, and the time allowed for rest, are dictated solely by the master. No bargain is made, no wages given. A pure despotism governs the human brute; and even his covering and provender, both as to quantity and quality, depend entirely on the master's discretion.

3. The slave being considered a personal chattel, may be sold, or pledged, or leased, at the will of the master. He may be exchanged for marketable commodities, or taken in execution for the debts, or taxes, either of a living, or a deceased master. Sold at auction, "either individually, or in lots to suit the purchaser," he may remain with his family, or be separated from them forever.

4. Slaves can make no contracts, and have no legal right or any property, real or personal. Their own honest earnings, and the legacies of friends belong, in point of law, to their masters.

5. Neither a slave, nor free colored person, can be a witness against any white or free man, in a court of justice, however atrocious may have been the crimes they have seen him commit: but they may give testimony against a fellow-slave, or free colored man, even in cases affecting life.

6. The slave may be punished at his master's discretion—without trial—without any means of legal redress,—whether his offense be real, or imaginary: and the master can transfer the same despotic power to any person, or persons, he may choose to appoint.

7. The slave is not allowed to resist any free man under any circumstances: his only safety consists in the fact that his owner may bring suit, and recover, the price of his body, in case his life is taken, or his limbs rendered unfit for labor.

8. Slaves cannot redeem themselves, or obtain a change of masters, though cruel treatment may have rendered such a change necessary for their personal safety.

9. The slave is entirely unprotected in his domestic relations.

10. The laws greatly obstruct the manumission of slaves, even where the master is willing to enfranchise them.

11. The operation of the laws tends to deprive slaves of religious instruction and consolation.

12. The whole power of the laws is exerted to keep slaves in a state of the lowest ignorance.

13. There is in this country a monstrous inequality of law and right. What is a trifling fault in the white man, is considered highly criminal in the slave; the same offences which cost a white man a few dollars only, are punished in the negro with death.

14. The laws operate most oppressively upon free people of color.

PROPOSITION 1. *Slavery is hereditary and perpetual.* In Maryland the following act was passed in 1715, and is still in force: "all negroes and other slaves, already imported, or hereafter to be imported into this province, and all children now born, or hereafter to be born, of such negroes and slaves, shall be slaves during their natural lives. . . ."

PROP. 3. *Slaves considered personal chattels, liable to be sold, pledged, &c.* The advertisements in the Southern papers furnish a continued proof of this; it is, therefore, unnecessary to go into the details of evidence. The power to separate mothers and children, husbands and wives, is exercised only in the British West Indies, and the *republic* of the United States!

PROP. 4. *Slaves can have no legal claim to any property.* The civil code of Louisiana declares: "*all that a slave possesses belongs to his master*—he possesses nothing of his own, except his peculium, that is to say, the sum of money or moveable estate, which *his master chooses he should possess.*"—"Slaves are incapable of inheriting or transmitting property."—"Slaves cannot dispose of, or receive, by donation, unless they have been enfranchised conformably to law, or are expressly enfranchised by the act, by which the donation is made to them. . . ."

In South Carolina "it is not lawful for any slave to buy, sell, trade, &c., without a license from his owner; nor shall any slave be allowed to keep any boat or canoe, for his own. . . ."

In Georgia, a fine of thirty dollars a week is imposed upon any master who allows his slave to hire himself out . . . and it is lawful for any person, and the *duty* of the Sheriff, to apprehend the slave. In Maryland, the master, by a similar offence, except during twenty days at harvest time, incurs a penalty of twenty dollars per month. . . .

In Mississippi, if a master allows his slave to cultivate cotton for his own use, he incurs a fine of fifty dollars; and if he license his slave to trade on his own account, he forfeits fifty dollars for each and every offence. Any person trading with a slave forfeits four times the value of the article purchased; and if unable to pay, he receives thirty-nine lashes, and pays the cost. . . .

PROP. 5. *No colored man can be evidence against a white man, &c.* The master is merely obliged to take the precaution not to starve, or mangle, or murder his negroes, *in the presence of a white man.* No matter if five hundred colored people be present, they cannot testify to the fact. . . .

The *Code Noir* merely allows a slave's testimony to be heard by the judge, as a suggestion which might throw light on other evidence, without amounting of itself to any degree of legal proof. . . .

PROP. 6. *The master has absolute power to punish a slave, &c.* "The revised code of Louisiana declares: 'The slave is entirely subject to the will of the master, who may correct and chastise him, though not with *unusual* rigor, nor so as to maim or mutilate him, or to expose him to the danger of loss of life, or to cause his death.'" Who shall decide what punishment is *unusual?*

PROP. 7. *The slave never allowed to resist a white man.* It is enacted in Georgia, "If any slave shall presume to strike *any* white man, such slave, upon trial and conviction before the justice, shall for the *first* offence, suffer such punishment as the said justice thinks fit, not extending to life or limb; and for the second offence, *death.*" It is the same in South Carolina, excepting that death is there the punishment of the *third* offence. . . .

PROP. 8. *Slaves cannot redeem themselves or change masters.* Stroud says, "as to the right of *redemption,* this proposition holds good in all the slaveholding States; and is equally true as it respects the right to compel a *change of master,* except in Louisiana. According to the new civil code of that State, the latter privilege may sometimes, perhaps, be obtained by the slave. But the master must first be *convicted* of cruelty—a task so formidable that it can hardly be ranked among possibilities. . . ."

PROP. 9. *Slave unprotected in his domestic relations.* In proof of this, it is only necessary to repeat that the slave and his wife, and his daughters, are considered as the *property* of their owners, and compelled to yield implicit obedience—that he is allowed to give no evidence—that he must not resist *any* white man, under *any* circumstances which do not interfere with his *master's* interest. . . .

PROP. 10. *The laws obstruct emancipation.* In nearly all slaveholding States, a slave emancipated by his master's will, may be seized and sold to satisfy *any debt.*

In Kentucky, Missouri, Virginia, and Maryland, greater facilities are afforded to emancipation. An instrument in writing, signed by two witnesses, or acknowledged by the owner of the slave in open court, is sufficient; the owner reserving the power to demand security for the maintenance of aged or infirm slaves. By the Virginia laws, an emancipated negro, more than twenty-one years old, is liable to be again reduced to slavery, if he remain in the State more than twelve months after his manumission. . . .

PROP. 12. *Whole power of the laws exerted to keep negroes in ignorance.* The city of Savannah, in Georgia, a few years ago, passed an ordinance, by which "any person that teaches a person of color, slave or free, to read or write, or causes such persons to be so taught, is subjected to a fine of thirty dollars for each offence; and every person of color who shall teach reading or writing, is subject to a fine of thirty dollars or to be imprisoned ten days and whipped thirty-nine lashes. . . ."

PROP. 13. *There is a monstrous inequality of law and right.* More than seven slaves walking or standing together in the road, without a white man, may receive twenty lashes each from any person. . . .

PROP. 14. *The laws operate oppressively on free colored people.* Free people of color, like the slaves, are excluded by law from all means of obtaining the common elements of education. . . .

A New-York paper, November, 1829, contains the following caution:

"*Beware of kidnappers!*—It is *well understood* that there is at present in this city, a gang of kidnappers, busily engaged in their vocation of stealing colored children for the Southern market! It is believed that three or four have been stolen within as many days. . . ."

Chapter VII. *Moral Character of Negroes*

The opinion that negroes are naturally inferior in intellect is almost universal among white men; but the belief that they are worse than other people, is, I believe, much less extensive: indeed, I have heard some, who were by no means admirers of the colored race, maintain that they were very remarkable for kind feelings, and strong affections. Homer calls the ancient Ethiopians "the most honest of men;" and modern travelers have given innumerable instances of domestic tenderness, and generous hospitality in the interior of Africa. . . .

Chapter VIII. *Prejudices Against People of Color, and Our Duties in Relation to this Subject*

There is another Massachusetts law, which an enlightened community would not probably suffer to be carried into execution under any circumstances; but it still remains to disgrace the statutes of this Commonwealth. It is as follows:

"No African or Negro, other than a subject of the Emperor of Morocco, or a citizen of the United States, (proved so by a certificate of the Secretary of the State of which he is a citizen,) shall tarry within this Commonwealth longer than two months; and on complaint a justice shall order him to depart in ten days; and if he do not then, the justice may commit such African or Negro to the House of Correction, there to be kept at hard labor; and at the next term of the Court of Common Pleas, he shall be tried, and if convicted of remaining as aforesaid, shall be whipped not exceeding ten lashes; and if he or she shall not *then* depart, such process shall be repeated, and punishment inflicted, *toties quoties*." Stat. 1788, Ch. 54. . . .

The state of public feeling not only makes it difficult for the Africans to obtain information, but it prevents them from making profitable use of what knowledge they have. A colored man, however intelligent, is not allowed to pursue any business more lucrative than that of a barber, a shoe-black, or a waiter. . . .

Every citizen ought to have a fair chance to try his fortune in any line of business, which he thinks he has ability to transact. Why should not colored men be employed in the manufactories of various kinds? If their ignorance is an objection, let them be enlightened, as speedily as possible. If their moral character is not sufficiently pure, remove the pressure of public scorn, and thus supply them with motives for being respectable. All this can be done. It merely requires an earnest wish to overcome a prejudice, which has "grown with our growth and strengthened with our strength," but which is in fact opposed to the spirit of our religion, and contrary to the instinctive good feelings of our nature. . . .

It has been shown that no other people on earth indulge so strong a prejudice with regard to color, as we do. It is urged that negroes are civilly treated in England, because their numbers are so few. I could never discover any great force in this argument. Colored people are certainly not sufficiently rare in that country to be regarded as a great show, like a giraffe. . . .

Mr. Garrison was the first person who dared to edit a newspaper, in which slavery was spoken of as altogether wicked and inexcusable. For this crime the Legislature of Georgia have offered five thousand dollars to any one who will "arrest and prosecute him to conviction *under the laws of that State*." An association of gentlemen in South Carolina have likewise offered a large reward for the same object. It is, to say the least, a very remarkable step for a State in this Union to promulgate such a law concerning a citizen of another State, merely for publishing his opinions boldly. . . .

Mr. Garrison is a disinterested, intelligent, and remarkably pure-minded man, whose only fault is that he cannot be moderate on a subject which it is exceedingly difficult for an honest mind to examine with calmness. Many who highly respect his character and motives, regret his tendency to use wholesale and unqualified expressions; but it is something to have the truth told, even if it be not in the mildest way. Where an evil is powerfully supported by the self-interest and prejudice of the community, none but an ardent individual will venture to meddle with it. Luther was deemed indiscreet even by those who liked him best. . . .

Our books, our reviews, our newspapers, our almanacs, have all been silent, or exerted their influence on the wrong side. The negro's crimes are repeated, but his sufferings are never told. Even in our geographies it is taught that the colored race *must* always be degraded. Now and then anecdotes of cruelties committed in the slaveholding States are told by individuals who witnessed them; but they are almost always afraid to give their names to the public, because the Southerners will call them "a disgrace to the soil," and the Northerners will echo the sentiment. . . .

We are told that the Southerners will of themselves do away with slavery, and they alone understand how to do it. But it is an obvious fact that all their measures have tended to perpetuate the system; and even if we have the fullest faith that they mean to do their duty, the belief by no means absolves us from doing ours. The evil is gigantic; and its removal requires every heart and head in the community. . . .

I know a lady in Georgia who would, I believe, make any personal sacrifice to instruct her slaves, and give them freedom; but if she were found guilty of teaching the alphabet, or manumitting her slaves, fines and imprisonment would be the consequence; if she sold them, they would be likely to fall into hands less merciful than her own. Of such slave-owners we cannot speak with too much respect and tenderness. They are comparatively few in number, and stand in a most perplexing situation; it is a duty to give all our sympathy to *them*. It is mere mockery to say, what is so often said, that the Southerners as a body really wish to abolish slavery. If they wished it, they certainly would make the attempt. . . .

The strongest and best reason that can be given for our supineness on the subject of slavery, is the fear of dissolving the Union. The Constitution of the United States demands our highest reverence. Those who approve, and those who disapprove of particular portions, are equally bound to yield implicit obedience to its authority. But we must not forget that the Constitution provides for any change that may be required for the general good. The great machine is constructed with a safety-valve, by which any rapidly increasing evil may be expelled whenever the people desire it. . . .

Under all circumstances, there is but on honest course; and that is to do right, and trust the consequences to Divine Providence. "Duties are ours; events are God's." Policy, with all her cunning can devise no rule so safe, salutary, and effective, as this simple maxim. . . .

We cannot too cautiously examine arguments and excuses brought forward by those whose interest or convenience is connected with keeping their fellow creatures in a state of ignorance and brutality; and such we shall find in abundance, at the North as well as the South. I have heard the abolition of slavery condemned on the ground that New England vessels would not be employed to export the produce of the South, if they had free laborers of their own. This deserves an answer. . . .

To "love our neighbor as ourselves," is, after all, the shrewdest way of doing business. . . .

If we are not able to contribute to African schools, or do not choose to do so, we can at least refrain from opposing them. If it be disagreeable to allow colored people the same rights and privileges as other citizens, we can do with our prejudice, what most of us often do with better feelings—we can conceal it. . . .

Sixty thousands petitions have been addressed to the English parliament on the subject of slavery, and a large number of them were signed by women. The same steps here would be, with one exception, useless and injudicious; because the general government has not control over the legislatures of individual States. But the District of Columbia forms an exception to this rule. *There* the United States have power to abolish slavery; and it is the duty of the citizens to petition year after year, until a reformation is effected. . . .

Source Note: Lydia Maria Child, *An Appeal in Favor of that Class of Americans Called Africans*, Boston, 1833. Edited with an introduction by Carolyn Karcher (Amherst: University of Massachusetts Press, 1996). Reproduced by permission of Bruce Wilcox, Director.

WILLIAM ELLERY CHANNING (1780–1842)

William Ellery Channing was born in Newport, Rhode Island, on April 7, 1780. He died in Bennington, Vermont, on October 2, 1842. His career was vigorous and varied, including writings on the state of our national literary scene, *Remarks on a National Literature* (1830), numerous books of collected sermons, and three works on the slavery issue: *Slavery* (1835), *The Abolitionist* (1836), and *The Duty of the Free States* (1842). In 1803, he was made pastor of the Federal Street Congregational Church in Boston, which he turned into one of the most powerful pulpits of antebellum New England, just as the Episcopal minister, Phillips Brooks, would dominate the second half of the nineteenth century from another Boston pulpit, Trinity Church in Copley Square.

Channing was the last great voice of the first wave of abolitionist thinkers, those who opposed slavery in principle but who were not committed to the Garrisonian ideal of immediate, unconditional, and total emancipation of the slaves. Also called "gradualists," the early abolitionists sought the emancipation of slaves through attrition, death, and colonization. Channing was regarded to be a theological liberal, and he became a New England leader of the Unitarian movement, the persuasion that deeply influenced Ralph Waldo Emerson, the Harvard literature professor Henry Wadsworth Longfellow, and the Supreme Court Justice Oliver Wendell Holmes. His participation in the antislavery movement was largely effected through his writings, particularly the three books; the excerpts here, taken from his 1835 work, *Slavery*, show the clarity of his thinking and the power of his rhetoric. Like many abolitionists, Channing relied less on Scripture precedent for proof and more on the moral power of his argument, his appeal to feeling, intellect, and reason. Channing was a compromiser, a conciliatory thinker, and his position on the slavery issue was also one of compromise. Channing urged Northerners to extend a peace offering to the South, showing that their slavery was "your calamity, not your crime, and we will share with you the burden of putting an end to it." This reasoning was not to survive in the climate of militant abolitionism, led by William Lloyd Garrison and Wendell Phillips, who called for an immediate and unconditional end to slavery in the South.

SUGGESTIONS FOR FURTHER READING

Dumont, Dwight Lowell. *Antislavery: The Crusade for Freedom in America*. Ann Arbor: University of Michigan Press, 1961.

Garrison, William Lloyd. *Thoughts on African Colonization; or, an Impartial Exhibition of the Doctrines, Principles and Purposes of the American Colonization Society*. Boston: Garrison and Knapp, 1832.

Mayer, Henry. *William Lloyd Garrison and the Abolition of Slavery*. New York: St. Martin's Press, 1998.

Mendelsohn, Jack. *Channing, the Reluctant Radical*. Boston: Little, Brown, 1971.

Robinson, David. "The Legacy of Channing: Culture as a Religious Category in New England Thought." *Harvard Theological Review* 74 (1981): 221–39.

Smith, James Ward, and A. Leland Jamison, eds. *Religion in American Life. Vol. I: The Shaping of American Religion*. Princeton: Princeton University Press, 1961.

Van Anglen, Kevin P. "'That Sainted Spirit': William Ellery Channing and the Unitarian Milton." *Studies in the American Renaissance* (1983): 101–27.

Slavery
by William Ellery Channing

The first question to be proposed by a rational being is, not what is profitable, but what is Right. Duty must be primary, prominent, most conspicuous, among the objects of human thought and pursuit. If we cast it down from it supremacy, if we inquire first for our interests and then for our duties, we shall certainly err. We can never see the Right clearly and fully, but by making it our first concern. No judgment can be just or wise, but that which is built on the conviction of the paramount worth and importance of Duty. This is the fundamental truth, the supreme law of reason; and the mind, which does not start from this in its inquiries into human affairs, is doomed to great, perhaps fatal error.

The Right is the supreme good, and includes all other goods. In seeking and adhering to it, we secure our true and only happiness. All prosperity, not founded on it, is built on sand. If human affairs are controlled, as we believe, by Almighty Rectitude and Impartial Goodness, then to hope for happiness from wrong doing is as insane as to seek health and prosperity by rebelling against the laws of nature, by sowing our seed on the ocean, or making poison our common food. There is but one unfailing good; and that is fidelity to the Everlasting Law written on the heart, and rewritten and republished in God's Word.

Whoever places this faith in the everlasting law of rectitude must of course regard the question of slavery first and chiefly as a moral question. . . .

The following remarks, therefore, are designed to aid the reader in forming a just moral judgment of slavery. Great truths, inalienable rights, everlasting duties, these will form the chief subjects of this discussion. Of late our country has been convulsed by the question of slavery. The consequence is, that not a few dread all discussion of the subject, and if not reconciled to the continuance of slavery, at least believe that they have no duty to perform, no testimony to bear, no influence to exert, no sentiments to cherish and spread, in relation to this evil.

There was never such an obligation to discuss slavery as at this moment, when recent events have done much to unsettle and obscure men's minds in regard to it.

Slavery ought to be discussed. We ought to think, feel, and write about it.

Slavery, indeed, from its very nature must be a ground of alarm wherever it exists. Slavery and security can by no device be joined together. But we may not, must not, by rashness and passion increase the peril. To instigate the slave to insurrection is a crime for which no rebuke and no punishment can be too severe. This would be to involve slave and master in common ruin. It is not enough to say, that the Constitution is violated by any action endangering the slave-holding portion of our country. A higher law than the Constitution forbids this unholy interference.

As men, as Christians, as citizens, we have duties to the slave, as well as to every other member of the community. On this point we have no liberty. The Eternal Law binds us to take the side of the injured; and this law is peculiarly obligatory, when we forbid him to lift an arm in his own defence.

This must triumph. It is leagued with God's omnipotence.

Slavery cannot stand before it. Great moral principles, pure and generous sentiments, cannot be confined to this or that spot. They are divine inspirations, and partake of the omnipresence of their Author.

To increase this moral power is every man's duty. To embody and express this great truth is in every man's power; and thus every man can do something to break the chain of the slave.

The great teaching of Christianity is, that we must recognize and respect human nature in all its forms, in the poorest, most ignorant, most fallen. We must look beneath "the flesh," to "the spirit." The spiritual principle in man is what entitles him to our brotherly regard. To be just to this is the great injunction of our religion. To overlook this, on account of condition or color, is to violate the great Christian law.

To recognize our own spiritual nature and God's image in these humble forms; to recognize as brethren those who want all outward distinctions, is the chief way in which we are to manifest the spirit of Him, who came to raise the fallen and to save the lost.

He who cannot see a brother, a child of God, a man possessing all the rights of humanity under a skin darker than his own, wants the vision of a Christian. . . .

These remarks are intended to show the spirit in which slavery ought to be approached, and the point of view from which it will be regarded in the present discussion.

1. I shall show that man cannot justly be held and used as Property.

2. I shall show that man has sacred and infallible rights, of which slavery is the infraction.

3. I shall offer some explanations to prevent misapplication of these principles.

4. I shall unfold the evils of slavery.

5. I shall consider the argument which the Scriptures are thought to furnish in favor of slavery.

6. I shall offer some remarks on the means of removing it.

7. I shall offer some remarks on abolitionism.

8. I shall conclude with a few reflections on the duties belonging to the times.

In the first two sections I propose to show that slavery is a great wrong, but I do not intend to pass sentence on the character of the slave-holder. These two subjects are distinct. Men are not always to be interpreted by their acts or institutions. The same acts in different circumstances admit and even require very different constructions. I offer this remark, that the subject may be approached without prejudice or personal reference. The single object is to settle great principles. Their bearing on individuals will be a subject of distinct consideration. . . .

Property

The slave-holder claims the slaves as his Property. The very idea of a slave is, that he belongs to another, that he is bound to live and labor for another, to be another's instrument, and to make another's will his habitual law, however adverse to his own.

A right, in a word, to use him as a tool, without contract, against will, and in denial of his right to dispose of himself or to use his power for his own good. "A slave," says the Louisiana Code, "is in the power of the master to whom he belongs."

Now this claim of property in a human being is altogether false, groundless. No such right of man can exist. A human being cannot be justly owned. To hold and treat him as property is to inflict a great wrong, to incur the guilt of oppression.

This position there is a difficulty in maintaining on account of its exceeding obviousness. It is too plain for proof. To defend it is like trying to confirm a self-evident truth.

The man, who, on hearing the claim to property in man, does not see and feel distinctly that it is a cruel usurpation, is hardly to be reached by reasoning, for it is hard to find any plainer principles than what he begins with denying.

As men we cannot justly be made slaves. Then no man can be rightfully enslaved. . . .

A man cannot be seized and held as property, because he has Rights. This truth has never, I believe, been disputed. It is even recognized in the every codes of slave-legislation, which, while they strip a man of liberty, affirm his right to life, and threaten his murderer with punishment. Now, I say a being having rights cannot justly be made property; for this claim over him virtually annuls all his rights. It strips him of all power to assert them.

Another argument against property is to be found in the Essential Equality of men. I know that this doctrine, so venerable in the eyes of our fathers, has lately been denied. Verbal logicians have told us that men are "born equal," only in the sense of being equally born. They have asked whether all are equally born. They have asked whether all are equally tall, strong, or beautiful; or whether nature, Procrustes-like, reduces all her children to one standard of intellect and virtue.

Be it also remembered, that these diversities among men are as nothing in comparison with the attributes in which they agree, and it is this which constitutes their essential equality. All men have the same rational nature, and the same power of conscience, and all are equally made for indefinite improvement of these divine faculties, and for the happiness to be found in their virtuous use.

That a human being cannot be justly held and used as property is apparent from the very nature of property. Property is an exclusive, single right. It shuts out all claim but that of the possessor. What one man owns cannot belong to another.

Our laws know no higher crime than that of reducing a man to slavery. To steal or to buy an African on his own shore is piracy. In this act the greatest wrong is inflicted, the most sacred right violated. But if a human being cannot without infinite injustice be seized as property, then he cannot without equal wrong be held and used as such.

He cannot be property in the sight of God and justice, because he is a Rational, Moral, Immortal Being; because created in God's image, and therefore in the highest sense his child; because created to unfold Godlike faculties, and to govern himself by a Divine law written on his heart, and republished in God's Word. His whole nature forbids that he should be seized as property.

Such a being was plainly made for an End in Himself. He is a person, not a Thing. He is an End, not a mere Instrument or Means.

We have thus seen that a human being cannot rightfully be held and used as property. No legislation, not that of all countries or worlds, could make him so. Let this be laid down, as a first, fundamental truth. Let us hold it fast, as a most sacred, precious truth. Let us hold it fast against all customs, all laws, all rank, wealth, and power. Let it be armed with the whole authority of the civilized and Christian world.

What! is human legislation the measure of right? Are God's laws to be repealed by man's? Can government do no wrong? What is the history of human governments but a record of wrongs? How much does the progress of civilization consist in the substitution of just and humane, for barbarous and oppressive laws? Government, indeed, has ordained slavery, and to government the individual is in no case to offer resistance. . . .

Rights

Man has rights by nature. The disposition of some to deride abstract rights, as if all rights were uncertain, mutable, and conceded by society, shows a lamentable ignorance of human nature. Whoever understands this must see in it an immovable foundation of rights. These are gifts of the Creator, not grants of society. In the order of things, they precede society, lie at its foundation, constitute man's capacity for it, and are the great objects of social institutions. The consciousness of rights is not a creation of human art, a conventional sentiment, but essential to and inseparable from the human soul.

Man's rights belong to him as a Moral Being, as capable of perceiving moral distinctions, as a subject of moral obligation.

It is said that in forming civil society the individual surrenders a part of his rights. It would be more proper to say that he adopts new modes of securing them. . . .

How absurd is it to suppose, that by consenting to be protected by the state, and by yielding it the means, he surrenders the very rights which were the objects of his accession to the social compact!

In all ages the Individual has in one form or another been trodden in the dust. In monarchies and aristocracies he has been sacrificed to One or to the Few; who, regarding government as an heirloom in their families, and thinking of the people as made only to live and die for their glory, have not dreamed that the sovereign power was designed to shield every man, without exception, from wrong.

Let not the sacredness of individual man be forgotten in the feverish pursuit of property. It is more important that the Individual should respect himself, and be respected by others, than that the wealth of both worlds should be accumulated on our shores. National wealth is not the end of society. It may exist where large classes are depressed and wronged. It may undermine a nation's Spirit, institutions, and independence. . . .

Slavery strips man of the fundamental right to inquire into, consult, and seek his own happiness. His powers belong to another, and for another they must be used. He must form no plans, engage in no enterprises, for bettering his condition. Whatever be his capacities, however equal to great improvements of his lot, he is chained for life by another's will to the same unvaried toil. He is forbidden to do for himself or others the work, for which God stamped him with his own best gifts.—Again, the slave is stripped of the right to acquire property. Being himself owned, his earnings belong to another. He can possess nothing but by favor.

Again, the slave is stripped of his right to his wife and children. They belong to another, and may be torn from him, one and all, at any moment, at his master's pleasure.—Again, the slave is stripped of the right to the culture of his rational powers. He is in some cases deprived by law of instruction, which is placed within his reach by the improvements of society and the philanthropy of the age. He is not allowed to toil, that his children may enjoy a better education than himself. The most sacred right of human nature, that of the developing of his best faculties, is denied.

He is subjected to the lash, by those whom he has never consented to serve, and whose claim to him as property we have seen to be a usurpation.

I will add but one more example of the violation of human rights by slavery. The slave virtually suffers the wrong of robbery, though with utter unconsciousness on the part of those who inflict it.

But it is not true that he owns nothing. Whatever he may be denied by man, he holds from nature the most valuable property, and that from which all other is derived, I mean his strength. His labour is his own, by the gift of that God who nerved his arm, and gave him intelligence and conscience to direct the use of it for his own and others' happiness. No possession is so precious as a man's force of body and mind.

The worth of articles of traffic is measured by the labor expended in their production.

To take by force a man's whole estate, the fruit of years of toil, would by universal consent be denounced as a great wrong; but what is this, compared with seizing the man himself, strength, and labor, by which all property is won and held fast? The right of property in outward things is as nothing, compared with the right to ourselves. . . .

The Evils of Slavery

The first rank among the evils of slavery must be given to its Moral influence. This is throughout debasing.

The slave is regarded and treated as property, bought and sold like a brute, denied the rights of humanity, unprotected against insult, made a tool, and systematically subdued, that he may be a manageable, useful tool. How can he help regarding himself as fallen below his race? How must his spirit be crushed! How can he respect himself? He becomes bound to Servility. . . .

I proceed to consider its Intellectual influence, another great topic. God gave us intellectual power, that it should be cultivated; and a system which degrades it, and can only be upheld by its depression, opposes one of his most benevolent designs. Reason is God's image in man, and the capacity of acquiring truth is among his best inspirations. To call forth the intellect is a principal purpose of the circumstances in which we are placed, of the child's connexion with the parent, and of the necessity laid on him in maturer life to provide for himself and others. The education of the intellect is not confined to youth; but the various experiences of later years do vastly more than books and colleges to ripen and invigorate the faculties.

Now, the whole lot of slave is fitted to keep his mind in childhood and bondage.

Should his eye chance to fall on "the Declaration of Independence," how would the truth glare on him, "that all men are born free and equal!" All knowledge furnishes arguments against slavery. From every subject light would break forth to reveal his inalienable and outraged rights. . . .

I proceed, now, to the Domestic influences of slavery; and here we must look for a dark picture. Slavery virtually dissolves the domestic relations. It ruptures the most sacred ties on earth. It violates home. It lacerates the best affections. The domestic relations precede, and, in our present existence, are worth more than all our other social ties.

The most precious burden with which the heart can be charged, the happiness of the child, he must not bear. He lives not for his family, but for a stranger. He cannot improve their lot. His wife and daughter he cannot shield from insult. They may be torn from him at another's pleasure, sold as beasts of burden, sent he knows not whither, sent where he cannot reach them, or even interchange inquiries and messages of love. To the slave marriage has no sanctity. It may be dissolved in a moment at another's will. His wife, son, and daughter may be lashed before his eyes, and not a finger must be lifted in their defence. He sees the scar of the lash on his wife and child. Thus the slave's home is desecrated. Thus the tenderest relations, intended by God equally for all, and intended to be the chief springs of happiness and virtue, are sported with wantonly and cruelly.

And let it not be said that the slave has not the sensibilities of other men. Nature is too strong even for slavery to conquer. Even the brute has the yearnings of parental love. . . .

Slavery produces and gives license to Cruelty. By this it is not meant that cruelty is the universal, habitual, unfailing result.

Slavery in this country differs widely from that of ancient times, and from which the Spaniards imposed on the aboriginals of South America. There is here an increasing disposition to multiply the comforts of the slaves, and in this let us rejoice. At the same time, we must remember, that, under the light of the present day, and in a country where Christianity and the rights of men are understood, a diminished severity may contain more guilt than the ferocity of darker ages. . . .

Slavery, above all other influences, nourishes the passion for power and its kindred vices. There is no passion which needs a stronger curb. Men's worst crimes have sprung from the desire of being masters, of bending others to their yoke. And the natural tendency of bringing others into subjection to our absolute will is to quicken into fearful activity the imperious, haughty, proud, self-seeking propensities of our nature. Man cannot, without imminent peril to his virtue, own a fellow-creature, or use the word of absolute command to his brethren. God never delegated this power.

The slaveholder, indeed, values himself on his loftiness of spirit.

I approach a more delicate subject, and one on which I shall not enlarge. To own the persons of others, to hold females in slavery, is necessarily fatal to the purity of a people. That unprotected females, stripped by their degraded condition of woman's self-respect, should be used to minister to other passions in men than the love of gain, is next to inevitable. Accordingly, in such a community the reins are given to youthful licentiousness. Youth, every where in perils, is in these circumstances urged to vice with a terrible power. And the evil cannot stop at youth. Early licentiousness is fruitful of crime in mature life. How far the obligation to conjugal fidelity, the sacredness of domestic ties, will be revered amidst such habits, such temptations, such facilities to vice, as are involved in slavery, needs no exposition.

A slave-country reeks with licentiousness. It is tainted with a deadlier pestilence than the plague.

But the worst is not told. As a consequence of criminal connexions, many a master has children born into slavery.

Our slave-holding brethren, who tell us that the condition of the slave is better than that of the free laborer at the North, talk ignorantly and rashly. They do not, cannot know, what to us is a matter of daily observation, that from the families of our farmers and mechanics have sprung our most distinguished men, men who have done most for science, arts, letters, religion, and freedom; and that the noblest spirits among us would have been lost to their country and mankind, had the laboring class here been doomed to slavery.

It is said, however, that the slave, if not to be compared to the free laborer at the North, is in a happier condition than the Irish peasantry. Let this be granted. Let the security of the peasant's domestic relations, let his church, and his schoolhouse, and his faint hope of a better lot pass for nothing.

But still we are told the slave is gay. He is not as wretched as our theories teach. After his toil, he sings, he dances, he gives no signs of an exhausted frame or gloomy spirit. The slave happy! Why, then, contend for Rights?

The slave happy! Then happiness is to be found in giving up the distinctive attributes of a man; in darkening intellect and conscience; in quenching generous sentiments; in servility of spirit; in living under a whip; in having neither property nor rights; in holding wife and child at another's pleasure; in toiling without hope; in living without an end!

That there are those among the free, who are more wretched than slaves, is undoubtedly true; just as there is incomparably greater misery among men than among brutes. The brute never knew the agony of a human spirit torn by remorse or wounded in its love.

But the slave, we are told, is taught Religion. This is the most cheering sound which comes to us from the land of bondage. We are rejoiced to learn that any portion of the slaves are instructed in that truth, which gives inward freedom.

Religion, though a great good, can hardly exert its full power over the slave. Will it now be taught to make him obedient to his master rather than to raise him to the dignity of a man? Is slavery, which tends so proverbially to debase the mind, the preparation for spiritual truth? Can the slave comprehend the principle of Love, the essential principle of Christianity, when he hears if from the lips of those whose relations to him express injustice and selfishness?

Scripture

Attempts are often made to support slavery by the authority of Revelation. "Slavery," it is said, "is allowed in the Old Testament, and not condemned in the New. Paul commands slaves to obey. He commands masters, not to release their slaves, but to treat them justly. Therefore slavery is right, is sanctioned by God's Word."

This reasoning proves too much. If usages sanctioned in the Old Testament and not forbidden in the New are right, then our moral code will undergo a sad deterioration. Polygamy was allowed to the Israelites, was the practice of the holiest men, and was common and licensed in the age of the Apostles. But the Apostles nowhere condemn it, nor was the renunciation of it made an essential condition of admission into the Christian church. Why may not Scripture be used to stock our houses with wives as well as with slaves?

What was slavery in the age of Paul? It was the slavery, not so much of black as of white men, not merely of barbarians but of Greeks, not merely of the ignorant and debased, but of the virtuous, educated, and refined. Piracy and conquest were the chief means of supplying the slave-market, and they heeded neither character nor condition. Sometimes the greater part of the population of a captured city was sold into bondage, sometimes the whole, as in the case of Jerusalem. Noble and royal families, the rich and great, the learned and powerful, the philosopher and poet, the wisest and best men, were condemned to the chain. Such was ancient slavery. And this we are told is allowed and confirmed by the Word of God!

Slavery, in the age of the Apostle, had so penetrated society, was so intimately interwoven with it, and the materials of servile war were so abundant, that a religion, preaching freedom to its foundation, would have armed against itself the whole power of the State. Of consequence Paul did not assail it. He satisfied himself with spreading principles, which, however slowly, could not but work its destruction. He commanded Philemon to receive his fugitive slave, Onesimus, "not as a slave, but above a slave, as a brother beloved;" and he commanded masters to give to their slaves that which was "*just* and equal;" thus asserting for the slave the rights of a Christian and a Man; and how, in his circumstances, he could have done more for the subversion of slavery, I do not see.

The perversion of Scripture to the support of slavery is singularly inexcusable in this country. Paul not only commanded slaves to obey their masters. He delivered these precepts: "Let every soul be subject unto higher powers. For there is no power but of God; the powers that be are ordained of God. Whosoever, therefore, resisteth the power, resisteth the ordinance of God; and they that resist shall receive to themselves damnation." This passage was written in the time of Nero. It teaches passive obedience to despotism more strongly than any text teaches the lawfulness of slavery.

The very course, which the Gospel takes on this subject, seems to have been the only one that could have been taken in order to effect the universal abolition of slavery. The gospel was designed, not for one race or for one time, but for all men and for all times. It looked not at the abolition of this form of evil for that age alone, but for its universal abolition. . . .

Means of Removing Slavery

In this country no power but that of the slaveholding States can remove the evil, and none of us are anxious to take the office from their hands. They alone can determine and apply the true and sure means of emancipation.

What, then, is to be done for the removal of slavery? In the first place, the slaveholders should solemnly disclaim the right of property in human beings. The great principle, that man cannot belong to man, should be distinctly, solemnly recognized. The slave should be acknowledged as a partaker of a common nature, as having the essential rights of humanity. This great truth lies at the foundation of every wise plan for his relief.

There is, indeed, a grandeur in the idea of raising more than two millions of human beings to the enjoyment of human rights, to the blessings of Christian Civilization, to the means of indefinite improvement.

The slave cannot rightfully and should not be owned by the Individual. But, like every other citizen, he belongs to the Community, he is subject to the community, and the community has a right and is bound to continue all such restraints, as its own safety and the well-being of the slave demand. It would be cruelty, not kindness, to the latter to give him a freedom, which he is unprepared to understand or enjoy. It would be cruelty to strike the fetters from a man, whose first steps would infallibly lead him to a precipice. The slave should not have an owner, but he should have a guardian. He needs authority, to supply the lack of that discretion which he has not yet attained; but it should be the authority of a friend; an official authority, conferred by the state, and for which there should be responsibleness to the state, an authority especially designed to prepare its subjects for personal freedom. The slave should not, in the first instance, be allowed to wander at his will beyond the plantation on which he toils; and if he cannot be induced to work by rational and natural motives, he should be obliged to labor; on the same principles on which the vagrant in other communities is confined and compelled to earn his bread.

There is but one weighty argument against immediate emancipation, mainly, that the slave would not support himself and his children by honest industry; that, having always worked on compulsion, he will not work without it; that having always labored from another's will, he will not labor from his own; that there is no spring of exertion in his own mind; that he is unused to forethought, providence in self-denial, and the responsibilities of domestic life; that freedom would produce idleness; idleness, want; want, crime; and that crime, when it should become the habit of numbers, would bring misery, perhaps ruin, not only on the offenders, but the state.

The great step, then, towards the removal of slavery is to prepare the slaves for self support. The colored man is not a savage, to whom toil is torture, who has centered every idea of happiness and dignity in a wild freedom, who must exchange the boundless forests for a narrow plantation, and bend his proud neck for an unknown yoke. Labor was his first lesson, and he has been repeating it all his life. Can it be a hard task to teach him to labor for himself, to work from impulses in his own breasts?

One of the great means of elevating the slave, in calling forth his energies is to place his domestic relations on new ground. This is essential. We wish him to labor for his family. Then he must have a family to labor for. Then his wife and children must be truly his own. Then his home must be inviolate. Then the responsibilities of a husband and father must be laid on him. No measure for preparing the slave for liberty can be so effectual as the improvement of the domestic lot. The whole power of religion should be employed to impress him with the sacredness and duties of marriage.

To carry this and all other means of improvement into effect, it is essential that the slave should no longer be bought and sold. As long as he is made an article of merchandise, he cannot be fitted for the offices of a man. While treated as property, he will have little encouragement to accumulate property, for it cannot be secure. While his wife and children may be exposed at auction, and carried, he knows not where, can he be expected to feel and act as a husband and father? It is time, that this Christian and civilized country should no longer be dishonored by one of the worst usages of barbarism. Break up the slave-market, and one of the chief obstructions to emancipation will be removed.

I have said nothing of colonization among the means of removing slavery, because I believe that to rely on it for this object would be equivalent to a resolution to perpetuate the evil without end. Whatever good it may do abroad, and I trust it will do much, it promises little at home. If the slaveholding States, however, should engage in colonization, with a firm faith in its practicableness, with an energy proportionate to its greatness, and with a sincere regard to the welfare of the colored race, I am confident it will not fail from want of sympathy and aid on the part of the other States.

I have said nothing of the inconveniences and sufferings, which, it is urged, will follow emancipation, be it ever so safe; for these, if real, weigh nothing against the claims of justice. The most common objection is, that a mixture of the two races will be the result. Can the slaveholder use the word "amalgamation" without a blush? That emancipation will have its evils we know; but the evils of slavery exceed beyond measure the greatest which contend its removal. . . .

Abolitionism

Of the abolitionists I know very few; but I am bound to say of these, that I honor them for their strength of principle, their sympathy with their fellow-creatures and their active goodness. As a party, they are singularly free from political and religious sectarianism, and have been distinguished by the absence of management, calculation, and worldly wisdom.

The abolitionists have done wrong, I believe; nor is their wrong to be winked at, because done fanatically or with good intention; for how much mischief may be wrought with good design! They have fallen into the common era of enthusiasts, that of exaggerating their object, of railing as if no evil existed but that which they oppose, and as if no guilt could be compared with that of countenancing or upholding it.

Very unhappily they preached their doctrine to the colored people, and collected these into their societies. To this mixed and excitable multitude, minute, heart rending descriptions of slavery were given in the piercing tones of passion; and slaveholders were held up as monsters of cruelty and crime. Now to this procedure I must object as unwise, as unfriendly to the spirit of Christianity, and as increasing, in a degree, the perils of the slaveholding States. Among the unenlightened, whom they so powerfully address, was there not reason to fear that some might feel themselves called to subvert this system of wrong, by whatever means?

I earnestly desire that abolitionism may lay aside the form of public agitation, and seek its end by wiser and milder means. I desire as earnestly, and more earnestly, that it may not be put down by lawless force. There is a worse evil than abolitionism, that is the suppression of it by lawless force. . . .

Source Note: William Ellery Channing, *Slavery* (Boston, 1835).

JAMES McCUNE SMITH (1813–1865)

James McCune Smith was one of the most prominent of the nineteenth-century black abolitionists. Born in New York City in 1813, he was, like Frederick Douglass, his contemporary, a man of mixed white and black parentage. He received an excellent education, but not all of it in the United States. First, he attended the African Free School in Manhattan. For his university education, he was compelled to emigrate to Great Britain, as most American universities were closed to African-Americans. He studied at the University of Glasgow, from which he received his B.A. in 1835, M.A. in 1836, and M.D. in 1837. After his medical residency in Paris, he practiced medicine in New York City for twenty-five years, while remaining active in the black abolitionist movement.

Because he was the first African-American to hold a medical degree, his medical practice in New York prospered; however, he is best remembered for his activism and writings as an abolitionist. "Smith's intellect, integrity, and lifelong commitment to abolitionism brought him state and national recognition. From the early 1840s, he provided leadership for the campaign to expand black voting rights in New York, although he initially refused to ally with any political party. In the 1850s, Smith continued his suffrage activity through the black state conventions. He eventually gravitated to the political antislavery views of the Radical Abolition party, and received the party's nomination for New York Secretary of State in 1857" (*Encyclopedia of Black Americans*, pp. 2493–95).

James McCune Smith was primarily a pamphlet writer; however, he authored several important books, including A *Lecture on the Haytien Revolutions; with a Sketch of the Character of Toussaint L'Ouverture* (1841) and *The Destiny of a People of Color* (1843). He also authored introductory essays to Frederick Douglass's *My Bondage and My Freedom* (1855), the second of Douglass's three autobiographical accounts, and Henry Highland Garnet's *Memorial Discourse* (1865). Smith was offered a teaching position at Wilberforce University, but his poor health (he suffered from heart disease) made it impossible for him to accept the position. In later life, he moved to Williamsburg, Long Island, New York, where he died on November 17, 1865.

SUGGESTIONS FOR FURTHER READING

Blight, David. "In Search of Learning, Liberty, and Self-Definition: James McCune Smith and the Ordeal of the Antebellum Black Intellectual." *African-Americans in New York Life and History* 9 (1985): 7–25.

"James McCune Smith." In *Encyclopedia of Black Americans*, ed. Augustus Low (New York: McGraw-Hill, 1981), pp. 2493–95.

Quarles, Benjamin. *The Black Abolitionists*. New York: Oxford University Press, 1969.

Ripley, Peter C., et al., eds. *The Black Abolitionist Papers*. Vol. 3: *The United States, 1830–1846*, and vol. 4: *The United States, 1847–1858*. Chapel Hill: University of North Carolina Press, 1991.

The Destiny of a People of Color
by James McCune Smith

But how shall we enquire into the future? With what line and rule shall we step beyond the bounds of the present and read with an intelligent eye the fate of men and empires? . . .

The rule is announced in the simple proposition: What hath been will be or like causes under like circumstances will produce like effects. This proposition is the very basis of all our belief, all our hope—it is the very essence of that Faith in the stability of things without which life would be made up of dismal, because uncertain, anticipation. Reposing on the belief that because our planet, for thousands of years, hath described its orbit round the sun, and that because day and night, seed-time and harvest, summer and winter, have run their successive course, therefore they will continue in the same, we live on free from apprehensions which would turn life into a curse. . . .

May we not, then, guided by a proposition so universal in its application, the basis at once of our faith and of our knowledge,—may we not venture upon the investigation of the probable destiny of those with whom we are more immediately linked? . . .

It has been asserted, by intelligent men, that the day will come when the colored population of these United States shall have entirely disappeared, and when the various nations of men that now make up our "chequered Union," shall, in the words of our national motto, "of many nations make one." The statistical reports seem to announce the slow but certain approach of such a time; for, the census of the United States, from 1790 to 1840 shows, that whilst the white population has maintained the same ratio of increase, the increase of the colored population has been by a gradually diminishing ratio. In other words, the whites are increasing more rapidly, relatively, than the colored people.

But, notwithstanding a time may come, when the descendants of our people shall no longer be distinguished by any physical peculiarity, yet it is clear, that a destiny awaits them which they must fulfil, and which will greatly affect whoever may live during and after its fulfillment. In order to investigate that destiny, it is necessary, first, to examine into our present position, by which our fate must necessarily be governed.

First: We are a minority held in servitude by a majority.

Secondly: That majority simulates a Republican form of Government.

Thirdly: We, the minority, held in servitude, are distinguished by a different complexion from the majority who holds us in thrall.

Such is our position. Men have been held in servitude in other times and places, under one or two of the above conditions, and the destiny of such men has been recorded; but until now, and in our case, there has not happened a concurrence of all these conditions in the position of any people upon the earth. . . .

Let us now take up the propositions which describe our condition. And first, let us enquire into the probable destiny of men enslaved, and who differ in complexion from their masters.

The white slaves on the coast of Barbary have as yet wrought out no general fact in history; as if slavery was natural to them, they have tamely remained in bondage, occasionally escaping by flight or ransom. But the Jews, held in slavery by the Egyptians, after suffering dreadful oppression, at length gathered themselves under a leader raised up by God, and migrated from the house of Bondage. A remarkable characteristic of this slavery was that there was no amalgamation between the masters and their slaves. Escape from slavery, by migration, was in this instance the law obeyed by the minority (the Jews) who differed in complexion from their masters. Can this law be applied to our destiny?

To a certain extent, we do escape from slavery in this manner. But thirty thousand, which is, in full, the number of people who have migrated to Canada, Liberia, and the West Indies, is too small a number from which to draw a general inference, it is only one eighty-third portion of our population. No! we are not a migrating people. The soil of our birth is dear to our hearts, and we cling to it with a tenacity which no force can unhinge, no contumely sever. . . .

Alike in servitude, and in being distinguished by complexion from our taskmasters, we act differently from the Israelites? Why? It must be for the accomplishment of some end different from what they effected. They emigrated from the scene of their slavery, and in the search for Liberty. "*Ubi libertas, ibi patria,*" is an expression of their rule of conduct; and from the time of their escape from the House of Bondage, until now, the persecuted, or oppressed few have for the most part fled from their homes in search of Liberty. By remaining upon the scene of our oppressions we are acting out the converse of their rule of conduct. We proclaim to the oppressed few, "*Ubi patria, ibi libertas,*" "Where our country is, there shall Liberty dwell!" . . . .

By remaining in this country, the scene of our enslavement, we shall overcome slavery, and consequently confute, by the resistless evidence of facts, the doctrines upon which slavery rests. This will do more for human Liberty than could be accomplished by emigration. By the latter course we might escape from, but would leave untouched an evil institution, which, by our present course, we are destined to overthrow.

But in overcoming the Institution of Slavery, we must by our conduct confute the doctrines on which it is based. One of these doctrines is that "Might makes Right." Because men have the power, therefore they have the right to keep other men enslaved. This doctrine has also been the basis of several modern revolutions. For when the dogma of the Divine Right of Kings, and the reign of superstition lost their influence upon the minds of the masses, these masses arose in their might, and relying upon their physical might, endeavored to obtain those rights which had been so long withheld from them. Their success has been only partial, because, perchance, their efforts were based upon an unstable foundation—mere might.

We are not in possession of physical superiority: yet we must overturn the doctrine "might makes right," and we can only do so by demonstrating that "right makes right." This very doctrine is contained in the American Declaration of Independence, which declares that "all men have certain inalienable rights." But the Constitution of these United States, professedly constructed on the above principles, hold that there are some "other persons"—besides all men—who are not entitled to these rights! It is our destiny to prove that even this exception is wrong, and therefore contrary to the highest interests of the whole people, and to eradicate from the Constitution this exception, so contrary to its general principles.

There is another doctrine which we are destined, nay, that we are daily illustrating by our conduct. It has been the History of nearly all great Revolutions, that Reformers have followed out the doctrine of returning evil for evil. So soon as the oppressed have found the opportunity and the power, they have retaliated upon the oppressor with a similarity of oppression. They have returned evil for evil. *We are destined to show the infinite superiority of returning Good for Evil.* Even at this hour, bound with bands of iron at the South, and the fetters of prejudice at the North, scorned, jeered at, tortured with the fangs of ferocious and malignant slanders, and with the merciless lash of the slave whip, we have refrained from deluging our country in blood. The beautiful edifices of our oppressors spring up on every side, gathering into villages, towns, and cities, and the broad rivers run by them, swollen with the tears of the oppressed, but untinged with the blood of the oppressors. They drive us from the magnificent temples which they erect for the worship of the Most High, as if He were a "respecter of persons."

In our humble way, we raise humble tenements in which we approach the footstool of our common Father, and we pray, not for vengeance, but for mercy on our oppressors, and we throw open the doors that all, even those who exclude us, all who thirst may come in and drink, that all who are heavily laden may unburthen themselves before altars erected to the Living Lord; in a word, in our every act, and all our relations we are already rendering Good for Evil, and what can be more glorious in the destiny of any people!

We are an oppressed minority, then, and are men of kindred power with those who oppress us. What has been the fate of oppressed minorities who have resisted oppression? History is full of evidence on this subject. The Jews, for example, in comparatively modern times have been persecuted and oppressed very much in almost every European kingdom. The Inquisition of Spain was specially instituted against them. They were expelled from country after country by a series of laws which are the prototypes or precedents of the Ohio-code. Even at this hour they are excluded from the privileges of citizenship in free, enlightened and philanthropic Great Britain. And yet we find that the Jews, the so pitilessly oppressed minority, now hold in their hands the rule, the very fate of some of the kingdoms which were formerly foremost in persecuting them. The very persecutions which they suffered drove them to amass that influence— MONEY—which enables them to rule their former oppressors.

Source Note: James McCune Smith, *The Destiny of a People of Color* (Boston, 1843). The allusion above to the "Ohio Code" specifically refers first, to the manly resistance of the people of color to mob violence in Cincinnati, and second, to the fact that in spite of the odious Black Code of Ohio, the colored people of Ohio had advanced more rapidly and energetically than the same population in any other state, according to McCune's calculations. (The non-violent and Christian doctrine of returning "good for evil" is of course an early expression of the doctrine that Martin Luther King, Jr., would adopt for the civil rights movement of the 1950s and 1960s.)

ANGELINA EMILY GRIMKÉ (1805–1879)
AND SARAH MOORE GRIMKÉ (1792–1873)

Angelina Emily Grimké and her sister, Sarah Moore Grimké, were nineteenth-century social reformers who were committed to abolitionism and the emerging women's movement. Born in Charleston, South Carolina, on February 20, 1805, Angelina grew up surrounded by wealth, privilege, and slavery. Both women instinctively disliked the institution on which the family's privilege was based, and they moved to New England, where both became Quakers and joined the abolition movement inspired by William Lloyd Garrison. Both sisters wrote passionately concerning slavery. Sarah authored *An Epistle to the Clergy of the Southern States* (1836). Angelina, who married the abolitionist Theodore Dwight Weld, wrote the longer treatise also excerpted here, *An Appeal to the Christian Women of the South* (1836), as well as *An Appeal to the Women of the Nominally Free States* (1837). Also excerpted here is Angelina Grimké's exchange of correspondence with Catharine E. Beecher (1800–74), which is her response to Beecher's 1837 book entitled *An Essay on Slavery and Abolitionism, with Reference to the Duty of American Females*. This dialogue over the roles of women in the antislavery cause marks a division in women's views of the fusion of suffrage and antislavery. Catharine Beecher, who always opposed women's suffrage, regarded abolitionists like Weld and Grimké to be excessive, and she deplored the entry of women into public discourse concerning slavery. As Beecher's publications indicate, she was deeply committed to the domestic roles of women. The exchange between Angelina Grimké and Catharine Beecher

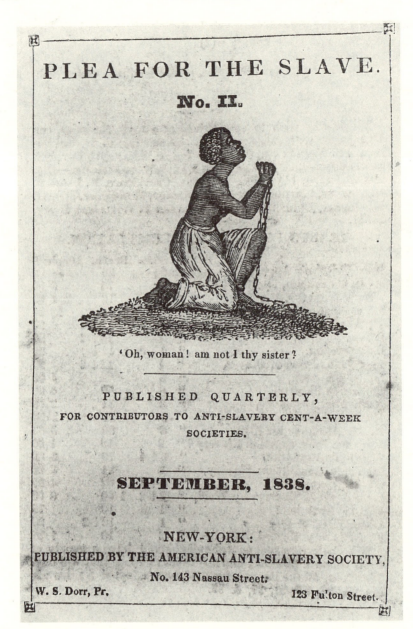

"Plea for the Slave," the American Anti-Slavery Society, New York, 1838.

constitutes yet another dimension of the antebellum slavery debates, the essential place of women in the rapidly fragmenting Union.

SUGGESTIONS FOR FURTHER READING

Ginzberg, Lori. *Women and the Work of Benevolence: Morality, Politics, and Class in the Nineteenth-Century United States.* New Haven: Yale University Press, 1990.

Grimké, Sarah Moore, and Angelina Emily Grimké. *The Public Years of Sarah and Angelina Grimké: Selected Writings, 1835–1839.* Ed. Larry Ceplair. New York: Columbia University Press, 1989.

White, Deborah Gray. *Ain't I a Woman: Female Slaves in the Plantation South.* New York: W.W. Norton, 1985.

Yellin, Jean Fagan. *Women and Sisters: the Antislavery Feminists in American Culture.* New Haven: Yale University Press, 1989.

——, and John Van Horne. *The Abolitionist Sisterhood: Women's Political Culture in Antebellum America.* Ithaca: Cornell University Press, 1994.

An Appeal to the Christian Women of the South
by Angelina Emily Grimké

> Then Mordecai commanded to answer Esther, Think not within thyself
> that thou shalt escape in the king's house more than all the Jews. For if
> thou altogether holdest thy peace at this time, then shall their enlargement
> and deliverance arise to the Jews from another place: but thou and thy
> father's house shall be destroyed: and who knoweth whether thou art come
> to the kingdom for such time as this. And Esther bade them return
> Mordecai this answer:—and so will I go in unto the king, which is not
> according to law, and *if I perish, I perish.*—Esther IV. 13–16.

Yes! Sisters in Christ I feel an interest in *you*, and often has the secret prayer arisen on your behalf, Lord "open thou their eyes that they may see wondrous things out of thy Law"—It is then, because I *do feel* and *do pray* for you, that I thus address you upon a subject about which of all others, perhaps you would rather not hear anything.

It is true, I am going to tell you unwelcome truths, but I mean to speak those *truths in love.* . . .

The *women of the South can overthrow* this horrible system of oppression and cruelty, licentiousness and wrong. Such appeals to your legislatures would be irresistible, for there is something in the heart of man which *will bend under moral suasion.* There is a swift witness for truth in his bosom, which *will respond to truth* when it is uttered with calmness and dignity. If you could obtain but six signatures to such a petition in only one state, I would say, send up that petition, and be not in the least discouraged by the scoffs and jeers of the heartless, or the resolution of the house to lay it on the table. It will be a great thing if the subject can be introduced into your legislatures in any way, even by *women*, and *they* will be most likely to introduce it there in the best possible manner, as a matter of *morals* and *religion*, not of expediency or politics. You may petition, too, the different ecclesiastical bodies of the slave states. Slavery must be attacked with the whole power of truth and the sword of spirit. Your must take it up on *Christian* ground, and fight against it with Christian weapons, whilst your feet are shod with the preparation of the gospel of peace. And *you are now* loudly called upon by the cries of the widow and the orphan, to arise and gird yourselves for this great moral conflict, with the whole armor of righteousness upon the right hand and on the left.

There is every encouragement for you to labor and pray, my friends, because the abolition of slavery as well as its existence, has been the theme of prophecy. "Ethiopia (says of the Psalmist) shall stretch forth her hands unto God." And is she not now doing so? Are not the Christian negroes of the south lifting their hands in prayer for deliverance, just as the Israelites did when their redemption was drawing nigh? Are they not sighing and crying by reason of the hard bondage? And think you, that He, of whom it was said, "and God heard their groaning, and their cry came up unto him by reason of the hard bondage," think you that his ear is heavy that he cannot *now* hear the cries of his suffering children? Or that He who raised up a Moses, an Aaron, and a Miriam, to bring them up out of the land of Egypt from the house of bondage, cannot now, with a high hand and stretched out arm, rid the poor negroes out of the hands of their masters? Surely you believe that his arm is *not* shortened that he cannot save. And would not such work of mercy redound to his glory? But another string of the harp of prophecy vibrates to the song of deliverance: "But they shall sit every man under his vine, and under his fig-tree, and *none shall make them afraid*; for the mouth of the Lord of Hosts hath spoken it." The *slave* never can do this as long as he is a *slave*; whilst he is a "chattel personal" he can own *no* property; but the time *is to come* when *every* man is to sit under *his own* vine and *his own* fig-tree, and no domineering driver, or irresponsible master, or irascible mistress, shall make him afraid of the chain or the whip.

Slavery, then, must be overthrown before the prophecies can be accomplished, but how are they to be fulfilled? Will the wheels of the millennial car be rolled onward by miraculous power? NO! God designs to confer this holy privilege upon *man*; it is through *his* instrumentality that the great and glorious work of reforming the world is to be done. And see you not how the mighty engine of *moral power* is dragging in its rear the Bible and peace societies, anti-slavery and temperance, Sabbath schools, moral reform, and missions? Or to adopt another figure, do not these seven philanthropic associations compose the beautiful tints in that bow of promise which spans the arc of our moral heaven? Who does not believe, that if these societies were broken up, their constitutions burnt, and the vast machinery with which they are laboring to regenerate mankind was stopped, that the black clouds of vengeance would soon burst over our world, and every city would witness the fate of the devoted cities of the plain! Each one of these societies is walking abroad through the earth scattering the seeds of truth over the wide field of our world. . . .

But I will now say a few words on the subject of Abolitionism. Doubtless you have all heard Anti-Slavery Societies denounced as insurrectionary and mischie-

vous, fanatical and dangerous. It has been said they publish the most abominable untruths, and that they are endeavoring to excite rebellions at the South.
Have you believed these reports, my friends? Have *you* also been deceived by
these false assertions? Listen to me, then, whilst I endeavor to wipe from the
fair character of Abolitionism such unfounded accusations. You know that I am
a Southerner; you know that my dearest relatives are now in a slave State. Can
you for a moment believe I would prove so recreant to the feelings of a daughter
and a sister, as to join a society which was seeking to overthrow slavery by
falsehood, bloodshed, and murder? I appeal to you who have known and loved
me in days that are passed, can you believe it. No! my friends. As a Carolinian, I
was peculiarly jealous of any movements on this subject; and before I would join
an Anti-Slavery Society, I took the precaution of becoming acquainted with
some of the leading Abolitionists, of reading their publications and attending
their meetings, at which I heard addresses both from colored and white men;
and it was not until I was fully convinced that their principles were *entirely
pacific*, and their efforts *only moral*, that I gave my name as a member to the
Female Anti-Slavery Society of Philadelphia. Since that time, I have regularly
taken the Liberator, and read many Anti-Slavery pamphlets and papers and
books, and can never read any account of cruelty which I could not believe.
Southerners may deny the truth of these accounts, but why do they not *prove*
them to be false. Their violent expressions of horror at such accounts being
believed, *may* deceive some, but they cannot deceive *me* for I lived too long in
the midst of slavery, not to know what slavery is. When I speak of this system,
"I speak that I do know," and I am not at all afraid to assert, that Anti-Slavery
publications have *not* overdrawn the monstrous features of slavery at all. And
many a Southerner *knows* this as well as I do. A lady in North Carolina remarked to a friend of mine, about eighteen month since, "Northerners know
nothing at all about slavery; they think it is perpetual bondage only; but of the
depth of degradation that word involves, they have no conception; if they had,
they would never cease their efforts until *so horrible* a system was overthrown."
She did not know how faithfully some Northern men and Northern women had
studied this subject; how diligently they had searched out the cause of "him who
had none to help him," and how fearlessly they had told the story of the negro's
wrongs. Yes, Northerners know *every* thing about slavery now. This monster of
iniquity has been unveiled to the world, her frightful features unmasked, and
soon, very soon will she be regarded with no more complacency by the American republic than is the idol of Juggernaut, rolling its bloody wheels over the
crushed bodies of its prostrate victims.

But you will probably ask, if Anti-Slavery societies are not insurrectionary,
why do Northerners tell us they are? Why, I would ask you in return, did
Northern senators and Northern representatives give their votes, at the last sitting of congress, to the admission of Arkansas Territory as a state? Take those
men, one by one, and ask them in their parlours, do you *approve of slavery*? Ask
them on *Northern* ground, where they will speak the truth, and I doubt not
every man of them will tell you, *no*! Why then, I ask, did *they* give their votes to

enlarge the mouth of that grave which has already destroyed its tens of thousands? All our enemies tell *us* they are as much anti-slavery as we are. Yes, my friends, thousands who are helping you to bind the fetters of slavery on the negro despise you in their hearts for doing it. . . . .

But you will say, a great many other Northerners tell us so, who can have no political motives. The interests of the North, you must know my friends, are very closely combined with those of the South. The Northern merchants and manufacturers are making *their* fortunes out of the *produce of slave labor*; the grocer is selling our rice and our sugar; how then can these men bear a testimony against slavery without condemning themselves? But there is another reason, the North is most dreadfully afraid of Amalgamation. She is alarmed at the very idea of a thing so monstrous, as she thinks. And lest this consequence *might* flow from emancipation, she is determined to resist all efforts at emancipation without expatriation. It is not because *she approves of slavery*, or believes it to be "the corner stone of our republic," for she is as much *anti-slavery* as we are; but amalgamation is too horrible to think of. Now I would ask *you*, is it right, is it generous, to refuse the colored people in this country the advantages of education and the privilege, or rather the *right* to follow honest trades and callings merely because they are colored? The same prejudice exists here against our colored brethren that existed against the Gentiles in Judea. Great numbers cannot bear the idea of equality, and fearing lest, if they had the same advantages we enjoy, they would become as intelligent, as moral, as religious, and as respectable and wealthy, they are determined to keep them as low as they possibly can. Is this doing as they would be done by? Is this loving their neighbors *as themselves*? Oh! That *such* opposers of Abolitionism would put their souls in the stead of the free colored man's and obey the apostolic injunction, to "remember them that are in bonds *as bound with them*."

You need not be surprised, then, at all, at what is said *against* Abolitionists by the North, for they are wielding a two-edged sword, which even here, cuts through the *cords of caste*, on one side, and the *bonds of interest* on the other. They are only sharing the fate of other reformers, abused and reviled whilst they are in the minority; but they are neither angry nor discouraged by the invective which has been heaped upon them by the slaveholders of the South and their apologists at the North.

Abolitionists understand the slaveholding spirit too well to be surprised at any thing that has yet happened at the South or the North. They know that the greater the sin is, which is exposed, the more violent will be the efforts to blacken the character and impugn the motives of those who are engaged in bringing to light the hidden things of darkness. They understand the work of Reform too well to be driven back by the furious waves of opposition, which are only foaming out of their own shame.

I can prove the *safety* of immediate Emancipation by history. In St. Domingo in 1793 six hundred thousand slaves were set free in a white population of forty-two thousand. That Island "marched as by enchantment towards its ancient splendor, cultivation prospered, every day produced perceptible proofs of its

progress, and the negroes all continued quietly to work on the different plantations, until in 1802, France determined to reduce these liberated slaves again to
bondage. It was at *this time* that all those dreadful scenes occurred, which we so
often *unjustly* hear spoken of, as the effects of Abolition. They were occasioned
not by Emancipation, but by the base attempt to fasten the chains of slavery on
the limbs of liberated slaves.

And why not try it in the Southern States, if it *never* has occasioned rebellion; if *not* a *drop* of *blood* has ever been shed in consequence of it, though it has
been so often tried, why should we suppose it would produce such disastrous
consequences now? "Be not deceived then, God is not mocked," by such false
excuses for not doing justly and loving mercy. There is nothing to fear from
immediate Emancipation, but *every thing* from the continuance of slavery.

Sisters in Christ, I have done. As a Southerner, I have felt it was my duty to
address you. I have endeavored to set before you the exceeding sinfulness of
slavery, and to point you to the example of those noble women who have been
raised up in the church to effect great revolutions, and to suffer for the truth's
sake. . . .

Source Note: Angelina Emily Grimké, *An Appeal to the Christian Women of the South*
(Boston, 1836).

An Epistle to the Clergy of the Southern States
by Sarah Moore Grimké

. . . "Let us make man in OUR IMAGE, after our likeness, and let him have
dominion over the *fish* of the sea, and over the fowl of the air, and over the
cattle, and over all the earth, and over every creeping thing, that creepeth upon
the earth." Here is written in characters of fire continually blazing before the
eyes of every man who holds his *fellow* man in bondage—In the image of God
created he man. Here is marked a distinction which can never be effaced between a man and a *thing,* and we are fighting against God's unchangeable decree
by depriving this rational and immortal being of those inalienable rights which
have been conferred upon him. He was created a little lower than the angels,
crowned with glory and honor, and designed to be God's vice-regent upon
earth—but slavery has wrested the sceptre of dominion from his hand, slavery
has seized with an iron grasp this God-like being, and torn the crown from his
head. Slavery has disrobed him of royalty, put on him the collar and the chain,
and trampled the image of God in the dust.

. . . Can any crime, tremendous as is the history of human wickedness, compare in turpitude with this?—No, the immutable difference, the *heaven-wide
distinction* which God has established between *that* being, whom he has made a
little lower than the angels, and all the other works of this wonderful creation,
cannot be annihilated without incurring a weight of guilt beyond expression
terrible.

. . . Permission ample was given to shed the blood of all inferior creatures, but of this *being, bearing the impress of divinity*, God said, "And surely the blood of your lives will I require, at the hand of every beast will I require it, and at the hand of man, at the hand of every man's brother will I require the life of man. Who so sheddeth man's blood, by man shall his blood be shed, for in the IMAGE OF GOD made he man." Let us pause and examine this passage— Man may shed the blood of the inferior animals, he may use them as *mere means*—he may convert them into food to sustain existence—but if the top-stone of creation, the *image of God* had his blood shed by a beast, that blood was required even of this irrational brute: as if Deity had said, over *any likeness* I will spread a panoply divine that all creation may instinctively feel that he is precious to his Maker—so precious, that if his life be taken by his fellow man—if man degrades himself to the level of a beast by destroying his brother—"by man shall his blood be shed."

This distinction between *man* and *things* is marked with equal care and solemnity under the Jewish dispensation. "If a man steal an ox, or a sheep, and kill it, or sell it, he shall restore five oxen for an ox, and four sheep for a sheep." But, "he that stealeth a man and selleth him or if he be found in his hand, he shall surely be put to death." If this law were carried into effect now, what must be the inevitable doom of all those who now hold man as property? If Jehovah were to exact the execution of this penalty upon the more enlightened and more spiritually minded men who live under the Christian dispensation, would he not instantly commission his most tremendous thunderbolts to strike from existence those who are thus trampling upon his laws, thus defacing his image?

. . . And here I cannot but advert to a most important distinction which God has made between immortal beings and the beasts that perish—No one can doubt that by the fall of man the whole creation underwent a change. The apostle says, "We know that the whole creation groaneth and travaileth in pain together." But it was for *man* alone that the Lord Jesus "made himself of no reputation and took upon him the form of a servant. . . ."

Mr. Calhoun of Norfolk, in a speech in the House of Delegates of Virginia, on the subject of negro slavery in 1832, speaking of our right to hold our colored brethren in bondage, says:

"As a Virginian, I do not question the master's title to his slave; but I put it to that gentleman, as a man, as a moral man, as a Christian man, whether he has not some doubts of his claim to his slaves, being as absolute and unqualified as that to other property. Let us in the investigation of this title go back to its origin—Whence came slaves into this country?—From Africa. Were they free men there? At one time they were. How came they to be converted into slaves?—By the stratagem of war and the strong arm of the conqueror; they were vanquished in battle, sold by the victorious party to the slave trader; who brought them to our shores, and disposed of them to the planters of Virginia. . . . The truth is, our ancestors had *no title* to this property, and we have acquired it only by legislative enactment."

. . . Another plea by which we endeavor to silence the voice of conscience is, "that the child is invariably born to the condition of the parent." Hence the law of South Carolina, says "ALL THEIR (THE SLAVES) ISSUE AND OFF-SPRING, BORN, OR TO BE BORN, SHALL BE, AND THEY ARE HEREBY DECLARED TO BE, AND REMAIN FOREVER HEREAF-TER, ABSOLUTE SLAVES, AND SHALL FOREVER FOLLOW THE CONDITION OF THE MOTHER." To support this assumption, recourse is had to the page of inspiration. Our colored brethren are said to be the descendants of Ham who was cursed with all his posterity, and their condition only in accordance with the declaration of Jehovah, that he visits the iniquities of the fathers upon the children—I need only remark that Canaan, not Ham, was the object of Noah's prophecy, and that upon his descendants it has been amply fulfilled.

. . . The present position of my country and of the church is one of deep and solemn interest. The times of our ignorance on the subject of slavery which God may have winked at *have passed away*. We are no longer standing unconsciously and carelessly on the brink of a burning volcano. The strong arm of Almighty power has rolled back the dense cloud which hung over the terrific crater, and has exposed it to our view, and although no human eye can penetrate the abyss, yet enough is seen to warn us of the consequences of trifling with Omnipotence. Jehovah is calling to us as he did to Job out of the whirlwind, and every blast bears on its wings the sound, Repent! Repent! God, if I may so speak, is waiting to see whether we will hearken unto his voice. He has sent out his light and his truth, and as regards us it may perhaps be said—there is now silence in heaven. The commissioned messengers of grace to this guilty nation are rapidly traversing our country, through the medium of the Anti-Slavery Society, through its agents and its presses, whilst the "ministering spirits" are marking with breathless interest the influence produced by these means of knowledge thus mercifully furnished to our land. . . .

What an appalling spectacle do we now present! With one hand we clasp the cross of Christ, and with the other grasp the neck of the downtrodden slave! With one eye we are gazing imploringly on the bleeding sacrifice of Calvary, as if we expected redemption through the blood which was shed there, and with the other we cast the glance of indignation and contempt at the representative of Him who there made his soul an offering for sin! My Christian brethren, if there is any truth in the Bible, and in the God of the Bible, *our hearts bear us witness* that he can no more acknowledge us as his disciples, if we willfully persist in this sin, than he did the Pharisees formerly, who were strict and punctilious in the observance of the ceremonial law, and yet devoured widows' houses. *We have added a deeper shade to their guilt, we make widows by tearing* from the victims of a cruel bondage, the husbands of their bosoms, and then devour the widow herself by robbing her of her freedom, and reducing her to the level of a brute. I solemnly appeal to your consciences. . . .

And this is the sin which the Church is fostering in her bosom—This is the leprosy over which she is casting the mantle of charity, to hide, if possible, the "putrefying sores"—This is the monster around which she is twining her maternal arms, and before which she is placing her anointed shield inscribed "holiness to the Lord"—Oh, ye ministers of Him who so loved the slave that he gave his precious blood to redeem him from sin, can ye any longer with your eyes fixed upon the Cross of Christ, plant your feet on his injured representative, and sanction and sanctify this heart-breaking, the soul-destroying system?

Source Note: Sarah Moore Grimké, *An Epistle to the Clergy of the Southern States* (Boston, 1836).

CATHARINE E. BEECHER (1804–1878)

Catharine Beecher was born into one of the most illustrious families of antebellum America. Her father was the well-known Lyman Beecher, not only a minister but also the president of Lane Theological Seminary in Cincinnati, Ohio. Her brother, Henry Ward Beecher, was also a Protestant minister of the Second Great Awakening, and her sister, Harriet Beecher Stowe, was the most influential author in America before the Civil War. Catharine Beecher was engaged to a young Yale professor who tragically died before their marriage; she devoted the rest of her life to the cause of women's education, although she was always an opponent of the women's suffrage movement. Moving to Cincinnati to accompany her father in his presidency of Lane Seminary, Catharine was active in the founding of several small women's colleges in the Midwest, which were living examples of her commitment to excellence in women's higher education. The text excerpted here, *An Essay on Slavery and Abolitionism, with Reference to the Duty of American Females* (1837), is an example of the rhetorical force of her antislavery argument, and the moral arguments embraced by the Beechers, who were committed to antislavery but who did not engage in direct ways in the political turmoil surrounding abolitionism. Catharine Beecher also authored several works on domestic economy and the roles of women in antebellum American society, listed below.

SUGGESTIONS FOR FURTHER READING

Beecher, Catharine. *The Duty of American Women to their Country*. New York, 1845.

———. *The Evils Suffered by American Women and Children: the Causes and the Remedy*. New York, 1846.

———. *Miss Beecher's Domestic Receipt Book*. New York, 1846.

———. *Physiology and Calisthenics for Schools and Families*. New York, 1856.

———. *A Treatise on Domestic Economy for the Use of Young Ladies at Home and at School* (1841). Introduction by Kathryn Sklar. New York: Schocken, 1977.

———. *Woman Suffrage and Woman's Profession*. Hartford, CT, 1871.

Dubois, Ellen Carol. *Feminism and Suffrage: The Emergence of an Independent Women's Movement in America, 1848–1869*. Ithaca: Cornell University Press, 1978.

Groneman, Carol, and Mary Beth Norton, eds. *To Toil the Livelong Day: America's Women at Work, 1780–1980*. Ithaca: Cornell University Press, 1987.

Kinney, James. *Amalgamation: Race, Sex, and Rhetoric in the Nineteenth-Century American Novel*. Westport, CT: Greenwood Press, 1985.

Morton, Patricia. *Disfigured Images: The Historical Assault on Afro-American Women*. Westport, CT: Greenwood Press, 1991.

————, ed. *Discovering the Women in Slavery: Emancipating Perspectives on the American Past*. Athens: University of Georgia Press, 1996.

Matthews, Glenna. *The Rise of Public Woman: Woman's Power and Woman's Place in the United States, 1630–1970*. New York: Oxford University Press, 1992.

Sklar, Kathryn Kish. *Catharine Beecher: A Study in American Domesticity*. New York: Norton, 1973.

Smith-Rosenberg, Carroll. *Disorderly Conduct: Visions of Gender in Victorian America*. New York: Oxford University Press, 1985.

An Essay on Slavery and Abolitionism, with Reference to the Duty of American Females
by Catharine E. Beecher

The Following are the circumstances which occasioned the succeeding pages. A gentleman and a friend, requested the writer to assign reason why he should not join the Abolition Society. While preparing a reply to this request, MISS GRIMKÉ'S *Address* was presented.

The writer then began a private letter to Miss Grimké as a personal friend. But by the wishes and advice of others, these two efforts were finally combined in the following Essay, to be presented to the public.

Addressed to Miss A. E. Grimké.

The object I have in view, is to present some reason why it seems unwise and inexpedient for ladies of the non-slave-holding States to unite themselves in Abolition Societies; and thus, at the same time, to exhibit the inexpediency of the course you propose to adopt.

Your remarks seem to assume, that the *principles* held by Abolitionists on the subject of slavery, are peculiar to them, and are not generally adopted by those at the North who oppose their *measures*. In this you are not correctly informed.

I know not where to look for northern Christians, who would deny that every slave-holder is bound to treat his slaves exactly as he would claim that his own children ought to be treated in similar circumstances; that the holding of our fellow men as property, or the withholding any of the rights of freedom, for mere purposes of gain, is a sin, and ought to be immediately abandoned.

The distinctive peculiarity of the Abolition Society is this: it is a voluntary association in one section of the country, designed to awaken public sentiment against a moral evil existing in another section of the country, and the principal point of effort seems to be, to enlarge the numbers of this association as a means of influencing public sentiment.

Experience has shown, that when certain moral evils exist in a community, efforts to awaken public sentiment against such practices, and combinations for the exercise of personal influence and example, have in various cases tended to rectify these evils. Thus in respect to intemperance;—the collecting of facts, the labours of public lecturers and the distribution of publications, have had much effect in diminishing the evil. So in reference to the slave-trade and slavery in England.

Clarkson, Wilberforce, and their coadjutors, commenced a system of operations to arouse and influence public sentiment, and they succeeded in securing the suppression of the slave trade, and the gradual abolition of slavery in the English colonies.

The second reason I would urge against joining the Abolition Society is, that its character and measures are not either peaceful or Christian in tendency, but they rather are those which tend to generate party spirit, denunciation, recriminations, and angry passions. . . .

I believe, that as a body, Abolitionists are men of pure morals, of great honesty of purpose, of real benevolence and piety, and of great activity in efforts to promote what they consider the best interest of their fellow men. I believe, that, in making efforts to abolish slavery, they have taken measures, which they supposed were best calculated to bring this evil to an end, with the greatest speed, and with the least danger and suffering to the South. I do not believe they ever designed to promote disunion, or insurrection, or to stir up strife.

I regard individuals among them, as having taken a bold and courageous stand, in maintaining the liberty of free discussion, the liberty of speech and of the press.

Although Abolitionists may be lauded for many virtues, still much evidence can be presented, that the character and measures of the Abolition Society are not either peaceful or Christian in tendency, but that they are in their nature calculated to generate party spirit, denunciation, recrimination, and angry passions.

Let us now look at the leaders of the Abolition movement in America. The man who first took the lead was William L. Garrison, who, though he professes a belief in the Christian religion, is an avowed opponent of most of its institutions. The character and spirit of this man have for years been exhibited in *The Liberator*, of which he is the editor. That there is to be found in that paper, or in any thing else, any evidence of his possessing the peculiar traits of Wilberforce, not even his warmest admirers will maintain. How many of the opposite traits can be found, those can best judge who have read his paper. Gradually others joined themselves in the effort commenced by Garrison; but for a long time they consisted chiefly of men who would fall into one of these three classes; either good men who were so excited by a knowledge of the enormous evils of slavery, that *anything* was considered better than entire inactivity, or else men accustomed to a contracted field of observation, and more qualified to judge of immediate results than of general tendencies, or else men of ardent and impulsive temperament, whose feelings are likely to take the lead, rather than their judgement.

The editors of *The Emancipator, The Friend of Man, The New York Evangelist*, and the other abolition periodicals, may therefore be considered as among the chief leaders of the enterprise, and their papers are the mirror from which their spirit and character are reflected. . . .

One of the first measures of Abolitionists was an attack on a benevolent society, originated and sustained by some of the most pious and devoted men of the age. It was imagined by Abolitionists, that the influence and measures of the colonization society tended to retard the abolition of slavery, and to perpetuate injurious prejudices against the coloured race. The peaceful and Christian method of meeting this difficulty would have been, to collect all the evidence of this supposed hurtful tendency, and privately, and in a respectful and conciliating way, to have presented it to the attention of the wise and benevolent men, who were most interested in sustaining this institution. . . .

. . . In public, the enterprise [the Colonization Society] was attacked as a plan for promoting the selfish interests and prejudice of the whites, at the expense of the coloured population. . . .

And the style in which the thing was done was at once offensive, inflammatory, and exasperating. Denunciation, sneers, and public rebuke, were bestowed indiscriminately upon the conductors of the enterprise, and of course they fell upon many sincere, upright, and conscientious men, whose feelings were harrowed by a sense of the injustice, the indecorum and the unchristian treatment, they received. . . .

. . . Compare this method of carrying a point, with that adopted by Wilberforce and his compeers, and I think you will allow that there was a way that was peaceful and Christian, and that this was not the way which was chosen.

The next measure of Abolitionism was an attempt to remove the prejudices of whites against the blacks, on account of natural peculiarities. Now, prejudice is an *unreasonable* and *groundless* dislike of persons or things. . . .

If the friends of the blacks had quietly set themselves to work to increase their intelligence, their usefulness, their respectability, their meekness, gentleness, and benevolence, and then had appealed to the pity, generosity, and Christian feelings of their fellow citizens, a very different result would have appeared. Instead of this, reproaches, rebukes, and sneers, were employed to convince the whites that their prejudices were sinful, and without any just cause. They were accused of pride, of selfish indifference, of unchristian neglect. This tended to irritate the whites, and to increase their prejudice against the blacks, who thus were made the cause of rebuke and exasperation. . . .

. . . Now, the question is not, whether these things, that were urged by Abolitionists, were true. The thing maintained is, that the method taken by them to remove this prejudice was neither peaceful nor Christian in its tendency, but, on the contrary, was calculated to increase the evil, and to generate anger, pride, and recrimination, on one side, and envy, discontent, and revengeful feelings on the other. . . .

. . . It was an entire disregard of the prejudices and properties of society, and calculated to stimulate pride, anger, ill-will, contention, and all the bitter feelings that spring from such collisions. Then, instead of adopting measures to soothe and conciliate, rebukes, sneers and denunciation, were employed. . . .

. . . The whole system of Abolition measures seems to leave entirely out of view, the obligation of Christians to save their fellow men from all needless temptations. If the thing to be done is only lawful and right, it does not appear to have been a matter of effort to do it in such a way as would not provoke and irritate; but often, if the chief aim had been to do the good in the most injurious and offensive way. . . .

. . . It is a fact, that Abolitionists have taken the course most calculated to awaken illegal acts of violence, and that when they have ensued, they have seemed to rejoice in them, as calculated to advance and strengthen their cause. The violence of mobs, the denunciations and unreasonable requirements of the South, the denial of the right of petitions, the restrictions attempted to be laid upon freedom of speech, and freedom of the press, are generally spoken of with exultation by Abolitionists, as what are among the chief means of promoting the cause. It is not so much by exciting feelings of pity and humanity, and Christian love, towards the oppressed, as it is by awakening indignation at the treatment of abolitionists themselves, that their cause has prospered. . . .

. . . The leaders of the Abolition Society disclaim all such wishes or intentions; they only act apparently on the assumption that they are exercising just rights, which they are not bound to give up, because other men will act unreasonably and wickedly.

Another measure of Abolitionists, calculated to awaken evil feelings, has been the treatment of those who objected to their proceedings. . . .

. . . The peaceful and Christian method of encountering such opposition, would have been to allow the opponents full credit for purity and integrity of motive, to have avoided all harsh and censorious language, and to have employed facts, arguments and persuasions, in a kind and respectful way with the hope of modifying their views and allaying their fears. Instead of this, the wise and good who opposed Abolition measures, have been treated as though they were the friends and defenders of slavery, or as those who, from a guilty, timid, time-serving policy, refused to take the course which duty demanded. . . .

Now there is nothing more irritating, when a man is conscientious and acting according to his own views of right, than to be dealt with in this manner. The more men are treated as if they were honest and sincere—the more they are treated with respect, fairness, and benevolence, the more likely they are to be moved by evidence and arguments. On the contrary, harshness, uncharitableness, and rebuke, for opinions and conduct that are in agreement with a man's own views of duty and rectitude, tend to awaken evil feelings, and indispose the mind properly to regard evidence. Abolitionists have not only taken this course, but in many cases, have seemed to act on the principle, that the abolition of Slavery, in the particular mode in which they were aiming to accomplish it, was of such paramount importance, that every thing must be overthrown that stood in the way. . . .

. . . Another measure of Abolitionists, which has greatly tended to promote wrath and strife, is their indiscreet and incorrect use of terms. . . .

. . . Now if men take words and give them a new and peculiar use, and are consequently misunderstood, they are guilty of deception, and are accountable for all the evils that may ensue as a consequence. . . .

. . . Now Abolitionists are before the community, and declare that all slavery is sin, which ought to be immediately forsaken; and that it is their object and intention to promote the *immediate emancipation* of all slaves in this nation. . . .

. . . The true and only proper meaning of such language is, that it is the duty of every slaveholder in this nation, to go immediately and make out the legal instruments, that, by the laws of the land, change all his slaves' freemen. . . .

. . . The meaning which the Abolitionist attaches to his language is this, that every man is bound to treat his slaves, as nearly as he can, like freemen; and to use all his influence to bring the system of slavery to an end as soon as possible. And they allow that when men do this they are free from guilt, in the matter of slavery, and undeserving of censure. . . .

The great mistake of Abolitionists is in using terms which inculcate the immediate annihilation of the relation, when they only intend to urge the Christian duty of treating slaves according to the gospel rules of justice and benevolence, and using all lawful and appropriate means for bringing a most pernicious system to a speedy end. . . .

But so long as they persevere in using these terms in a new and peculiar sense, which will always be misunderstood, they are guilty of a species of deception and accountable for the evils that follow.

One other instance of a similar misuse of terms may be mentioned. The word "manstealer" has one peculiar signification, and it is no more synonymous with "slave-holder" than it is with "sheep-stealer." But Abolitionists show that a slave-holder, in fact does very many of the evils that are perpetrated by a man-stealer, and that the crime is quite as evil in this nature, and very similar in character, and, therefore, he calls a slave-holder a man-stealer. . . .

. . . Abolitionism, on the contrary, is a system of *coercion* by public opinion; and in its present operation, its influence is not to convince the erring, but to convince those who are not guilty, of the sins of those who are. . . .

Now what is the evil to be cured?

SLAVERY IN THIS NATION.

That this evil is at no distant period to come to an end, is the unanimous opinion of all who either notice the tendencies of the age, or believe in the prophecies of the Bible. All who act on Christian principles in regard to slavery, believe that in a given period (variously estimated) it will end. The only question then, in regard to the benefits to be gained, or the evils to be dreaded in the present agitation of the subject, relates to the *time* and the *manner* of its extinction. The Abolitionists claim that their method will bring it to an end in the shortest time, and in the sagest and best way. Their opponents believe, that it will tend to bring it to an end, if at all, at the most distant period, and in the most dangerous way. . . .

The position then I would aim to establish is, that the method taken by the Abolitionists is the one that, according to the laws of mind and past experience, is least likely to bring about the results they aim to accomplish. . . .

It is the maxim then of experience, that when men are to turned from evils, and brought to repent and reform, those only should interfere who have the best right to approach the offender. While on the other hand, rebuke from those who are deemed obtrusive and inimical, or even indifferent, will do more harm than good.

It is another maxim of experience, that such dealings with the erring should be in private, not in public. The moment a man is publicly rebuked, shame, anger, and pride of opinion, all combine to make him defend his practice, and refuse either to own himself wrong, or to cease from his evil ways.

The Abolitionists have violated all these laws of mind and of experience, in dealing with their southern brethren.

Their course has been most calculated to awaken anger, fear, pride, hatred, and all the passions most likely to blind the mind to truth, and make it averse to duty.

They have not approached them with the spirit of love, courtesy, and forbearance. . . .

While Abolition Societies did not exists, men could talk and write, at the South, against the evils of slavery, and northern men had free access and liberty of speech, both at the South and at the North. But now all is changed. Every avenue of approach to the South is shut. No paper, pamphlet, or preacher, that touches on that topic, is admitted in their bounds. Their own citizens, that once laboured and remonstrated, are silenced; their own clergy, under the influence of the exasperated feelings of their people, and their own sympathy and sense of wrong, either entirely hold their peace, or become the defenders of a system they once lamented, and attempted to bring to an end. This is the record of experience as to the tendencies of Abolitionism, as thus far developed. This is no picture of fancied dangers, which are not near. The day has come, when already the feelings are so excited on both sides, that I have heard intelligent men, good men, benevolent and pious men, in moments of excitement, declare themselves ready to take up the sword—some for the defense of the master, some for the protection and right of the slave. There will be men from the North and West, standing breast to breast with murderous weapons, in opposing ranks. . . .

. . . Is not the South in a state of high exasperation against Abolitionists? Does she not regard them as enemies, as reckless madmen, as impertinent intermeddlers? Will the increase of their numbers tend to allay this exasperation? Will the appearance of a similar body in their own boundaries have any tendency to soothe? Will it not still more alarm and exasperate? . . .

When this point is reached, will the blacks, knowing, as they will know, the sympathies of their Abolition friends, refrain from exerting their physical power?

I only say, that if Abolitionists go on as they propose, such results are *more* probable than those they hope to attain.

I have not here alluded to the probabilities of the severing of the Union by the present mode of agitating the question. This may be one of the results, and, if so, what are the probabilities for a Southern republic, that has torn itself off for the purpose of excluding foreign interference, and for the purpose of perpetuating slavery? Can any Abolitionist suppose that, in such a state of things, the great cause of emancipation is as likely to progress favorably, as it was when we were one nation, and milling on those fraternal terms that existed before the Abolition movement began? . . .

Women in Society

It is the grand feature of the Divine economy, that there should be different stations of superiority and subordination, and it is impossible to annihilate this beneficent and immutable law. . . .

The master of a family the superior, the domestic a subordinate—the ruler a superior, the subject a subordinate. Nor do these relations at all depend upon superiority either in intellectual or moral worth. However weak the parents, or intelligent the child, there is no reference to this, in the immutable law. However incompetent the teacher, or superior the pupil, no alteration of station can be allowed. However unworthy the master or worthy the servant, while their mutual relations continue, no change in station as to subordination can be allowed. In fulfilling the duties of these relations, true dignity consists in conforming to all those relations that demand subordination, with propriety and cheerfulness. . . .

Heaven has appointed to one sex the superior, and to the other the subordinated station, and this without any reference to the character or conduct of either. It is therefore as much for the dignity as it is for the interest of females, in all respects to conform to the duties of this relation. And it is as much a duty as it is for the child to fulfill similar relations to parents, or subjects to rulers. But while woman holds a subordinate relation in society to the other sex, it is not because it was designed that her duties or her influence should be any the less important, or all-pervading. But it was designed that the mode of gaining influence and of exercising power should be altogether different and peculiar.

It is Christianity that has given to woman her true place in society. And it is the peculiar trait of Christianity alone that can sustain her therein. . . .

A man may act on society by the collision of intellect, in public debate; he may urge his measure by a sense of shame, by fear and by personal interests; he may coerce by the combination of public sentiment; he may drive by physical force, and he does not out step the boundaries of his sphere. But all the power, and all the conquests that are lawful to woman, are those only which appeal to the kindly, generous, peaceful and benevolent principles. . . .

Woman is to win every thing by peace and love; by making herself so much respected, esteemed and loved, that to yield to her opinions and to gratify her wishes, will be the free-will offering of the heart. But this it to be all accomplished in the domestic and social circle. There let every woman become so cultivated and refined in intellect, that her taste and judgment will be respected; so benevolent in feeling and action; that her motives will be reverenced;—so unassuming and unambitious, that collision and competition will be banished. . . .

But the moment woman begins to feel the promptings of ambition, or the thirst for power, her aegis of defence is gone. All the sacred protection of religion, all the generous promptings of chivalry, all the poetry of romantic gallantry, depend upon woman's retaining her place as dependent and defenceless, and making no claims, and maintaining no right but what are the gifts of honour, rectitude and love.

A woman may seek the aid of co-operation and combination among her own sex, to assist her in her appropriate offices of piety, charity, maternal and domestic duty; but whatever, in any measure, throws a woman into the attitude of a combatant, either for herself or others—whatever binds her in a party conflict—whatever obliges her in any way to exert coercive influences, throws her out of her appropriate sphere. If these general principles are correct, they are entirely opposed to the plan of arraying females in any abolition movement; because it enlists them in an effort to coerce the South by the public sentiment of the North; because it brings them forward as partisans in a conflict that has been begun and carried forward by measures that are any thing rather than peaceful in their tendencies; because it draws them forth from their appropriate retirement, to expose themselves to the ungoverned violence of mobs, and to sneers and ridicule in public places; because it leads them into the arena of political collision, not as peaceful mediators to hush the opposing elements, but as combatants to cheer up and carry forward the measure of strife. . . .

If petitions from females will operate to exasperate; if they will be deemed obtrusive, indecorous, and unwise, by those to whom they are addressed; if they will increase, rather than diminish the evil which it is wished to remove; if they will be the opening wedge, that will tend eventually to bring females as petitioners and partisans into every political measure that may tend to injure and oppress their sex. . . .

Then it is neither appropriate nor wise, nor right, for a woman to petition for the relief of oppressed females. . . .

In this country, petitions to congress, in reference to the official duties of legislators, seem, IN ALL CASES, to fall entirely without the sphere of female duty. Men are the proper persons to make appeals to the rulers whom they appoint, and if their female friends, by arguments and persuasions, can induce them to petition, all the good that can be done by such measures will be secured. But if females cannot influence their nearest friends, to urge forward a public measure in this way, they surely are out of their place, in attempting to do it themselves. . . .

We need *ten thousand* teachers at this moment, and an addition of *two thousand every year*. Where is this army of teachers to be found? Is it at all probable that the other sex will afford even a moderate portion of this supply? . . .

Will men turn aside from these high and exciting objects to become the patient labourers in the school-room, and for only the small pittance that rewards such toil? No, they will not do it. Men will be educators in the college, in the high school, in some of the most honourable and lucrative common schools, but the *children*, the *little children* of this nation must, to a wide extent, be taught by females, or remained untaught. . . .

And as the value of education rises in the public mind, and the importance of a teacher's office is more highly estimated, women will more and more be furnished with those intellectual advantages which they need to fit them for such duties.

By the concession of all travelers, American females are distinguished above all others for their general intelligence, and yet they are complimented for their retiring modesty, virtue, and domestic faithfulness, while the other sex is as much distinguished for their respectful kindness and attentive gallantry. There is no other country where females have so much public respect and kindness accorded to them as in America, by the concession of all travelers. And it will ever be so, while intellectual culture in the female mind, is combined with the spirit of that religion which so strongly enforces the appropriated duties of a woman's sphere.

But it may be asked, is there nothing to be done to bring this national sin of slavery to an end? . . .

To this is may be replied, that Christian females, can say and do much to bring these evils to an end. . . .

It is a sacred and imperious duty, that rests on every human being, to exert all his influence in opposing every thing that he believes is dangerous and wrong, and in sustaining all that he believes is safe and right. . . .

If the female advocate chooses to come upon a stage, and expose her person, dress, elocution to public criticism, it is right to express disgust at whatever is offensive and indecorous, as it is to criticise the book of an author, or the dancing of an actress, or anything else that is presented to public observation. And it is right to make all these things appear as odious and reprehensible to others as they do to ourselves.

In the present aspect of affairs among us, when everything seems to be tending to disunion and distraction, it surely has become the duty of every female instantly to relinquish the attitude of a partisan, in every matter of clashing interests, and to assume the office of a mediator, and an advocate of peace. And to do this, it is not necessary that a woman should in any manner relinquish her opinion as to the evils or the benefits, the right or the wrong, of any principle or practice. . . .

There are certain prominent maxims which every woman can adopt as peculiarly belonging to her, as the advocate of charity and peace, and which it should be her especial office to illustrate, enforce, and sustain, by every method in her power. . . .

Is a woman surrounded by those who favour the Abolition measures? Can she not with propriety urge such inquiries as these?

Is not slavery to be brought to an end by free discussion, and is it not a war upon the right of free discussion to impeach the motives and depreciate the character of the opposers of Abolition measures? When the opposers of the

Abolition movement claim that they honestly and sincerely believe that these measures tend to perpetuate slavery, or to bring it to an end by servile wars, and civil disunion, and the most terrific miseries—when they object to the use of their pulpits, to the emboldening of literary students, to the agitation of the community, by Abolition agents—when they object to the circulation of such papers and tracts as Abolitionists prepare, because they believe them most pernicious in their influence and tendencies, is it not as much persecution to use invidious insinuations, depreciating accusation and impeachment of motive, in order to intimidate, as it is for the opposers of Abolitionism to use physical force? Is not the only method by which the South can be brought to relinquish slavery, a conviction that not only her *duty*, but her highest *interest*, requires her to do it? And is not *calm, rational Christian* discussion the only proper method of securing this end? . . .

Is a woman among those who oppose Abolition movements? She can urge such inquires as these: Ought not Abolitionists to be treated as if they were actuated by the motives of benevolence which they profess? . . .

If Abolitionism prospers by the abuse of its advocates, are not the authors of this abuse accountable for the increase of the very evils they deprecate? . . .

The South, in the moments of angry excitement, has made unreasonable demands upon the non-slave-holding States, and has employed overbearing and provoking language. This has provoked re-action again at the North, and men, who heretofore were unexcited, are beginning to feel indignant, and to say, "Let the Union be sundered." Thus anger begets anger, unreasonable measure provoke equally unreasonable returns.

Abolitionists are men who come before the public in the character of *reprovers*. That the gospel requires Christians sometimes to assume this office, cannot be denied; but it does as unequivocally point out those qualifications which alone can entitle a man to do it. And no man acts wisely or consistently, unless he can satisfy himself that he possesses the qualifications for this duty, before he assumes it.

The first of these qualifications is more than common exemption from the faults that are reproved. . . .

For a man is to judge of himself, not by a comparison with other men, but as he stands before God, when compared with a perfect law, and in reference to all his peculiar opportunities and restraints. Who is there that in this comparison, cannot find cause for the deepest humiliation?. . . .

. . . A reprover, therefore, if he would avoid a quarrel and do the good he aims to secure, must be possessed of that meekness which can receive evil for good, with patient benevolence. And a man is not fitted for the duties of a reprover, until he can bring his feelings under his control.

The peculiar qualifications, then, which make it suitable for a man to be an Abolitionist are, an exemplary discharge of all the domestic duties; humility, meekness, delicacy, tact, and discretion, and these should especially be the distinctive traits of those who take the place of leaders in devising measures.

And in performing these difficult and self-denying duties, there are no men who need more carefully to study the character and imitate the example of the Redeemer of mankind. . . .

Source Note: Catharine E. Beecher, *An Essay on Slavery and Abolitionism, With Reference to the Duty of American Females* (Philadelphia, 1837).

Letters to Catharine E. Beecher, in Reply to an Essay on Slavery and Abolitionism
by Angelina Emily Grimké

Letter I. Fundamental Principles of Abolitionists

Brookline, Mass. 6 month, 12th, 1837

My Dear Friend: Thy book has appeared just at a time, when, from the nature of my engagements, it will be impossible for me to give it that attention which so weighty a subject demands. Incessantly occupied in prosecuting a mission, the responsibilities of which task all my powers, I can reply to it only by desultory letters, thrown from my pen as I travel from place to place. I prefer this mode to that of taking as long a time to answer it, as thou didst to determine upon the best method by which to counteract the effect of my testimony at the north—which as the preface of thy book informs me, was thy main design.

. . . The great fundamental principle of Abolitionists is, that man cannot rightfully hold his fellow man as property. Therefore, we affirm, that *every slaveholder is a man-stealer*. We do so, for the following reasons: to steal a man is to rob him of himself. It matters not whether this be done in Guinea, or Carolina; a man is a *man*, and *as* a man he has *inalienable* rights, among which is the right to personal *liberty*. Now if every man has an *inalienable* right to personal liberty, it follows, that he cannot rightfully be reduced to slavery. But I find in these United States, 2,250,000 men, women and children, robbed of that to which they have an *inalienable* right. How comes this to pass? Where millions are plundered, are there *no plunderers*? If then, the slaves have been robbed of their liberty, *who* has robbed them? Not the man who stole their forefathers from Africa, but he who now holds them in bondage; no matter *how* they came into his possession, whether he inherited them, or bought them, or seized them at their birth on his own plantation. The only difference I can see between the original man-stealer, who caught the African in his native country, and the American slaveholder, is, that the former committed *one* act of robbery, while the other perpetrates the same crime *continually*. Slaveholding is the perpetrating of acts, all of the same kind, in a *series*, the first of which is technically called man-stealing. The first act robbed the man of himself and the same state of mind that prompted *that act, keeps up the series*, having *taken* his all from him: it *keeps* his all from him, not only *refusing to restore*, but still robbing him of all he gets, and as fast as he gets it. Slaveholding, then, is the *constant or habitual perpetration of the act of man-stealing*. To *make* a slave is *man-stealing—the ACT itself*—to *hold* him as such is man-stealing—the *habit, the permanent* state, made up of *individual* acts. In other words—to *begin* to hold a slave is man-stealing—to *keep on* holding him is merely a *repetition* of the first act—a doing of the same identical thing *all the time.* A series of the same acts continued for a length of time is a *habit*—*a permanent state.* And the *first* of this series of the *same* acts that make up this *habit* or state is just like all the rest.

If every slave has a right to freedom, then surely the man who withholds that right from him today is a man-stealer, though he may not be the first person who has robbed him of it. Hence we find that Wesley says, "Men-buyers are *exactly on a level with* men-*stealers.*" And again—"Much less is it possible that any child of man should ever be *born a slave.*" Hear also Jonathan Edwards— "To hold a man in a state of slavery, is to be *every day guilty* of robbing him of his liberty, or of *man-stealing.*" And Grotius says—"Those are men-stealers who abduct, *keep,* sell or buy *slaves* or freeman."

If thou meanest merely that *acts* of that *same nature,* but differently located in a series, are designated by different terms, thus pointing out their different *relative* positions, then thy argument concedes what we affirm—the identity in the *nature* of the acts, and thus it dwindles to a mere philological criticism, or rather a mere play upon words.

These are Abolition sentiments on the subject of slaveholding; and although our principles are universally held by our opposers at the North, yet I am told on the 44th page of thy book, that "the word man-stealer has one peculiar signification, and is no more synonymous with slaveholder than it is with sheep-stealer." I must acknowledge, thou hast only confirmed my opinion of the difference which I had believed to exist between Abolitionists and their opponents. As well might Saul have declared, that he held similar views with Stephen, when he stood by and kept the raiment of those who slew him.

. . . But there is another peculiarity in the views of the Abolitionists. We hold that the North is guilty of the crime of slaveholding—we assert that it is a *national* sin: on the contrary, in thy book, I find the following acknowledgment: "*Most* persons in the nonslaveholding States, have considered the matter of southern slavery as one in which they were no more called to interfere, than in the abolition of the press-gang system in England, or the tithe-system in Ireland." Now I cannot see how the same principle can produce such entirely different opinions. "Can a good tree bring forth corrupt fruit?" This I deny, and cannot admit what thou art anxious to prove, viz., that "Public opinion may have been *wrong* on this point, and yet *right* on all those great *principles* of rectitude and justice relating to slavery." If abolition principles are generally adopted at the North, how comes it to pass, that there is no abolition action here, except what is put forth by a few despised fanatics, as they are called? Is there any living faith without works? Can the sap circulate vigorously, and yet neither blossoms put forth nor fruit appear?

Again, I am told on the 7th page, that all Northern Christians believe it is a sin to hold a man in slavery for *"mere purposes of gain"*; as if this was the *whole* abolition principle on this subject. I can assure thee that Abolitionists do not stop here. Our principle is, that *no circumstances can ever justify* a man in holding his fellow man as *property*; it matters not what *motive* he may give for such a monstrous violation of the laws of God. The claim to him as *property* is an annihilation of his right to himself, which is the foundation upon which all his other rights are built. . . .

Source Note: Angelina Emily Grimké, *Letters to Catharine E. Beecher, in Reply to an Essay on Slavery and Abolitionism, Addressed to A. E. Grimké* (Boston, 1838).

American Slavery As It Is: The Testimony of a Thousand Witnesses by Theodore D. Weld

[*See the headnote for Theodore D. Weld in chapter 4 of this volume.*]

Advertisement to the Reader.

A majority of the facts and testimony contained in this work rests upon the authority of SLAVEHOLDERS, whose names and residences are given to the public, as vouchers for the truths of their statements. That they should utter falsehoods, for the sake of proclaiming their own infamy, is not probable.

Their testimony is taken, mainly, from the recent newspapers, published in the stave states. Most of those papers will be deposited at the office of the American Anti-Slavery Society, 143 Nassau Street, New York City. Those who think the atrocities, which they describe, incredible, are invited to call and read for themselves. . . .

Introduction.

Reader, you are empanelled as a juror to try a plain case and bring in an honest verdict. The question at issue is not one of law, but of fact—"What is the actual condition of the slaves in the United States?" . . . You have a wife, or a husband, a child, a father, a mother, a brother, a sister—make the case your own, make it theirs, and bring in your verdict. The case of Human Rights against Slavery has been adjudicated in the court of conscience times innumerable. The same verdict has always been rendered—"Guilty;" the same sentence has always been pronounced, "Let it be accursed;" and human nature, with her million echoes, has rung it round the world in every language under heaven, "Let it be accursed. Let it be accursed." . . .

It is no marvel that slaveholders are always talking of their *kind treatment* of their slaves. The only marvel is, that men of sense can be gulled by such professions. Despots always insist that they are merciful. The greatest tyrants that ever dripped with blood have assumed the titles of "most gracious," "most clement," "most merciful," &c., and have ordered their crouching vassals to accost them thus. When did not vice lay claim to those virtues which are the opposites of its habitual crimes? The guilty, according to their own showing, are always innocent, and cowards brave, and drunkards sober, and harlots chaste, and pickpockets honest to a fault. Everybody understands this. When a man's tongue grows thick, and he begins to hiccough and walk cross-legged, we expect him, as a matter of course, to protest that he is not drunk. . . .

Slaveholders, the world over, have sung the praises of their tender mercies towards their slaves. Even the wretches that plied the African slave trade, tried to rebut Clarkson's proofs of their cruelties, by speeches, affidavits, and published pamphlets, setting forth the accommodations of the "middle passage," and their kind attentions to the comfort of those whom they had stolen from their homes, and kept stowed away under hatches, during a voyage of four thousand miles . . . .

As slaveholders and their apologists are volunteer witnesses in their own cause, and are flooding the world with testimony that their slaves are kindly treated; that they are well fed, well clothed, well housed, well lodged, moderately worked, and bountifully provided with all things needful for their comfort, we propose—first, to disprove their assertions by the testimony of a multitude of impartial witnesses, and then to put slaveholders themselves through a course of cross-questioning which shall draw their condemnation out of their own mouths. We will prove that the slaves in the United States are treated with barbarous inhumanity; that they are overworked, underfed, wretchedly clad and lodged, and have insufficient sleep; that they are often made to wear round their necks iron collars armed with prongs, to drag heavy chains and weights at their feet while working in the field, and to wear yokes, and bells, and iron horns; that they are often kept confined in the stocks day and night for weeks together, made to wear gags in their mouths for hours or days, have some of their front teeth torn out or broken off, that they may be easily detected when they run away; that they are frequently flogged with terrible severity, have red pepper rubbed in their lacerated flesh, and hot brine, spirits of turpentine, &c., poured over the gashes to increase the torture; that they are often stripped naked, their backs and limbs cut with knives, bruised and mangled by scores and hundreds of blows with the paddle, and terribly torn by the claws of cats, drawn over them by their tormentors; that they are often hunted with blood hounds and shot down like beasts, or torn in pieces by dogs; that they are often suspended by the arms and whipped and beaten till they faint, and when revived by restoratives, beaten again till they faint, and sometimes till they die; that their ears are often cut off, their eyes knocked out, their bones broken, their flesh branded with red hot irons, that they are maimed, mutilated and burned to death over slow fires. All these things, and more, and worse, we shall *prove*. Reader, we know whereof we affirm, we have weighed it well; *more and worse WE WILL PROVE*. Mark these words, and read on; we will establish all these facts by the testimony of *slaveholders* in all parts of the slave states, by slaveholding members of Congress and of state legislatures, by ambassadors to foreign courts, by judges, by doctors of divinity, and clergymen of all denominations, by merchants, mechanics, lawyers and physicians, by presidents and professors in colleges and *professional* seminaries, by planters, overseers and drivers. We shall show, not merely that such deeds are committed, but that they are frequent; not done in corners, but before the sun; not in one of the slave states, but in all of them; not perpetrated by brutal overseers and drivers merely, but by magistrates, by legislators, by professors of religion, by preachers of the gospel, by governors of states, by "gentlemen of property and standing," and by delicate females moving in the "highest circle of society." We know, full well, the outcry that will be made by multitudes, at these declarations; the multiform cavils, the flat denials, the charges of "exaggeration" and "falsehood" so often bandied, the sneers of affected contempt at the credulity that can believe such things, and the rage and imprecations against those who give them currency. We know, too, the threadbare sophistries by which slaveholders and their apologists seek to evade such testimony. If they admit that such deeds are committed, they tell us that they are exceedingly rare, and therefore furnish no grounds for judging of the general treatment of slaves; that occasionally a brutal wretch in the *free* states barbarously butchers his wife, but that no one thinks of inferring from that, the general treatment of wives at the North and West.

. . . The foregoing declarations touching the inflictions upon slaves, are not haphazard assertions, nor the exaggerations of fiction conjured up to carry a point; nor are they the rhapsodies of enthusiasm, nor crude conclusions, jumped at by hasty and imperfect investigation, nor the aimless outpourings either of sympathy or poetry; but they are proclamations of deliberate, well weighed convictions, produced by accumulations of proof, by affirmations and affidavits, by written testimonies and statements. . . .

We will first present the reader with a few Personal Narratives furnished by individuals, natives of slave states and others, embodying, in the main, the results of their own observation in the midst of slavery—facts and scenes of which they were eye-witnesses.

In the next place, to give the reader as clear and definite a view of the actual condition of slaves as possible, we propose to make specific points, to pass in review the various particulars in the slave's condition, simply presenting sufficient testimony under each head to settle the question in every candid mind. The examination will be conducted by stating distinct propositions, and in the following order of topics.

1. THE FOOD OF THE SLAVES, THE KIND, QUALITY AND QUANTITY, ALSO, THE NUMBER AND TIME OF MEALS EACH DAY, &C.
2. THEIR HOURS OF LABOR AND REST.
3. THEIR CLOTHING.
4. THEIR DWELLINGS.
5. THEIR PRIVATIONS AND INFLICTIONS.
6. *In conclusion*, a variety of OBJECTIONS and ARGUMENTS will be considered which are used by the advocates of slavery to set aside the force of testimony, and to show that the slaves are kindly treated. . . .

Source Note: Theodore Dwight Weld, *American Slavery As It Is: The Testimony of a Thousand Witnesses* (New York: The American Antislavery Society, 1839; reprint edition, 1968, The Ayer Co. for Arno Press, New York, 1991).

Cat-hawling
by Roy Sunderland

This information for the benefit of anyone who believes cats are benevolent, precious pets!!!

A whole gang of slaves had been flogged to make one of them confess that he had stolen a hog. Finally, one was fixed upon as the culprit, and the following method taken for his punishment:—

A boy was then ordered to get up, run to the house, and bring a cat, which was soon produced. The cat, which was a large gray tom-cat, was then taken by the well-dressed gentleman, and placed upon the bare back of the prostrate black man, near the shoulders and forcibly dragged by the tail down the back, and along the bare thighs of the sufferer. The cat sunk his nails into the flesh, and tore off pieces of the skin with his teeth. The man roared with pain of this punishment, and would have rolled along the ground had he not have been held in his place by the force of four other slaves, each one of whom confined a hand or a foot. As soon as the cat was drawn from him, the man said he would tell who stole the hog, and confessed that he and several others, three of whom were holding him, had stolen the hog—killed, dressed, and eaten it. In return for this confession, the overseer said he should have another touch of the cat, which was again drawn along his back, not as before, from the head downwards, but from below the hips to the head. The man was then permitted to rise, and each of those who had been named by him as a participator in stealing the hog, was compelled to lie down, and have the cat twice drawn along his back—first downwards, and then upwards. After the termination of this punishment, each of the sufferers was washed with salt water by a black woman, and they were then dismissed.

This was the most excruciating punishment that I ever saw inflicted on black people—and, in my opinion, it is very dangerous, for the claws of the cat are poisonous, and wounds made by them are very subject to inflammation.

Source Note: *An Antislavery Manual, Containing a Collection of Facts and Arguments on American Slavery by Rev. Roy Sunderland* (New York: Piercy and Reed, 1837).

GERRIT SMITH (1797–1874), ARTHUR TAPPAN (1786–1865), AND LEWIS TAPPAN (1788–1873)
by Melba Jensen

Gerrit Smith was born March 6, 1797, at Utica, New York. His father, Peter Smith, had amassed substantial land holdings in central and western New York, and Gerrit Smith began his career as the manager of his father's estate. Deterred from entering the ministry by this obligation, Smith remained a businessman for his entire life, but his social conscience and his financial assets enabled him to become a philanthropist. He supported a variety of organizations promoting Bible reading, Sunday School, temperance, and woman's suffrage.

His support of the antislavery movement evolved over time. In the early 1830s, he supported the American Colonization Society, but in 1835 he joined the New York State Anti-Slavery Society and worked with Lewis and Arthur Tappan's national organization, the American Anti-Slavery Society. After the AASS split in 1840, Smith charted a separate course and formed the Liberty Party, which ran antislavery candidates for state and national offices. He believed that the language of the U.S. Constitution forbade slavery and hoped that slavery could be voted out of the Union. In the early 1850s, he helped persuade Frederick Douglass to accept the Constitution as an antislavery document, which ended the possibility of a rapprochement between Douglass and William L. Garrison.

Smith was elected to the U.S. House of Representatives in 1852, and he was present for the Kansas-Nebraska debates. Disillusioned with what he saw and unwilling to remain in Washington, D.C., Smith resigned after the 1853–54 session and returned to New York. From this time, Smith's antislavery activities took a militant turn. He supported John Brown's militia activities in Kansas and was involved in planning Brown's raid on the federal arsenal at Harpers Ferry, Virginia. Smith continued to speak and write for emancipation and his other reform interests during and after the Civil War. He died on December 28, 1874.

Arthur and Lewis Tappan were two of ten children born to Benjamin and Sarah Homes Tappan in Northampton, Massachusetts. Arthur was born on May 22, 1786, and Lewis was born on May 26, 1788. Both pursued business careers. Arthur started a wholesale silk warehouse in New York, and Lewis joined his brother's business in 1828 to recover from financial reverses. Together, the two brothers pursued philanthropic and reform efforts. One of Arthur's first forays into antislavery activism was to pay William L. Garrison's fine for libel and secure his release from a Baltimore jail. Arthur was also attracted to educational reform. Initially, he attempted to start a manual labor school for free Africans at New Haven, Connecticut, but abandoned the effort in the face of opposition. His second effort to found an integrated school at Oberlin, Ohio, proved successful. Oberlin trained antislavery speakers and activists. The Tappans, working with Garrison, helped form the American Anti-Slavery Society, an umbrella organization that was based in New York City for the state antislavery societies. Lewis Tappan proved an astute publisher for the organization. He edited many of its publications and helped Gamaliel Bailey start one of the first national antislavery newspapers, *The National Era*.

Arthur's business suffered in the financial panics of the late 1830s, and he was disheartened by the schism of the AASS into Garrisonians advocating disunion and political parties like Gerrit Smith's Liberty Party. His efforts to form an alliance with abolitionists in England proved unproductive, and he gradually withdrew from the antislavery movement. Lewis, however, remained active. He was initially reluctant to support the Liberty Party, but Gerrit Smith persuaded him to assist the political reform efforts of the 1850s.

Arthur Tappan died on July 22, 1865, and Lewis Tappan died on June 21, 1873.

SUGGESTIONS FOR FURTHER READING

Barnes, Gilbert H. *The Anti-Slavery Impulse: 1830–1844*. New York: Harbrace, 1993.
Friedman, Lawrence J. "The Gerrit Smith Circle: Abolitionism in the Burned-Over District." *Civil War History* 26:1 (1980): 18–38.
Frothingham, Octavius Brooks. *Gerrit Smith: A Biography*. New York, Negro Universities Press, 1969.
Harlow, Ralph V. *Gerrit Smith, Philanthropist and Reformer*. New York: Holt, 1939.
Sorin, Gerald. *The New York Abolitionists: A Case Study of Political Radicalism*. Westport, CT: Greenwood Press, 1971.

THE NEW YORK ABOLITIONISTS
edited and introduced by Melba Jensen

The New York abolitionists—Gerrit Smith, Arthur Tappan, and Lewis Tappan—distinguished themselves by their willingness to pursue the end of slavery through political action. In New York City, Arthur and Lewis Tappan published antislavery newspapers including *The Anti-Slavery Record*. These papers injected antislavery thought into public debate, New York State politics, and eventually the legislative agenda of the U.S. Congress. In central New York State, Gerrit Smith organized antislavery voters into the Liberty Party. "There is power in the Constitution to abolish every part of American slavery," Smith argued, and he urged voters to support political candidates who believed that slavery was both illegal and unconstitutional. Smith's interpretation of the Constitution and the Tappans' editorial efforts to influence legislation evolved into a distinct form of political antislavery activism that functioned as a counterpoint to William L. Garrison's calls for "disunion."

Despite the willingness of Smith and the Tappan brothers to make political commitments, there were important differences in the form these commitments would take. Temperament and geographic location each gave different emphases to their antislavery work. Arthur Tappan was a taciturn, self-effacing man with a mercantile education who wrote brief letters and avoided giving public addresses. His opposition to slavery was an extension of his conservative Congregational Christianity, which emphasized a community's responsibility to assist each soul in its pursuit of salvation. In 1831, he attempted to start a manual labor school to teach trades to destitute Northern blacks. However, the concerted opposition forced him to abandon the plan and showed him the depth of Northern racism. In 1833, he helped form the American Anti-Slavery Society; he would be elected president of the organization each year until the organization split in 1840. Tappan was an excellent choice to head a parent organization for the state antislavery societies that composed the AASS, despite his lack of rhetorical or oratorical skill. He supplied $3,000 annually for the operation of the AASS from the profits of his wholesale-silk warehouse, and his reputation as both a businessman and a Christian reformer enhanced the AASS's credibility. To assist with the writing and speaking duties of his office, Arthur relied heavily on his brother Lewis and their New York City business associates. Under the leadership of the Tappans, the AASS would pursue the immediate abolition of slavery, but their preferred method was a persuasive appeal to moderation and morals. Where Garrison described the task of abolishing slavery as a contest between "gospel truth . . . and the deceptions of the Devil," Tappan stressed the need to follow the sentiments of the Declaration of Independence and the good example of the British in abolishing slavery.[1]

Gerrit Smith embraced more radical forms of antislavery activism than the Tappans, and the differences reflected the distance between New York City and central New York State. Central New York had been a sparsely settled forest when Gerrit's father, Peter Smith, came from New York City in 1789. Peter Smith belonged to the Revolutionary War generation. He was a Calvinist who wondered whether his soul was predestined to join the elect in eternal life, and he sought wealth as a sign of God's grace. Peter purchased a large tract of land from the Oneida Indians in a dubiously legal sale and, in 1806, established his estate, Peterboro, in the town of Smithfield. New York State had not yet eliminated slavery, and Peter used both indentured servants and slaves to break new fields around Peterboro. Young Gerrit's first exposure to slavery probably occurred when he was assigned to help with fieldwork. Gerrit was a gregarious, intelligent, and somewhat self-important child—frequently at odds with his dour father—and this early contact with slavery made a deep impression on him. Later in life, he recalled it as the moment he began to hate slavery.[2]

By the time Gerrit began to manage his father's estate in 1819, central New York had become a hotbed of religious and social reform. The state had abolished slavery and terminated indentures, and Peterboro lay on the edge of an area "burned over" by religious revivals and dotted with utopian communities. Among his neighbors, Gerrit found religious thinkers like Charles Grandison Finney. Finney, a lawyer turned preacher, emphasized the individual's ability to embrace salvation through an act of will. Communal prayer was still necessary, but the individual's own moral sensibility marked the path to God. "Truth," Finney wrote, "is employed to influence men, prayer to move God."[3] In this environment, Smith gradually put aside his father's beliefs in predestination and joined Christian reform organizations devoted to this world instead of the next. He supported Sunday schools to educate those who worked during the other six days, the Temperance Movement, Sunday observance, and various foreign missionaries. Smith possessed not only the wealth but also the personal attributes to became an influential reformer for revival-inspired audiences. He had matured into a persuasive public speaker. The child's gregariousness had become adult eloquence, and at six feet tall, he commanded the audience's attention on the platform. Smith raised money on a scale that few except Arthur Tappan could exceed. In the years between 1828 and 1835, Smith raised $9,000 for the American Colonization Society.[4]

Finney had also attracted Arthur Tappan's attention. Tappan wanted to start another school, but this time he wished to train antislavery speakers and organizers for the AASS. Oberlin College opened in the fall of 1835 with Finney on the faculty and Tappan as its financial backer. Arthur's commitment of time and money to Oberlin College had two long-term effects on the antislavery crusade in the United States. First, Oberlin incubated the methods by which antislavery ideas would be spread for the remainder of the decade. Tappan brought Finney, and an eloquent AASS agent, Theodore Weld, together with a cadre of students ready to train as antislavery agents. The milieu at Oberlin infused the antislavery message with a revival theology and a missionary's method. Slavery was a sin resulting from sloth, lust, and greed. By opposing it, Christians could both aid the slaves and perfect their own spirits. Antislavery activism promised more than social change: it offered a state of grace attainable in this life.[5]

The second effect of Arthur Tappan's Oberlin project was to increase Lewis Tappan's influence within the AASS. To cope with the demands of running the AASS while he dealt with Oberlin business, Arthur increased the responsibilities of his younger brother, Lewis Tappan, for the day-to-day activities of the organization. Lewis Tappan was as committed as Arthur to spreading the antislavery gospel, but he understood the technology of communication. Arthur depended on the personal charisma of the AASS speakers to convert Northerners to antislavery ideals. To support the speakers, the AASS supplied antislavery journals and pamphlets to the newly formed societies for their reading rooms. Lewis valued the journals as an opportunity to reach a wider audience. He particularly wanted to reach Southern audiences living where antislavery speakers were not welcome. In May 1835, he raised the capital necessary to issue antislavery literature using the new steam-driven rotary presses. These presses reduced the cost of printing a newspaper from over 6 cents to less than 1 cent by increasing the daily run to between 20,000 and 30,000 copies.[6] In a single month, Lewis Tappan demonstrated the AASS's new publishing capacity. He produced four journals—*Human Rights*, *The Anti-Slavery Record*, a monthly version of the *Emancipator*, and a children's paper called *The Slave's Friend*—as well as several pamphlets.[7]

These publications never reached Southern readers. In July 1835, Lewis Tappan shipped 20,000 pieces of antislavery literature to Southern cities including Charleston, South Carolina. Federal law guaranteed free delivery for newspapers, but the Charleston postmaster refused to distribute such "incendiary" literature. The journals remained in a warehouse until angry citizens seized and burned them. The uproar was based, in part, on a miscalculation. Tappan's actual investment in the journals was less than $200, but—using the old figure of 6 cents for a hand-printed paper—it appeared to be $1,200. From this figure, Southerners inferred the existence of a powerful antislavery organization with virtually unlimited financial backing, and they demanded that it be suppressed.

In the North, mobs responded to Southern demands by breaking up antislavery meetings—threatening the attendees with everything from egging to hanging.[8]

Gerrit Smith faced one of these mobs, and the experience convinced him that the existence of slavery endangered Northern political freedoms. On October 21, 1835, Smith attended the Utica Anti-Slavery Convention. He had gone to the meeting more out of curiosity than as a committed antislavery advocate. Officially, he still belonged to the American Colonization Society, but for the past year, he had urged the organization to accept emancipation without colonization. He was dissatisfied with the ACS's refusal, but he did not perceive the degree of Northern resistance to antislavery ideas that stood behind it. As he seated himself in the Second Presbyterian Church beside his wife Nancy, a score of men including a U.S. congressman gathered outside to disperse the meeting. As soon as the meeting was called to order, the unruly mob rushed into the church. They pushed through the crowd, shouting threats of eternal damnation and calling the convention attendees "traitors to their country." The nervous convention leaders quickly adjourned the meeting, but Smith persuaded them to reconvene the following day at his home in Peterboro.[9]

Smith's encounter with the mob convinced him that freedom of speech and assembly were incompatible with slavery, but he had to explain why this conviction took precedence over Southern assurances that slavery was protected by the Constitution. On October 22, Smith wrote: "Submitting to these restraints, we could not be what God made us to be . . . *men*. Laws to gag a man—to congeal the gushing fountains of his heart's sympathy—and to shrivel up his soul by extinguishing its ardor and generosity—are laws not to assist him in carrying out God's high and holy purposes in calling him into being; but they are laws to throw him a passive, mindless, worthless being at the feet of despotism." That morning, when Smith rose to address his guests seated on the gentle sweep of Peterboro's lawn, he had convinced himself that slavery could not be justified by divine or human law. "Is it said that the South will not molest our freedom, if we will not disturb their slavery—if we will not insist on the liberty to speak and write about this abomination? Our reply is, that God gave us the freedom for which we contend—that it is not a freedom . . . which we have received at the hands of the South;—not a freedom which stands, on the one hand, in the surrender of our dearest rights, and, on the other in the conceded perpetuity of the body and the mind and soul-crushing system of American slavery. We ask not, we accept not, we scornfully reject, the conditional and worthless freedom, which the South proffers us."[10]

After 1835, Smith advocated religious beliefs that reflected his experience in the antislavery movement, and he advocated antislavery principles as the litmus test for Christian doctrine. In 1837, Smith debated whether slavery could be divinely approved with the Reverend James Smylie of Mississippi. Smylie cited the Old Testament references to Abraham's and Isaac's slaves as proof that slavery was a benign institution and one of which God approved. Smith utterly rejected this treatment of the Hebrew patriarchs as something other than fallible individuals. To Smith, Abraham was just as inclined to mistake his own advantage for God's will as a Southern slaveholder. "We must continue to judge slavery by what is," Smith argued, "and not by what you tell us it will, or may be." Reliance on his own experience led him to challenge, and finally abandon, both denominations and theologies.[11]

In 1838, Smith also challenged abolitionists to improve their political parties. Under the aegis of the Liberty Party, the New York State Anti-Slavery Society questioned candidates for public office and endorsed those who answered satisfactorily. The process provoked angry resistance. Some objections came from abolitionists who were hesitant to risk what little influence they exerted on the Whig Party by threatening to withdraw their votes. Other objections came from moderate antislavery Whig candidates worried that seeking an endorsement would drive voters to support proslavery Democrats. Smith concluded that the established political parties were as guilty of perpetuating slavery as the churches. It was "a spurious religion," he wrote, that insisted on silence about "a system which is killing the bodies and . . . souls of millions of our enslaved countrymen," and "a spurious republicanism, which bids us vote for men who uphold that system."[12] After 1838, Smith made antislavery principles his litmus test for both religious organizations and political parties.

The mob opposition that had driven men like Smith to embrace the AASS abated in the late 1830s, but this proved a mixed blessing for the organization. Harsh criticism and threats of violence had suppressed internal disagreements even while the membership increased. After the external criticism diminished, the internal disagreements surfaced. The most public disagreement arose between Garrison and the Tappan brothers over the role of women in the AASS.

Women had already made substantial contributions to antislavery work. Angelina and Sarah Grimké had seized on the unique moral sensibility attributed to women in the mid-nineteenth century, and transformed it into the basis for social and political action. Sarah addressed herself directly to the Southern clergy and challenged them to acknowledge slaves as rational beings with immortal souls.[13] Angelina urged women to enact their reputation for moral discernment by petitioning their legislators.[14] Women responded to these calls. Through their churches or antislavery societies, they gathered signatures on petitions to eliminate slavery where it existed and prevent it from spreading into newly formed states.[15]

Despite these contributions, a disagreement arose between Garrison's and the Tappans' supporters over whether women could be voting members and officers. Garrison perceived both the contribution women were making to antislavery work and the inconsistency of having non-voting advocates for emancipation and suffrage. He lobbied the AASS to recognize women as voting members and permit them to serve on committees. Arthur Tappan and his colleagues opposed this plan. They clung to their vision of the AASS as a respectable organization pursuing a single goal—an end to slavery—not a multi-issue reform agenda.[16]

Garrison and Tappan's public debate revolved around the AASS Constitution. It stated that "any person" who accepted the society's principles and made a donation could be a voting member of the AASS. Garrison argued that since women were people, they were clearly eligible for membership. Arthur Tappan, who had been present when the document was written, argued that the original framers of the AASS Constitution intended "person" to mean a man.[17] The irony of this debate was that the AASS Constitution was modeled on the U.S. Constitution, and Arthur's arguments about the framers' intent were the same arguments that proslavery representatives to the U.S. Congress would make about the U.S. Constitution. Even within the antislavery movement, activists were struggling to assimilate the full implications of antislavery thought to their political process.

Lewis and Arthur Tappan withdrew from the vanguard of the antislavery movement after 1840. Neither approved of Garrison's reform agenda, nor did they feel entirely comfortable with Smith's Liberty Party. The irascible Arthur lacked the skills and temperament for electioneering or party politics. He understood reform as a Christian mission, and as the movement expanded in scope and method, his role diminished proportionally. His major contributions remained financing the AASS and training the men and women who sustained it through their speaking and writing. The younger Lewis adapted somewhat more successfully by fusing Arthur's methods with his own knowledge about publishing. In 1846, Lewis Tappan raised the funds to pay Gamaliel Bailey, an ambitious editor willing to start an antislavery newspaper in Washington, D.C. *The National Era* provided abolitionists with a window on federal politics and nurtured a constituency of antislavery voters by reporting Congressional debates on slavery.[18]

The National Era also provided a venue for antislavery literature. In 1852, Bailey agreed to publish Harriet Beecher Stowe's serial novel, *Uncle Tom's Cabin*, which had profound political consequences. Its antislavery arguments—embodied in memorable characters—gave legislators a graphic, antislavery rhetoric with which to characterize their proslavery opponents. The poem "Nebraska," published during the 1854 Kansas-Nebraska debates, is one example:[19]

> And joy on every Slaver's deck; and cheers and three time three
> Shouted for Pierce and Douglas now by "Loker" and "Legree."

It compares U.S. President Franklin Pierce and Senator Stephen Douglas— both instrumental in preserving the possibility of slavery in the Kansas and Nebraska Territories—to a mercenary slave catcher and a brutal plantation owner. Stowe's characters function as a political shorthand to accuse Pierce and Douglas of maintaining slavery for political profit.

Accusations of complicity with slavery carried particular weight, since Congress had enacted the Fugitive Slave Law of 1850. Under the provisions of the Fugitive Slave Law, a U.S. marshal could seize anyone accused of being an escaped slave. The alleged slave received a hearing in front of a commissioner of the Circuit Court, and the commissioner received $10 if he agreed the accused was an escaped slave but only $5 if he did not. Northern communities—annoyed to find U.S. marshals serving as "slave catchers" and commissioners given an incentive to profiteer—often obstructed enforcement. In Syracuse, New

York, Gerrit Smith helped thwart a deputy U.S. marshal's attempt to prove that a local cooper named William "Jerry" Henry was a fugitive slave. Smith and several other antislavery activists rushed Jerry from his hearing, pushed him into a waiting carriage, and sent him to Canada.

Smith turned the "Jerry Rescue" into an opportunity to publicize his views on the U.S. Constitution. Since the 1835 Utica Anti-Slavery Convention, Smith had realized that slavery was incompatible with the Constitution's guarantees of free speech and assembly. The abrogation of Jerry's right to a jury trial was another example of the way in which slavery was at odds with these constitutional guarantees. While reformers like Garrison regarded these contradictions as evidence that the framers of the Constitution intended to tolerate slavery, Smith focused on the document's language. He argued that constitutional guarantees of civil liberty proved that slavery was illegal and that the Fugitive Slave Laws were unconstitutional. To showcase his arguments, Smith charged the deputy with attempting to kidnap Jerry. The deputy's acquittal was a foregone conclusion, but Smith used the trial as a platform to revile the Fugitive Slave Laws and promote the Constitution as an antislavery document.[20]

In the wake of the trial's publicity, Smith ran for a two-year term in the U.S. House of Representatives. Smith was the Liberty Party's candidate, so he was assured of the antislavery vote, but local businessmen also found him attractive. They were anxious to finalize a reciprocity treaty with Canada that would eliminate tariffs on their goods and imported grains. Smith owned mills, and they trusted him to promote their mutual interests. The combination of abolitionist and free-trade voters was sufficient to place Smith in the House for the rancorous Kansas-Nebraska debates.

The Kansas-Nebraska debates became the crucible that tested Smith's arguments regarding the Constitution and prepared him for the final, violent phase of his antislavery activism. The debates began with an attempt to avoid discussing whether slavery would be permitted in the Nebraska Territory. Stephen A. Douglas—a pugnacious senator with aspirations to be president—had written that "all questions pertaining to slavery in the territories, and in the new States to be formed therefrom, are to be left to the people residing therein, through their appropriate representatives."[21] Smith, with his experience managing his father's land, recognized the implications of this language. Leaving the decision of whether a territory would permit slavery to an undetermined group of representatives elected by an unspecified group of residents at an undetermined time was a recipe for anarchy and violence.

The debate over the Nebraska territories offered Smith a national audience for his constitutional ideas. In his "Speech on the Nebraska Bill," he argued that the Constitution gave Congress the power to abolish the slave trade because it gave Congress the power to regulate commerce and to establish "uniform" rules of naturalization. The Constitution also gave Congress the responsibility to guarantee every State "a republican form of government" and the responsibility to deny no person "due process of law." Neither the powers nor the responsibilities of Congress could be fulfilled, Smith concluded, until slavery was eliminated.

Smith's speech to the U.S. House of Representatives was primarily a constitutional analysis, but it was also the statement of his antislavery creed. He knew that speaking against slavery would be "construed into hostility to the Union," but he loved the Union too well to let it go without a fight. "I prize the Union, because I prize the wisdom, courage, philanthropy, and piety, of which it was begotten. I prize it, because I prize the signal sufferings, and sacrifices, which it cost our fathers. I prize it, because I prize its objects—those great and glorious objects, that prompted to the Declaration of Independence; that were cherished through a seven years' war; and that were then recited in the preamble of the Constitution, as the objects of the Constitution. I prize it, for the great power it has to honor God and bless man. I prize it, because I believe the day will come, when this power shall be exerted to this end."[22]

Smith's contribution to the 1853–54 session of the House of Representatives is, in many ways, indicative of the unique contribution made by the New York abolitionists to the antislavery movement. In spite of the uncertainties inherent in attempting to reconcile his antislavery ideals with the constant compromise of representative democracy, Gerrit Smith served in Congress, and his service proved advantageous for the antislavery cause. By staking out a radical view of the Constitution in the debate over the Kansas-Nebraska Bill, Smith redefined the center. His argument that slavery was unconstitutional helped recruit other congressmen to support moderate antislavery measures.

Smith did not complete his term in the House of Representatives. His constitutional arguments proved no match for Senator Douglas's political threats and President Pierce's political patronage. The Kansas-Nebraska Bill passed. Disillusioned with political process and homesick for Peterboro, he resigned and returned to New York. Within a year, he met John Brown, a stern Calvinist who was headed for the Kansas Territory. Violent confrontations between pro-slavery and "free-state" settlers had erupted, and the hastily formed territorial government could not prevent them. Brown's sons had staked claims in the Kansas Territory, and John Jr. had written to his father asking him to bring weapons.[23] Brown brought the weapons, and on May 24, 1856, he led a retaliatory raid against his son's proslavery neighbors. Brown's raiders herded five men from their cabins in the middle of the night and hacked them to death with artillery broadswords. In the chaos that ensued, Brown escaped from Kansas and presented himself to eastern supporters as the defender of the free-state settlers. Smith admired Brown as a freedom fighter, and they began to discuss Brown's plan to foment a slave insurrection.

On October 17, 1859, John Brown, three of his sons, and eighteen other men stormed the engine house at the federal arsenal in Harpers Ferry, Virginia.[24] Brown had intended to start a slave insurrection which would spread from Virginia farther South. He hoped that slaves would flee North, and he intended to assist them by forming a network of military strongholds along the route. None of these hopes were recognizable in the result of the raid. Most of Brown's men were killed in the engine house by federal troops, while Brown was captured, tried for treason, and hanged. Only one of Brown's hopes was realized by his death. He had intended make Southern slaveholders fear for their safety, and they did when abolitionists honored Brown as a martyr in the cause of antislavery.

How much Smith knew about Brown's plans is a perplexing question. Smith certainly knew Brown's intention to start an insurrection, though how many details he knew is not clear. Smith's son-in-law and Brown's surviving sons destroyed much of their fathers' correspondence after John Brown's capture. John Brown, Jr., would later testify that Smith aided his father with "advice and money, and by counsel."[25] The more intriguing question is how much personal responsibility Smith accepted when he assisted Brown. One answer seems to be, more than he could bear. Two weeks after Brown's capture, Gerrit Smith entered the Utica State Asylum for the Insane suffering from nervous collapse—or from fear of being subpoenaed to testify at Brown's trial.

Gerrit Smith's partnership with Brown represents Smith's last and boldest antislavery gamble. It represents the culmination of his antislavery career, but not the majority of his work. Smith had participated all the phases of the antislavery movement. He had been an antislavery speaker, given and raised money, faced down mobs, organized political parties, resisted the Fugitive Slave Laws, and preached the antislavery Constitution in courts and Congress. His career shows remarkable variety in activity, but it shares the pragmatic and politically oriented character of Arthur and Lewis Tappan's antislavery work. The New York abolitionists were conservative of institutions and organizations whenever possible, and this tendency distinguished them from Garrison and other New England counterparts.

Speech in the Meeting of the New-York Anti-Slavery Society, Held in Peterboro, October 22, 1835
by Gerrit Smith

[*Gerrit Smith had been at the New York State Anti-Slavery Society meeting in Utica on the previous day when a mob forced the meeting to disband. Smith invited the participants to reconvene at his home in Peterboro, and as the host, was invited to give an address. Smith was not yet a member of the NYASS, and in his speech, he reminds the audience of this. However, facing the Utica mob deeply affected his understanding of slavery in two ways. Smith argues that if he were forced to give up writing and speaking about slavery then he would be no better than a slave himself. He is primarily concerned about the prospect of Northern whites losing their political liberties, rather than Southern blacks gaining their freedom. However, he uses the prospect of losing his right to free speech as a way to understand how much worse the Southern slave's experience might be. In this speech, Smith projects a tenuous empathy for the slave based on his experience at Utica.*]

Mr. Smith rose to move and advocate the adoption of the following Resolution:

Resolved, That the right of free discussion, given to us by God, and asserted and guarded by the laws of our country, is a right so vital to man's freedom, and dignity, and usefulness, that we can never be guilty of its surrender, without consenting to exchange that freedom for slavery, and that dignity and usefulness for debasement and worthlessness.

. . . At such a time as this, when you are nobly jeopardizing, for truth's sake, and humanity's sake, property and reputation and life, I feel it to be not only my duty, but my privilege and pleasure, to identify myself with you, as far as I conscientiously can, and to expose my property and reputation and life to the same dangers, which threaten yours.—Passing events . . . admonish me of the necessity there is, that the friends of human rights should act in concert: and, with all my objections to your society, it is not only possible but probable, that I shall soon find myself obliged to become a member of it.

. . . I love the free and happy form of civil government under which I live. . . . My reason . . . for loving a republican form of government, and for preferring it to any other—to monarchical and despotic governments—is, not that it clothes me with rights, which these withhold from me; but, that it makes fewer encroachments than they do, on the rights, which God gave me—on the divinely appointed scope of man's agency. . . . Take from the men, who compose the church of Christ on earth, the right of free discussion, and you disable them for His service. They are now the lame and the dumb and the blind. . . .

. . . There is one class of men, whom it especially behooves to be tenacious of the right of free discussion. I mean the poor. The rich and honorable, if divested of this right, have still their wealth and their honors to repose on, and to solace them. But, when the poor are stripped of this right, they are poor indeed. The unhappy men, who composed the mob in Utica yesterday, are of this class. May they yet learn, and before it is too late, how suicidal was the violence, TO WHICH THE LIPS AND PENS OF THEIR SUPERIORS STIMULATED THEM: and, that, in attacking this most precious right in your persons, they were most efficiently contributing to hasten its destruction in their own: a right too in respect to which the poor man is the equal of the richest and the proudest; and his possession of which is all, that saves him from being trampled upon in Republican America by the despotism of wealth and titles, as the despotism tramples upon him elsewhere, where he is not permitted to tell the story of his wrongs, and to resist oppression by that power, which even wealth and titles cannot withstand—the power of the lips and the Press. Let the poor man count as his enemy, and his worst enemy, every invader of the right of free discussion.

We are threatened with legislative restraint on this right. Let us tell our legislators in advance, that this is a right, restraints on which, we will not, cannot bear; and that every attempt to restrain it is a palpable wrong on God and man. Submitting to these restraints, we could not be what God made us to be; we could not perform the service, to which He has appointed us; we could not be men. Laws to gag a man—to congeal the gushing fountains of his heart's sympathy—and to shrivel up his soul by extinguishing its ardor and generosity—are laws not to assist him in carrying out God's high and holy purposes in calling him into being; but they are laws to throw him a passive, mindless, worthless being at the feet of despotism.

And to what end is it that we are called on to "hold" our tongues, and throw down our pens, and give up our influence? Were it for a good object, and could we conceive that such a sacrifice would promote it, there would be a color of fitness in asking us to do so. But, this is a sacrifice, which righteousness and humanity never invoke. Truth and mercy require the exertion—never the suppression, of man's noble rights and powers. We are called on to degrade and unman ourselves, and to withhold from others that influence, which we are bound to exert upon them, to the end that the victim of oppression may lie more quietly beneath the foot of his oppressor: to the end, that one sixth of our countrymen, plundered of the dearest rights—of their bodies, and minds and souls—may never know of those rights; to the end, that TWO MILLIONS AND A HALF of our fellow men, crushed in the iron folds of slavery, may remain in all their suffering and debasement and despair. It is for such an object—an object so wicked and inexpressibly mean—that we are called on to lie down beneath the slaveholders' blustering and menace, like whipped and trembling spaniels. We reply, that our Republican spirit cannot thus succumb; and, what is infinitely more, that God did not make us—that Jesus did not redeem us for such sinful and vile uses.

We knew before, that slavery could not endure, could not survive free discussion; that the minds of men could not remain firm and their consciences quiet under the continued appeals of truth, and justice, and mercy: but the demand, which slaveholders now make on us to surrender the right of free discussion, together with their avowed reasons for this demand, involves their own full concession, that free discussion is incompatible with slavery. The South now admits by her own showing that slavery cannot live, unless the North be tongue-tied. But we have two objections to being thus tongue-tied. One is, that we desire and purpose to fully exert all our powers and influence—lawfully, temperately, kindly—to persuade the slaveholders of the south to deliver our colored brethren from their bonds: nor shall we give rest to our lips or pens, until this righteous object is accomplished: and the other is, that we are not willing to be slaves ourselves. The enormous and insolent demands of the South, sustained, I am deeply ashamed to say, by craven and mercenary spirits at the North, manifest beyond all dispute, that the question now is, not merely, nor mainly, whether the blacks at the South shall remain slaves—but whether the whites at the North shall become slaves also. And thus, whilst we are endeavoring to break the yokes, which are on others' necks, we are to see to it, that yokes are not imposed on our own.

Is it said that the South will not molest our freedom, if we will not disturb their slavery—if we will not insist on the liberty to speak and write about this abomination? Our reply is, that God gave us the freedom for which we contend—that it is not a freedom bestowed by man;—not an ex gratia freedom, which we have received at the hands of the South;—not a freedom, which stands, on the one hand, in the surrender of our dearest rights, and, on the other, in the conceded perpetuity of the body and mind and soul-crushing system of American slavery. We ask not, we accept not, we scornfully reject, the conditional and worthless freedom, which the South proffers us.

It is not to be disguised, that a war has broken out between the North and the South.—Political and commercial men are industriously striving to restore peace: but the peace, which they would effect, is superficial, false, and temporary. True, permanent peace can never be restored, until slavery, the occasion of the war, has ceased. The sword, which is now drawn, will never be returned to its scabbard, until victory, entire, decisive victory is ours or theirs; not, until that broad and deep and damning stain on our country's escutcheon is clean washed out—that plague spot on our country's honor gone forever;—or, until slavery has riveted anew her present chains, and brought our heads also to bow beneath her withering power. It is idle—it is criminal, to hope for the restoration of peace, on any other condition. Why, not to speak of other outrages, which the South has practiced on the rights and persons of Northern men, who can read the simple and honest account, which Amos Dresser gives of his sufferings at the hands of slaveholders, and still flatter himself with the belief, that the North can again shake hands with slavery?—If the church members and Church elders, who sat in mock judgment on that young man's case, could be impelled by the infernal spirit of slavery to such lawless, ruffian violence; how can any reasonable hope remain, that, whilst the south remains under the malign influences of slavery, its general demeanor towards the North can be even tolerable? The head and front of Dresser's offending, was his connection with an Anti-Slavery Society in a distant state: and for this he was subjected by professors, and titled professors too, of the meek and peaceful religion of Jesus, to corporal punishment—public, disgraceful, severe. [*Amos Dresser was publicly whipped and given 24 hours to leave Nashville, Tennessee, after a citizen's committee found him guilty of possessing and distributing antislavery literature.*]

Who shall be mustered on our side for this great battle? Not the many. The many never come to such a side as ours, until attracted to it by palpable and unequivocal signs of its triumph. Nor do we need the many. A chosen few are all we need. Nor, do we desire those, who are skillful in the use of carnal weapons. For such weapons we have no use. Truth and love are inscribed on our banners, and "by these we conquer." There is no room in our ranks for the politician, who, to secure the votes of the South, would consent that American slavery be perpetual. There is no room in them for the commercial man, who, to secure the trade of the South, is ready to applaud the institution of slavery, and to leave his countrymen—his brethren—their children, and children's children—subjected to its tender mercies, throughout all future time. We have no room, no work for such. We want men, who stand on the rock of Christian principles; men who will speak, and write, and act with invincible honesty and firmness; men, who will vindicate the right of discussion, knowing that it is derived from God; and who, knowing this, will vindicate it against all the threats and arts of demagogues, and money worshippers, and in the face of mobs, and of death. There is room in our ranks for the old and decrepit, as well as the young and vigorous. The hands that are tremulous with years, are the best hands to grasp the sword of the spirit. The aged servants of God best know how "to move the arm which moves the world." Our work, in a word, is the work of God; and they are the best suited to it, who are most accustomed to do his work.

Source Note: Gerrit Smith, *Speech in the Meeting of the New-York Anti-Slavery Society, Held in Peterboro, October 22, 1835* (Peterboro, New York, 1835).

Letter to Rev. James Smylie, of the State of Mississippi, 1837
by Gerrit Smith

[*In his public debate with Gerrit Smith, the Reverend James Smylie argued that slavery was a benign institution. He cited the Old Testament story of Abraham's search for a wife for his son, Isaac. Smylie viewed Abraham's willingness to place the task in the hands of a servant as evidence of the trust and confidence that existed, or eventually would exist, between Southern masters and their slaves. In response, Smith argued that, even if one wished, no Southern slaveholder dared to entrust a slave with such a task. If one did, both slaveholder and slave risked violent retaliation for violating law or custom. Smylie's use of Abraham's story offered Smith a way to introduce the issues of literacy and marriage. Legally, slaveholders could not teach their slaves to read. Nor were slaves' marriages legally recognized. Abolitionists frequently cited these two issues as evidence that slavery was incompatible with living a Christian life.*]

. . . 3d. When I read your quotation from the twenty-fourth chapter of Genesis, made for the purpose of showing that God allowed Abraham to have slaves, I could not but wonder at your imprudence, in meddling with this chapter, which is itself, enough to convince any unbiased mind, that Abraham's servants held a relation to their master and to society, totally different from that held by Southern slaves. Have you ever known a great man in your state to send his slave into another to choose a wife for his son?—And, if so, did the lily white damsel he selected call the sable servant "my Lord?"—And did her family spare no pains to manifest respect for their distinguished guest, and promote his comfort? But this chapter, which you call to your aid, informs us, that Abraham's servant was honored with such tokens of confidence and esteem. . . .

5th. So Southern masters accord religious privileges and impart religious instruction equally to their slaves and their children? Your laws, which visit with stripes, imprisonment, and death, the attempt to teach slaves to read the Bible, show but too certainly, that the Southern master, who should undertake to place "his children and his household" on the same level, in respect to their religious advantages, as it is probable that Abraham did (Gen. 18:19), would soon find himself in the midst of enemies, not to his reputation only, but also to his life.

. . . After you shall have allowed, as you will allow, that slavery, as it exists, is a war with God, you will be likely to say, that the fault is not in the theory of it; but in the practical departure from that theory; that it is not the system, but the practice under it which is at war with God. . . . Well, you shall have the benefit of this plea, and I admit, for the sake of argument, that this theory of slavery, which lies far back, and out of sight of every visible and known thing about slavery, is right. And what does this admission avail you? . . .

We must continue to judge slavery by what it is, and not by what you tell us it will, or may be. Until its character be righteous, we shall continue to condemn it; but when you shall have brought it back to your sinless and beautiful theory of it, it will have nothing to fear from abolitionists. There are two prominent reasons, however, for believing that you will never present Southern slavery to us in this lovely character, the mere imagination of which is so dear to you. The first is, that you are doing nothing to this end. It is an indisputable fact that Southern slavery is continually getting wider and wider from God, and from an innocent theory of servitude; and the "good men at the South," of whom we have spoken, are not only doing nothing to arrest this increasing divergency, but they are actually favoring it. . . . The other of these reasons for believing that Southern slavery will never be conformed to your beau ideal of slavery, in which it is presupposed there are none but principles of righteousness, is, that on its first contact with these principles, it would "vanish into thin air," leaving "not a wreck behind." In proof of this, and I need not cite any other case, it would be immediate death to Southern slavery to concede to its subjects, God's institution of Marriage; and hence it is, that its code forbids marriage. The rights of a husband in the wife, and of the wife in the husband, and of the parents in their children, would stand directly in the way of that traffic in human flesh, which is the very life-blood of slavery; and the assumptions of the master would, at every turn and corner, be met and nullified by these rights. . . .

Source Note: Gerrit Smith, "Letter to Rev. James Smylie, of the State of Mississippi," New York, 1837.

Address of the American and Foreign Anti-Slavery Society
to the Friends of the Anti-Slavery Cause
throughout the United States and the World
by Arthur Tappan

[*In 1840, Arthur Tappan realized he could not prevent the AASS from electing a woman, Abby Kelley, to the business committee. The AASS Constitution said that "any person" who accepted the principles could become a voting member and, if elected, an officer. Unwilling to accept this innovation, Tappan and several others formed a new organization and published the "Address of the American and Foreign Anti-Slavery Society." The address is really Arthur Tap-*

pan's recollections of what the original authors of the AASS Constitution had intended when they used the word "person." Tappan argued that the authors intended to exclude women from the term "person." He also argued that the fact that no women had voted in the previous six years proved his assertion. The irony of Tappan's arguments about the framers' intent and precedent was that proslavery congressmen used them in a similar way. Abolitionists argued frequently that the Fifth Amendment to the U.S. Constitution—"No person shall . . . be deprived of life, liberty, or property without due process of law"—applied to slaves. In response, their opponents cited slavery's persistence as evidence that the framers intended "person" to exclude slaves.]

The American and Foreign Anti-Slavery Society was organized in the city of New York, by about three hundred members of the American Anti-Slavery Society, on the 15th of May, 1840. Many of you are familiar with the history of the *peculiar difficulties* which have embarrassed the anti-slavery cause in the State of Massachusetts during the last two years; and the *efforts* which were made, a year ago, in the business meetings of the American [Anti-Slavery] Society in this city, to procure the sanction of that institution to the new sectarian views, with respect to the part which it was assumed that females had a right to take in those meetings. . . . Our confidence in the integrity of those who had engaged with us in the momentous struggle against slavery, led us to hope, that whatever might be the *private* opinions of individuals, as to the *inherent sinfulness* of human government, and the sphere in which females ought to act, yet, that the American [Anti-Slavery] Society could never be identified with these views, or that its official sanction could, by any means, be obtained to principles so evidently foreign to any thing contemplated, or set forth in its Constitution. . . .

It is well known, that the convention, which formed that association, was composed of men only, and that it was not, at first, a mixed society of men and women. And it is equally well known, that it was then designed and understood, that its business should be conducted by men, as *is usual in the other benevolent societies of the age*; while, at the same time, it was expected and desired, that females should form auxiliaries, in the usual way, to the parent Institution. And this interpretation of the constitution, and the consequent practice, continued for six years, up to the annual meeting in 1839, without the least interruption. Hence, it is evident, that those of our numbers who have recently assumed to bring females into the business meetings to vote and speak, and also, that they should be appointed *officers* of the Society, as they were at the late annual meeting, are responsible for the difficulty which has produced division in the Society. It is true, the fourth article of the Constitution says that "any person," who consents to its principles, &c., may become a member of the Society, and be entitled to vote at its meetings. But, that this provision was not designed to signify any thing more than is implied in similar provisions in the constitutions of the other benevolent societies of the day, is *proved*.

1. From the understanding of those who took a part in forming the Society in 1833. No one then assumed, that the word "person" was to be understood out of the common way of interpreting constitutions.

2. From the *uniform practice* of the American Anti-Slavery Society, for six years, from the time when it was organized.

3. From the manifest absurdity of the contrary doctrine. For, if the word "person," in the Constitution, is to have the indiscriminate application contended for, then, it must, of course, include, not only women, but *children* also, thousands of whom have been in the habit of contributing to the funds of the Society.

It would, perhaps, be a sufficient refutation of this *new* interpretation of the word "person," in the Constitution, to know, that at the Convention in 1833, which formed the Society, two or three women, members of the Society of Friends, were present, to offer a few remarks, and leave was, accordingly, granted. Agreeably to the recommendation of that Convention, separate female societies were extensively formed; thus proving, that no one originally claimed it as a right, that females should debate in the public meetings, and much less that they should be appointed officers of the Society. And yet, in view of all these well known facts, at the recent meeting of the Society, the acting President nominated a woman on the business committee, associated with eleven men. . . . This was considered a test vote of the relative strength of the "woman's rights," and constitutional parties, assembled; and it was believed, that the act of placing a woman on the business committee, was merely an initiatory step to the introduction of other measures, FOREIGN to the original principles and designs of the anti-slavery enterprise, all tending to divert the minds of abolitionists from the cause of the poor slave, and the rights of the free people of color. It was thought, that it would be in vain to attempt a reversal of this decision, or to expect a change for the better; that meetings thus constituted would not consent to alterations of the Constitution defining the word "person" to mean men, or to substitute a representative system for the usual collection of members in this disproportionate number from one locality, thus leaving the door open (as was done this year) for a packed delegation; that persons of such different moral affinities could not, advantageously, labor together; and that Providence seemed to indicate that it was a duty, for peace sake, as well as for other considerations, to separate from those who seemed to be rendering the anti-slavery cause an object of dislike to a large number of influential and excellent citizens. . . .

Source Note: Arthur Tappan, *Address of the American and Foreign Anti-Slavery Society to the Friends of the Anti-Slavery Cause throughout the United States and the World* (New York, 1840).

Speech on the Nebraska Bill, April 6, 1854
by Gerrit Smith

[*The Kansas-Nebraska debates offered Gerrit Smith the opportunity to expound a complete antislavery reading of the U.S. Constitution. First, Smith deals with the issue of the framers' intent. Next, he examines the clauses most often cited by advocates of slavery: the apportionment clause, the migration and importation clause, and the clause on which the Fugitive Slave Laws were based. Finally,*

Smith argues that slavery is incompatible with many of the duties given to the federal government and that must, and will, be abolished.]

Much stress is laid on the intentions of the framers of the Constitution. But we are to make little more account of their intentions than of the intentions of the scrivener, who is employed to write the deed of the land. It is the intentions of the adopters of the Constitution, that we are to inquire after; and these we are to gather from the words of the Constitution, and not from the words of its framers—for it is the text of the Constitution, and not the talk of the Convention, that the people adopted. It was the Constitution itself, and not any of the interpretations of it, nor any of the talks or writings about it, that the people adopted.

. . . We begin with the Preamble of the Constitution. This, at least, is anti-slavery: and this tells us, that the Constitution is anti-slavery—for it tells us, that one thing, for which the Constitution was made, was "to secure the blessings of liberty"—not to inflict, or sustain, the curse of slavery. . . . I admit that the Preamble is not the Constitution.

I admit, that it is but the porch of the temple. Nevertheless, if, instead of the demon of Slavery coiled up in that porch, we see the Goddess of Liberty standing proudly there, then we may infer, that the temple itself, instead of being polluted with Slavery, is consecrated to Liberty. And we are not mistaken in this inference. As we walk through the temple, we find that it corresponds with the entrance. The Constitution is in harmony with the Preamble.

The first reference, in the Constitution, to slavery, is in the apportionment clause . . . it is nevertheless, a clause not to encourage, but to discourage slavery. The clause diminishes the power of a State in the national councils in proportion to the extent of its slavery. This clause is, in truth, a bounty on emancipation. Had it provided, that drunkards should each count, but three fifths of a man, it surely would not be called a clause to encourage drunkenness. Or, had it provided, that they, who can neither read nor write, should each count but three fifths of a man, it, surely, would not be called a clause to encourage illiterateness. In the one case, it would be a bounty on sobriety, and, in the other, on education.

The next clause of the Constitution, which we will examine, is that, which . . . empowers Congress to abolish the foreign slave-trade . . . [and] the provision, respecting "migration or importation," suspended the exercise of this power for twenty years. . . . [This] suspension could not destroy, nor, to any degree, impair, the essential anti-slavery character of the clause under consideration. On the contrary, the suspension itself shows, that the clause was regarded, by the makers of the Constitution, as potentially anti-slavery—as one that was capable of being wielded, and that probably would be wielded, to suppress the slave-trade. . . .

Manifestly, the clause of the Constitution, which imparts power to abolish the slave-trade, and not that, which briefly suspends the exercise of this power, gives character to the Constitution. If my neighbor deeds me his farm, only reserving to himself the possession of it for a month, (and a week in the life of an individual is longer than twenty years in the life of a nation,) it would, certainly, be very absurd to call it a transaction for continuing him in the owner-ship and possession of the farm. . . .

. . . We have, now, disposed of two of the three clauses of the Constitution, which are assumed to be pro-slavery, namely: the apportionment clause, and the migration and importation clause. The third refers to fugitive servants . . . ap-prentices, minor children, and others. . . . But slaves, by every American defini-tion of slaves, are as incapable of owing as are horses or even horse-blocks. . . . Says Justice Best, in case of Forbes vs. Cochran: "A slave is incapable of com-pact." . . And still another reason, why this clause is not to be taken as referring to slaves, is the absurdity of supposing, that our fathers consented to treat as slaves whatever persons, white or black, high or low, virtuous or vicious, any future laws of any State might declare to be slaves. Shall we of the North be bound to acquiesce in the slavery of our children, who may emigrate to the South, provided the laws of the South shall declare Northern emigrants to be slaves?

We have, now examined those parts of the Constitution, which are relied on to give it a pro-slavery character; and we find, that they are not entitled to give it this character. We proceed to glance at some, at only some, of those parts of the Constitution, which clearly prove its anti-slavery character; which are ut-terly incompatible with slavery; and which, therefore, demand its abolition.

. . . 3. "Congress shall have power to establish a uniform rule of naturalization."

But this power, if faithfully exercised, is fatal to slavery. For if our three millions and a half of slaves are not already citizens, Congress can under this power make them such, at any time. . . .

4. "The Congress shall have power to promote the progress of science and useful arts by securing for limited times to authors and inventors the exclusive right of their respective writings and discoveries."

This clause clearly authorizes Congress to encourage and reward the genius, as well of him who is called a slave, as of any other person. . . . Not so, how-ever, if there may be slavery. For the victim of slavery has no rights; and the productions of his mind, no less than the productions of his hands, belong to his master.

5. "Congress shall have power to declare war, grant letters of marque and reprisal—to raise and support armies—to provide and maintain a navy."

It necessarily follows, from the unconditional power to Congress to carry on war, that it can contract with whom it pleases—white or black, employer or employed—to fight its battles; and can secure to each his wages, pension, or prize money. But utterly inconsistent with this absolute power of Congress is the claim of the slaveholder. . . .

6. "The United States shall guaranty to every State in this Union a republican form of government."

How could the General Government be maintained, if in one State suffrage were universal, and in another conditioned on the possession of land, and in another on the possession of money, and in another on the possession of slaves, and in another on the possession of literary or scientific attainments, and in another on the possession of a prescribed religious creed, and if in others it were conditioned on still other possessions and attainments. . . . How speedy the ruin to our national and subordinate interests! In such circumstances, the General Government would be clearly bound to insist on an essential uniformity in the State Governments. But what would be due from the General Government then, is emphatically due from it now. Our nation is already brought into great peril by the slavocratic elements in its councils; and in not a few of the States, the white as well as the black, masses are crushed by that political element. Surely the nation is entitled to liberation from this peril; and . . . the enjoyment of a "republican form of Government."

7. "No State shall pass any bill of attainder."

But what is so emphatic, and causeless, and merciless a bill of attainder, as that, which attaints a woman with all her posterity for no other reason than that there is African blood in her veins.

. . . In the most benighted portions of the earth, the victims of such a system [slavery] would, in process of time, come to such a sense of their wrongs, and their power also, as to rise up and throw off the system. But that, here, such a system must be hurried to its end, is certain. For, here, it is entirely out of harmony with all the institutions around it, and with all the professions of those who uphold it. Here it is continually pressed upon by ten thousand influences adverse to its existence . . . the only question is, whether it shall die a peaceful or a violent death. . . .

. . . I shall be blamed for speaking unwisely on the subject of slavery . . . to speak against slavery in any manner, and, especially, in the national councils, is construed into hostility to the Union: —and hostility to the Union is, in the eye of American patriotism, the most odious of all offences—the most heinous of all crimes.

I prize the Union, because I prize the wisdom, courage, philanthropy, and piety, of which it was begotten. I prize it, because I prize the signal suffering and sacrifices, which it cost our fathers. I prize it, because I prize its object—those great and glorious objects, that prompted to the Declaration of Independence; that were cherished through a seven years' war; and that were then recited in the preamble of the Constitution, as the object of the Constitution. I prize it, for the great power it has to honor God and bless man. I prize it, because I believe the day will come, when this power shall be exerted to this end.

. . . I know that in the Divine Economy, no honest discharge of the conscience, and no faithful testimony of the heart, shall be suffered to go unrewarded. I know that, in this perfect and blessed Economy, no sincere words in behalf of the right are lost. Time and truth will save them from falling ineffectual. To time and truth, therefore, do I cordially commit all, that I have said on this occasion; and patiently will I wait to see what uses time and truth shall make of it.

Source Note: Gerrit Smith, *Speech on the Nebraska Bill, U.S. House of Representatives, 33rd Congress, 1st Session, April 6, 1854.*

1. Bertram Wyatt-Brown, *Lewis Tappan and the Evangelical War Against Slavery* (Cleveland: Press of Case Western Reserve University, 1969), pp. 106–7. The analysis of Arthur Tappan's contribution to antislavery follows Wyatt-Brown's closely.

2. George Thomas, Esq., *Personal Recollections of Gerrit Smith, Jan. 5, 1875* (mss., Madison County Historical Society).

3. Charles G. Finney, *Lectures on Revivals of Religion*, ed. William G. McLoughlin (Cambridge: Belknap Press of Harvard University Press, 1960), p. 52.

4. Ralph V. Harlow, *Gerrit Smith: Philanthropist and Reformer* (New York: Holt, 1939), 63.

5. Wyatt-Brown, *Lewis Tappan*, pp. 129–32.

6. Leonard L. Richards, *"Gentlemen of Property and Standing": Anti-Abolition Mobs in Jacksonian America* (New York: Oxford University Press, 1970), p. 72.

7. Wyatt-Brown, *Lewis Tappan*, p. 143.

8. Richards, *"Gentlemen of Property,"* p. 52.

9. Harlow, *Gerrit Smith*, p. 122.

10. Gerrit Smith, "Speech in the Meeting of the New York Anti-Slavery Society, Held in Peterboro, October 22, 1835" (ts., Gerrit Smith Papers, Syracuse University).

11. Gerrit Smith, "Gerrit Smith to Rev. James Smylie, of the State of Mississippi" (New York, 1837).

12. Harlow, *Gerrit Smith*, p. 141.

13. Sarah Moore Grimké, "An Epistle to the Clergy of the Southern States," 1836.

14. Angelina Emily Grimké, "An Appeal to the Christian Women of the South," 1836.

15. Richards, *"Gentlemen of Property,"* p. 57.

16. Henry Mayer, *All on Fire: William Lloyd Garrison and the Abolition of Slavery* (New York: St. Martin's Press, 1998), pp. 280–82.

17. Arthur Tappan, *Address of the American and Foreign Anti-Slavery Society* (New York, 1840).

18. Stanley Harrold, *Gamaliel Bailey and the Antislavery Union* (Kent, OH: Kent State University Press, 1986), pp. 81–83.

19. *New York Daily Tribune*, June 3, 1854.

20. Harlow, *Gerrit Smith*, p. 298.

21. Stephen B. Oates, *The Approaching Fury: Voices of the Storm, 1820–1861* (New York: HarperCollins, 1997), p. 147.

22. Gerrit Smith, *Speeches of Gerrit Smith in Congress* (New York: Mason, 1855), p. 208.

23. Oates, *Approaching Fury*, p. 171.

24. Harpers Ferry now lies in West Virginia.

25. Harlow, *Gerrit Smith*, p. 398.

WENDELL PHILLIPS (1811–1884)

Wendell Phillips was a superbly educated Bostonian, socially prominent, and well to do if not wealthy. His legal practice always took second place, however, to his passionate concern for his fellow man, whether it be in support of women's suffrage, the antislavery and abolitionist movements, or even prohibition. Together with William Lloyd Garrison and Lydia Maria Child, Phillips formed a prominent trio of Boston reformers who had powerful influence on the social problems of mid-century America. Like his contemporary, Garrison, Wendell Phillips was a pioneering reformer who championed a number of unpopular causes, including prison reform, the federal regulation of corporations, and an improvement in the federal policy toward displaced Native Americans. Unlike Garrison, Phillips advocated occasional violence in the cause of abolitionism. Both men called for unconditional emancipation and were critics of the U.S. Constitution as a proslavery document, and both men called for secession of the North from the slaveholding South and a rejection of the Compromise of 1850, which included the Fugitive Slave Law, viewed by most abolitionists as a compact with Satan. Unlike Garrison, Phillips was superbly educated, having attended the Boston Latin School and Harvard College, Class of 1831. He was also a graduate of the Harvard Law School (1834). As closely as they worked and as many issues as they agreed upon, Garrison and Phillips disagreed on several prominent questions and were eventually disunited in 1865 when the American Anti-Slavery Society elected Phillips as president to succeed Garrison. Phillips's achievement was in his writing and his oratory, not in his political acumen or elected positions. He is represented in this volume by his treatise, *The Constitution a Proslavery Compact* (1845), which engages the legalisms of Lysander Spooner's *The Unconstitutionality of Slavery* (1845), also antislavery but different in its approach to the issues. Phillips also wrote *The Philosophy of the Abolitionist Movement* (1854), which is a defense of abolitionism at a time when its principles were under assault not only in the South, but also by conservative abolitionists in the North. Phillips was a powerful speaker, perhaps, with Frederick Douglass, one of the two most effective orators in antebellum America. He died in Boston on February 2, 1884.

SUGGESTIONS FOR FURTHER READING

Colfax, Richard H. *Evidence against the Views of the Abolitionists, Consisting of Physical and Moral Proofs of the Natural Inferiority of Negroes.* New York: James T. M. Bleakley, 1833.

Davis, David Brion. *Slavery and Human Progress.* New York: Oxford University Press, 1984.

Dillon, Merton. *The Abolitionists: The Growth of a Dissenting Minority.* Dekalb: Northern Illinois University Press, 1975.

Dumond, Dwight Lowell. *Antislavery: The Crusade for Freedom in America.* Ann Arbor: University of Michigan Press, 1961.

Filler, Louis. *The Crusade against Slavery, 1830–1860.* New York: Harper, 1960.

Kraditor, Aileen S. *Means and Ends in American Abolitionism: Garrison and His Critics on Strategy and Tactics, 1834–1850.* New York: Pantheon, 1969.

Mayer, Henry. *William Lloyd Garrison and the Abolition of Slavery.* New York: St. Martin's Press, 1998.

McCaine, Alexander. *Slavery Defended from Scripture, Against the Attacks of the Abolitionists in a Speech Delivered before the General Conference of the Methodist Protestant Church, in Baltimore, 1842*. Baltimore: William Woody, 1842.

McPherson, James. *The Abolitionist Legacy*. Princeton: Princeton University Press, 1988.

Pease, Jane H., and William H. Pease. *Bound with Them in Chains: A Biographical History of the Antislavery Movement*. Westport, CT: Greenwood Press, 1972.

Perry, Lewis. *Radical Abolitionism: Anarchy and the Government of God in Antislavery Thought*. Ithaca: Cornell University Press, 1973.

———, and Michael Fellman, eds. *Antislavery Reconsidered: New Perspectives on the Abolitionists*. Baton Rouge: Louisiana State University Press, 1979.

Stewart, James Brewer. *Holy Warriors: The Abolitionists and American Slavery*. New York: Hill and Wang, 1976.

Walters, Ronald G. *The Antislavery Appeal: American Abolitionism after 1830*. Baltimore: Johns Hopkins University Press, 1976.

The Constitution, a Pro-Slavery Compact
by Wendell Phillips

Introduction

. . . These extracts develop most clearly all the details of that "compromise," which was made between freedom and slavery, in 1787; granting to the slaveholder distinct privileges and protection for his slave property, in return for certain commercial concessions on his part toward the North. They prove also that the Nation at large were fully aware of this bargain at the time, and entered into it willingly and with open eyes.

. . . The clauses of the Constitution to which we refer as of a pro-slavery character are the following:

ART. 1, SECT. 2. Representatives and direct taxes shall be apportioned among the several States, which may be included within this Union, according to their respective numbers, which shall be determined by adding to the whole number of free persons, including those bound to service for a term of years, and excluding Indians not taxed, *three-fifths of all other persons*.

ART. 1, SECT. 8. Congress shall have power . . . to suppress insurrections.

ART. 1, SECT. 9. The migration or importation of such persons as any of the States now existing, shall think proper to admit, shall not be prohibited by the Congress, prior to the year one thousand eight hundred and eight: but a tax or duty may be imposed on such importation, not exceeding ten dollars for each person.

ART. 4, SECT. 2. No person, held to service or labor in one State, under the laws thereof, escaping into another, shall, in consequence of any law or regulation therein, be discharged from such service or labor; but shall be delivered up on claim of the party to whom such service or labor may be due.

ART. 4, SECT. 4. The United States shall guarantee to every State in this Union a republican form of government; and shall protect each of them against invasion, and, on application of the legislature, or of the executive, (when the legislature cannot be convened) *against domestic violence.*

The first of these clauses, relating to representation, confers on a slaveholding community additional political power for every slave held among them, and thus tempts them to continue to uphold the system: the second and the last, relating to insurrection and domestic violence, perfectly innocent in themselves—yet being made with the fact directly in view that slavery exists among us, do deliberately pledge the whole national force against the unhappy slave if he imitate our fathers and resist oppression—thus making us partners in the guilt of sustaining slavery: the third, relating to the slave-trade, disgraces the nation by a pledge not to abolish that traffic till after twenty years, *without obliging Congress to do so even then,* and thus the slave-trade may be legalized tomorrow if Congress choose: the fourth is a promise on the part of the whole Nation to return fugitive slaves to their masters, a deed which God's law expressly condemns and which every noble feeling of our nature repudiates with loathing and contempt.

. . . A few persons, to be sure, of late years, to serve the purposes of a party, have tried to prove that the Constitution makes no compromise with slavery. Notwithstanding the clear light of history; the unanimous decision of all the courts in the land, both State and Federal; the action of Congress and the State Legislature; the constant practice of the Executive in all its branches; and the deliberate acquiescence of the whole people for half a century, still they contend that the Nation does not know its own meaning, and that the Constitution does not tolerate slavery!

Every candid mind, however, must acknowledge that the language of the Constitution is clear and explicit.

Its terms are so broad, it is said, that they include many others beside slaves, and hence it is wisely (!) inferred that they cannot include the slaves themselves? Many persons besides slaves in this country doubtless are "held to service and labor under the laws of the States," but that does not at all show that slaves are not "held to service;" many persons beside the slaves may take part "in insurrections," but that does not prove that when the slaves rise, the National Government is not bound to put them down by force. Such a thing has been heard of before as one description including a great variety of persons—and this is the case in the present instance.

But granting that the terms of the Constitution are ambiguous—that they are susceptible of two meanings, if the unanimous, concurrent, unbroken practice of every department of the Government, judicial, legislative, and executive, and the acquiescence of the whole people for fifty years do not prove which is the true construction, then how and where can such a question ever be settled? If the people and the Courts of the land do not know what they themselves mean, who has authority to settle their meaning for them?

If then the people and the Courts of a country are to be allowed to determine what their own laws mean, it follows that at this time and for the last half century, the Constitution of the United States has been, and still is, a pro-slavery instrument, and that any one who swears to support it, swears to do pro-slavery acts, and violates his duty both as a man and as an abolitionist. What the Constitution may become a century hence, we know not; we speak of it *as* it is, and repudiate it *as* it *is*.

But the purpose, for which we have thrown these pages before the community, is this. Some men, finding the nation unanimously deciding that the Constitution tolerates slavery, have tried to prove that this false construction, as they think *it*, has been foisted into the instrument by the corrupting influence of slavery itself, tainting all it touches. They assert that the known antislavery spirit of revolutionary times never *could* have consented to so infamous a bargain as the Constitution is represented to be, and has in its present hands become. Now these pages prove the melancholy fact, that willingly, with deliberate purpose, our fathers bartered honesty for gain, and became partners with tyrants, that they might share in the profits of their tyranny.

And in view of this fact, will it not require a very strong argument to make any candid man believe, that the bargain which the fathers tell us they meant to incorporate into the Constitution, and which the sons have always thought they found there incorporated, does not exist there, after all? Forty of the shrewdest men and lawyers in the land assemble to make a bargain, among other things, about slaves, after months of anxious deliberations they put it into writing and sign their names to the instrument, fifty years roll away, twenty millions, at least, of their children pass over the stage of life, courts sit and pass judgment, parties arise and struggle fiercely; still all concur in finding in the instrument just that meaning which the fathers tell us they intended to express: must not he be a desperate man, who, after all this, sets out to prove that the fathers were bunglers and the sons fools, and that slavery is not referred to at all?

Besides, the advocates of this new theory of the Anti-slavery character of the Constitution, quote some portions of the Madison Papers in support of their views; and this makes it proper that the community should hear *all* that these Debates have to say on the subject. The further we explore them, the clearer becomes the fact, that the Constitution was meant to be, what it has always been esteemed, a compromise between slavery and freedom.

If then the Constitution be, what these Debates show that our fathers intended to make it, and that, too, their descendants, this nation, say they did make it and agreed to uphold, then we affirm that it is a "covenant with death and an agreement with hell," and ought to be immediately annulled. [Thus] no abolitionist can consistently take office under it, or swear to support it.

But if, on the contrary, our fathers failed in their purpose, and the Constitution is all pure and untouched by slavery, then, Union itself is impossible, without guilt. For it is undeniable that the fifty years passed under this (anti-slavery) Constitution, show us the slaves trebling in numbers; slaveholders monopolizing the offices and dictating the policy of the Government; prostituting the strength and influence of the Nation to the support of slavery here and elsewhere, trampling on the rights of the free States, and making the courts of the country their tools. To continue this disastrous alliance longer is madness. The trial of fifty years with the best of men and the best of Constitutions, on this supposition, only proves that it is impossible for free and slave States to unite on any terms, without all becoming partners in the guilt and responsibility for the sin of slavery. We dare not prolong the experiment, and with double earnestness we repeat our demand upon every honest man to join in the outcry of the American Anti-Slavery Society,—

No Union With Slaveholders!

Source Note: Wendell Phillips, "The Constitution, a Pro-Slavery Compact: Selections from the Madison Papers, &c," *The Anti-Slavery Examiner—No. A7*. New York: American Anti-Slavery Society, 1845. In the Collection of the Widener Library, Harvard University, and the Boston Public Library.

Lysander Spooner (1808–1887)

Lysander Spooner was a Massachusetts constitutional theorist who argued, in print, against the viability of slavery under the charter agreement of the new nation. Born in western Massachusetts, he apprenticed to two lawyers in Worcester who were prominent in Massachusetts's politics. For a time, he practiced law in Grand Rapids, Ohio, and became a land speculator there; however, he returned to Massachusetts to engage in reform activity, including a scheme to break the monopoly of the U.S. Post Office by founding the American Letter Mail Company in 1844. Like UPS and FedEx today, Spooner's mail company was a financial success, but he was opposing the federal government, and his costs were enormous. Spooner's most prominent concern was slavery, and he became well established in the antebellum slavery debates by an early contest with Wendell Phillips, which is represented in this volume.

He vigorously opposed slavery and used legal reasoning to convince his readers that the Declaration of Independence, the constitutions of the various founding states, and the Articles of Confederation (which preceded the U.S. Constitution as the charter document of the new nation) were all documents that did not allow slavery. He did not agree with the Garrisonians, particularly Wendell Phillips, who saw in the Constitution an "agreement with Hell" and a "Proslavery Compact," as Phillips would call it. Spooner debated in print with Wendell Phillips and with Henry Bowditch, whose *Slavery and the Constitution* (1849) was a response to Spooner's *Unconstitutionality of Slavery* (1845). According to John Thomas, "As a trained lawyer, Bowditch was not impressed by Spooner's cranky and seemingly factitious argument. His own *Slavery and the Constitution* (1849) was intended as a rebuttal to Spooner's book based on an examination of the Constitution 'according to the common meaning of its terms' and establishing the 'uncontrovertible conclusion' that it legalized and upheld slavery" (Thomas, p. 115). Spooner's arguments may have held up as a burden of proof for constitutional theorists, but they did not have the widespread public appeal of Wendell Phillips's oratory. Phillips's *Constitution, A Pro-Slavery Compact* (1845), also an engagement with the Spooner argument, is excerpted here. Spooner's opposition to Phillips and the Garrisonians concerning the Constitution may have appeared conservative in relation to their militant position, but he became passionate about the condemned abolitionist, John Brown. According to Randy E. Barnett, Spooner had met Brown shortly before Brown's ill-fated raid on Harpers Ferry, and afterwards attempted to implement a plan in which radical abolitionists would kidnap the governor of Virginia and hold him hostage for Brown's release. The plan was never acted upon, though Spooner's associates had gone so far as to locate a boat and crew. Spooner also provided legal arguments to aid abolitionists charged with violating the Fugitive Slave Act, and his work on behalf of such defendants led him in 1854 to publish a book, *Trial by Jury*, in which he defended as essential to a free society the jury's role as triers of both fact and law—the position sometimes referred to as "jury nullification." Until his death in 1887 at the age of 79, Spooner eked out an impoverished existence as a writer, activist, and legal theorist. His writings were extensive, including a lengthy, though never completed, treatise defending intellectual property rights. Spooner is best remembered today for his conflict with Wendell Phillips, the abolitionist orator who with William Lloyd Garrison led the militant faction of abolitionism to regard the Constitution as a proslavery compact.

SUGGESTIONS FOR FURTHER READING

Barnett, Randy E. "Was Slavery Constitutional before the Thirteenth Amendment? Lysander Spooner's Theory of Interpretation." 28 *Pacific Law Journal* 977 (1997).

Bowditch, Henry Ingersoll. *Slavery and the Constitution* (Boston, 1849).

Mayer, Henry. *All on Fire: William Lloyd Garrison and the Abolition of Slavery.* New York: St. Martin's Press, 1998, pp. 428 ff.

Shively, Charles. "Critical Biography." In *The Collected Works of Lysander Spooner* (Weston, MA: M&S, 1971).

Spooner, Lysander. *The Unconstitutionality of Slavery* (Boston, 1845).

Thomas, John L., ed. *Slavery Attacked: the Abolitionist Crusade.* Englewood Cliffs, NJ: Prentice-Hall, 1969.

The Unconstitutionality of Slavery
by Lysander Spooner

Chapter VII, The Constitution of the United States

. . . Let us now look at the *positive* provisions of the Constitution, *in favor of liberty*, and see whether they are not only inconsistent with any legal sanction of slavery, but also whether they must not, of themselves, have necessarily extinguished slavery if it had had any constitutional existence to be extinguished.

And, first, the Constitution made all "the people of the United States" *citizens* under the government to be established by it; for all of those, by whose authority the Constitution declares itself to be established, must of course be presumed to have been made citizens by it. . . .

Who, then, established the Constitution?

The preamble to the Constitution has told us in the plainest possible terms, to wit, that "We, *the people* of the United States do ordain and establish this Constitution," etc.

By "the people of the United States," here mentioned, the Constitution intends *all* "the people" then permanently inhabiting the United States. If it does not intend all, who were intended by "the people of the United States?" The Constitution itself gives no such answer to such a question. It does not declare that "we, the *white* people," or "we, the *free* people," or "we, a *part* of the people"—that is, we the *whole* people—of the United States, "do ordain and establish this Constitution."

If the *whole* people of the United States were not recognized as citizens by the Constitution, then the Constitution gives no information as to what portion of the people were to be citizens under it. And the consequence would then follow that the Constitution established a government that could not know its own citizens.

. . . That the designation, "We the people of the United States," included the whole people that properly belonged to the United States, is also proved by the fact that no exception is made in any other part of the instrument.

If the Constitution had intended that any portion of "the people of the United States" should be excepted from its benefits, disenfranchised, outlawed, enslaved, it would of course have designated these exceptions with such particularity as to make it sure that none but the true persons intended would be liable to be subjected to such wrongs. Yet, instead of such particular designation of the exceptions, we find no designation whatever of the kind. But, on the contrary, we *do* find, in the Preamble itself, a sweeping declaration to the effect that there are no such exceptions; that the whole people of the United States are citizens, and entitled to liberty, protection, and the dispensation of justice under the Constitution.

. . . Again. If the Constitution was established by authority of all "the people of the United States," they are all legal parties to it, and citizens under it. And if they were parties to it, and citizens under it, it follows that neither they, *nor their posterity*, nor any nor either of them, can ever be legally enslaved within the territory of the United States; for the Constitution declares its object to be, among other things *"to secure the blessing of liberty to ourselves and our posterity."* This purpose of the national Constitution is a law paramount to all state constitutions; for it is declared that "this Constitution, and the laws of the United States that shall be made in pursuance thereof, and all treaties made, or which shall be made under the authority of the United States, shall be the supreme law of the land; and the judges *in every state* shall be bound thereby, any thing in the constitution or laws of any state to the contrary notwithstanding."

. . . But however clear it may be, that the Constitution, in reality, made citizens of all "the people of the United States," yet it is not necessary to maintain that point, in order to prove that the Constitution gave no guaranty or sanction to slavery—or if it had not already given citizenship to all, it nevertheless gave to the government of the United States unlimited power of offering citizenship to all. The power given to the government of passing of naturalization laws, is entirely unrestricted, except that the laws must be uniform throughout the country. And the government has undoubted power to offer naturalization and citizenship to every person in the country, whether foreigner or native, who is not already a citizen. To suppose that we have in the country three millions of native-born inhabitants, not citizens, and whom the national government has no power to make citizens, when its power of naturalization is entirely unrestricted, is a palpable contradiction.

Chapter XIII, The Children of Slaves Are Born Free

This law of nature, that all men are born free, was recognized in the Declaration of Independence. But it was not a new principle then. Justinian says, "Captivity and servitude are both contrary to the law of nature; for by that law all men are born free." But the principle was not new to Justinian; it exists in the nature of man, and is as old as man—and the race of man generally has acknowledged it. The exceptions have been special; the rule general.

The Constitution of the United States recognizes the principle that all men are born free; for it recognizes the principle that natural birth in the country gives citizenship—which, of course, implies freedom. And no exception is made to the rule. Of course, all born in the country since the adoption of the Constitution of the United States, have been born free, whether there were or were not any legal slaves in the country before that time.

Even the provisions, in the several state constitutions, that the legislatures shall not *emancipate* slaves, would, if allowed their full effect, unrestrained by the Constitution of the United States, hold in slavery only those who were then slaves; it would do nothing towards enslaving their children, and would give the legislatures no authority to enslave them.

It is clear, therefore, that on this principle alone, slavery would now be extinct in this country, unless there should be an exception of a few aged persons.

Source Note: Lysander Spooner, *The Unconstitutionality of Slavery* (Boston, 1845).

HORACE MANN (1796–1859)

The name Horace Mann is rightly associated with education, and numerous schools in the United States are named after him. In his sixty-three years, he succeeded in becoming a graduate of Brown University and the Litchfield

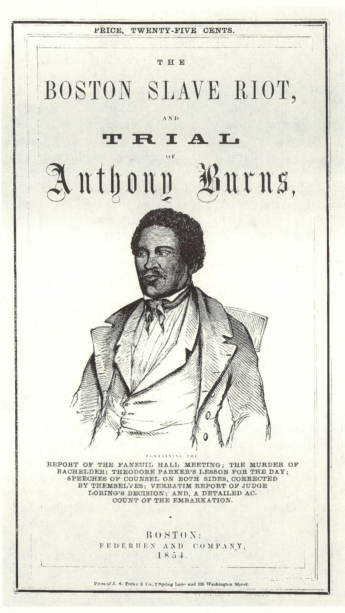

"The Boston Slave Riot and Trial of Anthony Burns," with a picture of Burns and a full description of his trial and circumstances.

School of Law, a practicing attorney, a Massachusetts state senator, and the president of Antioch College in Ohio. He is remembered for his fierce dedication to the improvement of the school systems of Massachusetts, which were disorganized and less effective in antebellum America than they had been in colonial times. Mann was an effective speaker, as his "Speech Delivered in the U.S. House of Representatives, on February 15, 1852," makes clear. He is also associated with the founding of the Common School movement in the United States, arguing for universal, free, public education for precollege young people. Although he eventually succeeded to the presidency of an institution of higher learning, his reputation was built on his lifelong support for public secondary education and his opposition to slavery. He was born in Franklin, Massachusetts, on May 4, 1796, and died in Yellow Springs, Ohio, on August 2, 1859.

Speech Delivered in the U.S. House of Representatives on the Subject of Slavery in the Territories, and the Consequences of Dissolution of the Union
by Horace Mann

If the word "Abolitionist" is to be used in a reproachful and contumelious sense, does it not more properly belong to those who would extend a system which in its very nature abolishes freedom, justice, equity, and a sense of human brotherhood? Does it not belong to those who would abolish not only social and political, but all natural rights; who would abolish "liberty and the pursuit of happiness;" who would close up all the avenues to knowledge; who would render freedom of thought and liberty of conscience impossible, by crushing out the faculties by which alone we can think and decide; who would rob a fellow-man of his parental rights, and innocent children of the tenderness and joys of a filial love; who would introduce a foul concubinage in place of the institution of marriage, and who would remorselessly trample upon all the tenderest and holiest affections which the human soul is capable of feeling? After Mr. Jefferson, in the Declaration of Independence, had enumerated a few oppressive deeds of the British king towards his American colonists, he denominated him "a prince whose character was marked by every act that could define a tyrant." There are now as many slaves in this country as there were colonists in 1776. Compare the condition of these three million slaves with the condition of the three million colonists. The conduct of that sovereign who was denounced before earth and heaven as having committed all the atrocities that could "define a tyrant" was mercy and loving-kindness compared with the wrongs and privations of three millions of our fellow beings, now existing among us. If the word "Abolitionist," then is to be used in a reproachful sense, let it be applied to those who, in the middle of the nineteenth century, and in defiance of all the lights of the age, would extend the horrors of an institution which by one all-comprehending crime towards a helpless race, makes it impossible to commit any new crime against them,—unless it be to enlarge the area of their bondage, and to multiply the number of the victims. . . .

If we were abolitionists, then we are abolitionists of human bondage; while those who oppose us are abolitionists of human liberty. We would prevent the extension of one of the greatest wrongs that man ever suffered upon earth; they would carry bodily chains and mental chains,—chains in a literal and chains in a figurative sense,—into realms where even half-civilized descendants of the Spaniard and the Indians have silenced their clanking. . . .

I know it is said that the *fact* of slavery always precedes the *law* of slavery; that *law* does not go before the institution and create it, but comes afterwards to sanction and regulate it. But this is no more true of slavery than of every other institution or practice among mankind whether right or wrong. Homicide existed before law; the law came in subsequently and declared that he who took an innocent man's life without law, should lose his own by law. The law came in to regulate homicide; to authorize the taking of human life for crime just as we authorize involuntary servitude for crime; and it may just as well be argued that murder is a natural right because it existed before law, as that slavery is a natural right because it existed before the law. *This argument appeals to the crime which the law was enacted to prevent, in order to establish the supremacy of the crime over the law that forbids it. . . .*

Having, as I trust, refuted the argument of the slaveholder, that the prohibition of slavery in the territories is an act of injustice to his rights, I will consider his next assertion, that it is an insult to his feelings. We are told that the exclusion of slavery from the territories is an affront to the honorable sensibilities of the south; and that acquiescence in the exclusion would involve their dishonor and degradation. . . .

There are two answers to this complaint. The first is, that among gentlemen, no insult is ever offered where none is intended. . . .

But there is another consideration,—one which appertains to the party supposed to be insulted, rather than the party charged with the insult. In his "Theory of Moral Sentiments," Adam Smith maintains that it is the judgment of men,—the opinion of the bystanders,—that gives us the pleasure of being approved, or the pain of being disapproved, on account of our conduct. Now, in this contest between the north and the south, on the subject of extending slavery, who are the bystanders? They are the civilized nations of the earth. We, the north and south, are contending in an arena. All civilized men stand around us. They are a ring of lookers-on. It is an august spectacle. It is a larger assemblage than ever witnessed any other struggle in the history of mankind; and their shouts of approbation or hisses of scorn are worthy of our heed. And what do these spectators say, in the alternations of the combat? Do they urge on the south to mightier efforts, to the wider spread of slavery, and the multiplication of its victims? Do they shout when she triumphs? When new chains are forged and riveted, when new realms are subdued by haughty taskmasters, and overrun by imbruted slaves, do their plaudits greet your ears and rouse you to more vehement efforts? All the reverse; totally the reverse. They are now looking on with disgust and abhorrence. They groan, they mock, they hiss. The brightest pages of their literature portray you, as covered with badges of dishonor; their orators hold up your purposes as objects for the execration of mankind; their wits hurl the lightnings of satire at your leaders. . . .

And do those gentlemen who make these threats soberly consider how deeply they are pledging themselves and their constituents by them? Threats of dissolution, if executed, become rebellion or treason. . . .

I cannot contemplate this spectacle without a thrill of horror. If the two sections of this country ever marshal themselves against each other, and squadrons rush to the conflict, it will be a war carried on by such powers of intellect, animated by such vehemence of resources, as the world has never before witnessed. "Ten foreign wars," it has been well said, "are a luxury compared with one civil war." But I turn from this scene with a shudder. If, in the retributive providence of God, the volcano of civil war should ever burst upon us, it will be amid thunderings above, and earthquakes below, and darkness around; and when that darkness is lifted up, we shall see this once glorious union,—this oneness of government, under which we have been prospered and blessed as Heaven never prospered and blessed any other people,—rifted in twain from east to west, with a gulf between us wide and profound, save that this gulf will be filled and heaped high with the slaughtered bodies of our countrymen; and when we reawaken to consciousness, we shall behold garments and the hands of the survivors red with fratricidal blood. . . .

And what is the object for which we are willing to make this awful sacrifice? Is it to redeem a realm to freedom? No! But to subjugate a realm to slavery. Is it to defend the rights of man? No! But to abolish the rights of man!

I know it is said that some of the Northern States are averse to the reception of blacks. Let us analyze this idea. There are now by estimation three million of slaves. Say one half of these are either too old or too young to have the strength or the intelligence to escape. A million and a half are left; five hundred thousand of these will have attachments to their own parents or children, or to their masters, too strong to be broken; or they may be so degraded as to be contented with bondage; for their contentment is always one of the measures of their degradation. This would leave a million for fugitives, consisting wholly of the most able bodied and intelligent. The Northern States comprise a territory of five hundred thousand square miles. A million of escaped slaves would give but two to a square mile, and this surely would not be a formidable number, even, where colorphobia is strongest. . . .

Southern gentlemen, when they threaten disunion cannot surely be so much at fault as to forget that slavery exists here as it never existed before in the world. In Greece there were slaves;—in some cases highly intelligent and accomplished slaves. They could have escaped if they would; but where should they escape to? All coterminous nations,—the whole circle round,—were barbarians. These slaves, therefore, had no place to flee to, where better institutions and juster laws prevailed. . . .

But it is said that if dissolution occurs, the "United States South" can form an alliance with Great Britain. And are there no instigators and abolitionists in England? Yes, sir, ten in England where there is one at the north. Frederick

Douglass has just returned from England, where he has enjoyed the honors of an oration. William Wells Brown, another fugitive slave, is now traveling in England. His journeys from place to place are like the "progresses" of one of the magnates of that land. . . .

Sir, every man who has traveled in England knows that there are large, wealthy, and refined circles there, no member of which would allow a slaveholder to sit at his table or enter his doors. Not only churches, but moral and religious men, the world over, have begun to read slaveholders out of their communion and companionship. If the south expects to rid itself of agitation and abolitionism by rupturing its bonds with the north and substituting an alliance with Great Britain for our present constitution they may envy the wisdom of the geese who invited the fox to the stand sentinel over them while they slept. . . .

I said that the slave does not know much of geography; but he understands enough of it to know where lies the free frontier. The slave does not know much astronomy; but there is one star in the firmament, which is dearer to him than all the heavenly host were to the Chaldeans. . . .

In the case of the *Amistad*, where a forgotten few ignorant, degraded wretches, fresh from the jungles of benighted Africa herself, seized upon the vessel in which they were transported, and compelled the master, under peril of his life, to steer for the north star,—that light which God kindled in the heavens, and which he will as soon extinguish as he will extinguish the love of liberty which he has kindled in every human breast?

And will they find a model of their manifesto in that glorious Declaration of American Independence which their own immortal Jefferson prepared, and to which many of the greatest of all their historic names are subscribed? Alas, they will have to read that Declaration, as the devil reads Scripture, backwards! I know not what may be the rhetorical terms and phrases of the Declaration but I do know that its *historic* form and substance cannot be widely different from this:—

We hold these truths to be self-evident, that men are not created equal; that they are not endowed by their Creator with inalienable rights; that white men, of the Anglo-Saxon race, were born to rob, and tyrannize, and enjoy, and black men, of the African race, to labor, and suffer, and obey; that a man, with a drop of African blood in his veins, has no political rights, and therefore shall never vote; that he has no pecuniary rights, and therefore whatever he may earn or receive, belongs to his master; that he has no judicial rights, and therefore he shall never be heard as a witness to redress wrong, or violence, or robbery, committed by white men upon him; that he has no parental rights, and therefore his children may be torn from his bosom, at the pleasure or caprice of his owner; that he has no marital rights, and therefore his wife may be lawfully sold away into distant bondage, or violated before his eyes; that he has no religious rights, and therefore he shall never read the Bible; that he has no heaven-descended, God-given rights of freedom, and therefore he and his posterity shall be slaves forever. We hold that governments were instituted among men to secure and fortify this ascendancy of one race over another; that this ascendancy has its foundation in force ratified by law and in ignorance and debasement inflicted by intelligence and superiority; and when any people, with whom we are politically associated, would debar us from propagating our doctrines or extending our domination into new realms and over free territories, it becomes our duty to separate from them, and to hold them, as we hold the rest of mankind,—friends when they make slaves, enemies when they make freemen.

I say, sir, of whatever words and phrases the southern "Magna Carta" may consist, this, or something like this, must be its substance and reality.

So a preamble to their constitution must run in the wise: "We, the people of the 'United States South,' in order to form a more perfect conspiracy against the rights of the African race, establish injustice, insure domestic slavery, provide for holding three millions of our fellow-beings, with all the countless millions of their posterity, in bondage, and to secure to ourselves and our posterity the enjoyment of power, and luxury, and sloth, do ordain and establish this constitution for the 'United States South.'"

Sir, should a civil war ensue between the north and the south, (which may God in his mercy avert,) in consequence of an attempt to dissolve this Union, and the certain resistance which would be made to such an attempt, it would be difficult to exaggerate the immediate evils which would befall the interests of New England and some other parts of the north. Our manufacturers and our commerce would suffer at least a temporary derangement. . . .

Source Note: Horace Mann, *Speech Delivered in the U.S. House of Representatives, February 15, 1852, on the Subject of Slavery in the Territories, and the Consequences of Dissolution of the Union* (Washington, DC, 1852).

ALEXANDER CRUMMELL (1819–1898)

Alexander Crummell was born in New York City on March 3, 1819, and died on September 10, 1898. Crummell was a "freeman," or "free African," although his father, a "Boston Crummell," was at one time a slave. According to his biographer, Wilson J. Moses, Crummell was a "passionate man with a keen, acerbic wit, but he was also a dark, brooding, Miltonic figure. He was optimistic concerning the future of black people in America and what he called 'the destined superiority of the Negro.' But he was also pessimistic about human nature and spoke repeatedly of human degradation and depravity" (Moses, *Destiny and Race*, p. 5). This habit of mind is perhaps best seen in some of his sermons, such as "The Day of Doom," preached in 1854, in which he reminds his listeners of the approaching Judgment and the Apocalypse that awaits the world of sinners, not only the slaveowners of the United States. "Crummell was a complex figure, whose significance cannot be understood so long as we cling to the standard cliches about African-American culture or stereotypes concerning the black preacher. Crummell absolutely rejected the 'get-happy' philosophy of 'feel-good religion.' His writings illustrate the existence of a strenuous black 'protestant' ethic that was later to be manifested in the Puritanical discipline of the Nation of Islam under Elijah Muhammad and Malcolm X" (Moses, *Destiny and Race*, p. 5). Crummell was celebrated by W. E. B. Du Bois in his classic work, *The Souls of Black Folk: Essays and Sketches*. Crummell was an exceptionally well educated man, and spent many years living in England, where in 1853 he received an earned, not an honorary, degree from Cambridge University. He traveled widely in Liberia and other parts of Africa, and returned to the United States to become pastor of St. Luke's Episcopal Church in Washington, D.C., from 1879 to 1894 (Moses, *Destiny and Race*, pp. 7–9). Crummell lived a very long life and contributed many essays to the literature of Reconstruction America, engaging in the same debates concerning the future of the African in America that would occupy Booker T. Washington and W. E. B. Du Bois at the turn of the century, shortly after Crummell's death in 1898. For example, his speech "Our National Mistakes and the Remedy for Them" was an apologia for the United States government delivered before the Common Council and the Citizens of Monrovia, Liberia, West Africa, on July 26, 1870, which was the Monrovian day of national independence. In another address, "The Destined Superiority of the Negro," Crummell preached a Thanksgiving sermon in November 1877, which critiqued the race-theory arguments of antebellum writers like Josiah Nott and George Gliddon, making the argument that the African Negro had in fact demonstrated, historically, a progress that is not characteristic of other oppressed races. "Wave after wave of a destructive tempest has swept over his head, without impairing in the least his peculiar vitality. Indeed, the Negro, in certain localities, is a superior man, today, to what he was three hundred years ago. With an elasticity rarely paralleled, he has risen superior to the dread inflictions of a prolonged servitude, and stands, today, in all the lands of his thralldom, taller, more erect, more intelligent, and more aspiring than any of his ancestors for more than two thousand years of a previous era." (Moses, *Destiny and Race*, p. 200). In another post-bellum speech, "The Black Woman of the South: Her Neglects and Her Needs," given before the Freedman's Aid Society of Ocean Grove, New Jersey, on August 15, 1883, Crummell fused the women's rights agenda with the further emancipation of the African from the Jim Crow culture of Reconstruction.

In the text that follows, Crummell focuses on the injustices of chattel slavery as an institution and on the degradation of the Negro that has historically followed the enslavement of Africans in America.

SUGGESTIONS FOR FURTHER READING

Du Bois, W. E. B. "Of Alexander Crummell." In *The Souls of Black Folk: Essays and Sketches* (Chicago: A. C. McClurg, 1903), vol. XII, pp. 215–27.

Moses, Wilson J. *Alexander Crummell: A Study of Civilization and Discontent.* New York: Oxford University Press, 1989.

———, ed. *Destiny and Race: Selected Writings [of Alexander Crummell], 1840–1898.* Amherst: University of Massachusetts Press, 1992.

An Address to the British and Foreign Anti-Slavery Society
by Alexander Crummell

Sir, it seems to me that the friends of the negroes in the United States, during the last *fifteen* or twenty years, have partially forgotten one great fact, namely, that the origin of slavery is not, perhaps, to be found so *much* in any particular laws, as in the weakness, the benightedness, and the degradation of that particular class brought into slavery. It is the disposition, on the part of the strong and selfish, to use and employ the weak and miserable part of creation as their own instruments. How is this to be remedied? I cannot ignore the other plans which have been proposed and enforced here this evening; for I regard each of them as good and feasible. Yet I think there is one other plan which should not be neglected. I do think, that if you wish to free a people from the effects of slavery, you must improve and elevate their character. And the Negro needs this improvement. I do not pretend to deny that the people to whom I belong in the United States are, as a whole, weak and degraded. How could it be otherwise? For upward of two centuries they have, for the most part, been deprived of all religious instruction; debarred from all the means and appliances of education; cut off from all participation in civil and political prerogatives; shut out beyond the pale of humanity! And what could be the result of such a regimen as this, but degradation and benightedness? Sir, it is one of the marvels of the world that they preserve so many of the high instincts of humanity as they do—that they have not become, long ere this, thoroughly brutalized and demented! But, Sir, it is full time now to begin to instruct this people, to cultivate their minds, and to instill into them good moral and religious principles. Extend to them the means of improvement, and allow them full opportunity for the development of their capacities, and oppression could not withstand the influence and power thereof. But Sir, there are great difficulties in the way of the cultivation even of the free colored race in America. In the Southern States, it is forbidden by cruel and oppressive laws. In the Northern States, the prejudice of the whites prevents a full participation in the advantages of schools and colleges; while, on the other hand, the poverty of the colored people makes them unable to secure to themselves these advantages to a desirable extent. From these circumstances arises the necessity that the friends of the African in America should interest themselves in the educational interests of the colored race in America. . . . [Opposing colonization, Crummell continues,] The idea that a colony, made up, as its advocates frequently assert, of ignorant, degraded, benighted slaves fresh from the slave-shambles and cotton plantations of the Southern States of America when once carried across the ocean, should become the hope of Africa! Sir, the idea is preposterous, upon their own showing, in the last degree that men, who have been degraded for centuries—that a people who have been made base and miserable by a most galling oppression—who had been almost brutalized, and kept almost godless; that these should be the men to lay the foundations of the great states on the coast of Africa, of dispelling the ignorance of the nations, and of propagating virtue. Where was there ever such a marvelous sight witnessed in all the history of the world? Take up the history of colonization, both ancient and modern, and on which of its many pages do you discover such a result, or can you find such a precedent? . . . The Negro is an exception to the general facts. I have been noticing, Sir, that the middle passage alone is enough to destroy any people. It has not destroyed the vitality of the Negro!! They have increased in mental and moral importance, and have made themselves felt. Yes, Sir, they have made themselves so much felt, that they have made their cause and their interests matters of great importance to the nation enslaving them. In many cases they have worked out their emancipation, for emancipation has not been merely a boon. It has been, also, an achievement on the part of the black man. When I notice the endurance of this race, their patience and hopefulness, their quiet perseverance and humility; when I contemplate their remarkable vitality and strong tenacity of life; when I see their gradual rise from degradation and enslavement, and their transition in many quarters from a state chattelism to manhood and freedom; when I behold the capable men of this people coming forward to vindicate and redeem their brethren in Africa and in other lands; when I observe the increased interest of the Christian world and especially of Christian England in Africa and the simultaneous interest of African chiefs and Africans in general, in the Gospel, and all the zealous efforts of the civilized world in behalf of this people I cannot but think that all these are the concurrent Providences of God for good; that they are all tending to some great fact—some glorious manifestation of African development in the future—a Fact so high and lofty in its moral significance that it may justly claim to be the realization of the poet's prediction, "Time's noblest offspring is the last."

Source Note: Alexander Crummell, "An Address to the British and Foreign Anti-Slavery Society," 1851, in Wilson J. Moses, ed., *Destiny and Race: Selected Writings. 1840–1898* (Amherst: University of Massachusetts Press, 1992), pp. 157–64. Reprinted by permission of Bruce Wilcox, director. Originally published in *The Anti-Slavery Reporter*, June 2, 1851.

ROGER BROOKE TANEY (1777–1864)

Roger Taney, chief justice of the Supreme Court of the United States, was born in Calvert County, Maryland, on March 17, 1777, and died on October 12, 1864. His career was distinguished by controversy and extremely conservative, even extremist, Supreme Court opinions. A graduate of Dickinson College, he became a practicing attorney in Maryland and married Anne Key, the sister of Francis Scott Key, who composed the "Star Spangled Banner." He belonged to the political party headed by Andrew Jackson, and as U.S. attorney general, he persuaded Jackson to veto the new Bank of the United States charter and pressed for the withdrawal of all federal deposits from the bank. Taney was so controversial that he was not confirmed by the Senate as Secretary of the Treasury, and in 1835, his nomination as associate justice of the Supreme Court was also rejected by the Senate. However, in 1836 he succeeded John Marshall on the Supreme Court and commenced a judicial career determined to deprive the

African of civil rights and to perpetuate the institution of slavery. In the Court's decision *re Dred Scott v John Sandford*, Taney argued first, that Scott had not been freed from slavery by residing in a free territory, thus enforcing the Fugitive Slave Act of 1850, and second, that a Negro could not sue in federal court, not holding citizenship in the United States. In a ruling, he declared that Congress had never possessed the authority to ban slavery from the Territories, which in effect declared the Missouri Compromise of 1820, which had already been seriously modified by the Compromise of 1850 and the Kansas-Nebraska Bill, to be unconstitutional. His extremism and personal arrogance joined his controversial Court opinions to arouse controversy, so that his death, in 1864, was not publicly mourned in Washington (*Dictionary of American Biography*). This excerpt is taken from the *Dred Scott v Sandford* decision of March 6, 1857.

Opinion of the Court in Dred Scott, Plaintiff in Error, v John F. A. Sandford
by Roger B. Taney

. . . The personal rights and privileges guarantied to citizens of this new sovereignty were intended to embrace only those who were then members of the several State communities, or who should afterwards by birthright or otherwise become members, according to the provisions of the Constitution and the principles on which it was founded.

It becomes necessary, therefore, to determine who were citizens of the several States when the Constitution was adopted.

[T]he legislation and histories of the times, and the language used in the Declaration of Independence, show, that neither the class of persons who had been imported as slaves, nor their descendants, whether they had become free or not, were then acknowledged as a part of the people, nor intended to be included in the general words used in that memorable instrument.

It is difficult at this day to realize the state of public opinion in relation to that unfortunate race, which prevailed in the civilized and enlightened portions of the world at the time of the Declaration of Independence, and when the Constitution of the United States was framed and adopted.

They had for more than a century before been regard as beings of an inferior order, and altogether unfit to associate with the white race, either in social or political relations; and so far inferior, that they had no rights which the white man was bound to respect; and that the negro might justly and lawfully be reduced to slavery. . . . He was bought and sold, and treated as an ordinary article of merchandise and traffic, whenever a profit could be made by it. This opinion was at that time fixed and universal in the civilized portion of the white race. It was regarded as an axiom in morals as well as in politics, which no one thought of disputing, or supposed to be open to dispute; and men in every grade and position in society daily and habitually acted upon it in their private pursuits, as well as in matters of public concern, without doubting for a moment the correctness of this opinion.

And in no nation was this opinion more firmly fixed or more uniformly acted upon than by the English Government and English people. They not only seized them on the coast of Africa, and sold them or held them in slavery for their own use; but they took them as ordinary articles of merchandise to every country where they could make a profit on them, and were far more extensively engaged in this commerce than any other nation in the world.

The opinion thus entertained and acted upon in England was naturally impressed upon the colonies they founded on this side of the Atlantic, and, accordingly, a negro of the African race was regarded by them as an article of property, and held, and bought and sold as such, in every one of the thirteen colonies which united in the Declaration of Independence, and afterwards formed the Constitution of the United States. The slaves were more or less numerous in the different colonies, as slave labor was found more or less profitable. But no one seems to have doubted the correctness of the prevailing opinion of the time.

The legislation of the different colonies furnishes positive and indisputable proof of this fact. . . .

The province of Maryland, in 1717, passed a law declaring "that if any free negro or mulatto intermarry with any white woman, or if any white man shall intermarry with any negro or mulatto woman, such negro or mulatto shall become a slave during life, excepting mulattoes born of white women, who, for such intermarriage, shall only become servants for seven years. . . ."

The other colonial law to which we refer was passed by Massachusetts in 1705. It is entitled "An act for the better preventing of a spurious and mixed issue," &c.; and it provides, that "if any negro or mulatto shall presume to smite or strike any person of the English or other Christian nation, such negro or mulatto shall be severely whipped. . . ."

. . . [T]hese laws . . . show, too plainly to be misunderstood, the degraded condition of this unhappy race. They were still in force when the Revolution began, and are a faithful index to the state of feeling towards the class of persons of whom they speak, and of the position they occupied throughout the thirteen colonies, in the eyes and thoughts of the men who framed the Declaration of Independence and established the State Constitutions and Governments. They show that a perpetual and impassable barrier was intended to be erected between the white race and the one which they had reduced to slavery, and governed as subjects with absolute and despotic power, and which they then looked upon as so far below them in the scale of created beings, that intermarriages between white persons and negroes or mulattoes were regarded as unnatural and immoral, and punished as crimes, not only in the parties, but in the person who joined them in marriage. And no distinction, in this respect was made between the free negro or mulatto and the slave, but this stigma, of the deepest degradation, was fixed upon the whole race.

We refer to these historical facts for the purpose of showing the fixed opinions concerning that race, upon which the statesmen of that day spoke and acted . . . in order to determine whether the general terms used in the Constitution of the United States, as to the rights of man and the rights of the people, was intended to included them, or to give them or their posterity the benefit of any of its provisions.

The language of the Declaration of Independence is equally conclusive:

> We hold these truths to be self-evident: that all men are created equal; that they are endowed by their Creator with certain unalienable rights; that among them is life, liberty, and the pursuit of happiness; that to secure these rights, Governments are instituted, deriving their just powers from the consent of the governed.

The general words above quoted would seem to embrace the whole human family, and if they were used in a similar instrument at this day would so be understood. But it is too clear for dispute, that the enslaved African race were not intended to be included, and formed no part of the people who framed and adopted this declaration; for if the language, as understood in that day, would embrace them, the conduct of the distinguished men who framed the Declaration of Independence would have been utterly and flagrantly inconsistent with the principles they asserted; and instead of the sympathy of mankind, to which they so confidently appeared, they would have deserved and received universal rebuke and reprobation.

Yet the men who framed this declaration were great men—high in literary acquirements—high in their sense of honor, and incapable of asserting principles inconsistent with those on which they were acting. They perfectly understood the meaning of the language they used, and how it would be understood by others; and they knew that it would not in any part of the civilized world be supposed to embrace the negro race, which, by common consent, had been excluded from civilized Governments and the family of nations, and doomed to slavery. They spoke and acted according to the then established doctrines and principles, and in the ordinary language of the day, no one misunderstood them. The unhappy black race were separated from the white by indelible marks, and laws long before established, and were never thought of or spoken of except as property, and when the claims of the owner or the profit of the trader were supposed to need protection.

This state of public opinion had undergone no change when the Constitution was adopted, as is equally evident from its provisions and language. . . .

[There] are two clauses in the Constitution which point directly and specifically to the negro race as a separate class of persons, and show clearly that they were not regarded as a portion of the people or citizens of the Government then formed.

One of these clauses reserves to each of the thirteen States the right to import slaves until the year 1808. . . . And by the other provision the States pledge themselves to each other to maintain the right of property and the master, by delivering up to him any slave who may have escaped from his service, and be found within their respective territories. . . . And these two provisions show, conclusively, that neither the description of persons therein referred to, nor their descendants, were embraced in any of the other provisions of the Constitution; for certainly these two clauses were not intended to confer on them or their posterity the blessings of liberty, or any of the personal rights so carefully provided for the citizen.

No one of that race had ever migrated to the United States voluntarily; all of them had been brought here as articles of merchandise. The number that had been emancipated at that time were but few in comparison with those held in slavery; and they were identified as a part of the slave population rather than the free. It is obvious that they were not even in the minds of the framers of the Constitution when they were conferring special rights and privileges upon the citizens of a State in every other part of the Union.

Source Note: Roger B. Taney, "Opinion of the Court in Dred Scott, Plaintiff in Error, v John F. A. Sandford," March 6, 1857.

HORACE BUSHNELL (1802–1876)

A leading nineteenth-century theologian and Congregational minister, Horace Bushnell was a man of exceptional talents, and a born reformer. Following his education at Yale College, he studied law and then theology at the Yale Divinity School, where he became a tutor. Bushnell was intellectually keen, and approached both social and theological problems as a scholar, as the sermon excerpted here clearly shows. He was, however, extremely conservative in some of his views, and unlike many of his abolitionist contemporaries, he argued against equal rights for women and men. Relatively late in his career, he collected some of his essays into a book, *Work and Play* (1864), where some of his conservative social views were expressed. In 1869, he authored a small book entitled *Women's Suffrage: The Reform against Nature*; as the title suggests, Bushnell here argued that motherhood and domesticity were appropriate roles for women. He followed the reasoning of Catharine Beecher, who had also composed conduct manuals for young women, and his views concerning women's rights were diametrically opposed to those of William Lloyd Garrison.

Although Bushnell lived in an era of intense social reform, he was more an abstract theologian than a practical reformer, and his real interests were in correcting the Calvinist notions of innate depravity and unconditional election. His *Christian Nurture* (1847 and 1861) was a groundbreaking argument that articulated the Romantic doctrine of childhood, namely, that children were born innocent and were to be "nurtured" either toward evil or good. This basic denial of the doctrine of innate depravity put Bushnell at odds with conservative Christianity, even by nineteenth-century standards, but his social conservatism estranged him from abolitionists and evangelists alike. Bushnell criticized the excesses of militant abolitionism, though he attacked the Fugitive Slave Law of 1850. He was essentially a "gradualist" in his approach to the abolition of slavery, but he saw the Civil War as an apocalyptic event through which the forces of good should eventually triumph over the forces of evil.

Bushnell was pastor of the North Church in Hartford, but regularly received invitations from educational institutions to become president. He declined both Middlebury College and the college that was to become the University of California at Berkeley, preferring to write and lecture about the changing doctrines of Christianity. He continued to write often-controversial books on theology and religious history, including *Nature and the Supernatural* (1858) and *God in Christ* (1849). These works showed his allegiance to a new European theology, a mystical romanticism, espoused by Schliermacher in Germany and Samuel Taylor Coleridge in England, whose *Aids to Reflection* (1825) was a work that influenced not only Bushnell, but also Ralph Waldo Emerson. Bushnell's works are a response to the Transcendentalism of Emerson and Thoreau, and articulate his belief in an organic relation between man's being and the spirit of God, a belief that Emerson had expressed in his concept of the "oversoul."

Bushnell's 1839 *Discourse on the Slavery Question* is represented here not because Bushnell was a leading abolitionist, for he was not. What he did do was enter the antebellum slavery debates at a critical moment and throw his support behind the antislavery cause. Although he opposed the Fugitive Slave Act and the Compromise of 1850, he did not choose to participate in the reform movements of his time. His primary radicalism is found in his new theology, based on a rejection of Edwardsean Calvinism and a belief in the essential, natural goodness of man, including children, who were free from innate depravity. These theological views deeply influenced his opinion of the essential nature of man, and no doubt contributed to his opposition to slavery in the United States.

SUGGESTIONS FOR FURTHER READING

Bushnell, Horace. *An Argument for "Discourses on Christian Nurture."* Hartford, CT, 1847.

———. *Christ in Theology* (1851). New York: Garland, 1987.

———. *God in Christ.* Hartford, CT, 1849.

———. *Nature and the Supernatural.* New York, 1858.

———. *Women's Suffrage: The Reform against Nature* (1869). Washington, DC: Zenger, 1978.

Cherry, Conrad. *Nature and Religious Imagination.* Philadelphia: Fortress, 1980.

———, ed. *Horace Bushnell, Sermons.* New York: Paulist, 1985.

Crosby, Donald A. *Horace Bushnell's Theory of Language.* The Hague: Mouton, 1975.

Cross, Barbara M. *Horace Bushnell: Minister to a Changing America.* Chicago: University of Chicago Press, 1958.

Edwards, Robert L. *Of Singular Genius, of Singular Grace: A Biography of Horace Bushnell.* Cleveland: Pilgrim, 1992.

Smith, H. Shelton, ed. *Horace Bushnell.* New York: Oxford University Press, 1965.

A Discourse on the Slavery Question, Delivered in the North Church, Hartford
by Horace Bushnell

As regards the matter of abolishing slavery in the Southern portions of our country, there are two great questions, which arise for discussion and settlement.

I. Whether such abolition is possible, or a duty obligatory on the Southern Legislatures. And,

II. What is our duty in reference to the subject; what measures, if any, ought we to adopt with a view to hasten the result. . . .

There are some three or four features in American slavery, which no Christian, no man who has the common feelings of humanity, can think of without pity, disgust, and shame. . . .

The obnoxious features in American slavery of which I speak are these. . . .

First and chief of all is the non-permission of the family state, by the denial of marriage rites; by tearing asunder those parents whom God, more merciful than the laws, has doubtless accepted in the rites of nature; by stripping their children from their arms; by disallowing, if I should not rather say, extinguishing every affection which makes life human. . . .

Another feature of American slavery is the absence of any real protection to the body of the slave, in respect to limb, life, or chastity. It is philosophically true, that there are no such statutes, and they are not to be named in making out the legal view of slavery. . . .

A third feature of American slavery, as a legal institution is that it nowhere recognizes, in the slave, a moral or intellectual nature. He exists for another;—in himself he is no man. He is a muscular being only, in the laws, or, rather I should say, he is a muscular tool, a thing composed of arms and legs and various integuments convenient to do work with. A frightful system of legalized selfishness has robbed him of himself. Light is denied him, the windows of his soul are shut up by express statute. As a creature of conscience, a creature of immortal wants, a creature in god's image, he has no legal existence. . . .

Now observe—when I fix upon these features of slavery and take my stand for abolition before them, I do by no means regard the view they present, as a picture of slavery in this life. The condition of the slave, thus deserted, is seldom as desperate as the law suffers it to be. In this matter, he depends entirely upon the mercy, or the caprice of his master. Sometimes, of course, he finds a parent in his master. For myself, I cannot think of slavery, in this view, knowing as I do, the selfishness, the ferocity, the demoralized passions of men, without such a sense of its woes and cruelties as I cannot restrain. It compels me to say—I will not reason the matter farther. No facts, no arguments, no apprehension of mischief in a change, shall put me at peace with these things. They ought to be, will be, must be put away. And this to me is the abolition of slavery. . . .

I say to the South, this institution is your own, not ours. Take your own way of proceeding. Modify your system as you please. But let me declare to you that, until you have established the family state and made it sacred, till you have given security to the body, till you have acknowledged the immortal mind and manhood of your slave, you do an offence to God and humanity, in the continuance of this institution, which we must condemn. In this sense, I am ready to go for the abolition of slavery, and I cannot think that any man in New England, is so lost to the spirit of liberty and humanity as to feel otherwise. . . .

I turn here, on the one hand, to our Southern brethren, and say, here is a force in motion which you cannot long resist. The law of human society is against you, and you can as easily drive back the sun. The moral position of the world begins to reflect a peculiar disgrace on your institutions. You feel it now; you will feel it more; you will be compelled to yield to the feeling. I make no doubt that you are now firmly resolved to face out the odium of the human race; but cannot hold that resolve. Man's will is stout enough for a short time, but it can no more hold out in a long strain, than the muscles of his arms of his leg. . . .

I turn on the other hand, to our Anti-Slavery brethren, and say, do not regard yourselves in the organization you have raised up. Neither conclude, too hastily, at the beginning of a movement for liberty that what you are doing is a real advantage or assume too much consequence to yourselves. The destruction of slavery will be accomplished, either with you, or without you; or, if you make it necessary, in spite of you. . . .

I am obliged to say that I do not anticipate any such bright destiny opening on the African race in their country, as seems to occupy the vision of our Anti-Slavery brethren. They cherish egregious expectations, in this matter, I am confident, and the zeal which actuates them is, so far, out of proportion. Their action would be more healthful, if they had a more moderate estimate of the good, which is probably to be accomplished, in behalf of the colored race. . . .

There is no example in history, where an uncultivated and barbarous stock has been elevated in the midst of a cultivated and civilized stock; and I have no expectation that there ever will be. . . .

My expectation is that the African races, in this country, would soon begin to dwindle towards extinction, in the same way, if emancipated. Some few persons would, of course, be much elevated by their new privileges; as we see in the case of individuals among our Indian tribes. I am far from thinking that the African is incapable of elevation. We have facts enough to prove the contrary. The difficulty is to elevate the race, *as a race*, among us. . . .

In attempting to elevate the African race among us, there is too great a disadvantage against them in the beginning, to allow any hope of success. They need five hundred or a thousand years of cultivation to give them a fair chance. They cannot maintain the competition, they will be preyed upon and overreached, they will, many of them, betake themselves to idleness, vice, and crime; by all these conjoint influences they will be kept down and gradually diminished in numbers. At present they are kept from a decline in population, only by the interest their masters have in them. . . .

If we suppose that Christian benevolence will undertake for the race and will rescue them from the doom, otherwise sure to overtake them, doubtless much will be attempted and much done in that way. But the work is so great, the amount of Christian instruction and patronage requisite, so far beyond the possible supply, as effectually to cut off all hope of success. . . .

Furthermore, I have facts to show the probable decline of our colored population in a state of freedom, which leaves us no need of speculation. Take the case of the Irish. It is not true, as many suppose, that they become an integral part of our nation to any considerable extent: They become extinct. It is very seldom that their children born in this country live to mature age. Intemperance and poor living sweep them away, both old and young together. If you will glance over the catalogues of our colleges and legislatures, the advertisements of merchants and mechanics, you will almost never find an Irish name among them, which shows you at least that they do not rise to any rank among us. At the same time, if you will search the catalogues of alms-houses, and prisons, and potter's fields, there you will find their names in thick order. . . .

If then slavery ought thus to be given up, or abolished by the South, let us inquire—

III. What is our duty, at the North, in reference to this subject; what measures, if any, ought we to adopt. . . .

Many, who are offended by the Anti-Slavery movements, do not stay to settle their own minds, as they ought, but declare at once, that we have nothing to do with the subject, and have even no right to touch it. But that is a doctrine which cannot be yielded to for a moment. . . .

Again we are linked with slavery, by duties of mutual aid and defence. Thus if an insurrection arises, we may be called, according to the constitution, to march down our troops and aid in restoring the laws. . . .

We have also a common character with the South, we are one nation, and have as dear a property in their good name, as they have in their own. . . .

A man's right hand cannot be a thief's and his left an honest man's. No more can a nation have its honor or its dishonor in single limbs and fragments. . . .

Then again our holy religion is a spirit of universal humanity and benevolence. By it we are constituted brothers of mankind. . . .

The first movement here at the North was a rank onset and explosion. . . .

The first sin of this organization was a sin of ill manners. They went to work much as if they were going to drive the masters—as they do their negroes. The great convention, which met at Philadelphia, drew up a declaration of their sentiments, in which they visibly affected the style and tone of the declaration of independence. . . .

The Union is undervalued, and its preservation is often spoken of with lightness!

The movements of our societies have not touched the consciences of the Southern people, as many would be glad to believe, when they see the heat that is excited. . . .

We have been greatly mistaken, as to the moral power of associations generally, but here they are specially impotent. If you wish to put a man of real weight quite out of the way, to *hide* him, or make his name a cipher, as regards this question, you need only put him into an Anti-Slavery association. He *will lie there sweltering* under the heated mass of numbers, like the giant under Aetna, and by men as little felt or regarded. . . .

The three great features of American slavery, which I have named, must be an offence to every principle of goodness in your hearts. I charge you, then, in every sphere of life, as citizens and as Christians, to justify your own consciences, and be true to your post, as friends of God and humanity. . . .

You cannot be indifferent to these weighty interests. You are the sons of New England; you are friends, too, of humanity, and lovers of your country. I invoke you also in the higher name of GOD and duty.—May He whose distinction it is, that he bringeth out of the land of Egypt and out of the house of bondage; the wheels of whose chariot were filled, of old, with the eyes of an all-inspecting and equal justice; who sent forth His Son, in the later ages, proclaiming liberty to the captives. . . .

Source Note: Horace Bushnell, *A Discourse on the Slavery Question, Delivered in the North Church, Hartford* (Hartford, 1839).

CHARLES SUMNER (1811–1874)

Born in Boston on January 6, 1811, Charles Sumner graduated from Harvard College in 1830 and the Harvard Law School in 1833. (Most Bostonians today remember him as namesake of the Sumner Tunnel, under Boston Harbor, leading to Logan Airport.) He was a privileged Bostonian, and among his friends were Harvard literature professor and poet Henry Wadsworth Longfellow, the Concord transcendentalist Ralph Waldo Emerson, the minister William Ellery Channing, and the educator Horace Mann. His mentor in the law was Justice Joseph Story, whose "Charge" is contained in chapter 2 of this volume.

In antebellum America, Sumner was a strong abolitionist and powerful speaker whose oratorical authority led to his repeated election to the U.S. Senate from Massachusetts. His views were often controversial, and after the Civil War he supported Reconstruction measures that would have granted full Negro suffrage throughout the South as a requirement for the readmission of those states that had seceded from the Union at the outbreak of the war. He openly opposed the Compromise of 1850 and its inclusion of the Fugitive Slave Law.

His oratory typically was of the nature of tirade; in vituperation he was peerless, and his uncompromising stand on slavery made him a favorite and most powerful abolitionist. He bitterly opposed the Kansas-Nebraska Bill in 1854 and in May 1856, in a [Senate] debate on the admission of Kansas, made his most famous address, "The Crime Against Kansas." He scorned the Kansas-Nebraska Act as a swindle and he heaped invective upon its authors, Senators Andrew Butler and Stephen A. Douglas, in the most vindictive terms. Two days later, while at his desk in the Senate chamber, he was set upon and severely beaten by Preston S. Brooks, a congressman from South Carolina who was a nephew of Butler. For three years, Sumner was unable to resume his official duties, but the outraged Massachusetts legislature re-elected him in 1857 despite his incapacitation. (*Webster's American Biographies*, p. 1008)

During his long absence from the Senate, his seat was held vacant as a reminder of his antislavery views and as a rebuke to the South Carolina congressman who had savagely attacked him. Sumner's significance as an abolitionist senator derived from his oratorical powers and in his ability to speak, often without notes, for hours at a time. Both his "Crime against Kansas" speech of 1856 and his "Barbarism of Slavery," excerpted here, lasted approximately four hours. According to his biographer, Frederick J. Blue, Charles Sumner "continued his crusade for full civil rights for blacks, even as the Congress and the country grew weary of the issue. His proposal to prohibit discrimination in schools, juries, transportation, and public accommodation was blocked by conservatives in the Senate. Only after his death did a much-weakened civil rights bill become law, in part as a gesture to his memory. The measure, which was far ahead of its time, was nonetheless a fitting tribute to Sumner, although few were surprised when the Supreme Court ruled much of it unconstitutional in 1883" (Blue, p. 139). On March 11, 1874, Sumner died in Washington, D.C., after a career filled with reform causes.

SUGGESTIONS FOR FURTHER READING

Blue, Frederick J. "Charles Sumner." In *American National Biography* (New York: Oxford University Press, 1999), p. 435.

Dumond, Dwight Lowell. *Antislavery Origins of the Civil War in the United States.* Ann Arbor: University of Michigan Press, 1961.

———. *Slavery: The Crusade for Freedom in America.* Ann Arbor, University of Michigan Press, 1961.

McKitrick, Eric L., ed. *Slavery Defended: the Views of the Old South.* Englewood Cliffs, NJ: Prentice-Hall, 1963.

Walters, Ronald G. *The Antislavery Appeal: American Abolitionism after 1830.* Baltimore: Johns Hopkins University Press, 1976.

The Barbarism of Slavery
by Charles Sumner

Dedication

To the young men of the United States, I dedicate this new edition of a speech on the barbarism of Slavery, in token of heartfelt gratitude to them for brave and patriotic service rendered in the present war for civilization.

. . . The election of Mr. Lincoln was a judgment against Slavery, and its representatives were aroused.

. . . It was under the shadow of this constitutional assumption that the assumption for Slavery grew into virulent vigor, so that, at last, when Mr. Lincoln was elected, it broke forth in open *war*; but the war was declared in the name of State Rights.

Therefore, there are two *apparent* rudiments to this war. One is Slavery and the other is State Rights. But the latter is only a cover for the former. If Slavery were out of the way there would be no trouble from State Rights.

The war, then, is for Slavery, and nothing else. It is an insane attempt to vindicate by arms the lordship which had been already asserted in debate. With mad-cap audacity it seeks to install this Barbarism as the truest civilization. Slavery is declared to be the "corner-stone" of the new edifice. This is enough.

The question is thus presented between Barbarism and Civilization; not merely between two different forms of Civilization, but between Barbarism on the one side and Civilization on the other side. If you are for Barbarism, join the Rebellion, or, if you can not join it, give it your sympathies. If you are for Civilization, stand by the Government of your country with mind, soul, heart, and might!

Such is the issue simply stated. On the one side are women and children on the auction-block, families rudely separated; human flesh lacerated and seamed by the bloody scourge; labor extorted without wages; and all this frightful, many-sided wrong is the declared foundation of a mock commonwealth. On the other side is the Union of our Fathers, with the image of "Liberty" on its coin and the sentiment of Liberty in its Constitution, now arrayed under a patriotic government, which insists that no such mock Commonwealth, having such a declared foundation shall be permitted in our territory, purchased with money and blood, to impair the unity of our jurisdiction and to insult the moral sense of mankind.

Therefore, the battle which is now waged by the Union is for Civilization itself and it must have aid and God-speed from all who are not openly for Barbarism. There is no word of peace, no tone of gentleness, no whisper of humanity, which does not become trumpet-tongued against the Rebellion. War itself seems to "smooth its wrinkled front" as it undertakes the championship of such a cause. The armed soldier becomes a minister of mercy.

Speech

By various voices, is the claim made for Slavery, which is put forward defiantly as a form of civilization—as if its existence were not plainly inconsistent with the first principles of anything that can be called Civilization—except by that figure of speech in classical literature, where a thing takes its name from something which it has not, as the dreadful Fates were called merciful because they were without mercy. . . .

Such are the two assumptions, the first an assumption of fact, and the *second* an assumption of constitutional law, which are now made without apology or hesitation. I meet them both. To the first I oppose the essential Barbarism of Slavery, in all its influences, whether high or low, as Satan is Satan still, whether towering in the sky or squatting in the road. To the second I oppose the unanswerable, irresistible truth, that the Constitution of the United States no-

where recognizes property in man. These two assumptions naturally go together. They are "twins" suckled by the same wolf. They are the "couple" in the
present slave-hunt. And the latter can not be answered without exposing the
former. It is only when Slavery is exhibited in its truly hateful character, that we
can fully appreciate the absurdity of the assumption, which, in defiance of the
express letter of the Constitution, and without a single sentence, phrase, or
word, upholding human bondage, yet it foists into this blameless text the barbarous idea that man can hold property in man.

. . . The Barbarism of Slavery appears; first in the *character of Slavery*, and
secondly in the *character of Slave-masters*. Under the first head we shall naturally
consider (1) the Law of Slavery and its Origin, and (2) the practical results of
Slavery as shown in a comparison between the Free States and the Slave States.
Under the *second* head we shall naturally consider (1) Slave-masters as shown in
the Law of Slavery; (2) Slave-masters in their relations with slaves, here glanc-
ing at their three brutal instruments; (3) Slave-masters in their relations with
each other, with society, and with Government; and (4) Slave-masters in their
unconsciousness. . . .

. . . 1.) I begin with the *Law of Slavery and its Origin*, and here this Barbarism paints itself in its own chosen definition. It is simply this: Man, created in
the image of God, is divested of his human character, and declared to be a
"chattel"—that is, a beast, a thing or article of property, its own chosen definition. That this statement may not seem to be put forward without precise authority, I quote the statutes of three different States, beginning with South
Carolina, whose voice for Slavery always has an unerring distinctiveness. Here is
the definition supplied by this State:

"Slaves shall be deemed, held, taken, reputed, and adjudged in law, to be
chattel personal in the hands of their owners and possessors and their executors,
administrators, and assigns, to all intents, constructions, and purposes whatsoever."—*2 Brev. Dig., 229.*

And here is the definition supplied by the Civil Code of Louisiana:

"A slave is one who is in the power of a master to whom he belongs. The
master may sell him, depose of his person, his industry, and his labor. He can do
nothing, possess nothing, nor acquire anything, but what must belong to his
master."—*Civil Code, Art. 35.*

In similar spirit, the law of Maryland thus indirectly defines a slave as an
article:

"In case the personal property of a ward shall consist of specific *articles, such
as slaves,* working beasts, animals of any kind, the court, if it deem it advantageous for the ward, may at any time pass an order for the sale *thereof.*"—
Statutes of Maryland.

Not to occupy time unnecessarily, I present a summary of the pretended law
defining Slavery in all the Slave States, as made by a careful writer, Judge
Stroud, in a work of juridical as well as philanthropic merit:

"The careful principle of Slavery—that the slave is not to be ranked among
sentient beings, but among *things*—*as* an article of property—a chattel per-

sonal—obtains as undoubted law in all of these (Slave) States."—Stroud's *Law of Slavery*.

. . . The slave is held simply for *the use of his master*, to whose behest, his life, liberty, and happiness are devoted, and by whom he may be bartered, leased, mortgaged, bequeathed, invoiced, shipped as cargo, stored as goods, sold on execution, knocked off at public auction, and even staked at the gaming-table on the hazard of a card or a die; all according to law. Nor is there anything, within the limit of life, inflicted on a beast which may not be inflicted on the slave. He may be marked like a hog, branded like a mule, yoked like an ox, hobbled like a horse, driven like an ass, sheared like a sheep, maimed like a cur, and constantly beaten like a brute; all according to law. And should life itself be taken, what is the remedy?

. . . *Secondly*. Slavery paints itself again in its complete *abrogation of marriage*, recognized as a sacrament by the church, and recognized as a contract wherever civilization prevails. Under the law of Slavery, no such sacrament is respected, and no such contract can exist. The ties that may be formed between slaves are all subject to the selfish interests or more selfish lust of the master, whose license knows no check. Natural affections, which have come together, are rudely torn asunder; nor is this all. Stripped of every defense, the chastity of a whole race is exposed to violence, while the result is recorded in the tell-tale faces of children, glowing with their master's blood, but doomed for their mother's skin to Slavery, through all descending generations. . . .

Thirdly. Slavery paints itself again in its complete *abrogation of the parental relation*, which God in his benevolence has provided for the nurture and education of the human family, and which constitutes an essential part of Civilization itself. And yet, by the law of Slavery—happily beginning to be modified in some places—this relation is set at naught, and in its place is substituted the arbitrary control of the master, at whose mere command little children, such as the Savior called unto him, though clasped by a mother's arms, may be swept under the hammer of the auctioneer. I do not dwell on this exhibition. Sir, is not Slavery barbarous?

. . . *Fourthly*. Slavery paints itself again *in closing the gates of knowledge*, which are also the shining gates of civilization. Under its plain unequivocal law, the bondman may, at the unrestrained will of his master, be shut out from all instruction; while in many places, incredible to relate! the law itself, by cumulative provisions, positively forbids that he shall be taught to read. Of course, the slave can not be allowed to read, for his soul would then expand in larger air, while he saw the glory of the North Star, and also the helping truth, that God, who made iron, never made a slave; for he would then become familiar with the Scriptures, with the Decalogue still speaking in the thunders of Sinai; with that ancient text, "He that stealeth a man and selleth him, or if he be found in his hands, he shall surely be put to death;" with that other text, "Masters, give unto your servants that which is just and equal;" with that great story redemption, when the Lord raised the slave-born Moses to deliver his chosen people from the house of bondage; and with that sublimer story, where the Savior died a cruel death, that all men, without distinction of race, might be saved—leaving to mankind commandments, which, even without his example, make Slavery impossible.

. . . This same testimony also found expression from the fiery soul of Jefferson. Here are some of his words:

> There must be an unhappy influence on the manners of our people, produced by the existence of Slavery among us. The whole commerce between master and slave is a perpetual exercise of the most boisterous passions, THE MOST UNREMITTING DESPOTISM on the one part, and degrading submission on the other; our children see this, and learn to imitate it. . . . *The man must be a prodigy who can retain his manners and morals undepraved by such circumstances.* And with what execration should the statesman be loaded, who, permitting one half the citizens thus to trample on the rights of the other, *transforms those into despots,* and these into enemies, destroys the morals of the one part, and the *amor patriae* of the other! With the morals of the people, their industry also is destroyed.

. . . In the recent work of Mr. Olmsted, a close observer and traveler in the Slave States, which abounds in pictures of Slavery, expressed with caution and evident regard to truth, will be found still another, where a Slave-master thus frankly confesses his experience:

> "I can tell you how you can break a nigger of running away, certain," says the Slave-master. "There was an old fellow I used to know in Georgia, that always cured his so. If a nigger ran away, when he caught him, he would bind his knee over a log, and fasten him so he couldn't stir; and then he'd take a pair of pincers, and pull one of his toe-nails out by the roots; and tell him, that if he ever run away again, he would pull out two of them; and if he run away again after that, he told him he'd pull out four of them, and so on, doubling each time. He never had to do it more than twice; it always cured them."—*Olmsted's Texas Journey, 105.*

Like this story, which is from the lips of a Slave-master, is another, where the master, angry because his slave had sought to regain his God-given liberty, deliberately cut the tendons of his heel, thus horribly maiming him for life.

. . . The enormity of the pretensions that Slavery is sanctioned by the Constitution becomes still more apparent, when we read the Constitution in the light of great national acts and of contemporaneous declarations. First comes the Declaration of Independence, the illuminated initial letter of our history, which in familiar words announces that "all men are created equal; that they are endowed by their Creator with certain unalienable rights; that among these are Life, *Liberty*, and the Pursuit of Happiness; that to secure these rights governments are instituted among men, deriving their just powers from the consent of the governed." "Let it be remembered, that it has ever been the pride and the boast of America, *that the rights for which she has contended were the rights of human nature.* By the blessing of the Author of *these rights*, they have prevailed over all opposition, and form THE BASIS of thirteen independent States." Now, whatever may be the privileges of States in their individual capacities, with their several local jurisdictions, no power can ever be attributed to the nation, in the absence of a positive unequivocal grant, inconsistent with these two national declarations. Here is the national heart, the national soul, the national will, the national voice, which must inspire our interpretation of the Constitution, and enter into and diffuse itself through all the national legislation. Such are the commanding authorities which constitute "Life, Liberty, and the Pursuit of Happiness," and in more general words, "the Rights of Human Nature," without distinction of race, or recognition of the curse of Ham, as the basis of our national institutions. They need no additional support.

Source Note: Charles Sumner, *The Barbarism of Slavery: Speech of Hon. Charles Sumner, on the Bill for the Admission of Kansas as a Free State, in the United States Senate, June 4, 1860* (Boston, 1860). Copy owned by the editor, the gift of his daughter, Susan R. Lowance.

Concluding Remarks and Alexis de Tocqueville
(1805–1859)

Henri Grégoire and Alexis de Tocqueville were two Frenchmen who contributed much to the antebellum slavery debates. Grégoire's *On the Cultural Achievements of Negroes* (1808) was an early discussion of racial equality and a challenge to the hierarchical theory of race classification, examined in chapter 7. Tocqueville's *Democracy in America* (1835), from which the excerpt that follows was taken, was widely read in Europe and the United States. Tocqueville acted as an enlightened commentator and observer of the new experiment in democracy, which was founded on English constitutional law but was unique in the world of the early nineteenth century. Chapter 10 of this work treats race relations in the new world, especially the character and destiny of the Africans who had been imported as slaves and were denied citizenship. Tocqueville accurately prophesied that the success or failure of the new democracy would in large measure depend on the successful political and social assimilation of the African into American society, whether or not full racial equality was ever achieved. His observations have often been cited as an indictment of the early American democracy which allowed slavery while professing that "all men are created equal." Although the Declaration of Independence, where these Jeffersonian words appear, was not a part of the Constitution later chartered by the founding fathers, it has long been a measuring rod for democratic principles, and was cited often by later abolitionist writers such as Frederick Douglass and Harriet Beecher Stowe; *Uncle Tom's Cabin* (1852) contains a similar prophetic judgment as a concluding jeremiad to her vast readership. Joseph Ellis, in his award-winning study of Jefferson, *The American Sphinx*, has argued that while Jefferson's words were nowhere incorporated into the actual charter document of the United States, the Constitution, the phrase nevertheless has the essential power of law because it undergirds many of the amendments to the Constitution, especially those based on equality of opportunity and prohibition against discrimination because of race, creed, color, gender, sexual preference, and national origin. The all-inclusive principle that "all men are created equal" has done more to shape the identity of citizens of the United States, a "nation of immigrants," than perhaps any other public pronouncement by an American. Indeed, it is this statement rather than the Constitution, against which many of the proslavery advocates in antebellum America, such as Thornton Stringfellow, would argue their cases.

In the Capitol building in Washington, D.C., there is an oil painting entitled "The First Reading of the *Emancipation Proclamation*," by Francis Bicknell Carpenter, painted in 1864. It represents the occasion of July 22, 1862, when

Abraham Lincoln declared: "I, as Commander and Chief of the Army and Navy of the United States, do order and declare that . . . all persons held as slaves . . . shall thenceforward and forever be free." President Lincoln went on to declare that "no national reunion should occur without the abolition of slavery," echoing William Lloyd Garrison's declaration that there should be no union with slaveholders. The *Emancipation Proclamation*, signed January 1, 1863, did not affect slaves in the border states. It did, however, directly address the status of those slaves held in the Confederacy which had seceded from the United States in 1861. This "first reading" was followed by a preliminary proclamation issued on September 22, 1862, following the Battle of Antietam, where the Union Army had been victorious, despite heavy losses on both sides. Slavery, and the attendant problem of racial inequality, so forcefully cited by Tocqueville in 1835, was not officially abolished until the ratification and adoption of the Thirteenth Amendment to the Constitution in 1865 and the subsequent passage of the Civil Rights legislation, which became the Fourteenth Amendment.

The two prominent abolitionists, Frederick Douglass and William Lloyd Garrison, had disagreed about the status of the U.S. Constitution, Garrison preferring its abolition and Douglass always arguing for the amendment process that eventually prevailed. However, as these events unfolded and Lincoln decreed emancipation followed by the Thirteenth and Fourteenth Amendments, Douglass rightly observed that "the work of freedom has only begun." As John Hope Franklin has argued in his masterful *From Slavery to Freedom*, a modern history of the African-American experience, these early prophets could not have foreseen the harsh injustices of Reconstruction and Jim Crow legislation such as the *Plessy v Ferguson* decision of 1896, in which the Supreme Court of the United States upheld the doctrine of "separate but equal" accommodations for interstate railroad travel, a decision which eventually spread to every segment of American society, including hotels, restaurants, and schools. The "work of freedom" had indeed only begun in 1863, and Frederick Douglass joined Harriet Beecher Stowe and Alexis de Tocqueville in prophetically declaring the future of democracy in the United States.

Tocqueville was, of course, not an American citizen. However, his perspective on the condition of Africans in America in the early decades of the nineteenth century was instrumental in articulating the fundamental contrast between the ideology of the founding fathers, that "all men are created equal," and the observed practice of the fledgling democracy as it struggled to clarify its objectives and sort out its fundamental principles. *Democracy in America* is by no means the final word on the resolution of this essential conflict between individual rights as guaranteed under the Constitution and the "commonweal" or "common good" that is sought through a system of amendments to that charter document. It is very clear from the history of the United States in the twentieth century, especially in its continued pursuit of civil rights for African-Americans led by Martin Luther King, Jr., in the 1950s and 1960s, that Tocqueville's observations are as relevant today as they were in 1835. Even now, racial discrimination is practiced throughout the United States in spite of federal laws prohibiting it, such as the Fair Housing Act of 1988, which prohibits discrimination of all kinds in the sale or rental of housing. The struggle for the acceptance of affirmative action guidelines, the widespread acceptance of *The Bell Curve* (1994), the failure of many American cities to effectively integrate their school systems even though this was mandated by the Supreme Court decision of 1954, *Brown v Board of Education of Topeka, Kansas,* and the persistence well into the last decades of the twentieth century of segregation by neighborhoods—in Chicago, Boston, Los Angeles, as well as Atlanta and Charlotte—all demonstrate that Tocqueville's fundamental observations were correct.

The struggle of the African-American to obtain voting rights took more than one hundred years following the passage of the Thirteenth Amendment to the Constitution in 1865; President Lyndon B. Johnson signed this civil rights legislation in 1965 with Dr. Martin Luther King, Jr., attending. The tableau recalled President Abraham Lincoln decreeing the "Emancipation Proclamation" or pressing for the Thirteenth Amendment with the ex-slave Frederick Douglass advising. The long segregationist influence of *Plessy v Ferguson* on transportation, accommodations, admission to educational institutions, movie theaters, restaurants, drinking fountains, public restrooms and other places of public access, including churches throughout the United States, was demonstrated in the second half of the twentieth century in such episodes as the Montgomery bus boycott, initiated when the heroic Rosa Parks refused to move to the back of the bus in 1954. Despite appearances to the contrary, "Jim Crow" was alive and well in the twentieth century. The entertainment industry helped to shape public attitudes and values just as the stereotypical minstrel shows of the nineteenth century had contributed to public assumptions about essential differences between blacks and whites. Indeed, in the early years of Hollywood, character actors such as Bill "Bojangles" Robinson, or Stepin Fetchit, or Oscar-winner Hattie McDaniel, who played Mammy in the 1939 film version of Margaret Mitchell's *Gone with the Wind*, perpetuated negative stereotypes of African-Americans that made the acceptance of "all men are created equal" even more problematic. D. W. Griffith's *Birth of a Nation,* a silent film that recreated the founding of the Ku Klux Klan (1866) by Confederate veterans of the Civil War, resurrected the antebellum anxiety about the emancipated African as a perpetual threat to the predominately white social order. The extremely popular Shirley Temple films, especially *Dimples* (1935), which, ironically, dramatized the story of an acting troupe in the 1850s that toured playing scenes from *Uncle Tom's Cabin*, provided popular cultural icons of African-American "otherness" that supported widely accepted views of African inferiority and white supremacy. On the radio, the popular *Amos and Andy Show*, where the lead characters were portrayed by white actors imitating African-American dialect and speech, was transformed into a television series that entertained audiences throughout the 1950s, just as the civil rights movement was gaining prominence. By 1965, this recreation of minstrel entertainment had been taken off the air in response to vigorous protests by the NAACP and other civil rights organizations.

Minstrel entertainment has provided a long-accepted satirical view of African-American society and culture, and these visions are as misleading as they are destructive of the Jeffersonian objective that "all men are created equal." The stereotyping of African-Americans as athletes (Michael Jordan) or entertainers (Sammy Davis, Jr.) or buffoons (Richard Pryor, Eddie Murphy) has a very long history that commenced when T. C. Rice adopted the blackface stage persona of Jim Crow in the 1820s, using burned-cork grease in much the same way minstrel characters were to do for over one hundred and fifty years. These powerful icons were slow to give way to an acceptance of the African-American's civil rights. Even the literary and cinematic pairing of a black and a white character to suggest human interdependence that transcends racial boundaries has not been able to overcome the impact of minstrel stereotyping. Images such as Ishmael and Queequeg from Herman Melville's *Moby-Dick* (1851), or Huck and Jim in Mark Twain's *Huckleberry Finn* (1885), or Uncle Tom and Little Eva in Harriet Beecher Stowe's *Uncle Tom's Cabin* (1852), and more contemporary examples such as Crockett and Tubbs from *Miami Vice*, Robert Culp and Bill Cosby in *Mission: Impossible*, and Sidney Poitier in Rod Steiger's *In the Heat of the Night*, and Tim Robbins and Morgan Freeman in *Shawshank Redemption*, show that writers and filmmakers have long struggled with American racial identity, just as Tocqueville prophesied that they would. It is significant that the armed forces of the United States were abruptly, not gradually, integrated in 1948, by a single decree from President Harry Truman, and that the 1950s films generated by World War II, such as John Wayne's *Sands of Iwo Jima*, have few African-American characters in them because during that war, the services were not integrated and combat units were kept separated. It is also significant that the Hollywood productions following the Vietnam War (*Full Metal Jacket; Born on the Fourth of July; For the Boys*, where four decades of military experience are traced; and *The Deer Hunter*, to name a few) showed a fully integrated military, with human interdependence clearly transcending all racial barriers.

Generally, Hollywood has elected to follow rather than shape American values, and the brief survey here shows a pattern of responding to public taste rather than attempting to shape or influence it. Occasionally, social protest films will appear—*A Gentleman's Agreement*, with Gregory Peck; *Guess Who's Coming to Dinner*, with Spencer Tracy and Sidney Poitier; and, very recently, Stephen Spielberg's *Amistad* and Oscar-winning *Schindler's List*. In 1989, the African-American director Spike Lee produced *Do the Right Thing*, which examines the many problems of African-American identity in a fully integrated low-income neighborhood, followed in 1991 by *Jungle Fever*, a film which explores problems of social identity and acceptance of an interracial couple who are both professionals. Lee's excellent historical treatment of the minstrel tradition is found in *Bamboozled* (2000), where modern acceptance of nineteenth-century minstrel stereotyping, set in a twentieth-century New York City national network studio, runs into direct conflict with powerful racial attitudes now found on both sides of the barrier. Like Tocqueville, these films of social protest join their literary counterparts in the nineteenth century, Melville, Twain, and Stowe, to suggest that unless reform comes soon, the ambitious plans of the United States to develop a harmonious society will ultimately fail. As Tocqueville put it, "Once one admits that whites and emancipated Negroes face each other like two foreign peoples on the same soil, it can easily be understood that there are only two possibilities for the future: the Negroes and the whites must either mingle completely or they must part. I have already expressed my conviction concerning the first possibility. I do not think that the white and black race will ever be brought anywhere to live on a footing of equality." This pessimistic vision, while dating from 1835, has uncanny relevance for the United States as we enter the twenty-first century.

Stowe was not much more optimistic in the "Concluding Remarks" of *Uncle Tom's Cabin*, but she does offer the alternative of repentance and salvation, the traditional Judeo-Christian paradigm, to an apocalyptic racial conflagration:

A day of Grace is yet held out to us. Both North and South have been guilty before God; and the Christian Church has a heavy account to answer. Not by combining together, to protect injustice and cruelty, and making a common capital of sin, is this Union to be saved—but by repentance, justice, and mercy; for, not surer is the eternal law by which the millstone sinks in the ocean, than that stronger law, by which injustice and cruelty shall bring on nations the wrath of almighty God!

These prophetic words, like the warnings of Alexis de Tocqueville issued only seventeen years earlier, could apply to the history of American efforts to assimilate the former slaves into the dominant white culture at any time during the more than two centuries since the words "all men are created equal" were first articulated. *A House Divided* traces the evolution of that ideology in a culture that has resisted its acceptance from the beginning. The primary documents that illustrate that resistance and articulate opposition to its acceptance show how the essential debate has characterized American identity since 1776.

Democracy in America
by Alexis de Tocqueville

Part II, Chapter 10 . . . *Some Considerations Concerning the Present State and Probable Future of the Three Races that Inhabit the Territory of the United States*

. . . Among these widely different people, the first that attracts attention, and the *first* in enlightenment, power, and happiness, is the white man, the European, man par excellence; below him come the Negro and the Indian.

These two unlucky races have neither birth, physique, language, nor mores in common; only their misfortunes are alike. Both occupy an equally inferior position in the land where they dwell; both suffer the effects of tyranny, and though their affections are different, they have the same people to blame for them. . . .

In one blow, oppression has deprived the descendants of the Africans of almost all privileges of humanity. The United States Negro has lost even the memory of his homeland; he no longer understands the language his fathers spoke; he has abjured their religion and forgotten their mores. Ceasing to belong to Africa, he has acquired no right to the blessings of Europe; he is left in suspense between two societies and isolated between two peoples, sold by one and repudiated by the other; in the whole world there is nothing but his master's hearth to provide him with some semblance of a homeland.

The Negro has no family; for him a woman is no more than the passing companion of his pleasures, and from their birth his sons are his equals. . . .

Plunged in this abyss of wretchedness, the Negro hardly notices his ill fortune; he was reduced to slavery by violence, and the habit of servitude has given him the thoughts and ambitions of a slave; he admires his tyrants even more than he hates them and finds his joy and pride in a servile imitation of his oppressors.

His intelligence is degraded to the level of his soul.

The Negro is a slave from birth. What am *I* saying? He is often sold in his mother's belly and begins, so to say, to be a slave before he is born.

Devoid both of wants and of pleasures, useless to himself, his first notions of existence teach him that he is the property of another who has an interest in preserving his life; he sees that care for his own fate has not devolved on him; the very use of thought seems to him an unprofitable gift of Providence, and he peacefully enjoys all the privileges of his humiliation.

If he becomes free, he often feels independence as a heavier burden than slavery itself, for his life has taught him to submit to everything, except to the dictates of reason; and when reason becomes his only guide, he cannot hear its voice. A thousand new wants assail him, and he lacks the knowledge and the energy needed to resist them. Desires are masters against whom one must fight, and he has learned nothing but to submit and obey so he has reached this climax of affliction in which slavery brutalizes him and freedom leads him to destruction. . . .

The Negro makes a thousand fruitless efforts to insinuate himself into a society that repulses him; he adopts himself to his oppressors' tastes, adopting their opinions and hoping by imitation to join their community. From birth he has been told that his race is naturally inferior to the white man and almost believing that, he holds himself in contempt. He sees a trace of slavery in his every feature, and if he could he would gladly repudiate himself entirely.

Situation of the Black Race in the United States; Dangers Entailed for the Whites by Its Presence

. . . Christianity had destroyed servitude; the Christians of the sixteenth century reestablished it, but they never admitted it as anything more than an exception in their social system, and they were careful to restrict it to one of the races of man. . . .

The immediate ills resulting from slavery were almost the same in the ancient as in the modern world, but the consequences of these ills were different. In antiquity the slave was of the same race as his master and was often his superior in education and enlightenment. Only freedom kept them apart; freedom once granted, they mingled easily.

Therefore the ancients had a very simple means of delivering themselves from slavery and its consequences, namely to free the slaves; and when they made a general use of this, they succeeded.

Admittedly the traces of servitude existed in antiquity for some time after slavery itself had been abolished.

A natural prejudice leads a man to scorn anybody who has been his inferior, long after he has become his equal; the real inequality, due to fortune or the law, is always followed by an imagined inequality rooted in mores; but with the ancients this secondary effect of slavery had a time limit, for the freedman was so completely like the man born free that it was soon impossible to distinguish between them. . . .

No African came in freedom to the shores of the New World; consequently all those found there now are slaves or freedmen. The Negro transmits to his descendants at birth the external mark of his ignominy. The law can abolish servitude, but only God can obliterate its traces.

The modern slave differs from his master not only in lacking freedom but also in his origin. You can make the Negro free, but you cannot prevent him facing the European as a stranger.

That is not all; this man born in degradation, this stranger brought by slavery into our midst, is hardly recognized as sharing the common feature of humanity. His face appears to us hideous, his intelligence limited, and his tastes low; we almost take him for some being intermediate between beast and man.

When they have abolished slavery, the moderns still have to eradicate three much more intangible and tenacious prejudices: the prejudice of the master, the prejudice of race, and the prejudice of the white.

Having had the luck to be born among men shaped by nature very like ourselves and equal before the law, it is very difficult for us to understand the insurmountable gap between the American Negro and the European. . . .

Turning my attention to the United States of our own day, I plainly see that in some parts of the country the legal barrier between the two races is tending to come down, but not that of mores: I see that slavery is in retreat, but the prejudice from which it arose is immovable.

In that part of the Union where the Negroes are no longer slaves, have they come closer to the whites? Everyone who has lived in the United States will have noticed the opposite.

Race prejudice seems stronger in those states that have abolished slavery than in those where it still exists, and nowhere is it more intolerant than in those states where slavery was never known. . . .

In almost all the states where slavery has been abolished, the Negroes have been given electoral rights, but they would come forward to vote at the risk of their lives. When oppressed, they can bring an action at law, but they will find only white men among their judges. It is true that the laws make them eligible as jurors, but prejudice wards them off. The Negro's son is excluded from the school to which the European's child goes. In the theaters he cannot for good money buy the right to sit by his former master's side, in the hospitals he lies apart. He is allowed to worship the same God as the white man but must not pray at the same altars. He has his own clergy and churches. The gates of heaven are not closed against him, but his inequality stops only just short of the boundaries of the other world. When the Negro is no more, his bones are cast aside, and some difference in condition is found even in the equality of death.

So the Negro is free, but he cannot share the rights, pleasures, labors, griefs, or even the tomb of him whose equal he has been declared; there is nowhere where he can meet him, neither in life nor in death.

In the South, where slavery still exists, less trouble is taken to keep the Negro apart: they sometimes share the labors and the pleasures of the white men; people are prepared to mix with them to some extent; legislation is more harsh against them, but customs are more tolerant and gentle. . . .

The farther south one goes, the less profitable it becomes to abolish slavery. There are several physical reasons for this which need to be explained. . . .

Tobacco, cotton, and sugar cane grow in the South only and are there the country's main wealth. If they abolished slavery, the southerners would be faced with one of these two alternatives: either they must change their system of cultivation, in which case they would find themselves in competition with the more active and experienced northerners, or they must grow the same crops without slaves in competition with other southern states still keeping theirs.

Therefore the South has particular reasons for preserving slavery, which the North has not. But there is yet another motive more powerful than all the rest. The South could, at a pinch, abolish slavery, but how could it dispose of the blacks? The North rids itself of slavery and of the slaves in one move. In the South there is no hope of attaining this double result at the same time.

In proving that servitude is more natural and more advantageous in the South than in the North, I have given sufficient indication that the number of slaves should be much greater there. Africans were brought to the South first, and ever since then the largest numbers have been imported there. The farther south one goes, the stronger is the prejudice glorifying idleness. . . .

In the state of Maine there is one Negro to every three hundred of the population; in Massachusetts, one in a hundred; in the state of New York, two in a hundred; in Pennsylvania, three; in Maryland, thirty-four; in Virginia, forty-two; and finally in South Carolina, fifty-five. Those were the comparative figures for the year 1830. . . .

It is clear that the most southern states of the Union could not abolish slavery, as has been done in the northern states, without running very great risks which did not face the latter. . . .

. . . But if this first dawn of freedom shone on two million people at the same moment, the oppressors would have reason to tremble.

Having freed the sons of their slaves, the Europeans in the South would soon be forced to extend that benefit to the whole black race. . . .

So by abolishing slavery the southerners could not succeed, as their brothers in the North have done, in advancing the Negroes gradually toward freedom; they would not be able to diminish the numbers of the blacks appreciably, and they would be left alone to keep them in check. In the course of a few years one would have a large free Negro population among an approximately equal white population.

Those same abuses of power which now maintain slavery would then become the sources of the greatest dangers facing the southern whites. . . .

As long as the Negro is kept as a slave, he can be held in a condition not far removed from that of a beast; once free, he cannot be prevented from learning enough to see the extent of his ills and to catch a glimpse of the remedy. . . .

Once one admits that whites and emancipated Negroes face each other like two foreign peoples on the same soil, it can easily be understood that there are only two possibilities for the future: the Negroes and the whites must either mingle completely or they must part.

I have already expressed my conviction concerning the first possibility. I do not think that the white and black race will ever be brought anywhere to live on a footing of equality. . . .

There are parts of the United States where European and Negro blood are so crossed that one cannot find a man who is either completely white or completely black; when that point has been reached, one can really say that the races are mixed, or rather that there is a third race derived from those two, but not precisely one or the other.

Of all Europeans, the English have least mingled their blood with that of Negroes. There are more mulatoes in the South of the Union than in the North, but infinitely fewer than in any other European colony; there are very few mulatoes in the United States; they have no strength by themselves, and in racial disputes they generally make common cause with the whites. One finds much the same in Europe when the lackeys of great lords behave haughtily to the people.

This pride of origin, which is natural to the English, is most remarkably increased in the American by the personal pride derived from democratic liberty. The white man in the United States is proud of his race and proud of himself. . . .

I confess that in considering the South I see only two alternatives for the white people living there: to free the Negroes and to mingle with them or to remain isolated from them and keep them as long as possible in slavery. Any intermediate measures seem to me likely to terminate, and that shortly, in the most horrible of civil wars, and perhaps in the extermination of one or other of the two races.

The southern Americans see the question from the point of view and act accordingly. Not wishing to mingle with the Negroes, they do not want to set them free.

It is not that all the inhabitants of the South think slavery necessary to the master's wealth; on that point many of them agree with the northerners and readily admit that slavery is an evil; but they think that they have to preserve that evil in order to live.

Increasing enlightenment in the South makes the people there see that slavery is harmful to the master, and the same enlightenment makes them see, more clearly than they had seen before, that it is almost impossible to abolish it. A strange contrast results from this: slavery is more and more entrenched in the laws just when its utility is most contested; and while this principle is gradually being abolished in the North, in the South increasingly harsh consequences are derive therefrom. . . .

The Americans of the South, who do not think that at any time the Negroes can mingle with them, have forbidden teaching them to read or write under severe penalties. Not wishing to raise them to their own level, they keep them as close to the beasts as possible. . . .

The Americans of the South have realized that emancipation always presented dangers, when the freed slave could not succeed in assimilating himself to his master. To give a man liberty but to leave him in ignominious misery, what was that but to prepare a leader for some future slave rebellion? . . .

There is no doubt that these evils are terrible, but are they not the foreseen and necessary consequences of the very principle of slavery in modern times? . . .

What is happening in the South of the Union seems to me both the most horrible and the most natural of consequences of slavery. When I see the order of nature overthrown and hear the cry of humanity complaining in vain against the laws, I confess that my indignation is not directed against the men of our day who are the authors of these outrages; all my hatred is concentrated against those who, after a thousand years of equality, introduced slavery into the world again.

Whatever efforts the Americans of the South make to maintain slavery, they will not forever succeed. Slavery is limited to one point on the globe and attacked by Christianity as unjust and by political economy as fatal; slavery, and the democratic liberty and enlightenment of our age, is not an institution that can last. Either the slave or the master will put an end to it. In either case great misfortunes are to be anticipated.

If freedom is refused to the Negroes in the South, in the end they will seize it themselves; if it is granted to them, they will not be slow to abuse it. . . .

Conclusion

Now I am approaching the end. Up to now, in discussing the future destiny of the United States, I have tried to divide my subject into various parts so as to study each of them more carefully.

It is time to take a general look at the whole from a single point of view. . . .

In truth, therefore, there are only two rival races sharing the New World today: the Spaniards and the English. . . .

The lands of the New World belong to the first man to occupy them, and dominion is the prize in that race. . . .

So then, it must not be thought possible to halt the impetus of the English race in the New World. The dismemberment of the Union, bringing war into the continent, or the abolition of the republic, bringing tyranny, might slow expansion down, but cannot prevent the people ultimately fulfilling their inevitable destiny. No power on earth can shut out the immigrants from that fertile wilderness which on every side offers rewards to industry and a refuge from every affliction. Whatever the future may hold in store, it cannot deprive the Americans of their climate, their inland seas, their great rivers, or the fertility of their soil. Bad laws, revolutions, and anarchy cannot destroy their taste for well-being or that spirit of enterprise which seems the characteristic feature of their race; nor could such things utterly extinguish the lights of knowledge guiding them.

Thus, in all the uncertainty of the future, one event at least is sure. At a period which we may call near, for we are speaking of the life of nations, the Anglo-Americans alone will cover the whole of the immense area between the polar ice and the tropics, extending from the Atlantic to the Pacific coast. . . .

Source Note: Alexis de Tocqueville, *Democracy in America* (Boston, 1835–39).